Managing Risk in Virtual Enterprise Networks:

Implementing Supply Chain Principles

Stavros Ponis
National Technical University of Athens, Greece

T0338665

A volume in the Advances in Logistics, Operations, and Management Science (ALOMS) Book Series

Director of Editorial Content:	Kristin Klinger
Director of Book Publications:	Julia Mosemann
Acquisitions Editor:	Lindsay Johnston
Development Editor:	Christine Bufton
Publishing Assistant:	Myla Harty
Typesetter:	Callie Klinger and Myla Harty
Production Editor:	Jamie Snavely
Cover Design:	Lisa Tosheff

Published in the United States of America by
Business Science Reference (an imprint of IGI Global)
701 E. Chocolate Avenue
Hershey PA 17033
Tel: 717-533-8845
Fax: 717-533-8661
E-mail: cust@igi-global.com
Web site: http://www.igi-global.com

Library of Congress Cataloging-in-Publication Data

Managing risk in virtual enterprise networks : implementing supply chain principles / Stavros Ponis, editor.
   p. cm.
  Includes bibliographical references and index.
  Summary: "This book deals with risk management in enterprise network formations, stressing the importance of risk management in enterprises organized in networks followed by the presentation of the researcher suggested approaches which most of the time emphasizes in a supply chain"--Provided by publisher.
  ISBN 978-1-61520-607-0 (hardcover) -- ISBN 978-1-61520-608-7 (ebook) 1. Risk management. 2. Social networks. 3. Business logistics. I. Ponis, Stavros, 1970- II. Title.
  HD61.M2654 2010
  658.7--dc22
               2010000040

This book is published in the IGI Global book series Advances in Logistics, Operations, and Management Science (ALOMS) Book Series (ISSN: 2327-350X; eISSN: 2327-3518)

British Cataloguing in Publication Data
A Cataloguing in Publication record for this book is available from the British Library.

All work contributed to this book is new, previously-unpublished material. The views expressed in this book are those of the authors, but not necessarily of the publisher.

Advances in Logistics, Operations, and Management Science (ALOMS) Book Series

John Wang
Montclair State University, USA

ISSN: 2327-350X
EISSN: 2327-3518

Mission

Operations research and management science continue to influence business processes, administration, and management information systems, particularly in covering the application methods for decision-making processes. New case studies and applications on management science, operations management, social sciences, and other behavioral sciences have been incorporated into business and organizations real-world objectives.

The **Advances in Logistics, Operations, and Management Science** (ALOMS) Book Series provides a collection of reference publications on the current trends, applications, theories, and practices in the management science field. Providing relevant and current research, this series and its individual publications would be useful for academics, researchers, scholars, and practitioners interested in improving decision making models and business functions.

Coverage

- Computing and Information Technologies
- Decision Analysis and Decision Support
- Finance
- Information Management
- Marketing Engineering
- Operations Management
- Organizational Behavior
- Political Science
- Production Management
- Services Management

IGI Global is currently accepting manuscripts for publication within this series. To submit a proposal for a volume in this series, please contact our Acquisition Editors at Acquisitions@igi-global.com or visit: http://www.igi-global.com/publish/.

Titles in this Series

For a list of additional titles in this series, please visit: www.igi-global.com

Outsourcing Management for Supply Chain Operations and Logistics Service
Dimitris Folinas (Department of Logistics, ATEI-Thessaloniki, Greece)
Business Science Reference • copyright 2013 • 596pp • H/C (ISBN: 9781466620087) • US $185.00 (our price)

Operations Management Research and Cellular Manufacturing Systems Innovative Methods and Approaches
Vladimir Modrák (Technical University of Kosice, Slovakia) and R. Sudhakara Pandian (Kalasalingam University, India)
Business Science Reference • copyright 2012 • 368pp • H/C (ISBN: 9781613500477) • US $185.00 (our price)

Fashion Supply Chain Management Industry and Business Analysis
Tsan-Ming Choi (The Hong Kong Polytechnic University, Hong Kong)
Information Science Reference • copyright 2012 • 392pp • H/C (ISBN: 9781609607562) • US $195.00 (our price)

Supply Chain Optimization, Design, and Management Advances and Intelligent Methods
Ioannis Minis (University of the Aegean, Greece) Vasileios Zeimpekis (University of the Aegean, Greece) Georgios Dounias (University of the Aegean, Greece) and Nicholas Ampazis (University of the Aegean, Greece)
Business Science Reference • copyright 2011 • 338pp • H/C (ISBN: 9781615206339) • US $180.00 (our price)

Quality Management for IT Services Perspectives on Business and Process Performance
Claus-Peter Praeg (Fraunhofer Institute for Industrial Engineering, Germany) and Dieter Spath (Fraunhofer Institute for Industrial Engineering, Germany)
Business Science Reference • copyright 2011 • 348pp • H/C (ISBN: 9781616928896) • US $180.00 (our price)

Managing Risk in Virtual Enterprise Networks Implementing Supply Chain Principles
Stavros Ponis (National Technical University of Athens, Greece)
Business Science Reference • copyright 2010 • 408pp • H/C (ISBN: 9781615206070) • US $180.00 (our price)

Service Science and Logistics Informatics Innovative Perspectives
ZongWei Luo (The University of Hong Kong, China)
Information Science Reference • copyright 2010 • 462pp • H/C (ISBN: 9781615206032) • US $180.00 (our price)

DISSEMINATOR OF KNOWLEDGE

www.igi-global.com

701 E. Chocolate Ave., Hershey, PA 17033
Order online at www.igi-global.com or call 717-533-8845 x100
To place a standing order for titles released in this series, contact: cust@igi-global.com
Mon-Fri 8:00 am - 5:00 pm (est) or fax 24 hours a day 717-533-8661

Table of Contents

Section 1
Concepts, Methods and Approaches

Chapter 1
Jan Husdal, Molde Research Institute, Norway

Chapter 2
Brian Squire, Manchester Business School, UK

Chapter 3
Burak Sari, Leiden Institute of Advanced Computer Science (LIACS), The Netherlands

Chapter 4
Samir Dani, Loughborough University, UK

Chapter 5
Ettore Bolisani, University of Padua, Italy

Chapter 6
Mohammad Ali Shalan, PMP, ITIL, CISA, CGEIT, Jordan

Section 2
Models and Applications

Detailed Table of Contents

Section 1
Concepts, Methods and Approaches

Chapter 1

Jan Husdal, Molde Research Institute, Norway

Is managing risk in Virtual Enterprise Networks (VENs) different from managing risk in supply chains? This chapter studies VEN risk management from the perspective of supply chain risk management and attempts a mapping between concepts related to supply chain risk e.g. vulnerability, robustness, flexibility, resilience, business continuity and their possible VEN counterparts. Conceptual in its approach, this chapter introduces four distinct groups of VENs, namely Constrained, Directed, Limited and Free and concludes that VEN risk management can and should learn from supply chain risk management.

Chapter 2

Brian Squire, Manchester Business School, UK

This exploratory chapter uncovers some of the network measures that may benefit risk identification and analysis within supply networks. In doing so, it follows a tradition within other fields that have used formal network measures to determine the robustness of their networks of interest and to understand the sources of extended enterprise or supply chain risk. In this chapter, the author argues that network measures can provide additional insight to uncover sources of risk that could remain hidden using 'traditional' measures alone and provides researchers and managers with a wide-ranging framework for risk identification.

Chapter 3

The social integration of virtual enterprise networks involves the creation of identities for the participating nodes, the building of trust and the sharing of tacit and explicit knowledge between them. In that context, and in the presence of new challenges such as cultural differences and missing face to face relationships, to name a few, trust emerges as a critical issue. This chapter discusses extensively the way of managing trust in virtual enterprise networks as a solution to mitigate collaboration and performance risk and presents the necessary conditions that are required to support trust building in a virtual collaboration context.

Chapter 4

The temporary nature of the relationships and the informal structures of Virtual Enterprise Networks (VENs) can be the source of various challenges and risks. Based on a synthetic literature review on the risks associated with Virtual Enterprise Networks, in this chapter it is argued that establishing a shared culture of innovation within the network and integrating innovation proactively within the product and service offerings of the network members, alleviates the risk management/mitigation process. The author supports these arguments by proposing a framework which supports risk mitigation under the perspective of VEN innovation

Virtual Enterprises (VEs) are business models characterized by the aggregation of co-operating firms that share a common goal such as a business opportunity or a project. In these structures, knowledge can be seen as a primary asset. This chapter provides a knowledge-based view of VEs and aims to study a rather underexplored area of VE operation, which is the management of risks associated to the exchange and sharing of knowledge. In doing that, the author explores the nature of knowledge flows in a VE and after studying the related managerial issues he determines the different knowledge-related risk factors and discusses the challenges raised by the need for their successful management.

Chapter 6

IT integration with the VE business model particularities is never a trivial task, thus calling for a special approach to discover and mitigate risks and apply controls related to the continuously growing of IT usage and support in a VE environment. The main objective of this chapter is to provide a comprehensive in depth analysis of risks and issues associated with the IT aspects of Virtual Enterprise Networks

(VENs) from technical and procedural point of view and to prescribe specific guidelines to mitigate the effects of the identified and analyzed risks, processes and consequences in the form of an IT Governance framework

Chapter 7

Simulation is not only a powerful decision-making aid for supply chain managers but also a powerful research tool for theory building and testing. The purpose of this chapter is to illustrate an approach toward modeling disruptions, risks and other crisis events in Virtual Enterprise Networks. It provides several illustrations from published literature, presents a framework for managers and researchers to better apply and gain from the strength of simulation modeling, identifies several common pitfalls to avoid during the process, and compiles extensive references for readers who want to further their knowledge in this specific area.

Chapter 8

Supply chain management under uncertainty and risk has become the target of extensive research. In this chapter, a theoretical framework of supply chain risk analysis is proposed. Within this framework, risks and possible disruptions that affect supply chain ability to function normally are determined and studied. Next, the implementation of the proposed framework is evaluated through the presentation of a simulation example while, as the authors declare, the future objective of the research presented in this chapter is the elaboration of a software solution for supply chain modelling and risk evaluation.

Section 2
Models and Applications

Chapter 9

The continued rise in global sourcing and manufacturing has significantly added to the complexity of contemporary supply chains, creating new challenges and risks. At the same time, there is now a growing realization that the supply chain 'begins on the drawing board', meaning that design decisions can dramatically impact the risk profile of the business. Thus, the primary purpose of this paper is to propose a design centric approach towards creating resilient and highly responsive enterprise networks. Furthermore, the authors validate their proposed approach by applying it in three case studies from different industry sectors where design is an important element in the success of final products.

Chapter 10

María Jesús Sáenz Zaragoza Logistics Center & University of Zaragoza, Spain
Maria Pilar Lambán, University of Zaragoza, Spain
Eva Navarro, Zaragoza Logistics Center, Spain

Organizations that remain flexible take advantage of new opportunities, explore new ways of working and resolve unanticipated consequences. In this chapter, a conceptual strategic framework for increasing value chain flexibility is proposed. This framework addresses issues such as the company's own strategy towards the supply chain partners, the organization strategy, the logistics approach, the market strategy, the production strategy and finally innovation. The feasibility and adaptability of the proposed research is supported by an empirical study of fifty seven companies of the Food and Beverage sector.

Chapter 11

Stavros Ponis, National Technical University, Greece
Epaminondas Koronis, University of Warwick, UK

Outsourcing has been and still is a very popular management strategy for companies entering the globalized manufacturing era. In this chapter, the authors attempt a categorization of risk sources during the outsourcing initiative, propose mitigating actions and introduce the concept: 'vicious cycle' suggesting that outsourcing, if not managed successfully, eventually leads to the addiction of the organization to 'buy' expertise and knowledge in spite of knowledge acquisition. The authors validate their findings through a case study analysis of four medium size pharmaceutical companies, all of them having implemented outsourcing strategies.

Chapter 12

Konstantinos Kirytopoulos, University of the Aegean, Greece.
Dimitra Voulgaridou, National Technical University Athens, Greece
Vrassidas Leopoulos, National Technical University Athens, Greece

The core objective of this chapter is the provision of a decision framework for enterprise formations organized as collaborative clusters, which according to the authors constitute a sophisticated form of a virtual enterprise network. This framework, based on the ANP-BOCR model, takes into account clusters' special characteristics the most important of which is that the supply chain entities do have a clear picture of strategies, policies, needs, strengths and weaknesses of one another. The whole approach is illustrated through a parapharmaceutical cluster case study which reveals that "common" knowledge and risks are very important in an environment where entities are sometimes partners and sometimes competitors.

In this chapter, it is argued that Internal Audit activities and controls can help virtual organizations to improve and operate in a more efficient manner. This chapter proposes a methodological approach for the design of the Internal Audit function for risk assessment and control identification of inter-organizational supply chain processes, using business process modeling techniques and an internal audit–oriented enterprise modeling tool. Both the proposed approach and business process modeling tool are tested in a case study of a Virtual Enterprise Network operating in the Electronics sector

In this chapter the effort to capture market dynamics of consumer products via Agent-based Models and apply the findings in the context of risk management focused in Virtual Enterprise Networks, is presented. The research efforts result in the development of a software tool that supports leveraging risks associated with price wars, or other aggressive strategies the players in a given market may choose to follow. In that context, the proposed tool supports risk management during purchasing and production planning and provides solid justification for decisions associated with the introduction of new products by a Virtual Enterprise Network in an existing market.

Foreword

As we enter the dawn of the first decade of the new millennium, at no point in time has it been as important as it is now for enterprises to contemplate and introspect their supply chains, identify the risks entailed in their operations, manage these risks and implement mitigating and loss control strategies. In our times, where crises outburst all over the world, no company is immune or should hope to remain unaffected. Therefore the importance of being risk aware and subsequently crisis prepared becomes an issue of critical importance and in some cases, the discriminating factor between resilience and business termination.

In that sense, this book edited by Dr. Stavros Ponis entitled "Managing Risk in Virtual Enterprise Networks: Implementing Supply Chain Principles" is contemporary and characterized by a very good timing. Furthermore, the research efforts presented in this book are, in my opinion, quite interesting, since they attempt exploring risk management applied on a rather overlooked scientific area residing in the intersection of two overlapping (for some authors, reciprocal) concepts: Supply Chain Management and Virtual Enterprises.

In our days, Operations Management is no longer confined to individual production facilities and thus intensive cooperation with supply chain partners has become an integral part of its functioning. In recent years, two further developments gained ground. On one hand, enterprises are specializing and concentrating on their core competencies with outsourcing as a consequence, on the other side globalization has widened the range of choice among suppliers. Increased dependence on suppliers asks for new forms of collaboration. Intensive partnerships between many enterprises demand a new quality of cooperative ventures. Strategic, legal and risk issues have to be considered and operations management has to include new sophisticated methods and techniques for managing contemporary supply chains increasing in both size and complexity. These developments have led to the concept of extended or virtual enterprise.

The extended enterprise depicts one of the global trends and needs for industrial evolution. Basically, the concept of the extended enterprise emphasizes cross boundary cooperation. The message is simple and clear. Without deep cooperation no single company can prosper. Neither small, local SME's, nor huge, global players can survive on their own. Specific problems may arise due to fast changing market requirements. Partnerships are being formed and dissolved in a very short time window: "Agility" is the relevant keyword. Partnerships may be limited to specific products or components. Increasingly an enterprise may be part of several logistics partnerships, which constitute together a complicated network. "Virtuality" has become the keyword for this trend.

But many questions remain to be answered in order to successfully stand up to the challenge offered by these developments. How to establish and maintain efficient ways of cooperation with many partners? How to repeatedly modify the structures of an enterprise in a rapidly changing environment? How to improve overall operational effectiveness in order to enhance competitiveness on a world scale?

The essence of the extended enterprise is straightforward: deep cooperation opens opportunities for fast, efficient and reliable fulfillment of end customer needs throughout the whole demand chain. Even though some research communities call this phenomenon as "virtual enterprise", the fundamentals of this phenomenon are nothing but virtual: it is the question of tangible phenomena with tangible returns. The fact that information and communication technologies are preconditions for the success of the implementation of the concept, does not, however, imply that the underlying rationality was about virtual reality, but the true reality itself. As companies move from being stand-alone entities which pass product one to another, to being links in an interactive, adaptive, extended enterprise which deals successfully with rapid change, an unprecedented level of integration of people, business processes and technology is required.

In summary, supply chain management is no longer a purely reactive activity seeking to improve the capacity of the organization to absorb potential external shock waves, primarily directed along a linear supply route, whilst seeking to minimize the disruptions. It is now a more proactive activity engaging a complex enterprise network of upstream and downstream partners, seeking collectively to enhance competitive advantage, added value, lean operations, agility and profitability at the same time as managing a more complex interaction of risks. Issues are now about the benefits and risks associated with multiple sourcing, sharing the consequences of risks across the enterprise network, sharing information, building relationships and establishing trust. The expectation of enterprise network members may extend beyond the quality of the supplied resources to those of dependability, reliability, security and responsiveness of the network to mitigate any dislocations wherever they happen in the chain.

The management of risk in supply chains has now become an established, albeit fairly recently, field. The essence of this book is the capture, interpretation and dissemination of the latest developments in research, practice and policy in what is proving to be a very rapidly developing field. This book, carefully edited by Stavros Ponis, will provide a wide audience of researchers, scholars, policy makers and practitioners alike with a general view on research questions and recent advancements on the impact of risk management in virtual enterprise networks, whilst seeking to ensure that what is presented is well grounded in robust empirical methodologies end evidence or accurately represents the structures, practices and processes employed by the industry.

Ilias Tatsiopoulos
Professor of Production and Logistics
National Technical University Athens

I. P. Tatsiopoulos *is a Professor in Production Planning and Control and Manufacturing Information Systems in SIMOR/NTUA. He holds a Degree in Mechanical and Electrical Engineering with emphasis in industrial engineering from NTU Athens (1978) and a Ph.D. in Operations Management and O.R. from the University of Lancaster, England (1983). He has served as editor of various scientific journals, head of SIMOR, governmental committees and institutions, as long as coordinator of several national and EU funded projects. Among his varied academic interests, he recently focuses on strategic competitive management, computer-aided production management, logistics and the design and implementation of knowledge management systems.*

Preface

INTRODUCTION

The 21st century's unstable and highly competitive business environment is calling for a fundamental reassessment of the way enterprises are doing business. Modern business entities, more like world class competing athletes that are constantly asked to run faster, jump higher and throw further, are continuously stressed by both competitors and customers to produce more customized products in low cost and high quality (Ponis et al., 2008). Inevitably, pressures imposed by this new and demanding environment have mobilized enterprises into seriously rethinking the way they are conducting business towards more flexible and cost effective forms of organization. This management switch has been further amplified by the momentum created by the emergence of Information and Communication Technologies (ICT) and in particular the Internet which acted as a catalyst to strategic thinking and new business model development in all industries. In that context literature has documented a management shift from well-defined, stable enterprises having limited relationships with other companies and focusing on internal efficiency towards open enterprises (Browne & Zhang, 1999), collaborating and establishing inter-enterprise networks in order to achieve a sustainable position in the market and ensure their survival and business success.

One of the most prominent organizational paradigms of this new era is undoubtedly the Virtual Enterprise conceptualized for the first time in the works of Miles & Snow (1986) back in the mid eighties followed by a series of more elaborated approaches by Davidow and Malone (1992), Nagel & Dove al., (1993) and Byrne (1993) to name a few. Since then, the Virtual Enterprise concept has been enriched with numerous perspectives and parallaxes most of them dealing with the strength, duration and level of formalism of the relationship between the members of the Virtual Enterprise Network (Ponis et al., 2008), resulting in a number of alternative business models, such as the extended enterprise (Browne et al., 1995), smart organizations (Filos, 2005) and Supply Chains (Stevens, 1998). In this book, four core characteristics are identified (Ponis et al., 2008) that distinguish a pure VE from a real, traditional brick and mortar enterprise. These are:

- Temporary existence: A VE is formed in order to pursue specific business objectives. Once these are satisfied the network is dissolved and the partner enterprises are free to identify and exploit other business ventures and opportunities.
- Agility: The team formation of a VE is subject to change at any given point in time. New enterprises may join the formation and others may just as easily depart whenever it is deemed necessary by the enterprise coordinating the VE, henceforth the VE coordinator.
- Flexibility: During the VE life cycle, customer requirements may change. The enterprise alliance should be flexible enough to respond to the new market needs rapidly but still cost efficiently.

- Capability of market switching: A VE should be agile enough to respond to emerging needs in the market it is functioning in, and still be able to pursue business opportunities in other vertical industries.

Managing an enterprise network with the above qualities has evolved toward utilizing numerous new practices such as lean manufacturing, low cost country sourcing and outsourcing, co-manufacturing and supplier rationalization, all targeted to the objective of reducing waste and minimizing costs throughout the supply chain, in an end-to-end fashion. However, none of these practices comes without consequences especially to what risk vulnerability is concerned. Stretching the supply chain to absorb inefficiencies, though tempting and gainful, removes defense mechanisms and safe cushions resulting in increased vulnerability to threats produced by even the smallest or least expected cause of disruption. Being anorexic, enterprise networks fail to react effectively to these risk-imposing events resulting in reduced revenues and market share, inflated costs, budget failures, production mismatches and in the end of the day, dissatisfied partners and customers.

In that context, the initial editorial idea for this book was to develop a collective volume carefully including research papers dealing with Risk Management in Virtual Enterprise Networks by creatively transferring well established Supply Chain Risk Management principles. The reason for setting that objective was the absence of research efforts in that area in contradiction with Supply Chain Risk Management which has gained significant attention from numerous authors in the last ten years (Jüttner et al., 2003; Finch, 2004; Christopher, 2004; Tang, 2006; Waters, 2007). It is interesting to note that a quick search in Google Scholar for the exact term "Supply Chain Risk Management" returned almost 800 results while those produced by a similar search on the term "Virtual Enterprise Risk Management" or "Risk Management in Virtual Enterprises" can be counted with the fingers of the editor's two hands. Although this small experiment is of no scientific value, if coupled with the exhaustive literature review conducted by the editor during the process of developing the book proposal and call, which more or less produced the same results, one can justly argue that Managing Risk in Virtual Enterprise Networks is a research area at its infancy.

So, after setting up the scientific terrain, in mutual agreement with the publisher, the 'call for chapter proposals' process was initiated. In the course of that quest, a satisfying number of two page proposals were summoned for reviewing and at that point the core criteria for inviting the authors to submit a contribution at a later stage was the adherence with the book theme and the quality and edge of the proposed research. Having filtered the proposals at hand, twenty two of them were compliant with the book theme and seemed interesting enough to proceed to the next process step which was the submission of the full chapters.

Deciding which chapters fulfilled the criteria for inclusion in the book was the next step of the process. During that cumbersome effort it became apparent that although virtual enterprises have been and still are a 'hot' topic of academic research and discourse, dealing – at a satisfactory grade –with issues penetrating the SCM thick surface into reaching the VE core and its discrete characteristics in conjunction with Risk Management was not a trivial task. This quality was the prime discriminating factor for the proposals that were finally accepted for proceeding in submitting a full chapter for review. Inevitably, this led to a wide variety of papers each one presenting a different perspective of risk management in virtual enterprises or supply chains presented with VE characteristics. The vast dispersion of risk management approaches of the candidate chapters called for a decision regarding the desired structure of the book. Does the editor want to include less interesting chapters in favor of a better book structure or should he include the most intriguing chapters at hand and then try to figure out the best possible structure for his publication? Truthfully, what I decided and implemented in the course of this book's development is to select those chapters that were presented with an interesting perspective of the book theme even if this was not at the service of the book structure. Then a procedure of 'guiding' the authors towards improving their chapters by digging deeper on their research surfacing the virtual enterprise dimension wherever this was deficient, was initiated.

After almost four months of reviewing and enhancing the chapters with the invaluable help of the body of reviewers, a set of 14 long chapters (most of them over 10.000 words) dealing with risk management in enterprise network formations was selected for publication, with the majority of them residing in the intersection of Supply Chain Management, Virtual Enterprise Management and Risk Management. The common denominator of all chapters is the attempt to stress the importance of risk management in enterprises organized in networks followed by the presentation of the researcher (s) approach which most of the time emphasizes in a supply chain dimension and the challenges it imposes to networked enterprises in regard of risk management and mitigation. In that sense this book is organized in two sections: a) Concepts, Methods and Approaches including contributions of a more theoretical approach and b) Models and applications including chapters providing empirical validation of their research efforts in one or more real life case study.

BOOK STRUCTURE AND CONTRIBUTIONS

The first chapter of this section by Jan Husdal can very well serve as an introduction to the whole book since it attempts to bridge the gap between the concepts of Virtual Enterprise Networks and Supply Chains by building on literature findings drawn from both research areas. Jan Husdal, provides the reader with a novel perspective on VENs and in doing so a new VE taxonomy is introduced. After a fruitful discussion on risk management in both VEN and supply chains, Husdal turns to the ultimate objective of this chapter, which is to propose a conceptual framework for Risk Management in VENs with a Supply Chain Risk Management perspective and provide well argued evidence that VEN risk management can and should learn from existing supply chain risk management initiatives.

Brian Squire, in the next chapter, deals with the common characteristic of both discussed enterprise formations this being their network structure. Squire takes an exploratory look at the use of formal network measures to further understand the sources of risk in enterprises organized in networks. This exploratory chapter uncovers some of the network measures that may benefit risk identification and analysis within supply networks. In doing so, it follows a tradition within other fields that have used formal network measures to understand the robustness of their networks of interest.

Trust as the means of mitigating risks in Virtual Enterprise Networks is the core research issue of the next chapter by Burak Sari. According to the author, trust is the shared belief that network partners can depend on each other to achieve a common goal and constitutes a critical structural and cultural characteristic that influences the network's success and performance. Being such, the author argues that the need for a contextualized view of building and managing trust in VEs, is imperative and that establishing a trusted environment can significantly reduce the level of the perceived relational and performance risk from network members.

In the next chapter by Samir Dani, the dynamic quality of innovation is discussed in the context of Virtual Enterprise Networks which, by nature, provide an excellent opportunity for organizations to come together to pool their skills and competencies and create innovation within their supply chains. In this chapter, it is argued that innovation, apart from being a critical issue for maintaining competitive advantage, is also an important capability to manage/ mitigate risks especially when applied to communications, technology and legal areas. To support his argument, the author proposes a risk management framework for Virtual Enterprise Networks based on innovation and the effective feed of its results back to the risk management process.

Knowledge is a resource of prime value for all organizations, a reality further amplified in the case of Virtual Enterprise Networks. In that context, Ettore Bolisani provides, with his chapter, a knowledge-based view of VENs and attempts an analysis and classification of the possible sources of risk associated to the management of knowledge in a Virtual Enterprise Network. For validating his arguments, the author utilizes a real life example drawn from the IT Software industry and based on it he argues that the cognitive management of a successful VEN raises a number of risk sources and risk factors that can be related to the general nature of knowledge as economic resource and to the particular aspects of Knowledge Management in a VEN. Finally, the author provides the reader with a set of guides and approaches to support the successful management of the risk categories previously identified.

It is true that IT Management in a Virtual Enterprise Network is asked to achieve the seemingly impossible, which is to simultaneously open and protect enterprise information effectively, balancing risks with opportunities, and at the same time efficiently satisfying the VE networks' particular demands. In the next chapter, Mohammad Shalan aims to provide a comprehensive in depth analysis of risks and issues associated with the IT aspects of Virtual Enterprise Networks (VENs) from technical and procedural point of view and to prescribe specific guidelines to mitigate the effects of the identified and analyzed risks, processes and consequences. Finally, the author proposes an IT risk governance framework addressing IT risks in the context of a Virtual Enterprise Network.

Simulation is an established technique for the analysis of traditional supply chain and logistics systems. In that sense, the next two chapters attempt to describe the usefulness and applicability of the simulation tool in risk and disruptive events' modeling and in understanding the impact of such fluctuations on the performance of the whole network. In her Chapter, Ila Manuj, presents a simulation model development process for modeling disruptions and other crises events in global virtual enterprise networks and supports her proposed methodology by providing the reader with an indicative modeling example. Finally, the author presents a framework for managers and researchers to better apply and gain from the strength of simulation modeling, identifies several common pitfalls to avoid during the process, and compiles extensive references for readers who want to further their knowledge in this specific area. On the other hand, in their chapter Klimov et al., present a framework of simulation-based supply chain risk analysis. The proposed framework provides a risk measurement system, which is based on the supply chain performance evaluation. In this way, many risky events or unexpected disruptions within supply chains can be analyzed in a single system. To support their framework, the authors display a simulation example in an attempt to demonstrate possible experiments which can be performed within the context of supply chain risk analysis and the support of simulation.

Section 2 of this book entitled "Models and applications" presents a series of chapters providing different perspectives of risk management in Virtual Enterprise Networks. Still, all the chapters of this section share a common characteristic which is the existence of empirical research and the validation of their research by its application on more than one case company of the same or different industrial sector.

In the first chapter of this section, Omera Khan and Alessandro Creazza, based on a systematic and structured literature review, highlight the importance of keeping product design at the centre of the entire business process and managing it concurrently with the supply chain, utilizing their suggested 4C approach. Next, the authors validate their research findings through a cross-industry study of three case companies. The case studies revealed how companies deal with the alignment of product design and the supply chain and how they confront relevant challenges such as supply chain risk management and responsiveness. The authors conclude by stating that product design is a crucial factor in determining supply chain and business performance and propose a roadmap towards the design-centric organization, based on five transformation processes.

The issue of flexibility and the determination of its effects on risk mitigation for supply networks are discussed in the next chapter by María Jesús Sáenz, Maria Pilar Lambán and Eva Navarro. After presenting the basic concepts and features of flexible companies the authors introduce a conceptual framework including a set of best practices which enable flexibility value to be created in the context of an inter-organizational network. In that context, special focus is put on uncertainties and risks companies –members of a supply network- face when striving to reach a certain degree of flexibility. Finally, the authors support their research findings with an empirical analysis of how these practices are implemented in 57 companies of the food and beverage sector.

Outsourcing adds complexity to the business system it is applied and thus propagates new risks and enhances or transforms older ones as a result of the differentiated business model. In the next chapter by me and Epaminondas Koronis the knowledge-related risks of outsourcing are studied. In doing that, the authors first identify and taxonomize the risk sources of the outsourcing initiative, pinpoint the related threats and propose mitigating actions. Then, the authors turn their focus on knowledge exchanges during outsourcing and introduce the concept of "vicious cycle" suggesting that outsourcing if not managed successfully eventually leads to the addiction of the organization to "buy" expertise and knowledge in spite of creating it. The authors validate their findings through a case study of four companies drawn from the pharmaceutical industry.

In the next chapter by Konstantinos Kirytopoulos, Dimitra Voulgaridou and Vrassidas Leopoulos clusters, as a sophisticated form of a Virtual Enterprise Network, are studied. After a thorough literature review on clusters that results in a comparison table with Virtual Enterprise Networks the authors introduce a decision support framework based on the ANP-BOCR model. The application of the proposed framework is focused on the supplier selection process which is critical for clusters where its members not only cooperate but also compete. The ultimate objective of the authors approach is to enable the decision maker to visualize the impact of various conflicting criteria in the final outcome and document the evaluation results in such way that they can be communicated to various stakeholders. To support the validity of their research efforts the authors apply the proposed model in a cluster of the Greek Para-pharmaceutical industry.

An interesting approach towards risk management in Virtual Enterprise Networks, based on the establishment of a network-wide Internal Audit function is introduced in the next chapter by Nikolaos Panayiotou, Stylianos Oikonomitsios, Christina Athanasiadou and Sotiris Gayialis. The authors' approach is supported by a set of specific templates connected with the existing organizational and inter-organizational processes and activities and by an internal audit oriented enterprise modeling tool for risk assessment and control identification. The elaborated toolset assists business process improvement and quality enhancement in the enterprise network and supports the extended role of Internal Audit as a facilitator of change towards the network's business objectives. Finally the authors present their findings from the application of their approach in a virtual enterprise network operating in the electronics sector.

The electronics sector is the application test bed for the research efforts presented in the next and last chapter of this book by Christos Manolarakis, Ioannis Christou and Gregory Yovanof. The authors attempt to capture market dynamics and provide Virtual Enterprise Network managers with a new insight on consumer segmentation regarding a specific product type which will help them avoid risks associated with changing pricing strategies and compute near-optimal counter-strategies in case of price-wars initiated by opponents (other virtual enterprises or single companies). The authors propose an Agent Based Modeling tool that allows the description and simulation of the evolution or interactions of social structures and approaches consumer behavior under the perspective of their perception for consumer products. In that sense, the aforementioned tool can potentially support risk management in purchasing and production planning and to decisions associated with the introduction of new products by a Virtual Enterprise Network in an existing market.

AIM OF THE BOOK AND TARGET AUDIENCE

As already indicated in the first section of this preface, managing Risks in Virtual Enterprise Networks is a rather underexplored and unstructured scientific area. While this stands as an impediment for researchers and practitioners that aim to study the field, it also provides an increased degree of freedom in the development of new concepts, models, methodologies etc. The overall objective of this book is to contribute to activities that will result in an increased awareness on the Risk Management discipline, its usefulness and importance, in the context of contemporary enterprise formations such as Virtual Enterprise Networks by providing a set of methods, approaches and models that can guide existing research efforts or ignite new ones by introducing concepts and perspectives not previously been studied by academicians all over the world. In that sense, this book is neither a textbook nor an encyclopedia but rather a first attempt to establish a first wave of research efforts targeting an overlooked scientific area. Hopefully, this book including more than a thousand scientific references will establish the necessary background for further research in the field, attract interest and create challenges for both researchers and practitioners, thus initiating a broad academic discourse. In that sense, this book aspires to set a point-of-reference for scholars and researchers in the fields of Virtual Enterprises and Supply Chain Management who are interested in studying the Risk Management dimension in a cross-disciplinary fashion by applying new ideas and synthetic thinking in already well established concepts. Furthermore, the reader-friendly nature of this book aims to attract both graduate and post-graduate students who will hopefully consider it as a valuable reference resource.

REFERENCES

Browne, J., Sackett, P. J., & Wortmann, J. C. (1995). Future manufacturing systems - towards the extended enterprise. *Computers in Industry*, *25*, 235-54.

Browne & Zhang (1999). Extended and Virtual Enterprises-similarities and differences. *International Journal of Agile Management Systems*, *1*(1), 30-36.

Byrne, J. (1993). The virtual corporation. *Business Week*, 36–41.

Christopher, M. (2004). Creating resilient supply chains. *Logistics Europe*, 14-21.

Davidow, W. H., & Malone M. S. (1992). *The Virtual Corporation*. New York: Harper Business.

Filos, E. (2005). Virtuality and the future of organisations. In Putnik G. & Cunha M.M. (Ed.), *Virtual enterprise integration: Technological and organizational perspectives*. Hershey, PA: Idea Group Publishing.

Finch, P., (2004). Supply Chain Risk Management, *Supply Chain Management: An International Journal*, *9*(2), 183-196.

Jüttner, U., Peck, H., & Christopher, M. (2003). Supply chain risk management: outlining an agenda for future research. *International Journal of Logistics Research and Applications*, *6*(4), 197-210.

Miles, R., & Snow, C. (1986). Organizations: New concepts for new forms. *California Management Review*, *28*(2), 68-73.

Nagel, R., & Dove, R. (1993). *21st century Manufacturing Enterprise Strategy*. Bethlehem, PA: Iacocca Institute, Lehigh University.

Ponis, S. T., Vagenas, G., & I. P. Tatsiopoulos (n.d.). Knowledge Management in Virtual Enterprises: Supporting Frameworks and Enabling Web Technologies. In Bolissani E. (ed), *Building the Knowledge Society on the Internet: Sharing and Exchanging Knowledge in Networked Environments*. Hershey, PA: Information Science Reference.

Stevens, J. (1998). Integrating the supply chain. *International Journal of Physical Distribution and Materials Management*, *13*(1), 37-56.

Tang, C. S. (2006). Perspectives in Supply Chain Risk Management. *International Journal of Production Economics, 103*, 451-488.

Waters, D. (2007). *Supply Chain Risk Management: Vulnerability and Resilience in Logistics*, London: Kogan Page.

Acknowledgment

Editing a book is a cumbersome, effortful and time consuming process that spans from the initial concept and its transformation to a book proposal to the final delivery of the manuscript and the related with the chapters paperwork. Having these qualities, book editing can never become a "one man show", on the contrary team work and collaboration with a large number of individuals is the most critical issue in a book project.

Therefore, I would like to acknowledge the support of all the people participated in the preparation of this book, starting from the IGI Global personnel whose contribution throughout the project lifecycle has been invaluable. Special thanks goes to Ms. Christine Bufton my editorial assistant who was always there on time when I needed guidance or feedback from the publisher.

I would like to thank the body of reviewers for their constructive and fruitful comments that supported the authors of the accepted chapters, and as I would like to think, those of chapters rejected as well. Special thanks go to the chapter authors that also served as reviewers of contributions by other authors. They all accepted the extra work with pleasure and I thank them for that.

I also want to thank the members of the Executive Advisory Board for their willingness to participate in this project proving their faith in this book, for their constructive comments during the reviewing process and for their feedback regarding the final structure of this book.

Finally, I would like to thank all contributing authors for trusting me with their work; it means a lot to me. Last but not least, I wholeheartedly thank all the people close to me that I 'tortured' for over one year but they still kept providing me with their patience and support, whenever I needed it.

Stavros Ponis
Editor

Section 1
Concepts, Methods and Approaches

Chapter 1
A Conceptual Framework for Risk and Vulnerability in Virtual Enterprise Networks

Jan Husdal
Molde Research Institute, Norway

ABSTRACT

Is managing risk in Virtual Enterprise Networks different from managing risk in supply chains? It is not unusual for firms in a supply chain to come together and act as a virtual enterprise network (VEN) and the supply chains of today's globalized and outsourced business environment exhibit many VEN-like features. Looking at VEN risk management from the perspective of supply chain risk management, current ideas on VENs will serve as a base onto which ideas on supply chain risk will be transposed. Many concepts related to supply chain risk will be explored and related to their possible VEN counterparts: risk, vulnerability, robustness, flexibility, resilience and business continuity. Conceptual in its approach and drawing from other areas of research, this chapter introduces four distinct groups of VENS, namely Constrained, Directed, Limited and Free VEN, and concludes that VEN risk management can and should learn from supply chain risk management.

INTRODUCTION

Today's unstable and highly competitive business environment has created a shift in how enterprises are established and managed. Past "traditional" enterprises are increasingly replaced by new "virtual" enterprises, forming temporary networks of independent companies or Virtual Enterprise Networks (VENs) that share skills, costs and access

to each other's market. While this kind of business formation is not without risks, managing risk in VENs is a rather underexplored and unstructured scientific area.

Driven by the advent of globally available skills and operational excellence (Sengupta, 2008) it is not unusual for firms in a supply chain to come together and act as a VEN, and it is from this perspective that the subject of risk management in a VEN will be explored. The purpose of the chapter is to approach the realm of VEN risk management from a

DOI: 10.4018/978-1-61520-607-0.ch001

supply chain risk management (SCRM) perspective, where ideas from the current literature on supply chain risk, supply chain vulnerability and supply chain disruptions in traditional enterprises will be linked to some of the prevailing ideas of how to ideally structure and organize a VEN. Essentially, current ideas on VENs, along the lines of Thompson (2008a), will serve as a base onto which traditional ideas on supply chain risk will be transposed.

Thus, the idea of this chapter is to serve as a descriptive rather than prescriptive concept or framework for how a VEN is exposed to risk and furthermore to explore how a VEN can deal with potential risks, using SCRM practices applied to a VEN environment.

BACKGROUND

It has been more than 15 years since the shape of today's virtual enterprise networks began to emerge when Snow, Miles, Coleman, & Henry (1992) identified 3 types of networks: 1) internal, 2) stable and 3) dynamic, the latter composed of "lead firms who identify new opportunities and then assemble a network of complementary firms that meet the market needs" (Child, Faulkner, & Tallman, 2005a,). From this starting point, the definition of what constitutes a virtual enterprise network, in literature, varies considerably.

Virtual Enterprises: A Special Form of Cooperative Strategy

Traditional enterprises can enter into various forms of cooperation without necessarily establishing what is called a VEN. Child et al. (2005a) describe six reasons why firms seek to establish cooperative networks: 1) certainty – by developing relationships with mutual solidarity, 2) flexibility – by being able to quickly allocate a range of resources, 3) capacity – by "outsourcing" work to other network members, 4) speed – by being able

to quickly respond to a wide range of business opportunities, 5) skills and competence – by gaining access to resources other than one's own, and 6) intelligence – by sharing market information.

Placing cooperative networks on a scale, going from independent to integrated, Child et al., describe five degrees of networks: 1) Equal-Partner Network, 2) Unilateral Agreements, 3) Dominated Network, 4) Virtual Corporation, and 5) Strategic Alliance. The virtual corporation is described as "a loosely coupled enterprise in which the parts are held together through the medium of sophisticated information technology packages". Interestingly, they note that the virtual corporation may be "a transitional stage of company development on the path to complete hierarchy", a statement that is somewhat contradictory to Nolan & Croson (1995), who foresaw networks emerging as the organizational forms of the future, replacing and transforming the traditional pyramid-shaped hierarchical organization.

The Concept of Virtual Enterprises in the Past

In the late 1980s the term 'virtual corporation' began to appear for the first time. In the beginning, "virtual" referred to invisible or virtual links between companies in the form of information and communication technology, aka ICT or computers. Virtual corporations were technology-driven corporations, using and sharing the same information systems:

The virtual corporation is a temporary network of independent companies – suppliers, customers, even erstwhile rivals – linked by information technology to share skills, costs, and access to one another's markets (Byrne, 1993).

Davidow and Malone (1993) describe virtual corporations as being able to apprehend customer needs and specifications and create new products instantaneously or on-the-fly, thus constantly reinventing themselves to accommodate or respond to the market fluctuations:

To the outside observer it will appear almost edgeless with permeable and constantly changing interfaces between company, supplier and customers [...] with traditional offices, departments and operating divisions constantly reforming according to need. Job responsibilities will regularly shift, as will lines of authority. (Davidow and Malone, 1993).

Goranson (1993) describes a "virtual enterprise (VE)" as "a temporary aggregation of core competencies and associated resources collaborating to address a specific situation, presumed to be a business opportunity". Goranson goes on to describe four different kinds of aggregations or VEs:

- An aggregation of firms formed in response to an opportunity
- A pre-existing aggregation of core competencies seeking new opportunities
- An existing supplier chain, responding to market needs
- A bidding consortium of conventional businesses acting as one

What these kinds of VEs have in common is that they are all designed for a certain purpose or certain business opportunity. The common denominator is the existence of a business opportunity of mutual interest to all parties involved, or a business opportunity that cannot be realized without forming said aggregations. In some cases the collaboration will end when the business opportunity has been fulfilled, in other cases it will continue.

Diverging from Goranson (1993), Bickhoff et al. (2003) depict a different set of four basic types of virtual corporations, all strongly linked by ICT in order to fulfill their business goals: 1) a cooperation among partners, governed by a central corporation, with a centralized hierarchical structure, 2) a cooperation among partners, governed by a one corporation offering central services to its partners, but with the same equal rights as the other partners, 3) a virtual corporation with an independent coordinator, a so called *third party institution* offering central services, and 4) a virtual corporation with a common coordination of all partners, the idealistic type of a virtual corporation with no central control.

While Goranson (1993) is concerned with the purpose of a VEN and differentiates them accordingly, Bickhoff et al. (2003) seems more concerned with *management* and *structure*, similar to the definition of a dynamic network in Snow et al. (1992). This distinction will become important later in this chapter.

The Concept of Virtual Enterprises Today

Although definitions and descriptions of virtual enterprises vary, as noted by Cunha & Putnik, (2006), the intensive use of ICT is a common feature that goes further than other features in making a virtual enterprise different from a more traditional cooperation between enterprises. As Child, Faulkner & Tallman (2005a) put it,

The virtual corporation [...] places its emphasis not primarily on how two or more firms can work together to their mutual advantage, but on how one firm can be created with flexible boundaries and ownership aided by the facilities provided by electronic data exchange and communication (Child et al., 2005a).

Thompson (2008a) employs a perhaps more generalized view, where he sees the VEN as a business tool that can connect individual enterprises into peer networks where appropriate collaboration practices and technologies enable them to have the same capabilities and competitive advantage as large corporations, and his definition will be used as the bedrock assumption for what a VEN is for the remainder of this chapter:

A Virtual Enterprise Network (VEN) is a voluntary and dynamic community of Small And Medium Enterprises that commit to working together for a set period of time, to collectively seek opportunities to participate in collaborative projects of mutual business interest. (Thompson, 2008a)

Thompson deviates thus from the focus on ICT as the binding glue of a virtual corporation and focuses on the organizational and co-operational characteristics of a VEN; a VEN is thus a time-limited and opportunity-limited construct for individual firms to cooperate in. A VEN is a collection of smaller firms that outwardly act as one while retaining their individual corporate identity. A VEN, as defined by Thompson, and as used in this chapter, is not a (primarily) *vertically integrated supply chain* in a *distributed* manufacturing or industrial environment, but rather a *laterally integrated network* of businesses.

Thompson even goes as far as saying that small enterprises alone can only take on other small enterprises; small enterprises in a VEN can take on large corporations. What this means is that small enterprises in a VEN can extend their market reach beyond their individually reachable core market; what this also means is that the VEN as a whole is exposed to larger risks than each small enterprise is exposed to individually. However, as we shall see, the resources available to a VEN in managing those risks are greater than they are for a large traditional enterprise.

Risks in Virtual Enterprises

What is clear from the aforementioned definitions is that a VEN is a time-limited structure; it has a set life-cycle, i.e. the duration of a project or opportunity in which the participating enterprises partake. This life cycle perspective poses certain challenges in how to manage VEN risks, since

the risks may change from project to project or opportunity to opportunity.

While in a traditional enterprise setting the overall risk exposure may have a more static nature even in the most dynamic business environment, in a virtual enterprise network the risks themselves are highly dynamic because of the shifting players within the network. A VEN is often described as the best of everything, and consequently, the VEN risk management must also be the best of everything, and in the case of this chapter, VEN risk management ought to be the best of everything supply chain risk management.

The question is, can traditional supply chain risk management assist in VEN risk management? In answering this, current ideas on how to establish, assess and develop a VEN, as exemplified by Thompson and Goranson and others will be used throughout this chapter as a backdrop for investigating risks in a VEN, as seen from a supply chain perspective. How does traditional supply chain risk management apply to a VEN, and how can VEN risk management be translated into VEN management in general?

FUNDAMENTALS OF A VEN

A VEN is a network of a number of member enterprises and their individual competencies. These two dimensions, number of members, and individual competencies or skills can be used to set up a classification scheme for VENs.

Four Basic Compositions of a VEN

One of the foremost abilities of a VEN is its ability to quickly react to change and adapt to new opportunities. According to Goranson (1992), this ability to change works along two dimensions: 1) the number or "types of change" an organization is able to undergo and 2) the "degree of change" an organization is able to undergo. The former he calls "scope", the latter he calls "robustness". The

Figure 1. Categorization of VENs based on number of members and individual member skills

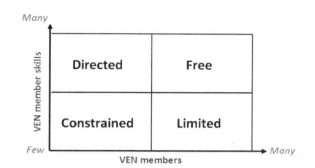

more robust an enterprise is, the more radical a change it can gracefully address.

In a VEN, each member brings with it the types of change and degree of change it can address on its own, individually contributing to the whole picture of overall business opportunities a VEN can participate in. The composition of a VEN as to types of change and degree of change is a determining factor in whether it will be successful or not; it is also a determining factor in the VENs degree of risk exposure.

A VEN consists of members and their individual skills. Some VENs are formed in response to a possible business opportunity, some may already exist as a result of a past business opportunity, some may be formed with the prospect of entering new opportunities, although no opportunities may exist at the present. Even though a VEN can have many members, there are maybe few differences in individual skills, which in turn may not open up too many different business opportunities. Conversely, a VEN can have few members with many individual skills; this will open up more diverse business opportunities, but potentially exhaust the VEN because of the overall work strain that is put on the few VEN members that possess the required skills by this business opportunity. For example, if a VEN wants to cater towards biomedical research, VEN members that possess innovation and creativity, along with laboratory facilities will likely be of

higher importance than perhaps VEN members with marketing skills. However, a VEN member with marketing skills can be potentially beneficial in a later business opportunity or in a later stage of the aforementioned biomedical enterprise.

The notion of skills in the VEN versus number of members in the VEN leads to the concept of four basic VEN compositions, as illustrated in Figure 1:

- Constrained
- Limited
- Directed
- Free

The concept is analogous to a similar concept used by Husdal (2009), who employed it to categorize supply chains based on the number of transportation modes and links within each mode. The more modes there are or the more links there are, the more diverse a transportation network is. Similarly, a VEN's outreach in terms of potential business opportunities is determined by the number of members and number of individual skills or competencies for each member (or vice versa: Number of member skills or competencies and number of individual members that possess this skill or competence)

In a *constrained* VEN there are only few members with few skills which the VEN has to depend on, it is therefore constrained in its scope. A VEN with many members, but with a small collective skill set can be seen as a *limited* VEN, because of the limited set of opportunities it can exploit despite the large number of its members. A VEN with few members, but with a wide range of individual skills can be seen as a *directed* VEN since it is highly dependent on or directed towards these members when seeking business opportunities. The ideal or *free* VEN is a VEN that has many members with a wide range of collective skills.

A constrained VEN can be seen as a worst-case scenario for a VEN, while a free VEN can be seen as the ideal scenario for a VEN. A constrained VEN can grow in three directions, it can add members or add skills, or ideally, both.

Admittedly, this may be seem like a simplistic concept, and obviously not all skills are created equal; vis-à-vis a business opportunity some skills will be of higher importance than others, and it is not so much the number of skills per se that counts.

Another note that must be made about Figure 1 is that, obviously, there is a lower and upper limit as to the number of VEN members. Thompson (2009) advocates no less than 10 and no more than 30 members for a VEN to function properly and to gain any synergy. It is not simply adding members and skills; it is adding the right members with the right skills. The different skills will also determine the different roles of the VEN members, as explained in the next section.

A similar argument as in Figure 1 can be made in relation to Goranson's definition of agility, and we can construct the same categorization using types of change and degrees of change, replacing *member skills* with *degrees of change* and the *number of VEN members* with *types of change*. The underlying assumption is that more members bring more competencies into the VEN and thus, more types of change and different opportunities are possible to the VEN. At the same time, each VEN member has a certain set of competencies, which determine the degree of change that is possible from opportunity to opportunity for each VEN member individually, and for the VEN as a whole.

In assessing the capabilities of a VEN, Thompson (2008a) suggests what he calls the "Ven Capability Heatmap Technique" in order to establish a VEN's collective capabilities vis-à-vis a business opportunity (pp. 142-144). This technique establishes a matrix of capability types and capability areas, with "Hot", "Warm", "Cool" and "Ice" zones, depending on the collective sum of each VEN member's type and area of capabilities. The Heatmap aims to be a strategic discussion starter, identifying areas where the network is strong or weak, where it may need new members, and where it needs to focus its efforts.

To some degree, Thompson's zones correspond to quadrants of Figure 1 above, where the "Hot" zone can be compared to the "Free" quadrant and the "Ice" zone compares to the "Constrained" quadrant.

Although rather crude in differentiation, these four different types of VENs possess different qualities, and consequently, require different risk management strategies.

Roles in a VEN

In addition to satisfying skill requirements, VEN members must also play specific organizational roles. Thompson (2008a) describes three basic roles that VEN members can take vis-à-vis a business opportunity: *lead*, (actively) *participate* or (passively) *contribute* (Thompson, 2008a). This is what Davidow and Malone (1993) mean when they say that "Job responsibilities will regularly shift, as will lines of authority". Figure 3 visualizes this concept. Here, ten VEN members out of 15 are part of three projects or business opportunities, with each member having same or different roles in the different projects, based on the individual set of skills a VEN member brings into the VEN.

In the example of Figure 2, the leader of Project 2 is also a participant in Project 1 and a

Figure 2. Roles in a VEN

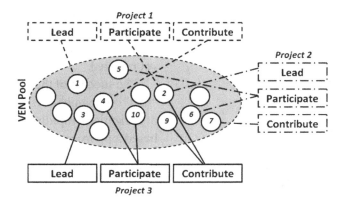

contributor in Project 3. The success of a VEN hinges on having enough VEN members that can play these roles in the various business opportunities the VEN may want to engage in. Not having enough flexibility would already make this VEN a constrained VEN, or at best a directed VEN that is highly dependent on few selected key members to provide the main thrust in fulfilling the business opportunities. Although this may not be of much concern in the early stages of VEN formation, such a directed or selected configuration of VEN members could potentially be detrimental to VEN survival as time progresses.

FROM A SUPPLY CHAIN TO A VEN

One way of looking at a VEN risk from a supply chain risk perspective is to convert a traditional supply chain to a VEN. Gunasekaran & Ngai

(2004) provide an excellent example, where the experiences of a near-VEN supply-chain are discussed with reference to the strategies, methods and technologies of a traditional supply-chain, but they do not mention supply chain risks. Hence, a new model is needed, and this chapter intends to develop such a model.

A traditional supply chain in its simplest form consists of a manufacturer, a supplier, and a customer. Mimicking the flow of goods and materials through the chain when assessing different parts of the supply chain, the manufacturer is often called the "focal" company, the supplier or supply-side is often seen as being upstream, while the customer or demand-side is seen as being downstream. The suppliers and customers on either side can be further structured into 1st, 2nd, 3rd and so on tiers (Harrison & Hoek, 2008). This creates a linear structure or chain, although the term supply network is probably more appropriate

Figure 3. A VEN seen from a traditional supply chain perspective

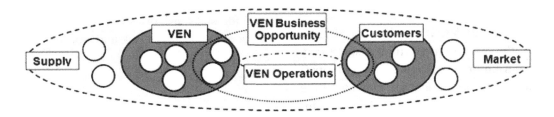

Figure 4. Four basic risk management strategies

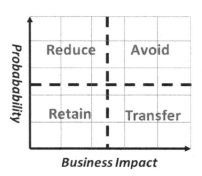

than supply chain in most cases in today's modern, globalized and interlinked business world.

Harland, Brenchley & Walker (2003) describe three different stages in the evolution of supply chains, the *In-house* model of the 1980s, the *Focused* model of the 1990s, and the *Virtual* model of today, where many supply activities are now completely outsourced and where the once core activity of manufacturing has been outsourced to contract manufacturers. Albeit not a full VEN, Harland's virtual model bears many of a VEN's hallmark signs, where supply networks become ever more complex, dynamic and fast-changing webs of relationships.

The traditional linear chain is not easily converted to a VEN perspective; nonetheless, an attempt is made in Figure 4, where a supply chain perspective has been replaced by a VEN perspective. The center of the VEN realm is made up of a VEN project or business opportunity, in this case linking two VEN members with one VEN customer, the linkage illustrated as VEN operations or VEN processes. The VEN itself is formed as a way to approach a set of certain business opportunities, here marked by a set of customers. Not all VEN members participate actively in the business opportunity; some may be mere contributors as in Figure 3, or participating in other projects or not at all. Outside of the VEN on the supply side are VEN member sup-

pliers or business contacts or other potential but not yet accredited VEN members. The market or demand side of the VEN is where we find other potential customers or business opportunities not yet realized.

The success of the VEN is tied to the ability of "real" companies (VEN members) to form virtual organizations rapidly to meet an emerging time-based opportunity (Goldman, 1995, p. 220). It must accommodate the likelihood that a company will be member of several virtual organizations (business opportunities) at the same time and will have a broad range of current and future partners. This implies that each VEN member will also be exposed to a broad range of risks that may or may not change from project to project.

FROM SUPPLY CHAIN RISK TO VEN RISK

Risk is an ambiguous concept, therefore there are many definitions of risk, depending on their specific application and on their situational context. One of the most common meanings is that of risk as a threat or danger. In addition, risk often implies the probability of a negative outcome. Harland, Brenchley & Walker (2003) define risk (R) as the product of the probability (P) of a loss (loss) and the significance or impact (I) of the loss, related to an event n (n):

$$R_n = P(loss)_n \times I(loss)_n$$

Technically speaking though, risk per se has neither a positive nor a negative value and is perhaps more related to uncertainty, where eventualities can be either beneficial or adverse. In order to understand risk in a VEN it is necessary to first look at the basics of risk and risk management.

The Risk Concept

One of the more interesting and also commonly used risk definitions is the one found in Kaplan (1997), later championed by Paulsson (2007). This definition splits the concept of risk into three different elements, together called *a triplet*. Each triplet identifies a risk *scenario*, involving a source, a likelihood and an impact:

- What can happen and what is the cause?
- How likely is it that it will happen?
- If it does happen, what are the consequences?

A risk can be seen as incompletely described unless all three elements are in place. An untrained individual or business entity often stops short after the first, or maybe the second question, without fully considering the third. In risk management, addressing the impacts is an important issue, which is why the consequences need to be considered along with the likelihood and source of risk.

Business Risks

Business risks, by their own nature, are as diverse as businesses are diverse and can arise from a number of external and internal sources. O'Hehir (2007), identifies five core groups of risks that a business has to face, while underlining that risks are dynamic and not mutually exclusive; there is no crisp borderline between the risk groups:

- Strategic
- Financial
- Operational
- Commercial
- Technical

Strategic Risk is related to the uncertainty of plans failing or succeeding. Financial Risk is the uncertainty of financial controls failing or succeeding, Operational Risk is the risk of human error or staff failing to perform. Commercial Risk is the risk of business relationships failing. Technical risk is the risk of physical assets failing or being damaged. This grouping of risks implies that risks have a long-term, forward-looking element (strategic risk) as well as a short-term, immediate element (operational risk).

While the above approach views risks from the point of business operations perspective, a different view is employed by Christopher & Peck (2004), building on Mason-Jones & Towill (1998), who summarize enterprise-wide risk into three groups, looking at where the risk source resides:

- Externally-driven or environmental risk
- Internally-driven or process risk
- Decision-driven or information risk

Externally-driven or environmental risks are related to external factors that can affect a firm's performance, such as competitors, customers, and regulations and technological advances. Internally-driven or process risks are related to manufacturing or production, operations and processing. Decision-driven or information risks are related to insufficient or erroneous decision support, along with contractual or legal issues.

Basic Risk Management

Risk reflects both the range of possible outcomes and the probabilities for each of the outcomes. Christopher (2005) advocates establishing a risk profile, with the purpose to establish where the greatest vulnerabilities lie and where the "greatest" risks are, based on the view that risk is the product of probability and impact.

A commonly used method for risk analysis is to plot unforeseen or unwanted events in a so-called risk matrix. The matrix axes can be divided qualitatively, where probabilities and impacts are subjective values, e.g. low/high and minor/major, or quantitatively, where probabilities and impacts are objective values, e.g. incident frequency and cost in monetary units.

The simplest form of risk management then uses this matrix to discern four possible management strategies (DeLoach, 2000), which can be illustrated using Figure 4.

- Avoid, in case of high probability/high impact
- Transfer, in case of high probability/low impact
- Reduce, in case of low probability/high impact
- Accept or Retain, in case of low probability/low impact

Avoid-risks are risks that no business can survive in the long run, if left unattended. That is why these risks need to be avoided. Transfer-risks are not as critical as the aforementioned, but still warrant attention due to their potential disastrous impacts. Transfer means pooling or sharing risks, and insurance is one central element here, since this transfers the risk to the insurer. Reduce-risks often relate to day-to-day issues and minor operational events, and although perhaps insignificant on their own, the aggregate impact of these risks can eventually compromise overall operational efficiency. Thus, the best way to deal with such risks is to reduce their likelihood, usually by means of "inspect and correct" (DeLoach, 2000).

Supply Chain Risk

Supply Chain Management has always perceived risk and uncertainty as important issues, although it is particularly in recent years that supply chain risk management has gained an increasing popularity as a separate field of study, even outside academic journals, as seen in Sheffi (2005), Christopher (2005) and Walters (2007).

However, despite the growing interest, or maybe because of it, different authors tend to address different types of supply chain risks and develop different classifications or taxonomies of risk. In a review of 208 journal articles on supply chain risk management published from 2000 to 2007, Vanany, Zailani & Pujawan (2009) classified the articles according to 15 industry sectors, 5 units of analysis, 3 types of risks and 4 stages of risk management, and unsurprisingly, did not find a consistent definition of supply chain risk. What this classification indicates, then, is that depending on your angle of approach, you are likely to come up with very different definitions of supply chain risk. Looking at VEN risk from the viewpoint of supply chain risk it seems clear that VEN risk too will not have one definition, but will depend on the individual VEN itself and the different VEN business opportunities that are explored in the VEN.

A business is exposed to risk by a potentially unlimited number of factors, which is perhaps one of the reasons why the supply chain risk literature seems inconsistent (Vanany et al.,2009). However, not all factors may have a significant impact, and the term risk driver is often used to distinguish important factors or risk sources from unimportant factors or sources (Jütner, Peck & Christopher, 2003). The notion of risk sources and drivers, as with risk itself, may depend on the user and the context. While the interest rate may be a driving factor vis-à-vis financial risk (risk source), a company's loan exposure could be a driving factor vis-à-vis changes in interest rate (risk source). Nonetheless, it is important to keep these two terms, sources and drivers, separated. Jütner et al. (2003) describe supply chain risk as a 4-fold construct:

- Risk sources
- Consequences of the risk sources
- Risk drivers that turn risks into consequences
- Strategies to address the risks

In addressing the risk, they identify four separate risk mitigating strategies: 1) Avoidance,

Figure 5. Risk management strategies need to be mitigative and contingent

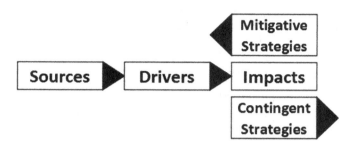

2) Control, 3) Co-Operation and 4) Flexibility. Following the view of Asbjørnslett (2008), flexibility can be both mitigative and contingent, although, the latter form of flexibility is what Goranson (1993) prefers to call agility rather than flexibility. Risk addressing strategies ought to be differentiated into mitigative strategies (risk exposure reducing) and contingent strategies (risk impact reducing). Figure 5 illustrates this concept, where mitigative strategies address drivers, while contingent strategies address impacts.

Christopher & Peck (2004) distinguish between three risk perspectives and five risk types, namely 1) Internal to the focal firm: a) Process risk and b) Control risk, 2) External to the focal firm: c) Supply risk and d) Demand risk, and 3) External to the supply chain: e) Environmental risks. Process risks relate to operations and manufacturing, while control risks relate to rules and systems governing the organization. Supply risks relate to the upstream flow of incoming supplies, while demand risks relate to downstream disruptions in outgoing product flows or incoming financial flows. Environmental risks relate to the outside world, regulatory or political changes, natural hazards or other disasters.

Actually, there is a fourth perspective, where both firm-internal and firm-external risks are contained: Internal to the supply chain (Process, Control, Supply and Demand). This is picked up by Jütner et al. (2003), where risks are divided into three groups: 1) Organizational Risk Sources, 2) Network Risk Sources, and 3) Environmental

sources. Here the network risk sources also contain the organizational risks related to each member in the supply chain or network. Both views (Jütner et al., 2003; Christopher & Peck, 2004) are summarized in Table 1.

It is noteworthy that the supply chain council (SCC), a global non-profit consortium, now has implemented supply chain risk into their SCOR model (Morrow, Wilkerson, & Davey, 2009). The SCOR reference model is a widely accepted framework for evaluating and comparing supply chain activities and their performance, and the SCOR supply chain risk framework uses the same four perspectives that are found in Jütner et al. (2003) and Christopher and Peck (2004), slightly renamed: 1) Internal-facing, 2) Customer-facing and 3) Supply-facing and 4) Environment-facing.

VEN Risk

One could argue that it is possible to transfer the views of Christopher & Peck (2004) into a VEN context by replacing *focal firm* with *VEN member* and *supply chain* with *VEN business opportunity*. Still, obstacles do exist especially due to the fact that that a supply chain, seen as one entity, is a vertically integrated system, while a VEN as an entity is a laterally integrated system.

The three-division perspective employed by Jütner et al. (2003) is probably the one best transferrable to a VEN setting, and the three supply chain risk sources can be translated into VEN risk

Table 1. Risk perspectives, risk types and risk sources

Perspective	Type	Source
Internal to the focal firm	Process risk Control risk	Organizational risk
External to the focal firm	Supply risk Demand risk (Environmental risk)	
Internal to the supply chain	Process risk Control risk Supply risk Demand risk	Network risk
External to the supply chain	Environmental risk	Environmental risk

Source: Jütner et al. (2003), Christopher & Peck (2005)

sources as follows: 1) Organizational risks that are internal to the VEN members and the customers in the business opportunity, 2) Network risks that relate to the overall processes in the business opportunity, starting with the VEN members and ending with the customer, and 3) Environmental risks outside of the structure of VEN – Customer – Business Opportunity.

There are other views and other differentiations of supply chain risks, many of which are interesting per se, but perhaps not so applicable to VENs. Worthwhile mentioning are Goshal (1987) and Manuj & Mentzer (2008). Further literature can also be found in the additional reading section at the end of this chapter.

Finally, there is the issue of whether we should view a VEN as one entity or as a set of individual members. In a supply chain *all* members work towards the same goal, in a VEN not all members are engaged in the same business opportunities at the same time, and thus, there will be an array of temporary "supply chains" or "networks" criss-crossing a VEN at any time. This makes VEN risk management a complex process where oversight is imperative.

Applying the risk understanding used in Jütner et al. (2003) to a VEN, VEN risks are the collective sum of internal and external circumstances that may influence the execution of VEN business opportunities and the operation of the VEN itself.

Supply Chain Vulnerability and VEN Vulnerability

Supply chain vulnerability is a concept that will help understand the analogous concept of VEN vulnerability. Starting with the Oxford Advanced Learner's Dictionary, "vulnerable is defined as "weak and easily hurt physically or emotionally". What is weak or easily hurt when it comes to a VEN?

In terms of supply chains, Christopher (2005) defines vulnerability as "an exposure to serious disturbance", arising from internal as well as external risks. This extends the definition of vulnerability to its causes, the risks, and its impact, a serious disturbance, but seems to omit the part of how easily hurt the supply chain is.

That perspective is provided by McManus, Seville, Brunsdon & Vargo, J. (2007) in the New Zealand research project "Resilient Organisations", who established a vulnerability matrix for evaluating and improving organizational resilience. Here, vulnerability is the product of criticality and preparedness. Criticality describes how severe the impact of a disruption is, should a given component of a system fail, and preparedness describes how well the organization can function, despite the failed component, e.g. a breakdown of ICT, which in most VENs would be nothing short of a disaster, while other failures may have lesser overall impacts. This definition of vulnerability contains the element of easily hurt, implying that a well-prepared organization can still function, and is not vulnerable, while an ill-prepared organization is likely to fail and is, thus, vulnerable. It is the preparedness then that determines the actual impact of disruptions.

Applied to a VEN environment, this perspective allows for the evaluation of critical VEN members or member skills and competencies, for every individual business opportunity as well as the VEN entity as a whole.

Supply Chain Networks vis-à-vis VENs

The view of a supply chain network that perhaps comes closest to a VEN is that of Peck (2005), where the "chain" is not a chain, but a complex web or network of interlinked businesses. Here, this network is seen as operating on four levels, where the links within one level may not match the links within the other levels.

At level 1, the supply chain is seen as a logistics pipeline, where the focus on lean and agile practices have made supply chain performance the overall goal but at the same time it has also exposed the supply chain to many risks. At level 2 the focus is on the supply chain as a carrier of goods and information from the source to the end customer. Supply chain vulnerability is determined by the intertwined connections in the transportation and communication networks that link production sites, distribution centers, warehouses, and retailers. At level 3 the view is further afield, looking at the supply chain from a strategic and management perspective, where organizational management, power-sharing, collaboration and competition become important factors in evaluating vulnerability. At level 4 the view is a broad macroeconomic perspective, political, economic, social, legal and technological factors, and disruptions or sudden changes in these factors are more often than not beyond the

control of the company, but must be dealt with accordingly, should they occur.

The 4-level model employed by Peck is easily transferable to a VEN environment and is an excellent tool for explaining the scope and dynamic nature of supply chain risk. It emphasizes that a resilient network involves much more than the design and management of robust supply chain processes. It is also important to recognize that by taking actions to reduce risk at one point within the four levels, at the same time the risk profile for the other levels is changed, including players and stakeholders not thought of in the initial risk assessment.

The 4-level model is also an excellent tool for seeing the difference between a VEN and a supply chain. On level 1 and 2 we find the flows of inventory and information, and the fixed and mobile assets of manufacturing and distribution. On level 3 and 4 we find the inter-organizational network and relationships and the wider environment (Ekwall, 2009). It can be argued that a supply chain in the traditional sense is primarily concerned with level 1 and 2, while a VEN, seen as one entity, is perhaps more concerned with level 3, and maybe, level 4. One implication that can be drawn from this argument is that VEN risk management is essentially different from supply chain risk management, and that while supply chain risk management often focuses on operations risks, VEN risk management should perhaps focus on relationship and network risks.

STRATEGIES FOR MANAGING VEN RISKS

In the recent literature, several "buzzwords" have been linked to supply chain risk and disruption management in various ways, among which are *robustness*, *flexibility*, *agility* and *resilience*. These concepts need to be explained both from a supply chain perspective as well as a VEN perspective.

Robustness, flexibility, agility and resilience stand out as four strategies or approaches towards supply chain disruptions. These four terms are distinctively different and which strategy works best would depend not only on the supply chain in question as a whole, but also on the part of the supply chain that may be vulnerable. A best-practice supply chain is likely to encompass all four, making it robust, flexible, agile and resilient at the same time.

In Rice & Canatio (2003) the focus is on security and resilience by upholding flexibility and redundancy as two methods with the greatest potential to create resilience. Flexibility can here be seen as a contingency action (actions taken in the event of a disruption) and redundancy can be seen as a mitigation action (actions taken in advance of a disruption, hence incurring a cost regardless of disruption), akin to the distinction between contingency and mitigation in Tomlin (2006), who also identified a third action: Passively accept (or willingly ignore) the disruption risk and the disruption itself. According to Tomlin this, more often than not, appears to be the default strategy, even when it is not appropriate.

Goranson (1992) differentiates between *agility* and *flexibility*. Flexibility is scheduled or planned adaption to unforeseen yet expected external circumstances. Agility is unplanned and unscheduled adaption to unforeseen and unexpected external circumstances. Interestingly, Sheffi (2005) employs flexibility as a means to achieve resilience, stating that "instead of relying solely on supply chain redundancy, a well-managed firm should develop resilience, by building flexibility that can be used to 'bounce back' from disruptions."(Sheffi, 2005).

The difference between robustness, flexibility, agility and resilience is illustrated in Figure 6, adapted from Husdal (2008).

Flexibility or agility, robustness and resilience are different sides of the same coin, yet at the same time distinctively different animals (Asbjørnslett, 2008). Flexibility or agility is the inherent capabil-

ity to modify a current direction to accommodate and successfully adapt to changes in the environment, whereas robustness refers to the ability to endure such changes without adapting. Resilience is the ability to survive despite withstanding a severe and enduring impact.

Lee (2004) introduces the "Triple-A" supply chain with the keywords agility, adaptability and alignment. Agility means to respond quickly to changes (and disruptions) in supply and demand, adaptability means to adjust to shifting markets and alignment implies an equitable sharing of costs, gains, risks, knowledge and information across the whole supply chain.

Christopher & Peck (2004) reason that resilience implies agility, and define supply chain agility as the ability to quickly respond to unpredictable changes in demand and supply. They also underline that the key to an agile and responsive supply chain is a presence of agile partners upstream and downstream of the focal firm.

The concepts of flexibility as a cross-enterprise undertaking is highlighted in Lummus, Duclos & Vokurka (2003) and later elaborated upon in Duclos, Vokurka & Lummus (2004). Here, cross-enterprise flexibility must be present in 6 components: 1) operations – the ability to configure assets and operations according to customer trends, 2) market – the ability to customize design and build close relationship with customers, 3) logistics – the ability to receive and deliver according to changes in supply and demand, 4) supply – the ability to reconfigure the supply chain, 5) organization – the ability to align labor force skills with customer or demand requirements and 6) information systems – the ability to match information systems architectures with changing information needs.

It can be argued that this view on flexibility is already present in a VEN, since it consists of many small units which are inherently more able to respond quickly to changes than a larger static organization. VENs are, by their own nature, robust, flexible, agile and resilient.

Figure 6. The concepts of robustness, flexibility/ agility and resilience

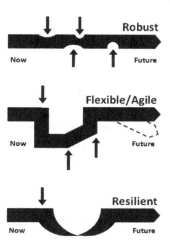

McManus et al. (2007) view resilience as a 3-fold construct, working in a complex, dynamic and interconnected fashion depending on 1) keystone vulnerabilities, criticality and preparedness, which has already been covered in a previous section of this chapter, 2) situation awareness, stemming from an assessment of the keystone vulnerabilities, and 3) adaptive capacity, which is nothing other than flexibility and agility. Resilience, in essence, is the ability to survive disruptive changes despite severe impact.

There is a distinct notion of different severity in these definitions, and in a business setting, the ability to survive (resilience) is likely to be much more important than the ability to quickly regain stability (robustness) or the ability to divert (flexibility or agility).

VEN CHARACTERISTICS AS DISRUPTION IMPACT PARAMETERS

Supply chain or VEN resilience is not only a function of organizational preparedness and adaptability; it is also a function of characteristics such as structure and design.

The notion that supply chain characteristics play a major role in supply chain disruptions is greatly underscored in Craighead, Blackhurst, Rungtusanatham & Handfield (2007), where the severity of supply chain disruptions is related to supply chain design characteristics (supply chain density, supply chain complexity and node criticality) and supply chain mitigation capabilities (recovery capability and warning capability). In brief: supply chain structure and supply chain organization. It is argued that supply chain disruptions and the associated operational and financial costs should be viewed as a normal more than an abnormal occurrence. However, there are specific factors that contribute to or dampen the severity of such disruptions.

These factors are presented in the form of 6 propositions: Firstly, propositions 1 to 3: *an unplanned event that disrupts a supply chain is more likely to have a severe impact if the supply chain structure is 1) dense or 2) complex or 3) contains critical nodes or bottlenecks.* Secondly, proposition 4 and 5: *an unplanned event that disrupts a supply chain is less likely to have a severe impact if the supply chain 4) has proactive or reactive recovery capabilities or 5) warning capabilities, as in detection and dissemination of critical information.* Thirdly, proposition 6, combining the previous 5 propositions: *an unplanned event disrupting a supply chain that is dense, complex and with many critical nodes is less likely to be severe if there is a capability to quickly detect and disseminate information about the event and thus respond and correct in a proactive or reactive manner.*

In a VEN context, proposition 1-2-3 can be seen as a related to the number of members and their skills and competencies, creating a situation similar to Figure 1. Proposition 4 and 5 can be seen as related to situation awareness and preparedness, along the lines of McManus et al. (2007).

Propositions 1-2-3 will differ from VEN to VEN. One could think of cases where the structure or design of the VEN is already pre-determined, with no room for maneuvering or adding new members or skills. In other words, proposition 1-3 stand, leaving proposition 4-5-6 as the key attack points for lessening the impact of disruptions on a VEN. Due to a VENs collective and collaborative structure, propositions 4 and 5 are likely to be inherent to most VENs, and VENs should fare better vis-à-vis disruptions than traditional supply chains.

VEN vulnerability, then, is the susceptibility to harm arising from impacts of internal and external risk sources and is determined by the VENs structural and organizational deficiencies, which may lead to an inadequate handling of aforesaid impacts.

A CONCEPTUAL FRAMEWORK FOR VEN RISK AND VULNERABILITY

Going back to the description of a VEN in Figure 3, and taking into account the views of Christopher and Peck (2004) and McManus et al. (2007), a conceptual framework for risk and vulnerability in VENs is proposed as illustrated in Figure 7. This Figure depicts how the vulnerability of a VEN is determined by its structural and organizational characteristics, and is analogous to the framework used in Husdal (2009), proposing a similar arrangement for risk and vulnerability in supply chains.

On one side, the VEN is subject to certain potential impacts, here termed "disruptions", coming from a set of risk sources. On the other side, the VEN has certain characteristics, which make up the VEN vulnerability.

The risk side is divided into four risk categories: 1) supply-side risk, 2) operational risks, 3) demand-side risks and 4) external risks. The vulnerability side is divided into two: 1) structural and 2) organizational characteristics. The term structural refers first and foremost to the four categories of VEN, while the term organizational refers to the VEN-internal preparedness, with

management and information technology as the binding force between structure and organization. These two elements, structure and organization, determine the degree of adaptability or the capacity the VEN possesses for dealing with or handling disruptions that might occur.

On the organizational side the individual members within the VEN may or may not be equipped with situation awareness, adaptive capacity and preparedness (McManus et al., 2007), on the structural side, the VEN may be unequipped in terms of skills and inadequate in member numbers. The organization holds the preparedness, while the structure holds the skills, the agility and the robustness. The warning capabilities are determined by the established protocol of system wide sharing of information on events relating to or important to the VEN, serving as a facilitator towards how disruptions are handled. VEN skills and competencies and VEN preparedness thus become two important factors in addressing VEN disruptions.

Although in most cases the structure and organization of a VEN are not haphazardly put together, the degree of order and focus in structure and organization will vary from company to company within the VEN. It can be said that the level of structural or organizational disorder that is present in a VEN equals the cost the company is willing to face vis-à-vis potential disruptions, while the level of organizational or structural order is the premium the VEN is willing to pay to insure itself against potential disruptions.

VEN RISK MANAGEMENT VIS-À-VIS BUSINESS CONTINUITY MANAGEMENT

In today's global and interwoven business environment, where supply chain disruptions can occur more or less frequently, the subsequent failure of one contributing participant in the supply network (or chain) can potentially lead to the

Figure 7. VEN risks and VEN vulnerability: A conceptual framework

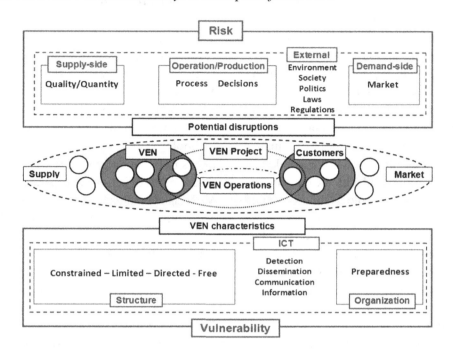

collapse of the whole network (or chain), since the individual members of the supply chain act in their own interest only. The untimely "death" of one member of the supply chain can lead to an unexpected growth or windfall for a different member of the supply chain and vice versa. It is a win-lose situation.

A VEN, as defined earlier in this chapter, using Thompson (2008), is a collaboration structure rather than a competition one, a collective effort rather than a set of individual efforts. The underlying idea of a VEN is that the individual VEN members act with the collective interest in mind, thus ensuring that the success of any business opportunity does not hinge on the efforts of an individual member alone, but hinges on all collectively supporting each other. The reason for this is that in a VEN there is no win-lose, only win-win or lose-lose relationship. Thompson's emphasis on collaboration and mutual interest is important here; should the individual VEN members decide to fight for positions or contracts or work solely

with their own interests in mind, they are basically undermining the VEN, and eventually this may bring on its demise. Consequently, if there can be only win-win or lose-lose, the term *business continuity management*, or maybe more appropriately, *VEN continuity management (VCM)* should be an integral part of VEN management.

BCM, or Business Continuity Management (Cornish, 2007), sometimes seen as a part of risk management, and sometimes vice versa, includes "the actions to be taken, resources required, and procedures to be followed to ensure the continued availability of essential services, programs and operations in the event of unexpected interruptions" (Normann & Lindroth, 2004). The main reason why supply chain risk management should be implemented with BCM in mind, is the fact that businesses are increasingly interconnected due the current trend towards outsourcing, globalization and consolidation (Christopher, 2005), and more often than not in the world of business these interconnections exist unknowingly and unintentionally to the players involved.

In consequence, this may leave businesses *without control of disruption sources*, and only *in control of disruption impacts*. It follows then that supply chain risk management must turn into enterprise risk management, in line with DeLoach (2000), where the enterprise risk management is seen as a natural evolution of operational risk management into a strategic process, with clear linkage to business opportunities, and with the purpose to align strategy, processes, people, technology and knowledge on an enterprise-wide basis (DeLoach, 2000). If supply chain risks are considered to be of a strategic nature, a well-handled supply chain disruption can translate into *business continuity*, while an ill-handled supply chain disruption can translate into *business dis-continuity*. This is illustrated no better than in the now classical, or rather infamous example of how to and how not to handle supply chain disruptions, in the Nokia versus Ericsson battle in the Albuquerque plant fire (Normann & Jansson, 2004), where Nokia through a proactive approach and a supply chain that was flexible and agile enough managed to minimize the disruption impacts, whereas Ericsson had a more reactive approach that eventually led to a disastrous financial loss.

A VEN is an interconnected enterprise in itself, but due to its set of members and skills, it has an inherent flexibility and redundancy should one or more of its members fail to fulfill their missions in the pursuit of a business opportunity. Thus, it may seem unlikely that a disruption within the VEN will cause the entire VEN collapse and result in a VEN discontinuity or even business opportunity discontinuity as in the example in the previous paragraph, Nonetheless, it is important to realize that managing supply chain disruptions in a VEN needs to take on a VEN-wide perspective, rather than focusing on the supply chain of a given business opportunity alone.

VEN MANAGEMENT

VEN management involves both strategic and operational processes (Walters, 2004). Is it possible to separate VEN risk management from VEN management itself? If we consider DeLoach (2000) it is not: In order to align business opportunities with strategy, processes, people, technology and knowledge, risk management needs to be an enterprise-wide undertaking, not discrete sets of actions in separate business areas. VEN risk management, thus, is an integral part of VEN management and VEN leadership.

VEN Leadership Roles

A VEN is a network of equal partners that will have different roles in different projects. While Thompson (2008a) uses three basic roles, this may not be enough for a VEN to fully function.

Katzy & Dissel (2001) describe six roles that are necessary for a virtual enterprise network to function: 1) Broker, 2) Competence Manager, 3) In/Outsourcing Manager, 4) Network Coach, 5) Project Manager and 6) Auditor. The broker's responsibility is to market the network vis-à-vis potential customers, while the competence manager oversees available technologies within the network on a general scale. The project manager supervises operations of the virtual enterprise in a certain business opportunity, assisted by the in/outsourcing manager, who interacts with the individual network partners on a more detailed level than the competence manager, handling the actual resources needed for a given business opportunity. The last two roles are more independent of the actual business opportunity: The auditor provides financial oversight and control, while the network coach assists in creating the necessary cooperative culture by setting business rules and routines and by managing conflicts within the network. If we take the six roles of Katzy & Dissel (2001) and align them with the flexibility components of Duclos et al. (2003) we could say that the broker oversees the market flexibility, the competence manager oversees information and organization flexibility, the project manager oversees operations flexibility, and the in/outsourcing manager oversees supply and logistics flexibility.

Child et al. (2005b) go further than simply dividing roles in a VEN. For a virtual organization also requires strategic direction. They state that a virtual corporation "needs a brain and a central nervous system". Its main task is to ensure the coordination, communication, knowledge management and governance among the partners. The third party institutions' core competence is the management and government of the virtual corporation, particularly process and project management. Kupke & Lattemann (2007) agree in such a strict separation of the virtual corporation's value chain in primary and supporting functions, where the third party acts as another partner in the network who is specialized on supporting functions, whereas the other partners are specialized on specific primary functions. They call this "the Strategic Virtual Corporation".

VEN Life Cycle Challenges

A VEN is a time-limited structure; it has a set life cycle. Thompson (2008b) describes VENs as bioteams or groups that exhibit the characteristics of a living system. Using an ant colony as example, Thompson contends that bioteams have four stages: 1) Founding Stage, 2) Ergonomic Stage, 3) Reproductive Stage, and 4) Terminal Stage.

This way of thinking is not completely new. Looking at supply chains from a systems perspective in her PhD thesis, Solvang (2001) describes a supply chain as having a life cycle with three stages: initiation, operation and cessation. The first part brings the system into being and deals with questions of how to design, structure, and develop the system. The second stage deals with operational issues, how to manage, maintain, support and upgrade the system, and so on. The third part steps in when the system is no longer needed or obsolete, and deals with how to retire, replace or deplete the system.

In a collaborative paper, Deng, Solvang & Solvang (2000) identify 5 phases in the supply chain life cycle: 1) identification of business opportunity, 2) selection of business partner, 3) formation of the supply chain, 4) operation of the supply chain, and 5) reconfiguration of the supply chain. This is a repetitive cycle. For every new business opportunity or product line these phases spring into action, thus creating a living and dynamic supply chain.

A supply chain life cycle, and likewise, a VEN life cycle can thus be separated into three basic stages: 1) formation, 2) operation and 3) extinction. Each step is critical to the next step, even extinction is critical to the next formation and the overall success for the supply chain and the overall continuity of the business, akin to Schumpeter's "creative destruction" (Nolan & Croson, 1995).

In a VEN, this life cycle repeats itself for every new business opportunity and can be a source of risk that is often overlooked: the lacking transfer of knowledge.

Knowledge Gap

One of the changes a VEN will face is termination or "death" (Thompson, 2008b) and this life cycle phase poses certain challenges. Although a VEN may not disband entirely upon the realization and fulfillment of a business opportunity, some of its members may leave, possibly seeking other VENs, or possibly going back to stand on their own.

Unlike a supply chain, a VEN is more loosely coupled and terminations of individual members may and will occur more frequently than in a traditional supply chain. With members leaving or not participating again in future projects, skills and competencies acquired during a business opportunity are not transferred from project to project. In O'Hehir's risk classification this would be termed commercial risk.

Members who leave a VEN may create a knowledge gap (Kupke & Lattemann, 2007). If this missing knowledge is an important prerequisite for the next business opportunity, the VEN may lose its competitive advantage, and miss out on potential new business opportunities. Thus, knowledge management (Buzon, Bouras, & Ouzrout, 2004; Simões & Soares, 2004) becomes an important issue in VEN risk management.

Here, the "competence" manager (Katzy & Dissel, 2001) holds a crucial role in keeping track of which knowledge is lost or not and how it can be replaced. The flexibility, agility, robustness and resilience of a VEN lies perhaps not so much in its structure or size, but in its reservoir of knowledge, skills and competencies. A potential loss of knowledge from one business opportunity to the other is probably one of the most challenging vulnerabilities a VEN must address in order to stay competitive.

VEN Risk Management

It is possible to take the four basic risk management strategies, namely Avoid, Reduce, Transfer and Retain and apply them to the four VEN types that were discussed earlier. By switching the placement of Retain and Avoid, and overlaying the risk management strategies matrix onto the VEN category matrix, this results in the following VEN risk management strategies:

- Constrained VEN – Avoid
- Directed VEN – Reduce
- Limited VEN – Transfer
- Free VEN – Retain

The constrained VEN is a situation that was earlier described as a worst-case scenario, and in terms of VEN risk management it definitely is an Avoid scenario. Conversely, a free VEN falls into the Retain or Accept category, since we can assume that such a VEN possesses the necessary resources to address the various risks

it is exposed to. Since a limited VEN has many members, risks can be pooled or shared, hence Transfer. Finally, the directed VEN, as mentioned in the beginning of this chapter, channels much of its resources towards few selected members, and we need to Reduce the individual risk each member is exposed to.

Approaching to a conclusion, a definition of VEN risk management is in place. Following Paulsson (2004) and Kajüter (2003), supply chain risk management can be described as the intersection of supply chain management and risk management. It has a collaborative and structured approach, and is included in the planning and control processes of the supply chain, to handle risks which might affect the achievement of the supply chain goals.

Based on the above, the following definition can be set up for VEN risk management: VEN risk management is the intersection of VEN management and risk management. It has a collaborative and structured approach, and is included in the planning and control processes of the VEN, to handle risks which might affect the achievement of the VEN goals, collectively for the VEN as a whole, or individually for the ongoing projects or business opportunities within the VEN.

A VEN, like any other business, is exposed to risk similar to supply chains. VEN risk management however, appears to have less in common with supply chain risk management and more in common with enterprise risk management or business continuity. It follows from the arguments made in this chapter that the third party mentioned in Kupke & Lattemann (2007) also ought to have the role of risk manager, providing strategic and operational insights for VEN risk management.

FUTURE RESEARCH DIRECTIONS

Abrahamson (2008) describes logistics as having evolved from transaction-based logistics to value-based logistics in four stages: 1) optimization of flows and specialization of tasks, 2) economies of scale with centralization of tasks, 3) economies of scope with flexibility in tasks, and 4) economies of integration with tasks interfacing directly with the end customer. This, he says, has readied the ground for an agile and "opportunity-driven" supply-chain. An opportunity-driven supply chain is only a small step away from a VEN, and it appears that the supply chain of the future will share many characteristics with a VEN. The congruence of virtual enterprise networks and supply chains or networks means that supply chain risks and VEN risks are likely to share much common research ground in the future.

The division of VENs into four distinct groups based on number of members and number of skills and competencies is of course a rough differentiation, and more refinement is required. What is needed is to collect relevant examples of "real" companies that may be associated with the categorization presented in Figure 1, and subsequently, it would be interesting to verify if the same companies fit the four risk strategies proposed above. This, in turn will help in further exploring the framework for risk and vulnerability (see Figure 7), particularly as to how the four categories influence the vulnerability of a VEN and how VEN preparedness plays a role in risk management.

Zsidisin (2003) suggests that managerial approach to risk from different perspectives is an area for future research in supply chain risk. This is not less important in a VEN. It is indeed important to understand what different people in an organization or across different organizations within a VEN perceive about VEN risks. Different perception about risks among the different VEN members could pose a conflict in deciding what actions to choose in a time of need.

In their appraisal of the virtual corporation, Child et al. (2005b) do not see the virtual corporation as the ultimate type of business cooperation. In most circumstances, so they say, the integrated corporation outperforms the virtual corporation.

This is particularly the case when it comes to the communication of tacit knowledge, where there is a need for industry standards and where the growth potential lies in extending existing markets rather than exploring new markets. However, in markets with considerable turbulence, where there is a need for response and flexibility across a global perspective, a single firm may not have the required resources, and that is when virtual corporations come into play. Virtual and integrated corporations are likely to exist side-by-side, with one becoming the selected winner in certain markets, but not in others. Somewhat outside the risk-related scope of this chapter, but one possible research alley would be to define these markets and why there is less risk for a virtual enterprise network in some markets as opposed to other markets.

Following up on Kupke and Lattemann (2007), the problem of the experience gap due to the frequent reconfiguration and retirement of partners poses a serious risk to VEN continuity. A VEN is a knowledge-driven undertaking and further work should concentrate on empirical analysis of this experience gap and – to rephrase Kupke and Lattemann (2007) – the concept of the Strategic Virtual Enterprise Network.

CONCLUSION

This chapter has attempted to interface supply chain perspectives with VEN perspectives, showing how risk management practices and approaches in supply chains can apply to risk management in VENs. The discussion has been kept at an executive level, and in a pondering manner sought to give strategic advice on the intersection of two much related research areas.

In conclusion it must be said that a VEN is a business entity, not a supply chain. Not necessarily not, one should add, since all businesses one way or the other and to a varying degree possess linkages to their suppliers and customers, which implies that all business opportunities in a VEN, like it or not, constitute some form of supply chain or supply network. With this in mind, ideas from supply chain risk management can very well aid in a fruitful discussion of VEN risk management.

Approaching VENs from a supply chain perspective can assist in defining the risks and challenges a VEN faces and how to manage them, particularly since many of the traditional supply chain risks stem from a lack of collaboration and visibility, the hallmarks of VENs, making a VEN perhaps the ideal setup for supply chains and making supply chain risk management practices a fertile ground for researching VEN risk management.

REFERENCES

Abrahamson, M. (2008). The Role of Logistics in Corporate Strategy. In Arlbjørn, J. S., Halldorson, A., Jahre, M., & Spens, K. (Eds.), *Northern Lights in Logistics & Supply Chain Management* (pp. 49–63). Copenhagen, Denmark: CBS Press.

Asbjørnslett, B. (2008). Assessing the Vulnerability of Supply Chains. In Zsidisin, G. A., & Ritchie, B. (Eds.), *Supply Chain Risk: A Handbook of Assessment, Management and Performance*. New York: Springer.

Bickhoff, N., Böhmer, C., Eilenberger, G., Hansmann, K.-W., Niggemann, M., & Ringle, C. (2003). *Mit Virtuellen Unternhemen zum Erfolg - Ein Quick-Check für Manager*. Berlin, Germany: Springer.

Buzon, L., Bouras, A., & Ouzrout, Y. (2004). Knowledge Exchange in a Supply Chain Context. In Camarinha-Matos, L. M. (Ed.), *Virtual Enterprises and Collaborative Networks* (pp. 145–152). Boston: Springer. doi:10.1007/1-4020-8139-1_16

Byrne, J. A. (1993, February 8). *The Virtual Corporation*. Business Week.

Child, J., Faulkner, D., & Tallman, S. B. (2005a). Networks. In *Cooperative Strategy* (pp. 145–163). Oxford, UK: Oxford University Press.

Child, J., Faulkner, D., & Tallman, S. B. (2005b). The Virtual Corporation. In *Cooperative Strategy* (pp. 164–189). Oxford, UK: Oxford University Press.

Christopher, M. (2005). Managing risk in the supply chain. In *Logistics and Supply Chain Management* (3rd ed., pp. 231–258). Harlow, UK: Prentice Hall.

Christopher, M., & Peck, H. (2004). Building the resilient supply chain. *International Journal of Logistics Management*, *15*(2). doi:10.1108/09574090410700275

Cornish, M. (2007). The business continuity planning methodology. In Hiles, A. (Ed.), *The Definitive Handbook of Business Continuity Management* (pp. 105–118). Chichester, UK: John Wiley & Sons.

Craighead, C. W., Blackhurst, J., Rungtusanatham, M. J., & Handfield, R. B. (2007). The Severity of Supply Chain Disruptions: Design Characteristics and Mitigation Capabilities. *Decision Sciences*, *38*(1), 131–156. doi:10.1111/j.1540-5915.2007.00151.x

Cunha, M. M., & Putnik, G. (2006). *Agile Virtual Enterprises: Implementation and Management Support*. Hershey, PA: Idea Group Publishing.

Dawidow, W. H., & Malone, M. S. (1993). *The Virtual Corporation*. New York: HarperBusiness.

De Loach, J. W. (2000). *Enterprise-wide Risk Management: Strategies for linking risk and opportunity*. London: Financial Times/Prentice Hall.

Deng, Z., Solvang, B., & Solvang, W. D. (2000). *Collaboration and Co-ordination of Virtual Supply Chain via Electronic Networking*. Paper presented at The 16h IFIP World Computer Congress, Beijing, China.

Duclos, L. K., Vokurka, R. J., & Lummus, R. R. (2003). A conceptual model of supply chain flexibility. *Industrial Management & Data Systems*, *103*(5/6), 446–456. doi:10.1108/02635570310480015

Ekwall, D. (2009). Managing the Risk for Antagonistic Threats against the Transport Network. Unpublished PhD thesis, University of Borås, Sweden.

Goldman, S. L., Nagel, R. N., & Preis, K. (1995). *Agile Competitors and Virtual Organizations - Strategies for Enriching the Customer*. New York: Van Nostrand Reinhold.

Goranson, T. (1999). *The Agile Virtual Enterprise*. Westport, CT: Quorum Books.

Gunasekaran, A., & Ngai, E. W. T. (2004). Virtual supply-chain management. *Production Planning and Control*, *15*(6), 584–595. doi:10.1080/09537 280412331283955

Harland, C., Brenchley, R., & Walker, H. (2003). Risk in supply networks. *Journal of Purchasing and Supply Management*, *9*(2), 51–62. doi:10.1016/S1478-4092(03)00004-9

Harrison, A., & van Hoek, R. (2008). *Logistics Management and Strategy: Competing Through The Supply Chain*. London: Prentice Hall.

Husdal, J. (2008). *Does location matter?* Paper presented at the International Conference on Flexible Supply Chains in a Global Economy, Molde, Norway.

Husdal, J. (2009). *Does location matter? Supply chain disruptions in sparse transportation networks*. Paper presented at the TRB Annual Meeting, Washington, DC.

Jütner, U., Peck, H., & Christopher, M. (2003). Supply Chain Risk Management: Outlining an Agenda for Future Research. *International Journal of Logistics: Research and Applications*, *6*(4), 197–210.

Kajüter, P. (2003). Risk Management in Supply Chains. In Seuring, S., Müller, M., Goldbach, M., & Schneidewind, U. (Eds.), *Strategy and Organization in Supply Chains*. Heidelberg, Germany: Physica.

Kaplan, S. (1997). The words of risk analysis. *Risk Analysis*, *17*(4), 407–417. doi:10.1111/j.1539-6924.1997.tb00881.x

Katzy, B. R., & Dissel, M. (2001). A toolset for building the virtual enterprise. *Journal of Intelligent Manufacturing*, *12*(2), 121–131. doi:10.1023/A:1011248409830

Kupke, S., & Lattemann, C. (2007). The strategic virtual corporation: bridging the experience gap. *International Journal of Web Based Communities*, *3*(1), 4–15. doi:10.1504/IJWBC.2007.013770

Lee, H. L. (2004). The Triple-A Supply Chain. *Harvard Business Review*, *82*(10), 102–112.

Lummus, R. R., Duclos, L. K., & Vokurka, R. J. (2003). Supply Chain Flexibility: Building a New Model. *Global Journal of Flexible Systems Management*, *4*(4), 1–13.

Mason-Jones, R., & Towill, D. R. (1998). Shrinking the supply chain uncertainty circle. *IOM Control*, *24*(7), 17–22.

McManus, S., Seville, E., Brunsdon, D., & Vargo, J. (2007). *Resilience Management: A Framework for Assessing and Improving the Resilience of Organisations (No. 2007/01)*. Christchurch, New Zealand: Resilient Organisations.

Morrow, D., Wilkerson, T., & Davey, M. (2009). SCOR for Supply Chain Risk Management. Retrieved March 14, 2009, from http://www.supply-chain.org/

Nolan, R. L., & Croson, D. C. (1995). *Creative Destruction: A Six-Stage Process for Transforming the Organization*. Boston: Harvard Business School Publishing.

Norman, A., & Lindroth, R. (2004). Categorization of Supply Chain Risk and Risk Management. In Brindley, C. (Ed.), *Supply Chain Risk* (pp. 14–27). Aldershot, UK: Ashgate.

Norrman, A., & Jansson, U. (2004). Ericsson's proactive supply chain risk management approach after a serious sun-supplier event. *International Journal of Physical Distribution & Logistics Management, 34*(5), 434–456. doi:10.1108/09600030410545463

O'Hehir, M. (2007). What is business continuity planning (BCP) stratetgy? In Hiles, A. (Ed.), *The Definitive Handbook of Business Continuity Management* (pp. 27–46). Chichester, UK: John Wiley & Sons.

Paulsson, U. (2004). Supply Chain Risk Management. In Brindley, C. (Ed.), *Supply Chain Risk*. London: Ashgate.

Paulsson, U. (2007). *On Managing Disruption Risks in the Supply Chain - the DRISC Model*. Unpublished PhD dissertation, Lund University, Lund, Sweden.

Peck, H. (2005). Drivers of supply chain vulnerability: an integrated framework. *International Journal of Physical Distribution & Logistics Management, 35*(3/4), 210–229. doi:10.1108/09600030510599904

Rice, J. B., & Caniato, F. (2003). Building a secure and resilient supply network. *Supply Chain Management Review, 7*(5), 22–30.

Sengupta, S. (2008). A Plan for Building a New Supply Chain. *Supply Chain Management Review, 12*(1), 46–52.

Sheffi, Y. (2005). *The Resilient Enterprise - Overcoming Vulnerability for Competitive Advantage*. Cambridge, MA: MIT Press.

Simões, D., & Soares, A. L. (2004). The Formation and Dissolution of Organizational Networks: A Knowledge Management Perspective. In Camarinha-Matos, L. M. (Ed.), *Virtual Enterprises and Collaborative Networks* (pp. 301–310). Boston: Springer. doi:10.1007/1-4020-8139-1_32

Snow, C. S., Miles, R. E., Coleman, H. J., & Henry, H. J. (1992). Managing 21st Century Network Organizations. *Organizational Dynamics, 20*(3), 5–21. doi:10.1016/0090-2616(92)90021-E

Solvang, W. D. (2001). Architecture *for supply chain analysis and methodology for quantitative measurement of supply chain flexibility*. Unpublished PhD dissertation, NTNU, Trondheim, Norway.

Thompson, K. (2008). *The Networked Enterprise*. Tampa, FL: Meghan-Kiffer Press.

Thompson, K. (2008b). *Bioteams*. Tampa, FL: Meghan-Kiffer Press.

Thompson. (2009, March). *Collaborating for New Business*. Presented at Connecting Innovation, Brighton, UK. Retrieved June 29, from bioteams.com/2009/05/20/the_networked_enterprise.html

Tomlin, B. (2006). On the value of Mitigation and Contingency Strategies for Managing Supply Chain Disruption Risks. *Management Science, 52*(5), 639–657. doi:10.1287/mnsc.1060.0515

Vanany, I., Zailani, S., & Pujawan, I. N. (2009). Supply Chain Risk Management: Literature Review and Future Research. *International Journal of Information Systems and Supply Chain Management, 2*(1), 16–33.

Walters, D. (2004). A Business Model for Managing the Virtual Enterprise. In Camarinha-Matos, L. M. (Ed.), *Virtual Enterprises and Collaborative Networks* (pp. 273–280). Boston: Springer. doi:10.1007/1-4020-8139-1_29

Walters, D. (2007). *Supply Chain Risk Management: Vulnerability and Resilience in Logistics*. London: Kogan Page.

Zsidisin, G. A. (2003). Managerial perceptions of supply risk. *Journal of Supply Chain Management*, *39*(1), 14–25. doi:10.1111/j.1745-493X.2003. tb00146.x

ADDITIONAL READINGS

Blecker, T., Kersten, W., Späth, H., & Koeppen, B. (2007). Supply Chain Risk Management: A Game Theoretic Analysis. In Wang, W. Y. C., Heng, M. S. H., & Chau, P. Y. K. (Eds.), *Supply Chain Management: Issues in the New Era of Collaboration and Competition* (pp. 355–386). Hershey, PA: Idea Group Publishing.

Cooper, M. C., Ellram, L. M., Gardner, J. T., & Hanks, A. M. (1997). Meshing multiple alliances. *Journal of Business Logistics*, *18*(1), 67–89.

Cousins, P. (2002). A conceptual model for managing long-term inter-organisational relationships. *European Journal of Purchasing & Supply Management*, *8*(2), 71–82. doi:10.1016/ S0969-7012(01)00006-5

Crossman, A., & Lee-Kelly, L. (2004). Trust, committment and team working: the paradox of virtual organizations. *Global Networks*, *4*(4), 375–390. doi:10.1111/j.1471-0374.2004.00099.x

Cueni, T., & Seiz, M. (1999). *Virtual organizations – the next Economic Revolution?* Unpublished paper. Swiss Federal Institute of Technology, EPFL, Lausanne, Switzerland. Retrieved June 29, from www.nubix.ch/vo/virtual.pdf

Das, T., & Teng, B. (2001). Trust, Control, and Risk in Strategic Alliances: An Integrated Framework. *Organization Studies*, *22*(2), 251–283. doi:10.1177/0170840601222004

Dorfman, M. S. (2002). Risk Management. In *Introduction to Risk Management and Insurance* (pp. 43–61). Upper Saddle River, NJ: Prentice Hall.

Gerber, A., Althaus, K., Dietzsch, M., Weidlich, D., & Steiner, R. (2004). Risk-Management of Product Development in Non-Hierarchical Regional Production Networks. In Camarinha-Matos, L. M. (Ed.), *Virtual Enterprises and Collaborative Networks* (pp. 509–516). Boston: Springer. doi:10.1007/1-4020-8139-1_54

Ghoshal, S. (1987). Global Strategy: An Organizing Framework. *Strategic Management Journal*, *8*(5), 425–440.

Giertz, E. (1999). *Säkra företagets flöden*. Stockholm, Sweden: Silfgruppen.

Holling, C. S., Berkes, F., & Folke, C. (2008). Science, sustainability, and resource management. In Berkes, F., & Folke, C. (Eds.), *Linking Social and Ecological Systems: Management Practices and Social Mechanisms for Building Resilience*. Cambridge, UK: Cambridge University Press.

Husdal, J. (2008b). Supply *Chain Risk: The dark side of Supply Chain Management*. Unpublished guest lecture. Molde University College. Retrieved February 28, 2009, from http://husdal. com/2008/11/12/supply-chain-risk/

IRM. (2002). *A Risk Management Standard*. Retrieved March 16, 2009, from http://www. theirm.org/publications/documents/Risk_Management_Standard_030820.pdf

Kaplan, S., & Garrick, B. J. (1981). On the quantitative definition of risk. *Risk Analysis*, *1*(1), 11–27. doi:10.1111/j.1539-6924.1981.tb01350.x

Kasper-Fuehrer, E. C., & Ashkanasy, N. M. (2001). Communicating trustworthiness and building trust in inter-organizational virtual organizations. *Journal of Management*, *27*(3), 235–254. doi:10.1016/ S0149-2063(01)00090-3

Kaye, D. (2008). *Managing Risk and Resilience in the Supply Chain*. London: BSI.

Kleindorfer, P. R., & Wassenhove, V. L. N. (2004). Managing risk in global supply chains. In Gatignon, H., & Kimberly, J. R. (Eds.), *The INSEAD-Wharton Alliance on Globalizing - Strategies for Building Successful Global Businesses* (pp. 288–305). Cambridge, UK: Cambridge University Press.

Koubatis, A., & Schönberger, J. Y. (2005). Risk management of complex critical systems. *International Journal of Critical Infrastructures, 1*(2/3), 195–215. doi:10.1504/IJCIS.2005.006119

Lau, H. C. W., Chin, K. S., Pun, K. F., & Ning, A. (2000). Decision supporting functionality in a virtual enterprise network. *Expert Systems with Applications, 19*(4), 261–270. doi:10.1016/S0957-4174(00)00038-5

Lau, H. C. W., Wong, C. W. Y., Ngai, E. W. T., & Hiu, I. K. (2003). Quality management framework for a virtual enterprise network: a multi-agent approach. *Managing Service Quality, 13*(4), 300–309. doi:10.1108/09604520310484716

Lin, A., & Patterson, D. (2007). An Investigation into the Barriers to Introducing Virtual Enterprise Networks. In Wang, W. Y. C., Heng, M. S. H., & Chau, P. Y. K. (Eds.), *Supply Chain Management: Issues in the New Era of Collaboration and Competition* (pp. 23–44). Hershey, PA: Idea Group Publishing.

Manuj, I., & Mentzer, J. T. (2008). Global Supply Chain Risk Management. *Journal of Business Logistics, 29*(1), 133–155.

Markus, M. L., Manville, B., & Agres, C. E. (2000). What makes a Virtual Organization Work? *MIT Sloan Management Review, 42*(1), 13–26.

Moshowitz, A. (1994). Virtual Organization: A Vison of Mangement in the Information Age. *The Information Society, 10*(4), 267–288.

Nemiro, J., Beyerlein, M., Bradley, L., & Beyerlein, S. (2008). *The Handbook of High-Performance Virtual Teams*. San Francisco: John Wiley & Sons.

Peck, H. (2006). Reconciling supply chain vulnerability, risk and supply chain management. *International Journal of Logistics: Research and Applications, 9*(2), 127–142.

Porter, M. E. (1985). *Competitive Advantage: creating and sustaining superior performance*. New York: Free Press.

Ritchie, B., & Brindley, C. (2007). Supply chain risk management and performance. *International Journal of Operations & Production Management, 27*(3), 303–322. doi:10.1108/01443570710725563

Sabbaghi, A., & Vaidyanathan, G. (2007). Integration of Global Supply Chain Management with Small and Medium Suppliers. In Wang, W. Y. C., Heng, M. S. H., & Chau, P. Y. K. (Eds.), *Supply Chain Management: Issues in the New Era of Collaboration and Competition* (pp. 127–164). Hershey, PA: Idea Group Publishing.

Svensson, G. (2000). A conceptual framework for the analysis of vulnerability in supply chains. *International Journal of Physical Distribution & Logistics Management, 30*(9), 731–749. doi:10.1108/09600030010351444

Svensson, G. (2004). Key areas, causes and contingency planning of corporate vulnerability in supply chains. *International Journal of Physical Distribution & Logistics Management, 34*(9), 728–748. doi:10.1108/09600030410567496

Tang, C. S. (2006). Perspectives in supply chain risk management. *Journal of Production Economics, 103*(2), 451–488. doi:10.1016/j.ijpe.2005.12.006

Wagner, S., & Bode, C. (2008). An empirical examination of supply chain performance along several dimensions of risk. *Journal of Business Logistics, 29*(1), 307–325.

Zsidisin, G. A., & Ellram, L. M. (2003). An Agency Theory Investigation of Supply Risk Management. *Journal of Supply Chain Management, 39*(3), 15–27. doi:10.1111/j.1745-493X.2003.tb00156.x

Chapter 2
Managing Supply Chain Risks:
Understanding the Impact of Network Characteristics

Brian Squire
Manchester Business School, UK

ABSTRACT

This chapter takes an exploratory look at the use of formal network measures to further understanding of the sources of extended enterprise or supply chain risk. It attempts to show that network measures can provide additional insight to 'uncover' sources of risk that could remain hidden using 'traditional' measures alone. More specifically, network measures of criticality, centrality, redundancy, distance and topology are combined with traditional measures of criticality, organisational slack, global sourcing and outsourcing to develop a more complete understanding on the determinants of the impact and/or probability of supply chain disruption. The measures identified provide researchers and managers with a wide-ranging framework for risk identification.

INTRODUCTION

Virtual Enterprises (VEs) can be defined as networks of suppliers, customers, engineers and other specialised service functions linked through advanced inter-organisational information technology in dynamic environments. This chapter is specifically focussed on the supply chain component of VEs and less on other aspects such information technology or their temporary nature.

In recent years the management of supply chain risks has risen to prominence within both academic and practitioner communities. A recent survey found that 80% of supply management executives had experienced disruptions in their supply chain within the past 24 months and that 75% predicted risks would increase over the next three years (Aberdeen Group, 2005). The increased probability of disruption can be ascribed to several factors, including the rise of global supply chains (Juttner et al, 2003), lean operations and supply (Sheffi, 2005), supply base complexity (Choi and Krause, 2006) and an excessive focus on outsourcing. Ironically, factors originally championed for driving better supply chain efficiency now appear to be creating greater vulnerabilities.

DOI: 10.4018/978-1-61520-607-0.ch002

Supply chain disruptions have been shown to have major implications for the profitability, survival and future growth of organisations. Previous research has estimated that supply disruptions cost an average of $50-100 million per day (Rice and Caniato, 2003) and that prolonged disruptions, such as the 18 day labour strike at a brake supplier factory for GM, can reduce earnings by as much as $900 million per quarter. Furthermore, recovery from disruption can often be prolonged. Event studies have shown that operating performance reduced can remain diminished by as much as two years (Hendricks and Singhal, 2005). These severe effects are often amplified by a lack of preparation within organisations. It has been estimated that a mere 5 – 25% of Fortune 500 companies have sufficient supply chain risk strategies in place and that approximately 50% of organisations lack formal metrics and procedures for assessing and managing supply risks (Mitroff & Alpasan, 2003; Aberdeen Group, 2005).

Critical to reducing vulnerability to disruptions is supply chain design. The same disruption can have very different implications depending on how organizations have designed their supply chain and planned for such an event. For example, take the responses of Apple and Dell to the earthquake that hit Taiwan in 1999. Dell was able to direct sales to products with available components through its direct order supply chain while Apple faced product backlogs due to its lack of supply chain flexibility and inability to change product configurations (Sheffi, 2005). This, and many similar examples, clearly demonstrates that supply chain design can have important implications to both the response and impacts of disruptions.

In an effort to help managers reduce disruptions, research has focused on actionable supply chain design variables that may help reduce firm level vulnerability. Studies have identified a range of pertinent variables but the most common include organizational slack, global supply chains, the level of outsourcing and sole sourcing arrangements (e.g. Chopra and Sodhi, 2004;

Kleindorfer and Saad, 2005). Whilst the literature has yielded significant insights into the phenomena of supply chain disruptions, existing models are somewhat limited in their explanatory power. For example, Wagner and Bode (2006) find that their predictor variables explain between 3 – 13% of the variance in various measures of supply chain vulnerability. Anecdotally, this is supported by evidence that suggests that although we now better understand the causes of disruptions, their frequency and impact still appear to be on the rise (Finch et al, 2009).

There is, therefore, a need to understand more fully what drives vulnerability within supply chains. It is the contention of this chapter that additional understanding may be obtained by combining extant predictors (such as those identified above) with network measures. By introducing formal network measures to the study of supply chain vulnerability, we can identify different causes of disruption that remain hidden when we follow what we could term as 'traditional' analysis. A similar argument is made by Choi and Kim (2008) who demonstrate how looking at the embeddedness of an organisation within its own network is important to explaining performance. An individual supplier should not be solely evaluated in isolation but also based on how that supplier is connected into the wider network. It also helps to formalise the work of Craighead et al. (2007) who recognised the importance of the network but without using formal network measures.

This exploratory chapter uncovers some of the network measures that may benefit risk identification and analysis within supply networks. In doing so, it follows a tradition within other fields that have used formal network measures to understand the robustness of their networks of interest. For example, Albert et al (2000) show that properties of a network have quite clear and distinct effects on the robustness of the Internet and the World Wide Web. Similar results have been found for many other forms of networks including organisational networks (Stanley et al, 1996), metabolic networks (Jeong et al, 2000), ecosytems (Camacho et al, 2002) and communication networks (Ebel et al, 2002).

The remainder of the chapter is structured as follows. The next section discusses the definition of supply chain risk and differentiates it from relational risk. The third section makes the case for a network level of analysis, providing background to the multilevel perspective as well as discussing the potential advantages over dyadic studies. The fourth section develops the conceptual model and specific propositions for each determinant of supply chain risk. The final two sections suggest directions for future research and provide conclusions respectively.

Table 1. Ten definitions of supply chain risk

References	Heading	Definition
Christopher et al. 2003	Understanding Supply Chain Risk: A Self-Assessment Workbook.	Supply chain risk is defined as "any risk to the information, material and product flow from original suppliers to the delivery of the final product".
Juttner et al. 2003	Supply Chain Risk Management: Outlining an agenda for future research.	Supply chain risk is defined as "the variation in the distribution of possible supply chain outcomes, their likelihood, and their subjective values".
Juttner 2005	Supply Chain Risk Management Understanding the Business Requirements from a Practitioner Perspective.	"Risk in the supply chain centres around the disruption of "flows" between organisations. These flows relate to information, materials, products and money".
Zsidisin et al. 2005	An Institutional Theory Perspective Of Business Continuity Planning For Purchasing And Supply Management.	Supply chain risk is defined as "the extent to which supply chain outcomes are variable or are susceptible to disruption, and thereby lead to detrimental effects on the firm".
Tang 2006	Perspectives in supply chain risk management.	Supply chain Risk is defined as "operational" risks and "disruption" risks. Operational risks are referred to the inherent uncertainties such as uncertain customer demand, uncertain supply, and uncertain cost. Disruption risks are referred to the major disruptions caused by natural and man-made disasters such as earthquakes, floods, hurricanes, terrorist attacks etc, or economic crises such as currency evaluation or strikes.
Gaonkar and Viswanadham 2007	Analytical Framework for the Management of Risk in Supply Chain.	Supply chain risk is defined by the distribution of the loss resulting from the variation in possible supply chain outcomes, their likelihood, and their subjective values. Supply chain risks comprise risks due to variations in information, material, and product flows, which originate at the original supplier and lead to the delivery of the final product to the end user.
Karningsih 2007	Risk Identification in Global Manufacturing Supply Chain.	Risk in supply chain is defined as "uncertain variation or disruption which could impede flow of information and resources in the supply network".
Wagner and Bode 2007	An Empirical Investigation into Supply Chain Vulnerability.	A supply chain disruption is defined as "an unintended, untoward situation, which leads to supply chain risk. Risk is equated with the detriment of a supply chain disruption, i.e. the realised harm or loss".
Klimov and Merkuryev 2008	Simulation Model for Supply Chain Reliability Evaluation.	Supply Chain risk is defined as internal and external risk. Risks referred to disruption such as earthquakes, floods, terrorist attacks, etc., or economic crises or strikes, are assigned to supply chain external group. Other risks are supply chain internal risks.
Manuj 2008	Global Supply Chain Risk Management Strategies.	Risk in a global supply chain context is defined as "the distribution of performance outcomes of interest expressed in terms of losses, probability, speed of event, speed of losses, the time for detection of the events, and frequency".

BACKGROUND TO SUPPLY CHAIN RISK

A review of the literature indicates no clear definition of supply chain risk. Table 1 includes a number of definitions selected from the literature.

As can be seen from this table, there are common elements in many of these definitions. Taking these elements, supply chain risk is defined in the context of this chapter as "the threat of disruption to supply chain continuity as measured by its impact and probability" where supply chain continuity refers to "the uninterrupted flow of materials, finances, and information forward and backward within the supply chain".

Differentiating Relational Risk from Supply Chain Risk

It is worth differentiating supply chain risk from the more established relational risk. Relational risk has been defined as "the degree to which decision makers are concerned with the partner's opportunistic behavior in cooperative efforts" (Das and Teng, 2001) and is a much studied concept in strategic alliances (e.g. Das and Teng, 1996; Nooteboom et al, 1997). The critical difference between the two concepts is that while relational risks examine deliberate acts of opportunism within the alliance, supply chain risks relate primarily, although not exclusively, to accidental failures occurring somewhere in the network. In other words, supply chain risks and their associated disruptions result from a whole range of factors that are not related to deliberate actions of a partner organization. Although relational risk is important to the continuity of buyer-supplier relationships, it is outside of the scope of this chapter where the focus is squarely placed on supply chain risks.

A Network Understanding of Supply Chain Risk

The concept of a network is extremely broad, however, at the core of network analysis is the application of a set of relations (or links) to a set of entities (or nodes)[1] (Monge and Contractor, 2003, p30). The choice of entity and relation depends on the specific objectives and questions of the study. For example, the entity could be an individual, a work group, or a division, and the relations could be based on communication, friendship, legal ties or competition. It is very important to make an explicit choice of entity and relation (Borgatti and Li, 2009), therefore in this chapter an entity refers to an organisation within the supply network and relation refers to a supply link[2].

The focus of network analysis is the relationship, which in its simplest form consists of the presence or absence of a link between two entities. This may be contrasted with traditional social science where the focus has been on the attributes, such as attitudes, opinions, or behaviour, of the entities themselves (Scott, 2005). Relations in network analysis are therefore not a function of the entities themselves but of the interactions between entities within a system. Having identified the presence of a link between two nodes, relations can be classified as directional or non-directional. Directional links have an origin and a destination i.e. they point from one node to another. On the other hand, non-directional links do not have an origin or a destination; they do not make the direction explicit (Monge and Contractor, 2003). In a supply network, our 'supply' relation between a buyer and a supplier is directional insofar as the components transfer from supplier to buyer[3]. Furthermore, links can also be measured by their strength, indicating the quantity of the relation (Monge and Contractor, 2003). In a supply network, strength could measure the quantity or value of the goods or service provided.

The properties of any given network can be analysed at various levels. Following Brass

Table 2. Determinants of supply chain risk

Level of Analysis	'Traditional'	'Network'	Contribution
Individual	Organisational Slack Criticality	Criticality Centrality	Uncovers 'chokepoints' outside tier one. Provides more complete measure.
Dyadic	Geographical distance	Distance Redundancy	Provides more complete picture of vulner-ability outside of tier one.
Global	Outsourcing/Vertical Integration	Topology	Shows it is not just the number of nodes but also their distribution that is important.

(1995), this study is interested in three levels: the individual; the dyadic; and the global. These refer to the organisation, the dyadic relation between two organisations and the entire supply network respectively. This multilevel analysis is important, as studies of networks that fail to include different levels will only be able to present a partial account of the topic of interest. For example, in a test of competing theories of careers' success, Seibert et al (2001) found that the inclusion of all three levels provides significantly more explanatory power than any one level alone.

From these fairly simple concepts, network scholars have been able to derive a considerable number of metrics or techniques that calculate the structural properties of a given network. Metrics provide clear and recognised definitions of various structural properties of networks from which researchers can build testable models (Wasserman and Faust, 1994). It is not the purpose of this chapter to provide a comprehensive overview of these measures and readers are referred to Wasserman and Faust, 1994; Brass, 1995; Scott, 2005; & Monge and Contractor, 2003 for further details. Instead, the focus is only on those metrics that have implications for levels of risk within networks which are developed in the proceeding section.

Framework of Determinants

This study adopts the focal firm's perspective to analyse how properties of a supply network influence supply chain risk. As previously stated,

supply chain risk is a function of both the probability of a disruption and the impact of a disruption. Thus there are two separate but inter-related dependent variables to this study. First, the *probability* that the focal node will be affected by a disruption occurring somewhere in the network and second, the *impact* this disruption will have on this node. These two variables are evaluated separately because individual determinants may affect one, or the other, or both.

To determine whether network analysis facilitates a more complete understanding of supply chain risk, the model includes both 'traditional' and 'network' measures. This means that the network measures will have to clearly demonstrate a potential additive benefit over and above the traditional measures alone. Although this chapter is purely conceptual, examples will be given of the network measures to help illustrate their usefulness. As suggested in the previous section, the framework will be constructed using measures at three levels: the individual, the dyadic and the global. The combination of all three levels will provide a more complete picture of supply chain risk determinants. Comparing 'traditional' measures with 'network' measures at the three levels of analysis helps shape the framework presented in Table 2.

It is not claimed that this list is exhaustive on either approach (traditional or network) or at each level. Rather, properties have been selected that have most commonly been identified as having important implications for supply chain risk to help make the case for including formal network measures in the analysis. Criticality is found in both traditional and network measures. This is intentional, the difference being the manner in which criticality is analysed and will be explained in more detail below.

Individual Level Determinants

Individuals are the various organisations within the supply network and include material suppliers, component and sub-assembly suppliers, third-party logistics, distributors and retailers. Individual level determinants of risk are widely studied in the 'traditional' literature and seek to understand how characteristics of an individual supplier can contribute to the risk profile of a buyer firm. The 'traditional' measures examined here are organisational slack and criticality, whereas the 'network' measures include centrality and criticality.

Organisational Slack

One of the primary reasons that supply chains are said to be more vulnerable than ever before is the focus (perhaps excessive) of organisations on driving cost out of the system (Stauffer, 2003). In striving for greater efficiencies, companies have reduced the buffer available to protect them from disruptions. This has lead many scholars of supply chain risk to call for greater recognition of the trade-off between cost efficiencies and business continuity. In particular, studies have highlighted the link between lean operations and the risk of disruption. Coleman and Jennings (1998) were one of the first to explicitly identify the potential disruptive influence of union strikes on organisations implementing lean JIT approaches. Since their publication, further managerial surveys have generally supported the view that lean inventories are one of the key drivers of supply chain risk (e.g. Juttner, 2005; Aberdeen Group, 2005).

In order to mitigate disruption, organisations are advised to build greater slack in the form of safety stock and excess capacity (Chopra and Sodhi, 2004). Wilding (2007) suggests that organisations retain inventory in as generic form as possible. This form of postponement increases responsiveness to disruption whilst reducing the risk of depreciating or redundant stock. Furthermore, inventory may be classified by the level of criticality to continuity (Elkins et al, 2005). By performing an ABC analysis of its stock (see Cousins et al, 2008, p50), an organisation can build slack for parts liable to disruption while retaining elements of the lean approach in less critical categories. Finally, the storage location of inventory is also important. For example, Toyota and Sears keep inventories of strategic stock at regional locations that can be shared among dealers and outlets in the event of a disruption (Tang, 2006).

The foregoing studies suggest that lean systems are more prone to disruption and take longer to recover. Accordingly, it is suggested that slack (in the form of inventory or capacity) will influence both the probability and the impact of a disruption. This leads to the first proposition.

Proposition 1: The probability and impact of a disruption are reduced when disruption involves a node with higher operational slack.

Node Criticality
Node Criticality is defined as the importance of a node within a supply network (Craighead et al, 2007). Traditionally, importance is gauged through portfolio management, i.e. positioning a supplier on the dimensions of complexity of the supply market and the impact on the business (Kraljic, 1983). The output from this exercise should be to position products and services into one of four categories: routine, leverage, bottleneck, and critical. This exercise helps buyers understand the importance of suppliers and is therefore a useful starting point for risk identification. In particular, organisations are recommended to

focus their resource allocation and risk management to suppliers positioned in either the critical or bottleneck categories.

The limitation of this 'traditional' measure is that it can be applied for the assessment of first tier suppliers only. Furthermore, it does not make any assessment of the links a supplier has with other organisations within the network. It may therefore be useful to use a 'network' measure to help demonstrate how criticality can be more than just a function of supply market complexity and the impact on the business.

Eigenvector Centrality[4] tells us that importance is not only a factor of the node itself, but also of the importance of the nodes to which it is connected (Newman, 2007). For example, if a critical supplier is directly connected to other critical suppliers, the importance of that supplier is higher than a critical supplier without these connections. In this case eigenvector centrality does not provide us with a different determinant, but demonstrates how the criticality may be measured in a more complete and informative manner than using the 'traditional' measure alone. It effectively allows the researcher to gauge the importance of a path as opposed to just a single supplier. Nodes with high eigenvector centrality have been shown to be important to the robustness and security of networks such as terrorist networks (Memon and Larsen, 2006), transport networks (Majima et al, 2007) and computing networks (Burgess et al, 2004). It is conjectured that similar effects may be found in supply networks.

Whether one uses traditional, network or both measures, node criticality will primarily affect the impact, rather than the probability, of a supply chain disruption. There is no inherent reason why a critical supplier is more likely to be disrupted, but if it were, the severity would be greater. This leads to the second proposition.

Proposition 2: The impact of a disruption is greater when it involves critical nodes in the network.

Node Centrality

The concept of centrality is one of the most common properties included in network analysis. Although centrality simply looks at the extent to which a node is central to a network (Brass, 1995), there are several different ways in which the concept can be measured (see Figure 1). First, *degree centrality* examines the number of direct links a node has with other nodes in the network. Degree centrality tends to be an important measure because nodes with more connections in a network have been shown to have greater job performance (Sparrowe et al, 2001), influence (Brass, 1984) and power (Burkhardt and Brass, 1990). Second, *closeness centrality* measures how easily or quickly a node can access all the other nodes in a network. Closeness centrality is linked to the efficiency with which a node can access information through direct and indirect connections within the network and therefore affects access to new innovations and business opportunities (Gulati et al, 2003). Finally, *betweenness centrality* examines the extent to which a node connects two other nodes that are not directly connected. In this sense, centrality relates to being the intermediary between two nodes and derives power through brokering information flows or opportunities between nodes (Mehra et al, 2001). In Figure 1, node C has the highest degree centrality, nodes G and F have the highest closeness centrality and node H has the highest betweenness centrality.

Of these three different measures, betweenness centrality is related to the impact of a disruption and degree centrality is related to the probability and impact of a disruption. A node with a high betweenness centrality score represents a bottleneck or choke point in the network and will therefore increase the impact of any disruption occurring upstream of that point. For example, a central node in a supply network might represent a port or third party distribution centre that links suppliers and customers that do not have a direct link. It represents a source of

Figure 1. Measures of centrality

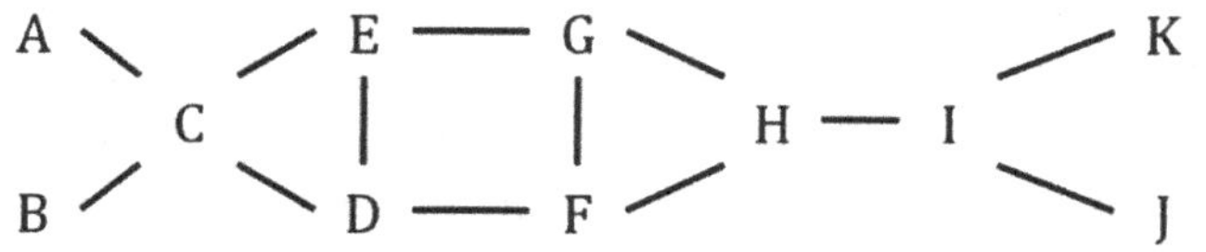

risk because any disruption to the central node will prevent the flow of materials along the supply chain. Arguably, these choke points would remain hidden unless a network analysis and an examination of the betweenness centrality of nodes for the SC is conducted. This leads to the third proposition.

Proposition 3a: The impact of a disruption is greater when it involves nodes in the network with a high level of betweenness centrality.

Degree Centrality has been shown to be a useful predictor of the risk of infection (Christley et al, 2005). The greater the number of links a person has with other individuals, the greater the chances of the disease being spread. Empirical evidence has shown this to be true for the spread of HIV (Neaigus et al, 1994; Bell, 1999) and various other forms of infection (Christley et al, 2005). For analogous reasons, it is suggested that nodes with higher degree centrality are more vulnerable simply because they have more inbound links in the network. In other words, degree central nodes have a higher probability of being 'hit' by the disruption simply as a function of their position and will create a greater impact where they can 'spread' the results of the disruption to a greater number of nodes. Degree centrality provides a useful indicator of inbound complexity, which has been previously linked to supply chain risk (e.g. Christopher and Lee, 2004). Furthermore, if the disruption was to occur at the central node, it is fairly apparent that the downstream disruption would be more severe than if it occurred at

a less central node. For these reasons it is suggested that:

Proposition 3b: The impact and probability of a disruption is greater when it involves nodes in the network with a high level of degree centrality.

Dyadic Level Determinants

Second, this study considers dyadic level determinants of supply chain risk. Dyadic determinants refer to measures that characterise the link between two nodes in the network (Monge and Contractor, 2003). A dyadic level of analysis is appropriate when examining the relations among organisations in the network (Mizruchi and Marquis, 2006) and is common to work examining inter-firm relations (e.g. Lamming, 1993; Gulati, 1995; Cousins, 2002). Dyadic properties have been shown to be important to study of supply chain risk where the same disruption can have very different implications depending on the relationship between the buyer and supplier organisations. For example, Petersen et al. (2008) cite the example of an executive in a North American Automotive Company who had realised the difference the dyadic relationship can have for long-term supply chain risk:

"We have to change the way we view suppliers. Instead of being hunters who seek to drive down prices, we need to become farmers, with the objective of cultivating and nurturing our supply base, in order to produce a healthy harvest"

This executive clearly realises that there is a balance that needs to be struck between squeezing a supplier to reduce cost and pushing them so far that they go out of business. This could not be clearer than in the current economic environment[5] where some forward thinking buyers are propping up key suppliers by reducing payment terms or actually paying them in advance of delivery. There is therefore a clear link between the dyadic relationship and supply chain risk. At a structural level, the dyadic determinants consist of geographical distance, distance and redundancy

Geographical Distance

There has been a dramatic rise in global sourcing over the past three decades (Monczka et al, 2005). Cost pressures within domestic markets, improved quality and delivery of global suppliers and the attractiveness of foreign markets has lead to global supply bases in most industries. Whilst there are benefits of global sourcing, there are also significant risks to supply continuity. For example, Juttner (2005) found that the terrorist attacks of 9/11 caused significantly greater disruptions for organisations with global supply chains than those who operated exclusively within the UK. This is supported by empirical evidence showing a relationship between global sourcing and supply-side risk (Wagner and Bode, 2006).

In studies of global sourcing and supply chain risk, the focus primarily relates to geographical distance between the buyer and the supplier. This distance has implications for the probability of supply chain disruption. In a qualitative study of global sourcing, Manuj and Mentzer (2008) found several reasons why distance may affect vulnerability. First, global sourcing introduces the risk of currency fluctuation that simply does not exist in domestic sourcing. Although some large organisations may be able to hedge against this, it does not remove the risk and is less common in small and medium size enterprises. Second, the transit time between buyer and supplier is

increased. Respondents to the authors study argued that it was not just the increase in mean time but also an increase in the standard deviation of the mean. Third, the increase in lead time leads to greater issues of forecasting. Respondents felt this reduced the accuracy of forecasts and induced bullwhip effects within the network. This leads to the fourth proposition.

Proposition 4: The probability of a disruption is greater when it involves geographically distant nodes in the network.

Distance and Redundancy

For any pair of nodes in a network there can be two types of links: direct and indirect (Monge and Contractor, 2003). Direct links are those connections that only involve two nodes, whereas indirect links are nodes that are connected only through other nodes. For example in Figure 2, nodes A and B have a direct connection (so do B and C), while A and C have an indirect connection. In the case of the latter, the connection is a two-step linkage or two degrees of separation. Thus a dyadic connection is no longer a straight connection between a buyer and a supplier but a link between any two nodes in a network. This change on how we perceive a dyadic linkage has some interesting consequences for supply chain risk.

First, and most obvious, we can say that the longer the number of steps in a network, the greater the probability of disruption. If we examine the average geodesic[6] of all paths that reach the buyer firm, we get an indication of the number of tiers within the network. It is argued that the greater the number of tiers the greater the possibility of

Figure 2. Direct and indirect links in a network

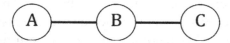

disruption at any stage. Second, we can also look at the redundancy within the network. Redundancy measures the number of alternative geodesics that connect the two nodes. Within a supply chain, this becomes critical when looking at transportation links as it gives a measure of the number of alternative routings or modes of transport should something go wrong. For example, the restrictions on air transportation and border crossings in the US after the terrorist attacks of 9/11 meant that lean supply chains were at risk of running dry. Ford was unable to react to the restrictions and subsequently had to close five of its plants until the barriers were lifted. On the other hand, Chrysler had redundant transport links that they were able to continue manufacturing without any stoppages (Sheffi, 2004). Both these measures are intuitively appealing, but without formal network measurement, an organisation does not have a way of knowing how exposed it is to disruption. This leads to the fifth set of propositions.

Proposition 5a: The probability of disruption is greater in networks with higher average geodesics.

Proposition 5b: The impact of disruption is greater in networks with low redundancy.

Global Level Determinants

The final set of determinants is derived from a network level of analysis. Network level analyses move beyond organisation and dyadic properties to examine the structure of the overall or global network. This level is important to the study of inbound supply risk because connections between a supplier's suppliers and between a supplier's customers can have important implications for disruptions. Indeed, it is often delays or failures within the second or third tier of supply networks that cause buyer disruptions. From a network perspective, network level properties can facilitate or impede an organisation's performance in areas

such as start up performance (Baum et al, 2000), innovation (Ahuja, 2000) and failure rates (Uzzi, 1997). Two properties of the network structure are considered important determinants of supply chain disruption. First, the size of the network, i.e. the number of nodes and second, the network architecture, i.e. the presence or absence of links between nodes in a network.

Number of Nodes[7]

The number of nodes within a supply network may vary for a number of reasons. Lamming et al (2000) find that product complexity increases the number of upstream suppliers citing the example of an automotive supply network (a complex product) that contains around 750 suppliers in comparison to a FMCG or pharmaceutical supply network (a less complex product) that contain fewer than 100 suppliers. Similarly, Choi and Hong (2002) find that more expensive product lines are more likely to be associated with a higher number of suppliers where the product requires more features and a greater number of steps in the fabrication process. Finally, outsourcing any activity will introduce at least one new node into an existing network.

The number of nodes will have an effect on the likelihood of a disruption. First, the increased number of suppliers creates leads directly to an increased number of hand-offs where each hand-off represents an opportunity for disruption. Second, the management of information flows becomes more difficult in larger networks (Lamming et al, 2000). The effect of information flows on inbound supply risk has a long history within the literature (Forrester, 1961; Lee, 1997). Paik and Bagchi (2007) have recently collected simulation data that demonstrates that increasing the number of echelons or length of the supply network has a significant impact on demand amplification and therefore on the risk of delays and stock outs. This leads to the fourth proposition.

Proposition 6: The probability of a disruption is greater in networks with a larger number of nodes.

Network Architecture

Structural properties of the network are also important to our analysis of risk. Ever since the seminal work of Erdös and Rényi in 1959, science has treated the structure of networks as being completely random. Models are based on a network of N nodes that are <u>randomly</u> connected with probability p. In such networks most nodes will have approximately the same number of links and the rate of decay is extremely rapid either side of the average. Thus the degree distribution[8] for the network will follow a Poisson distribution (see Figure 3 below).

In contrast to the random models of Erdös and Rényi, studies that have mapped the structure of 'real world' networks have found the degree distribution actually follows a power law (Barabási and Bonabeau, 2003). Power law distributions are very different from a Poisson distribution in that the peak of the graph is not at its average value and the rate of decay is much slower (Watts, 2004) (see Figure 3 below). The structure therefore includes a small number of 'hub' nodes that have an extremely large number of links and a large tail of nodes that have just a few links. Networks following a power law distribution have been termed scale-free (Barabási and Albert, 1999) and have

been observed in a number of real world networks including the WWW, citations of scientific papers, the collaborative network of Hollywood actors and the power grid of Western America.

More recent studies have begun to examine the degree distribution of supply chain networks. Initial empirical evidence of scale free properties has been found in supply chain distribution networks (Sun and Wu, 2005) and Liner Container Shipping Networks (Angeloudis et al, 2007). These findings are supported by an in depth structural analysis of the Guangzhou automotive supply chain network (Keqiang et al, 2008) where it is shown that the supply networks of Nissan, Honda and Toyota are all consistent will scale free distributions (see Figure 4). These findings make sense when we consider some of the trends within supply chain management over the past few decades. Firstly, there is ample evidence of a shift towards tiered sourcing configurations (Cousins, 2002). A tiered configuration creates a greater number of hubs within a network where work that was previously spread among a number of suppliers becomes concentrated and managed by a small number (possibly one) of so called 'mega suppliers'. Moreover, consolidation in both the 3PL sector (Berman, 2006) and the shipping of goods around the globe could also explain scale free distributions. Products are being consolidated in a smaller number of distribution hubs before being shipped to customers across the globe.

Figure 3. Random vs. scale-free networks (Adapted from Barabási and Bonabeau, 2003)

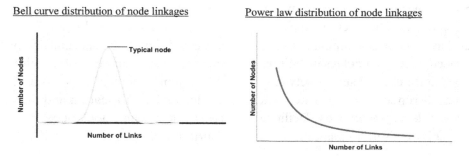

Figure 4. Topology of Guangzhou Automotive Supply Chain Network (© 2008, IEEE Computer Society. Used with permission)

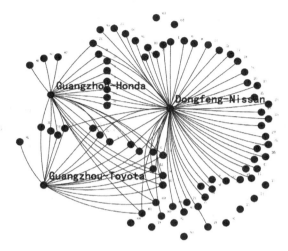

The degree distributions of networks are critical to any discussion of risk because the topology of the network can affect the probability and impact of a disruption. Scale free networks are thought to be robust against accidental failures but vulnerable to coordinated attacks (Barabási and Bonabeau, 2003). This is because random disruption is more likely to affect a node with few links simply because they are much more common than hub nodes. For a supply chain this means that accidental or random failure within the network is more likely to affect a supplier with fewer connections thereby reducing the probability of disruption to the overall network.

Proposition 7: The impact of a disruption resulting from accidental or random failure is reduced in supply chain networks that have scale free properties.

On the other hand, simulations have demonstrated that the removal of hub nodes has a quick and devastating effect on the network. For example, the Longshoreman union strike at a US West Coast port resulted in delivery delays of up to six months (Cavinato, 2004). In this example, the loss of a single node had a crippling effect on the supply chains of

many organisations precisely because it was a hub within the network. Thus 'coordinated attacks' on hub nodes will increase both the probability and impact of disruptions in scale free networks when compared to random networks:

Proposition 8: The impact of a disruption resulting from a co-ordinated attack is greater in supply chain networks that have scale free properties.

The foregoing discussion helps highlight the potential contribution of network measures to supply chain risk management. It is suggested that traditional and network measures provide complementary, and perhaps additive, perspectives to risk identification. Moreover, it appears useful to study determinants of supply chain risk from at least three levels, that of the individual, the dyadic and the global. One of the key objectives of this study is to provide a formal language and measurement system for supply chain risk management and to provide stimulation for further discussion and research. Based on its results, some preliminary suggestions for future studies are provided in the next section.

FUTURE RESEARCH DIRECTIONS

Businesses need to be able to identify and effectively mitigate vulnerabilities within their supply chains. Supply chain disruptions have been linked to reduced shareholder wealth (Hendricks and Singhal, 2005) and profitability. The first step of any risk management model is risk identification. This chapter proposes that already identified sources of risk might be broadened to include those identified through formal network measures. Using a conceptual analysis of formal network measures, this chapter considers the benefits of looking at measures of centrality, distance, redundancy and topology.

Mapping supply networks is never going to be an easy task but that does not mean it is not possible. Network maps of supply chains are starting to appear (e.g. Angeloudis et al, 2007; Keqiang et al, 2008) and are already starting to provide interesting findings. For example, a network analysis of the Mediterranean Port supply chain demonstrated that power within a supply chain was not solely attributable to firm-level characteristics but also to the position the firm occupied within the supply network (Cisic et al, 2007). Similarly, Battini et al (2005) mapped an Italian Industrial Group using a network analysis technique commonly found in ecology network studies. The authors found they could use this technique not only to map the network, but also to run simulations to help optimise the links between organisations.

A major concern is the boundary specification of the network[9] or which organisations should be in the population? Ideally this should be the outcome of a theoretically informed decision about what is significant to the research question under investigation (Scott, 2005). In other words, the research question should drive the choice of populations. A scholar looking at supply chain risk may conclude that the entire supply network forms a natural boundary, whereas a study of open

innovations means that the population would necessarily cut across supply networks. In the later case, membership of the project might be a better way to specify the boundary.

Of course, the size of this population may also be of concern to a supply chain researcher. Given that supply networks may incorporate tens of thousands of organisations, it may not be feasible to take measurements from all nodes. In this situation, the researcher will have to choose how they will sample from the overall population. Borgatti and Li (2009) offer some useful advice for supply chain researchers. First, they could use a snowball approach to identify the organisations within the network. Applying the snowball approach to supply chain management means that the first tier identifies the links they have with the second tier, the second tier identifies the links they have with the third tier and so on. Second, researchers could follow an aggregation strategy. Rather than ask respondents about their links to specific organisations, the aggregation strategy suggests that organisations identify their links to categories of others. For example, this could be categories of supplier (travel, stationary, critical module etc), industry codes and so on. Finally, the network could be defined as the ego network of the focal organisation. An ego network consists of the focal firm (ego), a set of organisations tied to the focal organisation (alters) and the ties between the alters.

Once researchers have gathered network data, they can start to model the various properties discussed in this chapter. It is beyond the scope of this chapter to provide details on the various metrics; however, well-established measures are available for centrality, geodesics, redundancy and topology. Interested readers are referred to Scott (2005) for an introduction to the field and Wasserman and Faust (1994) for in-depth discussion of the various metrics. Moreover, sophisticated network software, such as UCINET, Pajek and NetMiner, can aid analysis and visual representation of the data. Huisman and van Duijn (2005) provide an in-depth review of benefits and drawbacks of software for social network analysis.

Having established empirical support (if any) for the propositions in this chapter, it would be interesting to examine methods of mitigation. For example, scale-free properties indicate that a network is robust to accidental failure but vulnerable to co-ordinated attacked. This could have interesting implications for both the methods of mitigation and for the cost-benefit analysis of mitigation alternatives. In particular, firms may wish to add extra inventory or capacity at the hubs but may also wish to consider the probability of a co-ordinated attack. One could imagine the case where the risk of attack is so low that it reduces the necessity to add redundancy. However, this requires formal theorising and thorough empirical testing in the future.

Researchers could also start to look at the relationship between risk and other measures of networks. For example, studies of robust networks have been a major theme of research in fields such as computer science, biology and sociology. It would be interesting to see whether the same properties also apply to supply networks. This study has examined the benefits of specific network properties in reducing risk; a further stream of research could examine the trade-off for some of these measures. For example, the notion of redundant ties lends itself to a study of the trade-off between efficiency and resilience where more redundant ties are useful for risk reduction but also have a cost attached to them.

Finally, network measures could be built into methodologies for supply chain risk management. It is immediately apparent that the measures presented in this chapter could be used to help identify risks within a network. However, the use of network analysis could be extended to simulate the effects of various mitigation strategies. For example, having mapped the current supply network, researchers could examine the effect on robustness that inserting an additional supplier would have. This would provide a strong platform for the cost-benefit analysis of risk reduction strategies.

CONCLUSION

This chapter examines the potential contribution of formal network measures to the study and management of supply chain risks. The measures are primarily concerned with risk identification. In particular, network measures may help managers identify risks that remain hidden after traditional analysis where the focus is on geography and organization level. It is not argued that these measures are not important, indeed most of the traditional measures can be directly linked to the financial consequences of a disruption (Hendricks and Singhal, 2005), but rather that network analysis may have an additive impact on our understanding. Moreover, the formal methods of data collection and analysis might provide the means to communicate potential risks with analytical precision. This should appeal to the more established financial risk community where rigour and objectivity is highly valued. Finally, the combination of network analysis and supply chain risk management provides academics with rich research opportunities. There is much work to be done in terms of mapping supply networks, but the outcome could provide a deeper understanding of supply chain risk.

ACKNOWLEDGMENT

I gratefully acknowledge the financial support of the Engineering & Physical Science Research Council (Grant Number F063245). This chapter has benefited from the thoughtful insights and suggestions of the editor, Dr Stavros Ponis, and two anonymous reviewers.

REFERENCES

Aberdeen Group. (2005). *The Supply Risk Management Benchmark Report*. Boston: Aberdeen Group.

Ahuja, G. (2000). Collaboration networks, structural holes, and innovation: A longitudinal study. *Administrative Science Quarterly, 45*, 425–455. doi:10.2307/2667105

Albert, R., Jeong, H., & Barabasi, A.-L. (2000). Error and attack tolerance of complex networks. *Nature, 406*, 378–382. doi:10.1038/35019019

Angeloudis, P., Bichou, K., & Bell, M. G. H. (2007). Security and Reliability of the Liner Container-Shipping Network: Analysis of Robustness using a Complex Network Framework . In Bichou, K., Bell, M. G. H., & Evans, A. (Eds.), *Risk Management in Port Operations*. London: Informa.

Barabasi, A.-L., & Albert, R. (1999). Emergence of scaling in random networks. *Science, 286*, 509–512. doi:10.1126/science.286.5439.509

Barabasi, A.-L., & Bonabeau, E. (2003). Scale-Free Networks. *Scientific American*, (May): 50–59.

Battini, D., & Persona, A. (2007). Towards a use of network analysis: quantifying the complexity of Supply Chain Networks. *Int. J. Electronic Customer Relationship Management, 1*(1), 75–90. doi:10.1504/IJECRM.2007.014427

Baum, J. A. C., Calabrese, T., & Silverman, B. S. (2000). Don't go it alone: alliance network composition and startups' performance in Canadian biotechnology. *Strategic Management Journal, 21*, 267–294. doi:10.1002/(SICI)1097-0266(200003)21:3<267::AID-SMJ89>3.0.CO;2-8

Bell, D. C., Atkinson, J. A., & Carlson, J. W. (1999). Centrality measures for disease transmission networks. *Social Networks, 21*, 1–21. doi:10.1016/S0378-8733(98)00010-0

Berman, J. (2006). *3PL conslidation market is going strong*. Retrieved from http://www.logisticsmgmt.com/article/334621-3PL_consolidation_market_is_going_strong.php

Borgatti, S. P., & Li, X. (2009). On social network analysis in a supply chain context. *Journal of Supply Chain Management, 45*(2), 5–22. doi:10.1111/j.1745-493X.2009.03166.x

Brass, D. J. (1984). A structural analysis of individual influence in an organization. *Administrative Science Quarterly, 29*, 518–539. doi:10.2307/2392937

Brass, D. J. (1995). A social network perspective on human resources management. *Research in Personnel ang . Human Resource Management, 13*, 39–79.

Burgess, M., Canwright, G., & Engo-Monsen, K. (2003). A graph theoretical model of computer security. *International Journal of Information Security, 3*(2), 70–85. doi:10.1007/s10207-004-0044-x

Burkhardt, M. E., & Brass, D. J. (1990). Changing patterns or patterns of change: The effect of a change in technology on social network structure and power. *Administrative Science Quarterly, 35*, 104–127. doi:10.2307/2393552

Camacho, J., Guimera, R., & Amaral, L. A. N. (2002). Robust patterns in food web structure. *Physical Review Letters, 88*.

Cavinato, J. L. (2004). Supply Chain Logistics Risks. *International Journal of Physical Distribution & Logistics Management., 34*(5), 383–387. doi:10.1108/09600030410545427

Choi, T., Y., & Hong, Y. (2002). Unveiling the structure of supply networks: case studies in Honda, Acura, and DaimlerChrysler. *Journal of Operations Management, 20,* 469–493. doi:10.1016/S0272-6963(02)00025-6

Choi, T. Y., & Kim, Y. (2008). Structural embeddedness and supplier management: A network perspective. *Journal of Supply Chain Management, 44*(4), 5–13. doi:10.1111/j.1745-493X.2008.00069.x

Choi, T. Y., & Krause, D. R. (2006). The supply base and its complexity: Implications for transaction costs, risks, responsiveness, and innovation. *Journal of Operations Management, 24*(5), 637–652. doi:10.1016/j.jom.2005.07.002

Chopra, S., & Sodhi, M. (2004). Managing risk to avoid supply-chain breakdown. *MIT Sloan Management Review, 46*(1), 53–61.

Christley, R. M., Pinchbeck, G. L., Bowers, R. G., Clancy, D., French, N. P., & Bennett, R. (2005). Infection in Social Networks: Using Network Analysis to Identify High-Risk Individual. *American Journal of Epidemiology, 162*(10), 1024–1031. doi:10.1093/aje/kwi308

Christopher, M. (2003). *Creating resilient Supply Chains: A practical guide.* Bedford, UK: Cranfield University.

Christopher, M., & Lee, H. (2004). Mitigating Supply Chain Risk Through improved Confidence. *International Journal of Physical Distribution & Logistics Management, 34*(5), 388–396. doi:10.1108/09600030410545436

Cisic, D., Komadina, P., & Hlaca, B. (2007). Network analysis of the Mediterranian port supply chain structures. *Journal of Maritime Studies, 21*(1), 211–220.

Coleman, B. J., & Jennings, K. M. (1998). The UPS strike: Lessons for Just-In-Timers. *Production and Inventory Management Journal, 39*(4), 63–68.

Cousins, P. D. (2002). A Conceptual Model for Managing long-term inter-organisational relationships. *European Journal of Purchasing and Supply Management, 8,* 71–82. doi:10.1016/S0969-7012(01)00006-5

Cousins, P. D., Lamming, R. C., Lawson, B., & Squire, B. C. (2008). Strategic Supply Management: Principles, theories and practice. Harlow, UK: Pearson Education Limited.

Craighead, C. W., Blackburst, J., Rungtusanatham, M. J., & Handfield, R. B. (2007). The Severity of Supply Chain Disruptions: Design Characteristics and Mitigation Capabilities. *Decision Sciences, 38*(1), 131–156. doi:10.1111/j.1540-5915.2007.00151.x

Das, T. K., & Teng, B.-S. (2001). Trust, control, and risk in strategic alliances: An integrated framework. *Organization Studies, 22*(2), 251–283. doi:10.1177/0170840601222004

Ebel, H., Mielsch, L.-I., & Bornholdt, S. (2002). Scale free topology of e-mail networks. *Physical Review, 66.*

Elkins, D., Handfield, R. B., Blackburst, J., & Craighead, C. W. (2005). 18 Ways to Guard Against Disruption. Supply Chain Management Review, 46.

Finch, S. (2009). An upside to the downturn. *CPO Agenda, Spring.*

Forrester, J. W. (1961). *Industrial Dynamics.* Waltham, MA: Pegasus Communications.

Gaonkar, R. S., & Viswanadham, N. (2007). Analytical Framework for the Management of Risk in Supply Chain. *IEEE Transactions on Automation Science and Engineering, 4*(2), 265–273. doi:10.1109/TASE.2006.880540

Gulati, R. (1995). Does familiarity breed trust? The implications of repeated ties for contractual choice in alliances. *Academy of Management Journal*, *38*(1), 85–112. doi:10.2307/256729

Gulati, R., & Wang, L. (2003). Size of the Pie and Share of the Pie: Implications of Structural Embeddedness for Value Creation and Value Appropriation in Joint Ventures. *Research in the Sociology of Organizations*, *20*, 209–242. doi:10.1016/S0733-558X(02)20008-7

Hendricks, K. B., & Singhal, V. R. (2005). Association Between Supply Chain Glitches and Operating Performance. *Management Science*, *51*(5), 695–711. doi:10.1287/mnsc.1040.0353

Huisman, M., & van Duijn, M. A. J. (2005). Software for social network analysis . In Carrington, P. J. (Eds.), *Models and Methods in Social Network Analysis*. New York: Cambridge University Press.

Jeong, H., Tombor, B., Albert, R., Oltvai, Z. N., & Barabasi, A.-L. (2000). The large-scale organization of metabolic networks. *Nature*, *407*, 651–654. doi:10.1038/35036627

Juttner, U. (2005). Supply Chain Risk Management Understanding the Business Requirements from a Practitioner Perspective. *The International Journal of Logistics Management*, *16*, 120–141. doi:10.1108/09574090510617385

Juttner, U., Peck, H., & Christopher, M. (2003). Supply Chain Risk Management: Outlining an agenda for future research. *International Journal of Logistics: Research and Applications, 6.*

Karningsih, P. D., Kayis, B., & Kara, S. (2007). *Risk Identification in Global Manufacturing Supply Chain*. Jakarta, Indonesia: University of Indonesia.

Keqiang, W., Zhaofeng, Z., & Dongchuan, S. (2008). *Structure analysis of supply chain networks based on complex network theory*. Paper presented at the Fourth International Conference on Semantics, Knowledge and Grid.

Kleindorfer, P. R., & Saad, G. H. (2005). Managing Disruption Risks in Supply Chains. *Production and Operations Management*, *14*(1).

Klimov, R., & Merkuryev, Y. (2008). Simulation Model for Supply Chain Reliability Evaluation. *Technological and Economic Development of Economy Baltic Journal on Sustainability*, *14*(3), 300–311. doi:10.3846/1392-8619.2008.14.300-311

Kraljic, P. (1983). Purchasing Must Become Supply Management. *Havard Business Review (September-October).*

Lamming, R. C. (1993). Beyond partnership - Strategies for innovation and lean supply. London: Prentice-Hall.

Lamming, R., C., Johnsen, T., Zheng, J., & Harland, C. (2000). An intial classifcation of supply networks. *International Journal of Operations & Production Management*, *20*(6), 675–691. doi:10.1108/01443570010321667

Lee, H. L., Padmanabhan, V., & Whang, S. (1997). Information distortion in a supply chain: The bullwhip effect. *Management Science*, *43*(4), 546. doi:10.1287/mnsc.43.4.546

Majima, T., Katuhara, M., & Takadama, K. (2007). Analysis on transport networks of railway, subway and waterbus in Japan. *Studies in Computational Intelligence*, *56*, 99–113. doi:10.1007/978-3-540-71075-2_8

Manuj, I., & Mentzer, J. T. (2008). Global Supply Chain Risk Management Strategies. *International Journal of Physical Distribution & Logistics Management*, *38*(3), 192–223. doi:10.1108/09600030810866986

Martinez, M. T., Fouletier, P., Park, P. H., & Favrel, J. (2001). Virtual Enterprise – organization, evolution and control. *International Journal of Production Economics, 74*, 225–238. doi:10.1016/S0925-5273(01)00129-3

Mehra, A., Kilduff, M., & Brass, D. (2001). The social networks of high and low-self monitors: Implications for workplace performance. *Administrative Science Quarterly, 46*, 121–146. doi:10.2307/2667127

Memon, N., & Larsen, H. L. (2006). *Structural analysis and destabilizing terrorist networks.* Paper presented at the International Conference on Data Mining.

Mitroff, I., & Alpasan, M. (2003). Preparing for evil. *Harvard Business Review, 81*(4), 109–115.

Mizruchi, M. S., & Marquis, C. (2006). Egocentric, sociocentric, or dyadic? Identifying the appropriate level of analysis in the study of organizational networks. *Social Networks, 28*, 187–208. doi:10.1016/j.socnet.2005.06.002

Monckza, R. M., Trent, R. J., & Handfield, R. (2005). Purchasing & supply chain management (3 ed.). Mason, Ohio: Thomson South-Western.

Monge, P. R., & Contractor, N. S. (2003). *Theories of Communication Networks.* New York: Oxford University Press.

Neaigus, A., Friedman, S. R., Curtis, R., Des-Jarlais, D. C., Furst, S. T., & Jose, B. (1994). The relevance of drug injectors' social and risk networks for understanding and preventing HIV infection. *Social Science & Medicine, 38*, 67–78. doi:10.1016/0277-9536(94)90301-8

Newman, M. E. J. (Ed.). (2007). *The mathematics of networks.* Ann Arbor, MI: Center for the Study of Complex Systems.

Nooteboom, B., Berger, H., & Noorderhaven, N. (1997). Effects of trust and goverence on relational risk. *Academy of Management Journal, 40*(2), 308–338. doi:10.2307/256885

Paik, S. K., & Bagchi, P. (2007). Understanding the causes of the bullwhip effect in a supply chain. *International Journal of Retail and Distribution Management, 35*(4), 308–324. doi:10.1108/09590550710736229

Petersen, K. P., Handfield, R. B., Lawson, B., & Cousins, P. D. (in press). Buyer dependency and relational capital formation: The mediating effects of socialization processes and supplier integration. *Journal of Supply Chain Management.*

Rice, J., & Caniato, F. (2003). Building a secure and resilient supply chain. *Supply chain management review, 7*(5), 22-30.

Scott, J. (2005). Social Network Analysis (2 ed.). London: Sage Publications Ltd.

Seibert, S. E., Kraimer, M. L., & Liden, R. C. (2001). A social capital theory of career success. *Academy of Management Journal, 44*(2), 219–237. doi:10.2307/3069452

Sheffi, Y. (2005). *The Resilient Enterprise.* Cambridge, MA: The MIT Press.

Sparrowe, R. T., & Liden, R. C. (2001). Social networks and the performance of individuals and groups. *Academy of Management Journal, 44*(2), 316–325. doi:10.2307/3069458

Stanley, M. H. R., Amaral, L. A. N., Buldyrev, S. V., Leschhorn, H., Maass, P., & Salinger, M. A. (1996). Scaling behaviour in the growth of companies. *Nature, 379*, 804–806. doi:10.1038/379804a0

Stauffer, D. (2003). *Supply chain risk: Deal with it.* Harvard Business Review.

Sun, H., & Wu, J. (2005). Scale-free characterisitics of supply chain distribution networks. *Modern Physics Letters B, 19*(17), 841–848. doi:10.1142/S0217984905008797

Tang, C. S. (2006). Perspectives in supply chain risk management. *International Journal of Production Economics, 103*, 451–488. doi:10.1016/j.ijpe.2005.12.006

Uzzi, B. (1997). Social structure and competition in interfirm networks: The paradox of embeddedness. *Administrative Science Quarterly, 42*, 35–67. doi:10.2307/2393808

Wagner, S. M., & Bode, C. (2006). An Empirical Investigation into Supply Chain Vulnerability. *Journal of Purchasing and Supply Management, 12*, 301–312. doi:10.1016/j.pursup.2007.01.004

Wasserman, S., & Faust, K. (1994). *Social Network Analysis: Methods and Applications.* Cambridge, UK: Cambridge University Press.

Watts, D. J. (2004). *Six Degrees: The Science of a Connected Age.* London: Vintage Books.

Wilding, R. (2007). The Mitigation of Supply Chain Risk. *Institute of Supply Management, 18*(8), 12–13.

Zsidisin, G. A., Melnyk, S. A., & Ragatz, G. L. (2005). An Institutional Theory Perspective of Business Continuity Planning For Purchasing And Supply Management. *International Journal of Production Research, 43*(16), 3401–3420. doi:10.1080/00207540500095613

ADDITIONAL READINGS

Barabasi, A.-L. (2003). Linked. New York: Penguin Group (USA) Inc.

Blackhurst, J., Craighead, C. W., Elkins, D., & Handfield, R. B. (2005). An Empirically Derived Agenda of Critical Research Issues for Managing Supply- Chain Disruptions. *International Journal of Production Research, 43*(19), 4067–4081. doi:10.1080/00207540500151549

Blackhurst, J. V., Scheibe, K. P., & Johnson, D. J. (2008). Supplier Risk Assessment and Monitoring for the Automotive Industry. *International Journal of Physical Distribution & Logistics Management, 38*(2), 143–165. doi:10.1108/09600030810861215

Giunipero, C. L., & Eltantawy, R. A. (2004). Securing the upstream supply chain: a risk management approach. *International Journal of Physical Distribution & Logistics Management, 34*(9), 698–713. doi:10.1108/09600030410567478

Hendricks, K. B., Singhal, V. R., & Zhang, R. (2008). The Effect of Operational Slack, Diversification, And Vertical Relatedness On The Stock Market Reaction TO Supply Chain Disruptions. *Journal of Operations Management, 27*, 233–246. doi:10.1016/j.jom.2008.09.001

Khan, O., & Burnes, B. (2007). Risk and supply chain management: creating a research agenda. *International Journal of Logistics Management, 18*(2), 197. doi:10.1108/09574090710816931

Khan, O., Christopher, M., & Burnes, B. (2008). The Impact of Product Design on Supply Chain Risk: A Case Study. *International Journal of Physical Distribution & Logistics Management, 38*(5), 412–432. doi:10.1108/09600030810882834

Lee, H. L. (2002). Aligning Supply Chain Strategies with Product Uncertainties. *California Management Review, 44*(3).

Lee, H. L. (2004, October 1-12). *The Triple-A Supply Chain.* Harvard Business Review.

Monge, P. R., & Contractor, N. S. (2003). *Theories of Communication Networks*. New York: Oxford University Press.

Narasimhan, R., & Talluri, S. (in press). Perspectives on risk management in supply chains. *Journal of Operations Management*.

Ritchie, B., & Brindley, C. (2007). An Emergent Framework for Supply Chain Risk Management and Performance Measurement. *The Journal of the Operational Research Society*, 58.

Ritchie, R. (2007). Supply Chain Risk Management and Performance: A guiding framework for Future Development. *International Journal of Operations & Production Management*, *27*(3), 303–322. doi:10.1108/01443570710725563

Svensson, G. (2000). A Conceptual Framework for the Analysis of Vulnerability in Supply Chains. *International Journal of Physical Distribution & Logistics Management*, *30*(9), 731–750. doi:10.1108/09600030010351444

Svensson, G. (2004). Key Areas, Causes and Contingency Planning of Corporate Vulnerability In Supply Chain- A Qualitative Approach. *International Journal of Physical Distribution & Logistics Management*, *34*(9), 728–748. doi:10.1108/09600030410567496

Tang, C. S. (2006). Robust Strategies for Mitigating Supply Chain Disruptions. *International Journal of Logistics: Research and Applications*, *9*(1), 33–35.

Tomlim, B. (2006). On the Value of Mitigation and Contingency Strategies for Managing Supply Chain Disruption Risks. *Management Science*, *52*(5), 639–657. doi:10.1287/mnsc.1060.0515

Zsidisin, G. A. (2003). Managerial Perceptions of Supply Risk. *The Journal of Supply Chain Management*, 14-26.

Zsidisin, G. A. (2003). A Grounded Definition of Supply Risk. *Journal of Purchasing and Supply Management*, *9*, 217–224. doi:10.1016/j.pursup.2003.07.002

Zsidisin, G. A., Ellram, L., Carter, J. R., & Cavinato, J. L. (2004). An Analysis of Supply Risk Assessment Techniques. *International Journal of Physical Distribution & Logistics Management*, *34*(5). doi:10.1108/09600030410545445

ENDNOTES

[1] These terms are used interchangeably throughout.

[2] The author is aware that there may be other types of relation within the same supply network including informal information exchange, friendships, or membership of industry groups. However, this analysis is restricted to formal exchange that includes the provision of products and/or services in return for financial reward. In network terms, the study of one type of relation is called a uniplex study.

[3] In reality these links are bidirectional where product or services flow in one direction and finances flow the other way. Both directions could be important to the study of supply chain risk where cash flow and payment terms are very important to resilience of networks.

[4] More detail and other measures of centrality are found below. Google uses a technique similar to eigenvector centrality to rank its web pages.

[5] This chapter was authored in the midst of the so called 'credit crunch' in April 2009.

[6] The geodesic is the shortest distance between two points in a network.

[7] The number of nodes is different from the concept of complexity (see Choi and Krause, 2006) where there is a distinct focus on the

actual nodes and not on the links between them.

8   The degree of a node is the number of links it has to other nodes in the network (Wasserman and Faust, 1999). The degree distribution is the probability distribution of all the degrees across the network.

9   Readers are referred to Wasserman and Faust (1994), Scott (2005) and Laumann et al (1989) for in depth reading on the subject.

Chapter 3
Mitigating Risk through Building Trust in Virtual Enterprise Networks

Burak Sari
Leiden Institute of Advanced Computer Science (LIACS), The Netherlands

ABSTRACT

The emergence of virtual enterprise networks represents a dynamic response to the challenge of the hierarchical coordination of networked businesses. Therefore, the chapter's first aim is to provide justified answers to the question of why the virtual enterprise business model is getting so much attention and correlate these answers with the main business drivers that today's enterprises are facing. In virtual enterprises, the distributed tasks of the partners must be integrated over and above the barriers of missing face-to-face interactions and cultural differences. The social integration of the virtual network involves the creation of identities for the participating nodes, the building of trust and the sharing of tacit and explicit knowledge between them. The traditional organization already doing well in these areas seems to have an edge when going virtual. As a consequence, trust becomes more and more important in these types of virtual collaboration networks. Therefore, this chapter finally aims to discuss extensively the way of managing trust in virtual enterprise networks as a solution to mitigate collaboration and performance risk in varying business situations and also aims to present conditions for building trust in the virtual collaboration context.

INTRODUCTION

Companies of the 21st century are faced with increasing demands from the market. These demands are, among other things, derived from technological innovations and the corresponding development towards a global marketplace. Specific advantages created from operating in a global market appear to be exploitable only by agile organizations. Companies must find organizational solutions that allow them to cope with global business opportunities without suffering the effects of their limited resources or exposing themselves to the risk of direct investments. Literature reveals that many

DOI: 10.4018/978-1-61520-607-0.ch003

high tech enterprises have failed due to the lack of technical and management competencies (Berry, 1998). Companies are diversified through their competencies which are considered as a subset of resources and capabilities with the potential to lead the company to competitive sustainable advantages.

The increasing significance of the so-called 'new economy', also referred to as the digital and knowledge economy, pushes towards further concentration on corporate competencies while exploiting and developing these competencies in inter-organizational networks facilitated by advanced information and communication technologies (ICTs). In this context, the notion of the virtual enterprise is receiving increasing attention as a business model addressing these new business challenges. A virtual enterprise (VE), sometimes coined with the term virtual organization or business network, can be defined as a temporary network of companies that come together quickly to exploit fast changing opportunities (Davidow & Malone, 1992). It is based on the ability to create temporary co-operations and to realize the value of a short business opportunity that the partners cannot (or can, but only to lesser extent) capture on their own (Katzy & Schuh, 1998). The virtual enterprise has therefore the ability to recognize, rapidly react and cope with the unpredictable changes in the environment in order to achieve better responses to opportunities, shorter time-to-market, and higher quality with less investment (Goranson, 1999). The major challenges of VEs are the ability to share business processes and to establish supporting distributed IT systems which permit the effective utilization of flexible organizational structures and communication across the network and promotes the development of trust among members. Because of the pervasiveness of distributed IT systems and the shared processes, the interactions and interdependencies among VE members affect the performance of a VE. Those interdependencies are related to risk mitigation processes (Grabowski & Roberts, 1999). For instance, fluid organizational structures alone may or may not dampen risk in VEs; however, organizational structures that provide flexibility in response options as well as communication opportunities can better facilitate the risk mitigation process (Weick, 1993).

The success of a virtual enterprise is tightly related to the ability to set up a business formation uniquely tailored for a specific market delivery and composed of competencies from independent partners often not well acquainted. Besides, a crucial prerequisite for the existence of a virtual enterprise is the time it takes to deliver the solution, and as a part of this, the time it takes to set up the virtual enterprise itself. It is of no use being able to deliver a 'first class solution' if the time to market is not competitive. Until now, research into virtual enterprises and related business-to-business initiatives have generally focused on technological solutions and the linking of distributed information systems (Camarinha-Matos & Afsarmanesh, 2003; Filos & Ouzounis, 2003). However, technological solutions alone are not sufficient. Several other aspects need to be explored as well, such as the risk/uncertainty related to co-operating with new partners (are the partners trustworthy?) in a global environment.

In its conceptual form, the virtual enterprise creation is triggered by a specific customer need. Then, companies come together to share costs and skills that they could not undertake individually and create the solution requested by the customer (Sari *et al.*, 2007). However, this is easier said than done, since a set of challenges is related to the virtual enterprises business model. One of the most significant challenges is related to the dynamic aspect of a VE such as dealing with new and unknown partners on a more frequent basis. Thus, the first objective of this chapter is to clarify the virtual enterprise concept based on a thorough literature review and determine a business concept that suits the situation of industrial enterprises, i.e. the main challenges that were identified. That is, the chapter is expected to contribute with a new and more clarified understanding of the virtual enterprise concept. The intention is not to make a thorough examination of all relevant theories studying the VE business model but to support our statement that VEs can be the solution to business challenges which the contemporary companies are facing.

Before the set-up and operation of a VE, the partners first need to interact with each other. Since this process includes a relational risk (referred as the risk of the partner not cooperating in good faith), a need for trust gets essential between the partners (Das & Teng, 2001). Within this context, trust can be defined as the willingness to take risks (Mayer *et al.*, 1995). When setting up a VE, there is a risk that a potential partner is presented with low predictability about its future behavior due to lack of overview on his past experience. To minimize risk, VE initiators often limit their search for potential partners and focus on those partners that they already know and worked together in the past. However, the weakness of this strategy is that it limits the selection of good partners, with the risk that the best partner for cooperation is not taken into consideration, because he is not a member of the initiator's community. Thus, the second objective of this chapter is to address the role of trust in the formation of VE networks through understanding the prerequisites and key phases of building and managing trust in collaborative business networks. The relationship between trust and risk will be also explored by looking at the situation from a risk mitigation perspective.

BUSINESS CHALLENGES

In today's business environment corporations are faced with increasing requirements in terms of speed, quality, price, added value, and customer tailored products. The speed of change is increasing due to enhancements and innovations in infrastructure, transportation and technology especially information and communication technol-

ogy (ICT). This change puts the traditional stable business model under pressure in an increasing number of industries. Throughout the literature, the need for more dynamic enterprise forms is discussed (Filos & Banahan, 2003; Mowshowitz, 2002). More specifically, four interrelated major forces put additional requirements on today's enterprises:

- Globalization
- Focus on core competencies through outsourcing
- Customization
- Impact from the development in technologies.

As illustrated in Figure 1, these forces are not independent. For instance: the development in technologies enables companies to become more global. The globalization forces the competition and increases the risk, which in turn pressures companies to focus on their core competencies, which again enables them to provide more customized solutions to the market through networking and collaboration. These forces will be described separately in the following sub-sections.

Figure 1. Business drivers for virtual collaboration

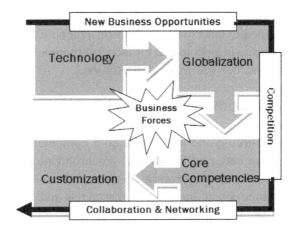

Globalization

The statement "the business-world is becoming smaller" although a cliché often heard, holds much truth. Enterprises co-operate more and more extensively with other enterprises in all the phases of a product's life cycle. Thus, organizations need to expand their scope to become global, and differentiate their patterns of cooperation to encompass collaborative activities. One of the implications of globalization is that it is no longer possible to base a business or a country's economic development on cheap labor (Drucker, 1999).

Therefore, to survive in the global world, companies have to be among the best in their particular field, a demand further enhanced by globalization which makes the competition and risk more global. Risks possess an inherent tendency towards globalization (Beck, 1992). A universalization of hazards accompanies for instance, industrial production, which has become independent of the place where products are actually produced: supply chains connect practically everyone on earth to everyone else. In other words, hazards linked to industrial production, for example can quickly spread beyond the immediate context in which they are generated.

As knowledge has grown, so has risk. Indeed, it could be argued that the social relationships, institutions and dynamics within which knowledge is produced have accentuated the risks involved. Risk has been globalized (Beck, 1999). Therefore, companies have to concentrate on their core competencies in order to face the increased competition and risk derived from globalization.

Core Competencies and Outsourcing

Outsourcing and a focus on core competencies require better collaboration, synchronization of processes, and appropriate handling of time and distance constraints. The increased risk and costs derived from globalization has lead companies to focus on their core processes and to outsource those

not vital for them. In some situations it even makes companies collaborate with their competitors and winning through that (Desbarats, 1999).

The notions of resources, capabilities and competencies have gained considerable attention from scholars of strategic management research as they attempt to explain why companies differ in organizational performance (Pedersen & Berg, 2001). Resources are defined as the inputs or factors available to a company through which it performs its operations or carries out its activities (Amit & Schoemaker, 1993). This generic definition includes resources of different kinds, physical, employee skills, patents, teams etc. Capabilities refer to a company's capacity, or ability, to deploy resources (Amit & Schoemaker, 1993). Competencies are a complimentary subset of resources and capabilities with the potential to lead to competitive sustainable advantages (Amit & Schoemaker, 1993). Whether a competitive advantage is sustainable or not is not defined by a period of calendar time, but by the inability of current and potential competitors to duplicate it (Barney, 1991). Another essential characteristic of a competence is that it does not get diminished when used; on the contrary it can be enhanced when it is applied and shared (Prahalad & Hamel, 1994).

In essence, one can argue that companies have to raise their awareness concerning their (core) competencies. They have to focus on what they do best (and leave the rest to other companies). Once the competence has been identified it should be nurtured and enhanced on an ongoing basis in order to ensure that the competitive advantage can be sustained. Corporations have to look out for applying their competencies in non-traditional ways (Prahalad & Hamel, 1994). That is, to maintain resources and capabilities as competencies and to improve existing competencies. The focus on the corporation's core competencies has lead organizations to downsize and outsource their non-core business.

Though outsourcing has proven to be effective, it brings significant risks that must be recognized and managed. In outsourcing, a company is relying on someone else to run certain business functions. If the outsourcing risks are not properly managed, they may negatively affect companies' operations and customers. The product or service can be outsourced, but the risk cannot. Some of the potential negative outcomes include (Quinn, 1999):

- On-time delivery performance and end-customer satisfaction levels may decline because of delays at third parties. This risk can be severely aggravated as the product/service is outsourced.
- Product or service quality may also suffer in outsourcing which may create a risk of affecting customer satisfaction. Companies must carefully select, qualify, contract and manage their outsourcing partners to ensure that quality does not deteriorate. This often requires adequate transition periods and/or parallel production as well as effective cross-training between companies. These aspects are often neglected because of cost-saving efforts.
- There is a risk that the outsourcing transition phase may also fail if schedules and budgets are not achieved because of insufficient planning and/or resources. Outsourcing is a replacement of production or service functions, and these functions have a direct bearing on the company's ability to meet its commitments to customers and shareholders.

Thus, as an answer to the globalization trend, companies are undergoing a transition towards a focus on their core competencies and at the same time towards outsourcing their non-core activities. In most situations, this requires collaboration with other partners possessing complementary competencies, and taking risks.

Customization

In addition to the globalization trend and the ongoing movement towards focusing on core competencies described above, companies have to adapt to an increasingly demanding market requiring more customized solutions.

The higher customization level is a consequence of the increased competition, derived from the increased globalization and focuses on core competencies, while also facilitated by the development of ICT. The higher the level of customization, the higher the risk will be, because the customized product has not been previously verified by the users. Likewise, the more the companies have to integrate their activities with the product supplier, the higher the risk will be.

Customization is based on the better access to knowledge about the needs and demands of the end customers. This knowledge may translate into significant cost reductions, like the elimination of distribution inventory, less product returns, reduced obsolescence or antiquated-fashion risks, mitigated product liability risks, and reduced cost of staffing to deal with post-sales product failures, complaints, liabilities, and loss of reputation (Kumar, 2004).

Treating customers as individuals can help establishing a long-term relationship with them, while getting inside knowledge about their preferences and future needs. If companies do not manage to establish individual relationships with their customers, they face the risk of losing them to a competitor (Flynn, 2003).

When dealing with customers and their expected lifetime values, the companies should also consider the potential risk associated to working with a specific customer(s). The issue of customer risk can be expressed as the probability of securing customer lifetime value through satisfying the customer needs and meeting their expectations (Dhar & Glazer, 2003). Hence, the company should consider composing a portfolio of customers to minimize long-term risk and to optimize their long-term earning (Camarinha-Matos & Afsar-manesh, 2003). In terms of the aforementioned competencies this means that companies need to find new ways of deploying their competencies in new business constellations by broadening the portfolio of end-products in which their competencies can contribute to (Camarinha-Matos & Afsarmanesh, 2003). Globalization and focus on core competencies can be seen as developments that enable and to some extent force companies to provide more customized solutions to their customers. Customization, globalization, and to some extent outsourcing and accompanying focus on core competencies trends are all facilitated by IT development.

Technology Impact

There is nothing particularly novel about industrial collaboration. Collaboration of some kind exists since the industrial revolution (Davidow & Malone, 1992). However, classification of the range and scope of cooperation has evolved with the advent of ICT tools. These tools have given manufacturers new means of sharing information and managing operations, thus blurring the organizational boundaries with suppliers, clients and even erstwhile competitors. The quality and efficiency issues extend well beyond the traditional enterprise boundary. Therefore, ICT tools have great impact on the emerging collaboration typologies (e.g. extended and virtual enterprises) and business paradigms (e.g. EC, i2i, b2b, and so on) (Jagdev & Browne, 1998; Jagdev & Thoben, 2001).

In the traditional marketplace value is usually created through aggregation of infrastructure, context and content. For example, a newspaper is an aggregated collection of content (news, business, sports etc), context (format, organization, editorial style), and infrastructure (printing plant including trucks and door-to-door delivery). Companies are under a transition from a traditional marketplace towards a combined marketplace and

a universal marketspace. ICT development enables enterprises to add or alter their content, changes the context of their interactions, and enables the delivery of various products and information in a variety of contexts over different infrastructures (Purdy & Safayeni, 2000). As a result, a new electronic market space has emerged which enables companies to do things differently and opens up opportunities to create new forms of values for their customers.

Still, the employment of new technologies, when combined with the desire for profit and the 'world-wide' access, entails significant risks. Indeed, Beck (1992) has argued that the gain in power from the 'techno-economic progress' is quickly being overshadowed by the emergence of risks. Risk in this sense is viewed as the probability of harm arising from technological and economical change. The evolution of technological innovation in addition to producing benefits also produces risks. The pervasive infusion of complex technologies and social life has created "ontologies of insecurity", i.e. risk has now become a part of reality, as opposed to something added or set apart from that reality (Beck, 1992). Thus, ICT should be seen as an enabler that broadens the market, facilitates communication, and collaboration but should be used cautiously so potential IT related risks fail to emerge.

In conclusion, one can argue that the business challenges described above impose tremendous pressures to contemporary companies, which have to subsequently change and evolve to survive. In other words, this means that companies, to a large extent, have to be global, focus on their core competencies and pursue collaboration with partners possessing complementary competencies thus enabling product manufacturing or service availability within a competitive 'time to market'. As a result, more dynamic business models are emerging such as the virtual enterprise (Sari *et al.*, 2008). This new enterprise form will be addressed extensively in the following section.

VIRTUAL ENTERPRISES AS NETWORKED BUSINESS

Literature sources describe new organizational forms such as: the fractal company (Warnecke, 1993), the agile enterprise (Goranson, 1999), the holonic organization (Sun & Venuvinod, 2001), the extended enterprise (Dyer, 2000), and the virtual enterprise (Mowshowitz, 2002). In the remainder of this section the focus will be on Virtual Enterprises.

Virtual Enterprises: Brief Introduction

As an actual term, virtual enterprises have only been around since 1990s. However, scholars have addressed some of the characteristics of the virtual enterprise earlier. In 1984, Miles and Snow introduced a new organization concept called "dynamic network" formed by an entrepreneur with the aid of brokers and maintained by a network of contractual ties facilitated by ICT as a basis to maintain trust and coordination (Miles & Snow, 1984).

Davidow and Malone were the first to use the term virtual in relation to an enterprise entity by introducing the term "Virtual Corporation" (Davidow & Malone, 1992). They claimed that the world was in the midst of a new business revolution and that the centerpiece of this business revolution was the virtual enterprise.

A significant contribution in the VE literature comes from Abbe Mowshowitz. In his article in 1994, Mowshowitz tries to identify what the principles that underlie successful firms, which he calls virtual organizations, are. He seeks to build a theory that can account for the phenomenon, particularly for providing a precise definition of a virtual enterprise. A central element in the definition and the accompanying theory is the distinction between conception and planning of an activity and its implementation (Mowshowitz, 1994). According to Mowshowitz, virtual enterprise is a goal-oriented enterprise (i.e., unit, func-

tion, activity) operating under meta-management (Mowshowitz, 2002). Thus, the realization of virtual enterprises requires a shift in the execution of management. One of these shifts is that management should establish a mature ability to switch. Conventional corporate management may switch between different options, but it normally does so on an ad-hoc basis, whereas switching is a standard operating procedure in VEs (Mowshowitz, 1997). The new business requirements pressure companies to become more flexible. Preparation is a way to systematize the ability to adapt quickly to new market demands. Thus, the ability to respond quickly to new possibilities related to changing environment becomes the path to success of a VE (Mowshowitz, 1997).

VE Characteristics and Challenges

As already indicated the virtual enterprise has received a lot of attention in the contemporary literature. However, no unified definition has been reached. The one defined in Sari *et al.* (2008) represents the different characteristics of VEs through a re-configurable, temporary and ICT-enabled customer solutions delivery system through the aggregation of different partner competencies which can function as a single organization

Based upon the literature review (Katzy & Schuh, 1998; Goranson, 1999; Cunha & Putnik, 2006; Sari *et al.*, 2007; Sari *et al.*, 2008), the general characteristics of a virtual enterprise and their association with risk are illustrated in Table 1:

Based on this table, one could get the impression that the virtual enterprise could be considered as a panacea solving all problems related to the new business challenges described previously. This however is an oversimplification of the truth.

The explosive expansion of ICT through the 1990s generated a lot of fuzz about the potential and the wonders of the emerging virtual world. As a respond, some authors such as Chesbrough & Teece (1998) claim that there was a tendency to over-emphasize the wonders of this new emerging

Table 1. VE characteristics

Characteristic	Description	Impact on Risk
Temporary nature.	Partnership will be less permanent, less formal and more opportunistic.	Trust issues exist, as partners do not know each other in advance.
Aggregation of partners.	Each partner contributes with its core competencies to the network.	Sharing of risk, cost and skills/competencies.
Supported/enabled by ICT.	Enabling virtuality and globalization.	Security related risks, global business risk.
Quick respond to a business opportunity.	Customization, from product towards solutions, reconfigurable and agility.	Reduced obsolescence or antiquated-fashion risks, mitigated product liability risks.

virtual world. The decentralized virtual company has the highest incentives to take risks and the lowest ability to settle conflicts and coordinate activities due to its decentralized nature. The integrated corporation is at the other end of the extreme and has the lowest incentives to take risks and highest ability to settle conflicts and manage the activities due to its centralized nature.. They also claim that virtual enterprises entail serious strategic hazards if applied for systemic innovations due to their requirements for information and coordinated adjustments throughout their entire development.

Last, but not least, the issue of trust when co-operating with new and unknown or less familiar partners, in the context of a VE, is of great significance. Literature proves that building a trustworthy relationship in practice is a very difficult process that may even last for years (Lewis, 1999). And the process becomes more stressful in the case of a strategic partner, with whom collaborative work and tight systems integration should take place.

TRUST IN VIRTUAL ENTERPRISES

The ways in which the partners identify one another, share power, communicate, collaborate and build trust in a virtual environment are important in achieving successful results. Effective partners not only fulfill the assigned task objectives but also, in the process, contribute to a trusting relationship among them. Trust is a critical structural

and cultural characteristic that influences the network's success, performance and collaboration. Without trust, building a true networked business is almost impossible (Duarte & Snyder, 1999). Indeed, the management literature is full of testimonials about companies that claim they benefited from building trust with suppliers or network partners (Duarte & Snyder, 1999; Dyer, 2000). Most research on trust is anecdotal, with little evidence of economic benefits. And even if the benefits are significant, how does a company proceeds in understanding the role of trust within its virtual enterprise network?

The Role of Trust in VEs

Trust is a shared belief that partners can depend on each other to achieve a common goal. In networked business, where the purpose is to get successful results that exceed the limited frame of an isolated transaction, trust also means that partners can depend on each other to contribute towards the common objective, which is network success (Lewicki *et al.*, 1998). That involves more than keeping promises, because it entails changes that can't be planned in advance. An alliance between Canon and Hewlett-Packard in the laser business illustrates this case (Lewicki *et al.*, 1998). In the late 1970s, HP was one of the few firms having computer expertise. At the same time, Canon had developed a laser technology for copying. Towards developing low-cost printer, HP received an invitation from Canon to combine HP's computer skills with Canon's laser know-how. After negotiations, they released their first desktop model which grew so fast that the alliance quickly became an important unit of each company's business. Since then, the partners have become major rivals in ink jet business, while their laser printer cooperation has kept its momentum. Today, their collaboration involves many products, but still they do not have a contract. It is based entirely on trust. Trust does not imply effortless harmony. Obviously, business is too complex to expect ready agreement on all issues. However, in a trusting relationship, conflicts motivate a probe for a deeper understanding of the situation and a search for constructive solutions. Trust creates good will, which sustains the relationship when one firm does something the other dislikes (Lewis, 1999). Having trust gives you confidence in a relationship and makes it easier to support and enhance it.

On the other hand, trust can also be defined as one party's confidence that the other party in the exchange relationship will fulfill its promises and commitments and will not exploit its vulnerabilities (Zaheer *et al.*, 1998). Without trust, commitment to the goals of the organization can waver, as members perceive the alliance as weak or disintegrating, fractured by misunderstanding or mistrust (McAllister, 1995). Trust is particularly important in VEs that require constant and close attention to shared commitments to safety and reliability, as well as a shared willingness to learn and adapt (Davidow & Malone, 1992). Trust permits a VE to focus on its mission, unfettered by doubts about other members' roles, responsibilities and resources, and to establish the belief that with trust, synergistic efforts in inter-organizational missions are possible (Grabowski & Roberts, 1999).

Conceptually, organizations are not able to trust each other in a VE; trust is mostly of individual nature. Trust can only be placed by one individual in another individual or between groups of individuals, such as partner organizations. However, individuals in an organization may share a trust orientation toward individuals within another organization. From this perspective, inter-organizational or VE trust describes the extent to which there is a collectively held "trust orientation" by organisational members toward another partner company in a VEN (Zaheer *et al.*, 1998). It is also important to note that the need for trust only arises in risky situations, because without risk involved, there is no need for trust. For example, VEs of the automotive industry are full of risks and vulnerabilities. The final product of this industry, the car, is a very complex structure with thousands of components that must work together as a system. Components are often tailored to specific models, and as a result partner companies (or suppliers) must make dedicated investments in terms of human resources, tools, equipment and so forth. Since these investments are not easily deployable to other uses, the partner companies are at high risk if the partners or the VE coordinator behave opportunistically. For example, after a partner has made an investment in a dedicated asset, the VE coordinator may try to renegotiate a contract based on the request coming from customers and threat to switch to another partner if the price is not lowered. Furthermore, the automotive industry is characterized by a high degree of market uncertainty, which increases both the risks associating with transactions and trust.

Developing trust in VEs requires small group activities among partners, because it is difficult to trust parties you do not know well, who you have not observed before, and who are not committed to the same goals (Handy, 1995). Trust plays an important role in VEs because it can leverage the ability and willingness to learn, thus affects its performance (Grabowski & Roberts, 1999). VEs with high levels of trust among their members can effectively utilize coordination and communication processes so members can learn from each other. High levels of trust also contribute to strengthening linkages among partner organizations (Grabowski & Roberts, 1999). Geographically dispersed organizations in VEs are truly eager to reduce their risk. Trust among organizational members is an important prerequisite for transforming linkages to alliances, thus mitigating risk, as organizations are reluctant to adopt alliance-like organizational structures that make them vulnerable to the uncertainties of the environment and to impacts from other organizations, without some assurances of shared vulnerability (Handy, 1995). More specifically, trust is very valuable within networked organizations, because it:

- Minimizes risk (Rasmussen & Wangel, 2007)
- Reduces uncertainty (Morris *et al.*, 2002)
- Contributes to the management of conflict and cooperation (Jarvenpaa *et al.*, 2004)
- Leads to superior knowledge sharing (Dyer, 2000; Morris *et al.*, 2002)
- Facilitates communication and coordination across companies (Duarte & Snyder, 1999)
- Lowers transaction costs (Dyer, 2000)

The research literature (Jarvenpaa *et al.*, 2004) confirms that VEs that have higher levels of trust outperform those with lower levels of trust. Trust reduces the need to formalize work or impose checks which slows down activity. Increased trust allows - as a consequence - work to be organized more quickly, with more creativity and higher motivation. When things go wrong, it allows higher levels of empathy in tackling co-operational problems. In summary, trust reduces hazards in working together either through increased creativity or the need for reduced control which then impacts productivity, while distrust is one of the major costs involved in transacting across boundaries. To counteract this, the task within companies is to reduce the perceived distances between organizations and individuals in VE networks by aligning thoughts and actions so partners understand each other better, use complimentary skills and have com-

mon goals. To do this, one needs to ask: what are the conditions for building trust in virtual environments?

CONDITIONS FOR TRUST FORMATION IN VES

Performance of successful networked businesses (e.g. VEs, supply chains etc.) is based on a high level of trust and a strong commitment among partners. Effective planning based on shared information and trust among partners is an essential requirement for successful collaboration. For example, Zineldin and Torbjorn (2003) found that over a third of strategic alliances end in failure. In a review of the extant collaboration literature, Bowersox *et al.* (2000) conclude that most of the problems and failures seem to occur in the implementation stage. These authors identify three main root causes of failures: inter-personal relationship; outcome performance; and organizational or structural reasons. The most commonly cited reason for failed inter-firm collaboration is the appearance of problems in the relationship between the participants such as: lack of trust; lack of commitment and ineffective information sharing among partners (Bowersox *et al.*, 2000; Zindeldin and Torbjorn, 2003). Information sharing sometimes requires a release of guarded financial, strategic and other operating information to partners who might have been and/or will be competitors, since effective information sharing is heavily dependent on trust beginning within the firm and ultimately extending to partners (Bowersox *et.al.*2000). It has also been argued that the issues of trust and risk can be significantly more important than in supply chain relationships, because supplier relationships in the case of VEs often involve a higher degree of interdependency between competitors.

Trust exists only under specific circumstances; such as having shared objectives. A systematic way to discover them is to understand the notion of trust in different contexts. While trust does not imply effortless harmony, in a trusting business relationship, conflicts motivate you to probe for deeper understandings and search for constructive solutions. This notion leads us to create a set of conditions for trust formation:

Mutual Need

The companies are coming together to form a VE, because most frequently it seems like a good idea or managers decide to make a deal based on an emerging need. Still, in theory, a VE is meant to establish a dynamic organization through the synergetic combination of dissimilar companies with different core competencies, thereby forming a best of everything consortium to perform a given business project and to achieve maximum degree of customer satisfaction (Sari *et al.*, 2008). An early step in building such an alliance is to determine whether it will serve an important value in the partner company. Next step is to determine how to achieve this objective in the best possible manner. The interested partner who is willing to participate in the VE network and the selection board (e.g. VE coordinator) should confirm to each other in advance whether they are the right parties for meeting each other's needs and expectations.

Thus, mutual need should be considered as a building block of trust. Because each partner brings a unique competence and value to the consortium, sufficient priority should be given in setting up mutual needs among the partners (Lewis, 1999).

Shared Objectives

Mutual need creates an opportunity to cooperate on the basis of mutually agreed-upon objectives (Smith *et al.*, 1995). Common objectives are surprisingly hard to develop and this task often gets little attention in the case of VENs. To appreciate this, clarifications are needed on how to find common objectives for individual organizations working towards building a joint vision in a strategic network (Lewis, 1999).

In VEs, a list of shared objectives should be defined, so partners come together under the same flag and thus easier persuaded to trust one another. The smartest way to create effective mutual objectives is to develop them from each firm's individual objectives (Smith *et al.*, 1995). The objectives must be sufficiently clear to serve as a practical decision guide for everyone in the network. Within this context, the partners should have common rules about keeping their relationship on a win-win basis. Based on these rules, the partners should develop specific objectives and create actions to meet these objectives at the business level.

Commitment

VE arises when each of the partner company offers its most esteemed core competences. Mutual need creates the potential for this, but does not ensure it. Such dedication can be expected if each of the partner firm believes that it is being treated as equal by the rest of the network members. This calls for allocating risks and benefits fairly, rather than using win-lose bargaining to let the partners get what they want. Before the partners agree to cooperate, they want to be sure that each of them would show a strong commitment to succeed (Gulati *et al.*, 2004; Lewis, 1999).

The networked businesses can run in unexpected events that shift the costs or benefits away from what it is fair. This fluctuation demands balance keeping, by restoring activities that will maintain the trust to its pre-disturbance level. Doing so is not altruism but enlightened self-interest.

Similar to VEs, in supply chains, successful relationship management also requires commitment among the partners, and such commitment is a critical element for trust (Handfield & Bechtel, 2002). The partner's asset specificity will increase the level of trust and information sharing among supply chain partners and by its nature will reduce the level of behavioral uncertainty for the partners. In other words, the greater the degree of specificity of the partners' resources in strategic alliances, the greater will be the increase in the level of trust between partners.

Interpersonal Relationship

VEs work through individuals – that is how all the partners come together and work towards a common objective. Deep trust – the essential ingredient for solving the most complicated problems – arises as an interpersonal relationship (Lewis, 1999). Good relationships enhance the performance of collaboration. Inside a VE, if partners can't resolve conflicts between each other, a higher authority may do so (Harrison & John, 1996).

On the other hand, sometimes trust might be based on the assumption that the other participants of the team are trustworthy, because they are employed in the same VE, or because they have been introduced by a third trusted partner. Thus, trust in VEs may be based not only on interpersonal relationships, but also on the degree to which it is assumed that the enterprise can control its employees as well as on the general reputation of the enterprise.

In summary, the conditions, which affect trust formation in VEs, are based on the effectiveness of interactions between partner companies, the level of interdependence and the degree of participation. The realization of these conditions is more difficult in VEs as there is a very limited face to face contact which is one of the most effective ways to build trust. So, the key question is how can trust can be built and managed in VEs?

BUILDING TRUST IN VES

Because virtual enterprises – especially project oriented ones – often form and disband quickly, trust has to be built immediately. The quality of the first interactions among members set the tone. Even one or two negative messages from a member have the potential to create distrust early in the network's life. The actions of the VE coordinator and partner companies that affect trust fall into three categories. Although trust is based on individual tolerances and experiences, the partners tend to trust others who perform competently, act with integrity, and display concern for the well-being of others (Lewis, 1999). All three factors should exist to ensure that a VE performs over a high level of trust. The following sections briefly explore those three factors:

Good Reputation

If an organization appears to have little or no experience or a reputation of underperformance, it may erode the trust that partner organizations have in the importance of the partnership and their belief that it can perform effectively (Shaw, 1997).

Timely follow-through on commitments is an important element in establishing a perception of performance and competence (Lewis, 1999). Promising something – whether it is information, a call, or an e-mail message – and then not delivering it, or not delivering it on time, erodes trust. Follow through may be more important to VE partners than to traditional alliances because VE partners have fewer clues by which to decide whether other partners are committed to the organization's performance. Developing a set of practices for follow through is one way for VEs to easily demonstrate a performance orientation. On the other hand, the ability to obtain resources also contributes to the perception of performance, especially for the VE coordinator. VE partners see coordinators who are able to obtain needed resources as performance oriented. For all VE partners, promising what they cannot deliver erodes trust.

Integrity

Integrity, the alignment of actions and stated values, creates a foundation for trust. VE partners monitor closely the VE operation to determine whether the other partners act in a manner that is consistent with what it is mutually agreed (Lewis, 1999). For example, VE partners who promise affirmative vote during a management board meeting, and do not act accordingly when the pressure is on, do not engender trust. In a virtual environment, such actions have an even worse effect than they do in a physical or co-located environment, because inconsistencies in behavior often are not explained by environmental or contextual issues.

The perception of integrity complements the perception of performance (Shaw, 1997). It is possible to believe that another organization is competent and will perform well but not to trust its integrity. Although there may be agreement and trust between two organizations in terms of coordinating and getting the work done, there may be less in areas having to do with inter-organizational relationships. Some VE partners find themselves working with organizations valued for their performance and effectiveness but not trusted in areas such as acting in alignment with their stated values or taking credit for the shared work on expense of a partner.

Integrity levels in a VE can be measured by two indicators, a) providing full support to the VE and all its members and b) maintaining a consistent and balanced communication (Lewis, 1999). Integrity has to do, in part, with managing perceptions of VE performance. Speaking poorly in public forums about VE's performance, about other VE members, or about the quality of the VE's product is not capable of destroying the VE's reputation alone, but signals a lack of judgment and integrity.

Perceptions of integrity are built into the communication process (Lewis, 1999). Ensuring that all VE members receive critical information at the same time can foster integrity. In a virtual environment, it is difficult for VE members to ascertain whether they have been systematically excluded by the coordinator or other VE members or just forgotten. In either case, trust can be eroded quickly when VE members wonder about the integrity of fellow members.

It is also important that communications provide a balanced picture of the current situation. Information that makes one party look better than another or produces biased assumptions can destroy trust.

Concern

In a VE, members trust members which are consistently responsive to their needs and to the needs of others in the organization (Lewis, 1999). One aspect of caring that appears to be critical to establishing and maintaining trust in a VE setting is the understanding of the impact that VE's actions have on people inside and outside the VE.

A crucial aspect of trust is the VE's awareness of its impact on other organizations, projects, functions and remote customers and sites (Shaw, 1997). VEs that are "organization-centric" and exhibit disregard for non-members may have difficulty in convincing potential VE members and others that they are trustworthy. A decision that adversely affects another organization in a VE may easily reduce trust in the organization. At the individual level, VE members who assess how their behaviors affect other VE members will most likely be perceived as having more concern for others. VE members who appear to be insensitive will be perceived as less trustworthy (Shaw, 1997).

Trust is predominantly built from ongoing interaction of people in a common context. Therefore, much effort should be put on finding indirect links to potential partners via contact persons whom the users trust and who can be asked for a quick evaluation of the potential partner (Lewis, 1999).

Better results in managing trust can also come from proper team set-up and from building a common understanding about rules and procedures in the early stages of collaboration. VE coordinators, who have good skills in facilitation, communication and coordination, will do better at managing trust. A specific role of the coordinator that's required in a VE is to maintain the partners' credibility, because the consortium will not inherently know about partners' past performance by reputation (McKnight *et al.*, 1998). The coordinator should put extra effort to establish, in a purposeful way, which partners are in the board, the nature of their expertise and the risk of placing them in the consortia. Then, on what basis –does trust relate with the risk?

RELATION BETWEEN TRUST & RISK IN VES

Risk in VEs

VEs are temporary networks of companies that come together quickly where complex products are exchanged along the production chain and where the product quality is difficult to analyze (Dyer, 1997). However, dynamic changes in the supply or demand situation repeatedly force companies to start new relations, to open new supply sources and to find new markets for their products. Business transactions with new partner companies in general involve various uncertainties and risks and developing co-operative and collaborative supplier relations requires a high degree of trust between parties (Handfield & Bechtel, 2002).

To reduce risk and uncertainties in transactions with a new partner, many different kinds of information need to be communicated between companies to create trust and confidence in the collaboration process. The concept of trust is globally well accepted since we experience and rely on it every day in our work environment. On the other hand, it is quite challenging to define trust

within the context of VE networks because of its use in different meanings which usually leads to confusion. For the purpose of understanding the relation between trust and risk in a business context, trust can be defined as the ability of one organization to depend on other organizations in a given situation entailing uncertainty and risk with the feeling of relative security, even though negative consequences are possible (Bachmann, 2001). This definition includes the basic ingredients of trust as it acknowledges its subjective nature.

Risk, risk perception, and risk management are acknowledged as critical strategy management initiatives (Beck, 1992). Risk is also an important aspect of managing VE networks because networks are risky ventures by nature. The failure rate of networks or alliances is higher than that of the single firm (Das & Teng, 1999). One big difference between the strategies of a single firm and networked organizations is the uncertainty of the cooperation among partners. When companies pursue business opportunities on their own, there is little risk to be concerned about the opportunistic behavior of other firms because they are involved only in market transactions. In the VE or supply chain literature, however, there is a general agreement that the concept of risk is made of two elements; the risk of partner not cooperating well (referred as relational risk) in addition to the risk of bad business performance (namely, performance risk) (Das & Teng, 1996).

In VEs, relational risk can be defined as the probability of not having fruitful or satisfactory cooperation. Conflicts arise because partner companies have their own individual interests which most of the times do not match precisely with those of their partners. Private benefits can be source of conflicts of interest and partners often have hidden agendas in the alliance which may create serious problems in interactions. Besides relational risk, there are many factors that may affect network performance. These factors include demand fluctuations, a lack of competence of the partners, changing policies, and rivalry among partners. These factors account for performance risk where objectives are not achieved, despite satisfactory cooperation among partner firms (Das & Teng, 1996).

TRUST AS A DETERMINANT OF RISK

Trust is a multilevel concept that exists at the personal, organizational, inter-organizational, and even international level. At the inter-firm level, researchers believe that trust is a key element in cooperative relationships (Lewis, 1999; Das & Teng, 1999). Many definitions of trust incorporate the element of risk since the idea is that trust is a relevant factor only in risky situations (Chiles & McMackin, 1996). Without uncertainty in the outcome, trust has no role of consequence and when trust exists in a relation, risk from cooperation is minimal.

In this chapter, it is argued that trust mitigates perceived relational risk in a VE network. If a partner company has a good reputation on managing its future, then VE coordinator is more confident that the partner firm will cooperate in good faith rather than in an opportunistic manner. Thus, trust reduces the perceived likelihood of opportunistic behavior, which in turn contributes to low costs. The necessary level of trust can be established over time through previous collaborations. Because trust suggests good intentions to make the alliance work, the network coordinator and partner firms will be less concerned about cooperation problems which eventually will lead to low collaboration risk in the network. Firms that have collaborated successfully in previous alliances tend to build a favorable reputation and thus will be easier selected from VE coordinators in future ventures (Das & Teng, 1999).

The required level of confidence for cooperation show changes according to the type of alliance (network). It is high in virtual enterprises (e.g. in the form of joint ventures) and low in non-equity al-

liances (e.g. co-marketing, licensing agreements) (Osborn & Hagedoorn, 1998). Since the partners in joint ventures work under the same umbrella, they are significantly dependent to each other in terms of various kinds of know-how. Thus, the acceptable relational risk is low. In that sense, unintended know-how loss is less likely in non-equity alliances, thus the partners in such alliances may proceed with high risk. On the other hand, partner firms in VE networks can afford only low levels of performance risk, because they are structurally more attached to the network. For instance, it is much more difficult and costly to exit a business network than a licensing agreement. On the other hand, partners of non-equity alliances accept high performance risk, as the cooperation does not need big investments and can be easily terminated. Hence, a high performance risk tends to be acceptable.

Trust may have unpleasant consequences (Jarvenpaa *et al.*, 2004). In other words, high levels of trust among partners do not necessarily imply increases in positive VE outcomes. Dirks and Ferrin (2001), state that high levels of trust may not always be justified because of the risk that others will take advantage of the situation. Under high levels of trust, the trust giving party is more likely to cooperate, put oneself at risk to the other party, and perceive the other party's actions in a positive light. This is because trust affects how the member interprets the past behavior of others, and a member with high initial trust may miss how partners are taking advantage of him or her, misinterpreting others' behavior. This can further fuel opportunistic behavior.

Although much discussion on risk awareness, risk management, business continuity planning and disruption handling can be found in the literature, the major focus of this discussion lies within the boundaries of a single firm (Beck, 1992; Juttner, 2005). Applying the knowledge gained from a single company perspective to a networked business context must be limited because it does not reflect an inter-organisational collaboration orientation

(Juttner, 2005). According to a literature - based study conducted by Mentzer *et al.* (2001), there seems to be a consensus that a VE at its simplest degree of complexity comprises three entities similar to a supply chain: a company, a supplier and a customer directly involved in the upstream and downstream flows of products, services, finances and information. A key characteristic of VE management is the coordination of activities between these interdependent organisations and can hence be defined as "the management of upstream and downstream relationships with partners and customers in order to create enhanced value in the final market place at less cost to the network as a whole" (Sari, 2009). Therefore, any approach to managing risks from a VE perspective must have a broader scope than that of a single organisation and provide insights regarding how the key processes have to be performed across at least three organisations. In a VE context, the coordination and joint effort rely on dependency, bargaining, negotiation and persuasion across organization borders in a similar to a supply chain manner. Because the traditional risk mitigation approaches, derived from a single company perspective, are not ideally suited to accommodate the requirements in a VE, supply chain principles has been applied to define an approach for understanding and mitigating risk in VE networks.

An example illustrating the differences between a single company perspective and a supply chain perspective is the risk analysis process. Identifying and assessing potential risks and their possible impact on operations is a complex and difficult task for a single organization (Juttner, 2005). However, to assess vulnerabilities in a supply chain context, companies must identify both direct risks and indirect risks, with the latter coming from the linkages between network members.

Risk mitigation in VEs should not be seen as an ad-on to the network (Grabowski & Roberts, 1999). It needs to be a process embedded into the VE set-up and operation. Indicative risk mitigation steps are the following (Peck, 2003):

- Building collaborative relationships: Collaboration is a key activity to risk mitigation. For instance, in global supply chains the large number of hand-overs within the supply pipeline can increase risk (Peck, 2003). Good collaborative supply chain relationships can ensure that intelligence within the supply chain can be shared and effectively disseminated enabling all members of the supply chain to react. Based on the studies of organizations who have managed supply chain risk effectively (Juttner, 2005), the collaboration may also be considered as a key condition to mitigate risk in a VE network.

- Creating agility: Agility in the supply chain is dependent on sound supply chain design and also effective collaboration (Lambert & Pohlen, 2001). It is founded on the need for high levels of transparency in all critical processes. Agility reduces uncertainty and enables the supply chain to be more demand driven rather than operations driven (Peck, 2003). Through high levels of transparency and increased velocity in information flows across the VE network, the risk can also be reduced.

- Creating risk mitigation culture: Risk mitigation needs to follow the culture of the organization (Chiles & McMackin, 1996). This culture can only be generated by board level involvement and the establishment of a cross disciplinary risk management team. A change in business strategy such as increasing the amount of items produced or sourced overseas can have a significant impact on the risk profile of an organization therefore risk mitigation process should be an integrated part of the decision making processes of the company (Wilding, 2003).

- Creating trust: As stated in the previous section, trust is a critical factor or determinant fostering risk in supply chains and all other types of alliances. The presence of trust generally improves the collaboration performance; for instance a lack of trust among supply chain partners often results in inefficient and ineffective performance as the transaction costs mount and risks arise (Jarvenpaa *et al.*, 2004).

In this section, it has been shown that collaborative relationships, agility, risk mitigation culture, trust and risk are interlinked and risk mitigation can be approached in a systematic manner. However, building trust has a more significant role in the risk mitigation process than other determinants. Risk mitigation in VEs is a complex endeavor that is related to specific types of trust. For instance, a firm's reputation in terms of goodwill trust should not be confused with its reputation for competence trust, because the goodwill leads to low relational risk while the latter helps to lower performance risk. Depending on the type of risk one is dealing with, different trust development mechanisms should be formulated as a systematic way to manage risk in VEs.

CONCLUSION

Enterprises face major challenges such as globalization, outsourcing, customization and exploitation of existing and future ICTs. In that context, the business vision is to rapidly set up customer-focused virtual enterprises which by utilizing partners with complementary competencies will be able to provide a product fulfilling customer needs. This chapter contributes towards that aim by increasing the theoretical understanding of the concept of VEs specifically in relation with the concept of trust and its risk related consequences in networked environments.

Indeed, the importance of trust has been increasingly recognized in virtual enterprises. On the contrary, the literature shows that businesses do not adequately articulate the value of trust, or share and formalize its critical components;

rather, they focus more on the codes of corporate governance. Moreover, few companies give trust a paramount role. This chapter illustrates that the specific effects of trust in business environments may mitigate risk.

As the business challenges move collaboration further into the form of VEs, it will become more essential for companies to have well-established trust protocols, i.e. setting high collaboration standards, instilling those standards in the corporate culture, and supporting that culture with aligned processes. A rigorous approach to establishing trust will enable companies to reap the full benefits of globalised, high technology environments. In this chapter, it is argued that the need for a contextualized view of building and managing trust in VEs, is imperative. Hereby, it is also suggested that trust can reduce the level of the perceived risk from network members. The dimensions of network risk were discussed as relational and performance risk. It is argued that trust is related to both risk dimensions and can be viewed as an active way of mitigating risk in VE networks. In addition, some key principles of supply chain management were suggested to mitigate risk in VE networks.

FUTURE RESEARCH DIRECTIONS

When the virtual enterprise concept emerged in the early 1990s, it initially received attention as a novel organizational form in the virtual marketplace where new and previously unacquainted partners could cooperate with the support of advanced ICTs. This chapter aims to discuss extensively the way of managing trust in VENs as a solution to mitigate risk in varying business situations and presents various conditions to support trust building in a networked business context. However, this does not mean that all aspects in relation to virtual enterprises have been addressed completely leaving no questions left for future research. On the contrary, in this chapter, it is argued that the task of preparing, setting up and operating virtual enterprises is a complex and comprehensive process building upon several disciplines. The results of the study presented in this chapter can be considered as the first step towards an effective realization of trust based and risk aware virtual enterprise systems.

On the other hand, trust is at the heart of today's knowledge economy. Based on trust, companies -or groups within a company- can share their know-how to achieve results which they cannot achieve individually. Unlike formal contracts or rigid hierarchies, trust liberates VE partners to respond together to the unexpected situations, which is essential for mutual creativity. Trust also fosters enthusiasm, ensuring the best performance from every partner. Trust must be constructed one step at a time and current literature lacks a methodological framework to support this process and determine where the partners fall in a trusty continuum. Therefore, the development of a toolbox for measuring the level of trust in virtual environments could help the partners to determine their ability to rely on each other and consists a future research activity of the highest priority.

REFERENCES

Amit, R., & Schoemaker, P. J. H. (1993). Strategic Assets and Organizational Rent. *Strategic Management Journal*, *14*, 33–46. doi:10.1002/smj.4250140105

Bachmann, R. (2001). Trust, Power and Control in Trans-Organizational Relations. *Organization Studies*, *2*, 341–369.

Barney, J. (1991). Firm Resources and Sustained Competitive Advantage. *Journal of Management*, *17*(1), 99–120. doi:10.1177/014920639101700108

Beck, U. (1992). *Risk Society*. London: Sage.

Beck, U. (1999). *What is Globalization?* Cambridge, UK: Polity Press.

Berry, M. (1998). Strategic planning in small high-tech companies. *Long Range Planning*, *31*(3), 455–466. doi:10.1016/S0024-6301(98)80012-5

Bowersox, D. J., Closs, D. J., & Stank, T. P. (2000). Ten Mega-Trends That Will Revolutionize Supply Chain Logistics. *Journal of Business Logistics*, *21*(2), 1–16.

Camarinha-Matos, L. M., & Afsarmanesh, H. (2003). Elements of a base VE Infrastructure. *Computers in Industry*, *51*(2), 139–163. doi:10.1016/S0166-3615(03)00033-2

Chesbrough, H. W., & Teece, D. J. (2009, March 3). When is Virtual Virtuous? Organizing for Innovation. *Strategic Management of Intellectual Capital. Harvard Business Review*, 27–36.

Chiles, T. H., & McMackin, J. F. (1996). Integrating variable risk preferences trust and transaction cost economics. *Academy of Management Review*, *21*, 73–99. doi:10.2307/258630

Cunha, M. M., & Putnik, G. D. (2006). *Agile Virtual Enterprises*. Hershey, PA: Idea Group.

Das, T. K., & Teng, B. S. (1996). Risk types and inter-firm alliance structures. *Journal of Management Studies*, *33*, 827–843. doi:10.1111/j.1467-6486.1996.tb00174.x

Das, T. K., & Teng, B. S. (1999). Managing risks in strategic alliances. *The Academy of Management Executive*, *13*(4), 1–13.

Das, T. K., & Teng, B. S. (2001). Relational risks and its personal correlates in strategic alliances. *Journal of Business and Psychology*, *15*(3), 449–465. doi:10.1023/A:1007874701367

Davidow, W. H., & Malone, M. (1992). *The Virtual Corporation*. New York: HarperBusiness.

Desbarats, G. (1999). The innovation supply chain. *Supply Chain Management*, *4*(1), 7–17. doi:10.1108/13598549910254708

Dhar, R., & Glazer, R. (2003, May). Hedging Customers. *Harvard Business Review*, 86–92.

Dirks, K. T., & Ferrin, D. L. (2001). The role of trust in organizational settings. *Organization Science*, *12*(4), 450–467. doi:10.1287/orsc.12.4.450.10640

Drucker, P. F. (1999). *Management Challenges for the 21st Century*. Oxford, UK: Butterworth Heinemann.

Duarte, D. L., & Snyder, N. T. (1999). *Mastering Virtual Teams: Strategies, Tools, and Techniques that Succeed*. San Francisco: Jossey-Bass.

Dyer, J. H. (1997). Effective interfirm collaboration: How firms minimize transaction costs and maximize transaction value. *Strategic Management Journal*, *18*(7), 535–556. doi:10.1002/(SICI)1097-0266(199708)18:7<535::AID-SMJ885>3.0.CO;2-Z

Dyer, J. H. (2000). *Collaborative Advantage: Winning through Extended Enterprises Supplier Networks*. Oxford, UK: Oxford University Press.

Filos, E., & Ouzounis, V. K. (2003). Virtual Organisations Technologies, Trends, Standards and the Contribution of the European RTD Programmes. *International Journal of Computer Applications in Technology*, Special Issue. *Applications in Industry of Product and Process Modelling Using Standards*, *18*(1), 6–26.

Flynn, D. (2003). *Information Systems Requirements: Determination and Analysis* (2nd ed.). New York: Mc Graw-Hill.

Goranson, H. T. (1999). *The agile virtual enterprise: cases, metrics, tools*. Westport, CT: Quorum Books.

Grabowski, M., & Roberts, K. H. (1999). Risk mitigation in virtual organizations. *Organization Science*, *10*(6), 704–721. doi:10.1287/orsc.10.6.704

Gulati, R., Khanna, T., & Nohria, N. (2004). Unilateral commitments and the importance of process in alliances. *Sloan Management Review*, 61–74.

Handfield, R. B., & Bechtel, C. (2002). The role of trust and relationship structure in improving supply chain responsiveness. *Industrial Marketing Management*, *31*, 367–382. doi:10.1016/S0019-8501(01)00169-9

Handy, C. (1995). Trust and the virtual organization. *Harvard Business Review*, *73*, 40–50.

Harrison, J. S., & John, C. H. (1996). Managing and partnering with external stakeholders. *The Academy of Management Executive*, *10*(2), 46–57.

Jagdev, H. S., & Browne, J. (1998). The extended enterprise — a context for manufacturing. *Production Planning and Control*, *9*(3), 216–245. doi:10.1080/095372898234190

Jagdev, H. S., & Thoben, K. D. (2001). Anatomy of enterprise collaborations. *Production Planning and Control*, *12*(5), 437–451. doi:10.1080/09537280110042675

Jarvenpaa, S. L., Shaw, T. R., & Staples, D. S. (2004). Toward Contextualized Theories of Trust: The Role of Trust in Global Virtual Teams. *Information Systems Research*, *15*(3), 250–267. doi:10.1287/isre.1040.0028

Juttner, U. (2005). Supply chain risk management: understanding the business requirements from a practitioner perspective. *The International Journal of Logistics Management*, *16*(1), 120–141. doi:10.1108/09574090510617385

Katzy, B., & Schuh, G. (1998). The Virtual Enterprise. In Molina, A., Kusiak, A., & Sanchez, J. (Eds.), *Handbook of Life Cycle Engineering - Concepts, Methods and Tools*. Dordrecht, UK: Kluwer Academic Publishers.

Kumar, A. (2004). Mass customization: metrics and modularity. *International Journal of Flexible Manufacturing Systems, 16*(4), 287–312. doi:10.1007/s10696-005-5169-3

Lambert, D., & Pohlen, Z. (2001). Supply chain metrics. *The International Journal of Logistics Management, 12*(1), 1–19. doi:10.1108/09574090110806190

Lewicki, R. J., McAllister, D. J., & Bies, R. J. (1998). Trust and Distrust: New Relationship & Realities. *Academy of Management Review, 23*(3), 438–454. doi:10.2307/259288

Lewis, J. D. (1999). *Trusted Partners: How Companies Build Mutual Trust and Win Together*. New York: Free Press.

Mayer, R. C., Davis, J. H., & Schoorman, F. D. (1995). An Integrative Model of Organizational Trust. *Academy of Management Review, 20*(3), 709–734. doi:10.2307/258792

McAllister, D. J. (1995). Affect and cognition based trust as foundations for interpersonal cooperation in organizations. *Academy of Management Journal, 38*, 24–59. doi:10.2307/256727

McKnight, D. H., Cummings, L. L., & Chervany, N. L. (1998). Initial Trust Formation in New Organizational Relationships. *Academy of Management Review, 23*(3), 473–490. doi:10.2307/259290

Mentzer, J., DeWitt, W., Keebler, J., Min, S., Nix, N., Smith, C., & Zacharia, Z. (2001). Defining supply chain management. *Journal of Business Logistics, 22*(2), 1–25.

Miles, R. E., & Snow, C. C. (1984). Fit failure and the hall of fame. *California Management Review, 26*(3), 10–28.

Morris, S. A., Marshall, T. E., & Rainer, R. K. (2002). Impacts of User Satisfaction and Trust on Virtual Team Members. *Information Resources Management Journal, 15*(2), 22–30.

Mowshowitz, A. (1994). Virtual Organization: A Vision of Management in the Information Age. *The Information Society, 10*, 267–288.

Mowshowitz, A. (1997). Virtual Organization. *Communications of the ACM, 40*(9), 30–37. doi:10.1145/260750.260759

Mowshowitz, A. (2002). *Virtual Organization, Toward a Theory of Societal Transformation Stimulated by Information Technology*. Westport, UK: Quorum Books.

Osborn, R. N., & Hagedoorn, J. G. (1998). Embedded patterns of international alliance formation. *Organization Studies, 19*(5), 617–638. doi:10.1177/017084069801900404

Peck, H. (2003). *Creating Resilient Supply Chains: A practical guide*. Cranfield, UK: Cranfield School of Management Publications.

Pedersen, J. D., & Berg, R. J. (2001). Supporting partner selection for Virtual Enterprises. In Mo, J., & Nemes, L. (Eds.), *Global Engineering, Manufacturing and Enterprise Networks* (pp. 95–102). Dordrecht, UK: Kluwer Academic Publishers.

Prahalad, C. K., & Hamel, G. (1994). Strategy as a field of study: Why search for a new paradigm? *Strategic Management Journal, 15*, 5–16.

Purdy, L., & Safayeni, F. (2000). Strategies for supplier selection: A framework for potential advantages and limitations. *IEEE Transactions on Engineering Management, 47*(4), 435–443. doi:10.1109/17.895339

Quinn, J. B. (1999). Strategic Outsourcing: Leveraging Knowledge Capabilities. *Sloan Management Review, 40*(4), 9–22.

Rasmussen, L. B., & Wangel, A. (2007). Work in the virtual enterprise – creating identities, building trust and sharing knowledge. *AI & Society, 21*, 184–199. doi:10.1007/s00146-005-0029-y

Sari, B., Kilic, S. E., & Sen, D. T. (2007). Formation of Dynamic Virtual Enterprises and Enterprise Networks. *International Journal of Advanced Manufacturing Technology, 34*(11-12), 1246–1262. doi:10.1007/s00170-006-0688-y

Sari, B., Kilic, S. E., & Sen, D. T. (2008). AHP Model for the Selection of Partner Companies in Virtual Enterprises. *International Journal of Advanced Manufacturing Technology, 38*, 367–376. doi:10.1007/s00170-007-1097-6

Shaw, R. (1997). *Trust in the Balance*. San Francisco: Jossey-Bass.

Smith, K. G., Carroll, S. C., & Ashford, S. J. (1995). Intra and Interorganizational Cooperation: Toward a Research Agenda. *Academy of Management Journal, 38*(1), 7–22. doi:10.2307/256726

Sun, H., & Venuvinod, P. K. (2001). The Human Side of Holonic Manufacturing Systems. *Technovation, 21*(6), 353–360. doi:10.1016/S0166-4972(00)00055-9

Warnecke, H. (1993). *The Fractal Company: A Revolution in Corporate Culture*. New York: Springer-Verlag.

Weick, K. E. (1993). The collapse of sense making in organizations: The Mann Gulch disaster. *Administrative Science Quarterly, 38*, 628–652. doi:10.2307/2393339

Zaheer, A., McEvily, B., & Perrone, V. (1998). Does trust matter? Exploring the effects of interorganizational and interpersoinal trust on performance. *Organization Science, 9*(2), 141–159. doi:10.1287/orsc.9.2.141

Zineldin, M., & Torbjorn, B. (2003). Strategic alliances: Synergies and challenges. *International Journal of Physical Distribution & Logistics Management, 33*(5), 449–464. doi:10.1108/09600030310482004

ADDITIONAL READINGS

Aulakh, P. S., Masaaki, K., & Sahay, A. (1996). Trust and performance in cross-border marketing partnerships: A behavioral approach. *Journal of International Business Studies, 27*, 1005–1032. doi:10.1057/palgrave.jibs.8490161

Barney, J. B., & Hansen, H. (1995). Trustworthiness as a source of competitive advantage. *Strategic Management Journal, 15*, 175–190. doi:10.1002/smj.4250150912

Berg, R. J., & Lieshout, J. M. (2001). Finding symbolons for cyberspace: addressing the issue of trust in electronic commerce. *Production Planning and Control, 12*(5), 514–538. doi:10.1080/09537280110042738

Das, T. K., & Teng, B. S. (1998). Resource and risk management in the strategic alliance making process. *Journal of Management, 24*, 21–42. doi:10.1016/S0149-2063(99)80052-X

Dowling, G. R. (1986). Perceived risk; The concept and its measurement. *Psychology and Marketing, 3*, 193–210. doi:10.1002/mar.4220030307

Dyer, J. H., & Chu, W. (2000). The Determinants of Trust in Supplier-Automaker Relationships in the U.S., Japan and Korea. *Journal of International Business Studies, 31*(2), 259–285. doi:10.1057/palgrave.jibs.8490905

Filos, E., & Banahan, E. (2001). Will the organisation disappear? The challenges of the new economy and future perspectives. In Camarinha-Matos, L. M., Afsarmanesh, H., & Rabelo, R. J. (Eds.), *E-business and Virtual Enterprises – Managing Business-to-Business Cooperation* (pp. 3–20). Kluwer Academic Publishers.

Fischhoff, B. (1985). Managing risk perceptions. *Issues in Science and Technology*, 2(1), 83–96.

Goldman, S. L., Nagel, R. N., & Preiss, K. (1995). *Agile competitors and virtual organizations: Strategies for Enriching the Customer*. New York: Van Nostrand Reinhold.

Gulati, R., Nohria, N., & Zaheer, A. (2000). Strategic Networks. *Strategic Management Journal*, 21, 203–215. doi:10.1002/(SICI)1097-0266(200003)21:3<203::AID-SMJ102>3.0.CO;2-K

Hosmer, L. T. (1995). Trust: The connecting link between organizational theory and philosophical ethics. *Academy of Management Review*, 20, 379–403. doi:10.2307/258851

Humphery, J., & Schmitz, H. (1998). Trust and Inter Firm Relations in Developing and Transition Economies. *The Journal of Development Studies*, 34(4), 32–61. doi:10.1080/00220389808422528

Katzy, B., Schuh, G., & Millarg, K. (1996). Die Virtuelle Fabrik – Produzieren im Netzverk. *TR Transfer*, 43, 30–34.

Kirby, J. (2003). Supply Chain Challenges: Building Relationships. *Harvard Business Review*, 81(7), 48–59.

Kortzfleisch, H., & Laham, A. A. (2001). Potentials and Restrictions of Knowledge Management. *Electronic Journal of Organizational Virtualness*, 1(1), 10–28.

Leimeister, J. M., Weigle, J., & Kremar, H. (2002). Efficiency of Virtual Organizations – The Case of AGI. *Electronic Journal of Organizational Virtualness*, 3(3), 145–152.

Lorenz, E. (1999). Trust, contract and economic cooperation. *Cambridge Journal of Economics*, 23, 301–315. doi:10.1093/cje/23.3.301

Luhmann, N. (1979). *Trust and power*. Chichester, UK: Wiley.

Oates, D. (1998). *Outsourcing and the Virtual Organization*. London: Random House.

Pavlou, P. A. (2003). Consumer acceptance of electronic commerce: Integrating trust and risk with the technology acceptance model. *International Journal of Electronic Commerce*, 7(3), 101–134.

Peteraf, M. A. (1993). The cornerstone of competitive advantage: resource based view. *Strategic Management Journal*, 14, 179–191. doi:10.1002/smj.4250140303

Riddalls, C. E., Johanson, B. I., Axtell, C. M., Bennett, S., & Clegg, C. (2002). Quantifying the Effects of Trust in Supply Chains during Promotional Periods. *International Journal of Logistics: Research and Applications*, 5(3), 17–29.

Sari, B., Schaffers, H., Kristensen, K., Loeh, H., & Slagter, R. (2007). Collaborative Knowledge Workers: Web Tools and Workplace Paradigms Enabling Enterprise Collaboration 2.0, eChallenges 2007, Vol. 4 Expanding the Knowledge Economy: Issues, Applications, Case Studies, Part 1, Edited by Paul Cunnigham and Miriam Cunningham, Part 1, The Hague, The Netherlands, (pp. 697-705).

Stuart, H. (1999). Towards a definitive model of the corporate identity management process. *Corporate Communications*, 4(4), 200–207. doi:10.1108/13563289910299328

Wigand, R., Picot, A., & Reichwald, R. (1998). *Information, Organization and Management: Expanding Markets and Corporate Boundaries.* Chichester, UK: John Wiley and Sons.

Zucker, L. G. (1986). Production of trust: institutional sources of economic structure. *Research in Organizational Behavior, 8*, 53–111.

Chapter 4
Managing Risk in Virtual Enterprise Networks:
A Supply Chain Innovation Perspective

Samir Dani
Loughborough University, UK

ABSTRACT

A virtual enterprise is a temporary relationship of participating members, which is formed for a specific objective or project and dissolved once the objective or project is fulfilled. The temporary nature of the relationship and the informal structure of the network can be the source of various challenges and risks. This chapter reviews the literature and investigates the risks associated with Virtual Enterprise Networks. It also argues that innovation is very important for managing/ mitigating risks and supports this argument by proposing a framework which defines a risk mitigation process under the perspective of supply chain innovation. This chapter also discusses ways to innovate within the virtual enterprise network and facilitating newfound innovation. The chapter ends with a brief discussion of future research areas and items of conclusion.

INTRODUCTION

In today's dynamic business environment supply chains and value chains are distributed globally, providing products and services to the customers in short lead times, emphasizing on low costs and high quality. The supply chains are designed and structured thoughtfully in order to optimize resource and skill capability. Sometimes, in order to reduce costs and bring innovation to the supply chain, larger organizations may bring onboard a network of organizations virtually collaborating on a temporary basis. This does not imply that only large organizations are leading the creation of these virtual networks. Some of the smaller organizations, who may have the innovative capabilities and skills but find it intimidating to transact on their own may form these networks to confront larger organizations. These networks can then provide the tools to take on tenders and projects which may have been available only to larger organizations. Thus a virtual enterprise is a temporary relationship of participating members,

DOI: 10.4018/978-1-61520-607-0.ch004

formed, operated, and dissolved to accomplish specific short- term goals (Reid, et. al., 1996). As supply chains are becoming more globalised and at the same time lean, they are also introduced to a number of uncertainties and risks which if not mitigated can cause severe problems sometimes leading to supply chain termination. Although the literature surrounding supply chain risks is growing, there is still place for more research in this area. Supply chain innovation is a capability that is being considered vital for both mitigating supply chain risks and for creating innovation for the supply chain. The temporary nature of the relationship and the informal structure of Virtual Enterprise Networks can lead to various challenges and risks for the network. It is important to understand these challenges and risks and try to mitigate them in order to create a better and more solid working environment. This chapter presents the challenges and risks involved, and explains how innovation can act as a mitigating and risk relief factor. The chapter also discusses ways of facilitating innovation within the context of a virtual enterprise network (VEN) and ends with a brief discussion regarding the future research areas and conclusion items.

BACKGROUND

Virtual Organizations

Davidow and Malone (1992) when considering the business organization of the future had suggested the development of virtual corporations i.e. a temporary network of companies coming together to quickly exploit market opportunities. This also provides the entities of the virtual corporation with an opportunity to share costs, skill sets and access to global markets. Globalization indeed changes the way business is conducted and supply chains spread across the globe bring organizations, large and small, together with one cause: fulfilling the customer requirements at short lead times, low

cost and high quality. Virtual organizations can be found in literature under various terms, e.g. Virtual Enterprises (Networks), Extended Enterprises, Supply Chains (Networks), Virtual Communities, etc. Camarinha-Matos (2002) has suggested that the trend towards creating virtual organizations is facilitated by the advances in information and communication technologies. The spread of the Internet and the development of tools to exploit the ever growing power of its power have brought business entities closer together to create organizations that now operate across national borders, invariably working in a boundary-less world. The working practices in industry are changing with organizations becoming more knowledge based and focusing upon their core competence, willing to share their unique skills in alliances with partner organizations. These alliances, often in the form of virtual networks, make much use of globally based team working. The virtual enterprise involves organizations and team members cooperating with globally dispersed partners in projects that often have a temporary nature lasting the duration of the contract. Zwegers, et. al. (2002) define Virtual Enterprise Networks as cooperative alliances of enterprises established to jointly exploit business opportunities. They suggest that the main purpose of the network is to prepare and manage the life-cycle of the virtual enterprise and establish mutual agreements among the network members on issues relating to common standards, procedures, intellectual property and information and communication technologies. Ahuja and Carley (1998) define a virtual enterprise network as a geographically distributed organization whose members, bound by a long-term common interest or goal, communicate and coordinate their work through information and communication technologies. However, Thompson (2008) suggests that the virtual enterprise network should connect Small And Medium Enterprises (SMEs) into peer networks, supported by appropriate collaboration practices and technologies, to give them the capabilities and competitive advantages similar to those of large, global enterprises. This definition of the virtual enterprise network suggests that the network can be more local than global in order to create a common competitive advantage. According to Barbini and D'Atri (2005) the virtual enterprise consisting of SMEs is usually informally organized and adopts non- hierarchical and modular configurations. This network of organizations acts as a single entity when dealing with the external environment. As represented by Lin and Patterson (2006) when discussing the initiatives introduced by Business Link South Yorkshire UK, a framework for a virtual enterprise network will outline the strategies available for government agencies and local SMEs to create virtual organizations amongst themselves to fulfill common goals. Lin and Patterson (2006) suggest that a virtual enterprise will achieve resource, market and process efficiency through mechanisms that develop relationships between companies.

The Main Characteristics of a VEN are Summarized by Barbini and D'Atri (2005) as Follows:

- The network is set-up to exploit a specific business opportunity.
- Each partner has to contribute towards value creation for the customer and the mutual interdependencies among members have to be identified and managed to create a unique combination of resources, skills and knowledge.
- The network allows members to connect and disconnect from it easily.
- Ideally, the network is not based on strategic partnership agreements and thus is not focused around a specific enterprise. Power sharing is a norm and it is possible to adapt to the markets without being inhibited by rigid legal and economic barriers.
- Members work together to integrate business processes and share data, information and knowledge resources.

- The virtual network aims to achieve short and medium term opportunities.
- The network allows members to protect their own private core information and knowledge assets from being accessed by others (D'Atri and Motro 2002).
- Members focus on their core business and the organizational structure is formed based upon the opportunity and characteristics of the members coming together to exploit the opportunity.
- Secure information and communication technology is required to facilitate communication and data sharing among the members.

DeSanctis and Monge (1999) have stressed the need for a common business culture, to allow members to 'speak a common language'. Camarinha-Matos and Afsarmanesh (2003) have suggested that open standards for communication should be adopted to allow autonomous information systems to be efficiently connected. It is also necessary to create on-line aggregation points where companies may get in touch, develop relationships and share information. In that context, knowledge is a prerequisite for stimulating the development of virtual inter-firm networks (Barbini 2003)

ISSUES AFFECTING VIRTUAL ENTERPRISE NETWORKS

When establishing a virtual enterprise network a number of challenges need to be attended to: control and supervision of work, awareness and coordination of efforts, and trust and collaboration (Lin and Patterson, 2006). In addition, network members may not feel part of the virtual enterprise especially when its boundaries are neither definite nor well defined (Pollock and Cornford, 2004). There are a number of issues affecting Virtual Enterprise Networks:

Trust: Virtual Enterprises depend upon trusting relationships developed quickly to obtain full benefit to be achieved from this style of cooperating. In this globally dispersed manner of working where contracts, rules and procedures may be difficult to apply, interpersonal trust becomes very important. "If we are to enjoy the efficiencies and other benefits of the virtual organization, we will have to rediscover how to run organizations based more on trust than on control. Virtuality requires trust to make it work: technology on its own is not enough" (Handy, 1995). Trust development in virtual teams also presents significant challenges because it is difficult to assess teammates' trustworthiness without ever having met them (McDonough, et. al. 2001). Moreover, as the life of many virtual teams is relatively limited, trust must quickly develop (Jarvenpaa and Leidner, 1999). Yet, trust development is deemed crucial for the successful completion of virtual team projects (Sarker, et. al. 2001). Trust in temporary systems seems to lead to a unique view of trust that is rapidly able to manage the issues of vulnerability, uncertainty, risk and expectations. Meyerson et al (1996) developed the concept of 'swift-trust' for temporary teams formed around a task that has a finite lifetime. Often globally dispersed teams are composed of members with diverse skills, limited history of working together and sometimes with limited prospect of working together in the future. If the team is highly culturally diverse and there are different objectives for group members then it is likely that the formation of trust will take longer. Jarvenpaa and Leidner's (1999) study suggests that 'swift trust' forms in global virtual teams with unique communication and behaviors. The initial communication via the earliest keystrokes begins to establish trust. Task communication maintains trust while social communications (and explicit statements of commitment, excitement, and optimism) strengthen trust.

Communication: According to Grabowski and Roberts (1999), trust and culture are important for obtaining reliability within virtual enterprises and to achieve reliability, the communication processes within the virtual enterprise must be the point of focus. Communication is a very important element of the virtual enterprise as it ensures that the members understand the goals, inculcate shared values and work together on solving issues. Berger (1987) suggests that people communicate to reduce uncertainty, thereby making their environments more stable. Grabowski and Roberts (1997) imply that communication about member responsibilities and relationships helps members to understand their roles and the differing levels of autonomy and interdependence within the virtual enterprise.

Conflict: Conflict is defined as "an expressed struggle between at least two interdependent parties who perceive incompatible goals, scarce rewards, and interference from the other party in achieving their goals" (Hocker and Wilmot, 1985). The source can vary from power issues, competition over scarce resources, tendencies to differentiate, ambiguity over responsibility or jurisdiction, to denial of one's self-image or characteristic identifications including values and sensitivities (Deutsch, 1969). Common forms of conflict can be defined as: relationship conflict or affective conflict, task or cognitive conflict and process conflict (Panteli and Sockalingam, 2005). Conflict will inevitably occur when two or more members of the virtual enterprise perceive the goals and the shared reward system differently. This may be due to poor trust, communication issues and different cultural values.

Culture: Grabowski and Roberts (1999) when discussing virtual organizations state that it is a challenging task to develop a strong and common organizational culture as most members will have their own culture. This may lead to a difference in shared values and can cause miscommunication. A number of virtual team studies have examined the role of cultural differences among team members. Cultural differences appear to lead to coordination difficulties (Kayworth and Leidner, 2000; Maznevski and Chudoba, 2001), and create obstacles to effective communication (Kayworth and Leidner, 2000; Sarker and Sahay, 2002; Van Ryssen, and Hayes Godar, 2000). A major challenge for virtual organizations is to decide when to have a strong unified culture for the enterprise and when to let each member operate based on its individual culture and organizational particularities.

Innovation: Paladino (2007) has considered the following definition when measuring innovation: "Innovation is a firm's ability to adopt new ideas, product and processes successfully". Bessant and Venables (2008) perceive the innovation process as involving two different strands being woven together, one being the *supply* strand of the knowledge of possible means and the other as the *demand* strand of the knowledge about needs. In terms of Virtual Enterprise Networks, innovation will be achieved through the collaborative efforts of the network members. The innovation may be a new product, process, technology or a practice fulfilling a need. The challenge is to create the necessary environment for facilitating innovation. As questioned by Barbini and D'Atri (2005) 'is it possible to justify and to assert the innovativeness of virtual enterprises just by claiming that they are made up of innovative "elements"? And furthermore does a sum of innovative features result to an innovative system?' In this chapter, it is argued that understanding the innovation environment within Virtual Enterprise Networks is imperative.

Risks: Uncertainties and risks are generally caused within virtual enterprises when conflicts of interest arise between network members as a result of various business interests, operations and cultures. These fluctuations are expected, since the temporary nature of the relationship prohibits trust building and enhances opportunism. Risks within virtual enterprises are discussed in detail in the next section. Lin and Patterson (2006) suggest that successful collaboration will take place if trust exists in the relationship and if the risks are effectively managed. According to them it is vital for the companies participating in the

virtual enterprise network to have an assurance for a mutual, trusting and long-term business partnership with others. Long term trust gained by the members can help to form temporary networks when an opportunity arises. This trust will enable members to perceive the collaboration as less risky and overlook concerns related to intellectual property violation. In the case of SME networks where no leading company does exist, resource allocation can be perceived as being an issue which can make the collaboration risky. Since SMEs have limited resources, network resource optimization is important. According to Lin and Patterson (2006), there is a need to create a mechanism to enhance the mutual trust within the network relationship.

RISKS ASSOCIATED WITH VIRTUAL ENTERPRISE NETWORKS

Definitions of risks associated with Virtual Enterprise Networks are based on whether the virtual enterprise network is a network of enterprises spanning various geographical locations working together with a common aim of providing goods / services to the final consumer, or whether it is a local/ regional network of SMEs working towards a common goal of providing goods / services to the final consumer. Although, both cases are generically similar with respect to the collaboration and objective, they are differentiated on account of location. In the case of enterprises based across various locations, the supply chains are exposed to a set of factors, which can create chaos and disruption. Local political turmoil, the increasing complexity and uncertainty of weather conditions, terrorism, counterfeiting, and other issues of that sort, create external risks threatening the supply chain. Supplier issues, strikes, quality problems, logistics issues, etc. lead to more internal operational risks, which need a different level of mitigation. In the case of local/regional networks, the situation is different since weather,

Table 1. Virtual enterprise network risk categories

Pooled information sources	Value/ supply chain: transaction risks	Networked system
Overgrazing: when some members of the network overuse the resources or information for their personal use thus limiting use to other members. *Contamination*: when some members of the network contaminate the information sources for their own gain. For example some members may try dumping of corrupt data, or allowing non-standard or unedited transactions onto the network, or unintentionally or intentionally infesting the system with viruses. *Poaching*: it is possible that one of the partners may attempt to collect and summarize information from the entire database, or monitor and analyze transactions over the common network to develop strategic information for private use. These actions might lead to Intellectual Property violation issues. *Stealing*: private information of individual members is used by some for their personal gain, IP issues, trust.	*Transaction specific capital risks*: investment by one party which is specific to a project and cannot be reused by other members. *Information asymmetry*: one/ or more network members having more or better information than the other members leading to opportunistic behavior. *Loss of resource control:* when resources are transferred as part of the relationship, and these resources cannot be returned or controlled in the event of termination of the relationship. The most important resources subject to loss of control are information and know-how, since it is very difficult to control access and subsequent utilization of such resources. For example when one member introduces its preferred supplier to the network and subsequently loses the supplier on account of poaching and opportunistic behavior of other members or the client.	Similar to transaction risks: These transactions are usually formed dynamically and often will not have a history of stable structures. In these cases, through mutual adjustment, the structure usually emerges incrementally and is a product of the network history, adaptive structuring process, and the cultural similarities/differences between the participating nodes in the relationship. The risks are on a more dynamic and incremental basis, further compounded by additional structural uncertainties and risks of cultural misunderstanding.

political and logistics issues etc. will be common for all enterprises. In both cases, information technology and communication tools will play an important part, however, in the case of local/ regional networks the dynamics of other forms of communication (including face to face) will have an additional effect on risk propagation and management. Grabowski and Roberts (1999) suggest that some of the factors that determine risk propensity within virtual organizations are similar to traditional organizations. Tasks and technology used, are inherently risky or can cause risks propagated by human and organizational errors. However, there are some factors that increase the complexity for risk propensity within virtual organizations, such as a) distributed organizational structures, b) different organizational cultures, c) uneven sharing of commitments and communication delays within the network with regards to risks- incidents and accidents.

Kumar and Dissel, (1996) when studying the sources of conflicts and coordination in inter-organizational systems suggested that risks could

be associated with three scenarios: pooled information sources, value/ supply chain and networked system. A transition of these scenarios in the context of Virtual Enterprise Networks provides the following risk categories as depicted in Table 1(based on Kumar and Dissel (1996)):

Considering inter-organizational relationships, Das and Teng (2001) examine two types of risks in strategic alliances; relational risk and performance risk. They explore the relationship between trust and risk in inter-organizational relationships. The risk of betrayal which ties in with the element of trust can to some extent be assuaged with sanctions and legal regulations, even if they remain latent (Bachmann, 2001). Although a virtual enterprise network is not necessarily similar to a supply network, when considering individual members within the network, their network position, their relationships and the rights and obligations that go with them (Turnbull et al., 1996) may have an effect on the risks that they will face. Since the position of an organization within the network can influence power and access to resources within the network, network position needs to be considered in assessing and managing risk. Zheng et al., (1998) suggest that in joint ventures or strategic alliances, risks and benefits are often shared through joint ownership with formal agreements such as obligation contracting, profit sharing schemes, property rights sharing, or ownership control, providing incentive systems for the parties to collaborate (Grandori and Soda, 1995). However, when comparing with virtual network enterprises where there are no clear rules of collaboration and partnership, there may not be such clarity of risk and benefit sharing. Also, since the network is a temporary collaborative agreement based on a specific project it will be difficult to form an agreement to ensure long-term commitment to allow sharing of sensitive information, knowledge and competences. Risk and benefit sharing is important for joint product/ service design, process design and supply chain innovation. The uncertain nature of these activities requires an open dialogue between parties to assess risk and benefits and agree on their theoretical allocation across the network. A mutually agreed measurement system is required to measure actual realization of risk, consequential losses, and benefits, and to enable renegotiation of the allocation of risks and benefits (Harland, et. al., 2003).

SUPPLY CHAIN RISKS AND INNOVATION

Supply Chain Risks

In his influential work "Risk, Uncertainty, and Profit", Frank Knight (1965) established the distinction between risk and uncertainty. According to Knight a phenomenon which is un-measurable is "Uncertainty" whereas one that is measurable is "Risk". Risk is defined as uncertainty based on a well grounded (quantitative) probability. Formally,

Risk = (the probability that some event will occur) X (the consequences if it does occur)

Genuine uncertainty, on the other hand, cannot be assigned such a (well grounded) probability. Furthermore, genuine uncertainty can often not be reduced significantly by attempting to gain more information about the phenomena in question and their causes (Lovkvist-Andersen, et. al., 2004). According to the Royal Society (1992, p4) "risk is the chance, in quantitative terms, of a defined hazard occurring". Deloach (2000) has defined business risk as the level of exposure to uncertainties that the enterprise must understand and effectively manage as it executes its strategies to achieve its business objectives and create value. Norrman and Jansson (2004) also express risk as: *Risk= Probability (of the event) × Business Impact (severity)*. They mention that while risks can be calculated, uncertainties are genuinely unknown. Chiles and McMackin (1996) observe that a manager's perspective of risk is associated with the notion of economic loss.

Supply chains, today, are exposed to factors, which can create chaos and disruption. Zsidisin (2003) suggested that risk in a supply chain context can be defined as the potential occurrence of an incidence associated with inbound supply in which the result is the inability of the purchasing organization to meet customer demand. Christopher and Peck (2003) taking inspiration from Mason-Jones and Towill (1998), have categorized supply chain risk into five categories: Internal to the firm: Process, Control, External to the firm but Internal to the Supply network: Demand, Supply, and External to the network: Environmental. Peck (2005, 2006) also suggests that the sources and drivers of supply chain risk operate at several different levels. The four levels suggested are:

- Level 1: value stream/product or process.
- Level 2: assets and infrastructure dependencies.

- Level 3: organizations and inter-organizational networks.
- Level 4: the environment.

Spekman and Davis (2004) have suggested dimensions for understanding supply chain risks incorporating some regular variables viz. movement of goods, information and money. However, they also stress the importance of secure IT systems, Corporate Social Responsibility (CSR) and relationships between supply chain partners. These dimensions were also resonated by Cavinato (2004) who identified risks and uncertainties in supply chains and furthermore added innovation to the dimension mix mentioned before. The concept of "resilience" is related to risk and vulnerability in a perspective that not all "risks" (hazards or threats) can be avoided, controlled, or eliminated. Instead, resilience focuses on the ability of the system to return to is original or desired state after being disturbed, i.e. its ability to absorb or mitigate the impact of the disturbance (Peck, 2006).

Supply Chain Innovation

Innovation is defined as "the introduction of something new", "a new idea, method, or device: a novelty" (Merriam- Webster Online). DTi, UK defines innovation as "the successful exploitation of new ideas" (DTi, 2003). Rothwell and Gardiner (1985) suggest that innovation is not only about a major technological advance (radical innovation) but also small-scale changes in technological know-how or processes (improvement or incremental innovation). In line with these definitions supply chain innovation is the process of introducing a new idea, method or device, either radically or incrementally, within the supply chain. The new idea may also be the application of existing tools in a new setting, which the supply chain has not previously experienced. According to UPS (2006) the greatest forces shaping global trade are supply chain innovations. Most supply chain innovations are created to increase efficiency, reduce lead times, reduce costs or improve quality. Supply chain innovations combine developments in information and related technologies to improve operational efficiency and enhance service effectiveness (Bello, et. al., 2004). However, there is also another reason, maybe not so apparent than the ones mentioned before, to innovate and that is to reduce / mitigate risks within the supply chain. According to Bello, et. al.(2004), some of the important supply chain innovations within the outbound supply chain are: efficient consumer response, continuous replenishment, Point Of Sale (POS) scanners, etc. These help in increasing the efficiency of the supply chain but also play a very important part in reducing/ mitigating 'Demand' risks. Similarly, some of the major supply chain innovations which have helped in improving supply chain operations and reducing supply chain risks are:

- Containerization: Malcolm Mclean introduced the container to the world in 1956 (Poston, 2006). Since then the transport system has been designed around containerized cargo. This has also helped the globalization boom, by facilitating the efficient transfer of goods from one country to another.
- RFID and satellite tracking systems: Useful for tracking the consignment, helps to reduce supply and demand risks, also helps to secure the supply chain.
- Vendor Managed Inventories: An inventory management technique that alleviates demand and supply risks.
- Postponement Strategies: A management technique that alleviates demand risks.
- Information and communication technologies: Technologies such as online bidding, electronic auctions, shared information and communication technology platforms help to manage information between supply

chain entities in an effective and efficient way and also help in reducing supply and demand side risks.

Franks (2000), specifically stresses the importance of continuous innovation in the supply chain. Citing the example of Compaq and Dell, it is depicted how Compaq was successful in innovating a new distribution system to gain market share, but lost out eventually to Dell who innovated a completely new business model for selling computers. Roy, et. al. (2004) proposed through their research that interactions between the buyer and the seller in supply chain relationships can lead to both incremental and radical innovations. This also highlights the importance of supply chain relationships in generating innovations and mitigating supply chain risks together. Supply chain innovations come from collaboration between a company's people and partners (UPS, 2006). Organizations such as Procter & Gamble, Dell, and Starbucks focus on supply chain innovation as an engine for growth (UPS, 2006).

MANAGING SUPPLY CHAIN RISKS THROUGH INNOVATION

Supply Chain risk management can be conducted for various organizational reasons: financial and corporate governance (Meulbroek, 2002), business continuity and crisis management (Adams et al., 2002), the ability to react quickly to ensure continuity (Van Hoek, 2003; Rowbottom, 2004), reputation management (O'Rourke, 2004), goal of reliability (Moore, 2002), and the achievement of the best trade-off between quality controls (through inspections) and process self-control (Svensson, 2002). Risk management entails identifying operational risks and developing mitigation procedures for maintaining operational performance. Along with considering supply chain risk management from an operational viewpoint, it is also beneficial to consider supply chain risk man-

agement from a strategic management perspective. Spekman and Davis (2004) have suggested that although interdependency between supply chain entities can increase risks in the supply chain, these can be effectively managed. Juttner et al., (2003) suggest that supply chain risk management is the process of identifying and managing risks in the supply chain through a coordinated approach amongst supply chain members in order to achieve the supply chain objectives. Rice and Caniato (2003) report that many firms have developed various risk assessment programmes that are intended to: a) identify different types of risks, b) estimate the likelihood of each type of major disruption occurring, c) assess potential loss due to a major disruption and d) identify strategies to reduce risk.

The basic process of managing supply chain risks consists of three stages: risk identification, risk assessment and risk management (Norrman and Lindroth, 2004). Literature and industry references report a plethora of tools that support each one of these stages. Still, companies are always in search of alternative methods to manage risk and one of them is by utilizing and introducing incremental innovations. Sometimes, innovations are so radical that they change the way the industry operates (e.g. containers). Zsidisin et al., (2000) and Zsidisin, (2003) present suggestions for minimizing risk from the supply perspective:

1) Carrying buffer stock and improving inventory management;
2) Using alternative sources of supply;
3) Use of contracts to manage price fluctuations and
4) Quality initiatives.

Although these suggestions may seem to be an industry norm at the moment, when first introduced they were nothing but "pure" innovation. Sheffi (2001) and Kleindorfer and Saad (2005) suggested the use of multiple suppliers as a way to reduce certain supply chain risks. Smeltzer and

Siferd, (1998) concluded that risks associated with poor selection of suppliers can be reduced by developing quality certification programs and auditing the suppliers to assure that they meet the required standards, whereas Lee and Whang (2003) developed a model to show how firms can reduce inventory due to less inspection time.

Various methods, ranging from formal quantitative models to informal qualitative plans, have been developed to assess and manage supply chain risks. These methodologies, models and concepts have tried to address different types of risks, ranging from demand to process and environmental risks. It is also important to consider whether risks are managed proactively or reactively. In order to setup the proactive or reactive risk management capability the organization will consider the levels of investment required, the impact of the risks, and the skill set of its employees. Some of these innovative solutions as put forth by various researchers are: Lean, six sigma, agile philosophies (Christopher and Rutherford 2004, Chapell and Peck, 2005), event management software (Malykhina 2005) and radio frequency identification (RFID) (Niemeyer et al. 2003). They all provide better visibility, velocity and more effective process control (Christopher and Lee 2001).

Some other approaches to supply chain risk management involve managing risks affecting: specific supply chain levels (Cavinato, 2004), systems inside and outside the chain, such as the information system (Finch 2004), specific projects (Halman and Keizer, 1994) with an aim to identify and manage risks that threaten the project's success (Ramgopal, 2003) and causes of project failure (Spekman and Davis, 2004). It can be argued, with reference to Cavinato (2004), that having the capability to manage risks within the innovational network of the supply chain will ensure that risks in the other networks of the supply chain can be managed. Building an innovative culture, innovative processes and innovation capability is the key to managing and mitigating supply chain risk scenarios. Virtual Enterprise Networks

form important links within the extended supply chain or in time the Virtual Enterprise Networks themselves may form into stable supply chains. It is also essential that companies within the virtual enterprise network also get the opportunity to utilize these innovations so that the network can operate seamlessly. Alternatively, the virtual enterprise network itself may be the entity which provides innovative solutions to the rest of the supply chain.

MANAGING RISKS IN VIRTUAL ENTERPRISE NETWORKS

Virtual Enterprise Networks are constantly faced with issues related to communication, trust and risks. These risks, as specified earlier in the chapter fall in three categories and constitute a manifestation of the nature of the enterprise network and the interaction of various humans and organizations within this network. In this chapter it is argued that risks associated with Virtual Enterprise Networks could be reduced/ mitigated by introducing innovations. The innovation process in Virtual Enterprise Networks is quite complex, because of the temporary nature of the network and the individual goals of each member.

Although some of the risks may emanate from external sources e.g. markets, most of them are internal to the network and are caused due to lack of trust, communication and cultural issues. Other causes are improper structures, lack of leadership, unshared goals, improper rewards systems, etc. Flexibility is the norm of the virtual enterprise network, but this should be supplemented by effective communication and processes to support shared values. The virtual enterprise lifecycle is composed of the following phases: creation, operation and dissolution. During its lifecycle the virtual enterprise has opportunities to transpose into the stage of: a) dissolution: the task is fulfilled and the virtual enterprise dissolves its temporary relationship, b) creating a new enterprise and c) transformation, where the temporary relationship turns into stable supply chains (Pires, et. al., 2001). The migration to one of these three alternatives also suggests that risks would change and so will the risk management methodology. Until the virtual enterprise network migrates to a more stable structure, it remains a temporary set-up of organizations coming together for a specific purpose and the risks need to be managed accordingly.

Grabowski and Roberts (1999) suggest that risks in systems can exist due to the system components being inherently risky or the components being safe but interacting in a way that increases risk. They also suggest that the success of a virtual organization hinges on shared, interdependent business processes that are designed to achieve shared business objectives. It is essential to create a common value chain and to support this initiative using the latest information technology. Also, due to the distributed, networked and shared nature of the Virtual Enterprise Networks, risks can migrate between the virtual enterprise network members making risk identification and mitigation difficult (Grabowski and Roberts, 1997). Effective communication is very important to the virtual enterprise network especially at the interfaces of the transacting organizations within the virtual enterprise network and the interface between the virtual enterprise network and the external environment. Communication across the interfaces will help to bring together the shared processes, interactions and interdependencies between the members and thus support risk management. When managing risks, it is also important to note that due to the shared interdependencies, change at one interface may have consequences at other interfaces within the virtual enterprise network. Since each virtual enterprise network will have a different dynamic it is important to understand the requirements of each virtual enterprise network and innovate accordingly. It is necessary to have systems in place within the virtual enterprise network to promote innovation.

The innovations do not always need to be radical and small incremental process innovations can instill good working practices, better communication and an increased level of trust. To manage Virtual Enterprise Network risks it can be inferred from the literature reviewed earlier in the chapter that innovations are necessary in the areas of communication, technology and also legal frameworks. These three areas are important on their own but more importantly need to be considered in their potential of interacting with each other. For example technology for communication, communication regarding new technology, legal procedures (contractual terms) regarding communication within the network, effective communication regarding the contractual terms to the members, use of technology for implementing contractual terms, contractual terms with regards to the use of technology. The three areas may also be considered together to create bespoke solutions to manage risks. The innovative solutions can take the form of new business models, new technological solutions and new organizational structures or a combination of either two or all three alternatives. Some of the areas for improvement and innovating are a) the development of better and secured modes of communication, b) the actualization of new models for sharing benefits, c) the establishment of new trust building mechanisms, d) the adaptation of new information and communication technologies and the use of concepts of open innovation for the design of network innovation models. Based on the discussion above, Figure 1 presents a framework for managing virtual enterprise network risks and a process to manage / mitigate risks. One of the important aspects of the framework is the feedback loop, which shows that Virtual Enterprise Networks operate in a dynamic environment. The innovative solution developed for managing a certain risk may in turn become a source for a further risk which will need to be managed/ mitigated.

The framework can be further described by adopting an example from the Environmen-

Figure 1. Managing risks in virtual enterprise networks

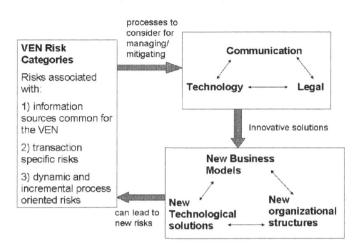

tal Technologies Cluster (ETC) (http://www. bioteams.com/etc_ven_case_study.pdf). The mission of the ETC is to protect and enhance the environment through the provision and implementation of collective, practical and innovative solutions. The cluster aims to harness and strengthen the combined expertise of members and provide industry with unique expertise and capacity on natural resource and environmental issues. The network comprises of fifteen core member companies within Northern Ireland with additional resources provided by business support and funding agencies. The main challenges for the cluster include establishing: good communication, shared objectives and trust, awareness of partner capabilities and competencies. It is clear that if the above challenges were not addressed the cluster would face risks in terms of information asymmetry. The cluster proactively took recourse to finding solutions to the future risks by setting an open communication channel with the help of an IT platform, series of workshops, conference calls and seminars. The group developed a process allowing for the development of ground rules, the evolution of partners to undertake key executive roles and the development of short term and long-

term goals and strategies. Although the developed solutions have considered new technology and a new organisational structure for the ETC, as these solutions are deployed there is a possibility that the rules set for engagement or improper use of technology may manifest into further risks.

Innovation is thus critical for the Virtual Enterprise Network both for mitigating risks within the network and for maintaining its competitive advantage. However, establishing an innovation process for the whole network is a very challenging task. As most networks get created for a specific project and disband immediately, it will not be possible for the network members to ruminate on the challenges as a team to generate innovative solutions. It may be necessary for a small network of organizations within the Virtual Enterprise Network to create a stable long term relationship so as to facilitate innovation. One of the biggest challenges when managing risks in Virtual Enterprise Networks is finding the champion for facilitating the innovation process. Since most Virtual Enterprise Networks are temporary in nature, it is difficult to assign the responsibility to specific members. Effective leadership to create an effective vision for the network is very important. The appropriate vision will also help in determining the level of resources required and the performance measures. To facilitate innovation, trust needs to be strengthened between the network members. This can be achieved by instilling a good communication platform and also a system for recognizing success. Barbini and D'Atri (2005) have suggested that innovation can be stimulated by allowing SMEs to concentrate on their core activities, supporting a continuous fine tuning of the task environment and facilitating the enhancement of technology developed by the members. It is also useful to establish co-opetitive (as proposed by Nalebuff, Brandenburger 1997) behaviors with other enterprises. Since innovation is sought only when risks happen or are predicted, a shared culture of innovation within the network will help to bring innovation proactively within the product and service offerings of the network members. Thus, alleviating risks should always be complimented by innovation as a group. Lin and Patterson (2006) suggest the mechanisms to develop relationships between companies: networking, special interest groups, one-to-one trading, recommending suppliers, nominating suppliers and partnering.

FUTURE RESEARCH DIRECTIONS

Virtual Enterprise Networks are important for a number of entities within today's business environments. For SMEs and local / regional enterprises it provides a platform for pooling resources and skill sets to work on projects for larger clients, if that is not possible on an individual level. For larger organizations, VENs provide access to vast resources and the advantage of forming temporary alliances for getting the task completed. In today's world of 'Wikinomics' (Tapscott and Williams, 2008) larger organizations may be able to use the principles of open innovation and by forming Virtual Enterprise Networks to create innovative business environments. In that context Virtual

Enterprise Networks should instil an innovative culture throughout the whole network in order to support risk mitigating. This is quite a difficult task, and more research needs to be conducted in the future to facilitate an innovation environment within Virtual Enterprise Networks. The challenges for the future are comprised of organizational, technological and legal issues. With respect to organizational issues, further research is needed on whether Virtual Enterprise Networks should have a specific structure than a loose temporary alliance of firms coming together and on the appropriate leadership styles that will foster innovation within the network. With regards to technology a significant issue that has to be addressed deals with determining the ICT mix that would foster higher levels of trust and communication within the virtual enterprise network. It is also necessary to consider legal issues in managing the Virtual Enterprise Networks in an attempt to answer the question of whether legal frameworks should be introduced within Virtual Enterprise Networks to overcome risks associated with 'pooled information sources' or not?. Finally, one of the challenges for future research is to investigate whether new business models of working and benefit sharing are essential and if not to propose roadmaps for their development

CONCLUSION

As larger organizations cut down on their resources and utilize the skills and resources of external organizations to innovate, Virtual Enterprise Networks provide an excellent opportunity for organizations to come together to pool their skills and competencies and create innovation within the supply chain. This chapter has provided an insight into risks experienced by Virtual Enterprise Networks and the management of these risks. The risks arise through the dynamics of shared relationships and responsibilities, resource and benefits allocation and mismatch of cultures. Some of the risks arise from opportunistic and dysfunctional behaviour shown by some of the network members. In this chapter, it is argued that innovation is an important capability to manage/ mitigate risks. To provide further insight into using innovation to manage risks a brief discussion regarding supply chain risks and supply chain innovation has been provided. There are various means of overcoming Virtual Enterprise Network risks and the focus within this chapter has been on developing innovation capability within the network to find solutions for risk management. A framework has been proposed which depicts the risk management process. Communication, Technology and Legal factors have been described as being important for finding innovative solutions to manage risks. The solutions will either be in the form of new business models, new organizational structures and/ or new technological solutions. Further research needs to be conducted to understand the issues and risks surrounding Virtual Enterprise Networks and to increase their capability to innovate.

REFERENCES

Adams, T. J., Austin, S. P., Soprano, R. S., & Stiene, L. M. (2002). Assessing the transition to production risk. *Program Manager, September*, 10-21.

Ahuja, M. K., & K. M. Carley (1998). Network structure in virtual organizations. *Journal of Computer- Mediated Communication 3*(4): Special Issue on Virtual Organizations.

Anon. (2009). *Northern Ireland cluster facilitators forum: case study*. Retrieved July 20, 2009, from http://www.bioteams.com/etc_ven_case_study.pdf

Bachmann, R. (2001). Trust, power and control in trans-organizational relations. *Organization Studies*, *22*(2), 337–365. doi:10.1177/0170840601222007

Barbini, F. M. (2003). Innovative Trade Fairs for Incubating Virtual Enterprises. In L. M. Camarinha-Matos, L.M. and Afsarmanesh, H. (eds.). Processes and Foundations for Virtual Organizations. Boston: Kluwer Academic Publishers.

Barbini, F. M., & D'Atri, A. (2005). How Innovative are Virtual Enterprises? In Bartmann D, Rajola F, Kallinikos J, Avison D, Winter R, Ein-Dor P, Becker J, Bodendorf F, Weinhardt C eds. *Proceedings of the Thirteenth European Conference on Information Systems*, 1091-1102, Regensburg, Germany.

Bello, D. C., Lohtia, R., & Sangtani, V. (2004). An institutional analysis of supply chain innovations in global marketing channels. *Industrial Marketing Management, 33*, 57–64. doi:10.1016/j.indmarman.2003.08.011

Berger, C. M. (1987). Communicating under uncertainty. In M. E. Roloff, & G. R. Miller (eds), Interpersonal Processes: New Dimensions in Communications Research, (pp. 39–62). Newbury Park, CA: Sage.

Bessant, J., & Venables, T. (2008) Creating Wealth from Knowledge. Cheltenham, UK: Edward Elgar Publishing Ltd.

Camarinha-Matos, L. M. (2002). *Virtual Organizations in Manufacturing: Trends and challenges*. International Conference on Flexible Automation and Intelligent Manufacturing 2002, Dresden, Germany

Camarinha-Matos, L. M., & Afsarmanesh, H. (2003). Elements of a Base VE Infrastracture. *Journal of Computers in Industry, 51*(2), 139–163. doi:10.1016/S0166-3615(03)00033-2

Cavinato, J. L. (2004). Supply chain logistics risks. *International Journal of Physical Distribution & Logistics Management, 34*(5), 383–388. doi:10.1108/09600030410545427

Chapell, A., & Peck, H. (2005). The application of a six sigma methodology to military supply chain processes. in *Operations and Global Competitiveness: Proceedings of the Euroma Conference*, (pp. 809–818).

Chiles, T. H., & McMackin, J. F. (1996). Integrating variable risk preferences, trust, and transaction cost economics. *Academy of Management Review*, *21*(1), 73–99. doi:10.2307/258630

Christopher, M., & Lee, H. L. (2001). Supply chain confidence: the key to effective supply chains through improved visibility and reliability. Global Trade Management, November, 1–10.

Christopher, M., & Peck, H. (2003). Building the Resilient Chain. *The International Journal of Logistics Management*, *15*(2).

Christopher, M., & Rutherford, C. (2004). Creating Supply Chain Resilience through Agile Six Sigma. *CriticalEye, Jun-Aug*, 24-28.

D'Atri, A., & Motro, A. (2002). VirtuE: Virtual Enterprises for Information Markets. In *Proc. European Conference on Information Systems*, Gdansk, Poland.

Das, T. K., & Teng, B. S. (2001). Trust, control and risk in strategic alliances: an integrated framework. *Organization Studies*, *22*(2), 251–283. doi:10.1177/0170840601222004

Deloach, J. W. (2000). Enterprise-wide risk management: Strategies for linking risk and opportunity Upper Saddle River, NJ: Prentice Hall

DeSanctis, G., & Monge, P. (1999). Introduction to the Special Issue: Communication Processes for Virtual Organizations. *Organization Science*, *10*(6), 693–703. doi:10.1287/orsc.10.6.693

Deutsch, M. (1969). Conflicts: productive and destructive. *Journal of the Social Sciences*, *25*, 7–41.

DTI. (2003). Competing in the Global Economy: The Innovation Challenge. London: Department of Trade and Industry

Finch, P. (2004). Supply chain risk management. *Supply Chain Management: An International Journal*, *9*(2), 183–196. doi:10.1108/13598540410527079

Franks, J. (2000). Supply Chain Innovation. *Work Study*, *49*(4), 152–155. doi:10.1108/00438020010330484

Grabowski, M., & Roberts, K. H. (1997). Risk mitigation in large scale systems: Lessons from high reliability organizations. *California Management Review*, *39*, 152–162.

Grabowski, M., & Roberts, K. H. (1999). Risk Mitigation in Virtual Organizations. *Organization Science*, *10*(6), 704–721. doi:10.1287/orsc.10.6.704

Grandori, A., & Soda, G. (1995). Inter-firm networks: antecedents, mechanisms and forms. *Organization Studies*, *16*(2), 183–214. doi:10.1177/017084069501600201

Halman, J. M., & Keizer, J. A. (1994). Diagnosing risks in product-innovation project. *International Journal of Project Management*, *12*(2), 75–81. doi:10.1016/0263-7863(94)90013-2

Handy, C. (1995). Trust and the virtual organization: how do you manage people whom you do not see? *Harvard Business Review*, *73*, 40–48.

Harland, C., Brenchley, R., & Walker, H. (2003). Risk in supply networks. *Journal of Purchasing and Supply Management*, *9*, 51–62. doi:10.1016/S1478-4092(03)00004-9

Hart, P., & Saunders, C. (1997). Power and trust: Critical factors in the adoption and use of electronic data interchange. *Organization Science*, *8*(1), 23–42. doi:10.1287/orsc.8.1.23

Hocker, J. L., & Wilmot, W. W. (1985). Interpersonal Conflict. 2nd edition, Dubuque, IA: William C. Brown.

Jarvenpaa, S. L., & Leidner, D. E. (1999). Communication and trust in global virtual teams. *Organization Science, 10*, 791–815 (also published as Communication and trust in global virtual teams, *Journal of Computer Mediated Communication, 3*[4], June 1998)

Juttner, U., Peck, H., & Christopher, M. (2003). Supply Chain Risk Management: Outlining an Agenda for Future Research. *International Journal of Logistics: Research and Applications, 6*(4), 199–213.

Kayworth, T., & Leidner, D. (2000). The global virtual manager: a prescription for success. *Eur. Managmt J., 18*(2), 183–194. doi:10.1016/S0263-2373(99)00090-0

Kleindorfer, P., & Saad, G. (2005). Managing disruption risks in supply chains. *Production and Operations Management, 14*, 53–68.

Knight, F. (1965). Risk, Uncertainty and Profit. New York: Harper & Row.(first published 1921).

Kumar, K., & Dissel, H. G. V. (1996). Sustainable Collaboration: Managing Conflict and Cooperation in Interorganizational Systems. *Management Information Systems Quarterly, 20*(3), 279–300. doi:10.2307/249657

Lee, H., & Whang, S. (2003). Higher supply chain security with lower cost: lessons from total quality management. Working paper, Graduate School of Business, Stanford University.

Lin, A., & Patterson, D. (2006). An Investigation in to the barriers to Introducing Virtual Enterprise Networks. Wang, W. Y.C., Heng M. S. H., Chau P. Y. K. (eds.), Supply Chain Management: Issues in the Era of Collaboration and Competition, Hershey, PA: IGI Global Publishing.

Lovkvist-Andersen, A., Olson, R., Ritchey, T., & Stenstrom, M. (2004) Developing a Generic Design Basis (GDB) model for extraordinary societal events using computer- aided morphological analysis. Retrieved April 10, 2009, from www.swemorph.com

Malykhina, E. (2005). The real time imperative. *Information Week, 3*(January), 1020, 43.

Mason-Jones, R., & Towill, D. R. (1998). Shrinking the supply chain uncertainty circle. Control,17-22.

Maznevski, M., & Chudoba, K. (2001). Bridging space over time: global virtual team dynamics and effectiveness. *Organization Science, 11*(5), 473–492. doi:10.1287/orsc.11.5.473.15200

McDonough, E., Kahn, K., & Barczak, G. (2001). An Investigation of the Use of Global, Virtual, and Collocated New Product Development Teams. *Journal of Product Innovation Management, 18*(2), 110–120. doi:10.1016/S0737-6782(00)00073-4

Merriam-Webster online (n.d.). Retrieved September 4, 2009, from http://www.merriam-webster.com/dictionary/innovation

Meulbroek, L. (2002). The promise and challenge of integrated risk management. *Risk Management & Insurance Review, 5*(1). doi:10.1111/1098-1616.00006

Meyerson, D., Weick, K. E., & Kramer, R. M. (1996). Swift Trust and Temporary Groups In *Trust in Organizations*, Thousand Oaks, CA: Sage Publications. Also presented at the conference of Trust in organizations, held at the Graduate School of Business, Stanford University, May 14-15th, 1994.

Moore, K. G. (2002). Six sigma: driving supply at Ford. Supply Chain Management Review, (July/August), pp.38–43.

Niemeyer, A., Pak, M., & Ramaswamy, S. (2003) Smart tags for your supply chain. *McKinsey Q.,* 4 Available online at: http://premium.mckinsey-quarterly.com

Norrman, A., & Jansson, U. (2004). Ericsson's proactive supply chain risk management approach after a serious sub-supplier accident. *International Journal of Physical Distribution & Logistics Management, 34*(5), 434–456. doi:10.1108/09600030410545463

Norrman, A., & Lindroth, R. (2004). Categorization of Supply Chain Risk and Risk Management. in Claire Brindley (ed). Supply Chain Risk. Pg. 20, Ashgate Publishing Ltd. UK

O'Rourke, M. (2004). Protecting your reputation. *Risk Management*(April).

Panteli, N., & Sockalingam, S. (2005). Trust and conflict within virtual inter-organizational alliances: a framework for facilitating knowledge sharing. *Decision Support Systems, 39,* 599–617. doi:10.1016/j.dss.2004.03.003

Peck, H. (2005). Drivers of supply chain vulnerability: an integrated framework. *International Journal of Physical Distribution and. Logistics Management, 35,* 210–232.

Peck, H. (2006). Reconciling supply chain vulnerability, risk and supply chain management. *International Journal of Logistics: Research and Applications, 9*(2), 127–142.

Pires, S. R. I., Bremer, C. F., De Santa Eulalia, L. A., & Goulart, C. P. (2001). Supply chain and virtual enterprises: comparisons, migration and a case study. *International Journal of Logistics: Research and Applications, 4*(3), 297–311.

Pollock, N., & Cornford, J. (2004). ERP systems and the university as "unique" organization. *Information Technology & People, 17*(1), 31–52. doi:10.1108/09593840410522161

Poston, T. (2006, April 25). *Thinking inside the box,* BBC News, 2006/04/25. Retrieved April 8, 2009, from http://news.bbc.co.uk/go/pr/fr/-/1/hi/business/4943382.stm

Ramgopal, M. (2003). Project uncertainty management. *Coastal Engineering, 45*(12), 21–24.

Reid, R. L., Tapp, J. B., Liles, D. H., Rogers, K. J., & Johnson, M. E. (1996, August 18-20). An integrated management model for virtual enterprises: vision, strategy and structure. In *Proceedings of the International Conference on Engineering and Technology Management,* IEMC 96, Vancouver BC.(pp. 522–527)

Rice, J., & Caniato, F. (2003). Building a secure and resilient supply network, *Supply Chain. Management Review, 7,* 22–30.

Rothwell, R., & Gardiner, P. (1985). Invention, innovation, re-innovation and the role of the user. *Technovation, 3,* 167–186. doi:10.1016/0166-4972(85)90012-4

Rowbottom, U. (2004). Managing risk in global supply chains. *Supply Chain Practice, 6*(2), 16–23.

Roy, S., Sivakumar, K., & Wilkinson, I. F. (2004). Innovation Generation in Supply Chain Relationships: A Conceptual Model and Research Propositions. *Journal of the Academy of Marketing Science, 32*(1), 61–79. doi:10.1177/0092070303255470

Royal Society. (1992). Risk Analysis, Perception and Management. London: Royal Society.

Sarker, S., Lau, F., & Sahay, S. (2001). Using an Adapted Grounded Theory Approach for Inductive Theory Building About Virtual Team Development. *The Data Base for Advances in Information Systems, 32*(1), 38–56.

Sarker, S., & Sahay, S. (2002). Information systems development by US–Norwegian virtual teams: implications of time and space. In *Proceedings of the Thirty-Fifth Annual Hawaii, International Conference on System, Sciences*, Hawaii, USA, pp. 1–10.

Sheffi, Y. (2001). Supply chain management under the threat of international terrorism. *International Journal of Logistics Management, 12*(2), 1–11. doi:10.1108/09574090110806262

Smeltzer, L. R., & Siferd, S. P. (1998). Proactive supply management: the management of risk. *International Journal of Purchasing and Materials Management, 34*(1), 38–45.

Spekman, R. E., & Davis, E. W. (2004). Risky business: expanding the discussion on risk and the extended enterprise. *International Journal of Physical Distribution & Logistics Management, 34*(5), 414–433. doi:10.1108/09600030410545454

Svensson, G. (2002). A conceptual framework of vulnerability in firms' inbound and outbound logistics flows. *International Journal of Physical Distribution & Logistics Management, 32*, 110–134. doi:10.1108/09600030210421723

Thompson, K. (2008). The Networked Enterprise: Competing for the Future Through Virtual Enterprise Networks. Tampa, FL: Meghan-Kiffer Press.

Turnbull, P., Ford, D., & Cunningham, M. T. (1996). Interaction, relationships and networks in business markets: an evolving perspective. *Journal of Business and Industrial Marketing, 11*(3/4), 44–62. doi:10.1108/08858629610125469

UPS. (2006, April 18-19). *Innovation and Global supply chain'- conference summary*. Retrieved July 17, 2009, from http://longitudes08.com/Barcelona08/research/conference_materials/Chicago06_Summary.pdf

Van Hoek, R. (2003). Are you ready? Risk readiness tactics for the supply chain. Logistics Research Network, London: Institute of Logistics and Transport.

Van Ryssen, S., & Hayes Godar, S. (2000). Going international without going international: multinational virtual teams. *J. Int. Managment, 6*, 49–60. doi:10.1016/S1075-4253(00)00019-3

Zheng, J., Johnsen, T., Harland, C. M., & Lamming, R. C. (1998, September 3-5). Initial conceptual framework for creation and operation of supply networks. In *Proceedings of the 14th IMP Annual Conference.* Turku, Finland.

Zsidisin, G. (2003). Managerial perceptions of risk. *Journal of Supply Chain Management, 39*, 14–25. doi:10.1111/j.1745-493X.2003.tb00146.x

Zsidisin, G. A., Ellram, L. M., Carter, J. R., & Cavinato, J. L. (2004). An Analysis of Supply Risk Assessment Techniques. *International Journal of Physical Distribution and Logistics Management, 34*(5), 397–413. doi:10.1108/09600030410545445

Zsidisin, G. A., Panelli, A., & Upton, R. (2000). Purchasing organization involvement in risk assessments, contingency plans, and risk management: an exploratory study. *Supply Chain Management, 5*(4), 187. doi:10.1108/13598540010347307

Zwegers, A., Wubben, H., & Hartel, I. (2002). Relationship Management in Enterprise Networks. In V. Marik, L.M. Camarinha-Matos & H. Afsarmanesh (eds.), Knowledge and technology integration in production and services – Balancing knowledge and technology in product and service life cycle, (pp. 157-164). Boston: Kluwer Academic Publishers.

ADDITIONAL READINGS

Berwanger, E. (1999, September). The Legal Classification of Virtual Corporation According to German Law. Organizational Virtualness and Electronic Commerce. In *Proceedings of the 2nd International VoNet Workshop*, Simowa Verlag Bern, (pp. 157-159).

Child, J., Faulkner, D., & Tallman, S. B. (2005). Cooperative Strategy. Oxford, UK: Oxford University Press.

Cunha, M. M., & Putnik, G. (2006). Agile Virtual Enterprises: Implementation and Management Support. Hershey, PA: IGI Global Publishing.

Davidow, W. H., & Malone, M. S. (1992). The Virtual Corporation: Structuring and Revitalizing the Corporation for the 21st Century. HarperBusiness, USA

Deloach, J. W. (2000). Enterprise-wide risk management: Strategies for linking risk and opportunity. Upper Saddle River, NJ: Prentice Hall

DTI. (2003). Competing in the Global Economy: The Innovation Challenge. London: Department of Trade and Industry.

Eckes, G. (2001). Six Sigma Revolution. New York: Wiley.

Gallivan, M. (2001). Striking a balance between trust and control in a virtual organization: a content analysis of open source software case studies. *Information Systems Journal*, *11*, 277–304. doi:10.1046/j.1365-2575.2001.00108.x

Jägers, H., Jansen, W., & Steenbakkers, W. (1998, April). Characteristics of Virtual Organizations. Organizational Virtualness. In *Proceedings of the VoNet Workshop*, Simowa Verlag Bern, (pp.65-76).

Jansen, W., Steenbakkers, W., & Jägers, H. (1999, September). Electronic Commerce and Virtual Organizations, Organizational Virtualness and Electronic Commerce. In Proceedings of the 2nd International VoNet Workshop, Simowa Verlag Bern, (pp. 53-66).

Knight, F. (1965). Risk Uncertainty and Profit. New York: Harper & Row. (first published 1921).

Mo, J. P. T., Zhou, M., Anticev, J., Nemes, L., Jones, M., & Hall, W. P. (2006). A study on the logistics and performance of a real "virtual enterprise. *Int. J. BusinessPerformance Management*, *8*(2/3), 152–169. doi:10.1504/IJBPM.2006.009034

Pantelia, N., & Sockalingam, S. (2005). Trust and conflict within virtual inter-organizational alliances: a framework for facilitating knowledge sharing. *Decision Support Systems*, *39*, 599–617. doi:10.1016/j.dss.2004.03.003

Putnik, G., & Cunha, M. M. (2005). Virtual Enterprise Integration: Technological and Organizational Perspectives., Hershey, PA: IGI Global Publishing.

Royal Society. (1992). Risk Analysis, Perception and Management. London: Royal Society.

Sheffi, Y. (2005). The Resilient Enterprise. Cambridge, MA: The MIT Press.

Sheffi, Y., & Rice Jr., J. B. (2005). Building the Resilient Enterprise. *MIT Sloan Management Review,* *47*(1).

Sydow, J. (1992). On the Management of Strategic Networks. In H. Ernste and V. Meier (Eds.), Regional Development and Contemporary Industrial Response, London, Pinter.

Sydow, J., Windeler, A. (1998). Organizing and Evaluating Interfirm Networks: A Structurationist Perspective on Network Processes and Effectiveness. *Organization Science,* *9*(3), Special Issue: Managing Partnerships and Strategic Alliances, 265- 284.

Tapscott, D., & Williams, A. D. (2008). WIKI-NOMICS: How mass collaboration changes everything. UK: Atlantic Books.

Tether, B. S. (2002). Who co-operates for innovation, and why An empirical analysis. *Research Policy*, *31*, 947–967. doi:10.1016/S0048-7333(01)00172-X

Thompson, K. (2008). The Networked Enterprise: Competing for the Future Through Virtual Enterprise Networks Tampa, FL: Meghan-Kiffer Press.

Thompson, K. (2008). Bioteams: High Performance Teams Based on Nature's Most Successful Designs. Tampa, FL: Meghan-Kiffer Press.

Tidd, J., & Bessant, J. (2009, March 3). *Managing Innovation: Integrating Technological, Market and Organizational Change*. New York: John Wiley & Sons; 4th Edition edition

Visser, E.-J., & Atzema, O. (2008). With or Without Clusters: Facilitating Innovation through a Differentiated and Combined Network Approach. *European Planning Studies*, *16*(9), 1169–1188. doi:10.1080/09654310802401573

Walters, D. (2000). Virtual organisations: new lamps for old? *Management Decision*, *38*(6), 420–436. doi:10.1108/00251740010373106

Chapter 5
Knowledge Assets in Virtual Enterprises:
Sources of Risk and Management Issues

Ettore Bolisani
University of Padua, Italy

ABSTRACT

Virtual Enterprises (VEs) are business models characterised by the aggregation of co-operating firms that share a common goal such as a business opportunity or a project. In these structures, knowledge can be seen as a primary asset. There is a subdivision of cognitive tasks among specialised companies, which exchange knowledge much before they even exchange goods or money. Assuming a knowledge-based view of VEs, implies the necessity to define appropriate methods to manage knowledge exchanges and the associated risks. The aim of this chapter is to explore the nature of knowledge flows in a VE and study the connected managerial issues to point out the different knowledge-related risk factors and to discuss the challenges posed by their successful management. To provide a practical example, the chapter also illustrates the findings of a real-life case-study.

INTRODUCTION

Due to the characteristics of the modern economy (such as the diffusion of Information And Communication Technologies - ICT, the increasing global competition, and the complexity of innovation processes), even the largest firms can't operate in isolation, but are embedded into international *networks of relationships*. For this reason, there have been significant efforts in the economic and mana-

gerial disciplines to identify the rising models of inter-organisational relationships, to describe their economic functioning, and to propose managerial guidelines. One of the models that have received significant attention is that of companies organised in the form of a *Virtual Enterprise* (VE). This model (whose definition will be discussed later in the paper) refers to large networks of companies that join in temporary but often repetitive relationships around a common business project. This model of inter-company collaboration may appear particularly appropriate in the current economy, which demands

DOI: 10.4018/978-1-61520-607-0.ch005

from companies to satisfy conflicting needs such as: efficiency and flexibility, subdivision and integration of tasks, innovation and stability, local and international presence, etc.

In the studies of the managerial challenges posed by the VE model, the literature on organisation science and strategic management is now intertwined with the more recent fields of knowledge management (KM) and knowledge economy, where knowledge is perceived as a core business resource. This has provided the opportunity for new perspectives on VEs, which can be seen as structures where companies share and exchange knowledge (Preiss, 1999; Malhotra, 2000), and consequently depend on one another in cognitive terms. In that context and in direct analogy with the subdivision of work in a manufacturing supply chain, a knowledge-based view of a VE identifies the *subdivision of cognitive tasks* among participating companies: each of them possesses specific elements of knowledge that have value only when they are exchanged and combined with the other companies' knowledge for the success of the entire project, for example the development of a new car model. This approach does not imply that physical activities disappear or are neglected; it just focuses on the knowledge developed, possessed and exchanged by the companies – and the mechanisms employed for this – to understand the functioning of a VE.

Assuming that no firm can possess all the knowledge that is necessary for conducting business, a VE can be seen as a structure to manage knowledge flows among the participating companies, in a way that enables co-operation (which represents the core characteristic of a VE) and also preserves independence (since each firm develops and possesses its own knowledge pool). The mechanisms and processes that govern the flows of knowledge become essential for the effective management of a VE (Kinder, 2003; Malhotra, 2000). This view requires a shift in VE management. For instance, rather than a problem of resource allocation among networked units

(Martinez et al., 2001) or of enabling ICT infrastructures (Kovacs and Paganelli, 2003), the focus should turn to the types and value of knowledge that is produced and exchanged by VE members and the mechanisms they employ for managing that knowledge.

This chapter considers a knowledge-based view of VEs and aims to study a rather underexplored issue of VE operation, which is the management of risks associated to the exchange and sharing of knowledge. Although there have already been some pertinent and supportive studies (see e.g. Loebbecke and van Fenema, 2000), this issue has been considered mainly from a general viewpoint. There is still the need for detailed analysis of the nature and typology of risks arising when knowledge is treated as an economic resource; in addition, the literature lacks empirical examples about the application of these concepts in practical situations.

The chapter is structured as follows:

- First, the proposed knowledge-based view of VEs is presented with the purpose to highlight the main issues deriving from a focus on knowledge and knowledge flows. The main references in that section are drawn from recent organisational and strategic studies on the VE model and the field of Knowledge Management. Then, a discussion is held in an attempt to integrate these contributions and highlight essential aspects of VE management under a knowledge perspective.
- Second, the management of risks associated with knowledge management in VEs is investigated and the combination of traditional elements of the risk management literature with those highlighted in the previous section is proposed.
- Finally, a practical application of the perspective illustrated to the analysis of a real-life case of VE (the *SAP ecosystem*) is presented.

BACKGROUND: KNOWLEDGE AS AN ECONOMIC ASSET FOR VES

A Functional Definition of VE

In this section, we discuss how VEs can be considered as structures for managing knowledge and, in doing that, effectively achieving business goals. When recalling the debate on the characteristics of VEs, two are the important points that have to be mentioned in the context of this chapter. First, the VE model can be placed in the general framework of *networks* (for a recent survey, see Todeva, 2006), which is an antecedent notion and has its roots in the studies of industrial organisation of the '80s (Jarrillo, 1986; Lorange and Roos, 1992). In particular, networking has been often seen as a special kind of inter-company coordination mechanism placed in the middle between *hierarchies and markets* (using Williamson's well known notions – Williamson 1985). Secondly, similarly to the VE, other terms are often used, both in the Operations Management and the Industrial Organisation literature, such as *extended enterprise*, *business network*, and others. All these terms refer to organisational models characterised by *aggregations of co-operating firms* that share a common goal, project, or value chain.

It is important to highlight the peculiarities of VEs when compared to other similar models. In particular, as regards the virtual vs. the extended enterprise model, the differences (Browne and Zhang, 1999) are sometimes not very substantial. Probably, the most discriminating characteristic is that the extended enterprise is often used to illustrate the evolutions of manufacturing supply chains towards agile or lean manufacturing (O'Neill and Sackett, 1994) a term often used in studies of manufacturing organisations, supply chain strategies, and operations management. Very often also, there is a focus on a special firm, that is supposed to create and coordinate the whole supply system (Childe, 1998). In general, the model

of extended enterprise is associated to long-term relationships in a particular supply chain.

Conversely, the VE model is associated to more temporary agreements among partners (Jagdev and Thoben, 2001) built around a *specific project* or market opportunity (Halaris et al., 2003) rather than the participation in a supply chain structure. Consequently, a VE is not necessarily created along a vertical supplier-customer relationship, but may involve *lateral* relations with other providers, and even with rival firms (Byrne, 1993). The partnership lasts as long as it is beneficial for the network as a whole (Franke, 2000). Finally, in a VE the single firm is considered more loosely linked to the others and the same firm can belong to different VE structures at the same time, although there are still some players that are considered *central* (Lefebvre and Lefebvre, 2002), like in the extended enterprise model.

A particularity of the term VE is the adjective *virtual*, which implies that relations among companies are essentially based on the exchange of *intangible* elements (i.e. information, knowledge). This does not mean that a VE can't include physical or monetary transactions, but there is a special emphasis on the intangible aspects of inter-firm relationships as an essential ingredient of the working of a VE. In association to this, there is also attention to the use of ICT as a way of connecting remote companies.

In this chapter, we will employ a definition of VEs based on our study of the relevant literature and we will adhere to it throughout this Chapter. According to this definition, a VE has the following characteristics: a) VE members specialise in different activities, and are not able to operate alone in a market or industry; b) VE members reach for external resources to reduce the risks of in-house development; c) as a whole, a VE is intended to design, produce and deliver products or services to the market; to do that, the members perform several exchanges that have an economic value, d) the co-ordination mechanisms of such aggregations are placed in the middle between market and hierarchy, e) the focus is on a specific project rather than on the belonging to a specific sector or supply chain, f) co-operation is organised in a way that enables a trade-off between overall flexibility and stability, utilizing a combination of temporary project-based relationships with regular or preferred interactions, g) intangible elements are the core aspect of inter-firm relationships, and h) VEs rely heavily on ICTs for favouring the effective sharing of information and knowledge.

VEs as Knowledge-Based Organisations

The literature has often considered the problem of managing VEs based on their *tangible* manifestations, i.e. by focusing on the assignment of tasks and the allocation of resources (Martinez et al. 2001; Kaihara, 2003) or on the design of IT infrastructures for connecting partners (Kovacs and Paganelli, 2003; Park and Favrel, 1999). These aspects are clearly relevant, but do not clarify all the basic mechanisms of VE operation.

This is the purpose of the proponents of a *knowledge-based view* of VEs, which extends the notion of knowledge-based firm initially proposed by Grant (1994) as a derivation of the resource-based theories (Wernerfelt, 1984; Barney, 2001). Some authors explicitly indicate VEs as *knowledge-based organisations*, in which distinct firms gather and exploit knowledge, and perform processes of knowledge transfer (Franke, 2000; Kinder, 2003; Preiss, 1999). In a VE, firms specialise in different cognitive domains, and are thus not able to operate alone in a market. This can be seen as the main reason for networking: companies reach for external cognitive resources to reduce the risks of in-house development. Their co-operation is organised in a way that enables a trade-off between overall flexibility and innovativeness (which are deemed essential ingredients in the current global competition) and stability. Firms can achieve this aim by means of intense flows

of knowledge, which today can also benefit from the use of ICTs (Browne and Zhang 1999).

In summary, knowledge can be seen as a primary resource in a VE: member firms participate in the development and delivery of goods and services with their peculiar knowledge, in order to satisfy customer needs and to improve product, process, and managerial practice (O'Neill and Sackett 1994; Preiss 1999; Venkatraman and Henderson 1998; Halaris *et al.* 2001). The literature highlights that the practical implementations of VEs are based on frequent exchanges of ideas, proposals, technical data, and other informational content across business units, firms, and value chains. Co-design/co-development teams and other formal/informal structures are commonly used to implement collaborative knowledge creating processes (Preiss 1999; Beesley 2004). ICT systems (e.g., shared databases, extended Enterprise Resource Planning - ERP systems, web-based services, etc.) are often used to connect remote partners and to facilitate structured knowledge contents (Zhuge 2006; Yoo and Kim 2002; Lillehagen and Karlsen 2001).

The cognitive implications of VEs are therefore related to both their internal *operation* and to the *co-ordination mechanisms* among the participating companies. In accordance to the classic Williamson's (1985) categorisation of *markets* vs. *hierarchies*, VEs are generally considered intermediate forms between market and hierarchy (Tuma, 1998), which has important implications from a knowledge-based perspective as well. The *return on investment* in a VE often grounds on the potential of each firm to concentrate on its own knowledge base and *let the others* develop complementary competencies that are essential to the effective functioning of the whole network. This requires a proper system to generate internal knowledge, exchange part of it with partners, acquire fresh knowledge from them, and finally combine distinct knowledge assets to pursue the overall goals of the VE and ensure the success of each VE member individually.

In a VE, the role of the leading organization, capable of co-ordinating the other trading partners (Childe, 1998, Lefebvre and Lefebvre 2002) can be also viewed from a cognitive perspective. The leading organization delivers critical tasks such as: *mapping* the knowledge currently scattered among dispersed organisations, managing transfers of relevant information among nodes in a trustworthy environment, setting common rules and language standards, and regulating knowledge exchanges with the external environment.

Another important issue is that of *trust*: since the effective operation of a VE requires limiting the opportunistic behaviour of participants, the reduction in knowledge *asymmetries* among parties is seen as a way to build a trustworthy environment (Spekman and Davis, 2004). According to Panteli and Sockalingam (2005), a trustworthy environment is the one that enables networked structures such as VEs to facilitate innovation and generation of fresh knowledge and, at the same time, to preserve the stability of interactions in a context where a certain degree of competitiveness coexists with collaboration.

The knowledge-based view of VEs also provides the researcher with the opportunity to integrate two fields of study that have been distant for a long time (Scarso et al. 2006): VEs and KM. Today there are many converging points: on the one hand, the recalled views of a VE as a knowledge-based structure (Franke, 2000), on the other hand, the studies of *knowledge inter-networking*. As regards this last point, although the KM literature has initially focused on the problems of managing knowledge inside an organisation (Nonaka and Tageuchi, 1995), the interactions between companies for accessing a wider pool of knowledge resources is considered essential to gain and sustain competitive advantages (Blecker and Neumann, 2000). In that sense, the resulting concept of *knowledge networks* (i.e.: formal or informal relations to share knowledge, explore innovations, and exploit new ideas - Peña, 2002; Inkpen and

Tsang, 2005) constitutes a distinctive feature of recent KM studies.

The integration of the VE and the KM fields of study provides fresh ideas for VE management. In this Chapter, in accordance with the book's main theme, we particularly consider the issue of risk management, which is an essential ingredient of management studies (Power, 2004) especially for multinationals (Miller, 1992). There have already been attempts to explore the idea of managing the risks of KM in VEs (Loebbecke C. and van Fenema, 2000), but this promising field still requires advancements. In the rest of the Chapter, a discussion on how the recent contributions in KM literature can provide the foundations for a study of risk factors in VEs will be conducted, followed by the illustration of the discussed concepts in a real life case scenario.

MANAGING KNOWLEDGE IN VES: FOUNDATIONS

Knowledge Flows and Knowledge Exchanges

A VE builds around the design, production and delivery of products or services to the market; to do that, the members perform several exchanges that have an economic value: for instance, suppliers produce components and deliver them to other companies that can assemble them, etc. Thus, in a VE, a firm is not considered *per se*: it produces value by interacting with other players (e.g. by trading) and exchanging knowledge with them.

In their seminal work, Cohen and Levinthal (1989) have already indicated that a firm's ability to assimilate and apply fresh knowledge coming from other companies (i.e. its learning or *absorptive* capacity) is essential. While their study mainly considers R&D activities, here we extend this idea by highlighting that companies not only learn from R&D but more broadly from all the operational or managerial activities implicating inter-firm interactions. Generally speaking, we might say that a transaction between VE members requires not only flows of *physical goods* (e.g. components sold to assemblers by suppliers) and *monetary flows* (i.e.: payments), but also an intense *transfer of knowledge*. For instance, in the project of development and commercialisation of a new product, there is often a complex exchange of knowledge among designers, engineers, suppliers, and all the other partners that are involved in the definition and manufacturing of the various components. Also, in the negotiation phase of a new supply, there is always the need for a complex exchange of knowledge, well before the partners can trade goods. We can thus argue that companies need to exchange a lot of knowledge before, during, and after the physical or monetary transfer.

Knowledge flows occur even regardless that a product is finally traded. Suppose, for instance, that in a VE a buyer and a supplier co-operate to design a new product (e.g. a core component of a new car), but the project eventually fails. In that case, there will be no physical or monetary exchanges, but the two companies have exchanged knowledge, and such knowledge has a value for both parties, because it becomes *useful experience* that can be exploited in future projects. Thus, *valuable knowledge* is exchanged even when the economic transactions are incomplete. In a VE, this mechanism becomes particularly important: managing the flows of valuable knowledge becomes a way to manage inter-company relationships and, by this way, to regulate the operation of the VE itself.

Knowledge as an Economic Asset

There is a need to understand knowledge flows in VE structures, and their economic meaning. Recent studies of KM can provide useful insights. A first step is to examine the exact nature of knowledge flows, which calls for a suitable definition of knowledge. This is not the place to recall a debate that has occupied philosophers

from the early beginnings of human history. We will rather focus on the economic nature that can be ascribed to knowledge when it is treated as object of exchange.

In the KM literature, the concept of knowledge grounds on the difference from data and information. While data are pure measures or elementary descriptions of facts or phenomena, and information is data that are organised and can assume a particular meaning, knowledge builds on information (and data), but is *much more* than this: Knowledge is generally intended as the *capability of using information to make business decisions or take actions*, or in other words as *workable* information (Tiwana, 2000). This is an operational definition that is functional in current KM practices.

It is not easy to transfer this definition into economic models for understanding the value of knowledge flowing between two companies. In the classic economic models, this aspect was often neglected. For example, information was generally assumed to be perfect (Stiglitz, 2002) and, thus, not an object which is worth further analysis. It was the development of the *information economics*, and more recently the studies of the so-called *Knowledge Economy* (Foray 2004) that started studying the nature of information and knowledge flows underpinning economic transactions.

However, when knowledge is treated as an economic object, several issues arise. First, economists have a rich toolbox of concepts, models, and even measures for physical assets, that seem inadequate when applied to knowledge (Foray, 2004). This has often resulted in knowledge being treated as an outcome (product) of R&D departments, assuming the tangible and treatable form of *patents*. The economic problem of knowledge exchange is then reduced to a question of *trading patents and licenses*. Today we know much about these mechanisms, but this is a substantial abstraction of the real problem: things are much more complicated when one considers the learning processes that individuals and organisations often perform well outside the boundaries of the R&D departments.

Also, in the above-mentioned views, knowledge is substantially treated as an *object* that can be detached from the individuals that manipulate it (i.e. an artefact that incorporates cognitive contents). But the nature of all the objects that can represent a manifestation of knowledge (documents, patents, procedures, know-how, but also experience, feelings, and even product and technologies) appears very heterogeneous, often unique, and surely not uniform. The boundary between one object of knowledge and another cannot be easily traced, and it is practically impossible to distinguish where or when one object ends and another starts: knowledge is rather a complex bundle of intertwined elements coming from various sources (Antonelli, 2007). In addition, when knowledge is treated as an object, it looks logical (and, not to mention, convenient) to assume that *knowledge objects can be accumulated*. But still, it is not clear how to measure such stocks (obviously neither in terms of number of units nor in terms of their acquisition cost or price), or how to define the mechanism which guides knowledge stock obsolescence over time (like a physical asset). It is obvious that an innovative and different approach towards knowledge modelling and handling is required.

A second problem is that, as some scholars (Iandoli and Zollo, 2007) underline, the valuable nature of knowledge also emerges when we consider it as a *process* and not an object: in other words, its value is not any longer an absolute and objective measure, but depends on the creativity of producers or on the learning processes of users. As Holsapple (2003) argues, we can define knowledge as a *representation* that a subject has of an object, procedure, phenomenon, etc. Given this definition, knowledge is never independent from the specific *processor* that possesses, delivers, elaborates, or acquires it. The processors' cognitive background, elaborative capability, interests,

behaviour and so on affect their representations of the world and, therefore, the nature and characteristics of knowledge handled and exchanged. Knowledge is thus not an *a priori* component that can be moved but, rather, depends on the context of usage and on the learning processes that come into play (Tyre & Von Hippel, 1997).

A particular attribute of knowledge is associated to the distinction between tacit (i.e. not codifiable, and mostly embedded in people) versus explicit (the one that can be codified and detached from its creator) form of knowledge. The existence of tacit components of knowledge is clearly connected to the above discussion on the degree to which the knowledge can be detached to the individuals. It is often difficult to apply this classification in practical terms since all knowledge includes a degree of tacitness along a continuum in which the one or the other dimension may dominate (Grant 2007). However, this distinction helps us to emphasise the core problem of knowledge exchange: explicit and codified knowledge, being in a form that is very close to an *object*, can be (more) easily transferred from a source to a receiver (sometimes by means of highly automated ICT systems - Bolisani & Scarso, 1999), or can be stocked somewhere for subsequent reuse. These are all properties that tacit knowledge, on the contrary, does not possess. Tacit knowledge is difficult to manipulate and transfer, and tends to remain embedded in the people who possess it.

If explicit knowledge is more appropriate for flowing from an organisation to another, one might say that there are very good reasons to convert tacit knowledge into explicit knowledge whenever feasible. To do that, a number of methods and mechanisms for *knowledge codification* (i.e. the process by means of which tacit knowledge is converted into explicit knowledge) are used in firms, such as: a) translating the experience, skills and know-how of employees into manuals, procedures, best practices, guidelines, etc., b) keeping track of the work of people and teams by means of formal reports, c) recording the activities of the firm by measuring technical or economic parameters, and so on.

The literature provides good reasons that can economically justify the effort of codification of knowledge by firms (Foray, 2004). Once codified, the knowledge tends to assume characteristics that are more similar to many physical goods: it can be described, valued, and even traded more easily; also, the costs of storage, replication, and dissemination of knowledge are low. In addition, to produce a continuous innovation flow the firms need to exploit an *organisational memory* of old projects reducing the costs of *reinventing the wheel* each time (Argote et al., 1990). This can be made more easily by using explicit knowledge items. Furthermore, the high turnover of today's companies requires measures to avoid the loss of useful experience of employees; especially in a multinational context, there is a need to set and disseminate compatible standards, best practices, and routines among all the dispersed units; last but not least, the potential of ICT technologies can be fully exploited only when knowledge is codified.

As some studies show (see e.g. Abramovitz & David, 1996), the impressive growth of countries like the United States can be explained by their capability to exploit the potential of codified knowledge. Still, knowledge codification is far from a trivial task and the process of codification of tacit knowledge into explicit knowledge always implies a *loss* in the content, since a part of this remains *stuck* to its source (von Hippel, 1994). Codification is also costly, since it involves the development of a model to represent knowledge in a formal way, the creation of a message that should be stored on an appropriate support, and the dissemination of a language to enable the decodification and the exploitation of knowledge by the prospective users.

Knowledge Markets

This discussion reveals another notion that is clearly important here: that of *knowledge market*. In practice, two types of knowledge markets can be identified, the inter-firm or *external* knowledge market and the internal market, namely inside the organisation. The first type is closer to the typical view of economic markets and is particularly important in the case of VEs. The implementation of formal or informal inter-firm agreements to exchange knowledge and, by this way, explore innovations and exploit new ideas (Millar et al., 1997; Warkentin et al., 2001; Peña, 2002) can constitute a challenging field.

The development of knowledge markets implies that firms accept to deliberately *trade* their knowledge items with another organization, a trade which involves a form of *compensation* in monetary or non-monetary terms. The attention is often put on the buyers of knowledge (i.e.: the receivers in a process of transfer), although firms can also consider the commercialization of their knowledge as part of their business strategy

Knowledge markets have unique characteristics, especially because knowledge is different from any other commodity that can be traded (Teece, 2003). An important distinction is between *public* and *private* knowledge. Once knowledge is discovered, coded, and made public, it becomes a public and non-rivalrous good. When that happens, its price should be equal to zero for an efficient diffusion, in accordance to the classic economic models (Foray, 2004).

In other cases knowledge can, however, be excludible: for instance when it is tacit, and its transfer is more difficult; or when it is embodied in a *carrier* (a code, an electronic packet, a book, someone who knows, etc.) on which there may be some form of control or *property protection*. Indeed, only purely disembodied knowledge (i.e.: common notions, general concepts, and other abstract objects of thought) can be totally non-excludible. But even in this case, it may be argued that the cost of processing and disseminating is not zero in the sense that the process of assimilation by people (learning) or the embodying in things (application) is costly in time and resources.

The institutional mechanisms that enable a firm to turn public knowledge into an excludible good (Teece, 2003), are the Intellectual Property Rights (IPR). The use of IPR is, however, neither easy nor always useful. As Stiglitz (1999) notes, protecting the property and use of knowledge – and, thus, making it an excludible good that can have a market price – cannot be done in the same way as protecting physical properties from theft, for example. And due to the complex bundled nature of knowledge items, there are some reasons why protecting knowledge would be even counter-productive. For instance, new ideas build on the work of others, and often draw from a common pool of pre-existing ideas. For example, it would be impossible (and possibly unfair) to impede the use of a mathematical theorem.

In addition, it should be noted that, from a receiver's viewpoint, public knowledge is important but, since it is public, there is no motivation to pay for it. In that context, no competitive advantage would be achieved from the use of public knowledge while, on the contrary, it can be said that it is tacit knowledge (for instance, the one embedded in the minds and experience of employees) that represents the grounds of the competitive advantage (Stiglitz, 1999). Under a knowledge perspective, the essential skill of a firm is, thus, to create, transfer, assemble, integrate and exploit knowledge assets in a way that transforms them into a competitive resource, i.e. difficult to imitate by competitors.

In that situation there is an intrinsic source of risk; while public knowledge is more easily transferred, it is tacit (or *non public*) knowledge that can have a recognised value in a knowledge market and, thus, can give motivations to companies for engaging in an exchange of knowledge. On the other hand, tacit knowledge cannot satisfy the essential property of homogeneity that characterises

competitive markets: each element of knowledge can be different from any other, and the essential aspects that identify goods in physical markets simply do not apply (quantity does not make any sense, and price is hard to establish). Also, the markets of tacit knowledge can fail since traders have to face several issues (Desouza and Awazu, 2003), such as the difficulty of signalling the features and contents of knowledge to the potential receivers. Knowledge has a perceived value based on experience (Choi et al., 1995), but if the source allows the receiver to experience a knowledge item (i.e. to read a book, or attend a lesson), then the latter has no need to pay for it.

The fact that in a knowledge market, evaluating the trading goods is difficult creates significant obstacles especially in the distribution of top quality offerings (this is the so called "risk of lemons" - Akerlof, 1970). *Trust* is an essential element here, but in a knowledge market, there may be the need for rules governing the establishment of a trustworthy climate. Also, a market needs liquidity, which means convincing enough people to buy and sell their knowledge, thus increasing the externalities of the participation in the market. This situation becomes particularly critical at the initial establishment of such a market.

KNOWLEDGE FLOWS AND RELATED RISK IN A VE

The concept of risk as a performance variance is widely used in finance, economics, and strategic management. Generally, the notion of risk refers to variations in corporate outcomes or performances that cannot be forecasted in advance. The major uses of the term are in reference to negative variations in business indicators such as revenues, costs, profit, market share, and so forth (Miller, 1992). Managers generally associate risk with negative outcomes (March and Shapira 1987), and consequently, risk can be quantified as the probability of an adverse event and the severity of its consequences (Mitchell,

1995). This notion, that can have direct applications in specific cases such as the insurance sector, has some limitations in a generic business context: the inherent problem of *measurement* (in particular, of probability of events) and, before that, the question of *identification* and *classification* of the sources and types of risk.

In this chapter, we specifically address the second element, i.e. the analysis and classification of the possible sources of risk associated to the management of knowledge in a VE. Nowadays, there is an increasing attention to the application of the notion of risk not only to an isolated company but also to *networked environments*. The interactions of a company with the global network of its partners are possible sources of risk (Clemons, 2000). A more recent area of study regards the implementation of approaches for managing risk in supply chains (Christopher and Lee, 2004; Gunipiero and Eltantawy 2004). For the development of approaches to managing risks in networked environments, there is the need to explore the nature of risk and risk management in the particular context represented by networked firms, which is essential for VEs as well. Based on the previous discussions, we summarize the basic points of this analysis, as follows:

- A VE consists of a number of companies that combine their specialised and complementary knowledge to achieve a common goal.

- In doing that, each firm generates original elements of knowledge and, by exchanging them with the other companies, contributes to the shared business project.

- These knowledge flows, which complement the physical and monetary transactions but can also occur independently from them, imply that each company is willing to draw knowledge contents from its internal *stocks* and to exchange them with others. Consequently, like any other economic exchange, this implies some *risk* that has to be managed.

In this chapter, we argue that this kind of risk should be recognised and managed properly in order to achieve the success of each VE member separately and of the VE as a whole. In particular, following previous studies (Loebbecke and van Fenema, 2000), we argue that, when knowledge is considered to be an economic asset, evaluating the risk of managing knowledge becomes an essential ingredient of the problem. In other words, the characteristics of *knowledge as economic asset* and the nature of *knowledge flows and knowledge exchanges* in a VE can help us to identify the *sources* of risk for the companies involved.

Several classifications of risk sources and categories can be found in the literature (Simons, 1999; Meulbrook, 2000; Smallman, 1996) complemented by taxonomies of the related losses (Harland et al. 2003). For our purpose, there are three main areas of risk that can be considered: the *financial* risk (e.g. Jorion, 2007) – i.e. the risk of failure of monetary investments; the *technical* risk (Wilson and McCutcheon, 2003) – i.e. the risk of failure of operational activities; and the *project management risk* (Barley, 2003), i.e. the risk of failure of the way a project is conducted. Although all these kinds can be associated to a financial loss in the end, their nature is different.

Connecting these definitions with the discussion that took place in the previous sections, we can propose a fundamental classification of *knowledge-related risks* in a VE environment. More specifically:

- *Technical risk* relates to the *appropriateness* of a particular kind of knowledge to the specific project that is conducted; here, the issues of source selection, communication language, conversion and integration of knowledge components appear to be critical.

- The *project management risk* relates to the failures in managing the processes of KM, such as the mechanisms for storing, retrieving, and communicating knowledge with others, as well as the technologies used to support the above processes

- The *financial risk* refers to the losses that a company may encounter in knowledge exchanges: for instance, when components of private knowledge flow to competitors and are imitated, resulting in a weaker competitive position, or when the exchange of knowledge with others does not give a valuable payback.

In the next section, we will illustrate how the aforementioned elements of risk can be identified in the current business practice, through the presentation of a real life VE example.

MANAGING THE RISK OF KNOWLEDGE FLOWS: PRACTICAL LESSONS

Here we examine the case of the *SAP ecosystem*. SAP is a Germany-based multinational company specialising in the development of ERP (Enterprise Resource Planning) software. The analysis conducted clarifies the mechanisms used in a VE to perform and manage the different kinds of inter-organisational knowledge flows, to highlight the risks that emerge in these situations, and to understand the management of the VE seen from a knowledge-based perspective. We will particularly assume the viewpoint of the leading firm (SAP), although remarks on the role of the other VE members will be provided as well.

Methodology and Research Questions

The main research questions that we addressed in the empirical study presented below are the following

- Is it possible to identify specific sources of risk associated to knowledge and

its management in a VE, following the schemes and concepts proposed in the previous sections?

- What are the practical problems and their possible solutions that emerge in the current practice?

To address these questions, the case study research instrument (Yin, 1989) is utilised. The unit of analysis is not the single firm but, rather, a VE. To identify a VE, the analysis started from the leading company, and then proceeded by identifying the principal other units with which the company interacts. Following the definition of VE previously discussed, the identification of these companies was based on the following criteria: since a VE is a project-based group of firms, the companies to consider were selected based on the fact that they collaborate to a specific project and in the specific case, those that work on a new implementation of ERP solution for a client. As collaborating companies we refer only to those that have sufficiently regular and non banal relationships, or it is better to say those that interact by means of a significant process of knowledge exchange. After a significant number of companies in the VE was identified, the knowledge flows occurring among them were analysed. This was done by examining each company, not focusing on the experience of the single firm itself but, rather, on the inter-company interactions. The knowledge flows between companies and the problematic aspects of their management were investigated.

The collection of empirical data was performed by means of systematic semi-structured interviews with managers, based on a check list that reflected the object of study. Supplementary information was obtained from other sources (e.g.: documental materials, literature and industry press, independent experts, etc.), which also allowed to make comparisons and cross-analysis of the data collected. Additional information about units of the VE not directly interviewed was also collected.

This was done with the help of the interviewed managers and experts coupled with the analysis of the existing literature and previous case-studies.

The questions that the interviews were trying to answer are the following:

- What are the knowledge specialisations of the company? What external specialisations are needed for the particular business? Why?
- How is knowledge generated and stored internally? What processes are used for this?
- How are interactions and knowledge exchanges with other companies conducted? What type of technology supports these interactions? What kind of communication underpins what kind of knowledge?
- How are the different kinds of knowledge used internally and externally to the company?

The SAP VE consists of SAP, which is the leading company, and the following business entities:

- Licensed dealers operating in the various local markets. These companies are mainly small IT service providers that participate in the implementation of a specific ERP system for a final client. There are hundreds of these partners all around the world; we will particularly report the cases of ICM.S and INFRACOM, two dealers that operate in northern Italy. Direct and indirect information was collected about other dealers.
- Providers of supplementary technologies (for instance, hardware systems) and competing vendors: these companies are often vital for the successful implementation of an ERP system;
- Clients themselves: although in principle it may be sound strange to consider these nodes as part of a VE (since these are the

companies that pay for the project), their inclusion in this analysis is important because the clients have a significant role in the completion of an ERP project, and they participate in the complex web of knowledge flows occurring in the VE. In this chapter, we explicitly consider three SAP customers of different sectors (Fashion Box – apparel company; Fiamm – car components; GIV – wine-maker), which are clients of the dealers mentioned above.

- The scientific organisations, including public labs and universities.
- Other service providers.

To give an idea of the structure analysed, the main VE nodes are reported in Figure 1. The grey shaded nodes were studied more directly, by means of specific semi-structured interviews to managers supported by the analysis of documental materials. The rest of the nodes were analysed by using documental sources, short interviews to managers and experts, or indirect sources. Arrows indicate the existence of direct relationships between the companies.

The Leading Node and the ERP Product

SAP (Systems Applications And Products In Data Processing) is a major software company specialising in ERP systems with a global sale organisation covering over than 50 countries. Founded in the '70s by five ex-IBM professionals, the company has grown steadily and currently employs about 51.000 people of 120 different nationalities, and amounts about 9 billion € of total sales. Created to sell specialised cost-accounting software for large customers, the company now sells its core ERP product comprising several modules for many industries and application fields, to both large and small clients all over the world. The last versions of SAP ERP include enhanced functionalities such as e-commerce functions and portal interfaces,

Figure 1. Nodes of the SAP VE

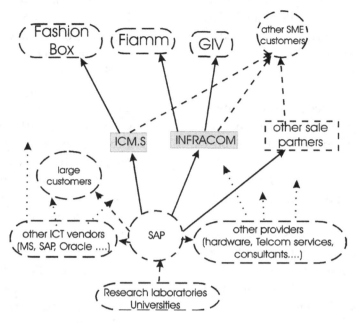

and are based on the most advanced technologies for business software production, such as SOA (Service Oriented Architecture). The company organisation has a strictly centralised R&D activity, while sales are managed by subsidiaries in various countries (and especially for the large clients). In addition, a network of local IT service firms - the SAP *ecosystem* in strict terms – act as independent licensees reselling SAP software and providing implementation services especially to small business customers.

Compared to other products and services, the sale of an ERP system has some peculiarities with significant cognitive implications. It comprises the sale of *something* (i.e.: a software licence) but also the provision of services (i.e.: process analysis, configuration, implementation, training, etc.); it has some standard components (namely, the core ERP modules), and on the other hand it implies much work of personalisation and customisation. There are different kinds of knowledge here. The *tangible* part of the product consists of knowledge embedded in an artefact (i.e. software), whose property is transferred to the client in the form of

licenses; the intangible part consists of tacit forms (i.e.: consulting, etc.) that need a direct supplier-customer contact. Indeed, an ERP implementation is a combination of both kinds of knowledge, tightly intertwined to one another.

For this reason, SAP has made huge organisational and technical investments with the purpose to find an effective way of managing these complex and conflicting characteristics of the ERP product. Although the single customer requires a specific ERP implementation that fits its processes, it would be too costly (and risky) for SAP to develop completely distinct ERP systems for every client. For this reason, an ERP project is always based on the combination and adaptation of distinct software modules that represent the *codification* of typical business processes. After decades of experience in the sector, SAP has been able to define an *ideal type* of company, to which the possible automation of processes was studied carefully. The results consist of a library of hundreds of modules representing typical business processes and their translation into software codes. These modules can be adapted, configured and combined to meet the needs of a specific final client. To conduct a new ERP implementation for a client, the SAP consultants analyse its processes, represent it in a formal way, and then find the appropriate software modules that best fit this set of processes.

In summary, the implementation of a SAP project rests on a sub-division of the product into *layers*. Each layer involves different knowledge items whose development requires different knowledge for each layer. This distinction appears useful to support the reduction of *technical risk*. At the lower level we find the *infrastructural* layer (i.e.: databases, operating systems, network components, etc.) where a highly technical specialisation is needed. At the *application* level, there are the so-called *building blocks*, configurable software modules that represent the translation into software of standard business processes: to define these modules, a deep knowledge of the business itself is needed, combined with a good knowledge of programming rules. The SAP people have rested on their long experience with the major ERP users for building their definition of the model of a generic company, whose processes have then been translated into software modules. Finally, at the *sales* level, the building blocks are selected and configured to meet the specific needs of a particular implementation: here, a profound knowledge of the single client and of the *specific* business processes of customers is necessary; as a matter of fact, the generic processes (which the building blocks refer to) have to be particularised to the case of the specific client.

Cognitive Vertical Integration vs. Risk of Networking

ERP sales require a wide range of knowledge, from technical issues to application aspects. These distinct components have to be combined together for the success of the project. Since any implementation is different from the others, the appropriate

chain of knowledge and competencies needs to be selected and activated appropriately.

In principle, SAP may have had two options that involve different management approaches to knowledge related risk: to pursue a *cognitive vertical integration*, which means the acquisition and development of all the knowledge needed to manage the entire development, production, and sale of the system, or to specialize in a specific portion of the knowledge chain and delegate 'non-core' competencies to other companies. The first option may seem to be the most appropriate choice, since it reduces the risk of *inconsistencies* in the management of the product and of opportunistic behaviours of partners that derive from a decentralisation policy. However, this option is still not risk free. The need for huge investments (in the form of skilled personnel, training, R&D, etc.) and the possibility of knowledge becoming obsolete are some of the main risks inherent in a vertical integration approach.

The particular nature of ERP systems (as described above) implies that a balance between conflicting risks should be found. This is what SAP attempted to do by pursuing an intermediate strategy that implies control over critical parts of the required knowledge and preserves the flexibility ensured by external partners. The implementation of the SAP VE appears to be a direct consequence of the application of this intermediate policy. SAP has developed advanced technical competencies of the application software (thus following an integration strategy), but left the rest of the technical competence (i.e.: hardware, operating systems, networking, etc.) to external providers. In that way, SAP tried to reduce the risks of obsolescence and avoided the huge investments it would otherwise need to establish the necessary knowledge platform. It should be noted here that SAP differentiates itself from the competition, since both Microsoft and Oracle are more vertically integrated.

At the same time, SAP keeps a strict control over the application software, and all the competencies that are needed to develop it (i.e.: high level programming, but also analysis of processes, market needs, etc.). To do that, proprietary technologies (including the ABAP programming language) have been developed, so that others can't have access to this core part of knowledge without permission.

In terms of the inter-organisational relationships, this involves a complex web of interaction with companies that are at the same time *competitors* and *business partners*. For instance, the SAP people need to exchange some technical knowledge with the Oracle team, because the ERP system builds up on an Oracle database; but on the other hand, the companies compete on the same market (since they both sell an ERP system). In that case, a careful identification of the knowledge components that should and can be shared, and those that need to remain private, is necessary to reduce the risk of imitation.

As to what sales competencies are concerned, again a mixed strategy is utilized. On the one hand, SAP keeps control over the sales to large customers, which represent an important part of the business and a *source* of application knowledge that supports the development of new releases. However, since the ERP market is highly fragmented but requires a direct provider-customer interaction, it would be risky to invest resources in a direct sales channel, especially in the case of small and medium sized customers. For this reason SAP developed its partner network. Local sales partners can contribute to a new ERP implementation with their knowledge of the specific customers but the risk of their opportunistic behaviour is reduced by preventing them from having direct access to the core technological components.

Risk of Knowledge Focalisation

One other aspect that has to be studied in terms of related risks is that of knowledge focalisation. SAP, is a company highly specialized in a specific product, this being the ERP system, and for

years it has based its entire market presence on this software. This is probably one of the basic ingredients of its success: the development of a complete ERP software would be impossible without the deep specialisation in a specific knowledge domain.

Still, cognitive focalisation implies some specific risk factors, such as the vulnerability of the company in case of sudden changes in the demand, of specific market difficulties that can hinder the exploitation of the product, or the rise of strong competitors that can reduce the market share. To face these risks, SAP needs to keep a high variety of supply even with a specialised product. This is achieved in collaboration with the VE sales partners by managing this special kind of *focalised variety*.

On the one hand, SAP develops and supplies a library of core modules of the system, which are fully interoperable and based on the same development framework. This *standard set* of tools builds on the focalised knowledge of the R&D team. On the other hand, each licensee has a specialised knowledge in a particular market/client/geographic area. It is the combination of all these focalisations that makes the sale of a *global but personalised software* like an ERP system possible.

Based on the above, one could argue that the organisation of the VE structure supports knowledge related risk mitigation. A core tool that supports risk mitigation is the SAP reference model, which represents the *codified language* that is assimilated and used by all the partners. The risk of *knowledge islands* (Franz et al., 2002), i.e. the creation of barriers that hinder the exchange of useful knowledge among partners, is thus reduced. By grouping the different experiences and competencies of all the companies and framing them into the common *SAP model*, the fruitful interaction between all players becomes possible. This also allows a *generation of variety*, because each VE member can retrieve the competence of the others and in turn, add its experience to the benefit of the whole network. The central node has the main role of collecting, storing and re-delivering the knowledge from external partners.

Private and Public Knowledge

A key aspect in the cognitive management of a VE is the boundary between the public components of knowledge and the parts that need to remain private. By analysing the modalities of knowledge exchange in the SAP VE three relevant aspects have to be noted:

- The cognitive specialisation that is necessary for reaching the excellence in the application areas of ERP systems.
- The logic of *community*, which allows the members to share the cognitive aspects that are of use for selling the SAP product in all the potential markets.
- The strict control by SAP on the core of the product.

An essential problem, in managing SAP's VE, is to identify what knowledge can or cannot be shared. As mentioned before, SAP has the strict control on the software code. On the other hand, since the market strength of SAP is grounded on the ecosystem of partners, keeping all the knowledge private can be problematic. As a matter of fact, SAP has a specific interest that the *SAP model* spreads largely, so that it becomes a standard that promotes itself. In addition, spreading the knowledge that is required for the success of ERP implementations (for instance, the way the processes are formalised, the functioning of the building blocks, etc.) enables the involvement of partners in the development of innovations to the SAP system, which enriches its knowledge stock. In other words, allowing controlled access to SAP's knowledge leads to a significant *cognitive payback* for the company as well.

Risk of Instability of the VE

Far from being a sort of *self-developed* system, the SAP ecosystem requires deliberate actions and measures to build and manage it. More specifically:

- *Orchestrated Evolution*: the sharing of knowledge is managed by SAP, which establishes the rules and standard languages for interactions, and certifies knowledge flows.
- *Partner Involvement*. For example, each accredited professional has access to the SAP portal and library, to retrieve documentation, suggestions, and even software components; also, the company organises courses and other training activities.
- *Involvement Of Different specialised players in the same network*: in the single project many companies can be involved; all these use the same language and cognitive reference;
- *Sharing of benefits*: all the members of the network can obtain benefits from the participation in the system.

These are factors of *stability* for the VE. However, there are also risks of instability. One risk relates to the complex co-operation/competition relationship among the partners. SAP lets different providers compete in the same market or geographical area. In other words, a customer willing to implement a SAP system can resort to a number of alternative competing providers. This is facilitated by the fact that partners can be (at least in part) interchangeable, because they work based on the same SAP standard.

This kind of *multiple channel* is necessary for SAP, to reduce the risk of losing market opportunities and the risk of opportunistic behaviour by a single *monopolistic* partner. This competition can however cause an increase in the risk of frictions and conflicts, which may influence network stability.

FUTURE RESEARCH TRENDS

The study raises a number of research issues that may be interesting to explore. Probably the most important one is the quantitative evaluation of the knowledge-related risk. This implies the need to assess the value of knowledge that is exchanged among the members of a VE. This is a critical but also a challenging point. Measuring the economic value of knowledge is still a debated question (Bolisani and Oltramari, 2009). Both theoretical and practical advancements are needed here.

As regards the empirical research presented here, there are evident limitations that can provide suggestions for future studies. A first problem is that one case study is not enough to provide robust empirical validations. There may be the need to conduct extensive research, and to shift from the exploratory stage to the formulation of hypotheses and their verification. A second limitation is the difficulty to reconstruct a VE starting from its nodes. In a network, there may be several informal relationships between individuals, which do not follow official channels. This aspect was not clearly analysed in the study, which was mainly limited to the level of the interaction between companies or project teams. It would be important to understand to what extent the informal individual-to-individual relationships are influential for the knowledge-based functioning of a VE and for the associated risks. This may also provide interesting suggestions from a managerial viewpoint.

CONCLUSION

The main objective of this chapter was to show that an appropriate reflection on the knowledge-related risk factors is significant for the operation of a VE. By considering the models that describe the mechanism of knowledge exchange between the different organisations that participate in a VE, it is possible to highlight that the cognitive management of a successful VE raises a number of risk sources and risk factors that can be related to the general nature of knowledge as economic resource and to the particular aspects of KM in a VE. More specifically we have identified:

a) Risks associated to the different *kinds of knowledge* (e.g.: tacit vs. explicit; private vs. public; knowledge of a specific domain, etc.);
b) Risks associated to the structure of the VE and the related *processes* utilized (e.g.: knowledge competition, vertical collaboration, etc.);
c) Risks associated to the mechanisms of *knowledge exchange* (e.g.: language settings, trust mechanisms, forms of payback, etc.)

Our study provides interesting lessons both from a theoretical and practical viewpoint. From a theoretical viewpoint, it allows us to understand the relationships between the concepts defined in the KM literature and the concept of economic risk, so that it becomes possible to assess the relevance and significance of risk-related issues in inter-company KM activities. From a practical viewpoint, it enables a better definition of specific problems and possible managerial solutions. As regards this last point, the various sources of risk lead to distinct problems of knowledge-based risk management, and consequent managerial practices that the companies might use.

The empirical research conducted in the context of this study had two main purposes: first, to introduce the concept of knowledge related risk management in VEs and second to provide interesting lessons for managerial approaches towards addressing the above issues. In particular, it is possible to classify the sources of knowledge-related risk and the possible approaches to their management, as follows:

- *Risk of inappropriateness of knowledge* (technical risk): this source of risk relates to the fact that for a specific project there is the need to integrate different components of knowledge. For instance, for a new ERP system there is the need to combine knowledge of hardware, operating systems, application software, business processes etc. Since in a VE, companies specialise in different knowledge components, the source of risk derives from the uncertainty that the knowledge which the participating companies need to share is really appropriate to that specific project. To mitigate that risk, several activities can be initiated, such as the development of a proper *language* to signal a company's specialisation to the rest of the network and the introduction of a mechanism to evaluate, identify and select partners based on their *cognitive appropriateness* for that project.
- *Risk of inappropriate processes of KM* (project management risk). The need for systematic management of knowledge is generally indicated as a practice to avoid *reinventing the wheel* in any new project or for avoiding the development of separate and idiosyncratic knowledge pools in an organisation (knowledge islands – Franz et al. 2000). The definition of KM processes and the choice of proper enabling technologies are essential ingredients to reduce the uncertainty associated with the management of knowledge. In the case analysed, each ERP implementation, despite of being different from one another, follows a similar project schedule. There is a clear relationship between the effort to preserve the variety of possible implementations and the efficiency of project management. This

can be interpreted in cognitive terms, because each stage of an implementation project requires different exchanges of knowledge between partners. To avoid implementation problems, these processes have to be tuned accordingly.

- *Risk of losses deriving from knowledge exchange* (financial risk): the critical point here is the different nature of knowledge as a public or private resource. As previously mentioned, in a VE there is always the need to share some components of knowledge, which eventually become public and thus less appropriable. The losses coming from leakages of knowledge that should instead be protected and remain private constitute a significant risk issue that has to be addressed by the VE leading company. Proper mechanisms to identify the components of knowledge that should remain private or become public, to evaluate the value of knowledge and the potential losses that may occur, and to protect private knowledge from the appropriation by others are essential parts of a knowledge-based risk management in a VE context. For example, in the case of SAP, the decision to keep the software core protected and to develop *building blocks* that can be shared with dealers is an example of a mechanism used to distinguish between the private and the public parts of knowledge and to manage them distinctly. It is always difficult to draw general conclusions from a single case. However, the use of the proposed classification may be extended to other situations where similar issues and sources of risk can be identified.

ACKNOWLEDGMENT

This paper contributes to the FIRB2003 project "Knowledge management in the Extended Enterprise: new organizational models in the digital age" funded by the Italian Ministry of University and Research. The author gratefully thanks the supportive suggestions of the Book Editor and of three anonymous reviewers.

REFERENCES

Abramovitz, M., & David, P. A. (1996). Technological Change, Intangible Investments and Growth in the Knowledge-based Economy: The US Historical Experience. In D. Foray & B.A. Lundvall (eds), Employment and Growth in the Knowledge-based Economy. Paris: OECD.

Akerlof, G. A. (1970). The Markets for "Lemons": Quality Uncertainty and the Market Mechanism. *The Quarterly Journal of Economics*, (August): 488–500. doi:10.2307/1879431

Antonelli, C. (2007). The Business Governance of Localized Knowledge. *Industry and Innovation*, *13*(3), 227–261. doi:10.1080/13662710600858118

Argote, L., Beckamn, S., & Epple, D. (1990). The Persistence and Transfer of Learning in Industrial Settings. *Management Science*, *36*(2). doi:10.1287/mnsc.36.2.140

Barley, B. (2003). Project Risk Management. New York: McGraw-Hill.

Barney, J. (2001). Resource-based theories of competitive advantage: a ten-year retrospective on the resource-based view. *Journal of Management*, *27*(6), 643–650. doi:10.1177/014920630102700602

Beesley, L. (2004). Multi-level complexity in the management of knowledge networks. *Journal of Knowledge Management*, *8*(3), 71–100. doi:10.1108/13673270410541051

Blecker, T., & Neumann, R. (2000). Interorganizational Knowledge Management - Some Perspectives for Knowledge oriented Strategic Management in Virtual Organizations, In Y. Malhotra (Ed), Knowledge Management and Virtual Organizations. Hershey, PA: Idea Group Publishing

Bolisani, E., & Oltramari, A. (2009, February 17-18). *Capitalizing flows of knowledge: models and accounting perspectives*, paper presented at the 4th International Forum on Knowledge Asset Dynamics – IFKAD, University of Glasgow.

Bolisani, E., & Scarso, E. (1999). Information Technology Management: a Knowledge-Based Perspective. *Technovation*, *19*, 209–217. doi:10.1016/S0166-4972(98)00109-6

Browne, J., & Zhang, J. (1999). Extended and virtual enterprises-similarities and differences. *International Journal of Agile Management Systems*, *1*(1), 30–36. doi:10.1108/14654659910266691

Byrne, J. (1993). The virtual corporation. *Business Week*, 98–102.

Childe, S. J. (1998). The extended enterprise-a concept of co-operation. *Production Planning and Control*, *9*(4), 320–327. doi:10.1080/095372898234046

Choi, S., Whinston, A., & Stahl, D. (1997). Economics of Electronic Commerce. Indianapolis, IN: Macmillan

Christopher, M., & Lee, H. (2004). Mitigating supply chain risk through improved confidence. *International Journal of Physical Distribution & Logistics Management*, *34*(5), 388–396. doi:10.1108/09600030410545436

Clemons, E. (2000, June 13). Gauging the power play in the new economy. *Financial Times*.

Cohen, W. M., & Levinthal, D. A. (1989). Innovation and Learning: the Two Faces of R&D. *The Economic Journal, 99*(397), 569–596. doi:10.2307/2233763

Desouza, K., & Awazu, Y. (2004). Markets in Know-How. Business Strategy Review, (Autumn), 59-65

Foray, D. (2004). The Economics of Knowledge. Boston: MIT Press.

Franke, U. (2000). The Knowledge Based view (KBV) of the Virtual Web, the Virtual Corporation and the Net Broker. In Y. Malhotra (Ed), Knowledge Management and Virtual Organizations, Hershey, PA: Idea Group Publishing

Franz, M., Freudenthaler, K., Kameny, M., & Schoen, S. (2002). The development of the Siemens Knowledge Community Support, In T.H. Davenport & and G.J.B. Probst, (Eds.), Knowledge Management Case Book, (147-159), New York: Wiley and Sons.

Giunipero, L. C., & Eltantawy, R. A. (2004). Securing the upstream supply chain: a risk management approach. *International Journal of Physical Distribution & Logistics Management, 34*(9), 698–713. doi:10.1108/09600030410567478

Grant, K. A. (2007). Tacit knowledge revisited – We can still learn from Polanyi. *Electronic Journal of Knowledge Management, 5*(2), 173–180.

Grant, R. M. (1996). Toward a Knowledge-Based Theory of the Firm. *Strategic Management Journal, 17*(Winter), 109–122.

Halaris, C., Kerridge, S., Bafoutsou, G., Mentzas, G., & Kerridge, S. (2003). An Integrated System Supporting Virtual Consortia in the Construction Sector. *Journal of Organizational Computing and Electronic Commerce, 13*(3/4), 243–265. doi:10.1207/S15327744JOCE133&4_06

Harland, C., Brenchley, R., & Walker, H. (2003). Risk in supply networks. *Journal of Purchasing and Supply Management, 9*(1), 51–62. doi:10.1016/S1478-4092(03)00004-9

Holsapple, C. W. (2003). Knowledge and its Attributes. In C.W. Holsapple (Ed.), Handbook of Knowledge Management (pp. 165-188). Berlin, Germany: Springer-Verlag

Iandoli, L., & Zollo, G. (2007), Organizational Cognition and Learning. Building Systems for the Learning Organization. Hershey, PA: IGI Global Publishing.

Inkpen, A. C., & Tsang, E. W. K. (2005). Social capital, networks and knowledge transfer. *Academy of Management Review, 30*(1), 146–165.

Jagdev, H. S., & Thoben, K. D. (2001). Anatomy of enterprise collaborations. *Production Planning and Control, 12*(5), 437–451. doi:10.1080/09537280110042675

Jarrillo, J. C. (1988). Strategic Networks: Creating the Borderless Organisation. Oxford, UK: Butterworth-Heinemann.

Jorion, P. (2007), Financial Risk Manager Handbook. New York: Wiley.

Kaihara, T. (2003). Supply Chain Management Multi-agent based supply chain modelling with dynamic environment. *International Journal of Production Economics, 85*(2), 263–269. doi:10.1016/S0925-5273(03)00114-2

Kinder, T. (2003). Go with the flow-a conceptual framework for supply relations in the era of the extended enterprise. *Research Policy, 32*(3), 503–523. doi:10.1016/S0048-7333(02)00021-5

Kovács, G. L., & Paganelli, P. (2003). A planning and management infrastructure for large, complex, distributed projects—beyond ERP and SCM. *Computers in Industry, 51*(2), 165–183. doi:10.1016/S0166-3615(03)00034-4

Lefebvre, L. A., & Lefebvre, E. (2002). E-commerce and virtual enterprises: issues and challenges for transition economies. *Technovation, 22*, 313–323. doi:10.1016/S0166-4972(01)00010-4

Lillehagen, F., & Karlsen, D. (2001). Visual extended enterprise engineering and operation-embedding knowledge management and work execution. *Production Planning and Control, 12*(2), 164–175. doi:10.1080/09537280150501266

Loebbecke, C., & van Fenema, P. C. (2000). Virtual Organizations that Cooperate and Compete: Managing the Risks of Knowledge Exchange. In Y. Malhotra (Ed), Knowledge Management and Virtual Organizations, Hershey, PA: Idea Group Publishing.

Lorange, P., & Roos, J. (1992). Strategic alliances: formation, implementation, and evolution. Cambridge, MA: Blackwell.

Malhotra, Y. (Ed.). (2000). Knowledge Management and Virtual Organizations. Hershey, PA: Idea Group Publishing.

March, J. G., & Shapira, Z. (1987). Managerial Perspectives on Risk and Risk Taking. *Management Science, 33*(11), 1404–1418. doi:10.1287/mnsc.33.11.1404

Martinez, M. T., Fouletier, P., Park, K. H., & Favrel, J. (2001). Virtual enterprise – organisation, evolution and control. *International Journal of Production Economics, 74*(1-3), 225–238. doi:10.1016/S0925-5273(01)00129-3

Meulbrook, L. (2000). Total strategies for company-wide risk control. *Financial Times (North American Edition)*, 9.

Millar, J., Demaid, A., & Quintas, P. (1997). Trans-organizational Innovation: A Framework for Research. *Technology Analysis and Strategic Management, 9*(4), 399–418. doi:10.1080/09537329708524294

Miller, K. D. (1992). A Framework for Integrated Risk Management in International Business. *Journal of International Business Studies, 23*(2), 311–331. doi:10.1057/palgrave.jibs.8490270

Mitchell, V. W. (1995). Organizational risk perception and reduction – a literature review. *British Journal of Management, 6*, 115–133. doi:10.1111/j.1467-8551.1995.tb00089.x

O'Neill, H., & Sackett, P. (1994). The Extended Manufacturing Enterprise Paradigm. *Management Decision, 32*(8), 42–49. doi:10.1108/00251749410069453

Panteli, N., & Sockalingam, S. (2005). Trust and conflict within virtual inter-organizational alliances: a framework for facilitating knowledge sharing. *Decision Support Systems, 39*, 599–617. doi:10.1016/j.dss.2004.03.003

Park, K. H., & Favrel, J. (1999). Virtual enterprise — Information system and networking solution. *Computers & Industrial Engineering, 37*(1-2), 441–444. doi:10.1016/S0360-8352(99)00113-8

Peña, I. (2002). Knowledge networks as parts of an integrated knowledge management approach. *Journal of Knowledge Management, 6*(5), 469–478. doi:10.1108/13673270210450423

Power, M. (2004). The Risk Management of Everything: Rethinking the Politics of Uncertainty. London: Demos.

Preiss, K. (1999). Modelling of knowledge flows and their impact. *Journal of Knowledge Management, 3*(1), 36–46. doi:10.1108/13673279910259376

Simons, R. L. (1999). How risky is your company? *Harvard Business Review, 77*(3).

Smallman, C. (1996). Risk and organisational behaviour: a research model. *Disaster Prevention and Management, 5*(2), 12–26. doi:10.1108/09653569610112880

Spekman, R. E., & Davis, E. W. (2004). Risky business: expanding the discussion on risk and the extended enterprise. *International Journal of Physical Distribution & Logistics Management, 34*(5), 414–433. doi:10.1108/09600030410545454

Stiglitz, J. (1999). Public Policy for a Knowledge Economy. *OECD Report*. Retrieved September 18, 2007 from http://www.worldbank.org/html/extdr/extme/knowledge-economy.pdf

Stiglitz, J. (2002). Information and the Change in the Paradigm in Economics. *The American Economic Review, 92*(3), 460–501. doi:10.1257/00028280260136363

Teece, D. J. (2003). Knowledge and Competence as Strategic Assets. In C.W. Holsapple (Ed.), Handbook of Knowledge Management (pp. 129-152). Berlin, Germany: Springer-Verlag.

Tiwana, A. (2000). The knowledge management toolkit. Upper Saddle River, NJ: Prentice Hall.

Todeva, E. (2006). Business networks. Strategy and structure. London: Routledge.

Tuma, A. (1998). Configuration and coordination of virtual production networks. *International Journal of Production Economics, 56-57*(1), 641–648. doi:10.1016/S0925-5273(97)00146-1

Tyre, M., & Von Hippel, E. (1997). The Situative Nature of Adaptive Learning in Organizations. *Organization Science, 8*(1), 71–83. doi:10.1287/orsc.8.1.71

Venkatraman, N., & Henderson, J. C. (1998). Real strategies for virtual organizing. *Sloan Management Review*, (Fall): 33–48.

Von Hippel, E. (1994). Sticky information and the locus of problem solving: Implications for innovation. *Management Science, 40*(4), 429–439. doi:10.1287/mnsc.40.4.429

Warkentin, M., Sugumaran, V., & Bapna, R. (2001). E-knowledge networks for inter-organizational collaborative e-business. *Logistics Information Management, 14*(1/2), 149–162. doi:10.1108/09576050110363040

Wernerfeld, B. (1984). A resource based view of the firm. *Strategic Management Journal, 5*(2), 171–180. doi:10.1002/smj.4250050207

Williamson, O. E. (1985). The economic institutions of capitalism. New York: Free Press.

Wilson, D., & McCutcheon, D. (2003), Industrial Safety and Risk Management. Edmonton, Canada: University of Alberta Press.

Yin, R. (1989). Case study research: Design and methods (Rev. ed.). Newbury Park, CA: Sage Publishing.

Yoo, S. B., & Kim, Y. (2002). Web-based knowledge management for sharing product data in virtual enterprises. *International Journal of Production Economics, 75*(1), 173–183. doi:10.1016/S0925-5273(01)00190-6

Zhuge, H. (2006). Knowledge flow network planning and simulation. *Decision Support Systems, 2*(2), 571–592. doi:10.1016/j.dss.2005.03.007

ADDITIONAL READINGS

Adler, P. S. (2001). Market, Hierarchy, and Trust: The Knowledge Economy and the Future of Capitalism. *Organization Science, 12*(2), 215–234. doi:10.1287/orsc.12.2.215.10117

Almeida, P., Song, Y., & Grant, R. M. (2002). Are Firms Superior to Alliances and Markets? An Empirical Test of Cross-Border Knowledge Building. *Organization Science, 13*(2), 147–161. doi:10.1287/orsc.13.2.147.534

Bolisani, E., Scarso, E., & Di Biagi, M. (2006). Economic issues of online professional communities. In E. Coakes & S. Clarke (eds), Encyclopedia of Communities of Practice in Information and Knowledge Management, Hershey, PA: IDEA Group.

Boyd, J., Ragsdell, G., & Oppenheim, C. (2007, September 6-7). *Knowledge Transfer Mechanisms: A Case Study from Manufacturing.* Paper presented at the 8th European Conference on Knowldege Management, Barcelona, Spain.

Brydon, M., & Vining, A. R. (2006). Understanding the failure of internal knowledge markets: A framework for diagnosis and improvement. *Information & Management, 43*, 964–974. doi:10.1016/j.im.2006.09.001

Cowan, R., & Foray, D. (1997). The Economics of Codification and the Diffusion of Knowledge. *Industrial and Corporate Change, 6*(3), 595–622.

Davenport, T., & Prusak, L. (1998). Working Knowledge: How Organizations Manage What They Know. Boston: Harvard Business School Press

Drucker, P. (1969). The Age of Discontinuity; guidelines to our changing society. New York: Harper & Row.

Garavelli, A. C., Gorgoglione, M., & Scozzi, B. (2002). Managing knowledge transfer by knowledge technologies. *Technovation, 22*, 269–279. doi:10.1016/S0166-4972(01)00009-8

Goranson, H. T. (2003). Architectural support for the advanced virtual enterprise. *Computers in Industry, 51*(2), 113–125. doi:10.1016/S0166-3615(03)00031-9

Kasper-Fuehrer, E. C., & Ashkanasy, N. M. (2001). Communicating trustworthiness and building trust in inter-organizational virtual organizations. *Journal of Management, 27*(3), 235–254. doi:10.1016/S0149-2063(01)00090-3

King, W. R. (2006). Knowledge Transfer. In D.G. Schwatz (Ed.) Encyclopedia of Knowledge Management. Hershey, PA: Idea Group.

Mowery, D. C., Oxley, J. C., & Silverman, B. S. (1996). Strategic Alliances and Interfirm Knowledge Transfer. *Strategic Management Journal, 17*, 77–91.

Nickerson, J. A., & Zenger, T. R. (2004). A Knowledge-Based Theory of the Firm – The Problem-Solving Perspective. *Organization Science, 15*(6), 617–632. doi:10.1287/orsc.1040.0093

Polanyi, M. (1967). The Tacit Dimension, Garden City, NY: Doubleday Anchor.

Quintas, P., Lefrere, P., & Jones, G. (1997). Knowledge Management: a Strategic Agenda. *Long Range Planning, 30*(3), 385–391. doi:10.1016/S0024-6301(97)90252-1

Steinmueller, W. E. (2002). Networked Knowledge and Knowledge-based Economies. *International Journal of Social Sciences, 171*, 159–173.

Stone, D. N., & Warsono, S. (2003). Does Accounting Account for Knowledge? In C.W. Holsapple (Ed.), Handbook of Knowledge Management (pp. 253-270). Berlin, Germany: Springer-Verlag

Takeishi, A. (2002). Knowledge Partitioning in the Interfirm Division of Labor: The Case of Automotive Product Development. *Organization Science, 13*(3), 321–338. doi:10.1287/orsc.13.3.321.2779

Teece, D. J. (1998). Capturing Value from Knowledge Assets: The New Economy, Markets for Know-how, and Intangible Assets. *California Management Review, 40*(3), 55–79.

Thorne, K. (2005). Designing virtual organizations? Themes and trends in political and organizational discourses. *Journal of Management Development, 24*(7), 580–607. doi:10.1108/02621710510608731

Chapter 6
Managing IT Risks in Virtual Enterprise Networks:
A Proposed Governance Framework

Mohammad Ali Shalan
PMP, ITIL, CISA, CGEIT, Jordan

ABSTRACT

Information Technology (IT) has proven to be a critical enabler for the formation and operation of Virtual Enterprises (VEs) and a provider of unique business enabling capabilities. Nevertheless, IT integration with VE business model particularities is never a trivial task, thus calling for a special approach to discover and mitigate risks and apply controls related to the continuously growing of IT usage and support in a VE environment. The main objective of this chapter is to provide a comprehensive in depth analysis of risks and issues associated with the IT aspects of Virtual Enterprise Networks (VENs) from technical and procedural point of view and to prescribe specific guidelines to mitigate the effects of the identified and analyzed risks, processes and consequences; In that context, this chapter also aims to promote and suggest an IT risk governance framework that will address the IT risks related to Virtual Enterprises following the recent trend of organic risk management.

INTRODUCTION

Historically, IT risk management practice has presented asthmatic behavior when it comes to keeping the pace with enterprise strategy and objectives. The first reason for that behavior is that too many executives tend to relegate IT risk to technical specialists outside the boardroom failing to recognize their importance and thus the need to be managed in a same fashion as traditional high profile risks that are incorporated into the strategic decision making process. The second reason is related to IT focus which has been on protecting the infrastructure and systems processing and storing the vast majority of information rather than in the information itself, its movement and flow. However, both approaches proved as too narrow to accomplish the level of integration, process assurance and overall protection that is now required especially for wide spread integrated platforms like virtual enterprises.

DOI: 10.4018/978-1-61520-607-0.ch006

Nowadays, this is changing. The recent control and audit laws and regulations are holding the enterprise executives as directly liable for any loss or legal implications result from IT risks and malfunctioning since IT is becoming a core element in enterprise performance directly affecting enterprise objectives and strategy. In addition, IT focus is currently shifted to the information itself, where IT and networking must achieve the seemingly impossible, to simultaneously open and protect enterprise information effectively balancing risks with opportunities, while responding to the requirements of emerging business models like VEs. All IT relevant activities should be completed in a full equilibrium to protect the enterprises most critical asset; information and reputation in a seamless business integration and continuous operation.

Managing IT risks is still a work in process, and in that context various attempts to develop risk management methodologies do exist in the literature (Walewiski & Gibson, 2003). Still, there are many potential risk avenues to explore and actions to be taken, especially where the existing approaches and frameworks are not up to the task. Efforts must be well organized across various stake holders including enterprise workers and executives, academia and regulatory bodies, as any individual and isolated approach will simply perpetuate the lack of consistency and increase the possibility that significant gaps will continue to exist if not grow. On the contrary, joint efforts illustrate coordinated efforts to bridge the gap between risk exposure and risk management practice, toward the age of organic risk management which aims to support risk management programs to manage the full range of IT risks as a compulsory part of the enterprise overall corporate governance, risk and compliance structure. IT risk governance is a framework that forms a strong basis to promote and support the organic risk concept, and also paves the road towards the new era of managing IT risks by integrating several existing risk and IT control frameworks.

The main objective of this chapter is to analyze and list the IT risks associated with virtual enterprise networks including technical and procedural risks, and then to provide guidelines for risk mitigation in the VE context. More importantly, this chapter aims to propose an IT risk governance framework that will address the IT risks related to Virtual Enterprises following the recent trend of organic risk management.

BACKGROUND

IT risk governance represents a fundamentally new way to conceptualize and manage IT risks especially when applied to virtual enterprise networks. Four major dimensions can be identified in literature, these being Information Technology, governance, risk management and virtual enterprises all evolving with plenty of research dedicated to each topic individually or bi-combined with another (Aven, 2008; De Haes & Grembergen, 2009; Goranson, 1999). Still, research correlating the four topics jointly is at its infancy.

Virtualization and IT transformations have reshaped significantly the business domains (Menken & Blokdijk, 2008). The information technology is increasingly recognized as a key enterprise asset, justifying what was stated by Peter Drucker (1999) that the diffusion of technology and the co-modification of information will transform the role of information into a resource equal in importance to land, labor and capital. This is obvious today with many enterprises establishing IT in the core of their operations or even going completely digital (Turban, 2008). Virtual enterprises constitute a live example of a digital domain where business is truly enabled by IT. That is why board members are being directly accountable for IT and requiring strong IT governance in analogy to their responsibility for enterprise objectives and key assets (Hardy, 2006). Such changes elevate the IT role in the enterprise development and shift the focus from managing IT resources -devices, applications and datasets- to service orchestration and workflows that define the business and ultimately deliver value to end users.

Virtual enterprises are an emerging platform where several challenges and opportunities exist. The term, and the concept, of the VE emerged in the beginning of nineties and could be seen as a further optimization of the basic ideas about dynamic networking. (Putnik & Cunha, 2005). VEs are connecting or interconnecting various stakeholders and business partners utilizing independent information systems and networks. In this chapter, it is argued that IT virtualization and VENs have the potential to become one of the most prominent business and IT paradigms of this century.

The governance concept has developed over the past few years, in a direct response to the financial crises and recent high-profile organizational failures coupled with significant disruption threats to information flow from hackers, worms and terrorists. In an earlier effort, during the past two decades, several legislatures and statutory authorities have created a complex array of new laws and regulations designed to force improvement in the organizational behavior, information security, controls and transparency (Brotby, 2006). Governance can be defined as the responsibility of senior executive management to maintain organizational transparency and objectives while establishing the enterprise processes, policies and the associated follow up mechanisms (Türke, 2008). A proper governance strategy combines controls to monitor and record business activities. It also measures compliance, and provides corrective actions where rules have been ignored or misconstrued (Brotby, 2006).

Risk Management is the process which enables the enterprise to set the risk tolerance, identify potential risks and prioritize them based on the enterprise's business objectives in association with internal controls (Crouhy, Galai & Mark, 2006; AAIRM, 2002). A broader and more inclusive

risk process means that opportunities and risks will be sought proactively (Hillson, 2008). Various risk definitions exist in text books, although some traditional risk definitions were inefficient and conceptually constricting. Plenty of books and articles have defined and discussed risks, the enterprise risk management and the risks associated with the VE paradigm (Brotby, 2006; Davis, Schiller, & Wheeler, 2006; Schlarman, 2009).

Virtualization spread and the IT role upgrade in modern business operations is accompanied by a shift in IT concepts and techniques. For example, in the past, the key network challenge was to keep the organization protected from the 'big bad world', through a clearly defined external perimeter, then focusing on IT systems and infrastructure inside the enterprise (Newman, 2004). Nowadays, the network physical perimeter has dissolved and the IT focus is spotted on information itself. Another issue posed by VENs is their breadth, both in terms of stakeholders involvement and technology where a single network structure that covers all kinds of communication devices, protocols, and techniques, does simply not exist (Camarinha-Matos, 2004; Menken & Blokdijk, 2008). Similarly it is widely accepted that it will be impossible to build complicated distributed systems that completely prevent unauthorized intrusions (Combs, 1999). Additionally, the introduction of virtualization concepts, e-business and associated processes have propagated additional research in IT, virtualization and infrastructure issues with a strong focus on security and integration. Currently there is a significant need to respond to wide spread technologies (Turban, Leidner, McLean & Wetherbe, 2008).

In summary, it can be argued that recent progress in supply chain networks, distributed systems, and audit environments has promoted research on enterprise risk management and risk governance the latter being a moderately new, but important and influential (Abram, 2009; Hardy, 2006) scientific area. Also, it is important to recognize that IT risk and governance issues related to VEs can't be addressed as a single technology or as a suite of applications in isolation from the business environment. Actually IT governance, risk and business regulations are continuously evolving towards the organic risk governance era (Schlarman, 2009).

IT CHALLENGES FOR VIRTUAL ENTERPRISE NETWORKS

Virtual enterprises constitute a moderately new architecture that is continuously adding new concepts, techniques and core competencies to the partnership and supports distributed operations phenomena. In a typical Virtual Enterprise example, research may be handled by a certain group at the headquarters, assembly can be done thousands of kilometers away, while production is outsourced to multiple partners in different countries while material or other parts are purchased from various geographically dispersed suppliers. This business model is leading to a massive increase in stakeholders who need to share processes, activities and enabling functions in a seamless but well controlled manner to facilitate integration, speed up the activities and avoid blockage. It is obvious that in such a business formation "stakeholders" have varying views on what is good or bad. In that context, different perspectives on the network's prosperity should be examined and the risks that they impose should be identified (Busby & Zhang, 2008).

In what concerns IT, networked enterprises need to advance and integrate backbone technologies to provide better services for VE stakeholders. This can be achieved by typically utilizing existing heterogeneous IT systems and networking platforms which combine traditional and advanced technologies that need to be shared virtually and made available to legal members. The key networking challenge encountered by VEs is to control risk concerns while fulfilling business requirements, thus having an inter-linked

network capable of managing enterprise security, organizational risks and associated impacts.

Being at the business core, information and networking technologies should be aligned with business strategy and goals to avoid strategy scattering. There are several causes for that, such as low-probability / high consequence information threats that occur due to insufficient descriptive and prescriptive aspects of decision making and stakeholders involvement and business partner complacency, where fully compatible services can restrict resources, while other services may create an environment contrary to the enterprise' benefits. Utilizing competitive technology advantages and embracing required changes will increasingly enable VENs to supply a broadening range of services, navigation capabilities and interactive information retrievals.

A TAXONOMY OF IT RELATED RISKS IN VENS

Risk analysis is a major component of any effective enterprise strategic plan and enterprise executives are the key stakeholders for risk appraisal as they determine the business directions, objectives and targets. Executives are consequently accountable for managing IT associated risks including network ones which -in contrary to what people might think - are not purely a technical issue. Risk appraisal for VENs is an evolving topic that is very crucial to setup and maintain a successful VEN, capable of supporting business and withstanding the rapid conceptual and technological developments. As of today, people have a limited understanding of VENs potential IT related risks in spite of their exponential spread into the marketplace.

In the text that follows, a VEN IT related risk taxonomy is proposed, aiming to serve as the basis for the IT risk governance framework that will be suggested later in the chapter.

Figure 1. A VEN IT related risk taxonomy

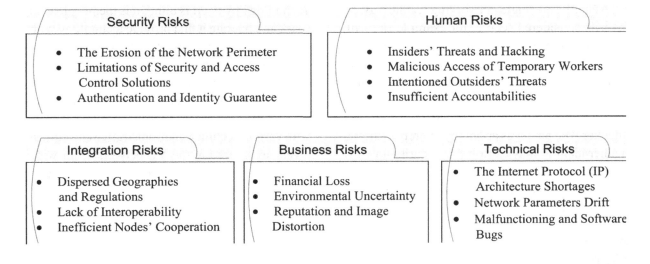

Security Risks

Security has been a major need for human beings since the beginning of existence and while its mechanisms and risks are being shifted following every breakthrough in humanity development, the current era of wide connectivity and great mobilization is unique in its security effects. Virtual enterprises are widely affected by these developments. The most prominent security related IT risks for VENs are described in brief in the following text.

The Erosion of the Network Perimeter

This phenomenon causes elimination of the trusted physical boundaries in order to enable around the clock information access and remote services for mobile users, partners and out-of-site staff. This erosion is caused by the need of the a) extended enterprise network to enable seamless sharing of information and services, b) mobile coverage to support in motion employees and to grant them with access from anywhere, c) wireless networking for seamless and flexible network access to be available within the offices and facilities and d) the need of IP convergence to produce a single converged enterprise network for data, voice and video. This erosion, although providing numerous advantages, is opening and integrating multiple communication elements, paths and technologies, exposing the network to an inherited risk caused by an increased probability of component, extension or configuration failure. That allows people more access privilege and the ability to log into unauthorized network zones or systems.

Limitations of Security and Access Control Solutions

Some communication protocols including the Internet Protocol (IP) are not secure as-is, thus they need additional security tools and mechanisms. Enterprises have traditionally employed network security solutions like firewalls, intrusion detection systems, and anti-virus software and network access control technologies like IP Security Box to protect their networks. However, such solutions are not sufficient for widely distributed heterogeneous VENs and do not prevent malicious or compromised nodes from accessing the network.

Actually, no single networking technology or layer is considered secure, for example firewall authentication relies on packet filtering and inspection to check the originating and destination addresses associated with a message. Thus, the main deficiency of the firewall technique is that it does not inspect the content of the messages. An attacker who achieves access by misrepresenting his/her identity may exploit this security hole by sending malicious content. As a conclusion, various authentication and authorization techniques should always be present for VENs.

Authentication and Identity Guarantee

In VENs, it is always crucial to know the identity of a communicating party, in order to decide whether to accept or deny the access request. A common authentication task is the verification of the identity of an entity, including the filtering of the claims made by parties in a secure environment. Two major categories of identity authentication protocols exist which are the trusted third party authentication that imposes a risk if the third party is corrupted or compromised and the authentication which utilizes an asymmetric cryptography without a trusted third party certificate. This second type is inefficient, and if a malicious entity intercepts the public keys being exchanged, it can replace them with different public keys and pose as one of the communication parties.

Data exchanged within a virtual enterprise needs to be authenticated, the claimed origins have to be verified and the content has to be validated against what its source claims to have transmitted. Additionally, application authentication is required to verify whether execution of the application on un-trusted servers is correctly performed or not. Still this being a post-execution method it might be an indication coming too late.

HUMAN RISKS

Technology by itself is blind, it is the people who spark and operate it that provide technology with direction, thus any "efforts that fail to consider how humans react to and use technology often do not deliver intended benefits" (Oliver, 2009, p. 5). This is more crucial in the case of virtual enterprises where a large number of stakeholders, with various technical, administrative and ethical levels are operating the VE network from wide spread geographies governed by different laws and regulations.

Insiders' Threats and Hacking

Internal hacking and malicious insiders are increasingly being able to leverage the vulnerabilities on enterprise networks as they attempt to gain unauthorized access to proprietary and regulated information. These attackers are constantly attempting to steal proprietary corporate information for espionage, extortion, identity theft, and other forms of industrial fraud. This is of particular importance in VENs were plenty of partners are interconnected and sometimes might have a conflict of interest.

The threats against business-technology systems have never been higher or armed with more sophisticated tools, than in our times. In recent years, employees, both current and former, have been suspected, indicted, and convicted of all types of crimes; selling of usernames and passwords, planting destructive logic bombs, sabotaging critical servers and applications, stealing credit reports and other personally identifiable financial information. "In addition, many enterprises see regulatory and security liabilities arising from employees using public communications services, especially instant messaging, e-mail, and other Internet-centric services lacking encryption and involving public servers or storage nodes" (Nortel Networks, 2004, p. 1).

Malicious Access of Temporary Workers

The threats and vulnerabilities are increasing as the workforce grows more diverse. Recent surveys are showing emerging trends to capture and sell business secrets to competitors and in that context entering company as a contractor is an easy way to collect such data. Often is the case of contractors who should have limited access for a certain period of time, but somehow manage to extend their access beyond the requested period; additionally many contractors are getting higher privileges than necessary.

In VENs particularly, information resources should be categorized, protected and the access rights should be restricted, otherwise un-trusted users may break down the system purposefully or even trusted users may, without any malicious intention, cause damage to the system by executing improper operations.

Intentioned Outsiders' Threats

Profit hacking has become a business in its own right, forming a good percentage of the network penetration and sniffing to steal proprietary corporate information, supplemented by other reasons like political, intelligence gathering and having fun. Malicious code can be purchased from various underground sources on the internet and then integrated in a completely modular fashion. Software robots called "Bot networks" may be rented out by the day, for the purpose of executing Distributed Denial Of Service (DDoS) attacks or for capturing credit card numbers and stealing identities.

The distributed natures of virtual enterprises with dispersed stakeholders make it easier for outsiders to penetrate the security controls and get an access foot inside. Armed with sophisticated tools, attackers constantly perform sniffing, spoofing, pharming, phishing, stealthiness and hacking among other techniques to compromise a network

and listen to required data. Such techniques can have a wide variety of effects, with varying levels of inconvenience to the user ranging from a subtle effect on the program's functionality to a complete systems crash or freeze in association with bypassing access controls in order to obtain unauthorized privileges, even worse it might cause a permanent damage. Such attacks might have enormous effects in VEs where the attacked point can be far away or even controlled by a distant business partner.

Insufficient Accountabilities

Lack of understanding, ownership and accountability within the enterprise is a major concern, even if strong security and standards are implemented. Executives and business employees' accountability and ownership form a cornerstone to ensure the security of information and systems which constitute the core of enterprise operation. Unfortunately a false assumption exists that the security of information and systems is the responsibility solely of the IT security office.

The accountabilities issue is very critical in VEs where partners or business units might adopt different measures leading to conflicting or even contradicting behaviors. This situation leads to potential risks and security weaknesses, which sometimes continue to exist for years, even if identified as repeating. Without the establishment of solid governance and controls, the large number of stakeholders involved in VEs can result in scattered efforts and in-efficient business involvement to assess the implementation and performance of key IT security processes which lead to the failure in adequate prioritization, funding decisions and remediation of significant weaknesses.

INTEGRATION RISKS

Integration is a key concept in virtual enterprises and most of the times it acts as a business enabler.

Achieving integration is neither straight forward nor risk free especially when activities and goals are diverse, as in the case of VENs. The most significant integration risks are explored and discussed in the text below.

Dispersed Geographies and Regulations

Often, VEs are geographically distributed business formations; meaning that VE will operate and exist in several cities, states or even countries. These geographies might have different, and sometimes, conflicting regulations, infrastructure and cultural background; additionally they typically establish different business processes and jurisdiction rules. With the lack of international harmonization, the current regulatory measures formatted on per-country basis deal with events based on cause-and-effect methodology without real consideration of the technology life cycle and the networking interactivities. Such dispersion in geographies and regulations are complicating VE integration, hindering the development of standardized networking, and might lead to inter-virtual enterprise competitive arbitrage.

Lack of Interoperability

Interoperability is defined as the ability of systems and networks to provide to, or accept services from other systems or networks without trust issues. This ability has a special importance to allow seamless information flow between enterprise members. Networking interoperability requires compatible communication paths, adequate signal clarity and scalable capacity.

Lack of interoperability imposes various risks on virtual enterprise networks operation such as:

a)   the inability to integrate disparate business processes and support multiple technology platforms,

b)   the increased networking cost and reduced systems agility

c)   the longer time to market, especially if network architecture and design is compromised. Additionally if the networks and/or systems are not connected, through an interoperability framework, security issues and threats are increased without sufficient countermeasures.

Inefficient Nodes' Cooperation

Smart and wireless environments represent the trend for future network automations related to sensory infrastructures and used extensively in enterprise virtualization and supply chain structures. In VEN topologies, nodes usually belong to different authorities and pursue different goals, thus nodes should cooperate in transmission and reception using many forms, in order to protect their valuable resources. Unfortunately, nodes tend to be selfish, and even worse, some nodes may be malicious whose objective is to degrade the network performance. Lack of cooperation will avoid the establishment of direct trust relations based on evidence related to the previous interactions of entities within a protocol. Lack of cooperation is seriously hurting and can lead to various risks, including the inefficiency in utilizing the constrained resources of mobile devices, such as power, computation ability and storage capacity. This causes performance degradation after limited life in service. This lack of cooperation can also cause inefficiency in discovering malicious nodes which are attacking the network. Malicious nodes compromise "good" nodes by retrieving their secret keys. Finally, active attacks might modify, delete, or inject data in the network.

BUSINESS RISKS

IT is an enabling factor for business development but on the other hand can impose direct or indirect risks that can harm business and destroy a long lasting heritage. Furthermore, IT is nowadays affecting business more than any other time in the past. In the following text, IT related risks directly affecting business development are described.

Financial Loss

Communication networks are forming the business backbone and therefore any network malfunctioning is affecting various company assets, violating cost controls and imposing legal and reputational implications resulting in direct or indirect asset impacts and financial loss. Networks are among products where higher utilization makes them more valuable. Network malfunctioning leads to subsequent service degradation and lower utilization, thus additional costs are required to safeguard transaction specific assets and re-implement options and resolutions. Network problems can add barriers between different communication systems and slow knowledge diffusion, thus leading to additional training and sometimes un-necessary travel and meeting costs. Furthermore, partner dissatisfaction can increase due to corrupted information and often legal disputes.

Environmental Uncertainty

Environmental uncertainty can be interpreted as the un-anticipated changes in circumstances surrounding the business. When environmental uncertainty is high, adaptability is crucial for business continuity and effectiveness. To enhance adaptability and provide quick remediation, IT and networking should be viewed as the core of business competitive strengths and not a simple supporting function. Additionally, inability to recognize and benefit from new technologies can lead to tightly coupled inter-firm relationships that will increase time and cost due to inefficient induction, communication and coordination.

Reputation and Image Distortion

Being more connected means that more information about your business is broadcasted to public, thus a risk of miss-interpretation and media damage is more likely to occur. Documentation, events and history tracking is more obvious today while effects are present even after a transaction is complete and results are propagated beyond the industrial and geographical boundaries.

Being part of a large virtual enterprise can result in leakage of more news and documentation either intentionally or by accident. Moreover the enterprise reputation will be affected by any service degradation conducted by other partners. Down time and system failures caused by IT can threat the efficiency of enterprise and might lead to lack of trust and discourage.

Technical Risks

Technical risks are the direct risks that typically require a technical expert to be resolved. The effect of technical risks can be system wide and catastrophic.

The Internet Protocol (IP) Architecture Shortages

Most of the internet activities are based on the Internet Protocol (IP) which was created originally to handle traffic on friendly basis utilizing the best-effort reach model. IP uses primitive controls and infrastructure management techniques and thus it is not secure and sufficient by itself. Today the IP infrastructure is complimented by various enhancements to raise its ability to survive but with increased risk factors.

IP networks are controlled by numerous institutions and operated in diverse environments to meet sophisticated network-wide objectives that force the creation of point solutions retro-fitted to the original box-centric architecture and enhanced with additional security tools and mechanisms.

For this reason IP networks have a bewildering complexity, with diverse state and logic distributed across numerous network elements and management systems.

Network Parameters Drift

Virtual enterprise networks hold unique characteristics related to traffic movements between various networks and topologies. This environment is magnifying typical network problems, such as delays related to the processing and propagation over the links or inside routing equipment overload, adding to the latency which is the time consumed by data to travel across the network. This is affecting the overall networking quality of service due to multiple errors and repetitions even on local connections.

Jitter and data-packet loss for example might cause unwanted variations of one or more characteristics of the periodic signal that results in a distortion which might damage the networking signal clarity. Jitter has a severe effect on streaming technologies like voice over IP and video-conferencing while affecting all other network applications.

Malfunctioning and Software Bugs

Technically defined, a malfunction is a partial or total failure of a device or application to operate as intended that might require an immediate action to stop damage while recovery is established. A software bug is an error, flaw, mistake, failure, or fault in a computer program that prevents it from behaving as intended. Bugs and malfunctioning has a special importance in VENs due to the unique VEN nature and characteristics.

The large volume of VENs stakeholders and users invite more bugs to arise from mistakes and errors made by people in using the program capabilities. Some bugs might also be produced in the source code or programs' design due to incomplete or contradicting requirements sub-mitted to the programmers. The ever changing environment of VENs requires continuous traffic prioritization and shaping because "all data units are created equal" in the conventional networks but quality features are utilized to promote data handling so that more important connections receive priority over less important ones. Such quality rules are updated continuously based on the changing business rules. The heterogeneous VENs environment, with simultaneous availability of the traditional and advanced technologies is a cause of malfunctioning, like the existence of wireless and regular Local Area Networks (LAN) where the traditional LAN has a quite effective physical security while wireless LAN must be treated as a network with much lower trust levels.

Following the description of the most apparent and important VENs risks in the above text, it is crucial touching some other elements that are playing significant role to mature the VENs risk analysis and governance structuring. Next few topics are exploring some risk vulnerabilities, VENs characteristics and related compliance standards to show correlations and enhance the understanding of VENs risk and governance.

RISK ARGUMENTS AND VULNERABILITIES

In the context of virtual enterprises, the classic case of game theory "the economic incentive of any decision maker to invest in protective actions thus depends on whether it expects others to follow suit" (Kunreuther, 2006, p. 19) applies, thus a risk faced by an enterprise depends not only on one's own choices but also on those of others. Any portion of the network is reliable as much as other parts are reliable, problems can propagate easily from one direction to another, and more interesting is that the motivation of any owner to invest in protection depends on how he expects others to behave. The weakest link risks are exaggerated where a network or portions of it opening for other partners are taking place without a full two way integration review and measures. This is also the case when insufficient research on both the descriptive and prescriptive aspects of decision making for low-probability, high consequence events is conducted.

One very critical aspect of IT security in a VE environment is that of employees who in the process of getting their work done, they perform all sorts of unwitting policy violations, such as mailing a confidential document to their webmail account so they can work at home, or printing out a screen-full of customer records to write notes on during lunch, or copying some product plans to a USB key to give to a teammate. In each case, there is potential for data loss and risk of penalty. Such behaviors create a risk of extending the network and data resources in an uncontrolled manner and put valuable enterprise information at risk. Risk severity will be even worse when the enterprise is virtualized and various users have different profiles.

Considering the fact that interconnectivity measures are typically probabilistic, dynamically expanding virtual enterprises must establish a solid change management foundation that can handle any network and systems modifications seamlessly without interruption for new enterprise elements that are coming across the board due to frequent technology and processes changes. In the contrary the lack of efficient change management processes might lead to increased downtime and degraded quality of networking and data transfer where changes are not properly tested and shaped to accommodate enterprise elements. Additionally lack of sufficient tracking of changes will make it difficult to roll back to a previous status if required and make it easier for vulnerability attacks to alter certain parameters without much questioning. In opposition, slow manual methods for adding or changing access privileges for users, additional service or resource that becomes available through the virtual enterprise will lead to duplicate or inconsistent information. Where changes to information in one source of data are not automatically propagated, data consistency, accuracy, and reliability cannot be assured.

VENS CHARACTERISTICS AND TRENDS

One important bearing for VE platforms is the multiple input and output channels, through which network entities are connected and interconnected. These channels are inviting synergy in virtual enterprises and provide a number of interlinks between the VE and the external world. The use of multiple channels presents some major risks to the enterprise network, such as:

- The opening of communication channels to enable intra-network communication regardless to infrastructure, technology or protocol variations.
- Enabling data flow and transaction volumes movement through the various channels seamlessly without delays, based on the network access policies and strategies.
- Providing availability and utilization of backup links to avoid loopholes, back door tracking and security breaches.

In such an interconnected platform, physical security does not prevent network layer attacks. For example securing the wireless device alone does not provide protection from those who would attack the communication infrastructure. Also to manage such environment effectively, enterprise systems management should extend beyond the traditional approaches to manage and handle features to support supply-chain management, customer relationship management, tracking functionalities and electronic commerce. Deficiencies in managing the traditional as well as the new technology channels and functions might deteriorate a cornerstone of a successful business.

Another trend that is highly associated with VEs is the usage of Open System Environments (OSE) and Service Oriented Architecture (SOA). These two concepts are increasingly utilized to bridge the gap and facilitate communication channels between virtual enterprise elements which are typically acquired from various vendors. OSE and SOA are means to provide unique and affordable techniques to allow different applications to exchange data with one another and loose the coupling of services with operating systems, programming languages and various technologies.

These technologies although deemed crucial for VEs are not risk free. The application of these paradigms in real-time systems affects the response time and human interface support. Additionally interoperability and trust issues between enterprise elements result typically from millions of messages that are generated by various interfacing services and open systems while interacting together.

HANDS ON RISK MITIGATION

This section is proposing a set of mechanisms to handle the particular security risks for VENs in a high level. Thus, it does not deal with the details for mitigating every risk category or group discussed earlier.

ENHANCING VENS RISK MANAGEMENT

In order to enhance the IT risk management in a VE environment, various mechanisms are required to build risk handling capabilities into core network fabric. These mechanisms should be enhanced with risk-mitigation strategy application and cascaded risk propagation avoidance mechanisms. Strategies need to be promoted where risks depend not only on the agent's own choices

but also on those of others. Correlation of data and processes related to virtual networks will be required also to identify combined threats, relation and power factors. The topics listed below constitute important factors supporting IT risk management in the VE environment.

Traffic Management

The goal of traffic management in VENs is to guarantee accessibility and performance according to a predefined service level helping network traffic to be protected by security measures. Traffic management combines various elements to achieve this goal starting with traffic filtering which allows passing traffic that is specifically permitted to flow through the network and traffic control which is used to pass traffic in such a way that guarantees availability and integrity. For example, it will ensure VoIP traffic gets the guaranteed Quality of Service requirements for good performance, while Instant Messaging traffic will be limited or blocked totally based on network status. Policy-based routing allows network access to resources, based on predefined policy rules and the user identity to ensure that the right security policy is enforced where high level of virtualization exist and security zones to physical devices is no longer sufficient.

Threat Controls

Controls are used to monitor network activities, detect attacks and patterns of attack and use autoremediation actions. All available data should be combined to make an intelligent analysis of network activities and detect threats at an early stage. Threat control combines intrusion detection used to detect and remedy of malicious network access, anomaly detection which utilizes a baseline of normal network behavior to recognize anomalous activities and suggest a resolution and event correlation which utilizes a system that collects, analyzes and correlates security event data from all over the network to mitigate distributed threats.

Security Management

Security management consists of a central management console that provides a control platform for all network devices, identity and policy repositories that are used as a central storage of the implemented users and policies. These repositories are updated and automated through a provisioning system and the analysis and comparison of various counter-measures are used to benchmark the VENs organizational, technological, managerial and procedural elements.

Endpoint Security

Endpoint security combines the identity-based access, where access is granted only after identity is proven, the endpoint integrity to check access device posture and verify its connection before access is granted, and the quarantine and remediation capabilities so that insecure devices are quarantined and given access to remediation tools or otherwise limited to strict pre-confined areas of the corporate network.

NETWORK AND INFORMATION METRICS

Measuring the network performance is playing a major role to define its performance and future situation. Among the most important metrics are:

- Confidentiality, where data or application code should be unintelligible to any non-entitled entity,
- Integrity, which aims to make the network and data free from unauthorized modification and damage

- Availability, which ensures that network and systems are available to stakeholders per the agreed terms in-spite of attacks or damages,
- Scalability, which confirms the ability to handle variable volume in client requests and network communication traffic.

IT AND RISK REGULATORY FRAMEWORKS

In response to growing involvement, various business aspects including IT and risk management have undergone many changes over the last two decades.

There exists a range of standards and regulations covering the risk and IT spectrum, with huge variance in requirements, target groups, objectives and outcomes. In this section the most important standards are described to broaden the readers' vision and also to prepare them for the next section. The Committee Of Sponsoring Organizations of the tread way commission (COSO) introduced the Enterprise Risk Management (ERM) Framework, known as COSO-ERM "as a response to many major corporations in the mid-70's that issued glowing financial reports followed by major losses or bankruptcy" (Moeller, 2008, p. 4). COSO ERM is addressing mainly legislation, quality control and security issues that need to be embedded in processes and products to create economic benefits (Davis, Schiller & Wheeler, 2006; Moeller, 2008).

The Risk Management Standard (AAIRM, 2002) published by the Institute Of Risk Management (IRM) in association with two other institutes aimed to describe the operation and functionality of risk management while maintaining a full cycle covering the organization's strategic objectives and monitoring the risk management model. The UK Office Of Government Commerce (OGC) has issued a model entitled "Management Of Risk:

guidance for practitioners (MoR)" which provides a generic framework for the management of risk across all parts of an organization. It incorporates all the activities required to identify and control the exposure to any type of risk, positive or negative, which may have an impact on the achievement of the organization's business objectives (OGC, 2002). The International Standards Organization is working on the development of a standard, named ISO 31000:2009, Risk Management— Guidelines on Principles and Implementation of Risk Management, which is being reviewed for publication (ISO, 2009). The importance of the proposed standard is that it provides a common language and model to be used by organizations to implement a risk management model that would be consistent, replicable and accurate.

Control Objectives for Information and related Technology (COBIT) framework that is managed by the IT Governance Institute (ITG) provides good practices across a domain structure and bridges the gaps among business risks, control needs and technical matters. COBIT framework acknowledges process owners' discharge of accountability and responsibility in the business continuum (Booker, Gardner, Steelhammer, & Zumbakyte, 2004; Davis, Schiller & Wheeler, 2006; Moeller, 2008). Information Technology Infrastructure Library (ITIL) is intended to describe approaches, functions, roles and processes, upon which organizations may base their own IT practices, it underpins but not dictates the business processes of an organization, thus an organization can't be marked as 'ITIL-compliant'. The role of ITIL is to give guidance at the lowest generally applicable level. Below that level, specific knowledge of the enterprise' business processes is required to tune with ITIL for optimum effectiveness (Davis, Schiller & Wheeler, 2006; Steinberg, 2005).

Several other standards exist in the IT and Risk Management domains that serve specific purposes and/or specific industries (Boyer, 2004; Cannon, Bergmann, & Pamplin, 2006; Humphreys,

2007). The plethora and diversity of approaches proves that a set of commonly accepted and well defined regulations and structures that support IT and Risk Management issues, in conjunction, simply does not exist. On the contrary, differences in regulations may complicate coordination and limit a harmonized approach towards IT risk management. Still, it is crucial to understand that in the current scope adhering to certain standards is compulsory to avoid falling behind the compliance rules and controls that is mandated by governments and regulatory bodies. The focus of IT risk governance is to associate best practices, coherent policies and regulatory frameworks to foster a self-regulated mechanism as an inherited technique for faster implementation and well justified business outcomes.

A PROPOSED RISK GOVERNACE FRAMEWORK FOR VENS

VEs are an emerging new platform with several challenges and opportunities. Risk governance is crucial to shape and facilitate the VE development as opportunities and risks will be sought more proactively (Hillson, 2008). This section is a step forward to setup a governance framework capable of handling and responding to risks that contemporary virtual enterprise networks are facing. The framework should manage the actual or potential risks posed to VENs, as well the stakeholders' perception of those risks. Its services should reflect a deep understanding of faced dilemmas and enable policy makers envision the future and plan correctly. The process to develop a risk governance framework for VENs is not easy, due to the facts that reliable technical and risk data is not yet mature and only few studies have been conducted to assess the full range of concerns. The suggested framework components are shown in Figure 2 and are detailed ahead in the remainder of this section.

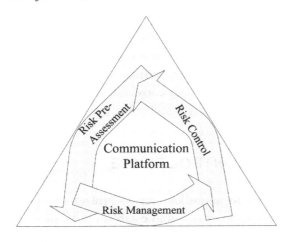

Figure 2. The proposed risk governance framework for VENs

RISK PRE-ASSESSMENT PHASE

This phase aims to collect and outline the special characteristics of the VENs and the potential risks they are facing and to identify concerns raised by major stakeholders. Areas of concern that might affect risk assessment include the need to discover, develop and implement best practices and regulatory policies. This step will be complemented by data collection in order to properly identify relevant information and enable risks analysis and reporting.

Exposure analyses need to be conducted to review evidences and standards related to VENs simulations and monitoring of actual status. Risk profile maintenance will establish necessary elements to build a complete and accurate overview of the actual risks incurred, associated with risk scenarios development and methods to describe risk factors and techniques. Conflicts documentation will identify potential conflicts and precautions in the development, regulation, and practice necessary to achieve an optimal balance between business progress and transparent risk management.

THE RISK MANAGEMENT PHASE

VENs are an emerging domain, where circumstances and technology are changing frequently making it very hard for researchers to follow the pace and conduct sufficient risk appraisals. Additionally, considering the dynamic nature of VENs development and the many different stakeholders involved in it, there is no single approach that can address all issues. Risks and concerns will vary among category groups and over time, and knowledge will continually expand. This situation makes risk management paramount in the efforts to address risk perceptions and stakeholders' concerns. Three main risk management phases are suggested due to the wide scope of risk management activities and involvements.

Risk Characterization

This phase aims to identify risk evidences and evaluate them by utilizing risk levels of tolerability and acceptability within predefined norms. Risks can be categorized in terms of available information, the cause and effect relationship understanding and of how controversial and ethically challenging the risk is perceived by stakeholders. Applying this approach will help creating a risk image based on stakeholders' views and needs; also it will categorize the risk into four initial groups as simple, complex, uncertain or ambiguous. The image and risk distinction are vital to ensure appropriate regulatory input and determine risk management strategies.

It is also fundamental to know that VENs are multidisciplinary, cross-sectored and involve numerous stakeholders, thus VENs risks' characterization may change over time as new knowledge emerges. Therefore it may be easier to focus on the dominant characteristics when deciding how to proceed. This approach will enable risk management teams to revise their decisions as new knowledge emerges, and perform necessary changes without much hassle and delay.

Response Categorization

Four risk response schemes are generally adopted and recognized namely risk avoidance, mitigation, transfer and acceptance (PMI, 2008). A risk is fitted into the appropriate response scheme based on the collective judgments of the responsible stakeholders propagated usually by matching the probability of an adverse event against the extent of its consequences. Risk reduction or mitigation are the actions most frequently used and require effort consuming activities to reduce the frequency or impact of a risk, or both, often by introducing a number of control measures.

Risk transfer aims to reduce the risk frequency or impact by transferring or otherwise sharing a portion of the risk with other external entities using common techniques such as insurance and outsourcing. Risk acceptance means that no action is taken relative to a particular risk and the loss or effect is accepted if it occurs. Risk acceptance is a mechanism to handle known risks and is different from just ignoring an unknown risk. Risk avoidance means avoiding the activities that give rise to risk. It is applied when no other risk response is adequate, the risk cannot be shared, and the risk is deemed un-acceptable by major stakeholders.

Response Planning

Response planning is defined as the process of developing options to respond to risk in a way that can minimize threats and maximize the identified opportunities that risk often creates. The response should be in-line with the significance of the risk, cost-effective, and realistic. Normally, a collaborative discussion needs to occur with consistent participation from all involved stakeholders and VENs research and development experts, in order for the response decision to take place.

Selecting the appropriate risk response is one of the most difficult tasks in risk governance especially in the context of insufficient evidences which is often the situation for VEs. Typically a combination of technical data, multi-stakeholder inputs and executives' support is utilized to choose a response. Risk response for VENs must be adaptable to new knowledge availability and circumstances change and must have the flexibility to perform necessary corrections and deal with a wide variety of risk scenarios.

RISK CONTROL PHASE

This is an important step to protect any given business process and to establish principles and guidelines for data modeling, risk integration, identification and measurement. "Risk control and monitoring is an iterative and continuous process to ensure that current risks are being mitigated, new risks are being identified and prioritized and risk databases are being structured and stored" (Kwak, 2003). Risk controls are necessary for a VEN risk governance framework, which helps to establish and maintain a common risk view and management methods, align policy with standard statements combining IT risk tolerance, promote risk awareness culture to make risk-aware business decisions and embed IT risk considerations in strategic business decision making.

These controls will contribute heavily to perform an enterprise-wide IT risk assessment and determine the broad amount of risk that is acceptable to the enterprise in pursuit of its objectives. This is achieved through defining risk tolerance thresholds, establishing a mechanism to prioritize IT risk response activities, tracking key IT risk decisions and establishing an enterprise-wide accountability for managing VENs' risks while coordinating IT and business risk strategy.

THE COMMUNICATION PLATFORM

Communication is an essential part of every governance framework act to elevate risk perception and stakeholder involvement. Effective communication must be located at the core of successful risk governance with an ultimate goal to assist stakeholders to understand the rationale of risk assessment and risk-related decisions thus helping them arrive at a balanced judgment. Stakeholders receiving risk information can be divided into two categories, those who are central to risk framing, appraisal or management and thus should be able to understand the meaning of the communicated messages (how they are to be involved, where appropriate, and what their responsibilities are), while the other group is combined of stakeholders outside the immediate risk appraisal process with a need to be informed and engaged in the process.

Effective communication practices are required throughout the whole risk handling chain to support informed decision making and broadcast issues and concerns to create mutual trust. A communication plan covers responsibilities, accountabilities, policies and procedures in one hand and the risk landscape including threats, controls, impacts, root causes and business decisions on the other with established filters for a clear, concise, communication that is directed to the right audiences.

Planning risk communication for VEs is a unique, high profile art that requires great attention to details and clear understanding of stakeholders' roles and enterprise hierarchy, relations and goals. Yet the benefits of open communication in VE platforms are very obvious, combining the spread of risk awareness and establishing risk acknowledgement as an integral part of the business. This will help stakeholders to respond to the adverse risks in full transparency knowing when, why and how to do it. In addition, stakeholders will be able to consistently prioritize IT and networking risk issues in a manner aligned with enterprise definitions and business strategies. Executive management will then steer the right resources to confront risk issues.

Poor risk communication has various consequences since it encourages the 'blame culture' in which business units tend to point the finger at IT and technical teams when targets are not achieved or outputs do not meet expectations. In VE platforms the risks under-reporting may spread a false sense of confidence at the top management on the degree of actual risk exposure. Such a status will reduce the trust level among business units or partners and result in a vague direction for risk management from the top down sometimes forming a perception that the enterprise is trying to cover up known risks from stakeholders. On the other hand, over communication may result in exposing risk related information to the external world which may deter potential clients or investors and generate unnecessary scrutiny from regulators.

FUTURE RESEARCH DIRECTIONS

Risk accompanies change, it is an inherited component of life and the willingness to take and accept risk is crucial for development and progress. The challenge of better risk governance is to enable stakeholders to benefit from change while minimizing the negative consequences of the associated risks. Risks are not confined to national borders; neither they are limited to a certain economy sector or technology platform. Thus they cannot be managed through the actions of a single sector or government. IT risk governance requires a global, systemic and integrated approach involving governments, non-governmental organizations, industry, academia and civil society. This opens a wide research terrain and some of the revealed research opportunities are discussed in the remainder of this section.

IT risk management in VENs is a scientific area still at its infancy, thus presented with large margins of research both in theories/concepts and in their application to real life case studies.

VE modeling is very important as well since the currently existing efforts are extensions of traditional enterprises and therefore the elaborated models could maximize the value of the VEs and networks by enhancing scalability, reducing costs, and simplifying network management through efficient, high-performance networking solutions.

VE IT and networks' optimization and acceleration techniques are required to organize various components in the VE platform including: virtualized routers, servers, data centers, and storage with minimized risks association and increased harmony. Plenty of recent VE platforms require enhanced levels of traffic performance management, which is critical for organizations to monitor and capture data and draw a baseline for the network management's challenges of virtualization, automation and security. Multi-Protocol Label Switching (MPLS) is an advanced way of managing heterogeneous or collected internet traffic by letting carriers merge different types of data traffic over one IP backbone, improving their ability to offer different classes of service. The integration of MPLS into VEN communications should be studied to discover the associated risks and enhance governance.

CONCLUSION

Supporting the introduction and justifying the acceptance of new research platforms is always difficult, both from the technical and the management perspective. Realizing the benefits of such platforms requires a willingness to accept some risk as a trade for progress. Although IT is, undoubtedly, the dynamic heart of VEs, practice has shown that network and technology risks are often not well understood by the enterprise's key stakeholders, including board members and executive management. Without a clear understanding of IT and associated issues, senior executives have no

point of reference for prioritizing and managing enterprise risks. This is a major drawback, since these are the people who should identify, monitor, control and govern major types of risk within the enterprise. Still, IT Risk Governance is being increasingly accepted as part of the future trend of organic enterprise risk and governance age. Governance is influenced by, and has an impact on, a wide variety of perspectives that contribute to the overall development, perception and acceptance of VEs. The scope of developing an IT risk governance framework for VEs is broad and will mature over the course of many years following several iterations

Virtual enterprises are continuously growing and are playing a major role in shifting the focus to information networks towards protecting the information itself, its movements and flow as a critical enterprise asset. Virtual enterprises are based on an IT structure forming a wide, multi-protocol and multi-technology environment with which various players and vendors daily interact. In this environment many risks result from integration and adaptation. This infrastructure has to achieve the seemingly impossible; to open and protect enterprise information effectively and balance risks with opportunities. The various risk types include security, humanity, integration, business and technical risks with every type consisting of various subcategories forming a large pool of risk elements and concern issues.

In this challenging environment, a strategy is needed to facilitate quality risk management decisions, support fact-based communication to lay the foundation for full risk assessment and disseminate a standardized methodology related to VEs and associated with the promotion of risk-related concepts. The development of an effective and acceptable IT risk governance framework for VEs is a challenge that requires the participation of a very wide range of stakeholders. This effort, in order to be successful, should be benefited from existing efforts to create common frameworks of understanding and practice. This chapter attempts to present such an effort and aspires to ignite fruitful discussion that will eventually lead to an increased number of research studies in the field of IT related Risk Management for Virtual Enterprise Networks.

REFERENCES

AAIRM. (2002). A risk management standard. London: The Institute of Risk Management.

Abram, T. (2009). The hidden values of it risk management. *Information Systems Audit and Control Association (ISACA) Journal*, (2), 40-45.

Aven, T. (2008). Risk analysis: Assessing uncertainties beyond expected values and probabilities. West Sussex, UK: John Wiely and Sons, Ltd.

Booker, S., Gardner, J., Steelhammer, L., & Zumbakyte, L. (2004). What is your risk appetite? The risk-it model. *Information Systems Audit and Control Association (ISACA) Journal*, *35*(2), 38–43.

Boyer, S. (2004). SCADA: supervisory control and data acquisition. Research Triangle Park, NC: Instrument Society of America.

Brotby, W. (2006). Information security governance: Guidance for boards of directors and executive management. Rolling Meadows, IL: IT Governance Institute.

Busby, J., & Zhang, H. (2008). How the subjectivity of risk analysis impacts project success. *Project Management Journal*, *39*(3), 86–96. doi:10.1002/pmj.20070

Cannon, D., Bergmann, T., & Pamplin, B. (2006). CISA certified information systems auditor study guide. New York: Wiley Publishing, Inc.

Combs, B. (1999). *The pseudo-internal intruder: A New access oriented intruder category*. Unpublished doctoral dissertation, University of Virginia, Virginia, USA.

Crouhy, M. Galai, D., & Mark, R. (2006). *The essentials of risk management*. New York: McGraw-Hill Inc.

Davis, C., Schiller, M., & Wheeler, K. (2006). IT auditing: Using controls to protect information assets. Emeryville, CA: McGraw-Hill Osborne Media.

De Haes, S., & Grembergen, W. (2009). Enterprise governance of information technology: Achieving strategic alignment and value. New York: Springer.

Drucker, P. (1999). Management challenges for the 21st century. New York: HarperCollins Publishers Inc.

Goranson, H. (1999). The agile virtual enterprise: Cases, metrics, tools. New York: Quorum Books.

Hardy, G. (2006). New roles for board members on IT. *Governance Journal*, *13*(151), 11–14.

Hillson, D. (2008). Why risk includes opportunity. *The Risk Register Journal of PMI's Risk Management Special Interest Group*, *10*(4), 1–3.

Humphreys, E. (2007). Implementing the ISO/IEC 27001 information security management system standard. Norwood, MA: Artech House Publishers.

ISO. (2009). ISO/FDIS 31000 Risk management - Principles and guidelines. *International Standards Organization (ISO) Technical Managemnt Board*. Retrieved May 30, 2009, from http://www.iso.org/iso/iso_catalogue/catalogue_tc/catalogue_detail.htm?csnumber=43170

Kunreuther, H. (2006). Risk and reaction: Dealing with interdependencies. *Harvard International Review: Global Catastrophe*, *28*(3), 17–23.

Kunreuther, H. (2008). *The weakest link: Risk management strategies for dealing with interdependencies* (Working Paper # 2008-10-13). Philadelphia, PA: University of Pennsylvania, the Wharton School.

Kwak, Y. (2003, September). *Perception and practice of project risk management.* Paper presented in the Project Management Institute Global Congress North America, Baltimore, MD.

Menken, I., & Blokdijk, G. (2008). Virtualization: The complete cornerstone guide to virtualization best practices. Brisbane, Australia: Emereo Pty Ltd.

Moeller, R. (2008, April). *Enterprise risk management and the project manager.* Paper presented at Project Summit & Business Analyst World, Philadelphia, PA.

Newman, M. (2004). Firewalls: keeping the big, bad world out of your firm. *San Fernando Valley Business Journal, 9*(18), 21–22.

Nortel Networks. (2004). Enabling real-time communications effectiveness for today's virtual enterprise. Research Triangle Park, NC: Nortel Networks.

Office of Government Commerce (OGC). (2002). *Management of risk: Guidance for practitioners.* London: Office of Government Commerce, Stationary office.

Oliver, D. (2009). *An introduction to the business model for information security.* Rolling Meadows, IL: Information Systems Audit and Control Association, (ISACA).

PMI. (2008). *A Guide to project management body of knowledge.* Newtown square. PA: Project Management Institute.

Putnik, G. (Ed.), & Cunha, M. (Ed.). (2005). *Virtual enterprise integration: technological and organizational perspectives.* Hershy, PA: Idea Group Publishing.

Ramirez, D. (2008). IT risk management standards: The bigger picture. *Information Systems Audit and Control Association (ISACA) Journal, 2008*(4), 35-39.

Schlarman, S. (2009). IT risk exploration: The IT risk management taxonomy and evolution. *Information Systems Audit and Control Association (ISACA) Journal, 2009*(3), 27-30.

Steinberg, R. (2005). Implementing ITIL: Adapting your it organization to the coming revolution in it service management. Victoria, BC: Trafford Publishing.

Turban, E., Leidner, D., McLean, E., & Wetherbe, J. (2008). Information technology for management: Transforming organizations in the digital economy. Hoboken, NJ: John Wiley and Sons Inc.

Türke, R. (2008). Governance: Systemic foundation and framework. Heidelberg, Germany: Physica-Verlag.

Walewski, J., & Gibson, G. (2003). *International project risk assessment: methods, procedures, and critical factor* (Research. Rep. No. 31). Austin, Texas: The University of Texas at Austin, Construction Industry Studies Centre.

ADDITIONAL READINGS

Biske, T. (2008). SOA governance. Birmingham, UK: Packt Publishing.

Bostrom, A., French, S., & Gottlieb, S. (Eds.). (2008). Risk assessment, modeling and decision support: Strategic directions. Heidelberg, Germany: Springer-Verlag.

Boyce, J., & Jennings, D. (2002). *Information assurance: Managing organizational IT security risks.* Woburn, MA: Butterworth-Heinemann.

Broder, J. (2006). Risk analysis and the security survey. Burlington, MA: Butterworth-Heinemann Elsevier.

Brown, B. (April, 2008). *Critical steps to reduce the risks associated with using external consultants on your projects.* Paper presented at Project Summit & Business Analyst World, Philadelphia, PA.

Camarinha-Matos, L. M. (Ed.). (2004). Virtual enterprises and collaborative networks. Norwell, MA: Kluwer Academic Publisher.

Dallas, G. (Ed.). (2004). *Governance and risk.* New York: McGraw-Hill companies Inc.

Dally, W., & Towles, B. (2004). Principles and practices of interconnection networks. San Francisco: Morgan Kaufmann.

Darby, J., & Kindinger, J. (September, 2000). *Risk factor analysis—A new qualitative risk management tool.* Paper presented at Project Management Institute annual seminar & Symposium, Houston, TX.

Fowler, D. (1999). Virtual private networks. San Francisco: Morgan Kaufmann Publishers Inc.

Grembergen, W. (Ed.). (2003). Strategies for information technology governance. Hershy, PA: Idea Group Publishing.

Hartman, B., Flinn, D. J., & Beznosov, K. (2001). Enterprise security with EJB and CORBA. New York: John Wiley & Sons.

Hassan, M., & Jain, R. (2003). High performance TCP/IP networking. Upper Saddle River, NJ: Prentice Hall.

Hoogervorst, J. (2009). Enterprise governance and enterprise engineering. Diemen, The Netherlands: Springer.

IT Governance Institute 'ITG'. (2008). *Enterprise value: Governance of IT investments - The Val IT framework 2.0.* Rolling Meadows, IL: Information Systems Audit and Control Association, (ISACA).

Jordan, E., & Silcock, L. (2005). Beating IT risks. West Sussex, UK: John Wiely and Sons, Ltd.

Kindinger, J. (2002). *A systems approach to project risk management.* Paper presented at the 6th International Conference on Probabilistic Safety Assessment and Management, Puerto Rico, USA.

Lientz, B., & Larssen, L. (2006). Risk management for IT projects. Oxford, UK: Butterworth-Heinemann.

McCumber, J. (2004). Assessing and managing security risk in IT systems: A structured methodology. Boca Raton, FL: Auerbach Publications.

Myerson, J. (Ed.). (2001). Enterprise systems integration. Boca Raton, FL: Auerbach Publications.

Niemann, K. (2008). *From Enterprise architecture to IT governance: Elements of effective IT management.* Wiesbaden, Germany: Vieweg & Sohn verlag.

Olifer, N., & Olifer, V. (2006). Computer networks: Principles, technologies and protocols for network design. West Sussex, UK: John Wiley and Sons, Ltd.

Peltier, R. (2005). Information security risk analysis. Boca Raton, FL: Taylor and Francis.

Renn, O. (2008). Risk governance: Coping with uncertainty in a complex world. London, UK: Earthscan Publications Ltd.

Renn, O., & Walker, K. (Eds.). (2007). Global risk governance: Concept and practice using the IRGC framework. Dordrecht, The Netherlands: Springer.

Sari, B. (2009). SME based virtual enterprises: Basics, concepts and methods. Saarbrücken, Germany: VDM Publishing.

Schekkerman, J. (2006). How to survive in the jungle of enterprise architecture frameworks. Victoria, BC: Trafford Publishing.

Schwarz, S. (2008, April). *Projecting Risk from stakeholder analysis using RACI.* Paper presented at Project Summit & Business Analyst World, Philadelphia, PA.

Taiwana, A., & Keil, M. (2006). Functionality risk in information systems development: An empirical investigation. *IEEE Transactions on Engineering Management, 53*(3), 412–425. doi:10.1109/TEM.2006.878099

Tarantino, A. (2008). The governance, risk, and compliance handbook. Hoboken, NJ: John Wiley and Sons Inc.

Theoharakis, V., & Serpanos, D. N. (Eds.). (2001). Enterprise networking: Multilayer switching and applications. London: Idea Group Publishing.

Thompson, J. (2003). Managing your virtual world: Internal controls for enterprise technology. *Government Finance Review, 19*(4), 46–51.

Thompson, K. (2008). The networked enterprise: Competing for the future through virtual enterprise networks. Tampa, FL: Meghan-Kiffer Press.

Vose, D. (2008). Risk analysis: A quantitative guide. West Sussex, UK: John Wiley and Sons, Ltd.

Wallace, M., & Webber, L. (2008). IT governance 2009: Policies & procedures. Gaithersburg, MD: Aspen Publishers Inc.

Warrier, S., & Shandrashekhar, P. (2006). *Enterprise risk management from boardroom to shop floor.* Paper presented in the Asia Pacific Risk and Insurance conference, Tokyo, Japan.

Westerman, G., & Hunter, R. (2007). IT risk: Turning business threats into competitive advantage. Boston, MA: Harvard Business School Publishing.

Chapter 7
Modeling and Simulating Disruptions and other Crisis Events in Virtual Enterprise Networks

Ila Manuj
The University of North Texas, USA

ABSTRACT

Simulation is not only a powerful decision-making aid for supply chain managers but also a powerful research tool for theory building and testing. In addition to incorporating stochastic situations, simulation also enhances decision making by offering the flexibility to understand system behavior when cost parameters and policies are changed in a timely, cost-effective, and non-disruptive manner. The purpose of this chapter is to illustrate an approach toward modeling disruptions, risks and other crisis events in virtual enterprise networks. It provides several illustrations from published literature, presents a framework for managers and researchers to better apply and gain from the strength of simulation modeling, identifies several common pitfalls to avoid during the process, and compiles extensive references for readers who want to further their knowledge in this specific area.

INTRODUCTION

The focus of managing business organizations has been shifting from enterprises with well-defined structures, limited external relationships, and a focus on internal optimization to enterprises that are interconnected with each other in a network, have tightly integrated yet dynamic relationships with their suppliers and customers, and pursue overall network optimization. In today's day and age,

these networks are no longer rigid combinations of enterprises; they are fluid structures comprising independent institutions, businesses, and specialized individuals. These member entities of a network collaborate with each other using information and communication technology to gain competitive edge and to create value for the end customer. Yet the membership of a network is not constant. Member entities join and leave as and when their product and/ or service offerings are required. The composition of these networks is dynamic, changes continually and forever seeks the next level of optimization

DOI: 10.4018/978-1-61520-607-0.ch007

both in terms of efficiency and value creation for the end customer. The means of collaboration are information and communication technology intensive and the networks span the entire globe. In effect, networks have transformed into global Virtual Enterprise Network (VEN) systems.

A virtual enterprise network may be defined as a temporary alliance of distributed independent enterprises that participates in the different phases of the life cycle of a product or service, and work to share resources, skills, and costs, supported by information and communication technologies, in order to take advantage of market opportunities (Ahuja & Carley, 1998). They are formed when new products are introduced and are dismantled when products are obsolete (Grefen et al., 2009). Typically, there may be a leading or a focal firm that is instrumental in guiding the structure of a virtual enterprise network. In sum, these virtual enterprise networks have dynamic and agile configurations.

These networks are attractive because they provide access to skilled manpower, low-cost labor and raw materials, better financing opportunities, larger product markets, superior technology, arbitrage opportunities to hedge or take advantage of events such as currency fluctuations, and additional inducements offered by host governments to attract foreign capital such as tax incentives. However, tied with these benefits are risks and disruptions related to currency, transit times, quality, safety, culture, opportunism, inventory ownership, intellectual property and several others. Some of the most severe disruptions can even jeopardize a company's survival. These include events such as supplier bankruptcy, production shut-down upstream or downstream the network, port strikes, wars, natural disasters and several others. It is critical to understand the impact of such disruptions on a network to ensure business continuity for all network members. Disruption at one entity in a network may put the entire network at the risk of a shut-down. Additionally, disruptions also

negatively impact the stock-value of companies (Hendricks & Singhal, 2005).

In a global virtual enterprise network, any decision is complex to arrive at, expensive to implement, and may need continual alterations as the network evolves, priorities are realigned, and environment changes. In such situations, it is difficult to assess the cost of risks in any decision and an incorrect choice can lead to expensive mistakes with sometimes disastrous consequences. For such situations, it is important to have good crises management plans (Kleindorfer & Saad, 2005). However, even better and of fundamental importance is linking risk assessment and quantification with risk management options ex ante. It is critical to understand the potential risks and disruptions and the extent of ultimate harm to the virtual enterprise network. In an absence of pro-active risk management, there might be a feeling of apprehension and an impression of unpreparedness and uncertainty in the firm and the virtual enterprise network. This will result in actions that are not necessarily directed towards the most effective strategies for managing risks and planning for disruptions. Rather, they are developed based on some short-term, myopic incentives. As one manager interviewed by the author said:

"...it's not that they (supply chain managers) don't want to (include risks in analyses). It's not that they don't know they should look at risk. But I think they don't because of the pressures they're under, the goals that they have to meet for the year. They probably figure, hey look, it's a low probability, probably won't happen and, frankly, my boss isn't asking me to look at it. So, why should I be a hero and miss my objectives? It's the right thing to do but they aren't rewarded for doing it. Maybe that's at the heart of this, is no one is compensated or incented in their day to day job to look at and evaluate the risks properly."

Table 1. Differences between traditional supply chain and virtual enterprise network

Element of Differentiation	Supply Chain	Virtual Enterprise Network
Structure and Configuration	Typically sequential vertical transactions in different stages of creation of value (Lazzarini et al., 2001). The aim is to integrate and manage the sourcing, flow, and control of materials using a total systems perspective across multiple functions and multiple tiers of suppliers (Mentzer et al., 2001).	Group of networks formed by horizontal ties among companies of a certain industry or sector, which in turn associate with other companies at other levels of the corresponding vertical chain (Lazzarini et al., 2001). The aim is to profitably and quickly exploit business opportunity by quickly establishing enterprise cooperation, communications links and configurations (Capo-Vicedo et al., 2008).
Sources of Value	Optimization of production and operations as the key source of value for the chain as a whole, reduction of transaction costs, and acquisition of value within the chain from innovation in other parts of the supply chain (Lazzarini et al., 2001).	Social structure (interpersonal relationships and the individual positions of the members of the network), development of 'local' and 'collective' knowledge and generation of external economies in the network that benefit the companies in the network as a result of total increase in value (Lazzarini et al., 2001).
Time Frame	Typically, exchanges and relationships are long term in nature (Georgantzas, 2001).	Each time there is a market opportunity, a new VE is configured (Capo-Vicedo et al., 2008). Typically, duration of exchange is relatively shorter than that in a supply chain (Georgantzas, 2001). Members are temporarily linked together and a VEN "dissolves" after a project is completed.
Communication	Information exchange reflects the formal break-up of activities and firm boundaries associated with the supply chain operations. Communication is predominantly vertical and formal.	Information and communication technologies allow coordinating all their processes virtually as one firm (Georgantzas, 2001). High degree of informal communication and predominantly horizontal information exchange.
Governance	A specific firm typically functions as a supply chain leader as a result of its size, economic power, customer patronage, comprehensive trade franchise, or initiation of the inter-firm relationships (Bowersox & Closs, 1996). Command and obedience of legally unequal parties (Georgantzas, 2001). Relatively formal relationships.	Participants attempt to establish a form of management and organization more 'democratic or federal' with regard to the management of the flows of information, goods, decisions and control (Capo-Vicedo et al., 2008). Lack of formal rules and procedures, and informal reporting relationships, and norms (Ahuja & Carley, 1999).

In addition to lack of incentives, the reason for ignoring risks and potential disruptions is the difficult process of understanding and quantifying risks and estimating their impact on the virtual enterprise network. Simulation modeling, described as a mathematical depiction of a problem, with problems solved for various alternatives and solutions compared for decision making, drawing insights, testing hypotheses, and making inferences (Keebler, 2006), is a powerful technique that offers significant assistance in such cases.

Simulation has for long been a tool for analysis of traditional supply chain and logistics systems. Virtual networks - though more dynamic than "traditionally-defined" linear and rather stable

supply chains - face some of the same critical issues and challenges. Moreover, there are some significant differences as detailed in Table I.

As is evident from the table above, several issues and challenges are similar, for both a supply chain and a VEN, such as the need to incorporate stochastic (uncertain) internal and external conditions in decision-making, the ability to understand the impact of a decision under a variety of cost parameters and policies (Rosenfield, Copacino & Payne, 1985) and the need to understand impacts of decisions (Chang & Makatsoris, 2001). However, what makes modeling more complex and different in a VEN context is the enhanced need for flexibility and agility, the shorter timeframe and the informal and transient governance structure. Making changes to the physical network structure, i.e., real life controlled experimentation of a virtual enterprise network system may be extremely difficult, disruptive to the network, and prohibitively expensive (Rosenfield, Copacino & Payne, 1985). In addition, another characteristic of a VEN that makes it different from a supply chain, particularly with regard to risk management, is that there are typically no historical data to refer to because of the ever-changing nature of VEN configuration. For example, a VEN established around a focal firm may be comprised of different members at different instances of time. Therefore, past data points may not be adequately reflective of the current VEN characteristics such as quality, lead times etc. Therefore, the main reliance is on the fuzzy experiences and subjective judgments of the personnel (Huang et al., 2008). This makes objective evaluations using simulation techniques an effective and important complement to subjective judgments.

The size and complexity of global virtual enterprise networks, their dynamic network of facilities and connecting linkages, their stochastic (uncertain) nature, the level of detail necessary for investigation, the changing membership and the complex inter-relationships between system components make simulation modeling a particularly appropriate approach to model risk and disruptive events and understand the impact of such disturbances on the performance of the whole network.

A powerful feature of computer-based simulation is the examination of a dynamic system such as a virtual enterprise network over time in short and long durations. Simulation runs representing years can be accomplished in a matter of hours thereby assisting in timely decisions (Chang & Makatsoris, 2001) that are informed with data and logic in addition to experience and feeling. For example, a quote from a senior manager from a leading home appliance manufacturing company illustrates this point in the context of an off-shoring decision:

"Compare that [domestic sourcing] to getting microwave ovens from China. You've got thirty days on the water alone. I mean, not on the water, but from point to point you've got thirty days of just transit time. You've got then the factory itself that is not nearly as flexible [as domestic facility] in that they have one month from schedules. So suddenly you are two months away from demand and that doesn't count the additional inventory that you're putting in the system as well. So you can see the enormous loss of flexibility that you have when you start globally sourcing versus our local factories. Our systems weren't prepared to deal with that kind of environment. We didn't know how to optimize it or really to deal with it. So certainly a number of projects that I've worked on, deal with that issue of how do you deal with a supply chain that is suddenly many times longer than it was, when we were just a domestically sourced business."

The cost of risk in the decision above could have been reasonably estimated a priori using simulation. However, this manager was elaborating on his concerns about risks in global supply chains and his inability to optimize and proactively deal with complex supply chain issues. With lack of simulation modeling to support decisions, managers typically select simple tools, rely on conventional judgment, and/or imitate other competing firms. This may not always result in effective decision making (Allen & Emmelhainz, 1984). In particular, for supply chain risk management, Sykes (2006, p.13) argues that, "The subject of supply chain risk is coming to the forefront of our profession today, and it has not adopted the mathematical and statistically driven methods of our professional counterparts in the fields of finance and insurance."

From both research methodology and practical application perspectives, computer-based simulation experimentation is most useful when a limited number of alternatives are considered, and the objective is to understand the effects

Figure 1. Virtual enterprise network - risk management simulation modeling framework

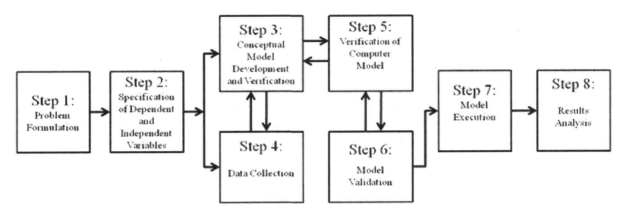

of change due to a limited number of variables (Rosenfield et al., 1985). Too many things varying at the same time may pose problems during interpretation of the results.

This chapter is organized as follows. First, an approach to modeling disruptions and risks in virtual enterprise networks is presented. Next, the approach is elaborated using a simple illustration followed by a set of questions that a modeler or a user of simulation models may utilize to maintain and/or ascertain the quality of a simulation model are presented. Finally, directions for future research are identified.

MODELING APPROACH

This section draws from and builds upon the works of Law (2006); Banks (1998); Manuj, Mentzer, & Bowers (2009) to suggest an eight-step discrete event simulation process for application specifically in the context of modeling disruptions, risks, and other crises events in virtual enterprise networks. The process is summarized in Figure I and referred to as the Virtual Enterprise Network - Risk Management Simulation Modeling (VEN-RMSM) framework. The eight steps in the VEN-RMSM framework may be implemented practically in the development of simulation mod-

els. Specific insights relevant to modeling risks in a virtual enterprise network are provided.

Before getting into the discussion on the simulation model, a few resources that may help a reader better understand and identify risks to a VEN may be useful. Chopra & Sodhi (2004) classify risks into those related with delays, disruptions, forecast inaccuracies, systems breakdowns, intellectual property breaches, procurement failures, inventory problems and capacity issues. Grabowski & Roberts (1999) provide an in-depth discussion on managing risks in virtual organizations. Hallikas et. al (2002) provide a list of supply risks in networks. Zsidisin et al. (2004) provide a description for assessment of supply risks. For a good description of demand risks, Fisher (1997) and Johnson (2001) may be consulted. For overall understanding, Manuj & Mentzer (2008) provide a description of risk management in a global supply chain context and Chopra & Sodhi (2004) provide a comprehensive list of risks. In terms of simulation, Li & Xiao (2006) provide an illustration of multi-agent virtual enterprise model using Swarm platform.

To demonstrate the process, examples of rigorous studies are provided for each step. Studies that are chosen as examples for a particular step report in detail on the step and provide insights into the measures taken to maintain the rigor of that step.

Step 1: Problem Formulation

This is one of the most critical and important steps of the process. The purpose of problem formulation, as the name says, is to completely and accurately state the problem. There are three things to keep in mind: first, what is the key concern that is driving the decision-maker to explore options; second, what is the decision that needs to be made based on the options evaluated using the simulation model, and third, what are the expected outcomes, i.e., what do we want to know at the end of the modeling process. For example, a senior executive may be concerned about the impact of a production disruption at the site of a sole-source supplier of a critical manufacturing component. She/he may want to make a decision on whether or not to contract with another back-up supplier. This manager may want to know the outcomes of disruption on total procurement cost and customer service levels over a two-week, three-month and six-month timeframe, and the cost and impact of contracting with an alternative supplier over a similar timeframe.

In general, this step leads to the definition of overall objectives and a list of specific questions to be answered by the simulation model. Most models fail to deliver on decision-makers' expectations because of inattention to this step (Keebler, 2006). Vague or confusing problem definition may result in incorrect analysis, lost time, incorrect inferences, bad or ineffective decisions, missed opportunities, and can cost money (Dhebar, 1993). Therefore, this step deserves utmost attention.

Oftentimes, problem definition is an iterative process. It is likely that the problem is not initially stated in precise terms. With the involvement of individuals and teams that are impacted directly or indirectly because of the problem, the main concerns can be separated from secondary issues, alternatives can be clearly articulated, complete understanding of the problem can be ensured, and that correct and relevant problem is addressed in totality may be ascertained. Once this step is adequately accomplished, the steps following this critical first step may be executed more efficiently (in terms of time and money invested) and effectively (in terms of accuracy achieved).

For example, Appelqvist & Gubi (2005) clearly formulate the problem under investigation as quantifying the benefits of postponement for a consumer electronics company as well as supply chain of Bang and Olufsen and other members in the supply chain. Furthermore, they used a qualitative pre-study to identify the range of products that could potentially benefit from a new manufacturing postponement concept.

Step 2: Specification of Dependent and Independent Variables

Once the problem is formulated, the next step is to identify the dependent and independent variables. Simply put, dependent variables are the variables that answer the third question identified in the previous section: what do we want to know at the end of the modeling process? In the example described above, total procurement cost and customer service levels were the dependent variables. The values of dependent variables depend upon the values of independent variables. Independent variables are system parameters the values of which are varied or manipulated and their effect on dependent variables is recorded and analyzed. Analyses of dependent variable values provide answers to the problem formulated in Step 1.

The outcome of a model depends on what is incorporated in the model including the dependent and independent variables. Therefore, the objective of the research or the business problem to be solved and the specific questions to be answered using the simulation model ought to guide the selection of dependent and independent variables. Depending upon the problem, all factors that influence the answers sought, i.e., affect the values of dependent variables, and need to be manipulated should be included as independent variables. Independent variables may include technical, legal, managerial, economic, psychological, organizational, monetary, and historical factors (Towill & Disney, 2008; Potter & Disney, 2006; Forrester, 1961). In a virtual enterprise network, disruption and other risk events will be a subset of independent variables. Examples of independent risk events may include currency fluctuations, quality risks, lead time variability risks, competitive risks, supplier bankruptcy risks, natural disasters, strikes, capacity shortages, wars etc.

Several sources may be consulted to identify the variables of interest. A good place to start is past research that addresses issues similar to the ones addressed in the current problem. Practitioners may want to enlist help of academics specializing in the area of interest. Another key group to involve in the process is the people who deal with the problem and whose job will be directly impacted by the decision under consideration. Subject matter experts - academics, consultants, or colleagues - may be referred to in order to ensure that all relevant and important variables are included.

In the specific case of modeling disruption and other crises events for virtual enterprise networks, it is important to include critical suppliers and customers to understand the vulnerabilities in their systems that might otherwise escape the attention of an internally-focused group. In a good example of study to estimate off-shoring risk for an automobile company, Canbolat et al. (2005) identified six key stakeholder groups in sourcing decision, namely purchasing, supplier technical assistance, product development, material planning and logistics, manufacturing, and finance. They interviewed four executives and at least one subject matter expert (SME) in each of the stakeholder groups. They discovered almost forty risk factors (independent variables) and relationships among risk factors. This ensured that all variables and relationships relevant to stakeholders and experts were included in the

model. They employed dollar value of risks, i.e., expected total costs after adjusting for risks, as the dependent variable.

As mentioned earlier, existing literature is a good source to validate the choice of variables. For example, Shang, Li & Tadikamalla (2004), who define their problem as identifying the best operating conditions for a supply chain to optimize performance, use total supply chain cost and service levels as dependent variables and employ several independent variables including extent of differentiation, extent of information sharing, capacity limit, reorder quantity, lead time, reliability of the suppliers, inventory holding costs, and demand variability. In a study by Holland & Sodhi (2004) to understand bullwhip effect, the authors employ an exhaustive range of independent variables such as demand autocorrelation, variance of forecast error, retailer's lead time, manufacturer's lead time, retailer's order batch size, manufacturer's order batch size, standard deviation of the deviation from the retailer's optimal order size, and standard deviation of the deviation from the manufacturer's optimal order size. They use observed variance of manufacturer's order size and observed variance of retailer's order size as dependent variables.

Step 3: Conceptual Model Development and Verification

A conceptual model is an abstraction of the real-world system under investigation using dependent and independent variables, and mathematical and logical relationships concerning the components and structure of the system (Banks, 1998). During this phase, it is important to list all assumptions and describe in detail the definitions of variables and the relationships between them to ensure that the simulation model develops in accordance with the problem statement. The validity of the outcome of a system and therefore the confidence of the users of the model in the findings depends on what is included during model development.

At times, there may be an overwhelming number of things that may be potentially included in a model. In such instances it is important to determine what should be included in and excluded from the model. Techniques such as Delphi and Failure Mode And Effects Analysis (FMEA) may also be employed to prioritize the elements that should go into the model.

The Delphi method allows people to arrive at a consensus on an issue of interest through a series of repeated interrogations of knowledgeable individuals. After the initial interrogation of each individual, usually by means of questionnaires, each subsequent interrogation is accompanied by information from the preceding one. Each participant is encouraged to reconsider and, if appropriate, change his/her previous reply (Makukha & Gray, 2004). Several rounds of anonymous discussions can be held using the Delphi Technique. Further, since the responses may easily be collected and shared in a manner that ensures the anonymity of the respondents, the process ensures that no one's opinion overtly influences the opinion of any other participant. When modeling disruptions and risk events in a virtual enterprise network, the Delphi technique may be used to reach a consensus on the probabilities and impacts of these disruptions and risks.

FMEA is often used in engineering design analysis to identify and rank the potential failure modes of a design or manufacturing process, and to determine its effect on other components of the product or processes in order to document and prioritize improvement actions (Sankar & Prabhu, 2001). Canbolat et al. (2005) employ FMEA to characterize the structure of risk for an automobile manufacturing company.

After the development of the conceptual model, it is important to verify the model prior to investing resources in the development of a computer model. Model verification ensures that conceptual model is an adequate and correct representation of the system under consideration. For conceptual model verification, a structured walk-through of the conceptual model may be undertaken before an audience that may include analysts, computer programmers, SMEs, decision stake-holders, users of the intended model, and senior management (Law, 2005). If possible, this step should include a few members who were not a part of the conceptual model development. Discussion during this stage typically includes items such as objectives, performance measures, model components and relationships between components, concepts, assumptions, algorithms, data summaries, and any other model aspects of interest. In the best case, input gathered during this step may be used to fine-tune the model that is correct and sufficiently detailed. In the worst case, it might lead a modeler back to the drawing board to rework the model. In sum, this step ensures that the representation of the problem entity is reasonable for the intended purpose of the model (Sargent, 2007).

Performing and documenting conceptual validation early in the model development process and describing the problem structure and the accompanying model in clear, simple language increases the credibility of the model researchers and practitioners (Law, 2005). In general, if researchers and modelers omit conceptual validation early in the model development process and attempt to validate the computer or computational model directly, it may be too late, too costly, or too time-consuming to fix errors and omissions in the computational model.

Step 4: Data Collection

Collecting data can be challenging as data may not be readily available, or not available in required formats, or not available at an appropriate level of detail. In the particular case of modeling disruptions and risks in virtual enterprise networks, there may be additional issues with the data such as the data required may not be available with a single entity and necessitates the cooperation of network members to obtain the data. It is also possible that because of its complexity, data on disruption and risk events is not captured at all or not captured in sufficient detail.

An important activity in this step is to establish data requirements to populate the conceptual model. In addition to the independent variables identified in Step 1, data is needed to specify model parameters, system configurations, policies such as inventory, sourcing, and transportation policies, and probability distributions of variables of interest.

Data collection may follow conceptual model development. However, data gathering is a long and tedious process. Therefore, for variables for which the requirements are definitively identified, data collection may proceed concurrently with conceptual model development. Data sources may include company databases, company annual reports, internal company reports such as performance tracking reports, industry reports published by independent consultants, government databases, interviews, past academic research, best practice reports, books, and other published sources. Before incorporation into the model, all data must be scanned for completeness, and accuracy, and to ensure that the data is available in its most current form. Data may need to be cleaned for errors, synchronized to remove discrepancies, and updated to account for missing data.

In case of disruption and risk management models, such as those for VENs, it is the author's experience that much of data needed for quantification of risks is available in qualitative form. Therefore, interviews and at times, group meetings, specifically designed and conducted for the problem, may be needed and are a valid and acceptable source of data. Techniques such as the Delphi technique discussed above may be used to convert qualitative data into quantitative data. In addition, securing the cooperation of multiple network entities is almost a prerequisite to ensure that the required data is collected in a timely manner.

In general, any independent variable may be manifested using one of three approaches (Banks,

1998). First, the variable may be deterministic in nature or not random, i.e., a set of other variables determine the variable of interest by the use of a function. Second, an independent variable may be operationalized by fitting a probability distribution to the observed data. This is useful when the actual data may be reasonably approximated by such commonly used distributions as normal, Poisson, exponential, or several others. For example, Shang, Li & Tadikamalla (2004) employ Bass (1969) for simulating demand. Third, a variable may be operationalized with an empirical distribution from observed data. In sum, a simulation provides an invaluable ability to incorporate stochastic variation.

In the example of a study for ascertaining the benefit of postponement strategy discussed earlier under Step 1, Appelqvist & Gubi (2005), based on interviews, previous work at the case company, and insights from the literature, developed three alternative delivery (or postponement) concepts and evaluated them using discrete-event simulation utilizing a mix of qualitative and quantitative data. They collected qualitative data by interviewing managers at Bang and Olufsen and its downstream intermediaries and used it to develop model operation policies. The data on other variables such as demand information was obtained from the company's ERP systems.

Step 5: Verification of Computer Model

For most situations, it is preferable that modeling begins simply and complexity is added gradually (Banks, 1998). Complexity in the form of additional variables and sub-models can be added until a model of acceptable detail and complexity is developed. Developing detailed flowcharts may also be useful but not always possible depending on the scope of the simulation model project. When developing a model, it is important to subdivide the entire problem into smaller manageable components. For each component, the objectives, the input and output variables, and the links to other components should be clearly specified.

Verification is the determination of whether the computer implementation of the conceptual model is correct. Verification includes examining the outputs of sub-models and complete simulation model to ensure that the models are executing and behaving acceptably by debugging any errors in programming logic and code.

Verification is a continuous process. It is a good practice to verify small pieces of model or sub-models of the model rather than attempting to verify the complete model in one go. Verification is likely to be more efficiently accomplished when carried out concurrently with model development. Waiting until the entire model is developed may result in patches to the original code, updating the codes in several modules, and at times, rewriting a significant piece of the code, all translated in lost time and money (Banks, 1998; Sargent, 2007). Waiting can also result in verification oversights and errors. In addition to helping with identifying unwanted system behavior, verification can also help in determining whether an analytical solution is more suitable or a simpler simulation substructure can be substituted for an existing complex one (Fishman & Kiviat, 1968).

Several programming languages and software packages exist to simulate logistics and supply chain systems. Simulation environment or programming platform used in past supply chain research include, among others, MS Excel with add-ins, ARENA, ExtendSIM, and Supply Chain Guru software package. In the literature reviewed, there is no evidence of preference for a particular software package that clearly outperforms others.

Model verification may be addressed in multiple ways. First, the code may be checked by at least one person other than the person who coded the model. This is important because there is a tendency to overlook mistakes if one is very familiar with the content. Second, if possible, the output of the parts of the model or sub-models may be compared with manually calculated solutions to determine acceptable behavior. By running a model using a variety of input values, results may be checked against reasonable, expected or calculated, or known output values. At times, it may be difficult to manually verify an actual complex model. In such cases, a simpler version of the model or sub-models may be tested with shorter pilot runs, employing relatively simpler scenarios or alternatives, and/or replacing stochastic values with deterministic values. The objective is to ascertain that both sub-models and the complete model behave acceptably.

A useful practice of developing detailed flowcharts along with detailed documentation of the model helps in delegating the verification process and thereby helps speed up model development. Animation is another powerful tool that may be used during the verification process. Sometimes visual cues are easier to observe and interpret as compared to data tables. The latest simulation software programs have built-in animation tools.

In summary, to develop a rigorous and valid model, it is critical that a model be thoroughly verified. To build user confidence in the model and to allow replication, modification, or extension of model, documentation of steps in the model development and verification process are invaluable. In an interesting application, Canbolat et al. (2005) use three case studies (one illustrated in their paper) to verify their model. Zhang & Zhang (2007) conducted statistical analysis comparing simulation results with theoretic (calculated) values at 5% level of significance.

Step 6: Model Validation

Model validation is the process of determining whether a simulation model is an accurate representation of the system under investigation (Law, 2006). A valid model can be used to make decisions similar to those that would be made if it were feasible and cost-effective to experiment with the system itself (Law, 2005). An invalid model may lead to erroneous conclusions and decisions.

The issue of validating a simulation model may be addressed in several ways, many of which are similar to those used to validate the conceptual model (Step 3) and in a way dependent on how well Step 3 was executed. Consultation with subject matter experts, including academic scholars, practitioners and intended users of the model during the conceptual development of model components and relationships between components will ensure the correct problem is solved and reality is adequately modeled (Law, 2006). After a computer model is developed, a structured walk-through of the model and a re-view of simulation results for reasonableness with a separate set of subject matter experts may be conducted. If the results are reasonably consistent with how the subject matter experts perceive the system should operate, the model is said to have face validity (Sargent, 2007). Particular attention should be made to bring on-board a few subject matter experts and/or managers who were not involved with the conceptual model development. Reviewing the literature for comparable simula-tion models and comparing the results against existing knowledge and findings is an additional means to ascertain model validity.

If feasible, computer-based simulation output may be compared with output data from the ac-tual system for input-output validation. This is also called results validation. Spectral analysis, a statistical technique used for analyzing actual or simulated time series, may be used for input-output analysis.

Results validation may not always be pos-sible, particularly in the case of virtual enterprise networks. The reasons may be that the model is a simpler representation of the actual system, that is, it employs fewer variables than those present in the real system. In such cases, it is difficult to isolate the impact of a few variables. In other cases, the problem under consideration is so new

that existing data to validate the model may not exist; or it may be difficult to find a company willing to share data on all variables included in this research. In such cases, partial datasets may be used to validate corresponding parts of the simulation model. Where no validation against actual output is possible, Fishman & Kiviat (1968, p. 192) suggest:

"While validation is desirable, it is not always possible. Each investigator has the soul-searching responsibility of deciding how much importance to attach to his results. When no experience is available for comparison, an investigator is well advised to proceed in steps, first implementing results based on simple well-understood models and then using the results of this implementation to design more sophisticated models that yield stronger results. It is only thorough gradual de-velopment that a simulation can make any claim to approximate reality"

During validation, additional important activi-ties may be performed using sensitivity analysis. First, it is critical to identify model parameters and independent variables that have the greatest impact on the performance measures. These need to be awarded careful attention during model-ing. Second, the stability of model needs to be tested. If certain extreme values of one or more independent variables generate bizarre values, those values and model behaviors needs to be identified and documented. This might also have implications for the ranges of independent vari-ables. This is especially critical when modeling disruption events and both the probability of a disruption event and the impact it has on a virtual enterprise network may be extreme in nature. Third, since any model is based on multiple as-sumptions, it is important to test the sensitivity of the analysis to changes in assumptions as this may have serious implications for the ap-plicability of the model. Systematic sensitivity analysis not only facilitates explicit recognition of the important assumptions and provides a useful way to identify and eliminate logical and methodological errors; it also improves the decision maker's understanding of the problem (Dhebar 1993).

Good examples of model validation are abundant in the literature. In an excellent example, Van der Vorst et al. (1998) developed a simulation model to improve performance of a food supply chain. A food supply chain has several clusters of sources of uncertainty such as order forecast horizon, input data, administrative and decision processes and inherent uncertainties. They conducted a case study using a simulation model to quantify the effects of alternative configurations and operational management concepts. To validate their model, they implemented one scenario at two retail outlets and measured the outcomes against a control outlet as well as simulated results. Appelqvist & Gubi (2005) conducted model validation using input-output transformation, i.e., comparing simulation data to real world data, on performance measures such as delivery times, delivery accuracy, and inventory levels; and also undertook a structured walk-through with company management. Shang, Li, & Tadikamalla (2004) compared simulation results with analytical models for simple known cases.

At this point, it is important to note that steps 3, 4, 5, and 6 do not always proceed sequentially. In fact, most of the time, the model development phase from conceptual model development to validation of the simulation model is an iterative process. For example, a problem discovered during model validation may necessitate a change in conceptual model. It is also possible that certain environmental changes may affect the values of independent variables. Therefore, a modeler should always keep an open mind about some changes to model at a later stage. This also implies that certain buffer times must be allocated to all steps in any simulation modeling project. As Pritsker (1998, p. 33) states very pertinently

"The secret to being a good modeler is the ability to remodel."

Step 7: Model Execution

An important decision once a model is ready and validated is to decide the sample size, run length, and warm-up period. Sample size is the number of independent model replications, i.e., how many times a given scenario or alternative be simulated. Since the input values of some or all independent variables may be stochastic, every repetition is likely to result in a different answer. Run length is the time-frame for each run and is usually dependent on the time-frame of the decision being considered. Warm-up period is the period that it takes for the model to stabilize and the independent and dependent variable values during this period are usually ignored.

Sample size determination is critical because of the presence of several risks in the virtual enterprise network, too many or too few runs of a simulation model may lead to erroneous conclusions. Too few runs may not account for all possible outcomes. Too many runs may also distort the results as the power of a statistical test to detect an effect increases with the number of replications (Mentzer & Gomes, 1991). Increasing the number of runs reduces the standard deviation of the sampling distribution, and therefore, for a given level of confidence, the half-width of the confidence interval decreases. This results in an increase in the absolute precision of the estimate of population of interest (where absolute precision is defined as the actual half-width of a confidence interval (Law, 2006)), but increasing the number of replications until statistically significant results are obtained makes the external validity of the results questionable.

An alternative to increasing absolute precision, as suggested by Bienstock (1996, p. 45) is "to let the number of replications be guided by a 'practical' degree of precision, i.e., a reasonable degree of precision, given the magnitude of population mean(s) that is (are) being estimated." A detailed discussion of this method called relative precision method can be found in Bienstock (1996), who contends that conclusions drawn from results in this manner are more meaningful both in terms of research goals and practical problem solutions. However, this technique is appropriate for successive independent replications of simulation runs; it is not appropriate for determination of achieved relative precision on subintervals of a single simulation run or in experimental designs that utilize variance reduction techniques (Bienstock, 1996). Bienstock & Mentzer (1999) adopt the relative precision method. Zhang & Zhang (2007) follow an iterative procedure by comparing output from scenarios under different combinations of run-length and number of replications. They use ANOVA and replication/deletion to ascertain the warm-up period, run length, and number of replications. Appelqvist & Gubi (2005) used the same demand data sets used for all replications. They suggest that this technique, known as correlated sampling, provides a high statistical confidence level.

It is important to note here that if an event has a very low probability and the objective is to determine if an event occurs, then a larger number of replications and longer simulation runs may be necessary. However, it is equally critical to remember that in real life, for a given event, a very large number of events may be practically impossible. In sum, it is the judgment of the modeler to identify whether the model is to determine if an event happens or to understand the impact of disruptions on the system and choose number of runs accordingly.

Step 8: Results Analysis

After the model executions are completed and results are collected, the final step is to analyze the data on performance measures or the dependent variables. This step includes two key activities. One is to interpret the results and the second is to analyze the differences between different model configurations (or alternatives) simulated.

Several analysis techniques are available such as visual inspection of graphical outputs; mean, lower and upper limits, standard deviation, percentage changes in and percentiles of dependent variables; response surface methodology (fitting regression models to simulation output); ANCOVA and ANOVA and different methods of multiple comparisons such as Tukey's, Scheffe's, and Fisher's methods. Modelers, reviewers, and practitioners should be aware of assumptions (e.g., normality or autocorrelation) that might affect the appropriateness of a given statistical technique for a given situation. The choice of analysis techniques varies considerably depending on the distribution of input and output variables. Therefore, if needed, the services of a statistician may be requested at this stage. Alexopoulos and Seila (1998) provide a good discussion on output data analysis.

An additional activity at this step is to document the result and the interpretation of the results. In addition to the final model results, the results of sensitivity analysis may provide interesting insights into the problem.

CASE STUDY EXAMPLE

The purpose of this section is to illustrate the VEN-RMSM process by using a simulation study designed to understand the impact of risks and disruptions on a virtual enterprise network when considering a postponement strategy. Postponement entails delaying the actual commitment of resources to maintain flexibility and delay the incurring of costs (Bucklin, 1965). There are two types of postponement – form and time. Form postponement includes labeling, packaging, assembly, and manufacturing. Time postponement refers to the movement of goods from manufacturing plants

Figure 2. Simulated supply chain

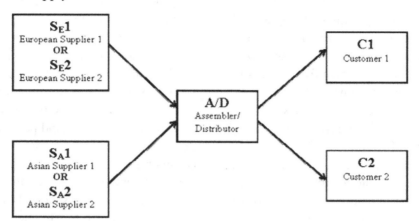

only after customer orders are received (Zinn & Bowersox, 1988). For this particular illustration, form postponement is employed.

Step 1: Problem Formulation

For illustration purposes, a simple VEN with four suppliers, a manufacturer/distributor, and two customers is conceptualized (see Figure II). There are two suppliers in Europe (SE1 and SE2) and two in Asia (SA1 and SA2). The assembler/distributor (A/D) and the two customers (C1 and C2) are based in the US. The A/D (and the decision maker) sells two products – Product A and Product B. Product A is composed of two components – A-Component (AC) unique to Product A and Common-Component (CC) shared between Product A and Product B. Product B is composed of two components – B-Component (BC) unique to Product B and Common-Component (CC). All four suppliers can supply components AC, BC, and CC. Currently, over 98% of the sourcing is from one Asian supplier with less than 2% business allocated to one European supplier on "as-needed" basis.

The key concerns for A/D are relatively higher quality issues and longer lead times of Asian supplier and its consequent impact of these issues on customer service and total procurement costs.

Moreover, there are various supply and demand risks in the network that further complicate decision making. A/D wants to work with two suppliers – one Asian and one European. A/D wants to make a decision which one of the two suppliers and which one of two Asian suppliers to select for a two-year framework. In total, four different supplier network configurations are possible. As an outcome, A/D wants to ascertain the impact of different break-ups of business between the two suppliers (e.g. 40-60, 30-70 etc.) on total procurement cost and customer service levels over a two-year timeframe under different combinations of supply and demand risks and in the event of disruption.

Step 2: Specification of Dependent and Independent Variables

To shortlist the important independent and dependent variables, extensive literature review and a qualitative research was based on data from in-depth qualitative interviews with the A/D firm and its customers and suppliers aiming to identify the most important risks involved in the decision discussed above in the problem formulation section. Additional interviews were conducted during simulation model development to collect data and validate the model. The description of the complete model is beyond the scope of this chapter; however the most important components of the model are described below.

Based on the qualitative study, the external supply chain environment comprised of supply and demand risks that were incorporated in the simulation model. Four types of environments were operationalized as combinations of high and low levels of supply and demand risks.

An assortment of risk events serves as the independent variables for this event-driven model. For supply and demand risks, over 30 risk events were identified in the literature and the qualitative study, for example wage rate changes, oil price changes and demand changes. For illustration purposes, this case study focuses on a small subset of the variables. Table 2 provides a list of all independent variables, their definitions, and values. Supply risk events are divided into supplier order processing time variability, cost variability, and quality variability. Disruption was modeled as a

30-day closure at the port of arrival in the US, due to union strike.

The decision is based on total supply chain profit that takes into account several other performance measures including total supply chain costs (inventory, transportation, and production costs), total supply chain revenues, and penalty costs from late deliveries. In addition, several other measures were recorded, including stockouts, total inbound lead time, fill rates, delays to customers, and average inventory, to help in the interpretation of results.

Step 3: Conceptual Model Development and Verification

To conceptually validate the model, subject matter experts were consulted and interviewed at every step. The primary review and consultation team consisted of four academics. After an acceptable level of detail and complexity was achieved as per

Table 2. Independent variables and supply risk events

Risk Factors	Definition Distribution	Asian (Low)	Asian (High)	European (Low)	European (High)
1. Supplier Order Processing Time Variability	Time from order placement to replenishment at the supplier facility Normal (Mean, SD)	N(15, 3) days	N(15, 6) days	N(15, 1.5) days	N(15,4.5)days
2. Cost Variability	Sourcing cost variability due to changes in exchange rates, wage rates, shortage of goods, natural disasters, oil price increases, and any other unforeseen reasons Triangular (Min, Mean, Max)				
	Component AC or Component BC ($)	T(15,16.5, 18)	T(15, 18.375, 21.75)	T(20, 21.5, 23)	T(20, 23, 26)
	Component CC ($)	T (35, 38.5, 42)	T (35, 42.875, 50.75)	T(50, 53.75, 57.5)	T(50, 57.5, 65)
3. Quality Variability/ Yield	Usable quantity (Total quantity-shortages due to losses, damages, and pilferage in-transit, communication errors, market capacity, war and terrorism, and natural disasters.) % usable	98	90	99	95

Table 3. Demand risk event

Risk Factor	Definition and Distribution	Low Risk	High Risk
Variability of demand	Average variation in daily demand Normal (Mean, SD)	N (1000, 300)	N (1000,500)

this primary review team, two business practitioners separately reviewed the conceptual model.

The following discussion elaborates on the model flow for this study. The numbers have been changed and the sources disguised to protect the identity of the manufacturer.

A model run is triggered by the generation of demand at the customer location. Demand is generated daily at both customer sites, C1 and C2. The demand is distributed normally with a mean of 1000 units per day per customer. The average demand for each customer is derived from secondary data of the manufacturer company. The standard deviation is set to 300 units for the low demand risk scenario and 500 units for the high demand risk scenario as per consultation with practitioners. Demand generated at customers is transmitted instantaneously to the manufacturer/distributor at the cost of $5/order. The order is due in 10 days.

Orders placed by customers are received instantaneously at the A/D, and order processing begins immediately. Processing at the A/D takes place 8 hours a day, 5 days a week. Order processing includes picking components, assembling, packing, and shipping goods. Order processing capacity is set to 150% of average daily demand or 1500 units per day. Goods are shipped to customers every day. For both products, picking and packing cost is $6/unit, assembly cost is $15/unit per unit, and shipping cost is $8/unit.

Quality variability, one of the independent variables, is operationalized using variable yields from different suppliers. Yields for suppliers are presented in Table 2. One supplier from each region must be chosen.

Inventory value of products and components is set at average purchase cost and accounts for the changing cost variability under different scenarios. Inventory carrying cost is set at 24% (Wilson, 2006).

As orders are processed, inventory levels for component parts AC, BC, and CC are checked twice a day. Whenever the inventory level for a given product or component goes below the Reorder Point (ROP), a replenishment order for a fixed quantity (Q) is placed with the supplier. Elaboration of the inventory policy is beyond the scope of this paper. The considerations for inventory policy included inventory carrying costs, order costs, lead times, container-load quantities, cost of stock-outs, annual demand and variability, and other things. Advanced methods of determining inventory policies may be found in Fricker & Goodhart (2000) and Silver, Pyke, & Peterson (1998).

The cost of components sourced from the Asian supplier was set to $15 for components AC and BC, and $35 for the component CC. Using a 25-30% cost differential, the component prices were set to $20 and $50 for the European supplier.

To operationalize the second aspect of supply risks, i.e., cost variability, the purchase cost of products and components from the Asian supplier was set to a high of 20% for low risk scenarios and a high of 45% for high risk scenarios. For European suppliers, cost variability was set to 15% for low risk and 30% for high risk suppliers.

Order processing times at the supplier facilities are provided in Table 2 and are based on consultations with the practitioners.

After a supplier processes the order, the goods are sent to the designated port using domestic transportation where they are loaded onto a ship. The ship travels from the supplier port to the designated port. At the port, the goods are cleared through customs and loaded onto a truck. Trucks transport the goods from the US port to the A/D. The transportation times from the European and Asian suppliers were based on estimates available from company databases and other secondary sources.

After the A/D processes the orders, goods are shipped daily to customers. The transit time to customers is a fixed 3 days. The goods are shipped with a charge of $10/unit. The transit times and cost figures are based on qualitative interviews and quotes from freight companies. Orders delivered late to customers are assessed a penalty cost of $35/unit. The selling price of the products is $150/unit based on the secondary data on gross margins of the industry.

Step 4: Data Collection

The data for this study came from the existing literature, secondary data sources, the qualitative study, and additional interviews with managers. This step also included cleaning, updating, and validating the data collected.

Step 5: Verification of Computer Model

This research used a simulation package designed specifically to model supply chains called Supply Chain Guru (SC Guru) by Llamasoft Corporation that combines full mixed-integer/linear programming optimization and discrete event simulation.

Although the primary researcher developed the models on her own, services of two programmers who are expert in modeling supply chains using SC Guru were employed to verify multiple aspects of the program. Continuous involvement of the experts also minimized the possibility of programming errors (bugs).

The output of parts of the model was compared with manually calculated solutions to determine if they behaved acceptably. The validation during this process included verification within a scenario of transportation times, queuing of shipments throughout the supply chain, supplier yields, and inventory policies. Simulation results for short pilot runs of simple cases for the complete model were compared with manual calculations to test whether the entire model (structure) behaved acceptably. The validation for final output for each scenario included total inbound container load/truckload costs of transportation, average purchase costs for average order processing and assembly costs at the A/D, picking and packing costs, outbound cost/unit of transportation, total cost, and total revenue. The model was built in stages where each sub-model was verified and gradually integrated into the main model.

Step 6: Model Validation

Subject matter experts, including academic scholars and practitioners, were consulted in the conceptual model development. A structured walkthrough of the model and a review of the simulation results for reasonableness with a separate set of subject matter experts.

Sensitivity analyses were performed on the programmed model that revealed that some model parameters had significant impact on the performance measures and, thus, they were reviewed again for correct modeling. For example, reorder quantities had a significant impact on performance outcome.

Step 7: Model Execution

Combinations of different selections of suppliers were used to generate four possible combinations of suppliers i.e. SE1 and SA1, SE1 and SA2, SE2 and SA1, and SE2 and SA2. Four different sourcing scenarios between Asian and European suppliers- 50-50, 60-40, 70-30, and 40-60 - were

Table 4. Summary of select results

Supply Risk	Demand Risk	Disruption	Result
Low	Low	No	Source does not have a significant impact.
High	Low	No	Higher share to European supplier as supply risks increase.
Low	High	No	Higher share to European supplier as demand risk increases.
High	High	No	Higher share to European supplier as demand risk increases.
Low	Low	Yes	Asian supplier is marginally better.
High	Low	Yes	Source does not have a significant impact.
Low	High	Yes	Source does not have a significant impact.
High	High	Yes	Higher share to European supplier as demand risk increases.

simulated with the first term representing the sourcing percentage from the Asian supplier and the second term from the European supplier. Each break-up was simulated for two levels of demand risk. Total number of scenarios were 32 i.e. 4 supplier combinations X 4 supplier business break ups X 2 demand risk levels. Each of the scenarios was replicated for a disruption leading to a total of 64 scenarios for the complete study. The relative precision procedure discussed earlier was used for sample size determination in this study. The run length was set to two years. All scenarios stabilized by the end of 45 days. Therefore, the warm-up period was set to 45 days. In addition, extensive sensitivity analysis was undertaken by varying the values of independent variables and select model parameters.

Step 8: Data Analysis

Elaboration of complete results is beyond the scope of this chapter, however a brief discussion on types of conclusions that may be drawn from a simulation model are presented. Results discussed here are based on consideration of high risk Asian and low risk European suppliers only. The other two suppliers, low risk Asian and high risk European, are excluded.

Main analyses were based on Tukey's multiple comparison of cell means. In addition, methods used to analyze the results included visual inspec-

tion of graphical outputs; mean, lower and upper limits, standard deviation, and percentage changes in performance measures.

Further sensitivity analysis was done by varying assembly costs. It turned out that reduction in assembly costs, faster assembly times that lead to lower penalty cost, or longer lead times to customers had greater impact on profits as compared to sourcing from more reliable high-cost suppliers.

CONCLUSION

This paper presented a simulation model development process for modeling disruptions and other crises events in global virtual enterprise networks and an illustration case study of its application. A detailed discussion of each step, along with examples drawn from simulation studies reported in leading logistics journals as well as specific issues for disruption and risk management in a virtual enterprise network were presented. To summarize the discussion, for modeling risks in a virtual enterprise network, important questions need to be answered for each step by all individuals collectively involved in model development. Table 5 provides a list of select questions.

Mathematical modeling (including simulation) is a widely used research method in the leading logistics and supply chain journals (Sachan &

Table 5. Summary of select questions

Step 1: Problem Formulation	
1	Have we involved, at the least, all direct stakeholders in the problem formulation?
2	Do we have a thorough and common understanding of the problem stated? Is the problem clearly formulated?
3	Have we clearly and consensually identified the key concerns, the decisions that need to be made, and the expected outcomes of the simulation model?
Step 2: Specification of Dependent and Independent Variables	
1	Have we involved all direct stakeholders and subject matter experts in the identification of important variables?
2	Are all relevant dependent and independent variables needed to solve the problem specified in Step 1 above included?
3	Is there evidence from prior literature on the importance of variables? If yes, have we looked into those studies for guidance?
4	Have we clearly defined all independent and dependent variables?
Step 3: Conceptual Model Development and Verification	
1	Have we laid out all important assumptions, algorithms, model components, mathematical and logical relationships between variables, data summaries and any other model aspects of interest?
2	Did we involve so-called "outsiders" such as colleagues from a different department, academics, or external consultants for conceptual validation of the proposed model?
3	Are we confident that the model is developing in accordance with the problem formulated in Step 1? Will this model provide the required answers?
4	Does the conceptual model reflect the collective opinion of important stakeholders? If not, techniques such as Delphi and FEMA may be employed.
5	Did we perform a structured walk-through of the model with knowledgeable audience?
6	Are we convinced that those who served as the audience have a reasonable and unbiased knowledge of the subject-matter?
7	Have we documented all important assumptions, algorithms, model components, and relationships between variables?
Step 4: Data Collection	
1	Do we have an exhaustive list of data required to specify model parameters, system configuration, operating policies, and independent variables?
2	Have we identified sources and/or owners of the date required? Do we have the cooperation of other outside entities that own the data? If any data is missing, how will we model it?
3	If we are using any computer-generated data, do we have a rationale for it?
4	Have we ensured that the data is complete, accurate, and up-to-date?
5	If some data is in qualitative form, how will it be quantified? Will we employ techniques such as Delphi and FMEA?
Step 5: Verification of Computer Model	
1	Have we broken down the problem into smaller model components such that the objective, the input and output variables, and the links to other components may be easily programmed?
2	Have we developed flowcharts that reflect the logical relationships in the model?
3	Were the model sub-components and the complete model adequately verified against manually calculated or exiting data?
4	Were the output of parts of the model (sub-structures) checked for reasonableness?
5	Was the computer model checked by at least one person other than the person who coded the model?
6	If tools such as animation are available, did we visually inspect the model operations?
Step 6: Model Validation	
1	Did we consult individuals other than those involved in model development and consulted during model validation?
2	Was a structured walk-through of the computer-based model performed with subject matter experts and intended users of the model?

continued on the following page

Table 5. continued

Step 1: Problem Formulation	
3	Were the reviewers of the simulation results convinced about the reasonableness of the results generated by the model?
4	What statistical techniques such as input-output transformation were used for model validation?
5	If results validation was not done, did we follow a rigorous model development process to be convinced of the validity of the model?
6	Was sensitivity analysis undertaken to identify the boundaries for the model?
Step 7: Model Execution	
1	What sample size, run length, and warm-up period were used?
2	Is the rationale for sample size, run length, and warm-up period stated?
Step 8: Results Analysis	
1	Which statistical techniques were used?
2	Are the analysis techniques statistically appropriate?

Adapted from: Manuj, Mentzer, and Bowers (2009)

Datta, 2005). Unfortunately, a review of the literature reveals that research in logistics and supply chain journals does not satisfactorily address and/ or report the efforts taken to maintain the rigor of simulation studies (Manuj, Mentzer & Bowers, 2009). Although simulation modeling is a powerful technique to model and understand system behavior, incorrect modeling can lead to costly and time-consuming mistakes. A review of logistics and supply simulation research reveals there are very few studies that report in detail on the eight steps identified in this chapter. Thus, there is no set standard for evaluation of simulation studies in logistics and supply chain journals.

To this end, this chapter provides a framework to design rigorous simulation studies to study risk and disruption events in virtual enterprise networks. For both reviewers and researchers, this chapter provides a comprehensive framework and checklist to establish the rigor of simulation research. Following this framework may better help a researcher convince the reader that the resultant models and conclusions are rigorous (i.e., trustworthy). For practitioners, this framework may assist in deciding whether to trust the results of such research and apply it to real virtual enterprise network situations. That said, it is important to note that some steps may not apply to a particular study. In such cases, it is up to the reviewer or user of a study to make judgment calls on whether each criterion has been satisfactorily addressed.

Based on the above discussion, certain inferences about the appropriateness of simulation methodology may be drawn. First, simulation should not be used when the goal is to generalize to a population of interest. Survey research is more appropriate in such cases. Second, simulation is usually not appropriate when an analytical solution is possible, or even preferable (Banks, 1998). Simulation models do not provide optimal results, but rather are best for comparing a fixed number of alternatives (Law, 2006). Another method called the Monte Carlo method that considers random sampling of probability distribution functions as model inputs to produce hundreds or thousands of possible outcomes may be more appropriate in certain cases. This method is useful when the number of factors affecting the outcome is large.

A note on the limitation of simulation models is also appropriate here. Simulation results may be difficult to interpret as most simulation outputs are essentially random variables and are based on random inputs. It may, at times, be difficult to interpret whether an observation results from system interrelationships or randomness (Banks, 1998). However, this last limitation may be adequately addressed by involving a knowledgeable statistician during the design and result-interpretation phases of model development.

FUTURE RESEARCH DIRECTIONS

There is a fair scope for improving the standard of simulation model studies published in leading journals. First, a review of the extant literature reveals that often the assumptions are not explicitly stated and it is left to the reader to infer them. Assumptions such as safety stock or sourcing policies may have significant implications on the applicability and limitations of simulation results. Thus, it is critical that all assumptions be clearly stated. Second, a thorough discussion of limitations not only minimizes misguidance but also opens doors for future research that may attempt to relax assumptions or extend the model to reduce limitations. Third, as mentioned earlier, there is a variety of simulation tools available to modelers. A brief discussion on the choice of a tool or a package, and its advantages and disadvantages should also be included to assist other researchers in making an informed choice.

REFERENCES

Ahuja, M. K., & Carley, K. M. (1998). Network structure in virtual organizations. Journal Of Computer- Mediated Communication. 3(4), Special issue on virtual organizations.

Alexopolous, C., & Seila, A. F. (1998). Output data analysis. In J. Banks (Ed.), Handbook of Simulation: Principles, Methodology, Advances, Applications, and Practice (pp. 225-272). New York: John Wiley and Sons.

Allen, M. K., & Emmelhainz, M. A. (1984). Decision support systems: an innovative aid to managers . *Journal of Business Logistics, 5*(2), 128–143.

Appelqvist, P., & Gubi, E. (2005). Postponed variety creation: case study in consumer electronics retail . *International Journal of Retail & Distribution Management., 33*(10), 734–748. doi:10.1108/09590550510622281

Banks, J. (1998). Principles of simulation. In J. Banks (Ed.), Handbook of Simulation: Principles, Methodology, Advances, Applications, and Practice (pp. 3-30). New York: John Wiley and Sons.

Bass, F. M. (1969). A new product growth model for consumer durables. *Management Science, 15*(5), 215–227. doi:10.1287/mnsc.15.5.215

Bienstock, C. C. (1996). Sample size determination in logistics simulations. *International Journal of Physical Distribution & Logistics Management., 26*(2), 43–50. doi:10.1108/09600039610113191

Bienstock, C. C., & Mentzer, J. T. (1999). An experimental investigation of the outsourcing decision for motor carrier transportation. *Transportation Journal., 39*(1), 42–59.

Bowersox, D. J., & Closs, D. J. (1996). Logistical Management: The Integrated Supply Chain Processes. New York: McGraw-Hill.

Bucklin, L. P. (1965). Postponement, speculation and the structure of distribution channels. *JMR, Journal of Marketing Research, 2*(1), 26–31. doi:10.2307/3149333

Canbolat, Y. B., Gupta, G., Matera, S., & Chelst, K. (2005). Analyzing risk in sourcing design and manufacture of components and subsystems to emerging markets. Paper presented at the annual conference of the Decision Sciences Institute, San Francisco.

Capo-Vicedo, J., Capo-Vicedo, J., Exposito-Langa, M., & Tomas-Miquel, J.-V. (2008). Creation of interorganizational networks of small and medium enterprises: virtual netchain concept. *The ICFAI Journal of Business Strategy.*, *5*(4), 23–39.

Chang, Y., & Makatsoris, H. (2001). Supply chain modeling using simulation. *International Journal of Simulation*, *2*(1), 24–30.

Chopra, S., & Sodhi, M. S. (2004). Managing risk to avoid supply-chain breakdown. *MIT Sloan Management Review.*, *46*(1), 53–62.

Dhebar, A. (1993). Managing the quality of quantitative analysis. *Sloan Management Review*, *34*(2), 69–75.

Fisher, M. L. (1997). What is the right supply chain for your product? *Harvard Business Review*, *75*(2), 105–116.

Fishman, G. S., & Kiviat, P. J. (1968). The statistics of discrete event simulation. *Simulation*, *10*(4), 185–195. doi:10.1177/003754976801000406

Forrester, J. W. (1961). Industrial Dynamics. Cambridge, MA: M.I.T. Press.

Fricker, R. D. Jr, & Goodhart, C. A. (2000). Applying a bootstrap approach for setting reorder points in military supply systems. *Naval Research Logistics*, *47*(6), 459–478. doi:10.1002/1520-6750(200009)47:6<459::AID-NAV1>3.0.CO;2-C

Georgantzas, N. C. (2001). Virtual enterprise network: the fifth element of corporate governance. *Human Systems Management.*, *20*(3), 171–189.

Grabowski, M., & Roberts, K. H. (1999). Risk mitigation in virtual organizations. *Organization Science*, *10*(6), 704–721. doi:10.1287/orsc.10.6.704

Grefen, P., Mehandjiev, N., Kouvas, G., Weichhart, G., & Eshuis, R. (2009). Dynamic business network process management in instant virtual enterprises. *Computers in Industry*, *60*(2), 86–103. doi:10.1016/j.compind.2008.06.006

Hallikas, J., Virolainen, V.-M., & Tuominen, M. (2002). Risk analysis and assessment in network environments: A dyadic case study. *International Journal of Production Economics*, *78*(1), 45–55. doi:10.1016/S0925-5273(01)00098-6

Hendricks, K. B., & Singhal, V. R. (2005). An empirical analysis of the effect of supply chain disruptions on long-run stock price performance and equity risk of the firm. *Production & Operations Management.*, *14*(1), 35–52.

Holland, W., & Sodhi, M. (2004). Quantifying the effect of batch size and order errors on the bullwhip effect using simulation. *International Journal of Logistics: Research & Applications.*, *7*(3), 251–261.

Huang, M., Ip, W. H., Yang, H., Xingwei, W., & Lau, H. C. W. (2008). A fuzzy synthetic evaluation embedded tabu search for risk programming of virtual enterprises. *International Journal of Production Economics*, *116*(1), 104–114. doi:10.1016/j.ijpe.2008.06.008

Johnson, M. E. (2001). Learning from toys: lessons in managing supply chain risk from the toy industry. *California Management Review*, *43*(3), 106–124.

Keebler, J. S. (2006). Rigor in logistics and supply chain models. Paper presented at the annual meeting of the Council of Supply Chain Management Professionals, San Antonio, TX.

Kleindorfer, P. R., & Saad, G. H. (2005). Managing disruption risks in supply chains. *Production & Operations Management.*, *14*(1), 53–68.

Law, A. M. (2005). How to build valid and credible simulation models. Winter Simulation Conference. pp. 24-32, Orlando, Fl. Retrieved April 1, 2009, from http://www.informs-sim.org/wsc05papers/004.pdf.

Law, A. M. (2006). Simulation Modeling and Analysis. New York: McGraw-Hill.

Lazzarini, S. G., Chaddad, F. R., & Cook, M. L. (2001). Integrating supply chain and network analyses: The study of netchains. *Journal of Chain and Network Science.*, *1*(1), 7–22. doi:10.3920/JCNS2001.x002

Li, H., & Xiao, R. (2006). A multi-agent virtual enterprise model and its simulation with Swarm.

Makukha, K., & Gray, R. (2004). Logistics partnerships between shippers and logistics service providers: the relevance of strategy. *International Journal of Logistics: Research & Applications.*, *7*(4), 361–377.

Manuj, I., & Mentzer, J. T. (2008). Global supply chain risk management. *Journal of Business Logistics.*, *29*(1), 133–155.

Manuj, I., Mentzer, J. T., & Bowers, M. R. (2009). Enhancing the rigor of computer-based simulation research in logistics and supply chain management. *International Journal of Physical Distribution and Logistics Management.*, *39*(3), 172–201. doi:10.1108/09600030910951692

Mentzer, J. T., Dewitt, W., Keebler, J. S., Min, S., Nix, N. W., Smith, C. D., & Zacharia, Z. G. (2001). Defining supply chain management. *Journal of Business Logistics.*, *22*(2), 1–26.

Mentzer, J. T., & Gomes, R. (1991). The strategic planning model: a PC-based dynamic, stochastic, simulation dss generator for managerial planning. *Journal of Business Logistics.*, *12*(2), 193–219.

Potter, A., & Disney, S. M. (2006). Bullwhip and batching: an exploration. *International Journal of Production Economics*, *104*(2), 408–418. doi:10.1016/j.ijpe.2004.10.018

Pritsker (1998). Principles of simulation modeling. In J. Banks (Ed.), Handbook of Simulation: Principles, Methodology, Advances, Applications, and Practice (pp. 31-51). New York: John Wiley and Sons.

Rosenfield, D. B., Copacino, W. C., & Payne, E. C. (1985). Logistics planning and evaluation when using 'what-if' simulation . *Journal of Business Logistics.*, *6*(2), 89–119.

Sachan, A., & Datta, S. (2005). Review of supply chain management and logistics research. *International Journal of Physical Distribution & Logistics Management.*, *35*(9), 664–704. doi:10.1108/09600030510632032

Sankar, N. R., & Prabhu, B. S. (2001). Modified approach for prioritization failures in a system failure mode and effects analysis. *International Journal of Quality & Reliability Management*, *18*(3), 324–335. doi:10.1108/02656710110383737

Sargent, R. G. (2007). Verification and validation of simulation models. In Proceedings of the 2007 Winter Simulation Conference, Washington, DC (pp. 124-37). Retrieved April 1, 2009, from http://www.informs-sim.org/wsc07papers/014.pdf.

Shang, J. S., Li, S., & Tadikamalla, P. (2004). Operational design of a supply chain system using the taguchi method, response surface methodology, simulation, and optimization. *International Journal of Production Research*, *42*(18), 3823–3849. doi:10.1080/00207540410001704050

Silver, E. A., Pyke, D. F., & Peterson, R. (1998). Inventory Management and Production Planning and Scheduling. New York: Wiley.

Sykes, S. R. (2006). Supply chain risk management - gaining a baseline grasp on an increasingly important challenge. *CSCMP Supply Chain Comment*, *40*(Jan/Feb), 12–13.

Towill, D. R., & Disney, S. M. (2008). Managing bullwhip-induced risks in supply chains. *International Journal of Risk Assessment & Management.*, *10*(3), 238–262. doi:10.1504/IJRAM.2008.021376

Van Der Vorst, J. G. A. J., Beulens, A. J. M., De Wit, W., & Van Beek, P. (1998). Supply chain management in food chains: improving performance by reducing uncertainty. *International Transactions in Operational Research*, *5*(6), 487–499. doi:10.1016/S0969-6016(98)00049-5

Zhang, C., & Zhang, C. (2007). Design and simulation of demand information sharing in a supply chain. *Simulation Modelling Practice and Theory*, *15*(1), 32–46. doi:10.1016/j.simpat.2006.09.011

Zinn, W., & Bowersox, D. J. (1988). Planning physical distribution with the principle of Postponement. *Journal of Business Logistics.*, *9*(2), 117–136.

Zsidisin, G. A., Ellram, L. M., Carter, J. R., & Cavinato, J. L. (2004). An analysis of supply risk assessment techniques. *International Journal of Physical Distribution & Logistics Management.*, *34*(5), 397–413. doi:10.1108/09600030410545445

ADDITIONAL READINGS

Arlbjørn, J. S., & Halldorsson, A. (2002). Logistics knowledge creation: reflections on content, context and processes. *International Journal of Physical Distribution & Logistics Management.*, *32*(1/2), 22–40. doi:10.1108/09600030210415289

Brindley, C. (2004). Supply Chain Risk. Burlington, VT: Ashgate Publishing.

Davis-Sramek, B., & Fugate, B. S. (2007). State of logistics: a visionary perspective. *Journal of Business Logistics.*, *28*(2), 1–34.

Handfield, R., & McCormack, K. (Eds.). (2008). Supply Chain Risk Management. Boca Raton, FL: Auerbach Publications.

Jüttner, U. (2005). Supply chain risk management. *International Journal of Logistics Management.*, *16*(1), 120–141. doi:10.1108/09574090510617385

Lee, Y. H., Cho, M. K., Kim, S. J., & Kim, Y. B. (2002). Supply chain simulation with discrete-continuous combined modeling. *Computers & Industrial Engineering*, *43*(1/2), 375–392. doi:10.1016/S0360-8352(02)00080-3

Longo, F., & Mirabelli, G. (2008). An advanced supply chain management tool based on modeling and simulation. *Computers & Industrial Engineering*, *54*(3), 570–588. doi:10.1016/j.cie.2007.09.008

McGrath, J. E. (1982). Dilemmatics: the study of research choices and dilemmas, In J. E. McGrath, J. Martin, & R. A. Kula (Eds.), Judgment Calls in Research. Beverly Hills, CA: Sage Publications, (pp.69-102).

Min, H., & Zhou, G. (2002). Supply chain modeling: past present and future. *Computers & Industrial Engineering*, *43*(1/2), 132–150.

Naylor, T. H., Wertz, K., & Wonnacott, T. H. (1969). Spectral analysis of data generated by simulation experiments with econometric models. *Econometrica*, *37*(2), 333–352. doi:10.2307/1913541

Norrman, A., & Jansson, U. (2004). Ericsson's proactive supply chain risk management approach after a serious sub-supplier accident. *International Journal of Physical Distribution & Logistics Management.*, *34*(5), 434–456. doi:10.1108/09600030410545463

Ross, S. M. (1993). Introduction to Probability Models. San Diego, CA: Academic Press.

Waters, D. (2007). Supply Chain Risk Management: Vulnerability and Resilience in Logistics. Philadelphia: Kogan Page.

Winter simulation conference website. Retrieved April 1, 2009, from http://www.informs-sim.org/wscpapers.html

Chapter 8
A Theoretical Framework for a Simulation–Based Analysis of Supply Chain Risk Management

Ruslan Klimov
Riga Technical University, Latvia

Yuri Merkuryev
Riga Technical University, Latvia

Juri Tolujew
The Otto von Guericke University of Magdeburg, Germany

ABSTRACT

Supply chain management under uncertainty and risk has become the target of extensive research. A review of the corresponding literature indicates mainly theoretical approaches, which attempt to provide solutions to certain problems. In this chapter, a theoretical framework of supply chain risks analysis is proposed. Within this framework, studied risks are determined by possible disruptions that affect supply chain ability to function normally. Thus, supply chain performance parameters are taken as a basis for a risk measurement system. Correspondingly, supply chain reliability parameters and performance fluctuations are studied in order to manage risks. A possible implementation of the proposed framework is discussed through the presentation of a simulation example. Still, the evaluation of the proposed framework's practical application remains an item of the future research agenda. The ultimate objective of the research presented in this chapter is the elaboration of a software solution for supply chain modelling and risk evaluation.

INTRODUCTION

Nowadays, the application of logistics techniques is becoming a common and important part of business management. Current logistics achievements which require the use of modern information technologies allow the creation of complex management systems that potentially provide a great profit. At the same time, these complex systems contain many risks that can seriously disrupt business activities.

Supply chain is perceived as a complex organizational form which is very sensitive to possible

DOI: 10.4018/978-1-61520-607-0.ch008

disruptions due to a high level of interdependencies between the activities of its member companies. On the other hand, cooperation between members provides a wide range of opportunities for supply chain disruption mitigation. Still, supply chain risk management is a quite new research area, which became the target of intensive research only a few years ago. An analysis of the corresponding literature reveals several approaches to supply chain risk management which mostly study how internal disruptions within firms can affect supply chain functionality. In addition, few are the studies that make good use of quantitative risk measurement systems.

This chapter proposes a theoretical framework for risk analysis in the context of supply chain management. The examined risks are connected with disruptions which are generally external to most supply chain members. First, the structure of a supply chain and basic performance parameters are the target of careful analysis. Then, a quantitative cost-based indicator which can be used for the effective measurement of identified risks is developed. In that sense, simulation is recognized as the most suitable instrument for studying the aforementioned performance parameters, which are used within the proposed risk analysis concept.

BACKGROUND

Literature regarding logistics and supply chain risk management is vast. A brief analysis indicates not only the large variety of risk management approaches, but also different types of risk perception within supply chain systems. This lack of standardization sometimes creates a relative confusion which attempts to address by providing a short but to the point discussion on supply chain risk management.

RISK AND UNCERTAINTY

First, the different perceptions on the terms of risk and uncertainty should be discussed. Though these terms have been the object of very extensive research in various scientific directions for many years, the clear and unique formulations of their meaning have not been stated yet (Brindley & Ritche, 2004). It is possible to define at least two basic schools of thought on the issue of whether risk and uncertainty have the same meaning. Some publications do not make a sharp distinction between the meanings of risk and uncertainty. Another way to distinguish between the two terms relies on the ability to make probability assessments: risk corresponds to events that can be associated with given probabilities; and uncertainty corresponds to events for which probability assessments are not possible (Chanvas, 2004; Borodzicz, 2005; Crouhy, Galai & Mark, 2006). This suggests that risks are easier to evaluate than uncertainties. It is also necessary to point out that unexpected profit is discussed as a possible risk variation in the context of financial management (Shapkin, A. & Shapkin, B., 2005). Still, these risks are beyond the scope of this chapter.

In the proposed research, any potential harm that may arise in the future due to current operation or some future events constitutes risk. It is suggested that any risk appears due to a changing environment formed by different uncertainties, and uncertainty is recognized as a negative characteristic of an environment (Cucchiela & Gastaldi, 2006; Waters 2007). Thus, the following risk definition is used: risk is any uncertainty that affects a system in an unknown fashion; its ramifications are unknown, but it brings great fluctuation in value and outcome (Mun, 2006). It should be noticed that each uncertainty can cause a risk event in the future, yet not all uncertainties produce risk for the operation of certain systems.

RISKS WITHIN SUPPLY CHAINS

Due to its specific nature, the definition and the meaning of risk can change within certain systems and their conditions (Christopher & Peck, 2004). Moreover, the potential complexity of supply systems increases the variety of risk perceptions. Thus, the precise formalization of studied risks is necessary for the implementation of correct management actions. It should be admitted that nowadays researchers use different interpretations of supply chain risk and consequently propose various risk mitigation approaches. Thus, some general discussions about supply chain risks, their definitions, classifications and management approaches are provided with the aim of research field recognition, within which the concept of risk management is proposed in the subsequent sections.

It can be acknowledged that the works of Zsidisin and et al. are some of the earliest studies in the area of supply chain risk management. According to Zsidisin & Ritchie (2008), supply chain risk is defined as:

- The potential occurrence of an incident or failure to seize opportunities with inbound supply in which its outcomes result in a financial loss for the firm.

In general, it is possible to classify supply risks in the following types (Tang & Tomlin, 2008):

- Supply cost risk –the risk that effective per-unit price can fluctuate over time due to variability in raw material prices and exchange rates, among other things;
- Supply commitment risk – the risk of unplanned costs due to restrictions of agreements with other partners;
- Supply continuity risk – the risk of material flow interruption due to disruptions related to quality, labour unrest, etc.

The classification below describes some examples of supply chain risks sources (uncertainties) mentioned by other researchers (Landeghem & Vanmaele, 2002; Jahns et al., 2006; Elkins et al., 2008; Melnyk et al., 2008), such as:

- Price fluctuations,
- Stochastic costs,
- Exchange rate,
- Supplier problems (lead-time, quality, loss of key supplier, etc.),
- Stochastic demand and customer regulations,
- Subcontracting availability and adverse changes in its financial conditions,
- IT systems failures,
- Available capacity and organizational failures,
- Political environment,
- Natural disruptions caused by nature, etc.

It is necessary to point out that Zsidisin's formalization of the term supply chain risk determines management goals mostly related to purchasing and supply processes (Faisal et al., 2007), i.e. physical problems with product delivery within a supply chain that have a detrimental financial effect on the firm. However, an alternative way to define supply chain risk is more connected with logistics activities (Norrman & Lindroth, 2005):

- risks that are related to the logistics activities in companies' flows of material and information.

Thus, many researchers recognize supply risks as a self standing supply chain management scientific area. For instance, the following supply chain risk groups are pointed out (Christopher & Peck, 2004; Juttner, 2005; Kersten et al., 2006; Bogataj, D. & Bogataj, 2007; Tang & Tomlin, 2008): supply risks, demand risks, process risks, control risks and environmental risks. Another definition of supply chain risk is as follows (Kersten et al., 2006):

- the damage – assessed by its probability of occurrence – that is caused by an event within a company, within its supply chain or its environment affecting the business processes of at least one company in the supply chain negatively.

The important thing is that the last definition specifies the following three risk event types by their area of affect: risks within a certain firm, risks within a whole supply system, and environmental risks. The supply chain risks mentioned above mostly affect the activities of a single company. At the same time, recent research indicates the necessity of identifying risks which might be external to any single company. These risks are associated with firms' dependencies and mostly relate to decisions made on strategic and tactical management level. Finally, environmental risks like natural disasters, adverse political changes, etc. are allocated to a separate group. Then, the general supply chain risks classification can be presented as follows (Christopher & Peck, 2004; Waters 2007):

- Internal to a particular firm,
- External to a firm, but internal to a supply chain (risks occur from interactions between members of the supply chain),
- External to a supply chain (risks arise from interactions with the environment).

The second risk group presented above is the target of our risk management concept. It should also be noted that risks which are internal to particular firms certainly affect the risks of the second group. Still, this effect, together with firms' interdependence links within a whole chain, should be considered from the point of view of a whole supply chain, not a single firm.

SUPPLY CHAIN RISK MANAGEMENT

It is fair to name Mathematical Economics and Financial Mathematics as the scientific fields with the most developed risk management techniques (Pike & Neale, 1999). Unfortunately, these techniques are hardly adoptable for supply chain risk management purposes. Nevertheless, the basic steps of risk management are similarly defined in most of the research efforts in different business areas, e.g. system analysis, risk identification, risk measurement, risk mitigation and monitoring. Generally, in the context of supply chains, risk measurement systems are mainly based on rank scales created by experts. The main problem is connected with difficulties in the mathematical evaluation of risk.

There are relatively few works on clearly defined risk management techniques. Generally, these works propose analytical supply chain models, where certain risks are defined as particular uncertainty parameters. Due to the potential complexity of supply systems, analytical modelling applications are very constrained by various simplifications and selective risk source considerations. For instance, Agrawal & Seshadri (1999) consider a single-period model of a simplified supply chain, where multiple retailers meet the classical newsvendor problem and deal with risk from the demand risk perspective only. This research was further enhanced by Chen & Seshadri (2006) who proposed an analytical model in an attempt to prove that the efficiency of a supply chain can be improved if the distributor utilizes less risky contracts to more risk averse retailers (instead of identical contracts to all retailers). Nagurney & Matsypura (2005) developed a complicated mathematical model of a global supply network. This model considers the decision-making (profit maximization) process, where supply and demand risks are taken as additional model constraints. Sodhi (2005) suggests a similar analytical model, in which a replenishment schedule for manufacturing is calculated on the basis of two risks metrics:

the risk of unmet demand and the risk of excess inventories at particular retailers. Here, the idea of risk measurement as expected costs (penalties) for a certain schedule should be noted. Demirkan & Cheng (2006) also consider an analytical model of a simple supply chain which provides end-customers with computer application services. The purpose of this research is to increase supply chain efficiency through coordination strategies in terms of risk and information sharing. Once again, risk is considered as the uncertainty of end-customer demand. In Chan & Kumar (2005), another model for supplier selection is proposed, which in a similar way to the research mentioned before, includes risk in the decision making system as an additional supplier attribute.. Chen & Zhang (2008) presented research on demand risk effects on the performance of a one-echelon supply chain. In this research, an annealing algorithm is used for resilient inventory policy determination. In their research, Brindley & Ritche (2004) consider risk as a function of particular variables - risk source types: environmental, industry, organizational, problem specific and decision-maker related variables. Similarly, Tsai et al. (2006) proposed a general risk indicator which can be calculated through different logistics risks, known as risk factors. The considered risks are classified into three groups: performance failure, organizational asset failure and market competition failure. The elaborated risk model considers the probability of occurrence of particular risks and the potential business losses. Similarly, a risk portfolio is described in Elkins et al. (2008). Faisal et al. (2007) suggested that for effective supply chain risk management, a risk mitigation environment should be created in which twelve risk mitigation variables and their interdependencies are considered. Then, graph theory and matrix method application are suggested for risk mitigation environment analysis. The obvious advantage of the proposed model is the opportunity to get quantitative results for evaluation of supply chain performance under risk. Finally, Kissani's (2006) research should be

mentioned, where interference theory is used for calculating acceptable supply chain reliability. The proposed analytical model represents the process of reliability improvement in case of uncertainties in supply and demand.

SIMULATION-BASED RISK MANAGEMENT

The idea of supply chain risk measurement is quite constrained by supply chain complexity. Once the number of considered risk factors is increased, the necessary analytical instrument becomes very sophisticated and not flexible enough for regular analysis. Moreover, classical analytical modelling is hardly adoptable for supply chain structural analysis in terms of additional risk identification. A good solution for various analyses of complex systems is the application of simulation techniques (Shannon, 1975). It is suggested that any network which consists of supply chain members, inter-related processes, various performance and risk parameters, can be represented by a simulation model.

There are many well-known benefits of simulation. For example, simulation allows one to evaluate outcomes of any decision before implementing them into real systems; simulation models are easier to understand than many analytical approaches; simulation allows one to create models whose analytical realization is impossible or complicated (Evans & Olson, 1998). It can be assumed that such advantages make simulation very useful for risk analysis. Today, simulation is used extensively in the context of logistic systems to model production and assembly operations, develop realistic production schedules, study inventory policies, analyze reliability and quality and equipment replacement problems, and design material handling systems. A good example of simulation-based supply chain risk management research can be found in Deleris & Erhun (2005), who developed the Monte Carlo simulation-based tool for risk measurement within supply chains. This model analyses the relation of supply chain performance to structural differences, and also evaluates potential losses originating in different risk events. In addition, Melnyk et al. (2008) suggest the application of discrete-event simulation in order to analyze the effect of supply chain disruptions on their performance. In the same path, Hennet et al. (2008) describe opportunities of discrete event simulation application in queuing networks and time-series models. These models aim to represent the occurrence of hazardous phenomena and their impact on supply chains.

In this chapter, an alternate simulation-based supply chain risk management approach is presented. It includes a supply chain performance measurement system which can be used for further disruption analysis and risk evaluation. The use of simulation permits the conduction of this analysis for supply chains with different structural parameters. In that sense, simulation models constitute a risk mitigation support tool, which is necessary for effective supply chain management under risk and uncertainty.

SUPPLY CHAIN RISK MANAGEMENT FRAMEWORK

This section presents a framework of simulation-based supply chain risk analysis. As already mentioned, the proposed idea is oriented toward risks which are external to particular supply members, but are internal to the supply network. At the same time, risks are considered in terms of vulnerability of total performance of the supply chain. In this way, both risks and rewards should be shared between the members of a supply chain (Norrman & Jansson, 2004).

According to Waters (2007), supply chain management is responsible for the movement of materials all the way from initial suppliers through to final customers. Thus, it is suggested that supply chain risk appears as any event that might affect

this movement and disrupt the planned flow of materials, i.e. the supply chain can't normally fulfil its main function. In a previous work of the authors (Klimov & Merkuryev, 2008), supply chain risk is defined as the possible disruptions that can affect supply chain's ability to function normally. In that sense, a risk analysis framework should consist of approaches for the study of fluctuations in supply chains with different structural abilities and in various cases of disruption.

SUPPLY CHAIN PERFORMANCE

According to the proposed definition, risk management is closely connected with supply chain performance. In the same way, Engelhardt-Nowitzki & Zsifkovits (2007) define that supply chain risks are positive or negative deviations from expected conditions that are manifested by means of relevant supply chain key performance indicators and originate from supply chain complexity. Thus, for effective supply chain risk management, a supply chain performance evaluation approach should be applied which can be used for further risk analysis. There are various alternatives in choosing appropriate performance parameters. A good categorization of supply chain performance metrics can be found in the definition of the SCOR (Supply Chain Operations Reference) model. (Bolstorff & Rosenbaum, 2003; Supply Chain Council, 2009):

- Supply chain delivery reliability,
- Supply chain responsiveness,
- Supply chain flexibility,
- Supply chain cost,
- Supply chain asset management efficiency,
- Profitability,
- Effectiveness of return.

In this chapter, we follow Kogan & Tapiero's (2007) suggestion that risks in a supply chain should be measured, valued and managed in terms of money i.e. by costs. Correspondingly, the category of supply chain costs is taken as a basis for the development of the proposed performance measurement system.

Let us consider an example of a supply chain. It consists of several raw material suppliers, manufacturers, transportation members and an end-client. Each member of the supply chain is imposed with numerous costs like: inventory holding costs, administrative costs, transportation costs, etc. Conditionally, supply chain performance can be represented by the summation (AC) of all local costs (LC) for all members of the supply chain:

$$AC = \sum\sum LC \qquad (1)$$

Still, taking into account the particularities of supply chain and risk management, the performance indicator should include an additional factor: the observation period. It is obvious that daily costs will change over time due to management policy factors, local disruptions, demand variations, etc. Thus, the costs parameter should be considered in a long time interval (T):

$$TC = \sum_{t=1}^{T} AC \qquad (2)$$

In order to utilize equation 2, local costs should be defined in more detail. Still, the previous discussion points out difficulties in supply chain analytical modelling. In most mentioned cases, supply chain risk analysis is constrained by the complexity of the applied mathematical instrument which leads to serious structural simplifications of the studied supply chain, ignorance of existing interdependencies between supply chain members, etc. Thus, it is proposed to use simulation as an instrument for supply chain performance values modelling.

It is suggested that a modern simulation-based tool can provide managers with supply chain

models which can pass over the above-mentioned difficulties, and at the same time, can be easily modified. All necessary supply chain cost computations can be substituted by simulation processes. The proposed framework, suggests three phases in simulation model development and application. First, the main structure of a supply chain is customized. Then, general and particular (at particular supply chain members) planning policies are determined. Finally, input data to the simulation model is entered and initialized (see Figure 1).

It should also be noted that use of simulation applications in analyzing the reliability of supply systems with different structural characteristics has already been discussed in a previous work of the authors (Klimov & Merkuryev, 2008). It is suggested to use discrete-event simulation, which is very common in supply chain modelling practice. After model development and execution of the simulation experiment, the output statistics can be used for further risk analysis, which should include a precise risk measurement system. It is important to note that the use of simulation is dictated by the necessity of obtaining stochastic data, i.e. there is no need to look for a simulation-based optimization scenario for a supply chain.

SUPPLY CHAIN RISK MEASUREMENT

Equation 2 represents the objective function which is used as a basis for the measurement of supply chain performance vulnerability. Correspondingly, within our research, risk analysis is considered through vulnerability expectations, but necessary statistics are collected using simulation techniques. In our case, only two types of costs are considered: inventory holding costs and backordering costs. Moreover, according to previously defined supply chain functions, costs, which don't affect supply chain total

Figure 1. Simulation-based analysis

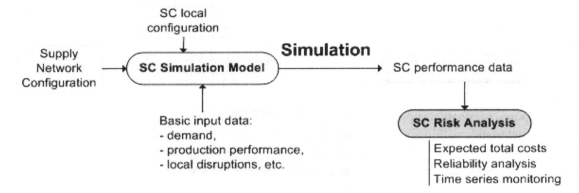

costs directly, are not taken into account. Thus, backordering costs are considered only for the retailer (market).

The proposed approach utilizes several risk management techniques within the context of a simulation example, which are described in the remainder of this section.

Expected Total Costs

- Let us consider a simple example of a supply chain (see Figure 2). It is assumed that several alternatives in supply chain configuration (or reconfiguration) are available, such as:. Different structure of the supply network,

- Different raw material suppliers with custom supply services and costs,

- Different transport organization alternatives,

- Various production planning strategies at particular manufacturing nodes, etc.

Each alternative of a supply chain configuration represents a unique scenario which can be characterized by its operational cost. Still, in cases of uncertain environment, stochastic processes should be studied i.e. expected performance values fluctuations should be analyzed. One simple way to perform stochastic output data analysis is

to apply a technique similar to "Value-At-Risk" (widely used in financial mathematics). According to this technique, risk is considered as the maximal possible negative outcome for a certain studied time period. Thus, "Value-at-Risk" for a supply chain ($VaRTC$) can be defined as the value l where the probability that the total costs L exceed l is not larger than $(1-\alpha)$, where α defines a chosen level of confidence.

$$VaRTC = \inf \{l \in R: P(L>l) \leq 1-\alpha\} \qquad (3)$$

As already mentioned, the "Value-at-Risk" technique is widely used in the practice of finance institutions, where it proved to be a very effective and easy way of risk evaluation (for shorter time periods). Still, a few critical disadvantages are reported by experts. For our discussion, it can be pointed out that such a technique does not consider risks continuously. Thus, it cannot represent the impact of particular disruptions and failures in a supply chain. This means that risk is measured for a scenario without any serious variations, thus "what-if" analysis cannot be performed.

Reliability Analysis

By using the measurement of maximal losses, it is difficult to understand how irregular disruptions (or even small failures) affect supply chain performance and which of them have the most influence on it (or which time periods have negative performance aspects). Therefore, an analysis of continuous changes of a supply chain performance within the time period has to be performed, and reliability characteristics of a supply chain have to be studied.

It is proposed to consider supply chain performance characteristics within short time periods. As an example, costs can be measured at each modelled time moment (daily) according to Equation 1. Still, taking into account supply chain specifics, some periodic fluctuations (in a similar way to seasonality) can be relevant to evaluation of such costs. Daily costs will change over time due to management policy factors, local disruptions, demand variations, etc. Thus, it is necessary to implement a wider observation time period (W), which should be chosen by a supply chain expert according to the specific supply chain characteristics. Then, at each time moment (c), supply chain performance can be characterized by an average value of the chosen time horizon:

$$TCa = (AC_{c-W} + AC_{c-W+1} + ... + AC_c) / W \quad c \geq W \quad (4)$$

$$TCa = (AC_1 + AC_2 + ... + AC_c) / c \quad 0 < c < W \quad (5)$$

As a result, supply chain performance is represented by average daily costs. The next step is to apply these values for risk analysis. According to the definition adopted in this chapter, risks correspond to any deviation from normal functioning. Thus, it is suggested to analyze intensive decreases of the monitored performance value. For this purpose, in risk management practice, it is possible to define several conditional states ($X(t)$) for a system: normal state, emergency and crisis (Borodzicz, 2005). Normal condition defines normal functioning of a supply chain, when material, financial and information streams flow through the system within predefined tolerances, which results in normally expected values of the performance indicator. The long term decrease

of this parameter leads to an emergency state, which involves the necessity of a thorough situation analysis. Further decrease equals crisis, i.e. gross losses, which can fatally affect supply chain functioning:

X(t) = {normal state, emergency, crisis} = F(TCa) (6)

The management activities should be directed at holding the system in the normal state. Accordingly, the system will always try to reach the normal state. In this way, performance pattern can be easily studied in a graphical form. Finally, statistical data can be used for the evaluation of system reliability characteristics.

It should be noticed that a simplified reliability analysis of a supply chain is also made in a previous work by the authors, where mathematical reliability evaluation and simulation application rationalization were discussed (Klimov & Merkuryev, 2008). The developed simulation model consisted of identical supply chain "nodes", whose "failure rates" were used as model input data. Correspondingly, output results showed probabilities of fatal interruption of material flow (similarly to reliability analysis in electric circuits). The cost-based performance measurement system of this chapter, is more objective, e.g. no expert-based "failure rates" values are needed. At the same time, the impact of supply chain disruption is represented in a more easily absorbed form. A more detailed discussion about the current model will be provided in the next sections.

Time Series Monitoring

Analysis of simulation results can provide risk managers with a vision of supply chain performance fluctuations. In this way, an early risk prediction system can be developed. For this purpose, techniques for comparing subsequent time series should be studied. Let us consider a chosen supply chain management scenario which is simulated several times. The output data can be represented in the form of time series $(S_1, S_2 ...)$ of length n:

$$S_1 = s_1, s_2, ... s_p ... s_n \qquad (7)$$

These time series should be generalized in a single data sequence (S) of the same length n that characterizes the functioning trends of a supply chain. Now, let us introduce conditionally real data in the form of time series (Q) with a shorter length m $(n>m)$:

$$Q = q_1, q_2, ... q_p ... q_m \qquad (8)$$

The following comparison should indicate whether Q was a subsequence of the generalized data sequence (S). Then, if the studied subsequence matches a part of the simulated data sequence, further supply chain performance characteristics can be forecasted. For instance, a rapid grow of regular costs and crisis establishment can be predicted. For the purposes of our example, simple time series comparison techniques were used and the comparison process was realized within a "sliding window" of length m. Thus, for $(n-m)$ times, the differences of considered data sets were analysed within each time interval i. For evaluation of the difference, the following simple summation metrics were used:

$$\sum_{p=1}^{m} abs \left[s_{p+i} - q_p \right] \text{ and } \sum_{p=1}^{m-1} \left[\left(s_{p+i} - s_{p+i+1} \right) - \left(q_p - q_{p+1} \right) \right]$$
for all $i = (1;n-m)$ \qquad (9)

The detection of similarities between the studied real data set and forecasted performance fluctuation graphs can notify the adequacy of a chosen management strategy, and can support the determination of further system development trends. More detailed and complicated discussions of data set comparison can be found in Chu et al., 2002.

AN EXAMPLE OF SIMULATION-BASED SUPPLY CHAIN RISK ANALYSIS

In this section, a simulation example is discussed in an attempt to demonstrate possible experiments which can be performed within the context of supply chain risk analysis.

SUPPLY SYSTEM DETERMINATION

The supply chain displayed in Figure 2 is considered as an example of simulation implementation. The system under study supplies end-customers with a specific product consisted of raw materials (R.M.) and components (C). For the sake of analysis only two cost categories are considered: inventory holding and back-ordering costs.

There are three different types of raw materials: RM1 and RM2 are used for component production while RM3 together with components (C) are used in end product manufacturing. The final products are sold on a single market. Correspondingly, the supply chain consists of three raw material suppliers (S1, S2, S3), two manufacturers (P1, P2) and the market. The types of material that flow through the chain are the following: RM1, RM2, RM3, C and End-products (P). The first manufacturer spends 14 units of RM1 and 18 units of RM2 to produce 5 units of component C. The second manufacturer uses 3 units of C and 12 units of RM3 to produce 5 units of P. Additionally, all necessary transportation is executed by five transport companies (T1, T2 ... T5). However, transportation processes are tightly simplified. In cases of unmet demand (i.e. the quantity of the end-product is less than the sum of demand and backorders), backorders are registered and generate additional backordering costs. It can be noticed once again that, according to the defined conception of a supply chain, only daily backorders (B) of the client market are taken into account. On the other hand, costs of inventories are measured at each particular supply

Figure 2. Supply chain example

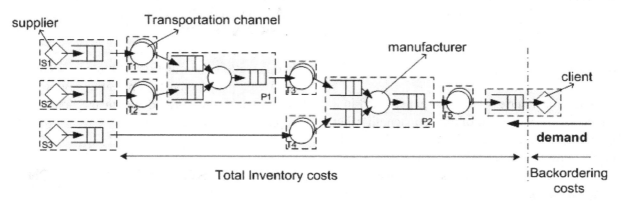

chain member (except raw material suppliers). Inventory holding costs (C^I) and backordering costs (C^B) per unit are defined separately for each supply chain member. According to Equation 1, supply chain performance is calculated by the following expression:

$$AC = B*C^B + \sum I*C^I \qquad (10)$$

In our example, basic suppliers' warehouses replenishment systems are independent of the studied network. Thus, for modelling purposes, each supplier inventory level increases every day for a random value determined by a triangular distribution function. Raw materials are transported from the suppliers to manufacturers using transportation channels. Each transportation channel is characterized by a lead time, which is also determined by a normal distribution function. There are no limitations to the number of available transportation channels, i.e. any material can be sent through any transportation channel at any time. New orders from the manufacturers can be made according to "Min-Max" inventory replenishment policies at their warehouses. Similarly, components from the first manufacturer (P1) warehouse are ordered following the "Min-Max" inventory replenishment policy at the second manufacturer (P2). On the other hand, end products from the second manufacturer are

transported to the market warehouse in batches of determined size, if current market inventory level is less than 20 units. The end demand from the market is determined by an exponential distribution function. The full list of studied costs and used distribution functions are presented in Table 1. Finally, manufacturing failures of the third supplier (S3) and second manufacturer (P2) are determined for use within the third simulation experiment.

In the remainder of this section, an example of risk analysis based on simulation-model output data for one year of supply chain operation is presented.

SIMULATION MODEL

The model is created with the support of ARENA (version 8.0) Discrete Event Simulation (DEV) software. The main objective of the simulation is to examine supply chain daily costs for a one year time period. The simulation process is described as follows:

- Activities of the first supplier (S1) are initialized: The level of inventories in the corresponding warehouse (see Figure 2) is increased by a finite number of units as determined by the predetermined

Table 1. Supply chain parameters

Supply chain member	Parameters
Costs	
First manufacturer (P1)	Inventory holding costs for: - RM1, - RM2, - C.
Second manufacturer (P2)	Inventory holding costs for: - RM3, - C, - P.
Market	Inventory holding costs for P. Backordering costs.
Inventory Replenishment Policies and Delivery Times	
Raw material suppliers (S1, S2, S3)	Warehouse daily replenishment follows the triangular distribution.
Manufacturers (P1, P2)	Warehouse Replenishment follows the "Min-Max" policy.
Transportation channels (T1, T2 … T5)	Delivery times follow the normal distribution.
Market	The single market is regularly replenished in batches of determined size. Daily demand follows the exponential distribution function.
System disruptions extensity and duration	
Raw material supplier (S3) and second manufacturer disruption extensity (P2)	Disruption extensities follow the exponential distribution function.
Raw material supplier (S3) and second manufacturer disruption duration (P2)	Disruption times follow the normal distribution.

distribution function. Then, raw materials are sent to P1's warehouse, provided that replenishment policy produces a demand signal. It is reminded that replenishment in the manufacturing level (P1, P2) follows a "Min-Max" policy.

- Delivery through transportation channel (T1): If a new order for raw materials from S1 is initialized, it is placed in the simulation block (T1), which represents a transportation channel. The delivery time for each order is defined by a normal distribution function. After that time elapses, the inventory level of the corresponding warehouse at the P1 is increased.
- Activities of the second supplier (S2) are initialized: Same as in the case of S1.

- Delivery through transportation channel (T2): Same as in the case of T1.
- Activities of the third supplier (S3) are initialized: The inventories of S3 are replenished in accordance with a triangular distribution function. If necessary, a quantity of raw materials is sent to P2. The necessary quantities are determined by a "Min-Max" inventory replenishment policy.
- Delivery through transportation channel (T3): Ordered quantities from S3 are placed in channel T3, where orders are delayed in accordance with defined transportation times. After the necessary delay is performed, the corresponding inventory level is increased.

- Activities of the first factory (P1) are initialized: If production resources of this block are not busy, and the factory has enough raw material inventories to start component production, the level of raw material inventories is decreased (minus 14 units of RM1 and minus 18 units of RM2) and a new semi-product unit production is initialized (production resources become busy). The production time follows a normal distribution function. When production finishes, the level of C inventory is increased by 5 units and production resources become available. Then, produced components are sent to the second factory (P2), if the applied policy (Min-Max) has created a demand signal.
- Delivery through transportation channel (T4): Ordered quantities are placed in channel T4 and are delayed in accordance with defined transportation times. After that, the corresponding inventory level at P2 is increased.
- Activities of the second factory (P2) are initialized: If production resources of this block are not busy, and the factory has enough component and RM3 inventories to start end-product production, the level of raw material and components is decreased (minus 3 units of C and minus 12 units of RM3) and new end-product production is initialized (production resources become busy). The production time follows a normal distribution function. When production finishes, the level of corresponding inventories is increased by 5 units and production resources become available.
- Delivery through transportation channel (T5): Ordered quantities are placed in channel T5 and are delayed in accordance with defined transportation times. After that, the level of market inventory is increased.
- Demand Fulfilment: If a warehouse has enough end products to fulfil the exponentially distributed demand and backorders then it does and inventory is decreased accordingly. If it can fulfil demand and part of the back ordered items, then inventory falls to zero and back order level increases accordingly
- Critical Supply Chain parameters and the supply chain performance indicator are evaluated (equations 4 and 5). Then, the simulation process starts over.

SIMULATION SCENARIOS

Risk analysis attempts an estimate of possible losses for certain configurations of the supply chain and supports the decision about the most appropriate network configuration. At the same time, planning of simulation experiments is an essential part of the risk analysis process. In the current chapter three simulation experiments (scenarios) are discussed. The first experiment represents the initial configuration of the supply chain as described in the previous section. In that scenario, it is assumed that all raw material suppliers and the component manufacturer are located significantly far from final production (P2) and the market. The second experiment assumes that final production facilities are moved closer to the suppliers. Finally, the third experiment provides additional modelling of physical disruptions, which can affect suppliers' ability to replenish their inventories. In Table 2, the input parameters of the proposed simulation study, for the three different operating scenarios, are presented.

In order to evaluate each scenario, a cost performance system is utilised, based on the following simulation output data:

- Daily inventory and backordering costs for the whole supply chain (see equation 10).
- Summation of all costs for a period of 365 days.

All three experiments realize 100 replications. Each replication is started with "warm-up" period of 3600 days (evaluated graphically).

The analysis of output data is taking place in three phases. First, maximal expected costs are evaluated that provide basic performance characteristics for a particular supply chain configuration. Then, an analysis of supply chain performance fluctuations within experiments is performed. Here, the variance of the collected data is the main analysis target: long periods of operation with high costs marks on bigger potential losses. At this point, a graphical representation is very important. Finally, a study of the available performance history graph is executed in order to validate possible forecasts and make additional statements about future system behaviour.

RESULTS

The simulation results consist of daily and annual total costs of the studied supply chain for each replication and scenario. The high number of replications in each experiment is crucial due to the necessity to perform adequate "Value-at-Risk" type evaluation. The output statistics should fit the normal distribution as much as possible. For

the purposes of the current example, one year *VaRTC* with α equal to 95% was evaluated using a historical modelling technique. So, according to Equation 3, the maximum expected total losses are equal to 34.000 cost units for the first experiment, 32.400 for the second experiment and 33.300 for the third one. Based on these results, one could easily conclude that there are benefits from second manufacturer relocation. At the same time, simulated disruptions of manufacturing process, point out profit decrease. Still, as mentioned earlier in the chapter, the proposed measurement system is more suitable for performance measurement and actually has restrictions in detailed analysis of disruptions effects. Thus, regular performance variation should be studied more carefully. In order to understand main trends in system performance development, smaller time periods should be considered. Equations 4, 5 and 10 were used to evaluate the indicator of supply chain performance within seven days ($W = 7$ days) and to create relevant graphs. Performance variations for each experiment are shown in Figure 3.

At this point, it should be noted that due to the large variation of obtained time series, statistical processing of the data sets for all replications is not performed in this chapter. Subsequently, within our demonstrative example, only one replication

Table 2. Input parameters for different simulation experiments

Experiment number:		1	2	3
Daily costs (€ per unit):				
First factory (P1)	Holding Cost (RM1)	0.15	0.15	0.15
	Holding Cost (RM2)	0.15	0.15	0.15
	Holding Cost (C)	0.35	0.35	0.35
Second factory (P2)	Holding Cost (C)	0.35	0.35	0.35
	Holding Cost (RM3)	0.15	0.15	0.15
	Holding Cost (P)	0.60	0.60	0.60
Market	Holding Cost (P)	0,60	0.60	0.60
	Backordering Cost	1.5	1.5	1.5

continued on the following page

Table 2. continued

Experiment number:			1	2	3
Component (5 units) and end-product (3 units) production times:					
First factory (P1)	Normal distribution		norm (1.6,0.5)	norm (1.6,0.5)	norm (1.6,0.5)
Second factory (P2)			norm (1.7,1)	norm (1.7,1)	norm (1.7,1)
Material and production delivery times:					
Transportation channels	Channel 1 (T1)		norm (12,0.5)	norm (12,0.5)	norm (12,0.5)
	Channel 2 (T2)		norm (13,0.5)	norm (13,0.5)	norm (13,0.5)
	Channel 3 (T3)		norm (9,1)	norm (3,0.2)	norm (3,0.2)
	Channel 4 (T4)		norm (5,0.7)	norm (5,0.7)	norm (5,0.7)
	Channel 5 (T5)		norm (3,0.2)	norm (9,1)	norm (9,1)
Inventory replenishment policies:					
First factory first warehouse	"Min-Max"	(20 to 200)		(20 to 200)	(20 to 200)
First factory second warehouse		(30 to 150)		(30 to 150)	(30 to 150)
Second factory first warehouse		(10 to 70)		(10 to 70)	(10 to 70)
Second factory second warehouse		(30 to 100)		(30 to 100)	(30 to 100)
Market	Constant size orders	10		20	20
Replenishment for the first raw material supplier (S1)	Triangular distribution	tria(1,2,4)		tria(1,2,4)	tria(1,2,4)
Replenishment for the second raw material supplier (S2)		tria(1,4,5)		tria(1,4,5)	tria(1,4,5)
Replenishment for the third raw material supplier (S3)		tria(2,5,8)		tria(2,5,8)	tria(2,5,8)
Daily demand representation:					
Market	Exp. distribution		expo (2,9)	expo (2,9)	expo (2,9)
System disruptions extensity and duration:					
(S3) failure extensity	Exp. distribution		-	-	expo (258)
(S3) failure duration	Normal distribution		-	-	norm (2,0.5)
(P2) failure extensity	Exp. distribution		-	-	expo (240)
(P2) failure duration	Normal distribution		-	-	norm (5,1)

for each experiment is considered for further risk evaluation.

Figure 3, represents a possible trend in the variation of supply chain performance (as it is defined in this chapter). Risk events correspond to high costs (spikes in the graph). In order to explore system operation abilities and to escape from non sufficient cases, conditional states for a supply chain should be determined (these states should be defined by risk managers): normal

Figure 3. Risk analysis graphical interpretation

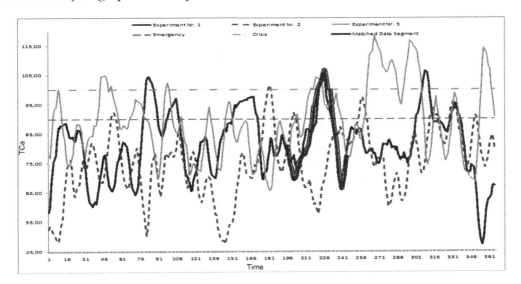

operation, emergency state and crisis state (see Figure 3). That means that managers should be aware of emergency and crisis situations while managing real systems and should forecast the probability and their duration. At the same time, after determination of thresholds for crisis and emergency states, system reliability parameters can be measured and used within risk management. In our case, following the simulation results of the first experiment, emergency and crisis thresholds were set on 90 and 100 costs units/day respectively. Based on that and by examining the graphs of Figure 3, the following results were obtained for the first experiment:

- The system operates in the emergency state for 15.34% (56 days) / year;
- The system, within a period of one year, regularly reaches the emergency state. Still, emergency has been transformed into crises only three times, i.e. the overall probability to get into crisis state from emergency is equal to 6.25%;
- The longest period of time, when system operates only in the emergency and crisis states, is equal to 20 days;

- The overall probability to get into emergency state from normal operation is equal to 2.07%.

A more detailed discussion about evaluation of reliability parameters for supply chain risk analysis can be found in Klimov & Merkuryev (2008).

In the same fashion and after the necessary modifications have been made, simulation experiments two and three were executed and the results are shown in the graphs of Figure 3. According to these results, conditions of experiment two result to a decrease of inventory holding and back order costs while experiment three which includes the impact of an external SC disruption, increases the overall cost of the supply chain under study. Additionally, traditional output data can be analyzed:

- Inventories (inventory holding costs) at particular warehouses;
- The level of unmet demand (backorders), etc.

The final step of our approach is forecasting supply chain performance for a certain period of time. In our example, an additional replication is performed for the first simulation experiment. The segment of output data set (time period of 50 days), which represents supply chain performance variations in this replication, is used as conventional replacement for a real data set. Then, this segment is compared with the results of the first replication. The comparison is based on equation 9. Additionally, segment matching can be defined graphically as it is shown in Figure 3. The data segment (presented by a heavy doubled line) fits closely the first experiment data graph (presented by a black line) starting from the 196th day. Thus, it is possible to assume about the real data set probable behaviour beyond the time-horizon of 50 days. For instance, the assumption about the growth of the performance value for another 10 days (until it becomes equal to 85) is made. In that way, simulation can be used as a tool that supports supply chain design and risk mitigation decisions about performed forecasts based on real performance data sets.

FUTURE RESEARCH DIRECTIONS

This chapter provides a theoretical framework of supply chain risk management, whose further development and application can be enhanced by both theoretical and practical research efforts. First of all, a supply chain performance measurement system which is used for risk determination should be validated in order to increase risk measurement adequacy. It is needed to determine the necessary supply chain parameters that will be included in this system. Performance attributes and categories should be discussed more carefully in order to implement the most significant ones into the risk measurement system. At the same time, the range of end-customer demand and the impact of its fluctuations should be analyzed. Then, mathematical techniques used for simulation output data analysis should be validated within the created systems.

It is also should be mention again that de-scribed model application requires the contribution of simulation specialists. Thus, additional practical research should be directed towards the development of a tool which might be used for autonomic model creation and the analysis of simulation results based on a description of the general parameters of the supply chain. The tool should consist of all the necessary techniques for risk evaluation and regular monitoring, and at the same time, it should give supply chain managers an opportunity to create their own structures of supply systems.

CONCLUSION

In this chapter, the theoretical framework of simulation-based analysis of supply chain risks is considered. Based on the discussion on risk perception and supply chain goals, supply chain risk is defined and potential techniques for supply chain risk management are presented. It is stated that usual risk measurement systems becomes quite constrained because of supply chain complexity and thus they are not flexible enough for regular analysis in supply chains. Thus, risk managers study supply chains with simplified structures and usually focuses their analysis on a few particular risks. The advised theoretical framework provides the risks measurement system, which is based on the supply chain performance evaluation. In this way, many risky events or unexpected disruptions within supply chains can be analyzed in a single system. Since most of the developed approaches for supply chain risk management have strong mathematical restrictions, the use of simulation is suggested. The simulation techniques provide necessary flexibility and ease for analysis of complex supply chains.

The discussed example consists of three simulation experiments which consider the supply chain with different structural and functional parameters. Based on the performance analysis of these experiments, each configuration of the supply chain is evaluated in terms of discussed supply chain risk analysis framework. Risk analysis procedures demonstrate the main advantages of the framework, which are the numerical risk interpretation, the graphical representation of the results and the ease of the supply chain structural and changing during the analysis. Still, the theoretical framework has shortcomings, which determination is stated as the target for future research.

REFERENCES

Agrawal, V., & Seshadri, S. (1999). Risk intermediation in supply chains. *Journal IIE Transactions*, *32*, 819–831.

Bogataj, D., & Bogataj, M. (2007). Measuring the supply chain risk and vulnerability in frequency space. *International Journal of Production Economics*, *108*, 291–301. doi:10.1016/j.ijpe.2006.12.017

Bolstorff, P., & Rosenbaum, R. (2003). *Supply chain excellence: a handbook for dramatic improvement using SCOR mode*.New York: Amakon.

Borodzicz, E. (2005). Crisis & security management. Atrium, UK: John Wiley & Sons Ltd.

Brindley, C., & Ritche, B. (2004). Introduction. In C. Brindley (Ed.), Supply chain risk (pp. 1-13). Hampshire, UK: Ashgate.

Chan, F., & Kumar, N. (2005). Global supplier development considering risk factors using fuzzy extended AHP-based approach. *The International Journal of Management Science*, *35*, 417–431.

Chanvas, J. (2004). Risk analysis in theory and practice. London: Elsevier Inc.

Chen, X., & Zhang, J. (2008). Supply chain risk analysis by using jump-diffusion model. In *Proceedings of the 2008 Winter Simulation Conference*, 638-646.

Chen, Y., & Seshadri, S. (2006). Supply chain structure and demand risk. *Journal of IFAC*, *42*, 1291–1299. doi:10.1016/j.automatica.2005.11.008

Christopher, M., & Peck, H. (2004). Building the resilient supply chain. *The International Journal of Logistics Management*, *15*, 1–14. doi:10.1108/09574090410700275

Chu, S., Keogh, E., Hart, D., & Pazzani, M. (2002). Iterative deepening dynamic time warping for time series. In *Proceedings of the 2nd SIAM International Conference on Data Mining*. 195-212.

Crouhy, M., Galai, D., & Mark. R. (2006). *The essentials of risk management*. New York: The McGraw-Hill.

Cucchiella, F., & Gastaldi, M. (2006). Risk management in supply chain: a real option approach. *Journal of Manufacturing Technology Management*, *16*, 700–720. doi:10.1108/17410380610678756

Deleris, A., & Erhun, F. (2005). Risk Management in Supply Networks Using Monte-Carlo Simulation. In *Proceedings of the 2005 Winter Simulation Conference*, (pp. 1643-1649).

Demirkan, H., & Cheng, H. (2006). The risk and information sharing of application services supply chain. *European Journal of Operational Research*, *187*, 765–784. doi:10.1016/j.ejor.2006.03.060

Elkins, D., Kulkarni, D., & Tew, J. (2008). Identifying and assessing supply chain risk. In B. Handfield & K. McCormack (Eds.), Supply chain risk management: minimizing disruptions in global sourcing (pp. 51-56). London: Auerbach Publications.

Engelhardt-Nowitzki, C., & Zsifkovits, H. (2007). Complexity-induced supply chain risks – interdependencies between supply chain risks and complexity management. In W. Kersten & T. Blecker (Eds.), Managing risks in supply chains (pp. 37-56). Berlin, Germany: Verlag.

Evans, J., & Olson, D. (1998). Introduction to Simulation and Risk Analysis. Upper Saddle River, New Jersey: Prentice-Hall.

Faisal, M., Banwet, D., & Shankar, R. (2007). Quantification of risk mitigation environment of supply chains using graph theory and matrix methods. *European Journal of Industrial Engineering, 1*, 22–39. doi:10.1504/EJIE.2007.012652

Hennet, J., Mercantini, J., & Demongodin, I. (2008). Toward an integration of risk analysis in supply chain assessment. In *Proceedings of the 20th European Modelling & Simulation Symposium*, (pp. 255-260).

Juttner, U. (2005). Supply chain risks management: understanding the business requirements from a practitioner perspective. *Journal of Logistics Management, 16*(1), 120–141. doi:10.1108/09574090510617385

Kersten, W., Boger, M., Hohrath, P., & Spath, H. (2006). Supply chain risk management: development of a theoretical and empirical framework. In W. Kersten & T. Blecker (Eds.), Managing risks in supply chains (pp. 3-17). Berlin, Germany: Verlag.

Kissani, I. (2006). Reliability improvement in supply chain design under demand and supply uncertainties. In W. Kersten & T. Blecker (Eds.), Managing risks in supply chains (pp. 57-75). Berlin, Germany: Verlag.

Klimov, R., & Merkuryev, J. (2008). Simulation model for supply chain reliability evaluation. *Journal: Technological and Economic Development of Economy, 14*, 300–311. doi:10.3846/1392-8619.2008.14.300-311

Kogan, K., & Tapiero, C. (2007) Supply chain games: operations management and risk valuation. New York: Springer.

Landeghem, H., & Vanmaele, H. (2002). Robust planning: a new paradigm for demand chain planning. *Journal of Operations Management, 20*, 769–783. doi:10.1016/S0272-6963(02)00039-6

Melnyk, A., Rodrigues, A., & Ragatz, G. (2008). Using simulation to investigate supply chain disruptions. In G. Zsidisin (Ed.), Supply chain risk: A handbook of assessment, management and performance (pp. 104-122). New York: Springer.

Mun, J. (2006). Modeling risks: applying Monte Carlo simulation, real options analysis, forecasting, and optimization techniques. Atrium, UK: John Wiley & Sons Ltd.

Nagurney, A., & Matsypura, D. (2005). Global supply chain network dynamics with multicriteria decision-making under risk and uncertainty [Electronic version]. *Journal of Transportation research, 41*, 585-612.

Norrman, A., & Jansson, U. (2004). Ericsson's proactive supply chain risk management approach after a serious sub-supplier accident. International . *Journal of Physical Distribution & Logistics Management, 34*, 434–456. doi:10.1108/09600030410545463

Norrman, A., & Lindroth, R. (2004). Categorization of supply chain risk and risk management. In C. Brindley (Ed.), Supply chain risk (pp. 14-27). Hampshire, UK: Ashgate. Jahns, C., Hartmann, E. & Moder, M. (2006). Managing supply risks: a system theory approach to supply early warning systems. In W. Kersten, & T. Blecker (Eds.), Managing risks in supply chains (pp. 195-212). Berlin,Germany: Verlag.

Paulson, U. (2004). Supply chain risk management. In C. Brindley (Ed.), Supply chain risk (pp. 79-96). Hampshire, UK: Ashgate.

Pike, R., & Neale, B. (1999). Corporate finance and investment: decisions and strategies. Upper Saddle River, NJ: Prentice-Hall.

Ritche, B., & Brindley, C. (n.d.). SCRM and performance – Issues and Challenges. In G. Zsidisin (Ed.), Supply chain risk: A handbook of assessment, management and performance (pp. 249-270). New York: Springer.

Shannon, R. (1975). System simulation. The art and science. Upper Saddle River, NJ: Prentice-Hall.

Shapkin, A., & Shapkin, B. (2005). Risk theory and risk situation modelling. Moscow: Dashkov&Co.

Sodhi, M. (2005). Management demand risk in tactical supply chain planning for a global consumer electronics company. *International Journal of Production and Operations Management, 14,* 69–79.

Tang, C. (2006). Perspectives in supply chain risk management. *International Journal of Production Economics, 103,* 451–488. doi:10.1016/j. ijpe.2005.12.006

Tang, C., & Tomlin, B. (2008). How much flexibility does it take to mitigate supply chain risks? In G. Zsidisin (Ed.), Supply chain risk: A handbook of assessment, management and performance (pp. 155-174). New York: Springer.

Tsai, M., Hung, S., & Han, C. (2006). Key risk factors for logistics outsourcing – a case of retailing industry in Taiwan. In W. Kersten & T. Blecker (Eds.), Managing risks in supply chains (pp. 179-192). Berlin, Germany: Verlag.

Waters, D. (2007). *Supply Chain Risk Management: Vulnerability and Resilience in Logistics.* London: Kogan Page Limited.

Zsidisin, G., & Ritchie, B. (2008). Supply chain risk management – developments, issues and challenges. In G. Zsidisin (Ed.), Supply chain risk: A handbook of assessment, management and performance (pp. 1-11). New York: Springer.

ADDITIONAL READINGS

Banks, J., Carson, J., Nelson, B., & Nicol, M. (2005). Discrete-event system simulation. Upper Saddle River, NJ: Prentice-Hall.

Brundschuh, M., Klabjan, D., & Thurston, D. (2003). *Modeling robust and reliable supply chains. Optimization Online e-print.* Retrieved June 25, 2009, from http://www.optimization-online.org/db_html/2003/07/679.html

Chen, Y., Naxcimento, M., Chin Ooi, B., & Tung, A. (2007). SpADe: On Shape-based Pattern Detection in Streaming Time Series. In *Proceedings of the 23rd ICDE,* (pp. 786-795).

Chopra, S., & Meindel, P. (2007). Supply chain management: strategy, planning, and operation. Upper Saddle River, NJ: Prentice-Hall.

Christopher, M. (2005). Logistics and supply chain management: creating value-adding networks. Upper Saddle River, NJ: Prentice-Hall.

Kelton, D., Sadowski, R., & Sadowski, D. (2007). Simulation with Arena. New York: McGraw-Hill.

Law, A. (2007). Simulation modeling and analysis. New York: McGraw-Hill.

Pruyt, E. (2007). System dynamics and uncertainty, risk, robustness, resilience and flexibility. In *Proceedings of the 25th International Conference of the System Dynamics Society and 50th Anniversary Celebration.*

Robinson, S. (2004). Simulation: The practice of model development and use. Atrium, UK: John Wiley & Sons Ltd.

SCOR. (n.d.). *SCOR Supply chain council.* Retrieved July 30, 2009, form http://www.supply-chain.org/

Zeigler, B., Praehofer, H., & Gon Kim, T. (2000). Theory of Modeling and Simulation. London: Elsevier Inc.

Section 2
Models and Applications

Chapter 9
Aligning Product Design with the Supply Chain:
Towards a Responsive and Resilient Enterprise

Omera Khan
University of Manchester, UK

Alessandro Creazza
Università Carlo Cattaneo LIUC, Italy

ABSTRACT

The continued rise in global sourcing and manufacturing has significantly extended supply chains for many companies and has added to their complexity, often implying business fragmentation and virtualization, and thus increase supply chain risk. At the same time, there is now a growing realization that the supply chain 'begins on the drawing board'; meaning that design decisions can dramatically impact the risk profile of the business. Historically, most organizations have been functional in their structure with responsibility for each stage in the value chain, including design being separate from the other. In today's challenging markets these 'silo' type structures have been found wanting as typically they are not capable of rapid response to fast-changing requirements. This paper is focused on the need to bring design into the heart of supply chain management to achieve a more responsive - and hence competitive - organization. Thus, the primary purpose of this paper is to propose that one of the ways to achieve a more responsive and resilient enterprise is by better aligning product design with the supply chain and hence developing a concurrent design strategy. The recommendations suggest ways in which managers and key decision makers can adopt a more 'design centric' approach to their supply chain, which has been shown to enhance the resilience and responsiveness of a firm.

INTRODUCTION

The globalization of supply chains and the trends to outsourcing and offshore manufacturing in search for lower costs have paradoxically exposed businesses to new risks and supply chain risk management has fast become a subject of heightened interest both in academic research and businesses world-wide (Cranfield, 2003). At the same time there is growing

DOI: 10.4018/978-1-61520-607-0.ch009

realization that the supply chain begins on 'the drawing board'; meaning that design decisions can dramatically impact the risk profile of the business (Krishnan & Ulrich, 2001). Hence, it is vital that design activities are integrated into the wider remit of supply chain management to increase a firm's resilience. As supply chains are longer and based on wider geographical areas, companies should find ways in which they can be more responsive and resilient. This requires more than simply introducing tools and techniques which can be useful in managing the day-to-day operations. It requires more strategic and organizational changes for better coordinating the supply chain processes with its product design processes as design is inextricably linked to supply chain risk. Therefore managing the alignment of product design and supply chain can bring significant benefits to supply chain performance, but likewise the misalignment could be disastrous for the supply chain. For example transportation costs and lead times can be affected by early design decisions and risk can be increased by being locked-in single source components (Burkett, 2006). Early involvement of supply chain professionals at the design stage could highlight and eliminate some of the risks that may creep up later in the supply chain when the costs to re-engineer the product or re-design the supply chain will be significantly higher, not to mention a major barrier to responsiveness. Unfortunately the evidence seems to be that, too often, product design decisions do not consider the through-life implications for the supply chain leading to obsolete stock in pipelines, market failures because of late product introductions and ultimately having dire consequences on a firm's ability to achieve market success.

A key challenge facing organizations in which design is a critical function is to integrate design and supply chain management in order to effectively meet customer needs and manage supply chain risk. The failure to do so could create problems at the manufacturing or logistics stages in the supply chain and thus, increase the risk of

supply chain disruption. These ideas signify that we must regard design as much more than just an activity which creates novel solutions or brings stylistic changes to products. There is in fact a more strategic role for design which impacts the total supply chain (Abeccassis, 2006; Ragatz et al, 1997).

The purpose of this paper is to understand the strategic relationship between product design and supply chain performance and how better alignment between the functions contributes towards building a more responsive and resilient supply chain. We first build a conceptual framework by reviewing the literature of the key areas using a structured and evidence-informed approach (Tranfield et al, 2003). This approach enables us to identify, select and analyze secondary evidence which contains any of the pre-defined research terms that were developed when we started the research. The major advantage of a structured literature approach is that it allows the researcher to undertake an in-depth and focused analysis of data which is most specific to the research. We then present the findings of three companies that were investigated to further explore the alignment between product design and the supply chain and to identify how the alignment contributes to a responsive and resilient enterprise. Following on from our cross-case examination we develop some general prescriptions and recommendations on aligning product design and the supply chain and illustrate this with a roadmap which we have developed from the research findings.

THE IMPORTANCE OF DESIGN: A CREATIVE TOOL TO ENHANCE COMPETITIVE ADVANTAGE

"Design is the second most important ingredient of success for rapidly growing businesses, 50% of manufacturers say that design is increasingly important to their competitive edge" (Design Council, 2004-2005).

It is evident that low prices should not be considered as the only strategy to respond to supply chain risks. Product design is recognized as a major source of differentiation in an increasingly competitive marketplace and it has been recognized as a strategic tool (Kotler & Rath, 1984). Porter (1985) refers to design as a discrete but value adding activity that allows a firm to perform activities more cheaply and better than its competitors. Design is a multifaceted concept, but in this paper we focus on product design as it embodies the supply chain, firstly because all products created by design have to be manufactured and transported through a supply chain and secondly because if the design of a product can offer quality and value for money in the perception of the consumer it can contribute to the competitiveness and success of the business.

The Cox Report, which was commissioned by the UK government in 2005, was fundamental in promoting the importance of design as a creative tool for increasing competitive advantage against the growing threat from emerging economies and their rapid pace of design and technology development. The Cox Report provided a number of guidelines to invest in design and for designers to focus on effective design management strategies across organizational boundaries with the aim to 'to bring high value-added products and services quickly and effectively to the market' (Cox Report, 2005). However, in order to fulfill this aim a more strategic approach for managing design process in the extended enterprise is required, one which is supported by agile and quick response strategies.

ALIGNING PRODUCT DESIGN WITH THE SUPPLY CHAIN

Design is an essential process for the supply chain because, through it, ideas can be profitably transformed into products for customers (Doyle & Broadbridge, 1999). This is especially true when fast-moving markets are regarded: consumer requirements are likely to rapidly and unpredictably change and if companies are focused on ensuring high effectiveness with high efficiency as well, they must adapt to these changes in a timely manner or they risk market failure. Concurrently managing product design and the supply chain is critical in solving this problem. In fact, the foundation of an effective response is not just having the design competence to identify what the customer wants but the ability to work with suppliers to ensure that they can deliver it at the right time, to the right quality and at the right cost.

Good supply chain management practice requires businesses to integrate processes such as procurement and logistics along with design to fully reap the benefits of a design driven supply chain. With customers increasingly demanding greater variety in products at lower costs, design has become an important means by which companies can gain a competitive advantage in their supply chains. For example, the design of products has a huge impact not only on market success, but also on the sourcing of components, production, and distribution and even on how final products will be displayed to customers in retail outlets. Therefore the way that the design process is managed and organized can have an impact on time-to-market. An important supply chain consideration is whether or not products can be manufactured to the desired specifications and with the right materials in adequate supply and whether that final product is packaged and transported in the most efficient manner, which makes design an important pre-cursor to supply chain decisions and highlights the need for better design-supply chain co-ordination

Fisher (1997) argued that the root cause of the problems plaguing many supply chains is a mismatch between the type of product and the type of supply chain. As a result, Fisher proposed a prescriptive framework for choosing the right supply chain for a certain product and for avoiding a mismatch between product design and the supply chain. In the same way, early studies by Hayes & Wheelwright (1979, 1984) proposed a product-process matrix, aimed to identify the best fit between product and process designs. We can consider the proposed matrix as an "ancestor" of Fisher's model, i.e. a first attempt to examine the importance of product design for choosing appropriate supply chain solutions, aligning product design and the supply chain. More recent research indicates that there could be considerable benefits in designing supply chains taking into account the dynamics of the supply chain as well as the design of the product and the design of the manufacturing processes used in the supply chain (Blackhurts et al, 2005). Taps & Steger-Jensen (2007) suggest aligning supply chain design with manufacturing strategies to reduce supply chain complexity and the empirical evidence from their research highlights the need to contrast supply chain design with product innovations. Van Hoek & Chapman (2006 & 2007) analysed the drawbacks from the misalignments between new product development and the supply chain as lost opportunities to leverage supply chain capabilities and product launch effectiveness. Research conducted into the apparel sector by Kincade et al. (2007) describes the benefits of designers and manufacturers from realigning their strategies. By working more simultaneously they can compress product lead times compared to the traditional linear approach, which is more typical of this sector.

TOWARDS A RESILIENT SUPPLY CHAIN: MANAGING SUPPLY CHAIN RISKS

It is clear that design is not just concerned with the appearance and functionality of products, but it also has an important role to play in the coordinated efforts to manage supply chain risk. In fact, the changing features of the global competitive landscape requires companies to be efficient and effective in managing needs for growing product proliferation and shorter technology life-cycles and with time-to-market becoming a critical issue for cost control (Van Hoek & Chapman, 2006). Other changes such as the rise of globalization and the shift from supplier-driven to demand-driven supply chains have forced companies to focus on developing product-led supply chains to mitigate supply chain risk, in a context characterized by growing unpredictability (Khan, 2008). This suggests the need to include supply chain issues early at the design stage, in order to consider the design implications to the total supply chain in terms of product/supply availability or capacity constraints. This clearly highlights the importance of the product design function in developing the appropriate supply chain strategies and the need for a better alignment between design and the supply chain.

Integrating logistics management with the design process can prove beneficial. For example, if product design decisions can take account of transport and storage requirements, then significant improvements to lifetime profits might result. For this reason, the integration between logistics and product design is acknowledged as crucial (Mather, 1992). Having logistics management involved early in the design process may well lead to the identification of potential problems if components or packaging materials with long replenishment lead times are being considered (Christopher & Peck, 2003). Similarly, it can help in anticipating constraints in product development and in managing the supply chain in order to control and minimize logistics management costs, whilst improving customer service level and logistics performance (Mather, 1992).

A consideration for logistics at the design stage means that product modifications can be made, for example in the shape and packaging of products which can be stored and transported more efficiently. A practical and recent example of the impact of product design on supply chain and logistics activities is represented by the introduction of the new Coca Cola can: the different size of its base has modified the shape and as a result improved transportation economies. Hence, the physical characteristics of the product, product architecture (i.e. the scheme by which the function of the product is allocated to physical components) can be considered as the key to solve the tradeoffs between product, process and supply chain design (Ulrich & Eppinger, 2000; Ulrich, 1995); furthermore product architecture influences supply chain performance (Baiman et al., 2004).

Besides logistics and supply chain managers being involved early in the development process, it has been suggested that having early supplier involvement (ESI) is equally important and helps in identifying problems linked with product and component supplies early on in the supply chain, when changes to design specification can still be made, whilst the percentage of invested costs are low and without disrupting the supply chain flow (Ragatz et al, 1997; Zsidisin & Smith, 2005). By assessing the outcomes of supply chain configuration decisions in the early phases of the product design process, it will be possible to concurrently consider other supply chain costs and not only the ones related to product design issues. In order to involve suppliers and supply chain managers in the design process, it is highly advisable to implement the physical integration of the design teams. Although, the global dimension makes it more difficult to accomplish this task, due to the physical dispersion of human resources, this obstacle must be overcome. One idea suggested in the literature is to establish 'virtual workspaces' to manage the integration of the design process beyond single companies' boundaries. This is the idea of "virtually co-located product design teams" (Sharifi & Pawar, 2002). This solution can grant significant benefits to product design process in terms of resource collaboration and integrated development, hence including the entire value chain departments. Some of these benefits are the easier solution of queries and misunderstandings, the reduction of re-iterations in the design process and the information and continuous ideas sharing (Sharifi et al, 2006).

TOWARDS A RESPONSIVE SUPPLY CHAIN: MANAGING AGILITY AND SUPPLY CHAIN RISKS

The integration of design within the extended supply chain is a critical way to mitigate the risk that can arise through lengthy time-to-market and extended replenishment lead times. Thus, the design-supply chain interface enables a firm to achieve greater agility and reduce the impact of supply risk. A key to exploit early suppliers' involvement is represented by concurrent engineering (O'Neal, 1993). Fine (1998) has highlighted the need to concurrently engineer not just the product, but also the processes and – most critically – the supply chain. This idea he calls 3DCE (three dimensional, concurrent engineering). In order to be agile and responsive, it is essential to share information with suppliers as mentioned earlier and this can be achieved through information systems, which can support multifunctional teams in the development of new product and supply chain strategies (Lau & Lee, 2000). The ability to respond to rapid and unexpected changes is the aim of agility and many managers are adopting agile practices (Christopher & Peck 2003; Collin & Lorenzin, 2006). In order to be customer driven and at the same time manage the complexity of the product design process, businesses must develop strategies which enable higher levels of responsiveness over a product life cycle.

Postponement enables delaying the start of activities until the time real demand can be ascertained, so that some parts of the manufacturing or logistics operations can be postponed until final customer commitments have been ascertained, hence reducing risk and uncertainty. Postponement certainly offers much more flexibility to markets which are characterized by turbulent demand fluctuations, short product life-cycles, large amount of product varieties and a need for customized solutions (Collin & Lorenzin, 2006). The selected postponement strategy also determines the position of order penetration point or decoupling point in the supply chain. For an agile supply chain, strategic inventory is held in a generic form as far upstream as possible at the point at which information on real final demand penetrates and hence, reduces distortion in demand (Christopher & Towill, 2000).

Coordinating supply and demand during the transition from one generation of products to another can be difficult and costly. In this case managing product transition through the product design process is crucial, identifying cost drivers and risks (including supply risks). In this case, supply chain, product and process features, and managerial policies should be integrated in the product design transition. This can be critical in enhancing supply chain agility in terms of flexibility and responsiveness (Erhun et al., 2007) whilst reducing supply chain risk. In fact, fast introduction of new products represents one of the variables affecting company's customer sensitivity. Therefore conducting supply chain risk assessment concurrently with product characteristics assessment is essential (Faisal et al., 2006). In this way, it will be possible to design supply chains coherently to improve responsiveness and resilience.

Changes in product design and in production processes also represent sources of supply chain risks, further exacerbated by the availability of lower cost alternatives (Spekman & Davis, 2004). Therefore supplier selection, supplier involvement and supply chain design are critical to ensure risks to the supply chain arising from the introduction of the new products and technologies are mitigated (Balasubramanian, 2004). Product complexity is another design-related impact on the supply chain. Much of the complexity is embodied in the product at the design stage. For example, if each new model launched has a unique bill of materials (BOM) then the impact on inventory costs will be significant and will remain throughout the life of that product. In order to manage this issue, it is possible to configure BOMs with the aim to make them coherent with the supply chain. In particular, Huang et al. (2005) suggest a generic bill of

materials (GBOM) aimed at managing product complexity and at minimizing total supply chain costs through a platform commonality approach. By moving towards a standardization of components or materials across a range, or by moving towards modular design or common platforms, significant reductions in supply chain complexity can be achieved (Ulrich & Eppinger, 2000).

Process and product design modularity has been suggested as an approach for companies to reduce their supply chain risks and to achieve a high degree of flexibility (Kleindorfer & Saad, 2005). Furthermore, in innovative, high margin and uncertain markets, agility can be a powerful tool aimed at managing product complexity and at mitigating risks. With this purpose in mind, collaborative product design can increase agility and improve responsiveness and flexibility, and consequently pave the way to reduce time to market. This particular need is felt by companies operating in global demand driven chains, such as the textile and fashion industry (Masson et al., 2007).

In such cases, it follows that design is the platform on which the effectiveness of the total supply chain rests. If design takes the lead in working with suppliers, the risks involved will be reduced. However, if design requirements are filtered through the supply chain, problems may well occur. Nevertheless, design is often seen in isolation from other functions in the supply chain and it is often neglected in the strategic management of the business (Doyle & Broadbridge, 1999; Kotler & Rath, 1984). Therefore, a key challenge facing organizations in which design is a critical function is to integrate design and supply chain management in order to effectively meet customer needs and manage supply chain risk. The failure to do so could create problems at the manufacturing or logistics stages in the supply chain and thus, increase the risk of supply chain disruption. The challenge is to find ways in which product development times can be reduced, feedback from the market place made more rapid and replenishment time's compressed (Christopher & Peck, 1997). However, the paradox is that over the years as supply chains have become global in the search for lower costs, lead times have in fact lengthened. And as increasingly more products are being manufactured so far from the end customer, the risks of failed products in the market place are high, subsequently increasing total costs not reducing them!

RESEARCH THEMES EMERGING FROM THE LITERATURE REVIEW

The literature introduces many subjects of discussion, but all of them seem to be centred around a common idea, represented by the need to integrate product design process with all other business processes and functions, such as supply chain management, logistics, procurement, manufacturing and engineering, marketing management, quality control, etc. The need for integrating product design with the other business processes requires companies to re-think their organizational structure. Companies should enable the integration of resources by establishing cross-functional teams and developing a product-design oriented supply chain organizational structure. We refer to this as the 4C approach to organisational change and we have illustrated this in Figure 1. This approach requires cooperation and co-location of cross-functional teams with product champions to over-look, lead and be responsible for the process. The 4C's of a design centric business are described as:

Champion for product range: A product champion is an individual who takes responsibility for the management of the interface between design and supply chain functions and ensures good visibility between design and supply chain in the extended enterprise. The product champion will overlook the concurrent design process and ensure a match between product architecture and supply chain design.

Cooperation in the extended enterprise: All parties internally and externally to the firm cooperate and understand the implications of product design on supply chain design. The focal firm and suppliers cooperate to mitigate design-supply chain related risks and ensure the smooth transition of products through the supply chain to the end customer through early supplier involvement at the product design-supply chain interface.

Co-location of concurrent design teams: Concurrent design teams which are multi-disciplinary in nature, where all the functions contribute to the design and development of the product are physically co-located together or if geographically dispersed virtually co-located with information transfer on a daily basis to ensure the smooth transition of products from drawing board to market.

Cross-functional teams: To enable the integration of resources, teams are multi-disciplinary consisting of individuals representing different functions contributing to the product design development process. This will also involve first and second tier suppliers to benefit from early supplier involvement.

All the key themes seem to highlight the necessity to carry out product design process in a highly integrated way, thus involving all the business functions in a concurrent approach. Consequently, the keys to integration are deemed to be concurrent engineering and concurrent design, supported by wide information sharing amongst all the involved players. Indeed, concurrent engineering is considered as the interface between new product development process, supply chain management and also supply chain risk. It allows the development of all the relevant aspects connected to product design feature decisions and supply chain design decisions, while taking into account also the supply chain risks arising from the product design process. Concurrent engineering and design are aimed at building a fully comprehensive and wide approach to the product design process.

Figure 1. 4C Approach to organizational change

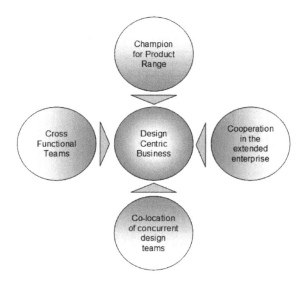

Conceptual Conclusions

In conclusion, the analysis of the structured literature review highlights the importance of keeping product design at the centre of the entire business process and managing it concurrently with the supply chain, through the suggested 4C approach illustrated in Figure 1 which could be seen as the first step towards aligning product design and the supply chain to develop a more 'design centric business process' which could contribute towards a more responsive and resilient organization. Figure 2 describes our conceptual framework.

METHODOLOGY

To understand how the alignment between product design and the supply chain is managed in industry and how this can enhance resilience and responsiveness an exploratory case study approach was used. Case studies are a well-recognized methodology for exploring areas where theory is still developing and for surfacing and understanding emerging phenomena whose dimensions are not yet fully understood (Yin, 1994).

Three case studies from different industry sectors where design has an important element in the success of final products were undertaken. Two of the organizations we interviewed are SME's and have manufacturing activities in the UK and a global supply chain. The third company we chose is a large global business with a strong design and supply chain capability. We chose this organization to compare and contrast our findings with the results from the SME's and to see what insights we can gain from 'best practice'. Hence, we maintained consistency through three key factors in our choice of samples:

1. Design is a critical element in the success of end products
2. The companies have manufacturing facilities in Europe
3. The companies have global supply chains

This helped to provide clarity of the key product design-supply chain issues and identify the differences between industries. Other techniques such as examining company documentation also provided an insight into the level of interface between product design and the supply chain and strategies for managing supply risk and approaches to enhance supply chain agility. All the case organizations were visited on site by the research team and information was gathered through a series of unstructured and semi- structured interviews with relevant staff (product design and development managers, supply chain and sourcing managers, operation managers, technical managers, marketing managers). The interview protocol enabled an exploration of how product design, supply chain, agility and risks were managed. Each interview was tape recorded, transcribed and interview reports were produced to enable the data analysis.

The data was analyzed using the principles of thematic analysis, often referred to also as template analysis (Crabtree & Miller, 1999; King, 2004;

Figure 2. A conceptual framework derived from the structured literature review

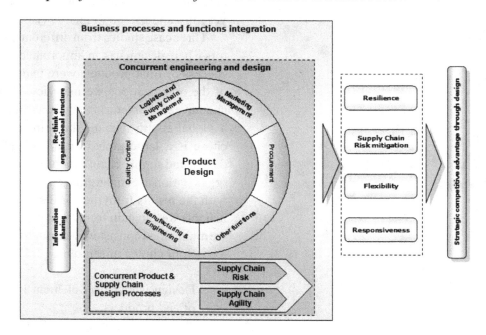

Miles & Huberman, 1994). Thematic analysis provides a framework to capture the richness of the data but also to help organize the data collected into a structure. As case transcripts are long, they can often be overwhelming to format and to tease out the depth of data. Thematic analysis enables researchers to organize the data into codes and themes and therefore assists in managing the data by developing templates from the themes and codes. Thematic or template analysis works particularly well with small data sets and when comparing 2 or 3 data sets or when the researcher knows what issues she or he is searching for (King, 2004). Therefore this methodology was appropriate for this particular study, since the researcher had an a priori insight into how better management of the interface between product design and supply chain could assist in reducing supply chain risk and enhance supply chain agility. Furthermore the study aimed to capture an in-depth insight into three cases by cross examining the data collected and highlighting the key themes which emerged from the template analysis and subsequently the

cross case examination. Before the cross-case examination we briefly outline a description of each case company.

Tileco is an SME manufacturing ceramic tiles. The company is mainly focused on the production of wall tiles. The tiles sector is characterized by a high concentration of a small number of big companies, because of the growing presence of foreign importers (mainly low-cost producers) and the maturity of the industry and of the manufacturing technology. The company grounds its competitiveness on its strong manufacturing legacy. Tileco's products are specifically developed for retailers, house developers and homeowners. Retailers represent 60% of its market, while 40% is constituted by contract customers.

Luxco, is an SME manufacturing fine quality cashmere, woolen knitwear and accessories. The product range includes cashmere garments and blankets, as well as merino, silk and cotton products. In the 19th century Luxco began the production of Estate Tweeds and pioneered the weaving of luxury wool fibers (cashmere and vicuna). Luxco runs the UK's last remaining vertical woolen mill, which carries out all processes from raw fiber to finished garment on one site. Today's competitive environment is dominated by the presence of low-cost country manufacturers. Quality, design, fashion and a strong brand name represent the key drivers in Luxco strategy.

Fabrico is a large multinational enterprise manufacturing plastic polymer materials. Virtually all its products are based on this material, engineered for a number of industries ranging from medical to textiles. The company employs approximately 7,500 associates at 45 facilities worldwide. Fabrico's UK division produces materials for garment manufacturers: membranes and laminates for sport, workforce, law enforcement and military gear. Fabrico's fabric division operates in a sector characterized by high concentration. This division does not compete directly with textile firms, but with material and technology providers, and with fluoropolymer product manufacturers.

From the cross-case examination we uncovered five recurrent key themes in relation to the objectives of the research (Product Design Strategy, Supply Chain Configuration, Supply Chain Risk Management, Supply Chain Agility and the Product Design-Supply Chain Interface), which will be discussed in detail.

PRODUCT DESIGN STRATEGY

Product design strategy in all the examined cases was found to be a critical issue: all the companies included in the sample indicated that design had a key role over the entire business process and was a major tool for sustaining a competitive advantage. For instance, Luxco gives product design the role of enabler for introducing product differentiation, achieving the target to make its products unique against commodities, which tend to be quite diffused in the market by now. For Tileco it is equally crucial because tiles are a mature product, and design can be the order

winning element. In Fabrico product design has a more decisive role, as an enabler for obtaining the best quality products, high performance and reliability. Through innovation, technology and design, Fabrico aims to keep a leading position at the top end of its market.

Considering that product design is a crucial factor, Luxco invested in increasing the size of the product design team: over fifteen years the company hired twelve designers, implementing a training program to allow them to gain a wider overview of the entire business process. In detail, the company created a "product specialist" role, and established "product range managers", creating a (missing) link between the management of the design function and the management of the supply chain. The new roles are given the task to coordinate the product design process at the same time as managing the impact and performance of the supply chain.

The product design strategy in Luxco is impacted by lengthy and capital intensive processes. Time-to-market is critical for Luxco, but it is constrained by long and fixed manufacturing processes typical of the textile supply chain. For example raw materials have to be sourced and scheduled for production ahead of each sales season, booking the necessary capacity and dealing with a one year long pipeline because of the labour and capital intensive manufacturing processes of textiles. In Tileco, the development process is triggered by a meeting of the design function with sales department, and only afterwards the other functions get involved (manufacturing, costing and accounting, supply chain and quality control). In this case, it is possible to highlight sequential product design and development processes. The consequence of such a process configuration is that the development of the product could restart over and over depending on the feedback provided by the supply chain functions. In Fabrico the product design process is largely dependent on orders placed by customers, which usually represent the start of the product development process. The product development process is tailored in function of the complexity of the product to be designed. For example, for brand new and technically complex products, it is possible to have a 2 year development pipeline, with many loops with the customer (the garment manufacturer for Fabrico and the retailer or consumer for Luxco). But when standard products are produced, the development process can be completed within 4 months, fitting in with the sale season's timing.

SUPPLY CHAIN CONFIGURATION

The challenge of combining low cost & high volume production with quality, fashionable and innovative products drives the decisions taken by Tileco in terms of supply chain configuration. For achieving this result, Tileco performs a segmentation of its supply chain according to the different types of products: for commodities (e.g. plain white tiles) the supply chain is driven by cost-effectiveness, whereas for premium collections design and quality become the main drivers. In contrast, Luxco struggles with balancing the supply chain according to its business requirements. In fact, the company operates at the top end of the market and consequently the main drivers for configuring the supply chain must be quality, service and design, even for their "low profile" or standard products. Fabrico adopted a strategy aimed at reconfiguring its supply chain into a demand chain for its customized products. The company recently shifted away from the focus on the manufacturing costs towards design issues and the relevance of its impact on the entire business. By offering tailored and customized products to its customers the company is able to better respond to demand, recognizing the risks, costs and dealing with more flexible and reliable lead times.

In determining their supply chain configuration, companies must effectively manage their sourcing strategy. As far as Tileco is concerned, the company directly manufactures 80% of its products, while the production of the remaining 20% (special size and variously decorated tiles) is outsourced to manufacturers located in Turkey, Spain, Italy, China, Indonesia and Bulgaria. Depending on which type of product needs to be externally sourced, purchasing cost, availability, sourcing lead times or quality determines the choice of the suppliers. However, Luxco considers quality of materials as the main driver leading the sourcing strategy, with respect to finished products. The company manufactures most of its range in Scotland, however some raw materials are sourced in Mauritius, where Luxco owns a spinning mill. No sourcing strategy for finished products is implemented by Fabrico, which manufactures the entire range in-house.

With respect to sourcing raw materials, all three companies have a distinct strategy. Tileco procures its raw materials (basically clay, sand and limestone) from local sites or from suppliers located in the UK. Furthermore, the company recently undertook a rationalization process of its supply base, with the aim to progressively adopt a single sourcing approach for each kind of raw material. On the contrary, Luxco deals with the sourcing of very precious raw materials (i.e. vicuna and cashmere wools), sourcing them directly from their native countries, which increases the complexity of its global supply base. Fabrico's raw materials are essentially represented by polyester: in this case the main driver determining the procurement strategy is price. So, the company sources from global suppliers (e.g. Taiwan instead of local suppliers), sometimes following their customers' strategic choices. But, in contrast to the SMEs, Fabrico secures its supply chain and is able to manufacture and deliver products by building partnerships with a few selected suppliers only.

SUPPLY CHAIN RISK MANAGEMENT

In order to achieve one of the primary targets of this research, we asked the interviewees to identify the main risks they have to confront within their supply chain, and to discuss the solutions adopted in order to mitigate them. In doing this, we wanted to examine how companies can exploit product design as a tool for mitigating supply chain risks and thus increasing resilience.

First, we analyzed the supply chain risks pertaining to the production/manufacturing process. One of the major risks faced by Tileco is represented by capacity limitations and constraints for planning the production and for reacting to changes to the production schedules, i.e. poor flexibility. Moreover, technical aspects related to the manufacture of tiles hinder flexibility for Tileco: for example, the temperature of the oven and the production throughput time require manufacturing process to be precisely scheduled. This issue is shared by Luxco, mainly because of the limited capacity in weaving worsted fabrics (one mill only left in Italy), along with some problems for scheduling the production. It must also contend with the fixed set-up times which have a high impact of changing the kind of product manufactured on all the various machines, i.e. decontamination process. In comparison, Fabrico is more flexible towards changes in the production plan, being able to cope with disruptions in the manufacturing and delivery processes. However, Fabrico confronts a series of critical issues as well and a critical point in the manufacturing process is represented by the dyeing and the finishing sections which are often very time consuming, with special lamination procedures which can add up to 4 weeks extra lead time.

The cross-case examination revealed that one of the major supply chain risks identified by all three companies is the quality of supplies. Tileco identifies the disruptions deriving from bad quality supplies, especially with few alternative sourcing points. For Luxco, the quality of the raw materials

is the main priority from their supply network and cost comes second, being committed to manufacturing luxury garments. A series of drawbacks are underlined by the companies with respect to the downstream section of the supply chain: in fact, the companies often feel "uncomfortable" in their relationship with their customers, mostly because of frequent changes in their requirements, causing high costs for both Tileco and Luxco, in particular when large samples have already been produced. Of course, these pitfalls have a series of implications for the product design and supply chain processes, particularly in terms of costs to incur and time to spend for implementing last minute changes required by customers. This makes both SMEs (Tileco & Luxco) feel less certain of the control on their internal design process, becoming unable to plan and perform it in an optimal way and being over dependent on their customers. Interestingly, Fabrico claims that downstream relationships are the cause for major delays and bottle necks in the supply chain and product design process.

It is remarkable to underline that companies state that the complexity of the supply chain is increased by the characteristics of the products, which act as a source of potential disruptions in the supply chain. The complexity can impact on the customer service level as well as on the time to market. This is the case when a new product is designed with a set of features implying a misalignment with the production system's capability or with the sourcing process.

Risks arising from the demand side are systemic and created by the companies own decisions. A strategy adopted by Tileco is represented by an increase of product variety, to appeal to a wider market, by means of a segmentation of the product range. Luxco confronts demand risks related to the progressive shift towards women's wear and lightweight garments: the first choice implies a considerable risk, due to the necessity to follow a high variability in the demand, while the latter require the use of worsted fabric, a material very difficult to source. Luxco has been forced to undertake this shift because of the climate change effects leading to warmer weather. In order to mitigate the 'new' risks, Luxco undertook a process aimed at reducing the number of product SKUs, whilst increasing the number of component SKU (such as labeling and packaging) in order to provide a customized service to their customers. Particular requirements from customers increase the complexity for Fabrico, in terms of innovation management and for the development of new products. The company often struggles with unrealistic requirements from customers (mostly about the technical performance of their garments) causing a slowdown for the whole product design and supply chain processes. In order to avoid this pitfall, Fabrico have introduced collaborative design, innovation and supply chain planning to help alleviate some of the major barriers they face in meeting their customer requirements.

A particularly significant outcome of the data collection process about supply chain risk is represented by the fact that, even though companies succeeded in accurately identifying the supply chain risk they have to face, no particular tool or technique was being used. In fact, they tend to exploit a series of actions aimed at mitigating the impact and the occurrence of risks with contingency plans to recover from disruptions. Tileco reacts to the disruptions connected with capacity constraints by outsourcing part of the production to its subsidiaries located in the UK. Luxco tries to gain more control over the business process complexity by means of a standard costing methodology aimed at guiding the business in a comprehensive way. Fabrico manages risks by means of integration with suppliers and with the design teams of customers.

SUPPLY CHAIN AGILITY

Supply chain agility emerged as a primary topic for the case companies. The first issue emerging from the case companies regards the management of product development lead times. In fact, the lead time necessary to develop new products is an essential element in bringing innovation to the market in a faster and timely way, and to react to new trends. The constraints affecting the time for developing new products are basically represented by the availability of resources and the structure of the product design process. Tileco manages the first issue by obtaining temporary extra resources, procured from one of its subsidiary companies, while Luxco has progressively increased the number of resources devoted to design. In contrast Fabrico, in a more structured way, manages the resources according to the complexity of the product to be developed: to this aim, an assessment of the number of designers and of the required time is performed. In order to better manage the development lead time, Fabrico was able to reach an agreement with its customers, and launch products at intervals thereby shortening lead times, while the SMEs were not able to significantly reduce the whole pipeline.

The strategies implemented to ensure responsiveness represents another key element. For example, the way Tileco pursues a higher degree of responsiveness is by segmenting its sourcing strategy, according to the demand pattern of the products and materials: the company procures items characterized by demand volatility from closer, cost neutral countries to the UK (Turkey, Spain, Italy), in order to be more responsive and sources the basic or stable items from China. Similarly, Luxco focuses on agility by producing their volume lines in a spinning mill in Mauritius as well as in Scotland and Fabrico manufactures in Asia but in Europe as well, in order to balance the problems connected with global transportation. Luxco adopts other strategies for improving the company's responsiveness by moving towards make-to-order and postponement of the dyeing activity (often by means of hand dyeing, to quickly respond to customers' color requirements). Likewise, Fabrico is introducing a system for color matching in the dyeing process, pursuing an enhanced responsiveness also through the production of smaller batches. Collaborative and partnership approaches with customers and suppliers are other solutions implemented by Fabrico in order to achieve a higher degree of responsiveness, through fast and direct communication and information sharing.

Furthermore, the case companies identified a series of barriers to enhanced agility. One main barrier is represented by the nature of the manufacturing process, which to some extent is a direct consequence of the choices about the characteristics of the products. For instance, Tileco and Fabrico manufacturing processes are characterized by frozen schedules and capacity constraints, hindering the possibility to widely modify the production plans. Equally, change-over times on the looms are a constraint for Luxco, which inhibits the firm from speeding up manufacturing processes without compromising the quality of the product. In addition, Fabrico highlights the difficulty to remove unpredictable delays in the production process, often resulting from bad management practices such as mitigating risks by means of time buffers. The sourcing process can be considered as a further barrier to enhanced agility: Tileco and Luxco both reported that the long lead times for sourcing products and the availability of materials is often a problem (e.g. the availability of yarn for Luxco). For Luxco and Fabrico, operating in the textile sector, some elements of the business are absolutely fixed, and consequently they have to cope with these structural elements, inhibiting improvements to agility (e.g. seasonality). A significant barrier is represented by the lack of communication. Tileco and Luxco highlight how this element and in particular the lack of internal and external communication, along with poor integration and information sharing represents a barrier to agility. Solutions such as partnerships with suppliers and shared development teams with customers allow Fabrico to resolve this issue,

even if the retailers do not integrate with garment manufacturers' buyers.

THE PRODUCT DESIGN-SUPPLY CHAIN INTERFACE

In the previous sections we gathered empirical information in order to describe the issues and the challenges the companies have to confront with respect to the product design strategy, the supply chain process, the supply chain risks and agility: thus, it is possible to provide an assessment and a description of the development of the interface between product design and the supply chain.

First, we wanted to describe the scope of the interface, and so we started from the analysis of the level of integration between the supply chain functions. The two SMEs show a fairly poor functional integration, even if a certain degree of communication between the various supply chain functions can be seen, especially in Tileco, while in Luxco the presence of product designers acting as project managers proves a certain commitment for developing products in a comprehensive and integrated process. On the contrary, Fabrico is characterized by a high degree of integration, with the presence of product specialists and product range managers. Besides, cross functional teams, including suppliers and customers ensures a high degree of integration between functions. This strategy is put into action through the implementation of a "lattice-amoebic organizational structure", as defined by the company itself.

The adoption of concurrent practices in product development can be a measure of how well the product design-supply chain interface is managed. The two SMEs show a low level of adoption, with the product development process being rather sequential, with no ESI (Early Supplier Involvement) approach and a late involvement of the various functions. In fact, the early decisions are essentially taken by product design and marketing functions only. This implies a number of loops and feedbacks coming from other supply chain functions, requiring changes in order to make the production and launch of a new product feasible and cost-effective. Even though the presence of designers acting as project managers could be seen as integration in the product development process in Luxco, the various phases remain substantially independent. On the contrary, the establishment of cross functional teams allows Fabrico to develop products in a concurrent way, although complex and special products will often create lengthy loops for aligning the development with customers (without losing the consistent concurrent approach). In fact, the first early decisions about products are shared by all the functions through

Figure 3. The interface between product design and the supply chain – Tileco

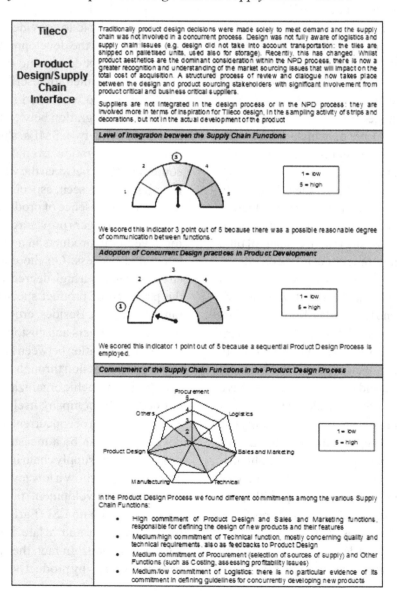

co-location of the design teams and coordination of the process to ensure high communication in the development.

Another measure of the development of the product design-supply chain interface is represented by the commitment of the various supply chain functions in the development process. In Tileco, sales and marketing and product design are the only functions to get highly involved in the design process, with medium commitment of technical and procurement departments, and with logistics simply informed about the decisions taken about the design of new products. Similarly, in Luxco the design function is highly committed, but there less involvement of procurement, technical and manufacturing functions and logistics. On the other hand, the organizational structure adopted in Fabrico is more integrated due to the

Figure 4. The interface between product design and the supply chain – Luxco

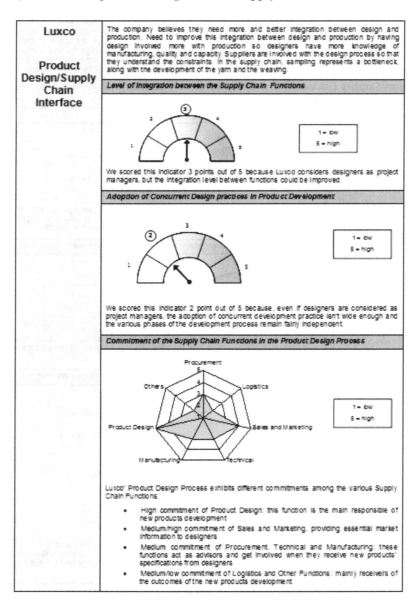

presence of cross functional development teams, led by product specialists and range managers, including suppliers and customers' designers as well. All the functions are involved in the product design process since the early phases. Figures 3, 4 and 5 illustrate the level of interface between product design and the supply chain in each case company.

SOLUTIONS AND RECOMMENDATIONS

The cross-case examination and the structured literature review have highlighted key insights on the interface between product design and the supply chain. In Figure 6 we present a summarizing chart of the key empirical findings. The chart shows the outcomes of our empirical research,

Figure 5. The interface between product design and the supply chain – Fabrico

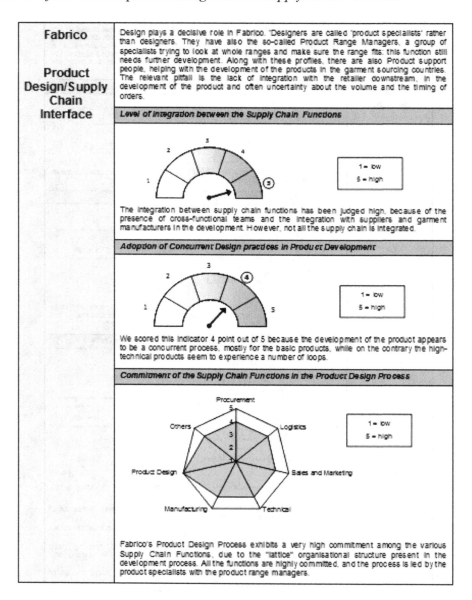

providing evidence of the practical implications and impact on the companies' business processes in terms of the interface between product design and the supply chain.

Based on the summary of the results presented in Figure 6, we underline that the case studies confirm the issues emerging from the literature on the importance of product design as a crucial factor in determining supply chain and business performance. In fact, the cross-case examination shows that companies give design an essential role in their business. However, research results also show poor alignment between product design and the extended supply chain. This situation is determined by a number of reasons, as we discussed before. The case companies appear to be conscious of the need for alignment, and some measures are undertaken to improve this process.

Key outcomes of the cross-case examination can be drawn, with respect to the development of the product design-supply chain interface. In the two SME's a lack of collaboration in the supply chain can be observed. In fact, the companies don't manage the supply chain in an integrated way: suppliers and customers are rarely included in the process. This can entail a series of problems concerning the continuity and the quality of the supplies (crucial factors for companies, as pointed out) with respect to the upstream section. On the other hand, a lack of integration downstream can lead to misalignments with the market and these can result in delays for effective launches of new products. But this issue regards also the integration of the supply chain with the other functions. In contrast with these findings, Fabrico proved that the establishment of cross-functional teams entails prominent benefits for achieving a higher integration of the functions, outside the boundaries of the company. Though, downstream in the supply chain Fabrico, Tileco and Luxco all struggle for enhancing the level of integration, and this is particularly true when retailers are considered.

A general lack of integration is tightly connected to a poor adoption of concurrent practices in the development of products: in fact, a disconnected and sequential development process is fairly usual amongst the companies. This implies a negative impact on time-to-market and on the responsiveness of the development process, due to the difficulty in providing an integrated and "direct" response to the potential changes to be implemented. The adoption of concurrent practices, as shown by Fabrico, shows it is possible to stick to the deadlines for the launch of a collection, gaining the possibility to further compress the time necessary for the development of the product. The poor adoption of concurrent practices in the development of the products is a

Figure 6. Summarizing chart of the outcomes of the research

Design –Supply Chain Transformation Process...		
From	**To**	**How do we get there?**
Design as a stand alone function	Design as part of a cross-functional approach	"T" shaped skills, training, "boundary less" business-organisational change
Supply chain as an after thought – for a design orientated business	Supply chain starts on the drawing board	Supply chain involvement at the product design stage
Designers "design"	Designers integrate across the "concept to delivery" process	Designers lead the orchestration of the product development process
Free "unconstrained" design	Constrained design	Range architectures aware of supply chain constraints, possibilities
Design for manufacturing/assembly	Design for supply chain	Establish appropriate de-coupling points – how far do we make a vanilla product before we stop? Balance design strategy against supply chain impact.

sign of a de-balanced commitment of the various business functions: if on one hand it is reasonable to have product design as a leading function in the development process, on the other hand having the other functions poorly involved or just informed about the design decisions has significant drawbacks, with the product design function often not really aware of logistics, transportation and supply chain implications. For this reason, the presence of cross functional teams, involving members from all the functions, creates a more integrated product development process, and a higher degree of responsiveness to the company. In fact, achieving agility appears to be a top priority for the case companies: responsiveness is sought by means of lead time compression, in order to be able to quickly react to uncertainties and changes and thus mitigating supply chain risks. The adoption of concurrent practices in a more integrated environment enables companies to move towards the achievement of this result, as confirmed by some short case examples of world-class companies.

Zara, the world famous clothing company, operating in the 'fast fashion' industry, achieved paramount success by means of aligning product design and the supply chain. In particular, the company forwards commit to fabric supply to break out from the long lead time framework (Ferdows et al. 2004, Birtwistle et al., 2003). In fact, 'Zara only commits up to 20% six months in advance of the season, a commitment, which increases up to 50% by the start of the season. This permits the other 50% to be decided once the season has been launched'. A similar strategy is implemented by fast fashion retailers in the UK such as New Look (Khan, 2008NL). Overall integration and alignment were adopted by Hewlett Packard, who studied and implemented the interfaces between cost accounting, process control and product design for finished products and for components as well (Patell, 1987). Moreover, the company pursued the alignment of product design with the supply chain by means of a strategy called "design for

localization", which means that design processes take into account operational and delivery considerations for multiple markets (Lee et al., 1993). This was the first step the company made from Design For Manufacturability approach towards a wider Design For Supply Chain Management strategy: the product line structure, bill of materials and customisation processes of a product are designed to optimize logistics costs and customer service performance (Lee & Sasser, 1995), thus obtaining a higher degree of responsiveness and consequently mitigating the traditional supply chain risks related to product design. Another company able to achieve world-class success through the integration between product design and the supply chain is represented by Dell, which was worth 12 billion dollars in less than 13 years. In particular, by means of the "virtual integration" concept, which offers the advantages of a tightly coordinated supply chain, benefiting from the focus and specialization that drive virtual corporations, Dell implemented the early supplier involvement strategy: suppliers are effectively considered as partners, assigning their engineers to Dell's design team and becoming part of the company (Magretta, 1998). Besides the ESI approach, Dell aligned product design and the supply chain by means of postponement, integrating the distribution channel and configuring products only when they are bought by customers at the on-line shop (Christopher & Towill, 2000). In this way, through an optimal delayed configuration, Dell achieved positive benefits in terms of compliance with the actual market requirements and hence obtained a higher responsiveness.

We also examined the risks related to product design and defined them in terms of threats the companies are facing, with respect to supply chain and product design. Specifically we showed how these risks are present in all the supply chain stages, from upstream in the supply side, to downstream in the demand side. Furthermore, we showed that most of the criticalities are present at the point of interface between the various stages of the supply chain. And the manufacturing side seems to be especially impacted, experiencing disruptions caused by both supply and demand side.

After having considered all the issues, it is possible to draw some prescriptions and recommendations about the importance of developing the interface between product design and the supply chain and how companies could achieve this strategic objective. The structured literature review and empirical case findings indicate that companies should exploit the paramount benefits deriving from the alignment of product design and the supply chain. But how, from a practical point of view, can companies move towards the alignment of product design and the supply chain?

First of all, the outcomes of this research, summarized in Figure 6, suggest that companies could move towards the adoption of the approach proposed by Fabrico, i.e. managing product development in an integrated and concurrent way, aligning the supply chain operations with the design process, for achieving enhanced agility and for mitigating supply chain risk through improved responsiveness and resilience. In fact, by adopting such a strategy, it is possible to increase the capability to react to market uncertainty. Moreover, it will be possible to reduce the inefficiencies in the supply chain, such as excessive inventories at the points of interface in the supply chain, withdrawals, and eventually mark-downs or lost sales. Efficiency is particularly significant, due to the current situation of recession and economic turmoil.

From a practical point of view, the integration of the supply chain in the product development process means that supply chain design should be directly undertaken on the drawing board, by involving supply chain managers in the very early phases of product design process. To reach a full integration of the development process, all the other business processes and functions related to product innovation, such as logistics, procurement, manufacturing, engineering, marketing management and quality control should be early

involved as well. However, this objective could not be reached without undertaking a significant organizational change, breaking down the traditional functional 'silo's' and moving towards a greater degree of cross-functional working where information is shared in a concurrent design environment. The cross case analysis showed that product design should be placed at the centre of the business, driving the development of new products coherently, concurrently and in an aligned way with supply chain design and business requirements, therefore we propose that by adopting a more "design centric" approach contributes towards developing a more responsiveness and resilient supply chain.

In order to give recommendations for pragmatically moving towards a responsive and resilient enterprise, we have developed a roadmap for the "Design Centric Business" (Figure 2). By adopting this approach we propose that products will be designed more concurrently to the supply chain therefore keeping account of the implications on the supply chain upstream and downstream in the very early stages of the development process and significantly improve their responsiveness and resilience. In order to achieve these results, a number of changes in the organization and in the management of product design and supply chain processes are needed. In order to link our literature and empirical findings with the practical issues, companies need to confront in order to become truly 'design-centric', we developed our roadmap suggesting a number of fundamental transformations for companies (Figure 7).

Our proposed transformation processes are:

1. Moving from design as a standalone function to a cross-functional approach. Whilst design as a function is not typically seen as being a part of the supply chain management activity, we argue that it should be. As cross functional teams are increasingly being utilized to manage end-to-end processes, their scope should be enlarged to include design.

Figure 7. A Roadmap for the Design Centric Business

	Tileco	Luxco	Fabrico
Company Industrial Sector	Manufacture of ceramic tiles	Manufacture of woollen knitwear	Manufacture of technical textiles
Company Size	SME (240 employees)	SME (200 employees)	Large (475 employees)
Organisational Structure	Functional	Functional	Lattice amoebic
Product Design Strategy	Design as enabler for order winning mature products	Design for introducing product differentiation	Design for best quality, high performance, reliability
Supply Chain (SC) key Drivers	SC cost balance with low cost & high volume production with quality and innovation	Quality, service, design	Demand chain for customised products
Major SC and Design Risks	Sources of Supply, Fluctuating Demand, Technical and quality requirements, Low flexibility of the production process	Bottlenecks in the pipeline, Loom downtime and changeover, Poor production flexibility, Shift towards lightweight garments with variable demand	Reduction of Supply base, Wrong forecasts, Set-up times, Shortage of capacity, Late changes in customer orders
Level of integration between SC functions	◑	◑	●
Adoption of concurrent practices in product development	○	◔	◕
Commitment of SC functions in the product design process	◑	◑	●
Most involved functions	Product design, Marketing	Product design, Marketing	Product design (as leading function)
Least involved functions	Logistics	Logistics and accounting	None
Degree of alignment between product design and the SC	◑	◑	●

○ Low ⟶ ● High

Clearly such a development could require a still further broadening of the scope of supply chain management with consequent implications for training and development. In particular, employees, designers and supply chain managers should be trained to become "T" shaped people, i.e. "people whose body is within their function but whose arms reach out within the process" (Wilding, 2003). This means that employees should be trained to become open-minded and to be able to collaborate with colleagues on the same project, broadening the scope of their function. Besides, physical and/or virtual co-location of development teams could help in expanding this approach. Moreover, this entails the need for reviewing the organizational structure of the company, in order to leave the traditional "silo" structure and move towards a lattice amoebic organization, with information sharing and product development progress sharing.

2. From supply chain to an afterthought to a recognition that the supply chain begins on the drawing board. Since a large part of the total life costs of a product are 'designed in' it is critical that the supply chain implications of product design decisions be clearly understood. The choice of materials, components and packaging has significance for replenishment lead times as well as possible future supply chains vulnerabilities. The physical characteristics of the product will also impact on space utilization and hence

on distribution and transport costs. To ensure that these issues are understood and factored into the new product development process it is vital that supply chain management and design work together, since the very early phases of the design process. This implies that, once the decision to develop a new product is undertaken, cross-functional teams including supply chain managers, key business functions and suppliers should be established as soon as possible to work together in order to understand all the implications of the design concept on the cost efficiency of the supply chain and on the limitations on the effectiveness of the proposed solutions.

3. Extending the role of the designer to become a new product development orchestrator. A case can be made for extending the role of the designer into the coordinator and orchestrator of the complete new product development process. In other words the designer should take responsibilities for ensuring that all the 'through life' cost implications are understood and that the supply chain consequences of new product decisions are factored in at the start. As we envisage that the end-to-end process will be managed by a team, then the designer might be seen as the orchestrator of the different elements of the process, becoming a real project manager for the development of new products. For this reason, companies should invest in training designers, in order to enable them understand and manage all the complexities related to the development of a new product, keeping into account all the implications deriving from the implementation of a particular product concept. Thus, companies should drive designers towards the adoption of the managerial tools typical of project management topic, beyond the scope of their traditional design activity. Moreover, also in this case, an effort towards

a change in the organizational structure is required: from rigid functional structures, companies should move to more flexible cross-functional settings, where designers could have the necessary visibility on key data, information and resources.

4. Moving from 'unconstrained' to 'constrained' design. In many design-led businesses there is a tendency to see design as a creative process and to avoid inhibiting that creativity. However, with the realization that supply chain efficiency and effectiveness is vital to business profitability and continuity, the argument for a 'constrained' approach to design becomes stronger. In other words the designer must work within a prescriptive brief, the parameters of which reflect the supply chain sensitivities to cost and risk. Of course, the creative nature of design should be preserved, but, considering that designers should act as project managers, they must be aware of the implications their choices can have on the supply chain and business processes, and for this reason they should keep into account a series of beneficial limitations. In this case as well, companies should invest in training designers and in changing the organizational structure, with a cross-functional approach aimed at allowing positive information exchanges between supply chain and design functions.

5. Changing from a philosophy of design for manufacturing or assembly to one of design for supply chain. Many organizations have tended to look at the design decision from a manufacturing perspective. In other words the priority has been to ensure that products are designed in such a way that manufacturability or assembly is enhanced. Whilst these considerations are clearly important, it can now be argued that the wider supply chain performance should now drive the design decision. In fact, besides manufacturing, all the implications deriving from the choice of

the sources of supply and from the issues related to the distribution process should be taken into account. For this reason, the establishment of cross-functional development teams should push to the fore the role of supply chain decision makers, orchestrated by designers-project managers and involving production directors as well, in order to develop new products with a broader and more comprehensive scope. In particular designing products to reduce complexity and increase agility through postponement strategies should be the goal wherever possible.

CONCLUSION

In the present paper we addressed the investigation of the strategic relationship between product design and supply chain performance and how a better alignment between these two functions contributes towards building a more responsive and resilient supply chain. We first performed a literature review on the key identified areas, building a conceptual framework which enabled us to draw some considerations about the benefits achieved through the alignment of product design and the supply chain, in terms of better supply chain risk mitigation and responsiveness. The 4C Approach to Organizational Change (Figure 1) suggests the first steps to move towards this strategic alignment. We also illustrated how engineering and design can help in moving towards the alignment between product design and supply chain (Figure 2). The case studies revealed how companies deal with the alignment of product design and the supply chain and how they confront relevant challenges such as supply chain risk management and responsiveness. They also enabled us to see how companies invest in product design, how they manage the new product development process and the level of interface between product design and the supply chain. We summarized and categorized the information in a series of templates and in

a chart from which we concluded that product design is a crucial factor in determining supply chain and business performance for companies. We developed a roadmap towards the design-centric organization, based on five transformation processes. These are associated with a re-design of the organization, placing design at the centre of the business, through a cross-functional approach where designers are project managers conscious of all the implications on the business deriving from design choices, along with a wide awareness of the fact that the supply chain begins on the drawing board. The transformation processes include a series of practical indications, for helping companies in achieving the benefits deriving from the alignment of product design with the supply chain, in terms of enhanced agility and supply chain risk management. These benefits are widely described in the literature and in the presented short examples of world-class enterprises, proving the practical value of our proposed framework for achieving a superior degree of resilience and responsiveness in virtual networks.

FUTURE RESEARCH DIRECTIONS

This study was built on a small sample of companies. It was based on a sound, systematic, and structured literature review which enabled the researchers to develop a series of research questions characterized by general validity. We addressed the research questions with a rigorous and consistent research methodology which permitted us to derive reliable and grounded findings, applicable and transferable to other companies and sectors. However, further developments of our research could be represented by the opportunity to extend the sample of companies, and to study the critical issues for designing products keeping into account all the factors and decisions impacting on the business at an early stage of the product development process. A particular focus on the integration between business functions in the product design process remains the founding concept of the future development of the research. In doing so, it could be interesting to further extend the research to explore the impacts of product architecture on supply chain design and to examine its impact on organizational change.

REFERENCES

Abecassis, C. (2006). Integrating Design and Retail in the Clothing Value Chain: An Empirical Study of the Organisation of Design International. *Journal of Operations and Production Management, 26*(4), 412–428. doi:10.1108/01443570610650567

Baiman, S., Fischer, P. E., & Rajan, M. V. (2001). Performance measurement and Design in supply chains. *Management Science, 47*(1), 173–188. doi:10.1287/mnsc.47.1.173.10673

Balasubramanian, R. (2001). Concurrent Engineering – A Powerful Enabler of Supply Chain Management. *Quality Progress, 34*(6), 47–53.

Birtwistle, G., Siddiqui, N., & Fiorito, S. S. (2003). Quick response: perception of UK fashion retailers. *International Journal of Retail & Distribution Management, 31*(2), 118–128. doi:10.1108/09590550310462010

Blackhurts, J., Wu, T., & O'Grady, P. (2005). Pcdm a decision support modelling methodology for supply chain, product and process design decision. *Journal of Operations Management, 23*(3), 325–343. doi:10.1016/j.jom.2004.05.009

Burkett, M. J. (2006). Design for Supply: An Evolutionary Path. *Supply Chain Management Review, 10*(8), 11–16.

Christopher, M. (2005). Logistics and Supply Chain Management, Creating Value Adding Networks - 3rd Edition, London: Prentice Hall.

Christopher, M., Aitken, J., & Towill, D. (2002). Understanding, Implementing and Exploiting Agility and Leanness. *International Journal of Logistics, 5*(1), 59–74. doi:10.1080/13675560110084139

Christopher, M., & Peck, H. (1997). Managing logistics in fashion markets. *The International Journal of Logistics Management, 8*(2), 63–74. doi:10.1108/09574099710805673

Christopher, M., & Peck, H. (2003). Marketing Logistics - 2nd Edition. Oxford, UK: Butterworth Heinemann.

Christopher, M., & Towill, R. D. (2000). Supply Chain Migration From Lean and Functional to Agile and Customised. *Supply Chain Management: An International Journal, 5*(4), 206–213. doi:10.1108/13598540010347334

Collin, J., & Lorenzin, D. (2006). Plan for supply chain agility at Nokia: Lessons from the mobile infrastructure industry. *International Journal of Physical Distribution & Logistics Management, 36*(6), 418–430. doi:10.1108/09600030610677375

Cox, G. (2005), Cox Review of Creativity in Business: Building on the UK's Strengths, London: HMSO.

Crabtree, B. F., & Miller, W. L. (1999). Doing qualitative research. Thousand Oaks, CA, Sage Publications.

Cranfield (2003). Creating Resilient Supply Chains: A Practical Guide. *Report produced by the Centre of Logistics and Supply Chain Management, Cranfield School of Management. Research Funded by Department for Transport.*

Design Council. (2004/2005). Design in Britain Internal Report by the Design Council.

Design Council. (2005). *Brown Backs Design.* Retrieved from www.design-council.org

Design Council. (2005/2006) Design in Business Internal Survey Report by the Design Council.

Doyle, S. A., & Broadbridge, A. (1999). Differentiation by design: the importance of design in retailer repositioning and differentiation . *International Journal of Retail & Distribution Management, 27*(2), 72–82. doi:10.1108/09590559910258571

Faisal, M. N., Banwet, D. K., & Shankar, R. (2006). Mapping supply chains on risk and customer sensitivity dimensions . *Industrial Management & Data Systems, 106*(6), 878–895. doi:10.1108/02635570610671533

Ferdows, K., Lewis, M., & Machuca, J. A. D. (2004). Zara. *Supply Chain Forum . International Journal (Toronto, Ont.), 4*(2), 62–67.

Fine, C. H. (1998). Clockspeed, New York: Perseus Books.

Fisher, M. (1997). What is the right supply chain for your product? *Harvard Business Review, 75*(2), 105–116.

Hayes, R. H., & Wheelwright, S. C. (1979). The dynamics of process-product life cycles . *Harvard Business Review, 57*(22), 127–136.

Hayes, R. H., & Wheelwright, S. C. (1984). Restoring Our Competitive Edge: Competing Through Manufacturing. New York: Wiley

Huang, G. Q., Zhang, X. Y., & Liang, L. (2005). Towards integrated optimal configuration of platform products, manufacturing processes and supply chains. *Journal of Operations Management, 23*(3/4), 267–290. doi:10.1016/j.jom.2004.10.014

Khan, O., Christopher, M., & Burnes, B. (2008). The impact of product design on supply chain risk: a case study. *International Journal of Physical Distribution and Logistics Management, 38*(5), 412–432. doi:10.1108/09600030810882834

Kincade, D. H., Regan, C., & Gibson, F. Y. (2007). Concurrent engineering for product development in mass customization for the apparel industry . *International Journal of Operations & Production Management, 27*(6), 627–649. doi:10.1108/01443570710750295

King, N. (2004), Using interviews in qualitative research, In Cassell, C., & Symon, G. (eds.), Essential guide to qualitative methods in organizational research, Thousand Oaks, CA: Sage Publications. (pp. 11-22).

Kleindorfer, P. R., & Saad, G. H. (2005). Managing Disruption Risks in Supply Chains . *Production and Operations Management, 14*(1), 53–68.

Kotler, P., & Rath, G. A. (1984). Design: A Powerful but Neglected Strategic Tool . *The Journal of Business Strategy, 5*(2), 16–21. doi:10.1108/eb039054

Krishnan, V., & Ulrich, K. (2001). Product development decisions: a review of the literature . *Management Science, 47*(1), 52–68. doi:10.1287/mnsc.47.1.52.10665

Lau, H. C. W., & Lee, W. B. (2000). On a responsive supply chain information system . *International Journal of Physical Distribution & Logistics Management, 30*(7/8), 598–610. doi:10.1108/09600030010346242

Lee, H. L., Billington, C., & Carter, B. (1993). Hewlett-Packard Gains Control of Inventory and Service through Design for Localization. *Interfaces, 23*(4), 1–11. doi:10.1287/inte.23.4.1

Lee, H. L., & Sasser, M. (1995). Product universality and design for supply chain. *Production Planning and Control, 6*(3), 270–277. doi:10.1080/09537289508930279

Magretta, J. (1998). The Power of Vertical Integration: an Interview with Dell Computer's Michael Dell. *Harvard Business Review, 76*(2), 73–84.

Masson, R., Iosif, L., MacKerron, G., & Fernie, J. (2007). Managing complexity in agile global fashion industry supply chains . *International Journal of Logistics Management*, *18*(2), 238–254. doi:10.1108/09574090710816959

Mather, H. (1992). Design for Logistics (DFL) - The Next Challenge for Designers . *Production and Inventory Management Journal*, *33*(1), 7–11.

Miles, M. B., & Huberman, A. M. (1994). Qualitative data analysis, Thousand Oaks, CA, Sage Publications.

O'Neal, C. (1993). Concurrent engineering with early supplier involvement: a cross functional challenge . *International Journal of Purchasing and Materials Management*, *29*(2), 3–9.

Patell, J. M. (1987). Cost Accounting, Process Control, and Product Design: A Case Study of the Hewlett-Packard Personal Office Computer Division. *Accounting Review*, *62*(4), 808–839.

Porter, M. E. (1985). Competitive Advantage: Creating and Sustaining Superior Performance, New York: The Free Press.

Ragatz, G. L., Handfield, R. B., & Scannel, T. V. (1997). Success factors for integrating suppliers into new product development . *Journal of Product Innovation Management*, *14*(3), 190–202. doi:10.1016/S0737-6782(97)00007-6

Sharifi, H., Ismail, H. S., & Reid, I. (2006). Achieving Agility in Supply Chain Through Simultaneous 'Design of' and 'Design for' the Supply Chain . *Journal of Manufacturing Technology*, *17*(8), 1078–1098. doi:10.1108/17410380610707393

Sharifi, S., & Pawar, K. S. (2002). Virtually co-located product design teams: Sharing teaming experiences after the event? International Journal of Operations & Production Management, 22(6), 656–679. doi:10.1108/01443570210427677doi:10.1108/01443570210427677

Spekman, R. E., & Davis, E. W. (2004). Risky business: expanding the discussion on risk and the extended enterprise. International Journal of Physical Distribution & Logistics Management, 34(5), 414–433. doi:10.1108/09600030410545454doi:10.1108/09600030410545454

Taps, S. B., & Steger-Jensen, K. (2007). Aligning supply chain design with manufacturing strategies in developing regions. Production Planning and Control, 18(6), 475–486. doi:10.1080/09537280701495021doi:10.1080/09537280701495021

Tranfield, D., Denyer, D., & Smart, P. (2003). Towards a Methodology for Developing Evidence-Informed Management Knowledge by Means of Systematic Review. British Journal of Management, 14(3), 207–222. doi:10.1111/1467-8551.00375doi:10.1111/1467-8551.00375

Ulrich, K. T., & Eppinger, S. D. (2000). Product design and development, New York: McGraw Hill.

Van Hoek, R. I., & Chapman, P. (2006). From tinkering around the edge to enhancing revenue growth: supply chain-new product development, Supply Chain Management: an international journal, 11(5), 385-389.

Van Hoek, R. I., & Chapman, P. (2007). How to move supply chain beyond cleaning up after new product development, Supply Chain Management: an international journal, 12(4), 239-244.

Wilding, R. D. (2003). The 3 Ts of highly effective Supply Chains. Supply Chain Practice, 5(3), 30–41.

Yin, R. K. (1994), Case Study Research: Design and Methods. Applied Social. Thousand Oaks, CA: Sage Publications.

Yin, R. K. (2003), Case Study Research: Design and Methods, 3rd edition, Thousand Oaks, CA: Sage Publications.

ADDITIONAL READING

Appelqvist, P., Lehtonen, J. M., & Kokkonen, J. (2004). Modelling in Product and Supply Chain Design: Literature Survey and Case Study. *Journal of Manufacturing Technology Management, 15*(7), 675–686. doi:10.1108/17410380410555916

Ellram, L. M., Tate, W. L., & Carter, C. R. (2007). Product-process-supply chain: an integrative approach to three-dimensional concurrent engineering. *International Journal of Physical Distribution and Logistics Management, 37*(4), 305–330. doi:10.1108/09600030710752523

Khan, O. (2008). New Look – Competing through the Design-Supply Chain Interface, ECCH Case Study Bedford, UK: Cranfield School of Management.

Khan, O. (2008, September 10-12). The Product Design-Supply Chain Interface: A Driver for Competitive Advantage. In *Proceedings from the Logistics Research Network Annual Conference*, Liverpool, UK.

Khan, O., & Burnes, B. (2007). Risk and Supply Chain Management: Creating A Research Agenda. *International Journal of Logistics Management, 18*(2). doi:10.1108/09574090710816931

Khan, O., Christopher, M., & Creazza, A. (2009, June 14-17). The Responsive and Resilient Enterprise: Aligning Product Design with the Supply Chain, In *Proceedings from the 16th Annual EurOMA Conference*, Goteborg, Sweden

Khan, O., & Creazza, A. (2009). Developing a Roadmap to the Design Centric Business. *International Journal of Logistics and Physical Distribution Management, 39*(4), 301–319. doi:10.1108/09600030910962258

Khan, O., & Creazza, A. (2009, May 1-4). New Look: Aligning Product Design with the Supply Chain for Responsiveness and Resilience. In *Proceedings from 20th Annual Production and Operations Management Society Conference*, Orlando, FL.

Khan, O., & Cutler-Greaves, Y. (2008). Managing Risks in Agile Supply Chains: Lessons from a UK Retailer. *International Journal of Agile Systems and Management, 3*(3/4).

Lee, H. L. (2004). The triple A supply chain. *Harvard Business Review, 82*(6), 102–112.

Parker, D. B., Zsidisin, G. A., & Ragatz, G. L. (2008). Timing and extent of supplier integration in new product development: a contingency approach. *Journal of Supply Chain Management, 44*(1), 71–83. doi:10.1111/j.1745-493X.2008.00046.x

Zsidisin, G. A., & Smith, M. E. (2005). Managing supply risk with early supplier involvement: A case study and research propositions. *The Journal of Supply Chain Management, 41*(4), 44–57. doi:10.1111/j.1745-493X.2005.04104005.x

Chapter 10
Flexible Supply Chains:
A Boost for Risk Mitigation?

María Jesús Sáenz
Zaragoza Logistics Center & University of Zaragoza, Spain

Maria Pilar Lambán
University of Zaragoza, Spain

Eva Navarro
Zaragoza Logistics Center, Spain

ABSTRACT

Organizations that remain flexible take advantage of new opportunities, explore new ways of working and resolve unanticipated consequences. When the focus is on integrating company strategies and operations in the same supply chain, flexibility is unarguably a very promising concept but at the same time, a concept very hard to implement, a cumbersome process with numerous uncertainties and risks along the way. In this chapter, a conceptual strategic framework for increasing value chain flexibility is proposed. This framework addresses issues such as the company's own strategy towards the supply chain partners, the organization strategy, the logistics approach, the market strategy, the production strategy and finally innovation. To support the validity of our proposed framework, an empirical study is presented followed by the conclusions propagated by this study and a description of future research prospects.

INTRODUCTION

Over the years, companies' strategies for improvement in their sectors have changed. These changes included cycle time reduction, which in the 1970s brought about a new strategy known as "responsiveness" to customer demand (Lewis, 1970). In the 1990s, a movement was created called "supply chain management" (Supply Chain Council) that moved

companies' focus away from internal management to managing across enterprises.

In the literature, flexibility theory and flexibility practices have focused most of the time on internal manufacturing. In the last decade, new practices related to flexibility in the supply chain (Vickery et al., 1999; Duclos et al., 2003) have begun to appear due to its positive effect on companies' competitiveness. When they integrate these strategic approaches in their operations, flexible firms take advantage of new opportunities, study

DOI: 10.4018/978-1-61520-607-0.ch010

new ways of working and resolve unanticipated consequences.

But when we talk about supply chain flexibility, one of the key questions is how do companies achieve it in a profitable way? The answer is by reducing the cycle time all while implementing a pull-based replenishment process. When cycle times are reduced, firms become stronger and are able to respond more quickly to changing market requirements and by utilizing pull-based replenishment, they are able to synchronize production with demand (Garber & Sarkar, 2007).

This chapter approaches one of the main drivers of supply chain efficiency within a strategic context, this being flexibility. In that context the concepts and features of flexible companies are analyzed. Then, the inter-organizational point of view is introduced through a description of supply chain flexibility and a presentation of the corresponding conceptual framework followed by an analysis of the driving features of value chain flexibility. The framework presents certain actions associated with encouraging greater relational integration. These actions are identified as best practices which enable flexibility value to be created in the context of the supply chain. An analysis of how supply chain actors must jointly innovate from an inter-organizational point of view while implementing flexible strategies is also presented.

The main uncertainties and risks that companies face when striving to reach a certain degree of flexibility in the supply chain are also analyzed. These risks are generally associated with the ability to achieve a dynamic alignment among supply chain agents in light of unexpected changes. On the other hand, as we will outline, the supply chain flexibility strategy that must be implemented depends on the type of uncertainties to be confronted. In addition to the analysis of flexibility best practices, a panel of key performance indicators (KPI) is presented, classified according to a prominent tool in supply chain process analysis- the SCOR (Supply Chain Operations

Reference) model endorsed by the Supply Chain Council. This panel enables constant monitoring of these processes and underlying activities that have an impact on supply chain flexibility and at the same time can support the early detection of risks and their subsequent mitigation.

The study presented in this chapter is complemented with an empirical analysis of how these practices are implemented in 57 companies of the food and beverage sector. The empirical analysis is carried out from the standpoint of the integration of supply chain actions by buyer-supplier agents. This analysis demonstrates how supply chain competitiveness is achieved through joint strategies among the members of the supply chain, with flexibility being a major strategy in the relationship between buyers and suppliers.

The chapter ends with a discussion on the feasibility and adaptability of our research approach and finally feedback, on the relative priority companies participating in our study give to the future need to implement these practices, is provided. The managerial implications of our study are also discussed in the end of this chapter.

FLEXIBLE COMPANIES

The first step of our approach includes a thorough understanding of the concept "flexible company" from an individual company's point of view. This introduction on flexible companies begins with what different, yet complementary, expert authors think about flexibility. Upton (1995) perceives flexibility as the capacity of an organization to adapt to changes. Gunasekaran et al. (2001) suggest that being flexible refers to the availability of products/services to satisfy customer demand.

Throughout the years, different dimensions of flexibility have been developed by various authors. One of the most distinguished and well-cited authors on flexibility publications is Gerwin (1993), who provides a basis for identifying specific dimensions of flexibility and the manner in which they may limit the effectiveness of the manufacturing process. Utilizing Gerwin's approach, in combination with what is proposed by Vickery et al. (1999), flexibility dimensions can be grouped into six different categories:

- *Product Flexibility*: the ability to customize products to meet specific customer demands. For example, postponement practices that entail a delay in decision making regarding customizing the product to the client's needs.
- *Volume Flexibility*: the ability to adjust capacity to meet changes in customer quantities. One example of this type of business practice is increasing the availability of inventory.
- *New Product Flexibility*: the ability to launch new or revised products, such as handling a range of products or variants with quick set-ups.
- *Distribution Flexibility*: the ability to provide widespread access to products by, for example, doubling product availability in several locations.
- *Responsiveness Flexibility*: the ability to respond to target market needs. Standard practices in this sense involve being continuously aware of competition in the market, together with suppliers, in order to discover these needs in advance.

Upton (1995) defined flexibility as the capacity of a firm to change or react in an intelligent way as regards time, effort, cost or performance. He considered flexibility to be the result of different dimensions, where each one should appear at a different time interval and where three different components define flexibility: Range, as the ability to design, make and distribute different products, Mobility, as the rapidity in which a firm can change from one product to another and Uniformity, as the ability to preserve standard products as a firm changes its products. Sanchez (1995) proposed that

flexibility from a strategic point of view (a flexible organization gains and maintains a competitive advantage in a dynamic environment) is composed of two main complementary dimensions: resource flexibility and coordination flexibility.

Given the many different contexts that can arise in industry today, it is difficult in the terms described herein to generalize the factors that determine whether or not a company is flexible, as this is limited by its sector of activity or economic situation, among others. However, if we had to outline the factors that determine an optimal level of flexibility and keeping in mind that they should be specified a posteriori for each individual supposition, the authors argue that these factors are the following:

- The product life cycle: it determines how often the production processes should be changed and the usage of similar or different procedures.
- The variety of products: with a greater variety, the supply chain has to be capable of working with more components.
- The distribution system: it has to be capable of adopting different policies depending on the type of consumer.
- The stability of consumers' orders: three factors affect the degree of flexibility required, these being; a) the natural variability of the demand for each product, b) the degree of uncertainty regarding demand forecasts and, finally c) the frequent changes in the characteristics of client orders.
- The similarity of components: it permits the usage of the same component in different products.
- The similarity of processes: the system should be more or less flexible depending on whether or not the different products go through similar processes.
- The capacity and attitude of the supply chain agents to integrate their strategies and operations: This provides a greater

joint reaction capacity for adaptation and alignment in light of changes generated either by the entire chain or by one of its agents or by the market itself.

CONCEPTUAL MODEL OF SUPPLY CHAIN FLEXIBILITY

As the supply chain extends beyond the company, supply chain flexibility must also extend beyond the single firm's internal flexibility (Duclos et al., 2003). To achieve the level of flexibility that provides customers with added value, supply chain organizations must look beyond operational flexibility, in manufacturing for instance, and integrate value chain flexibility from a strategic point of view.

Different definitions for supply chain flexibility can currently be found in the literature. Beamon (1999) describes it as the ability to respond to the uncertainty of a changing environment. For Duclos et al. (2003), it includes all flexibility within a supply chain, such as that of suppliers, carriers or internal departments. Kumar et al. (2006) define SC flexibility as the ability of supply chain partners to restructure their operations, align their strategies and share the responsibility of rapidly responding to customer demands at each link in the chain in order to produce a variety of products in the quantities, at the costs and with the qualities the customers expect all while still maintaining high performance. Das and Abdel-Malek (2003) define supply chain flexibility as the "elasticity" of the buyer-supplier relationship under changing supply conditions. As regards the drivers and sources of flexibility in the supply area, Mendonça and Giménez (2007) analyse two main strategies: improve supplier responsiveness and flexible sourcing, depending on the type of uncertainty the focal company faces. Zhang et al. (2002) argue that value chain flexibility can provide a variety of innovative, low-cost, high-quality products reliably and quickly, and that

it involves a difficulty to imitate and substitute which leads to a sustained competitive advantage by integrating flexibility along the supply chain. This study applies the competence and capability theory, which adds a systematic resource-based view of a firm's value chain flexibility. There are some generic principles drawn from the above theories that can be applied to the supply chain context. These are the following (Stevenson & Spring, 2007): a) flexibility is multi-dimensional, b) different elements of flexibility are more important in certain environments than in others and c) flexibility is a capability that does not have to be demonstrated. In accordance with the above definitions, the conceptual framework proposed in this chapter focuses on how a firm can build value chain flexibility by aligning its strategy with its supply chain partners under changing supply chain conditions. Within this framework, the focus is on integrating the strategies in the supply chain when flexibility becomes an important component of the system. By attaining this value chain flexibility, the firm is able to gain a sustained competitive advantage.

Different research on flexibility conceptual frameworks has been carried out which could be applied to the supply chain context (Gerwin, 1993; Sanchez, 1995; Vickery et al., 1999 or Stevenson & Spring, 2007). Considering the focus and the scope of this study, we are going to take into account the research of Beach et al. (2000), Zhang et al. (2002), Duclos et al. (2003) and Kumar et al. (2006) for our model. These frameworks have a common goal: to identify the different issues that must be considered in order to implement and manage value chain flexibility successfully. The focus of each framework and the reasons why they have been chosen for analysis in this research will now be explained.

The first one, by Beach et al. (2000), analyzes the relationship between business strategy, environmental uncertainty and manufacturing flexibility. It integrates these relationships with the necessary system performance measurements

Table 1. Characteristics of supply chain flexibility

Characteristics	Beach et al. (2000)	Zhang et al. (2002)	Duclos et al. (2003)	Kumar et al. (2006)
Competitive Advantage	X	X	X	X
Environmental Uncertainty	X	X		X
Production Strategy	X		X	X
Market Strategy			X	X
Corporate Culture	X			
Organizational Strategy			X	X
Value Chain Flexibility		X		X

between the manufacturing strategy and the business strategy, which allow us to have more control over a flexible supply chain.

The second one, by Zhang et al. (2002), explores the relationship between environmental uncertainty, value chain flexibility and competitive advantages. The authors focused their research on finding out "the flexible capabilities that impact relationships with customers and the flexible competences that support these capabilities". There are various reasons for using Zhang's research in this chapter. First of all, it focuses on the company's strategic approach and on how to combine a firm's capabilities with the resource-based view of a firm's value chain flexibility. Zhang's framework supports our knowledge on how flexibility in customer service becomes relevant, as well as how a firm can improve by establishing flexibility strategies in the organization.

The third one, by Duclos et al. (2003), explains how flexibility strategies must extend beyond the firm's boundaries and not just involve intra-firm flexibility, as many authors have asserted. The authors analyze the relationship between a firm, its suppliers and customers through different flexibility-related components, such as operations systems, the market, logistics, supply, organizational and information systems flexibility.

Finally, in this chapter we argue that the supply chain should be viewed from the entire value-adding chain, as Kumar et al. (2006) do in their research. This study suggests a three-stage approach for implementing and managing supply chain flexibility: a) flexibility identification, where the company should establish its mission and organizational competitive strategies, b) implementation and shared responsibility, and finally c) feedback and control through supply chain performance measurement.

Table 1 summarizes the main characteristics of each one of the four frameworks that are going to be used in elaborating our proposed conceptual framework:

The Proposed Framework

Based on the theoretical frameworks previously explained and considering the abovementioned strategic focus and the previously established scope, a new adapted framework has been developed which presents strategic flexibility within the supply chain context. At first, we have proposed a set of antecedents and a set of strategies that focus on creating Value Chain Flexibility, as depicted in Figure 1. The proposed antecedents, some external and others internal, will influence the development of competitive strategies that focus on improving supply chain flexibility, as well as the very process of implementing a new, more flexible supply chain. These antecedents are:

Figure 1. Conceptual framework of flexibility in the supply chain context

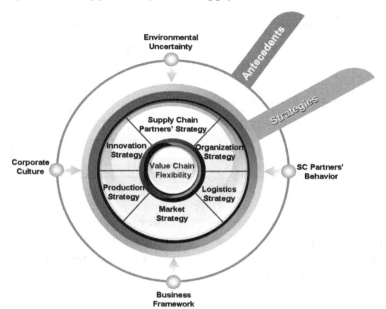

- *Environmental Uncertainty*: forces an organization to establish contingency plans that are to be incorporated into the organization's business strategy (Kumar et al., 2006; Gerwin, 1993). Knowledge of these types of external uncertainties will help the company to be prepared to react to these risks or mitigate them. This in turn, will lead an organization to conceive and implement different types of flexibility, based on the threats it may face.

- *Supply Chain Partners Behavior*: It is important to know the characteristics of all SC partners involved, such as their mutual trust or attitude towards change. This knowledge will support the organization in the coordination of the various supply chain agents and the subsequent alignment of their business strategies. In that sense, managers can understand the needs, strengths and potentials of their partners more comprehensively and thus, be able to encourage more efficient innovations (Duclos et al., 2003; Kumar et al., 2006).

- *Business Framework*: Reflects the acknowledged relationships between the business strategy formulation and the manufacturing process (Beach at el, 2000). The organization has to know product features, such as the product life cycle, the product strategy and the end-product characteristics.

- *Corporate Culture*: The cultural norms of an organization that help direct its behavior when making strategic decisions (Calentone et al., 2002), such as for example, cultural competitiveness or risk aversion are relevant. Some authors specifically mention the influence of this aspect, which is in turn related to business strategy (Beach et al., 2000). Companies' attitudes to corporate culture flexibility, with distributed decision-making and communications at all levels, can create a resilient enterprise (Sheffi, 2005).

With prior knowledge of the abovementioned antecedents, the company must encourage and develop competitive strategies that focus on improving flexibility in the supply chain. By doing so, it will obtain competitive advantages for the whole supply chain. These strategies are:

- *Supply Chain Partners Strategy*: Once the supply chain partners' capacities and behavior is known, strategic negotiations with suppliers and/or customers must be undertaken that will encourage coordination actions and enhance continuous improvement. It will also allow the company to know what the supply chain partner's flexibility capacity is and get this partner to commit to a certain extent of this flexibility capacity for the benefit of the supply chain (Mendonça & Giménez, 2007).
- *Organization Strategy*: It targets the flexibility that can be achieved through workforce manipulation and guides the organizational structure, the business practices and the culture under which that workforce operates (Duclos et al., 2003).
- *Logistics Strategy*: This refers to the ability to receive, produce and deliver in a cost-effective manner as supply sources and customers change (Duclos et al., 2003). In this framework of action, logistics will give the company a "distinct value to distinct customers" (Fuller et al., 1993).
- *Market Strategy*: This is the responsiveness to changes in market conditions and customer needs; for instance, the ability to customize products to meet specific customer demands or the ability to launch new or revised products as well as their components (Duclos et al., 2003).
- *Production Strategy*: Companies have to be able to reconfigure their production processes in accordance with holistic supply chain planning and according to the changes in demand. There is an extensive body of literature on manufacturing flexibility strategy, from which this specific strategy can draw (Gerwin, 1993; Beach et al., 2000; Narain et al., 2000).
- *Innovation Strategy*: Supply chain agents must be continuously on the lookout for innovation opportunities that enable optimizing the processes with common visions. These visions should be part of the joint collaboration strategy (Zhang et al., 2002; Saenz et al., 2008).

The value chain flexibility concept views two types of dimensions as different, but complementary: capability and competence (Zhang et al, 2002). These dimensions allow companies to gain competitive advantages. The dichotomy in value chain flexibility allows managers to identify which flexible capabilities are critical to their relationships with customers and flexible competences that support these capabilities. Flexible competences, which are internally focused, provide the processes and infrastructure that enable firms to achieve the desired levels of flexible capabilities, which are externally focused. It also helps firms cultivate the corresponding flexible competence that supports the customer-valued flexible capability. Flexible competence ensures a competitive edge.

These characteristics support the determination of how and where improvements can be made throughout the supply chain so as to add value to flexibility. This does not mean that the greatest possible flexibility must be achieved. What is important, is that each company finds its own flexibility framework; in other words, each company studies each one of the characteristics and verifies what improvements can be made considering the specific circumstances of the organization or group of organizations. When a flexibility strategy is designed, in the supply chain context, the company must control the effectiveness and efficiency of the supply chain. As Beach et al. explain (2000), it is necessary to have different controls in place throughout the theoretical framework which assist the researcher to verify the influences of flexibility management or the evolutions of the antecedents as environmental uncertainties or supply chain behaviors.

In accordance with all of the above, the proposed strategic conceptual framework would be as follows:

RISK MITIGATION IN A FLEXIBLE SUPPLY CHAIN

Nowadays, companies are confronted with numerous risks, most of them propagated by the reduced ability to provide a dynamic alignment among the various supply chain agents. One of the major problems when trying to confront supply chain risks is the lack of confidence among the partners. This can affect the supply chain in different ways, such as order cycle time, current order status, demand forecasts given, suppliers' capability to deliver, manufacturing capacity, quality of the products, transportation reliability and services delivered.

The more disorganization and decision risks in a supply chain, the less confidence there is among the partners, which means failure will be more likely. So, it's necessary to find a way to decrease this lack of confidence as the supply chain has to have visibility and control (Christopher & Lee, 2004):

- Visibility: It implies increased sharing of information among partners. By sharing information, there will be less uncertainty and the systems will become more responsive.
- Control: the ability to take control of supply chain operations.

It can be said that there are three different manager's attitude towards risk (March & Sharpira, 1987). First of all, managers do not understand or, perhaps do not trust probability estimates of possible outcomes. Second, they tend to focus on critical performance targets and because of this

attitude, manager's behavior becomes more risk averse when their performance is above a certain target. Finally, companies tend to reward managers for obtaining "good outcomes" and not for making "good decisions". Despite managers' attitude toward risk, their standpoint towards initiatives for managing risk must also be analyzed. Companies invest little time or resources to mitigating supply chain risks. The difficulty in obtaining an accurate probability of the occurrence of any particular disruption makes it complicated for firms to justify risk contingency plans. This inherent risk management characteristic results in firms underestimating disruption risk in the absence of accurate supply chain risk assessment.

In order to depict information related to supply costs and risks within the product/service level, a graph where risk and value are related is elaborated. This graph depicts four quadrants, labeled a) Bottleneck, b) Critical, c) Generic and d) Leverage. A high level of risk and high level of value appears as "critical", where the performance and value of the product/service is in the customer's hands. The opposite will be "generic", where costs, time and effort are in the acquisition process. If the risk is high, but its value is low, this is known as "bottleneck", which involves risks of non-availability, downtime costs and plant utilization rates. Finally, "leverage" implies low risk and high value which leads to price and delivery, supply chain investments, costs and processes (Cavinato, 2004).

In his book *The Resilient Enterprise*, Sheffi (2005) describes methods that support companies to increase security and reduce the likelihood of a disruption, such as layered defenses, the tracking and analysis of "near-misses", the fast detection and close collaboration with government agencies, trading partners and even competitors. One of the objectives of this chapter is to establish guidelines that will support risk mitigation. Given the fact that many different applications can arise in industry today, establishing a series of general guidelines is very complicated and sometimes

Figure 2. The risk – value quadrants

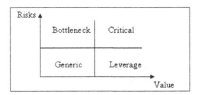

useless. Therefore, we shall attempt to establish some guidelines on how to mitigate risks although this would require a specific analysis of the sector or context under study in order to analyze the results obtained and how they are applied.

In the remainder of this section, an explanation of the six major types of supply chain risks (adapted from Tang and Tomlin, 2008; Zsidisin & Ritchie, 2008; Cavinato, 2004) that regularly appear in this strategic context as well as strategies to mitigate them, is provided:

- *Supply Risks*: The main goal is to reduce the cost of managing multiple suppliers and to foster better supplier relationships. Although managing a small number of suppliers is more efficient, the supply risks increase. Three types of supply risks have been described: supply cost risks, supply commitment risks and supply quality. These risks can be mitigated with strategies that involve multiple suppliers and flexible supply contracts.
- *Process Risks*: Firms have invested in programs such as total quality management, lean manufacturing and six sigma to improve internal quality and capabilities. Process risks include quality, time and capacity risks associated with in-bound and out-bound logistics and in-house operations. Using strategies for flexible manufacturing processes, the negative impact of the risk can be deteriorated.

- *Demand Risks*: Many firms sell their products in multiple countries to increase revenue. Demand risks are associated with demand uncertainty. Firms can follow the strategies of postponement to mitigate risks and responsive pricing.
- *Intellectual Property Risks*: They are difficult to mitigate when a multinational firm outsources its manufacturing operations to another country under certain contractual agreements. Supply chain innovations are particularly sensitive to these issues. One way to mitigate these risks is to establish agreements and contracts which on the one hand, allow for certain flexibility in the collaboration and on the other hand, establish limits on the flow of information.
- *Behavioral Risks*: The level of visibility and control is reduced when the number of partners increases. It is important to mitigate these risks by knowing the partners in the supply chain and by assuring that the objectives of the other agents in the relationship are satisfied. At the same time, it is essential to know what the company's behaviors are as far as corporate culture.
- *Political/Social Risks*: A global supply chain can become part of a political disturbance in the country of origin of any one of its members. With regards to this risk, it is important to be aware of the political and economic movements under which the activity is carried out and as soon as there is reason to believe that this can have an effect on the supply chain, collaborative relationships must be established to mitigate these risks.
- *Financial Risks*: These risks include a lack of cost visibility throughout the supply chain and improper investments. Precise knowledge of the costs throughout the supply chain, the establishment of business objectives and collaboration between

Table 2. Framework attributes as they relate to risk types

Risk Type	Framework Attribute
Supply Risks	• SC partners Strategy • Innovation Strategy • Logistics Strategy
Process Risks	• Production Strategy • Logistics Strategy
Demand Risks	• Market Strategy • Logistics Strategy
Intellectual Property Risks	• SC partners Strategy • Innovation Strategy
Behavioral Risks	• SC partners Strategy • Organizational Strategy
Political/Social Risks	• SC partners Strategy • Organizational Strategy
Financial Risks	• SC partners Strategy • Organizational Strategy • Production Strategy • Logistics Strategy

agents will help mitigate these risks.

The following table shows the relationships between supply chain risks and the elaborated theoretical framework (as shown in Figure 1):

As companies may not be able to assess the performance cost and conduct an elaborated return on investment analysis to justify the contingency plans, it's difficult for firms to implement supply chain strategies to mitigate risks. According to Tang (2006), if these strategies include efficiency and resiliency, firms will become more willing to implement them because both of them ensure profitability and business continuity.

The direct benefits of effective supply chain risk management (Zsidisin & Ritchie, 2008) include the following:

- The ability to anticipate and respond promptly to external trends and developments;
- A focus on the uncertainties rather than the certainties;
- Greater influence over the supply chain partners;
- Greater mutual understanding of the interests and problems of all supply chain partners;
- A better balance between opportunities and threats;
- Management which is not based on the cost factor alone;
- A competitive edge through the acceptance of controlled risks.

KEY PERFORMANCE INDICATORS OF SUPPLY CHAIN FLEXIBILITY

Performance indicators or metrics are measurements that are used to check how a process, plan or project is working. Their purpose is to provide information on the actual state of a program (description function) or to add "value judgment" to the previous function based on objective precedents (evaluative function).

Many authors have done research on metrics planning and designing systems to measure performance, all of which are in line with the company's strategies. Fitzgerald et al. (1991), suggest that there are two types of measurements: those related to results (competitiveness, financial performance) and those that focus on how the results are determined (quality, flexibility, utilization of resources and innovation). Beamon (1999) established three major types of performance measures: a) resource measures, which include inventory levels, personnel requirements, equipment use, energy use and costs, b) output measures, which include customer responsiveness as far as the quality and quantity of the finished product and c) flexibility measures. Furthermore, he stated that, in an uncertain environment, the supply chain must be capable of having a measuring system, including at least one individual measure for each one of these three types. Additionally these measures should be aligned with the organization's strategic goals.

In search for an integrated measurement system, Neely et al. (1995) present a conceptual framework for designing performance measurement systems, which is structured into three different levels of analysis: individual measures, the performance measurement system as an entity and the relationship between this measurement system and the environment in which it operates. In their research work, the concept of performance measurement is defined as a metric that is used to quantify the efficiency and/or effectiveness of an action and the concept of performance measurement system as all of the metrics used to quantify the efficiency and/or effectiveness of an action. They also mention the importance of alignment among the metrics used and the company's strategies. Gunasekaran et al. (2001) establish that the metrics used to measure a company's performance in the context of the supply chain must represent a balanced focus that could be classified into levels such as strategic, tactic and operational, and they may be financial or non-financial. Morgan (2004) also places importance on maintaining consistency between the strategy adopted by a company and its measurement system. In his analysis, he outlines three main requirements that a supply chain performance measurement system must meet: a) It must be linked to the organization's strategy, b) be part of an integrated control system and c) be internally valid and allow for proactive management. Furthermore, he proposes that it must be dynamic, inter-connectable, focused and useful.

There are many different and complementary reasons to propose a supply chain measurement system, including:

- The lack of measures that represent performance throughout the entire supply chain;
- The obligation to go beyond internal results and adopt a supply chain perspective;
- The need to determine the interrelationship between the performance of each individual company and the performance of the supply chain;

- The complexity of managing the supply chain;
- The need to align activities and share information on performance measures in order to implement strategies that make it possible to attain the supply chain objectives;
- The need to differentiate the supply chain in order to obtain a competitive advantage;
- The challenge of rewarding collaborative behavior through corporate functions and through supply chain firms.

The work of Lambert and Pohlen (2001) indicates the need for both financial as well as non-financial metrics in order to measure the performance of the strategic alliance established between supply chain agents. This alliance should be able to record the results obtained from the collaboration and joint projects to a joint profit. Additionally, loss account plays a very important role in knowing who is benefiting most from the new relationship, who is assuming more costs and how to distribute the increased profits (or charges) from the decisions taken in the supply chain in a way that is fair to all partners.

There is great divergence in the literature as far as how the authors measure flexibility. Slack (1983) identifies three factors that make measuring the flexibility of a production system difficult: a) flexibility is a measurement of potential, b) flexibility must be applied to other objectives besides production such as volume, delivery or the supply and c) flexibility has many dimensions both in range as well as response.

Gerwin (1987) continues with the manufacturing perspective, as regards flexibility, and identifies different types of flexibility. He also suggests some metrics for each one of the identified types, including:

- *Mix Flexibility*, which is defined as the number of different components manufactured with a certain piece of equipment. Possible measures: the range of characteristics of the handled components, the ratio of the number of components processed by the equipment out of the total number processed by the company, etc.

- *Design Changeover Flexibility*: measures the number of component substitutions made in a given period for a given piece of equipment. A possible measure would be calculating the investment ratio for the new product in the equipment out of the total investment (Gustavsson, 1984).
- *Modification Flexibility*, which is defined as the number of changes made to component designs over a period of time.
- *Rerouting Flexibility*: refers to rerouting the production when a machine must be replaced. One possible measure proposed is the rate of production decline when a machine stops working (Buzacott, 1982).
- *Volume Flexibility*: needs to be considered both on a component aggregate level as well as on the individual level. It can be measured in terms of the average volume fluctuations that occur in a given period divided by the capacity limit.

Due to the many dimensions of flexibility and the fact that it represents a measurement of potential, in order to situate the measures, the SCOR (Supply Chain Operations Reference) model has been used as a reference. It is a management tool that is known and approved world-wide by many logistics organizations of excellence and was developed by the Supply Chain Council. This reference model makes it possible to approach the various processes of the supply chain in accordance with their functions and interconnections. The model features a strategic process called "Global Plan", which covers the most operational processes known as "Source Plan", "Make Plan" and "Delivery Plan".

Flexibility performance metrics are presented below in accordance with the SCOR reference model and considering the metrics presented by other authors such as Zhang et al. (2005), Chopra

and Meindl (2007), Koste and Malholtra (1999) and Lummus et al. (2003). The metrics are presented in two tables. Table 3 details strategic level metrics and Table 4, operational. Strategic metrics are related with demand management flexibility, organizational flexibility and information system flexibility. Operational metrics' are related with supply planning, manufacturing planning and delivery planning. It is important to keep in mind that although the focus of this chapter is on studying flexibility in the supplier-buyer relationship as it applies to a more strategic context, in order to be able to quantify a certain performance measure, it is sometimes necessary to look at the operational context. The tables indicate the metrics under the corresponding SCOR process, the flexibility dimension, the relationship with the conceptual model proposed in Figure 1, the supply chain risks related to the metrics proposed and finally, the metrics and authors that have proposed them or their origin of adaptation. In doing that, a connection is established between the possible risks explained in the previous section and the metrics that can identify and measure the effectiveness of implementing the supply chain strategies that help mitigate these risks.

EMPIRICAL EVIDENCE REGARDING THE IMPLEMENTATION OF FLEXIBILITY BEST PRACTICES

The proposed framework for supply chain flexibility is complemented by an empirical analysis conducted in 57 companies of the food and beverage sector.

Study Methodology

Considering the scope of this chapter on supply chain flexibility, the focus of the empirical study is to analyze the dyadic buyer-supplier relationship from a production or processing company's point of view.

Table 3. Flexibility metrics - strategic level

SCOR Process	Flexibility	Relationship with the Model	Relationship with Risk	Metrics	Author
Global Plan	Demand Management Flexibility	*Production Strategy *Market Strategy *SC Partners Strategy	*Supply Risks *Process Risks	Variety of customer needs that can be served.	Zhang (2005)
			*Demand Risks	Time and cost to respond to various customer requests.	Zhang (2005)
				Quality of service across the various customer requests.	Zhang (2005)
	Organizational Flexibility	*SC Partners Strategy *Organizational Strategy *Innovation Strategy	*Supply Risks *Intellectual property Risks *Behavioral Risks *Political/social Risks	Number of shared flexibility objectives, metrics and plans jointly developed by buyer-supplier and buyer-customer.	Adapted from Lummus et al. (2003) / Koste and Malhotra (1999)
				Time and cost dedicated to developing the shared objectives, metrics and plans.	Adapted from Lummus et al. (2003) / Koste and Malhotra (1999)
				Shared plans implemented out of the total proposed.	Adaptated from Lummus et al. (2003) / Koste and Malhotra (1999)
				Number of members of the buyer-supplier and buyer-customer SC teams as well as the internal SC teams for each SC node.	Adaptated from Lummus et al. (2003) / Koste and Malhotra (1999)
				Dedication to joint plans as far as time and cost are concerned.	Adaptated from Lummus et al. (2003) / Koste and Malhotra (1999)
	Information System Flexibility	*SCPartners Strategy *Innovation Strategy *Production Strategy *Logistics Strategy	*Supply Risks *Demand Risks *Intellectual Properties Risks	Total time and cost involved in calculating long-term forecasts for the entire SC. Quality of the forecast.	Adaptation of Chopra S. and Meindl P. (2007) / Koste and Malhotra (1999)
				Quality and Compatibility of the information technology tools used by SC partners.	Adaptation of Lummus et al. (2003) / Koste and Malhotra (1999)

This study was designed to meet three objectives:

- Investigate the interrelationship between potential drivers for successful supply chain management such as flexibility strategies and their innovative capacity as well as their strategic components.
- Investigate to what degree learning and innovation are favored in buyer-supplier relationships and whether or not these determine business success.
- Find out how important the actions indicated in each answer are from an expert point of view.

A tool that is based on a questionnaire directed at manufacturing and processing companies in the food and beverage sector asking about the buyer-supplier relationship as it applies to the

Table 4. Flexibility metrics - operational level

SCOR Process	Flexibility	Relationship with the model	Relationship with risks	Metrics	Author
Source Plan	Physical flexibility of internal supply	* Logistics Strategy * Production Strategy * SC Partners Strategy * Market Strategy	*Supply Risks *Process Risks	The variety of production supply materials and the variety of materials returned by production or customer.	Adapted from Zhang (2005)
				Time and efficiency of different materials moved	Zhang (2005)
				Quality and supply dependability across the various incoming materials	Zhang (2005)
				Average Inventory	Adapted from Chopra and Meindl (2007)
				Average replenishment batch size	Adapted from Chopra and Meindl (2007)
				Average Safety Inventory	Adapted from Chopra and Meindl (2007)
	Purchasing flexibility	* Logistics Strategy * SC Partners Strategy	*Supply Risks *Process Risks *Behavioral Risks *Financial Risks	Different types of materials purchased	Zhang (2005)
				Time and cost to fill the different requests	Zhang (2005)
				Quality of materials purchased and quality of the process	Zhang(2005)
Make Plan	System operation flexibility	* Production Strategy * Organizational Strategy	*Process Risks	Capacity	Adapted from Chopra and Meindl (2007)
				Utilization	Adapted from Chopra and Meindl (2007)
Delivery Plan	Physical distribution flexibility	* Logistics Strategy * Production Strategy * Market Strategy * SC Partners Strategy	*Supply Risks *Process Risks *Demand Risks *Behavioral Risks *Financial risks	Different types of packaging and the number of modes of transportation	Adapted from Zhang, (2005)
				Time and cost to use different modes of transportation and different packages	Zhang (2005)
				Quality and dependability of the delivery of various products dispatched.	Zhang (2005)

supply chain was used as the research methodology. The person responsible for purchasing and/or supplies or where appropriate, the person who has a relationship with the most strategic supplier answered the survey. The survey was conducted by means of questionnaire shipment and the response rate was 10.2%.

In order to ensure that the data collection tool fulfilled its purpose and in order to have greater confidence in the results, the basic pre-requisites for designing questionnaires were followed: a) a correct definition of the problem being researched, b) a precise formulation of the hypothesis, and c) an appropriate specification of the variables and corresponding measurement scales (Santesmaes, 2005). In addition, the questionnaire was tested in two ways. Firstly, a panel of experts made up of 3 scholars and 5 professionals who hold positions as required by the respondent profile evaluated the quality and clarity of the propositions. Secondly, the IT tool SQP (Survey Quality Prediction) was used to determine the validity and reliability of the questionnaire (Saris & Gallhofer, 2007). Both showed positive results. Data was collected from June 2008 to March 2009.

Sector Analysis

The food and beverage sector has a strategic role within the socio-economic context of any country. Today, there are many risks and uncertainties that affect it: the impact of the increased costs of raw materials, the increase in the price of fuel, the recent and new legal requirements for food and environmental safety, as well as new threats as a result of globalization. On the other hand, there is a large number of companies with a variety of interests and strategies creating supply networks with coordination needs while at the same time, seeking efficiency. The food and beverage sector is made up of eight sub-sectors: fruits and vegetables, fats and oil, meat industry, beverage industry, milk industry, flour industry, fish transformation and other foodstuffs.

As for the size of the companies in the population, the food and beverage sector in Spain is a very fragmented sector and is mainly comprised of small businesses. In 2007, companies with less than 50 employees represented 96.60% of the sector's population (Spanish Agro-food Statistical Yearbook).

Data Gathering

Before beginning with the analysis, we shall provide the different statements on the survey along with their corresponding code which will be referred to later on in the statistical analysis. These questions are listed and classified according to the characteristics of the theoretical model previously described in Figure 1.

We must bear in mind that the questionnaire attempts to gather information from the companies on the level of implementation of the different proposed practices as well as the importance they place on each one of them. Therefore, each statement is assessed from two points of view as shown below:

Level of Implementation Importance

For the most part, the companies that participated in the study were in the beverage industry sub-sectors (40%). This sample is made up of important Spanish beer, soft drink and wine production companies. The next largest group that participated in the survey is from the other foodstuffs sector (23%), which is made up of companies that produce pastry and confectionery-related products. The percentages of each company type in the survey sample are shown in Figure 3.

The following Figure shows the companies included in the sample broken down by size, which corresponds to less than 10 employees for Micro-sized companies; from 10 to 50 for Small-sized companies; from 50 to 250 for Medium-sized; and more than 250 employees for the Big-sized ones:

Descriptive Statistics

Initially, the reliability of the results of the model was examined through the use of Cronbach's alpha parameter. This parameter examines the degree of homogeneity between the study items, with a value between 0 and 1. Greater reliability will be obtained when Cronbach's alpha parameter is closest to 1. Anything below 0.5 is considered to show a weak level of covariance between the variables. Since values of 0.84 for the degree of implementation and 0.86 for the importance were obtained in this empirical study, there is a high degree of homogeneity between the items. Therefore, the results can be considered reliable.

Table 5. Survey statements

SC Partners St.	
Pa1	We share performance indicators with our suppliers
Pa2	There is good coordination with our supplier's activity
Pa3	We maintain frequent communication with our supplier
Logistics St	
L1	We share a common vision that intends to obtain more efficient options for moving from our customer to our supplier
L2	We share a common vision that intends to achieve an efficient flow of information from our customer to our supplier
L3	My firm has increased its inventory turnover
Innovation St.	
I1	We regard innovation as key in the collaboration strategy
I2	We work by a philosophy of continuous improvement along with our providers
Organizational St.	
O1	We share a strategy to continuously improve the quality of service and the quality of the product delivered to our customers
O2	My firm has been able to anticipate the needs of the market due to the collaboration
Production St.	
Pr1	There is willingness from our suppliers to be agile and efficient when required
Pr2	We have developed or improved existing protocols for good production, practices or action manuals in the event of any incidences with our supplier
Pr3	We have improved processes with our supplier such as production, transportation, supply or forecast
Market St.	
M1	We share a common vision that intends to adopt production processes capable of rapidly responding to changes in product diversification
M2	We share a common vision that intends to adopt production processes capable of rapidly responding to changes in demand volume
M3	We share a common vision that intends to rapidly respond to the market by designing new products or components that satisfy our new needs
Flexibility	
F1	Our supplier collaborates with us to improve the lead times and final product quality
F2	We share a common vision that intends to shorten the cycle times of our production processes and those of our suppliers
F3	We share a common vision that intends to design production processes that allow postponing product customization or packaging
F4	We have the ability to reduce replenishment times with our strategic supplier
F5	The product life cycle of our products has shortened

The study analysis begins with the descriptive statistics of all the importance and implementation variables. The average response, standard deviation and the percentage of companies that gave the highest rating in each case are indicated. This data is presented in the following tables (Figure 5). The first table shows the results of the descriptive statistics for the level of implementation and the second shows those related to the importance (both rated in Table 6).

Figure 3. Subsectors and their participation in the sample

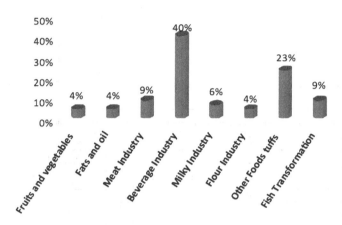

Figure 4. Participating companies by size

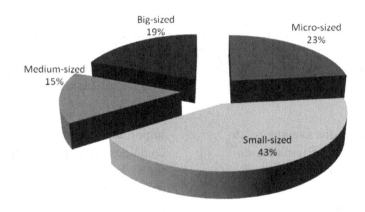

The descriptive characteristics of each one of the practices listed on the questionnaire, corresponding to each statement, are indicated below based on their average, their deviation and the percentages obtained for the responses with the greatest values. This analysis allows us to see how the sector adopts collaborative and flexible supply chain practices.

- Pa2: *There is good coordination with our supplier's activity.* We observed that 71% of the companies that completed the questionnaire have implemented coordination or are in the process of implementing it. This coincides with the fact that 70% of the companies believe it is very important. Given this data, it is clear that the averages here also stand out above the rest of the

Table 6. Response rating.

1	2	3	4	5		1	2	3	4
Not planned	Has been discussed	It is planned	We are implementing it	Totally implemented		Non important at all	Of little importance	Somewhat important	Very important

Figure 5. Table of descriptive statistics for implantation (left) table of descriptive statistics for importance(right)

	Average	Standard Desviation	% answer 4	% answer 5
Pa1	2.965	1.439	28%	16%
Pa2	4.088	1.123	21%	51%
Pa3	4.439	0.824	25%	61%
L1	3.702	1.180	33%	30%
L2	3.035	1.426	18%	21%
L3	3.193	1.329	39%	14%
I1	2.684	1.311	25%	9%
I2	3.877	1.226	28%	40%
O1	3.912	1.258	30%	42%
O2	3.053	1.274	16%	18%
Pr1	4.298	0.886	39%	49%
Pr2	2.807	1.457	21%	16%
Pr3	3.456	1.310	35%	23%
M1	3.193	1.302	37%	14%
M2	3.439	1.150	37%	18%
M3	3.404	1.266	39%	19%
F1	3.684	1.325	42%	30%
F2	2.930	1.348	32%	11%
F3	2.298	1.210	19%	2%
F4	3.596	1.178	39%	23%
F5	3.474	1.241	30%	25%

	Average	Standard Desviation	% answer 4
Pa1	2.965	0.886	32%
Pa2	3.649	0.612	70%
Pa3	3.667	0.546	70%
L1	3.316	0.890	54%
L2	2.789	1.114	28%
L3	3.175	0.947	44%
I1	2.702	1.034	25%
I2	3.368	0.794	54%
O1	3.579	0.731	70%
O2	3.035	0.963	37%
Pr1	3.772	0.423	77%
Pr2	2.772	1.035	26%
Pr3	3.158	0.960	44%
M1	2.947	0.934	28%
M2	3.088	0.892	35%
M3	3.158	1.014	47%
F1	3.246	0.931	47%
F2	2.825	1.054	30%
F3	2.158	0.996	12%
F4	3.386	0.840	56%
F5	2.877	1.070	35%

questions: in importance, the average is 3.6 out of 4; whereas in level of implementation, it is 4.1 out of 5. Finally, the deviation, which in both cases shows the lowest values, indicates uniformity in the values of this question.

- Pa3: *We maintain frequent communication with our supplier.* The percentages of importance (70%) and implementation (61% and 25%) with averages of 4.4 and 3.7, respectively, along with the deviations which indicate values that are close to the averages, demonstrate how much communication is valued between suppliers and companies.
- Pr1: *There is willingness from our suppliers to be agile and efficient when required.* Just as with the previous question, the

importance companies place on this (77%) coincides with the fact that its average is the highest out of all the questions with 3.8 and minimal deviation (0.4). At the same time, the percentage of companies that believe it has already been implemented in their process (49%) or that are implementing it (39%) is one of the highest with an average of 4.3 and a deviation which indicates uniformity among the data (0.9).

In addition, the strategies reflected in "We regard innovation as a key collaboration strategy" (I1) with an average of 2.7 and an assigned importance of 2.7 stand out due to its low level of implementation. This low rating is surprising considering that supply chain management incorporates continuous improvement among partners as one of the main values. The strategy "We share a common vision that intends to design production processes that allow postponing product customization or packaging" (F3), was also rated fairly low in both the value of implementation (with an average of 2.3) as well as its importance (average of 2.2), but this can be justified as it is a strategy that is more typical of other sectors such as the textile sector.

Correlation Analysis

The purpose of this analysis is to compare the characteristics of our proposed model with the characteristics of flexibility. This is done so that we can find out the level of influence of each one of the practices analyzed in comparison with those that place value on flexibility.

To check whether or not there is a dependency among variables, we apply a correlation among all of them. Those with a value near 1 are dependent and the closer they are to 0, the less of a relationship there is. This is combined with the p-value analysis which indicates the significance level. The closer the p-value is to zero, the more confidently we can affirm the correlation between the variables.

The dependent variables in this study are related to the implementation of flexibility by the firm in the supply chain. Further analysis has shown that the five flexibility implementation measures (F1 to F5) have a moderately high level of covariance (Cronbach's alpha = 0.64). Accordingly, we have summed up the five implementation measures to create the Flexibility F index and used this index as the dependent variable for the study.

The independent variables are the implementation measures for the practices that describe the conceptual model components: supply chain partners strategy, organization strategy, logistics strategy, market strategy, production strategy and innovation strategy. In addition, we also analyzed the relationships that exist given the importance

that the professionals assigned to the different practices.

A summary of what was explained above follows, where the correlation indexes are presented for both the level of implementation section (Table 7) as well as for the importance section (Table 8). Both tables highlight the values that compare with the integrated Flexibility Index F and its components (F1 to F5). Moreover, the values that feature a high degree of correlation between variables with a high degree of significance are shown in bold in these tables.

As can be observed in Table 8, the variables L2 and F1 show a positive correlation both as regards the level of implementation as well as importance (0.62, $p < 0.05$ and 0.53, $p < 0.05$). This indicates that the companies that share a common vision on how to achieve an efficient flow of information from the customer to the supplier, can benefit from an improvement in lead times and final product quality. Furthermore, positive correlation (0.52, $p < 0.001$) also exists between this variable L2, which describes the logistics strategy as far as the flow of information and F3, which is related to postponement strategies for product customization.

On the other hand, significant positive correlation (0.50, $p < 0.001$) was found between the variables M1 and F2. This result shows that the companies share a common vision on how to adopt production processes that are capable of rapidly responding to changes in demand volume. This would lead to shortening the company's and its suppliers' production process cycle times.

As indicated above, the Flexibility index F reflects the measures for the flexibility descriptive variables. Particularly noteworthy here is the correlation that exists with the variable Pa1 (0.44, $p < 0.001$), which describes the strategy where performance indicators are shared with the company's suppliers. This sharing would make it possible to more quickly respond to unexpected changes, as well as know the circumstances and capacities of one's supply chain partner in order to

Table 7. Correlation analysis for implementation

N=57	SC Partners			Logistics			Innovation		Organization		Production Strat.			Market Strat.			Flexibility					
	Pa1	Pa2	Pa3	L1	L2	L3	I1	I2	O1	O2	Pr1	Pr2	Pr3	M1	M2	M3	F1	F2	F3	F4	F5	F
Pa1	1.00																					
Pa2	0.32	1.00																				
Pa3	0.22	0.46	1.00																			
L1	0.16	0.36	0.38	1.00																		
L2	0.45	0.17	0.26	0.28	1.00																	
L3	0.06	0.04	-0.06	0.21	0.20	1.00																
I1	0.37	0.19	0.01	0.28	0.35	0.24	1.00															
I2	0.31	0.54***	0.37	0.30	0.23	0.30	0.30	1.00														
O1	0.34	0.28	0.33	0.43	0.36	-0.12	0.30	0.31	1.00													
O2	0.31	0.05	0.10	0.19	0.24	0.31	0.31	0.19	0.27	1.00												
Pr1	0.15	0.57***	0.50***	0.24	0.18	-0.02	0.13	0.23	0.23	0.08	1.00											
Pr2	0.38	0.13	-0.02	0.02	0.06	0.26	0.42	0.15	0.10	0.40	0.09	1.00										
Pr3	0.36	0.00	0.03	0.03	0.25	0.21	0.18	0.11	0.22	0.29	0.13	0.35	1.00									
M1	0.25	-0.01	0.09	0.46	0.35	0.21	0.19	0.07	0.25	0.31	0.01	0.16	0.28	1.00								
M2	0.34	0.23	0.25	0.59**	0.51***	0.14	0.33	0.31	0.37	0.29	0.15	0.16	0.22	0.56***	1.00							
M3	0.26	0.00	0.12	0.43	0.46	0.11	0.15	-0.01	0.42	0.23	0.08	0.09	0.45	0.59***	0.45	1.00						
F1	0.35	0.13	0.34	0.28	0.62*	0.09	0.43	0.20	0.22	0.14	0.19	0.17	0.22	0.42	0.42	0.44	1.00					
F2	0.35	-0.08	-0.04	0.16	0.27	0.41	0.18	0.32	0.08	0.19	-0.07	0.17	0.32	0.50***	0.35	0.18	0.18	1.00				
F3	0.43	-0.03	-0.12	0.03	0.52***	0.16	0.24	0.01	0.15	0.16	-0.03	0.08	0.04	0.29	0.26	0.32	0.34	0.48	1.00			
F4	0.13	0.05	0.15	0.13	0.31	0.05	0.17	-0.01	-0.02	-0.01	0.24	-0.04	0.25	0.26	0.20	0.45	0.44	0.27	0.25	1.00		
F5	-0.03	0.09	0.21	-0.13	0.04	0.20	0.06	0.16	0.08	0.30	0.12	0.39	0.10	-0.02	-0.02	0.03	0.09	0.16	0.17	0.09	1.00	
F	0.44***	0.11	0.09	0.20	0.51***	0.30	0.40	0.23	0.10	0.22	0.12	0.19	0.23	0.39	0.38	0.37						1.00

*p<0.05 **p<0.01 ***p<0.001

Table 8. Correlation analysis for importance

N=57	SC Partners			Logistics			Innovation		Organization		Production Strat.			Market Strat.			Flexibility				
	Pa1	Pa2	Pa3	L1	L2	L3	I1	I2	O1	O2	Pr1	Pr2	Pr3	M1	M2	M3	F1	F2	F3	F4	F5
Pa1	1.00																				
Pa2	0.37	1.00																			
Pa3	0.16	0.29	1.00																		
L1	-0.10	0.17	0.22	1.00																	
L2	0.37	0.20	0.24	0.25	1.00																
L3	0.22	0.02	0.08	-0.15	0.05	1.00															
I1	0.38	0.14	0.04	0.26	0.24	0.27	1.00														
I2	0.22	0.42	0.41	0.16	0.31	0.36	0.14	1.00													
O1	0.23	0.22	0.45	0.21	0.24	0.26	0.11	0.40	1.00												
O2	0.40	0.26	0.33	0.01	0.26	0.23	0.26	0.31	0.15	1.00											
Pr1	-0.02	0.10	0.36	0.19	-0.03	0.06	0.17	0.15	0.26	0.06	1.00										
Pr2	0.36	0.15	0.15	-0.02	0.21	0.19	0.37	0.06	-0.01	0.42	0.04	1.00									
Pr3	0.22	-0.03	0.24	-0.04	0.33	0.42	0.30	0.16	0.27	**0.52*****	0.27	0.47	1.00								
M1	0.11	-0.10	0.00	0.30	**0.52***	0.05	0.22	0.17	0.20	0.10	-0.03	0.04	0.25	1.00							
M2	0.28	0.16	0.24	0.37	**0.65*****	-0.02	0.30	0.31	0.17	0.33	0.10	0.20	0.28	**0.56*****	1.00						
M3	0.01	-0.05	0.16	0.22	0.49	0.18	0.13	0.19	0.45	-0.02	0.29	0.10	0.43	**0.59*****	0.32	1.00					
F1	0.18	0.00	0.37	0.10	**0.53***	0.07	0.23	0.26	0.18	0.17	0.19	0.24	0.42	0.41	0.38	0.41	1.00				
F2	0.11	-0.10	0.08	0.16	0.45	0.07	0.25	0.21	0.02	0.18	-0.05	0.22	0.26	**0.61*****	**0.61*****	0.31	0.41	1.00			
F3	0.41	0.15	0.07	0.12	0.48	0.08	0.36	0.31	0.04	0.27	-0.08	0.05	0.16	**0.51*****	0.41	0.29	0.27	**0.55*****	1.00		
F4	0.04	-0.11	0.40	0.31	0.24	0.05	0.26	0.05	0.15	0.05	0.30	0.04	0.12	0.12	0.29	0.28	0.33	0.30	0.10	1.00	
F5	0.16	0.31	0.17	0.23	0.41	0.16	0.27	0.24	0.07	0.39	0.06	0.26	0.38	0.17	0.35	0.18	0.37	0.30	0.27	0.35	1.00

*p<0.05 **p<0.01 ***p<0.001

bring about greater joint flexibility. Moreover, the flexibility index F is positively related to variable L2 (0.51, p<0.001), which describes the strategy for achieving an efficient flow of information along the supply chain. Other correlations that are significant will not be discussed herein as the relationships are quite obvious in most cases.

Regression Analysis

The following tables (Figures 6 and 7) present the results of the multiple regression analysis using the flexibility index F as the dependent variable and the variables that describe strategies about SC partners, logistics, innovation, organization strategy, production strategy and market strategy, as independent variables. Given that the objective of this study is to find out the descriptive level of the independent variables on the variation of the dependent variable, flexibility, the data related to the level of implementation has been chosen.

The data obtained on the descriptive level of the model chosen is specifically shown in Figure 6. The model is highly significant at p<0.01 and explains a great deal of the variance in flexibility in the supply chain context ($R^2 = 0.75$ and adjusted $R^2 = 0.62$). This means that 75% of the variance

in flexibility can be explained by the practices detected in this study, according to the opinions of the professionals on the implementation of these practices within these companies. This percentage is significant in this kind of studies. The F-Snedecor statistic for 16 and 30 degrees of freedom has a value of 5.6, which indicates that the explanation for the variance in the dependent variable obtained through the regression model is statistically significant at the level of 0.01.

Finally, with the t-Student study we verified which independent variables have the most significant effect on the dependent variable Flexibility F in the study, as is shown in Figure 7. After analyzing the regression coefficients, we observed that the greatest influence is on the descriptive variables for the supply chain partners and logistics strategies, as opposed to the remaining strategies mentioned in the model: innovation, organization strategy, production strategy and market strategy. In other words, strategies like sharing KPI with suppliers, activity coordination and frequent communication support the achievement of a higher level of flexibility. From a logistics point of view, sharing common visions regarding efficient options for transportation along the supply chain as well as efficient flows of information will lead to an

Figure 6. Table of regression analysis data

N	57
Multiple correlation coef	**0,87**
R²	**0,75**
Adjust R²	**0,62**
α	**0,88**
F- Snedecor	**5,61**

Figure 7. Table of regression analysis coefficients

VARIABLE	SC Partners			Logistics			Innovation		Organization		Production Strat.			Market Strat.		
	Pa1	Pa2	Pa3	L1	L2	L3	I1	I2	O1	O2	Pr1	Pr2	Pr3	M1	M2	M3
Regress. Coef.	0,187	0,217	0,155	0,157	0,110	-0,136	-0,097	-0,059	0,051	0,051	0,072	0,036	-0,017	0,006	0,005	-0,005
t-Student	1,55	-1,36	0,30	-0,05	2.01¬	2.02¬	0,76	0,58	-0,20	-0,87	0,55	0,09	0,06	2.31*	-0,97	2.21*

¬   p<0.1   *   p<0.05   **   p<0.01

increase in flexibility capabilities. In addition, we observed that the sign of influence of the logistics variable L3 is negative in the regression analysis. In other words, when a company increases its inventory turnover, it becomes negative in order to achieve a greater degree of flexibility. This is expected given the fact that the immediate availability of the product is lower, resulting in less capacity to respond to unexpected changes and to a lower potential for value chain flexibility.

CONCLUSION

Businesses nowadays are ever more sensitive to interpreting, finding out and considering the environment that surrounds them when making decisions regarding the market they must respond to, the suppliers they depend on and the competitors that threaten them. In such a vulnerable environment, being prepared for the uncertainties and risks that surround an organization, as well as having the knowledge and capacities to be flexible and adapt to changing circumstances, are critical for ensuring the organization's competitiveness. In this new business focus, not only the internal operational capacities of a company should be integrated, but also the dynamic and strategic alignment of the company with respect to the supply chain in which it participates. In other words, the ability to maintain a flexible and responsive supply chain is a strategically important capability.

Considerable effort has been directed in literature towards the operational aspects of flexibility without much attention being given to the strategic context or the supply chain. This chapter covers the aforementioned gap and offers a guide to support business professionals complement their operational knowledge on manufacturing flexibility and provides them with strategic knowledge on how to direct flexibility practices in the supply chain. More specifically, our study presents the conceptual framework that first analyzes the antecedents the company must consider, both external and internal, such as: environmental uncertainty, supply chain partners behavior, the business strategy as well as the corporate culture. Based on all of these characteristics, the company must plan and develop competitive strategies which focus on improving flexibility in the supply chain, such as: the company's own strategy towards the supply chain partners, organization strategy, the logistics approach, market strategy, production strategy and finally, innovation.

Out of the many possible risks that must be considered, the following potential risks have been identified and classified as applied to the supply chain and defining more efficient flexibility strategies: supply risks, process risks, demand risks, intellectual property risks, behavioral risks, political/social risks and financial risks. The corresponding strategies to mitigate them have also been indicated.

When identifying an area of action in the supply chain both strategically as well as operationally, the key element is knowing how the process, plan or project involved works. This is done by designing a panel of key performance indicators that help constitute value judgments. To this regard, the chapter describes the metrics that are most relevant to flexibility measurement. Moreover, the relationship between these indicators and the characteristics and strategies of the framework proposed by this study is presented.

This chapter presents an empirical study for the purpose of verifying the validity of the conceptual framework presented from the perspectives of implementing the proposed strategies and of the importance detected that is placed on each one of the strategies proposed by food and beverage sector professionals. This study has revealed that the strategies focusing on logistics and associated to supply chain partners are the most influential and consequently constitute key actions for boosting risks mitigation as described in the corresponding section. More specifically, sharing an efficient flow of information, a common vision of the movement of products and goods, sharing key performance indicators, frequent communication and tight coordination of activities, are actions which help attain a greater level of flexibility as they make it possible to know how the alignment of a company's capacities with those of the agents in its supply chain can be jointly adapted to environmental changes. The empirical regression study shows that the practices analyzed are capable of explaining 75% of the variance in the flexibility variable, which is significant for this kind of studies.

In summary, this chapter provides a general view of flexibility in the strategic context of the supply chain. It is up to each professional to make use of the results of this study in order to specifically adapt them to the circumstances or characteristics of the sector or supply chain in which she/he participates and to implement the proposed strategies in accordance with the tools in hers/his possession. In conclusion, we argue that promoting a culture of flexibility, both to the company and the supply chain level, which transcends the merely operational tools and daily activities, helps establish the norms and criteria for action when defining organizational strategies.

FUTURE RESEARCH

Much of the existing theoretical research on flexibility has been criticized for its narrow view and for focusing on manufacturing. Empirical research has been largely conducted by means of cross-sectional studies in order to expand this view, without exploring the supply chain framework and the firm approach from a dyadic relationship perspective.

Different research exists that presents score cards with performance indicators covering the inter-business context in the supply chain. However, the focus of these approaches, as far as measuring flexibility based on the interaction of two or more supply chain agents, is limited. More in-depth research in this field would support companies in determining a system of reference that would allow them to react more quickly when faced with the need to be flexible. With regards to this issue, one area of future research that would further contribute to this chapter would be a pilot study on the implementation of the metrics proposed in section 5 and a follow-up of their evolution. The implementation of these metrics, which are aligned with the company strategy, would provide the companies with a complementary signaling function that would help them to detect potential supply chain risks on time. These signals, together with the corresponding action or emergency plans, can substantially contribute to effective risk mitigation.

Moreover, recent literature on supply chain management has detected that one of the aspects with the greatest impact on its performance success is the dynamic alignment of the agents and the establishment of shared visions in order to jointly become more flexible. Facilitators of this approach can be found in strategies such as applying inter-organizational learning practices or promoting a change management culture, just to name two. Consequently, further research focus is needed on how aspects related to the behavior of key decision makers could create more efficient and synergistic flexibility.

REFERENCES

Beach, R., Muhleman, A., Price, D., Paterson, A., & Sharp, J. (2000). A review of manufacturing flexibility. *European Journal of Operational Research*, *122*, 41–57. doi:10.1016/S0377-2217(99)00062-4

Beamon, B. M. (1999). Measuring supply chain performance. *International Journal of Operations & Production Management*, *19*(3), 275–292. doi:10.1108/01443579910249714

Buzacott, J. (1982). *The fundamental principles of flexibility in manufacturing systems*. Paper presented at the meeting of the International Conference of Flexible Manufacturing Systems. Amsterdam: Elsevier.

Calantone, R., Dröge, C., & Vickery, S. (2002). Investigating the manufacturing–marketing interface in new product development: does context affect the strength of relationships? *Journal of Operations Management, 20*(3), 273–287. doi:10.1016/S0272-6963(02)00009-8

Cavinato, J. (2004). Supply chain logistics risks; From the back room to the board room. *International Journal of Physical Distribution & Logistics Management, 34*(5), 383–387. doi:10.1108/09600030410545427

Christopher, M., & Lee, H. (2004). Mitigating supply chain risk through improved confidence. *International Journal of Physical Distribution & Logistics Management, 34*(5), 388–396. doi:10.1108/09600030410545436

Das, S. K., & Abdel-Malek, L. (2003). Modelling the flexibility of order quantities and lead-times in supply chains. *International Journal of Production Economics, 85*, 171–181. doi:10.1016/S0925-5273(03)00108-7

Duclos, L., Vokurka, R., & Lummus, R. (2003). A conceptual model of supply chain flexibility. *Industrial Management & Data Systems, 103*(6), 446–456. doi:10.1108/02635570310480015

Fitzgerald, L., Johnston, R., Brignall, S., Silvestro, R., & Voss, C. (1991). Performance Measurement in Service Business. London: Chartered Institute of Management Accountants.

Fuller, J. B., O'Conner, J., & Rawlinson, R. (1993). Tailored logistics: the next advantage. *Harvard Business Review, 71*(3), 87–98.

Garber, R., & Sarkar, S. (2007). Want a more flexible supply chain? *Supply Chain Management Review, 62*, 28–33.

Gerwin, D. (1987). An agenda for research on the flexibility of manufacturing processes. *International Journal of Operations & Production Management, 7*(1), 38–49. doi:10.1108/eb054784

Gerwin, D. (1993). Manufacturing flexibility: a strategic perspective. *Management Science, 39*(4), 395–410. doi:10.1287/mnsc.39.4.395

Gunasekaran, A., Patel, C., & Tirtiroglu, E. (2001). Performance measures and metrics in a supply chain environment. *International Journal of Operations & Production Management, 21*(1-2), 71–87. doi:10.1108/01443570110358468

Gustavsson, S. O. (1984). Flexibility and productivity in complex production processes. *International Journal of Production Research, 22*(5), 801–808. doi:10.1080/00207548408942500

Koste, L. L., & Malhotra, M. K. (1999). A theoretical framework for analyzing the dimensions of manufacturing flexibility. *Journal of Operations Management, 18*(1), 75–93. doi:10.1016/S0272-6963(99)00010-8

Kumar, V., Fantazy, A., & Kumar, U. (2006). Implementation and management framework for supply chain flexibility. *Journal of Enterprise Information Management, 19*(3), 303–319. doi:10.1108/17410390610658487

Lambert, D. M., & Pohlen, T. L. (2001). Supply Chain metrics. *International Journal of Logistics Management, 12*(1), 1–19. doi:10.1108/09574090110806190

Lewis, C. D. (1970), Scientific Inventory Control. New York: American Elsevier Publishing Company.

Lummus, R. R., Duclos, K. L., & Vokurka, R. J. (2005). Delphi study on supply chain flexibility. *International Journal of Production Research, 43*(4), 1–13.

March, J., & Sharpira, Z. (1987). Managerial perspectives on risk and risk taking. *Management Science, 33*, 1404–1418. doi:10.1287/mnsc.33.11.1404

Mendonça, E., & Giménez, C. (2007). Drivers and sources of supply flexibility: an exploratory study. *International Journal of Operations & Production Management, 27*(10), 1115–1136. doi:10.1108/01443570710820657

Morgan, C. (2004). Structure, speed and salience: performance measurement in the supply chain. *Business Process Management Journal, 10*(5), 522–536. doi:10.1108/14637150410559207

Narain, R., Yadav, R. C., Sarkis, J., & Cordeire, J. J. (2000). The strategic implications of flexibility in manufacturing systems. *International Journal of Agile Management Systems, 2*(3), 202–213. doi:10.1108/14654650010356112

Neely, A., Gregory, M., & Platts, K. (1995). Performance measurement system design. *Manufacturing Engineering Group, 15*(4), 80–116.

Saenz, M. J., Barillas, D., & Lamban, M. P. (2008, July). *Innovation Strategies in Supply Chain Management and their relationship with Flexibility and Customer Service.* Paper presented at the meeting of the International Congress on Project Engineering, Zaragoza, Spain.

Sanchez, R. (1995). Strategic flexibility in product competition. *Strategic Management Journal, 16*(5), 135–159. doi:10.1002/smj.4250160921

Santesmaes, M. (2005). Dyane, version 3, design and analysis of survey in social and market researches. Madrid, Spain: Piramide.

Saris, W. E., & Gallhofer, I. (2007). Estimation of the effects of measurement characteristics on the quality of survey questions. *Survey Research Methods, 1*(1), 29–43.

Sheffi, Y. (2005). The Resilient Enterprise, Overcoming vulnerability for competitive advantage. Cambridge, MA: The MIT Press.

Slack, N. (1983). Flexibility as a manufacturing objective. *International Journal of Operations & Production Management, 3*(3), 4–13. doi:10.1108/eb054696

Stevenson, M., & Spring, M. (2007). Flexibility from a supply chain perspective: definition and review. *International Journal of Operations & Production Management, 27*(7), 685–713. doi:10.1108/01443570710756956

Supply Chain Council. (n.d.). *Supply-Chain Operations Reference-model.* Retrieved from www.supply-chain.org

Tang, C. (2006). Perspectives in supply chain risk management. *International Journal of Production Economics, 103*(2), 451–488. doi:10.1016/j.ijpe.2005.12.006

Tang, C., & Tomlin, B. (2008). The power of flexibility for mitigation supply chain risks. *International Journal of Production Economics, 116*, 12–27. doi:10.1016/j.ijpe.2008.07.008

Upton, D. M. (1995). What really makes factories flexible? *Harvard Business Review, 73*(4), 74–81.

Vickery, S., Calantone, R., & Drogue, C. (1999). Supply chain flexibility: an empirical study. *Journal of Supply Chain Management, 35*(3), 16–24. doi:10.1111/j.1745-493X.1999.tb00058.x

Zhang, Q., Vonderembse, M. A., & Lim, J.-S. (2002). Value chain flexibility: a dichotomy of competence and capability. *International Journal of Production Research, 40*(3), 561–583. doi:10.1080/00207540110091695

Zhang, Q., Vonderembse, M. A., & Lim, J.-S. (2005). Logistics flexibility and its impact on customer satisfaction. *The International Journal of Logistics Management, 16*(1), 71–95. doi:10.1108/09574090510617367

Zsidisin, G. A., & Ritchie, B. (2008). Supply chain risk. A Handbook of Assessment, Management and Performance. New York: Springer.

ADDITIONAL READINGS

Chopra, S., & Meindl, P. (2007). *Supply Chain Management Strategy, Planning and Operation.* Upper Saddle River, NJ: Pearson Prentice Hall.

Fawcetrt, S. E., Calantone, R., & Smith, S. R. (1996). An investigation of the impact of flexibility on global reach and firm performance. *Journal of Business Logistics, 17*(2), 167–196.

Fisher, M. (1997). What is the right supply chain for your product. *Harvard Business Review*, (Mar-Apr): 105–116.

Forrester, J. (1958). Industrial Dynamics. *Harvard Business Review*, 37–66.

Giunipero, L. C., Denslow, D., & Eltantawi, R. (2005). Purchasing/supply chain Management flexibility: moving to an enterpreneurial skill set. *Industrial Marketing Management, 34*, 602–613. doi:10.1016/j.indmarman.2004.11.004

Jack, E. P., & Raturi, A. (2002). Sources of volume flexibility and their impact on performance. *Journal of Operations Management, 20*, 519–548. doi:10.1016/S0272-6963(01)00079-1

Kleindorfer, P. R., & Saad, G. (2005). Managing disruption risks in supply chains. *Productions and Operations Managemen, 14*(1), 53–68.

Krajewski, L., Wei, J. C., & Tang, L. L. (2005). Responding to schedule changes in build to order supply chains. *Journal of Operations Management, 23*, 452–469. doi:10.1016/j.jom.2004.10.006

Lummus, R. R., Duclos, L. K. & Vokurka, R. J. (2003). Supply chain flexibility: building a new model. *Global Journal of Flexible Systems management, 4*(4), 1-13.

Oke, A., & Gopalakrishnan, M. (2009). Managing disruptions in supply chains: A case study of a retails supply chain. *International Journal of Production Economics, 118*, 168–174. doi:10.1016/j.ijpe.2008.08.045

Peck, H. (2005). Drivers of supply chain vulnerability: an integrated framework. *International Journal of Physical Distribution and Logistics Management, 35*(4), 210–232. doi:10.1108/09600030510599904

Perez, M. P., & Sanchez, A. M. (2001). Supplier relation and flexibility in the Spanish automotive industry. *Supply Chain Management, 6*(1), 29–38. doi:10.1108/13598540110381272

Petroni, A., & Bevilacqua, M. (2002). Indentifying manufacturing flexibility best practices in small and medium enterprise. *International Journal of Operations & Production Management, 22*(8), 929–947. doi:10.1108/01443570210436217

Sheffi, Y., & Rice, J. B. Jr. (2005). A supply view of the resilient enterprise. *MIT Sloan Management Review, 47*(1), 41–48.

Svensson, G. A. (2000). Conceptual framework for the analysis of vulnerability in supply chains. *International Journal of Physical Distribution and Logistics Management, 30*(9), 731–749. doi:10.1108/09600030010351444

Zsidisin, G., Ellram, L., Carter, J., & Cavinato, J. (2004). An analysis of supply risk assessment techniques. [t]. *International Journal of Physical Distribution and Logistics Management, 34*(5), 397–413. doi:10.1108/09600030410545445

Chapter 11
Managing the Risk of Knowledge Transfer in Outsourcing Organizations

Stavros Ponis
National Technical University, Greece

Epaminondas Koronis
University of Warwick, UK

ABSTRACT

The rhetoric of outsourcing as well as the importance of organizational knowledge have both been popular issues thoroughly examined in contemporary business literature. Still, combinatory studies on the effects of outsourcing, positive or negative, on the creation and maintenance of organizational knowledge and the related risks and consequences of outsourcing, remain scarce. Given the popularity of both fields of organizational analysis we consider the lacking of combinatory studies as striking. In this paper, we present the findings drawn on a multiple case study analysis of four medium size pharmaceutical companies, all of them having implemented outsourcing strategies. The chapter attempts a categorization of risk sources during the outsourcing initiative, proposes mitigating actions and organizes the findings of the research on the case companies by proposing a model of 'vicious cycle' suggesting that outsourcing, if not managed successfully, eventually leads to the addiction of the organization to 'buy' expertise and knowledge in spite of knowledge acquisition. While we identify the conflicting strategies and rhetoric, we also attempt to come up with a set of guidelines, which could help organizations avoid the knowledge negative side effects of outsourcing.

BACKGROUND

It was the early 80's when outsourcing began to receive significant attention by both the research community and industry practice as a result of a management switch of focus towards vertical disintegration. After a long lasting period of management literature exploring vertical integration (Bain, 1968; Williamson, 1975; Harringan, 1984,1986; Grossman & Heart, 1986) the merits of 'buy' rather than 'make' started to gain increasing interest. Williamson (1975) heralded the trend towards vertical disintegration, followed by authors such as Walker and Weber (1984), Kumpe and

DOI: 10.4018/978-1-61520-607-0.ch011

Bolwjin (1988), Venkatesan (1992), Ford et al., (1993) and Fine & Whitney (1996) all provided evidence of increased incidence of "buy" rather than "make" strategies (Harland et al., 2005) while early theories such the transaction cost theory (i.e. Williamson, 1975) and the resource-based view of Wernerfelt, (1984) dominated the initial outsourcing scientific terrain.

Since then and till now, outsourcing has gained exponential growth of the scientific interest. As argued in Johnson (1997:4-6), the term 'outsourcing' can be considered as a big umbrella covering all forms of contracted work provided by outsiders and implies all forms of assigning work to outsiders such are formal outsourcing, out-tasking and sub-contracting. The use of outsourcing has been constantly increasing in the last decades (Hendry, 1995; Takeishi, 2002), especially in terms of outsourcing IT functions (Quinn, 1992), logistics, financial auditing, consulting and human resources management (Vanson, 2001). Busi and McIvor (2008) in their efforts to set the outsourcing research agenda attempted to scan the Internet and the ISI Web Of Knowledge database for instances of the term outsourcing and compare these numbers with those returned from a query of both sources on the term 'Supply Chain Management'. Though, they admit this is not a scientifically sound approach, they believe that their results provide a valuable insight into the interest outsourcing has generated in the 'real world' as opposed to that which has generated in the scientific world, and the imbalance existing between research-led and industry-led contributions in the literature in this area. Their main arguments to support their approach was that WWW can be considered as a digital representation of real world trends while ISI Web of Knowledge is one of the most comprehensive databases of scientific articles. To update their argument we ran a quick scan of internet sources using Google, Google Scholar and ISI Web of knowledge which returned approximately 32.000.000, 261.000 and 2.700 results respectively. These updated figures

confirm the gap between practice and theory in favour of practice; still they narrow its breadth by including Google Scholar a far less discriminating scientific database than ISI Web of Knowledge.

Despite the wide spread of the outsourcing concept in contemporary literature, Gilley and Rasheed (2000) argue that there is still much debate on the concept's definition. According to Embleton & Wright, (1998), outsourcing is the use of outsiders and contracted work or the use of an external agent's services in order to fulfil operations that should normally take place 'in-house'. In Harland et al., (2005) a broad definition is used, inspired by Gilley and Rasheed who argue that outsourcing is the act of procuring something that was either originally sourced internally or could have been sourced internally notwithstanding the decision to go outside. This includes arrangements and concepts such as contracting out, subcontracting, make or buy etc. In this chapter, we will use the generic definition of Power et al., (2006) who argue that outsourcing is made up of two words, 'out' and 'sourcing', where sourcing refers to the act of transferring work, responsibilities and decision rights to someone else. Thus, outsourcing is the act of transferring work, responsibilities and decision rights to an entity outside the enterprise.

Summarizing the key elements from literature (Johnson, 1997; Hendry, 1995; Yakhlef, 2002) we would argue that outsourcing has the following characteristics: it is considered as a management tool, it places an emphasis on what is to be done rather than how it will be done, work takes places mainly or entirely off site, supplier provides all resources and the employee relations are managed by the supplier. It therefore becomes arguable that outsourcing is mainly based on contractual agreements and does not qualify as strong synergistic relationships which evolve into dynamic and strong ties among organizations (in the Nohria & Eccles, 1991 sense). On the contrary outsourcing should be mainly seen as a client-customer relationship where the mutual short-term satisfaction of both parties is essential (Johnson, 1997:

102). Despite the fact that outsourcing partners' relationships might be endurable and sustainable, temporality runs through the relationship. In that sense, outsourcing shares similar characteristics with the Virtual Enterprise concept.

INTRODUCTION

Under the current neo-liberal model, in most capitalistic economies, organizations focus on short-term results and neglect certain aspects of long-term planning (Whitley, 1999; Lazonick & O' Sullivan, 2000). In this respect, the downsizing of organizations towards more flexible and lean modes of organization has been and remains popular among strategic analysts and corporate decision-makers. Under this short term perspective, which has been often criticized as 'myopic', organizations have been increasingly using outsourcing and enterprise networks in the last decade as a mean to manage their operations economically and efficiently (Jarillo, 1988; 1993). Many studies reveal that the reasons for using outsourcing policies are mainly financial (Budros, 1999; Quinn, 1992; Jarillo, 1993) and knowledge oriented (Takeishi, 2002; see Chan, 1994 for a classification of outsourcing reasons). Indeed, Takeishi argues that "collaboration with external organizations could bring a firm such benefits as reducing the fixed costs, gaining flexibility and capitalizing on specialists' expertise" (2002: 321; see also Kanter & Mayers, 1991). Moreover, the business press and shareholders constantly place emphasis on the need for organizational economies and react positively to the adoption of flexible forms of organizing.

According to Misawa and Hattori (1998) in most leading Western companies more than half of the engineering tasks will be outsourced in the near future. Indeed, it is obvious that organizations in the modern competitive environment use outsourcing as part of their constant effort to economize and reduce expenses as well as to acquire expertise

in an attempt to stay in the market. Seufert et al. (1999) study on inter-organizational networks reveals that manufacturing industries, publishers, biotechnological industries, service industries, retailers and transportation firms choose to rely on wide inter-organizational networks or business deals in order to fulfill organizational goals and tasks (ibid: 181-182). Such business trends seem not paradoxical, given the intense pressure for organizational performance and the developed literature on the benefits of the lean and flexible corporation (Van de Ven, 2000) which sometimes evolves into an anorexic organization.

Organizational changes, towards flexible modes of organizing do not leave the management of knowledge unaffected, particularly since it is precisely the lack of know how that is one of the reasons managers decide to rely to outsiders in order to handle their tasks (Choo, 1998). Quintas (2002: 7) argues that, "it is certainly the case today that all organizations are being reformed and they are increasingly dependent on external sources of knowledge". In modern organizations emphasis on networks is given at the expense of investment in 'in house' development of knowledge capacities and intellectual assets despite the fact that survival of organizations depends on their ability to create, preserve and exploit knowledge (Edvisson & Malone, 1997).

But while outsourcing clearly provides noticeable and important consequences for the management and maintenance of organizational knowledge, combinatory views are relatively scarce by both managers and theorists. The first seem to deploy both policies for knowledge management and downsizing and outsourcing and share little concern for any possible contradictions between these rhetoric devices. Theorists, on the other hand, have provided little research evidence as to how organizations are affected as regards knowledge creation and learning mechanisms by the adoption of outsourcing practices. Despite the fact that some articles are concerned about the connection of outsourcing with organizational knowledge

(Misawa & Hattori, 1998; Takeishi, 2002; Hendry, 1995) it can be argued that not much has been said about how outsourcing practices affect organizational knowledge processes. Such lacking seems important given the increasing use of outsourcing and subcontracting by many enterprises (Chan, 1994; Hendry, 1995: 193; Johnson, 1997) and if we take into consideration that organizations seem willing to outsource crucial knowledge-intensive operations (such as manufacturing know how and research and development activities) rather than simply assigning operations of low knowledge value.

It is precisely the aim of this chapter to explore the relationship between outsourcing and knowledge management, to analyze how outsourcing relationships are developed and to determine the consequences for the internal organizational activities and relations. The logic behind the research is that there is a chain of internal organizational changes produced and initiated by the outsourcing practices which have a deep impact on the knowledge processes as well. Considering knowledge as a social value embedded in cultures and organizational identities (Blackler, 1995; Wenger, 1998; Tsoukas & Vladimirou, 2001; Brown & Duguid, 1991) this chapter's aim is to investigate the changes and pressures in organizational realities and relations, caused by outsourcing as well as the implications for knowledge circulation.

Our research findings, from an investigation on SME pharmaceutical firms, take the form of a complete knowledge pathology, which is resulted by the intensive reliance on outsourcing and subcontracting practices. Evidence reveals that outsourcing fundamentally changes employees' perceptions of their role while creating sequential effects of 'admiration' and then 'alienation'. The corrosion of identities also leads to a progressive although silent disintegration of communities of practice while daily habits of knowledge sharing and informal flows of information have given space to more formalistic approaches on knowl-

edge and the distancing of employees from the field of knowledge action. Such tendencies have been amplified by both outsiders' avoidance to share knowledge as well as by employees' reluctance to enter a learning process. Moreover, the organizations in question have all been implicated in a vicious cycle of dependence; the more they used outside knowledge the more they tended to lose their absorptive capacity which eventually leads them to additional reliance on outside expertise. While documented knowledge would be expected to facilitate knowledge transfer, its contribution was minimal.

The structure of the paper follows our rationale. In the following section we provide a detailed but not exhaustive documentation on risk sources of the outsourcing initiative based on a thorough study of the contemporary literature. Next, a summary on knowledge management is presented. We then move on to a combinatory approach addressing the questions and referring to existing literature. After we describe our research strategy, we dedicate three sections to the presentation of our findings, namely the corrosion of identities, the disintegration of communities of practice and finally the development of a vicious cycle of knowledge pathology. We then discuss the findings and refer to the role of documented knowledge and information flows while we attempt, in the final section, to explore the implications and come up with some ideas as to whether organizational tactics might lead to a minimization of knowledge effects when outsourcing.

OUTSOURCING AND RISK MANAGEMENT

Outsourcing adds an extra layer in a company's supply network and inevitably leads to a more complex business situation that has to be managed effectively in order to produce the anticipated – from the initiative - positive results. Adding complexity to any system propagates new risks and enhances or transforms older ones as a result of the differentiated business model. In that sense, risk management is not an option and every outsourcing initiative should be guided by a well-thought risk management process throughout the outsourcing initiative life cycle. In this chapter we build upon the work of Power et al., (2006) who dissect the outsourcing life cycle in seven discrete stages, these being: (a) strategic assessment, (b) needs analysis, (c) vendor assessment, (d) negotiation and contract management, (e) project initiation and transition, (f) relationship management and (g) continuance, modification or exit strategies. We do that by merging the above stages and creating three larger outsourcing methodological steps namely 1) Design – Plan, 2) Implement, 3) Monitor – Control and Support. Next, based on a thorough analysis of the outsourcing literature with special focus on risks emerging during the outsourcing initiative (Harland and Knight, 2005; Mc Ivor, 2000; Busi and Mc Ivor, 2008; Power et al., 2004; Power et al., 2006; Madsen et al., 2008; Moses and Ahlstrom, 2008; Jiang et al., 2006; Zsidisin, 2003; Li and Barnes, 2008; Oke

and Maltz, 2009; Brenner, 2009) we present a detailed list of risk sources, potential threats that risks impose and indicative mitigating actions, categorized by lifecycle stage. Our taxonomy of risk sources is visualized in Figure 1 below.

Finally, in the tables that follow, a detailed description of risk sources, potential threats and risk mitigation actions is provided. It is noted that these tables are not exhaustive but they constitute a solid base for initiating discussion and creating awareness to managers that are implicated in an outsourcing initiative and are in search of a methodological approach toward dealing with outsourcing related risks and the effects these may impose to the outsourcing process establishment and operation.

KNOWLEDGE MANAGEMENT: THE SOCIAL DIMENSION

In our days there is an unambiguous recognition by academics, researchers and practitioners about the importance of knowledge as a critical

Figure 1. Risk sources throughout the outsourcing initiative lifecycle

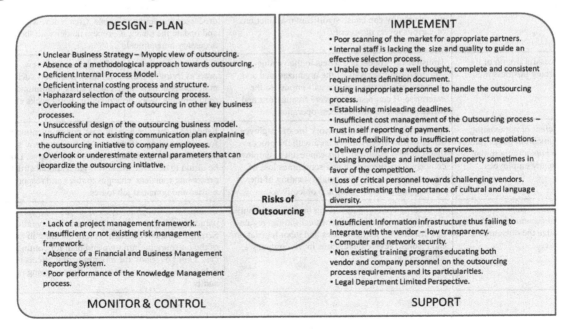

Table 1. Risks, threats and mitigating actions – design & plan stage

Risk Source	Potential Threat	Risk Mitigation Actions
Unclear Business Strategy – Myopic view of outsourcing.	Introducing an outsourcing initiative without prior securing management commitment and resolving business issues that may lead the whole venture to failure.	Secure management commitment, justify the need for the outsourcing initiative and determine its long term effects on the overall business strategy.
Absence of a methodological approach towards outsourcing.	Forget that outsourcing is not just hype but a very complex business strategy and thus demands a consistent methodological approach. Ignorance or worse arrogance can have catastrophic results to an otherwise potentially successful outsourcing venture. The need for a solid methodological approach is further amplified when no previous outsourcing experience at an international level exists.	Study both academia and industry research results regarding outsourcing. Evaluate the alternatives by seeking best practices and success testimonials from the industry. Select your approach and if unsure don't be hesitant in seeking consultation from outsourcing expert institutions, firms or professionals. In other words don't be afraid to outsource the support of your outsourcing process.
Deficient Internal Process Model.	Deciding to outsource a process which is not accurately documented affects both the outsourcing process selection and the process knowledge transfer during outsourcing. The first results in poor vendor selection while the latter can lead to inferior product/service to the customers.	Elaborate a detailed and consistent business model of business processes including workflow, roles, responsibilities, authorizations, systems and documents used.
Deficient internal costing process and structure.	Poor justification of the financial incentives for outsourcing a process. It can result in misleading figures that will create a gap of expectations during outsourcing implementation, a feeling of disappointment and a need for initiating the 'finger-pointing' behavior.	Execute a detailed cost analysis of your processes, especially focusing on the outsourcing candidates. Try to pinpoint from the start costs well hidden in the cost structure and determine rising costs that the outsourcing process will create upon its termination.
Haphazard selection of the outsourcing process.	Selecting the wrong process to outsource not only can lead to poor performance but furthermore can empower the competition as a result of critical knowledge leakage from the vendors.	Determine the core competences of the organization and decide whether financial benefits can outperform inherent risks of outsourcing the process. For non critical processes decide based on anticipated financial benefits and long term ramifications in product/service attributes such as quality, flexibility and improvement.
Overlooking the impact of outsourcing in other key business processes.	Processes designed and executed in organizations for years create a large network of interdependencies with other processes, critical or not. Overlooking this reality can cause significant malfunctions of various levels of severity.	Based on an updated version of the company's process model elaborate an impact analysis trying to assess the resulting effects of outsourcing in the processes remaining in-house. Create new workflows and update the business process model with the necessary amendments.
Unsuccessful design of the outsourcing business model.	Transferring process and assets to the vendor without a prior analysis of the organizational and financial effects this transfer will impose to the enterprise. It can result in severe fluctuations and increased costs of the business operation.	Conduct a detailed what-if analysis of the new process trying to include all its new aspects such as material/asset provision and its costs, communication requirements, work flow potential bottlenecks etc.
Insufficient or not existing communication plan explaining the outsourcing initiative to company employees.	Outsourcing will affect the work life of employees directly or indirectly implicated with the process that will be outsourced. This can result in employee demotivation, discontent and sometimes loss of key personnel due to a misunderstanding of the outsourcing process' goals and objectives.	Establish a detailed and 'honest' communication plan for disseminating information on the company's goals and objectives from the outsourcing initiative. Don't be afraid to describe the new organizational structure presenting transfers, changes to roles and responsibilities and potential job losses.
Overlook or underestimate external parameters that can jeopardize the outsourcing initiative.	Proceeding with an outsourcing initiative without studying the vendor's geo-political setting, regulatory framework particularities and labor legislation can result to severe disruptions in the company's supply chain.	Conduct a thorough analysis of all the external parameters that can affect the enterprise operation. Scrutinize the environment before deciding in favor of the outsourcing initiative and plan for contingencies. Don't overlook the environmental effects of the outsourcing decision and plan for overcoming relative audits.

Table 2. Risks, threats and mitigating actions – implement stage

Risk Source	Potential Threat	Risk Mitigation Actions
Poor scanning of the market for appropriate partners.	Selecting the outsourcing partner based on instinct or other personal criteria and not on a thorough market analysis rarely provides a positive outcome.	Conduct a thorough market analysis collecting information on vendors that have the necessary capacity, experience, know-how and reputation for getting the job done. Enrich your analysis with approved vendors from the company's supplier portfolio and then evaluate.
Internal staff is lacking the size and quality to guide an effective selection process	Selecting the right vendor for outsourcing can be a cumbersome process. Not all companies have the personnel with the appropriate qualities to outperform this challenge, a phenomenon which is further amplified in the case of SMEs and can lead to poor selection, inferior product or service delivery and ultimately customer dissatisfaction and loss of competitive advantage and reputation.	Word of mouth, market intelligence and industry testimonials can act as quick-fix to this shortcoming while hiring outsourcing specialists to perform a financial and business due diligence on the short-listed vendors seems like a most suitable but alas, more costly solution.
Unable to develop a well thought, complete and consistent requirements definition document.	A hastily prepared and not well thought requirements definition document will create loose ends that can potentially undermine both the contract negotiation and the outsourcing implementation process.	Prepare a detailed requirements definition document using a cross-functional team consisted of executives from all the affected departments. Utilize techniques such as round-table meetings and brainstorming in an effort to reveal all the hidden aspects of the outsourcing process. Complete all the necessary stages until you are ready to disseminate a call and receive requests for proposals.
Using inappropriate personnel to handle the outsourcing process.	The personnel that is called to support outsourcing does not have the necessary experience, process knowledge or maybe currently demotivated or in labor inertia.	Try to appoint employees with a good knowledge of the process and a fairly good level of inter-organizational communication skills. Create a cross-functional team. Communicate the message that this appointment is a job enhancement rather than a 'no man's land' mission.
Establishing misleading deadlines.	Setting up unrealistic milestones and deadlines that the vendor is unable to keep up with, even though he is dedicated and works in good faith. This can cause significant fluctuations in the outsourcing relationship especially if these deadlines are set at the early stages, thus leading to loss of confidence and mistrust.	Try to be realistic in your time plan and always keep in mind that know-how transfer is not an out of the box process. The absorptive capacity of your vendor is not always directly related with delivering. Provide some time for proof of good faith and substantial delivery results in the initial stages of the relationship.
Insufficient cost management of the Outsourcing process – Trust in self reporting of payments.	Inability to monitor and control the costs related to the outsourced process and trust in self reporting of payments can lead significant increases in the cost of outsourcing overwhelming the cost of the initial process executed internally.	Establish a financial reporting system able to monitor the outsourcing transactions' activities. Set up alarms / notifiers for when the process cost is getting higher than the predefined tolerances.
Limited flexibility due to insufficient contract negotiations.	Processes are the most dynamic part of an organization and are being constantly evaluated, challenged and improved. Inability to impose changes to the outsourced process due to contractual constraints has a significant effect on process flexibility, sometimes referred in literature as process stiffening.	A well thought contract providing space for process changes in a way that none party is negatively influenced is a good mitigation policy. Still, if this is not the case, preserving good faith and fair relationship with your vendor is always a good practice. The key here is to attach the vendor to the process in a fashion that secures a win-win situation produced from process improvements. When doing that try to impose a bi-directional flow of process improvements, thus avoiding being insulated from advancements created by the vendor.

Table 2. continued

Risk Source	Potential Threat	Risk Mitigation Actions
Delivery of inferior products or services.	For many, this is the number one threat when discussing outsourcing hazards and can also be found in literature under the term shirking. It can appear early in the relationship as a result of vendor inexperience or lack of the needed skills or worse in later stages alerting for the decaying quality of the relationship. Common results include contract disputes, involvement of legal departments, delayed deliveries and customer dissatisfaction.	Mitigating actions for this threat are directly connected with the execution of a superior vendor selection process and a thoughtful contractual agreement. After the signature of the contracts and the initiation of the outsourcing relationship a pragmatic approach should be adopted in investigating the root causes of delivery failure. If shirking is not the reason then ways should be examined for vendor support, before assigning legal departments to the case. If malice is detected then legal departments should initiate relationship dissolution activities and emergency plans for handling disruptions should be put to use.
Losing knowledge and intellectual property sometimes in favor of the competition.	The knowledge related risks entailed in outsourcing are numerous. To name some here, we pinpoint the threat of losing knowledge and intellectual property, the leakage of critical knowledge in favor of the competition, vendor using the company knowledge for his own profit etc. All these threats can have severe results to a company's growth and position to the market.	Knowing exactly 'what is proper to outsource' plays a significant role in minimizing the loss of knowledge during outsourcing. Establishing a bidirectional knowledge flow and a win-win business situation enhanced by well thought contractual agreements is a good mitigation practice.
Loss of critical personnel towards challenging vendors.	Close contact with the vendor reveals an alternative source of employment for those employees that excel in the works of the outsourcing relationship. Dissatisfied employees implicated in outsourcing can become an easy prey for vendors of all sizes, while distinguished and highly qualified employees are usually attracted by larger, industry established vendors.	Using first class, motivated and satisfied personnel from the start creates barriers in personnel leakage. Still, the exhibition of these individuals by definition creates inherent risks of loss to a well established and healthy vendor.
Underestimating the importance of cultural and language diversity.	Overlooking cultural differences and naively believing that a foreign vendor has the same perspective on the outsourcing relationship. This is almost never the case and the cost of this misalignment can be very high, with most obvious results being process delays and discrepancies in delivered products/services while both sides believe they have done everything right. Language diversity can also delay the whole process by creating misunderstandings and unnecessary disputes.	Personnel involved in the outsourcing process should be trained in understanding and dealing with the vendor's cultural particularities. Creating joint training programs with participation of the vendor's personnel is a great idea that could lead into effective team building that will guide the outsourcing initiative throughout its life cycle. Needless to say that the utilization of personnel that speaks the vendor's native language is an asset. Still, this is not always possible, so good communication skills in the mutually agreed "project language" is imperative.

resource for organisations (Foucault, 1980; Leonard & Sensiper, 1998). In that context managing knowledge has become an imperative in order to survive in this new unstable and fierce business environment (Davenport et al., 1998). More recent efforts (Davenport and Prusak, 1998; Liebowitz et al., 2000) have shown that knowledge and its effective management are major factors in determining the level of an organisation's performance and its degree of competitiveness (Holsapple and Jones, 2005). Indeed, organizations are implicated in a constant effort to improve their capacity to

Table 3. Risks, threats and mitigating actions – monitor, control and support stages

Risk Source	Potential Threat	Risk Mitigation Actions
Lack of a project management framework.	Outsourcing is widely considered and undoubtedly is a business strategy. Outsourcing a process is the materialization of this strategy in business actions and thus constitutes a strategic and critical project. Consequently, failing to manage it as such will axiomatically lead to poor performance if not a disaster.	A strategic approach towards outsourcing demands the utilization of a detailed project management framework, including all crucial outsourcing project attributes such as the description of the goals and objectives, the stakeholders of the initiative, the budget, the timeline of the project, the quality management procedures, the decision hierarchy, the communication plan etc.
Insufficient or not existing risk management framework.	Outsourcing by definition adds another layer in your existing supply chain and thus new risks are created. Overlooking this new 'reality' and failing to pinpoint the risks it entails is a recipe for failure. The Risk Management process is excluded from the Project Management Framework where often resides due to its significance in the outsourcing initiative.	Update or create from scratch a thorough risk management plan including all the new risks involved in your outsourcing decision. Evaluate the threats, the probability of their occurrence and their severity. Create contingency plans and always manage against potential disruptions. Avoid failing into the vendor lock-in trap by determining alternatives.
Absence of a Financial and Business Management Reporting System.	Monitoring and constantly evaluating the financial and business performance of the vendor is imperative. In absence of such a system, visibility is decreased, transparency is minimized and alert signals come always too late. This results in situations that maybe either irrecoverable or demand costly, copious and effortful mitigating actions instead of fine tuning that was needed in the first place.	Including vendor's obligations of management reporting in the detailed requirements definition document is the best mitigating action in that case. In absence of such premeditation, a company always has the choice of maintaining a healthy, win-win situation with its vendor, which makes negotiations on the establishment of a solid report management system easier.
Poor performance of the Knowledge Management process.	Outsourcing implies the transfer of large amount of information and knowledge to a third party in such a way that will permit this third party to (at least initially) duplicate this process to its premises, using its own equipment, personnel and sometimes material. Poor performance of the knowledge transfer process can have devastating results directly damaging product/service quality and customer satisfaction, thus leading to loss of market share and reputation.	Establish and initiate a knowledge management system that will safely guide the process to its journey to the vendor while minimizing the unavoidable losses and the knowledge orphanization phenomenon. Knowledge collection, maintenance, update, codification, transfer and translation if needed are some of the core processes of such a system.
Insufficient Information infrastructure thus failing to integrate with the vendor – low transparency.	In the era of Internet and E-Business not having the necessary technological infrastructure to support the outsourcing process is a recipe for disaster.	Bidirectional communication of information through integrated (at least at a good level) systems should be established coupled with ICT support which secures continuous operation and crush/ disaster recovery support.
Computer and network security.	Protecting confidential information and data is crucial for maintaining any relationship, between humans or businesses. In that sense security breaches that jeopardize confidentiality of business data, transactions or trade / marketing policies are unacceptable.	ICT departments on both ends of the line should jointly work on a security system that insures data integrity and confidentiality. On top of that, special policies should be established and disseminated to personnel regarding new media of communication such as e-mail, USB sticks and portable hard drives.
Non existing training programs for educating both vendor and company personnel on the outsourcing process requirements and its particularities.	Untrained personnel are unable to efficiently and effectively support the outsourcing process thus leading to poor performance, demotivated employees, rising of unnecessary disputes thoughtlessly brought up to the next level and ultimately dissatisfied customers.	Initiate outsourcing training programs throughout the life cycle of the project. Special emphasis should be put in training employees for cultural awareness.
Legal Department Limited Perspective.	Outsourcing at an international level increases the threat of a legal department with a limited, nation-wide knowledge of legislation and regulatory frameworks.	Country and region specific legal systems and regulatory frameworks should be studied with the objective to guide effectively and most importantly without surprises the outsourcing process from the negotiations and contract agreement phase to the relationship dissolution.

absorb knowledge (Cohen & Levinthal, 1990), to create new knowledge and innovate as well as to best maintain and manage its existing intellectual capital (Stewart, 1997). Particular streams of knowledge management have provided a functional consideration of knowledge, treating it as a resource and an organizational strategic goal. Theorists of Intellectual Capital have conceptualized knowledge as an asset thus a measurable and manageable entity which can be accumulated (Boudreau & Ramstad, 1997; Bukh et al., 2001; Stewart, 1997; Edvisson & Malone, 1997).

On the other hand, other theorists took a different path in revealing the complexity of tacit knowledge and consequentially treating knowledge as a social-based phenomenon which is socially constructed and embedded within the context of organizational practice (Nonaka, 1994; Nonaka & Takeuchi, 1995; Choo, 1998; Tsoukas, 1996). In this respect, knowledge does not constitute an asset or an objective reality, but should be viewed as a continuous process of social construction of meanings (Berger & Luckman's paradigm, 1966; Dant, 1991) where culture, common practices, ethics and routines play a very important role. Organizational knowledge has been conceptualized as interrelated with the social capital of organizations (Nahapiet & Goshal) and as embedded in organizational norms and cultures (Teece, 2001: 126; Weick, 1995; see also Blackler, 1995). It has been considered as consisting of meanings which are established and communicated via the discursive practices and utterances in an organization (Henriksson, 1999: 65; Yakhlef, 2002). As Bell et al. (2002) argued, "....the context in which the whole knowledge transfer is embedded has a major impact on the learning practice and its outcome".

In this respect, knowledge is socially constructed and maintained within the social processes of the organization (Wenger, 1998; Tsoukas & Vladimirou, 2001). In the most prominent approach of this stream of thinking, J.S. Brown and Paul Duguid (2000; 2001) have developed a view of knowledge as fundamentally associated with particular communities of practice understanding knowledge as being negotiated and internalized within social networks which establish their own sense making mechanisms (Weick, 1995). Under this perspective, we understand knowledge as a social process well related with the organizational environment. Such understanding requires further investigation of cases where the social capital of organization affects knowledge management and intellectual capital. We therefore attempt, in the next section, to examine the effects of outsourcing for knowledge management by focusing on social and organizational realities and effects.

KNOWLEDGE MANAGEMENT IN OUTSOURCING ORGANIZATIONS

Both the aforementioned streams of organizational development have been and remain popular among business theorists and practitioners. While preservation and development of knowledge has been a considerable organizational asset, processes of flexible organizing and the use of outsourcing, in particular, allow organizations to gain access to expertise and improve the efficiency of operations. What is striking though is that very few studies have been dedicated in researching the mutual interdependence between knowledge management and outsourcing. Research on the particular knowledge implications of outsourcing is still lacking. Such research gap seems striking taking into consideration that organizations increasingly rely on subcontracted services and outsourcing. Logically speaking, the relationship is open to multiple theorizations. For instance, one would argue that there is a positive relation in that outsourcing allows the organizations to 'learn' from outsiders but such claim could be contradicted by those arguing that access to external knowledge operates at the expense of organizational knowledge creation and maintenance.

Such claims and many more require adequate clarification along with a set of managerial advice as to how organizations may combine both outsourcing and knowledge capital preservation. It is precisely the aim of this chapter to contribute to these research questions and to provide an account of knowledge implications in outsourcing organizations. We seek to explore how organizational knowledge is affected and taking a social dimension of knowledge to explore the possible advantages or pitfalls. We are particularly interested in researching the absorptive capacity of organizations and to examine the mechanisms of knowledge creation, mainly seeking to explore whether the outsourcing organization may simultaneously be the knowledge organization.

RESEARCH METHODOLOGY AND DESIGN

Our research was conducted following the principles of a 'case study' approach (Yin, 1994), and in fact it is based on a 'multiple case study' analysis (Eisenkhart, 1989). The case study approach has certain advantages, especially for knowledge management research. It provides the researcher great opportunities to explore deeply

the organizational realities and to identify the reasons and causes of certain phenomena (Yin, 1994; Blaikie, 2000:215). Additionally the case study approach allows the researcher to use a mix of qualitative and quantitative data (Yin, 1994; Stake, 1994), although "qualitative methods are of primary importance" (Gillham, 2000: 10). For our study we focused on a set of pharmaceutical firms, of small and small-medium size in Greece, all of which have been using outsourcing practices while also being challenged to create, maintain and accumulate knowledge capital, this being a fundamental operation for the Pharma sector. Research also included a study within the subcontactoring companies, raising the number of companies under study to eleven (11).

In practical terms, choosing to do a case study is to choose to search for an explanation of the organizational realities and phenomena and requires a process of reasoning. In fact, case study is not a technique but more or less a mode for organizing data and evidence (Gillham, 2000), a perspective on how to see and explain social facts.

Since a social perspective of knowledge was used, during research, emphasis was given to people, their everyday life and how they work and think. Emphasis has also been given to the comparison between the past (company that doesn't

Figure 2. Research process for all eleven (11) companies

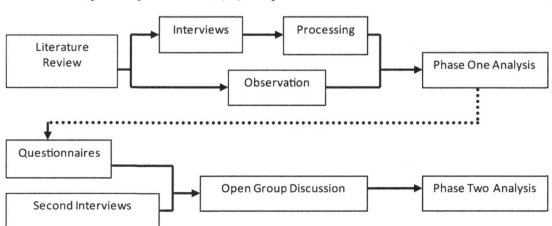

outsource) with the present one (outsourcing company). Amaratunga & Bauldry (2001) support the common idea that a complete case study research design should include a variety of research techniques, which could help the researcher to secure the conclusions and generalize the findings. In this respect, several research methods have been used, including observation, interviews and finally a small number of focus groups. The aim of the research design was to gather information from the interviewees from all companies and to return and cross check their first opinions with questionnaires and second interviews. Then a last open group discussion was designed to provide a final feedback from the organization about the issues that have arisen during the research.

Research has finally included three (3) medium sized pharmaceutical companies and their sub-contractors. The subjects of research are summarized in Table 4.

OUTSOURCING PRACTICES IN THREE MEDIUM SIZED PHARMACEUTICAL INDUSTRIES

Research findings indicate a large number of problems in knowledge management resulted by the extensive usage of outsourcing. Paradoxically, even in cases of successful collaborations, employees have been generally willing to agree that particular knowledge has not been distributed within the organization. Interview material revealed that it was mainly due to communication problems that employees failed to construct an atmosphere of knowledge sharing. It is interesting that some employees even denied the term 'loss of knowledge' arguing that 'to lose something, you must have it first'.

Lack of communication has been a problem in departments where operations are outsourced. Even in cases where contractors had to be physically present to the organization's environment (accounting consultants, software developers), sharing of knowledge was highly problematic while in cases where operations were taking completely outside the physical boundaries of the company, knowledge sharing has been even lower (sales and promotions, production). Indeed, geographical issues and space sharing seem to be correlated with the levels of knowledge sharing between employees and outsiders, a phenomenon well described by one of the interviewees in the following quotation *"When they are sitting on the desk, well then at least we can talk to them, ask questions and put some pressure. Otherwise it is impossible"*

It was also generally observed that collaboration failed to evolve into essential partnerships of mutual interest (Doz, 1996; Mowery et al., 1996). On the contrary it has been obvious that relations between staff and outsiders were focused on the contractual obligations. Lack of time (McDermott & O'Dell, 2001) and the politics of contractors to protect their role and knowledge (Scarborough, 1995) lead to an important gap in communication. It is definitely the case that there was no will to exchange knowledge while the social environment would not assist such efforts.

Table 4. Matrix showing contractual relations of outsourcing among the eleven (11) companies

Company/ Sub-contractors	Accounting & Consulting	Promotion operations	Information Systems	Some Manufacturing processes
PROEL SA	Thesis Ltd	Independent Group of salesmen (A)	Q-Logic SA	PH&T Italy
IAPHARM Ltd	(In-house)	Independent Group of salesmen (A)	Infinitum Software Solutions Ltd	ANFARM PROEL SA
MEDION Ltd	Large Auditing Company (Anonymous)	Independent Group of salesmen (B)	(Mostly In-house)	PROEL SA

Figure 3. Pathology of knowledge management when outsourcing operations

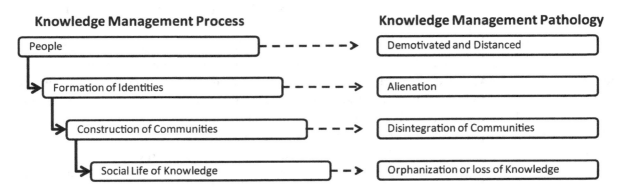

More or less, as Hendry (1995) also argues, outsourcing created risks for the maintenance of the corporate culture and the structure of the organization. Outsourcing defines a particular type of inter-firm relations; drawing results from PROEL and Iapharm, it is argued here that the nature of such relations does not facilitate the creation of a knowledge transfer social environment (Nahapiet & Goshal, 1998; Hall, 2001; Simonin, 1999; Bell et al., 2002).

Providing a critical evaluation of the conditions required it has been observed that:

a.   The contractors were not willing to share knowledge.
b.   Social conditions for learning and knowledge exchange have not existed and informal communication was not enough to promote knowledge exchanges.
c.   People of the company have become reluctant to participate to organizational processes, to see and learn from the outsiders.

ORGANIZATIONAL IDENTITIES

Given that knowledge management is based on social values and the accumulation of intellectual capital is well related with the quality of social capital (Stewart, 1997; Nahapiet & Goshal, 1998), it is not surprising that the findings presented in the previous section initiate certain effects for

knowledge management as well. The lack of communication, the concentration on contractual agreements and the absence of an environment of mutual exchange and collaboration combined with the distancing of employees from organizational processes produced negative effects for the accumulation and management of knowledge in the organization. Individuals themselves have been distanced from the actual practice, thus they have become observers of particular aspects of organizational life. Managers and employees described such changes as a process of organizational re-construction where new roles have been assigned to outsiders and where the individual lost its fundamental role as a primary resource for problem-solving. In most cases, top management failed to maintain a balance between employees and subcontractors thus establishing the image of outsiders as the most credible speakers in domains of their expertise. In certain cases, top management has adopted a purely technocratic discourse arguing that the evolution of subcontractors into dominant organizational actors is unavoidable.

Studying the literature on communities of practice focusing on the processes of social construction of knowledge, we are called to pay particular attention at the importance of group culture in knowledge processes. Research in outsourcing organizations has clearly revealed a set of pathologies of knowledge management which flaw the processes of communities of practice and the knowledge residing in the organization's social environment. Such pathology is analyzed in different phases, first as the demotivation of individuals, their alienation from the actual domains of organizational practice, the disintegration of communities and finally the loss of knowledge, or better said, the loss of knowledge opportunity.

Starting from the observed reality of alienation and employee's de-motivation (see also Hendry, 1995; Embleton & Wright, 1998) it is argued that such effects caused the disintegration of communities of practice in the organization and led to a dual loss of knowledge. Knowledge has been lost because of the deconstruction of communities (Lave & Wenger, 1993: 82) but also other parts of organizational knowledge have been marginalized since employees took a certain distance from the organizational processes (orphan knowledge, see Caddy, 2000). The next sections describe these knowledge implications, which are finally presented as a 'vicious cycle' of effects.

INDIVIDUALS' IDENTITIES

A primary finding during the research in companies was that the outsourcing of certain activities had a dramatic effect on people and their identity in the organization. Employees and managers' role has become less important and people who were close to the processes in the past seemed to take a certain distance from the situation. Most of them expressed the concern that not only did they lose part of their power in the organization but that in a way they have been marginalized and have been unable to understand their role; a form of alienation has been observed (Wheeler, 1996). It has been seen that the lack of effective communication with contractors caused the alienation of employees (Levinson, 1973; Erikson, 1990; Dukerich et al., 1998) who were isolated physically (geographical distancing of outsourcing, Takac, 1993) and culturally (Hendry, 1995; Embleton & Wright, 1998).

DISINTEGRATION OF COMMUNITIES AND SOCIAL CAPITAL PATHOLOGY

It is arguable then that in PROEL, the traditional groups of people dealing with issues have been dissolved; teams which had the responsibility for doing the job have been replaced by teams from outside the firm (Lin, 2000). As analyzed in previous chapters, communities of practice require a certain degree of cohesion and must be concentrated on certain goals, to have a specific identity (Lave & Wenger, 1991). Previous section's evidence presented, show that the individuals' identities have been affected and so were the identities of workgroups and teams; it is argued here that such process leads to the disintegration of communities while new ones have not been created. As a result, when managers started using outsourcing practices, the work teams and the individuals in the organization did not have enough incentives to learn and to explore methods and practices. The disintegration of communities lead to less dialogue in the enterprise, people of the outsourcing companies became less involved and finally lost the opportunity to learn by seeing (Raelin, 1997), by analyzing, by experimenting (Chailkin & Lave, 1993) and even by failing (Hall, 2001). The outsourcing of tasks has actually lead to the outsourcing of knowledge; additionally it can be argued that orphan knowledge has been created, in other words certain skills and expertise have been marginalized (see Caddy et al., 2001) since people's skills and experience or know-how stopped being used.

ADDICTION TO OUTSOURCING: LOSING THE ABSORPTIVE CAPACITY

While outsourcing has affected identities and as a result the formation and the role of communities, it has also produced effects for organizational learning and for the maintenance of knowledge itself.

What was found to be very important is that not only companies did lose parts of knowledge but that the disintegration of communities of practice, the lack of observation and experimentation (see Barley, 1996; Orr, 1990) combined with the poor social environment created dynamics for further and continuous worsening of the situation. The disintegration of learning processes in the organization took the form of a snow slide.

It is argued here that these effects are well related to the increasing reluctance of employees to become involved in outsourced processes and the obvious lack of participation (Hendry, 1995). In the past, employees even in their free time had interest on what was going in the company; the 'family' character of the organization also triggered such behaviour. Things changed though: "I myself used to check the pay-checks and the salaries and I spent hours and hours with other people discussing how we could change things. Now, simply there is no point, the administration relies on other people for these things" (from interview of Senior Accountant of PROEL).

SECONDARY EFFECTS: EXPLORING THE VICIOUS CYCLE OF KNOWLEDGE DEPENDENCE

The above situation produces secondary negative effects for the organization as a whole and it has been shown in our cases that the loss of absorptive capacity and the disintegration of knowledge in communities lead to further negative results. A main effect is the one of organizational dependence since the three (3) outsourcing companies are now relying on firms and outsiders to maintain their business activities. As argued in Fine (1998) and Takeishi (2002), relying to the knowledge of outsiders creates an expected level of dependence of the company. What was seen from our research was an increased dependence from the outsiders' knowledge and skills. During the research it was possible to identify certain cases where lack of organizational knowledge and the inability of the organization to have access to specific know-how resulted in losses in terms of time and money. Most incidents have been presented to the companies in matrix forms. To a certain extent what was also

Figure 4. A summary of effects of outsourcing for knowledge management in organizations

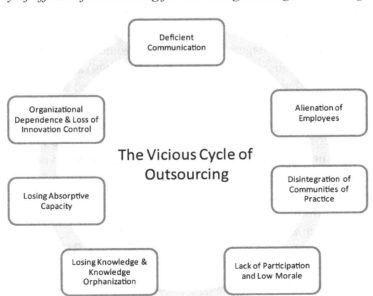

observed, as a result of dependency, was a raising insecurity (Embleton & Wright, 1998; Hendry, 1995; Takeishi, 2002) and a lack of trust in organizational capabilities to face specific problems; such situation is still creating an increasing dependence from those who know how to do the job. In other words, outsourcing has become a one-way process to import knowledge in the organizational boundaries and solve problems.

Yakhlef (2002) suggests that knowledge requirements themselves are formulated by the discursive relationship between the companies. In PROEL and Iapharm it has been noticed that the external agents, especially the promotion teams, usually have the ability to pass their views on management and executives of their clients. They possess, or have convinced that they possess, three levels of knowledge: what is required (what should be done), what can be done and what-if scenarios analysis. So both companies seem to lose progressively the ability to know "what is needed to know" or what kind of knowledge is required. Either because the contractors maintain a 'social closure policy' (Scarborough, 1995) or because the nature of knowledge itself is discursive and based on power relations (Yakhlef, 2002), it seems that only the consultants, marketers and information engineers are lately in position to suggest to the company what must be done and therefore they do control the innovation of management practices and activities. We have observed that the orphanization of knowledge has produced a dynamic increase of outsourcing needs. The above findings could be described as a 'vicious cycle' of effects which have the form of a continuous chain reaction, as presented in Figure 4.

So, a main issue is that the use of outsourcing initiates further needs for outsourcing within the same department or even in different operations. Both organizational dependence and innovation outsourcing have created to most managers the impression that the company could not survive without the contractors' knowledge; an interesting issue coming out of the questionnaires is that most of them would approve more outsourcing because "it seems that we do a better job when being in position of control instead of doing things" (Sales Manager of Iapharm). This idea of recycled outsourcing, missing from current literature, is very interesting and should be further studied and elaborated.

CONCLUSION

The vicious cycle of outsourcing effects should be considered as the main implication of this research. It has been shown that the use of outsourcing and subcontracting initiates certain social effects which finally produce further changes to the organizational life and to the intellectual capital of the organization. A continuous process of alienation (Erikson, 1990; Wheeler, 1996), disintegration of communities (Lave & Wenger, 1991; Wenger, 1998) and organizational de-identification (Dukerich et al., 1998) takes place while the company is transformed from a learning entity (Easterby-Smith, 1999) into an expertise purchaser (Chan, 1994). This study takes a negative stand against outsourcing, critically objecting the focus of management and shareholders on downsizing and reducing costs, neglecting important long-term aspects of organizational life (Lazonick & O'Sullivan, 2000; Kasey, 1995; Whitley, 1999) and the importance of knowledge management and accumulation. It is argued that before transforming the policy of outsourcing into specific management decisions, a consideration of issues concerning the organizational culture, identities and finally knowledge should take place (Embleton & Wright, 1998; Chan, 1994; Vanson, 2001; Hendry, 1995).

FUTURE RESEARCH

Elimination of the negative effects should be studied further and should be based on the principle that knowledge sharing and exchange of intellectual capital is primarily based on the development of social capital (Nahapiet & Goshal, 1998; Hall, 2001) and the motivation of employees (Leonard & Sensiper, 1998). Additionally, we argue that there are three typical approaches which can be followed:

a. Building and supporting inter-organizational mixed teams and communities.
b. Transforming the nature of relationship, several studies argue for a conversion of outsourcing contracts into strategic alliances.
c. Formalizing knowledge in order to achieve conversion of tacit and experience knowledge into typical, codified information flows.

However, the above propositions need to be further analyzed and empirically tested. Further research, currently conducted by the authors, focuses on specific organizational or functional mechanisms, which would assist the company to preserve and accumulate knowledge concurrently with changing the internal structure, while outsourcing or downsizing.

Further research is needed not only in order to clarify the field but also in order to avoid what has been seen during our research as a process of conflicting strategies and rhetoric. While managers have understood knowledge as an important asset their policies have been leading to the opposite results. Such conflicting strategies are sometimes not obvious to managers and it is the aim of research to further reveal the pathologies and propose solutions.

REFERENCES

Amaratunga, D., & Baldry, D. (2001). Case study methodology as a means of theory building: performance measurement in facilities management organizations. *Work Study, 50*(3), 95–104. doi:10.1108/00438020110389227

Bain, J. S. (1968). Industrial organization. New York: Wiley.

Barley, S. R. (1996). Technicians in the workplace: ethnographic evidence for bringing work into organizational studies. *Administrative Science Quarterly, 41*(3), 404–441. doi:10.2307/2393937

Bell, D. G., Giordano, R., & Putz, P. (2002). Interfirm sharing of process knowledge: exploring knowledge markets. *Knowledge and Process Management, 9*(1), 12–22. doi:10.1002/kpm.131

Berger, P. L., & Luckmann, T. (1966). The social construction of reality. London: Allen Lane The Penguin Press

Bhatt, G. D. (2000). Information dynamics, learning and knowledge creation in organizations. *The Learning Organization, 7*(2), 89–98. doi:10.1108/09696470010316288

Bhatt, G. D. (2001). Knowledge management in organizations: examining the interaction between technologies, techniques and people. *Journal of Knowledge Management, 5*(1), 68–75. doi:10.1108/13673270110384419

Blackler, F. (1995). Knowledge, knowledge work and organizations: an overview and interpretations. *Organization Studies, 16*(6), 1021–1046. doi:10.1177/017084069501600605

Blaikie, N. (2000). Designing social research: the logic of anticipation. Cambridge, UK: Polity Press.

Boudreau, J. W., & Ramstad, P. M. (1997). Measuring intellectual capital: learning from financial history. *Human Resource Management, 36*(3), 343–356. doi:10.1002/(SICI)1099-050X(199723)36:3<343::AID-HRM6>3.0.CO;2-W

Brown, J. S., & Duguid, P. (1991). Organizational learning and communities of practice: toward a unified view of working, learning and innovation. *Organization Science, 2*(1), 40–57. doi:10.1287/orsc.2.1.40

Brown, J. S., & Duguid, P. (2000). The social life of information. Boston, MA: Harvard Business School Press.

Brown, J. S., & Duguid, P. (2001). Knowledge and Organization: a social practice perspective. *Organization Science, 12*(2), 198–213. doi:10.1287/orsc.12.2.198.10116

Budros, A. (1999). A conceptual framework for analyzing why organizations downsize. *Organization Science, 10*(1), 69–82. doi:10.1287/orsc.10.1.69

Bukh, P. N., Larsen, H. T., & Mouritsen, J. (2001). Constructing intellectual capital statements. *Scandinavian Journal of Management, 17*, 87–108. doi:10.1016/S0956-5221(00)00034-8

Busi, M., & Mc Ivor, R. (2008). Setting the outsourcing research agenda: the top-10 most urgent outsourcing areas. *Strategic Outsourcing: An International Journal, 1*(3), 185–197. doi:10.1108/17538290810915263

Caddy, I. (2000). Intellectual assets and liabilities. *Journal of Intellectual Capital, 2*(1), 129–146. doi:10.1108/14691930010377469

Caddy, I., Guthrie, J., & Petty, R. (2001). Managing orphan knowledge: current Australasian best practice. *Journal of Intellectual Capital, 2*(4), 384–397. doi:10.1108/14691930110409679

Chailkin, S., & Lave, J. (1993). Understanding practice. Cambridge, UK: Cambridge University Press.

Chan, K. C. (1994). Learning for total quality. *The Learning Organization, 1*(1), 17–22. doi:10.1108/09696479410053403

Choo, C. W. (1998). The knowing organization: how organizations use information to construct meaning, create knowledge and make decisions. Oxford, UK: Oxford University Press.

Cohen, W. M., & Levinthal, D. A. (1990). Absorptive capacity: a new perspective on learning and innovation. *Administrative Science Quarterly, 35*(2), 128–152. doi:10.2307/2393553

Dant, T. (1991). Knowledge, ideology and discourse: a sociological perspective. London: Routledge.

Doz, Y. L. (1996). The evolution of cooperation in strategic alliances: initial conditions or learning processes. *Strategic Management Journal, 17*, 55–83. doi:10.1002/(SICI)1097-0266(199601)17:1<55::AID-SMJ788>3.0.CO;2-B

Dukerich, J., Kramer, R., & McLean-Parks, J. (1998). The dark side of organizational identification. In Whetten, D. A., & Godfrey, P. C. (eds), Identity in organizations: building theory through conversations (p. 245-256). London: Sage Publications.

Easterby-Smith, M., Araujo, L., & Burgoyne, J. (1999). Organizational learning and the learning organization: developments in theory and practice. London: Sage Publications.

Edvisson, L., & Malone, M. S. (1997). Intellectual Capital. London: Piatkus Publications.

Eisenhardt, K. M. (1989). Building theories from case study research. *Academy of Management Review, 14*(4), 532–550. doi:10.2307/258557

Embleton, P. R., & Wright, P. C. (1998). A practical guide to successful outsourcing. *Empowerment in Organizations*, *6*(3), 94–106. doi:10.1108/14634449810210832

Erikson, K. (1990). On work and alienation. In Erikson, K. & Valls, P. (eds), The nature of work: sociological perspectives (pp.19-35). New Haven, CT: Yale University.

Fine, C. H. (1998). Clockspeed: winning industry control in the age of temporary advantage. Reading, MA: Perseus Books.

Fine, C. H., & Whitney, D. E. (1996). Is the make-buy decision process a core competence? Working paper no. 3875-96, February, MIT Center for Technology, Policy, and Industrial Development, Cambridge, MA.

Ford, D., Cotton, B., Farmer, D., Gross, A., & Wilkinson, I. (1993). 'Make-or-buy decisions and their implications. *Industrial Marketing Management*, *22*(3), 207–214. doi:10.1016/0019-8501(93)90007-T

Foucault, M. (1980) The Archaeology of Knowledge, London: Polity Press

Gilley, K. M., & Rasheed, A. (n.d.). Making more by doing less: An analysis of outsourcing and its effect on firm performance. *Journal of Management*, *26*(4), 763–790. doi:10.1016/S0149-2063(00)00055-6

Gillham, B. (2000). Case study research methods. London & New York: Continuum Editions.

Good, W. J., & Hatt, P. K. (1952). Methods in social research. New York: Mc Graw Hill.

Grandori, A., & Soda, G. (1995). Inter-firm networks: antecedents, mechanisms and forms. *Organization Studies*, *16*(2), 183–214. doi:10.1177/017084069501600201

Grossman, S. J., & Hart, O. D. (1986). The Costs and Benefits of Ownership: A Theory of Vertical and Lateral Integration. *The Journal of Political Economy*, *94*(4), 691–719. doi:10.1086/261404

Hakansson, H. (1989). Corporate technological behaviour: cooperation and networks. London: Routledge.

Hakansson, H., & Johanson, J. (1988). Formal and informal cooperation strategies in international industrial networks. In Contractor, F. J., & Lorange, P. (eds), Cooperative strategies in international business. Lexington, UK: Lexington Books.

Hale, R., & Whitlam, P. (1997). Towards the virtual organization. London: McGraw Hill International.

Hall, H. (2001, April). *Social exchange for knowledge exchange*. Paper presented in the Conference "Managing Knowledge: conversations and critiques", Leicester University Management Center, UK.

Hamel, G. (1991). Competition for competence and inter-partner learning with international strategic alliances. *Strategic Management Journal*, *12*, 83–103. doi:10.1002/smj.4250120908

Harland, C., & Knight, L. (2005). Outsourcing: Assessing the Risks and Benefits for Organizations, Sectors and Nations. *International Journal of Operations & Production Management*, *25*(9), 831–850. doi:10.1108/01443570510613929

Harringan, K. R. (1984). Formulating vertical integration strategies. *Academy of Management Review*, *9*, 638–652. doi:10.2307/258487

Harringan, K. R. (1984). Matching vertical integration strategies to competitive conditions. *Strategic Management Journal*, *7*, 535–555.

Hendry, J. (1995). Culture, community and networks: the hidden cost of outsourcing. *European Management Journal*, *13*(2), 193–200. doi:10.1016/0263-2373(95)00007-8

Henriksson, K. (1999). The collective dynamics of organizational learning. Lund, Sweden: Lund University Press.

Holsapple, J., & Jones, K. (2005). Exploring Secondary Activities of the Knowledge Chain. *Knowledge and Process Management, 12*(1), 3–30. doi:10.1002/kpm.219

Jarillo, J. C. (1988). On strategic networks. *Strategic Management Journal, 9*, 31–41. doi:10.1002/smj.4250090104

Jarillo, J. C. (1993). Strategic Networks. New York: Butterworth – Heinemann.

Jiang, B., Frazier, V., & Prater, E. L. (2006). Outsourcing effects on firms' operational performance: An empirical study. *International Journal of Operations & Production Management, 26*(12), 1280–1300. doi:10.1108/01443570610710551

Johnson, M. (1997). Outsourcing (in brief). Boston: Butterworth Heinemann Editions. Israel, J. (1971). Alienation. New York: Allyn and Bacon Editions.

Kanter, R. M., & Mayers, P. S. (1991). Inter-organizational bonds and intraorganizational behavior: how alliances and partnerships change the organizations forming them. In Etzioni, A. & Lawrence P. (eds), Socio-Economics: towards a new synthesis. New York: Armonk

Kaplan, J. (2002, January 14). The realities of outsourcing. *Network World*, 12-13.

Korman, A. K. (1970). Towards a hypothesis of work behaviour. *The Journal of Applied Psychology, 56*, 31–41. doi:10.1037/h0028656

Kumpe, E., & Bolwjin, P. T. (1988)... *Harvard Business Review*, 75–81.

Lane, P. J., & Lubatkin, M. (1998). Relative absorptive capacity and inter-organizational learning. *Strategic Management Journal, 19*, 461–477. doi:10.1002/(SICI)1097-0266(199805)19:5<461::AID-SMJ953>3.0.CO;2-L

Lankford, W. M., & Parsa, F. (1999). Outsourcing: a primer. *Management Decision, 37*(4), 310–316. doi:10.1108/00251749910269357

Lave, J., & Wenger, E. (1991). Situated learning. Legitimate peripheral participation. Cambridge, UK: Cambridge University Press.

Lazonick, W., & O'Sullivan, M. (2000). Maximizing shareholder value: a new ideology for corporate governance. *Economy and Society, 29*(1), 13–35. doi:10.1080/030851400360541

Leonard, D., & Sensiper, S. (1998). The role of tacit knowledge in group innovation. *California Management Review, 40*(3), 112–132.

Levinson, D. (1973). Role, personality and social structure in the organizational setting. In Salaman, G., & Thompson, K. (eds), People in organizations, (pp. 222-237). Milton Keynes, UK: Open University Press.

Li, X., & Barnes, I. (2008). Proactive supply risk management methods for building a robust supply selection process when sourcing from emerging markets. *Strategic Outsourcing: An International Journal, 1*(3), 252–267. doi:10.1108/17538290810915308

Liebowitz, J., Montano, B., McCaw, D., & Rednik, K. (2000). The Knowledge Audit. *Journal of Knowledge and Process Management, 7*(1), 208–212.

Lin, J. (2000). Vertical integration versus outsourcing: a knowledge based reconciliation. In *Proceedings of the Midwest Academy of Management Conference.*

Lonsdale, C. (1999). Effectively managing vertical supply relationships: a risk management model for outsourcing. *Supply Chain Management: An International Journal, 4*(4), 176–183. doi:10.1108/13598549910284499

Madsen, E. S., Riis, J. O., & Waehrens, B. V. (2008). The Knowledge Dimension of Manufacturing Transfers: A Method for Identifying Hidden Knowledge. *Strategic Outsourcing: An International Journal, 1*(3), 198–209. doi:10.1108/17538290810915272

Mc Ivor, R. (2000). A Practical Framework for Understanding the Outsourcing Process. *Supply Chain Management: An International Journal, 5*(1), 22–36. doi:10.1108/13598540010312945

McDermott, R., & O'Dell, C. (2001). Overcoming cultural barriers to sharing knowledge. *Journal of Knowledge Management, 5*(1), 76–85. doi:10.1108/13673270110384428

Milgate, M. (2001). Alliances, outsourcing and the lean organization. Praeger.

Misawa, K., & Hattori, K. (1998). R&D outsourcing to create core competence. *Kenkyu Kaihatsu Manejimento, 8*(6), 4-13. Translated by J. K. Keaton, Retrieved from http://www.jkl.org/rd_research

Mishler, E. G. (1991). Representing discourse: the rhetoric of transcription. *Journal of Narrative and Life History, 1*, 255–280.

Morey, D., Maybury, M., & Thuraisingham, B. (Eds.). (2000). Knowledge Management: classic and contemporary works. Cambridge, MA: The MIT Press.

Moses, A., & Par, A. (2008). Dimensions of change in make or buy decision processes. *Strategic Outsourcing: An International Journal, 1*(3), 230–251. doi:10.1108/17538290810915290

Mowery, D. C., Oxley, J. E., Silverman, B. (1996). Strategic alliances and interfirm knowledge transfer. *Strategic Management Journal, 17* (Winter Special Issue), 77-91.

Nahapiet, J., & Goshal, S. (1998). Social capital, intellectual capital and the organizational advantage. *Academy of Management Review, 23*(2), 242–266. doi:10.2307/259373

Nohria, N., & Eccles, R. G. (1992). Networks and organizations. Boston, MA: Harvard Business Press.

Nonaka, I. (1994). A dynamic theory of organizational knowledge creation. *Organization Science, 5*(1), 14–37. doi:10.1287/orsc.5.1.14

Nonaka, I., & Takeuchi, H. (1995). The knowledge creating company: how Japanese companies create the dynamics of innovation. Oxford, UK: Oxford University Press.

North, D. C. (1990). Institutions, institutional change and economic performance. Cambridge, UK: Cambridge University Press.

Oke, A., & Maltz, A. (2009). Criteria for sourcing from developing countries. *Strategic Outsourcing:An International Journal, 2*(2), 145–164. doi:10.1108/17538290910973367

Orr, J. (1990). Sharing knowledge, celebrating identity: war stories and community memory in a service culture. In Middleton, D. S., & Edwards, D. (eds), Collective remembering: memory in society. Thousand Oaks, CA: Sage Publications.

Power, M., Bonifazi, C., & DeSouza, K. C. (2004). The Ten Outsourcing Traps to Avoid. *The Journal of Business Strategy, 25*(2), 37–42. doi:10.1108/02756660410525399

Power, M. J., Desouza, K. C., & Bonifazi, C. (2006). The Outsourcing Handbook: How to implement a successful outsourcing process. Philadelphia: Kogan Page.

Quinn, J. B. (1992). Intelligent Enterprise. New York: Free Press.

Quintas, P. (2002). Managing knowledge in the new century. In Little, S., Quintas, P., Ray, T. (eds), Managing knowledge: an essential reader. London: The Open University in Association with Sage Publications.

Raelin, J. A. (1997). A model of work-based learning. *Organization Science*, *8*(6), 563–578. doi:10.1287/orsc.8.6.563

Scarborough, H. (1995). Blackboxes, hostages and prisoners. *Organization Studies*, *16*(6), 991–1019. doi:10.1177/017084069501600604

Seufert, A., von Krogh, G., & Back, A. (1999). Towards Knowledge Networking. *Journal of Knowledge Management*, *3*(3), 180–190. doi:10.1108/13673279910288608

Simon, H. A. (1991). Bounded rationality and organizational learning. *Organization Science*, *2*(1), 125–134. doi:10.1287/orsc.2.1.125

Simonin, B. L. (1999). Ambiguity and the process of knowledge transfer in strategic alliances. *Strategic Management Journal*, *20*, 595–623. doi:10.1002/(SICI)1097-0266(199907)20:7<595::AID-SMJ47>3.0.CO;2-5

Spender, J. C. (1996). Making knowledge the basis of a dynamic theory of the firm. *Strategic Management Journal*, *17*, 45–62.

Stake, R. E. (1994). Case studies. In Denzin, N. K. & Lincoln, Y.S. (eds), Handbook of qualitative research. Thousand Oaks, CA: Sage Publications.

Stewart, T. A. (1997). Intellectual Capital: the new wealth of organizations. London: Nicholas Brealey Publishing.

Sveiby, K. E. (1997). The new organizational wealth: managing and measuring knowledge based assets. San Francisco: Berrett-Koehler.

Szymankiewicz, J. (1994). Contracting out or Selling out? *Logistics Information Management*, *7*(1), 28–35. doi:10.1108/09576059410052368

Takac, P. F. (1993). Outsourcing Technology. *Management Decision*, *31*(1), 25–38. doi:10.1108/00251749310023157

Takeishi, A. (2002). Knowledge partitioning in the interfirm division of labor: the case of automotive product development. *Organization Science*, *13*(3), 321–338. doi:10.1287/orsc.13.3.321.2779

Teece, D. J. (2001). Strategies for managing knowledge assets: the role of firm structure and industrial context. In Nonaka, I. & Teece D., Managing industrial knowledge: creation, transfer, utilization. London: Sage Publications.

Tsoukas, H. (1996). The firm as a distributed knowledge system: a constructionist approach. *Strategic Management Journal*, *17*, 11–25.

Tsoukas, H., & Vladimirou, E. (2001). What is organizational knowledge? *Journal of Management Studies*, *38*(7), 973–993. doi:10.1111/1467-6486.00268

van de Ven, A. H. (1992). Suggestions for studying strategy process: a research note. *Strategic Management Journal*, *13*, 169–191. doi:10.1002/smj.4250131013

Vanson, S. (2001). Challenge of outsourcing human resources. Oxford, UK: Chandos Publishing.

Walker, G., & Weber, D. (1984). A Transaction cost approach to make or buy decisions. *Administrative Science Quarterly*, *29*, 373–391. doi:10.2307/2393030

Wang, E. T. G., Barron, T., & Seidmann, A. (1997). Contracting structures for custom software development: the impacts of informational rents and uncertainty of internal development and outsourcing. *Management Science, 43*(12), 1726–1744. doi:10.1287/mnsc.43.12.1726

Weick, K. (1995) Sensemaking in organizations. Thousand Oaks: Sage Publications.

Wenger, E. (1998). Communities of practice. Cambridge, UK: Cambridge University Press.

Wernerfelt, B. (1984). A resource-based view of the firm. *Strategic Management Journal, 5*(2), 171–180. doi:10.1002/smj.4250050207

Wheeler, R. (1996). Double Lives and Emotional Labour in Legal Firms. *Human Relations, 32*(3), 190–207.

Whitley, R. (1999). Divergent Capitalisms: the social structuring and change of business systems. Oxford, UK: Oxford University Press.

Williamson, O. E. (1975). Markets and Hierarchies: Analysis and Antitrust Implications, New York: The Free Press.

Yakhlef, A. (2002). Towards a discursive approach to organisational knowledge formation. *Scandinavian Journal of Management, 18*, 319–339. doi:10.1016/S0956-5221(01)00015-X

Yin, R. K. (1994). Case study research: design and methods. Thousand Oaks, CA: Sage Publications.

Zsidisin, G. A. (2003). A grounded definition of supply risk. *Journal of Purchasing and Supply Management, 9*, 217–224. doi:10.1016/j.pursup.2003.07.002

ADDITIONAL READINGS

Alexander, M., & Young, D. (1996). Strategic outsourcing. *Long Range Planning, 29*(1), 116–119. doi:10.1016/0024-6301(95)00075-5

Ashton, D. (1998). Systematic risk and empirical research. *Journal of Business Finance & Accounting, 25*(10), 1325–1356. doi:10.1111/1468-5957.00240

Brenner, R. (2009). Mitigating Outsourcing Risks Part I & II. *Point Lookout, 15*(9). Retrieved August 8, 2009, from http://www.chacocanyon.com/pointlookout/090415.shtml

Canez, L., Platts, K., & Probert, D. (2000). Developing a framework for make-or-buy decisions. *International Journal of Operations & Production Management, 20*(11), 1313–1330. doi:10.1108/01443570010348271

Christopher, M., & Lee, H. (2004). Mitigating supply chain risk through improved confidence'. *International Journal of Physical Distribution & Logistics Management, 34*(5), 388–396. doi:10.1108/09600030410545436

Davenport, T. H., & Prusak, L. (1998). Working Knowledge: How organizations manage what they know. Boston, MA: Harvard Business School Press.

Desouza, K. C., & Evaristo, J. R. (2005). Managing knowledge in distributed projects. *Communications of the ACM, 47*(4), 87–91. doi:10.1145/975817.975823

Freytag, P., & Kirk, L. (2003). Continuous strategic sourcing. *Journal of Purchasing and Supply Management, 9*(3), 135–150. doi:10.1016/S1478-4092(03)00006-2

Harland, C., Brenchley, R., & Walker, H. (2003). Risk in supply networks. *Journal of Purchasing and Supply Management, 9*(1), 51–62. doi:10.1016/S1478-4092(03)00004-9

Jennings, D. (1997). Strategic guidelines for outsourcing decisions. *The Journal of Strategic Change, 6*(2), 85–96. doi:10.1002/(SICI)1099-1697(199703)6:2<85::AID-JSC260>3.0.CO;2-U

Juttner, U., Peck, H., & Christopher, M. (2003). Supply chain risk management: outlining an agenda for future research'. *International Journal of Logistics: Research and Applications, 6*(4), 197–210.

Kakabadse, N., & Kakabadse, A. (2000). Outsourcing: a paradigm shift. *Journal of Management Development, 19*(8), 670-728.

Lonsdale, C., & Cox, A. (1997, July 3). Outsourcing: risks and rewards'. *Supply Management*, 32-4.

March, J. G., & Shapira, Z. (1987). Managerial perspectives on risk and risk taking. *Management Science, 33*(11), 1404–1418. doi:10.1287/mnsc.33.11.1404

Nonaka, I., & Takeuchi, H. (1995). The Knowledge-creating company: How Japanese companies create the dynamics of innovation. New York: Oxford University Press.

Norrman, A., & Jansson, U. (2004). Ericsson's proactive supply chain risk management approach after a serious sub-supplier accident'. *International Journal of Physical Distribution & Logistics Management, 34*(5), 434–456. doi:10.1108/09600030410545463

Peck, H. (2006). Reconciling supply chain vulnerability, risk and supply chain management. *International Journal of Logistics: Research and Applications, 9*(2), 127–142.

Prahalad, C. K., & Hamel, G. (1990). The core competence of the corporation. *Harvard Business Review*, (July-August): 79–91.

Shapira, Z. (1995). Risk Taking: A Managerial Perspective. New York: Russell Sage Foundation.

Venkatesan, R. (1992). Strategic sourcing: to make or not to make. *Harvard Business Review*, (November-December): 98–107.

Zsidisin, G. A., Ellram, L. M., Carter, J. R., & Cavinato, J. L. (2004). An analysis of supply risk assessment techniques. *International Journal of Physical Distribution & Logistics Management, 34*(5), 397–413. doi:10.1108/09600030410545445

Chapter 12
Upgrading Effectiveness in VEs:
Decision Framework Based on the Benefits, Opportunities, Costs and Risks (BOCR) Model

Konstantinos Kirytopoulos
University of the Aegean, Greece

Dimitra Voulgaridou
National Technical University Athens, Greece

Vrassidas Leopoulos
National Technical University Athens, Greece

ABSTRACT

Due to the rapid evolution of information technology, supply chain integration is nowadays easier than in the past. Moreover, the need for economic efficiency leads suppliers and customers to closely co-operate in pursuit of, what seems to be the holy grail of modern supply chain management, end to end optimization. The core objective of this chapter is the provision of a decision framework for enterprise formations organized as collaborative clusters, which is a sophisticated form of a virtual enterprise network. This framework, based on the ANP-BOCR model, takes into account clusters' special charac-teristics the most important of which is that the supply chain entities do have a clear picture of strategies, policies, needs, strengths and weaknesses of one another. The whole approach is illustrated through a parapharmaceutical cluster case study which reveals that "common" knowledge and risks are very important in an environment where entities are sometimes partners and sometimes competitors.

INTRODUCTION

Recent trends in global production have both increased supply chain complexity and reinforced the notion that logistics strategies and practices are essential elements of business strategy (Pe-rona & Miragliotta, 2003). Logistics complexity has increased as organizations have moved from centralized, vertically integrated, single-site manufacturing facilities to geographically dis-persed networks of resources that collectively create value for their customers (Tatsiopoulos et al., 2004). In such a business environment,

DOI: 10.4018/978-1-61520-607-0.ch012

networking is almost an inevitable solution to help companies respond rapidly to market changes (Hallikas et al., 2004). A common framework of enterprise networks appears to be the formation of enterprise clusters. Clusters can be defined as "*geographic concentrations of interconnected companies, specialized suppliers, service providers, firms in related industries, and associated institutions (for example, universities, standard agencies, and trade associations) in particular fields that compete but also co-operate*" (Porter, 1998). In other words, companies participating in a cluster are on the one hand competitors as they are selling the same product at the same market, but on the other hand act as partners collectively trying to increase that market by exploiting common strategies so as to offer faster, better and cheaper products.

A typical cluster example, is that of the tourism industry where actors (e.g. hotels, restaurants, public authorities and stores of a specific territory) are co-financing advertisement or the installment of hot-spots that serve the market base of the whole cluster.

Clusters are generally built up spontaneously by the local business players, who want to take advantage of several factors existing in their geographic area, such as the presence in large numbers of suppliers and customers, the access to information and know-how, the availability of resources and low transactions and communication costs due to geographical proximity.

Development of clusters may easily provide the spark for the development of virtual enterprise networks (Rowe, Burn & Walker, 2005). A virtual enterprise network is formed by a group of suppliers, service providers and other specialized players who are interacting while trying to optimize the delivery of a product to satisfy customer needs. When the interaction among the actors of a virtual enterprise network, takes the form of integra-

tion of processes (e.g. supply chain processes) with the use of information technology, then the virtual enterprise network leads to collaborative commerce (c-commerce).

Collaborative commerce is a term that has emerged to describe a fundamental shift in the way companies interact. It is a set of techniques allowing companies to better manage their virtual enterprise networks. A fundamental parameter for achieving improvements in such complex systems is appropriate decision making. This chapter focuses on decision making within the context of clusters and c-commerce.

Within this new, highly demanding and complex system (virtual enterprise networks using c-commerce within a cluster), the decision making process is a complicated issue and as organizations become more and more dependent on their suppliers, the direct and indirect consequences of poor decision making become more critical (Chan & Kumar, 2007). Decision making in such systems is complex as the decision makers have to take into account numerous of contradicting criteria and circumstances. A short example of these criteria and circumstances would be the fact that the decision maker is more or less obliged to maintain good relationship among its suppliers and that all the actors of the chain share common knowledge of the strengths and weaknesses of one another. In a nutshell, taking decisions within such environments is quite complex and requires that both qualitative and quantitative criteria must be taken into consideration.

In this context, the present chapter proposes a multicriteria method, able to handle the aforementioned complexity and further supports it with an illustrative paradigm residing in the supply chain of the Greek parapharmaceutical industry. The parapharmaceutical supply chain comprises a cluster whose members engage in c-commerce activities (referred as collaborative cluster from this point forward), as defined above. The proposed method utilizes the Analytic Network Process

Model With Benefits, Opportunities, Costs And Risks (ANP - BOCR model) in order to cope with the multicriteria decision problem, with dependencies and feedback. Although it is highly customized for the parapharmaceutical industry, due to the specific nature of the products, its framework and general concept can be applied to various regions and industries which face the complex problem of evaluating and selecting suppliers' offers.

The rest of the chapter is organized as follows: First, a literature review of the main scientific fields (supply chain, networking and virtual enterprises, clusters and c-commerce, multicriteria decision making and ANP - BOCR method) related with the present study is presented. Then, the case study section provides a detailed description of the parapharmaceutical collaborative cluster environment and its basic business processes. In the same section, the implementation of the proposed ANP - BOCR model is illustrated. Finally, conclusions are drawn and issues that could spark further research are highlighted.

BACKGROUND – THEORETICAL FRAMEWORK

This chapter explores a very specific form of decision making for organizations operating as virtual enterprise networks using c-commerce within a cluster environment. The whole concept is presented for the supply chain of the Greek parapharmaceutical industry. Thus, the following literature review which supports the theoretical framework resides on general concepts of supply chain, networking and virtual enterprises, clusters and collaborative commerce and finally multicriteria decision making.

Supply Chain – General Concepts

The obscurity with the term 'supply chain' lays in the fact that there are too many definitions, which are not necessarily contradictory but each one of them focuses on different perspective or characteristics of this scientific field. Christopher (1992) provides a generic definition by describing the supply chain as *a network of organizations which interact, through upstream (e.g. suppliers) and downstream (e.g. distributors) links and add value to products and services, aiming to the greater possible customers' satisfaction.* More recent studies (e.g. Ritchie & Brindley, 2001) suggest the inclusion of the information and financial flow in supply chain's definition, reflecting the development of the Information And Communication Technology (ICT). Akkermans et al. (2003) by the term 'supply chain' refer to *all these procedures concerning the physical flow (spanning from raw materials to products), along with the bidirectional informational flow that accompanies them.*

According to Marsden (1997), supply chain can be seen in three different perspectives. The *limited or basic supply chain* focuses on the links of an enterprise with its direct suppliers and/or customers. A great volume of supply chain research is dedicated to these binary relationships. The term *extended supply chain* refers to the organizations that are connected with the whole network of suppliers and customers. The *ultimate supply* chain incorporates the series of processes from raw materials to the consumer and all the relevant services that add value to the customers.

On the other hand, the supply chain perspectives as seen by Ritchie & Brindley (2001), Cooper, Lambert and Pugh (1997) or Porter (1985) are somehow different. They identify four perspectives; structural, systems, strategic and relationship. The *structural perspective* seems to be the most typical, despite the numerous and radical changes that have taken place through the development of more amorphous structures with multidimensional relationships which have replaced the previous linear patterns (Ritchie & Brindley, 2001). The *systems perspective* focuses on the efficiency of the system in terms of transition of resources from raw materials to finished goods (Cooper, Lambert & Pugh, 1997). Many researchers state that this perspective coincides with the applications of logistics, aiming to enhance efficiency in processing, storage and transportation. The *strategic perspective* mainly concerns the development and maintenance of competitive advantage through positioning the organization in relation to its supply chain members and seeking to maximize the value to the consumer (Porter, 1985). More recent developments in the field of supply chain management suggest a new *relationship perspective* (Ritchie & Brindley, 2001) that focuses on building and managing the relationships at both strategic and operational level. Although these perspectives are different, all of them provide deeper insights into the same set of issues and problems with a clear common goal of improving the overall supply chain efficiency.

Networking and Virtual Enterprises

Networking is a common characteristic of contemporary supply chains. Harland (1996) defines the supply network as *a specific form of relationship which interconnects a predefined set of persons, objects and events*. According to Hakansson and Johanson (1993) a network is *consisted of actors, resources and activities, tightly interconnected*. Networking has had a strong influence on organizations' strategy formation. Concentration on core competencies and outsourcing less critical activities has increased the strategic importance of capabilities and resources on the outside of firm's boundaries. Reve (1990) suggests that companies need to concentrate on core competencies and skills in order to respond to the changing environment. This stresses the need for considering the dynamic aspects of relationship development as companies have to make continuous strategic

sourcing decisions based on the changes of external and internal business conditions.

Gadde and Hakansson (2001) distinguish between high and low involvement relationships. They state that low involvement leads to significant hidden costs and offers limited opportunities to gain cost and revenue benefits. On the other hand, high involvement offers significant benefits but increases the relationship handling costs. Doz and Hamel (1998) argue that due to growth opportunities in global markets and wider skills required by new technologies, companies have to turn to strategic partnerships and alliances with other companies to be able to get access to resources and capabilities and to pursue new opportunities. Furthermore, the ability of an organization to exploit external knowledge is an important capability of innovation and thus, a substantial source of corporate development.

Pfohl and Buse (2000) suggest that attention should be paid to strategic networks and virtual enterprises, which are dynamic and non-hierarchical in nature. Virtual enterprises represent dynamic networks, while strategic networks can be seen more stable in nature. The tiers in the network make coordination difficult as the responsibilities must be shared among the first-tier and the multi-tier suppliers. Additionally, the logistics transactions between the buyer and the first-tier supplier make the network structure more complex. In a virtual enterprise, companies no longer produce complete products in isolated facilities. Instead, they operate as nodes in a network of customers, suppliers, service providers and other specialized partners. The main objective of a virtual enterprise is to allow a number of organizations to rapidly develop a common operating environment and focus on customers' needs. Finally, another important characteristic of virtual enterprises is their strong dependence on information systems (Camarinha-Matos et al., 1998; 2009).

Clusters and Collaborative Commerce

A special form of virtual enterprise networks are the enterprise clusters, which encompass all characteristics of virtual enterprises but they require the geographical proximity of their members. These structures, although identified many years before, have gained special attention of policy-makers all over the globe and have been adopted by many developing countries since nineties. Generally speaking, through networking the firms aim at reducing financial and technological risks and improving their competitive advantage through deeper specialization. The increasing challenges due to shortening time to market and lead times generally, the fast developing technologies and the globalization trend have made enterprise clusters an emerging concept in business.

In recent years there has been a growing interest in the role of location in the global economy. Some have argued that globalization, especially the creation of borderless markets, the mobility of capital, the rise of transnational firms, and the transition to an information economy, signals the 'end of geography' (O'Brien, 1992), the 'death of distance' (Cairncross, 1997), and the 'delocalization' of economic and social relationships (Gray, 1998). The main claim is that globalization is rendering the significance of location for economic activity increasingly irrelevant. Others, however, support the opposite view that globalization is actually increasing rather than reducing the importance of location, that it is promoting greater regional economic distinctiveness, and that regional economies rather than national economies are now the key to wealth creation and world trade (Ohmae, 1995; Coyle, 1997, 2001; Krugman, 1997; Porter, 1998; Scott, 1998,2001; Fujita, Krugman & Venables, 2000). Thus, as the business economist Michael Porter (1998) puts it: "*In a global economy – which boasts rapid transportation, high speed communications and accessible markets – one would expect location*

to diminish in importance. But the opposite is true. The enduring competitive advantages in a global economy are often heavily localized, arising from concentrations of highly specialized skills and knowledge, institutions, rivalry, related businesses, and sophisticated customers". This is why interest in clusters has not been limited to either the academic research or practitioners. Indeed, over the past few years, the cluster concept has found a favoring audience amongst policy-makers at all levels, from the World Bank, to national governments, to regional development bodies, to city authorities. All of them were keen to find a new form of industrial policy or activism in which the focus is firmly on the promotion of successful, competitive economies. Porter's own work has been one factor stimulating this policy interest. Porter (1998) argued that while co-location is not sufficient for cluster formation, it 'supercharges' and magnifies the power of domestic rivalry which is the major motive to continuous innovation and improvement.

Clusters affect competition in three main ways (Trends Business Research, 2001). First, they raise productivity by providing access to specialized inputs and employees and make information sharing and technology upgrading easier. Furthermore, being part of a cluster, a company, is able to extend its specialized supplier base and by sourcing locally instead from distant suppliers it lowers transactions costs. In addition, it minimizes the need for inventory and eliminates importing costs and delays.

Moreover, developing close relationships fosters trust and facilitates the flow of information, which results in the formation of strong, knowledge-based networks that exist for generating, transferring and applying knowledge, and subsequently train and educate others in that knowledge (Martinus et al., 2005). Moreover, benefits arise from complementarities, which appear in many forms, such as the fact that linkages among cluster members result in a sum of value added transactions greater than the sum of its parts (Porter, 1998). For instance, it is not only the transactions themselves that offer added value but also the relationships built in parallel to these transactions. The dependency of cluster members assures that the good performance of one member can boost the success of the others. A cluster frequently enhances the reputation of a particular industry, making it more likely that buyers will turn to a vendor originated from the same cluster. The Italian fashion cluster and the Japanese technology cluster are living examples of how these enterprise structures have managed to boost the reputation of these industries by attracting customers worldwide (Porter, 1985). Clusters' members also seem to realize their buying risk to be lower than typical. This is because being based at a location where several suppliers exist, it is easier either to multisource or to switch vendors if the need arises.

Clusters play a vital role in a company's ability to innovate, as they increase the diffusion of technological knowledge and best practices within the cluster very rapidly, thus directly affecting competition. Companies inside clusters have a better perspective of the market than isolated competitors do and they are obliged to develop innovative strategies and develop the necessary capacities to implement them. In a cluster, enterprises voluntarily or involuntarily learn from each other and imitate each other. Actually, clusters do more than make opportunities for innovation more visible. They also provide the capacity and the flexibility to act rapidly, since a member of the cluster can source what it needs to implement innovations much easier (Guerrieri & Pietrobelli, 2000).

The third way for affecting competition is that clusters stimulate higher rates of establishing new companies, providing growth and long-term business dynamics. New companies grow up easier within an existing cluster rather than at isolated locations, as they lower their risks and can easier locate market opportunities. Furthermore, the members of a cluster are able to perceive gaps

and limitations of their industry in products and services and react vigorously by the formation of new businesses.

In order to better understand the structure and the operations of the enterprise clusters and highlight the differences between enterprise clusters and enterprise networks, such us extended enterprises, virtual enterprises and strategic networks, a comparison is presented in Table 1 (Voulgaridou, 2008). Although these terms are often used indiscriminately, they appear to encompass essential differences concerning their real meaning, their dynamics and their strategic or business goals (Rosenfeld, 2001). The first important difference is located in the reasons for their emergence and the factors which drive their formation. Enterprise clusters emerge as a result of the market forces and the intense competition among regional rivals. On the contrary, enterprise networks are usually formal partnerships among companies aiming to achieve a specific business objective. This difference leads to the outcome that although enterprise clusters are based mainly on informal relationships, enterprise networks are formed as a result of formal agreements and their relationships and transactions base is fully described in contracts (Rosenfeld, 2001).

An additional variance concerns the number of their members. In the case of enterprise networks the number of the members is limited (Håkasson & Snehota, 1998), while in an enterprise cluster, the number of the partners is theoretically infinite. Another difference of clusters is the diversified origin of their participants, spanning from related industries and universities to trade unions.

Further, the diffusion of information and technology within the cluster is fostered by their close collaboration and simultaneous development. This diffusion is enhanced by the exchange of personnel among partners, the comparison of their business strategies and the development of a common business culture. On the other hand, despite the usual exchange of information between cooperating parties, the main exchange

Table 1. Differences between enterprise networks and clusters (Voulgaridou, 2008)

Characteristics	Enterprise Networks	Enterprise Clusters
Base of transactions (Rosenfeld, 2001)	Contracts – usually short to mid-term business objectives	Informal relationships – usually related to a common business vision
Number of members (Håkasson & Snehota, 1998)	Limited	Unlimited
Composition (Porter, 1998)	Enterprises	Miscellaneous structure, great range of organizations
Relationships (Porter, 1998)	Collaboration	Collaboration and competition
Strategy/Policy (Cooke, 2001)	Common business goals	Common business vision, development of the region
Exchange of information and Knowledge (Cooke, 2001; Rosenfeld, 2001)	Predetermined by the contract	Spontaneous based on common business culture

of information and knowledge within enterprise networks is strictly predetermined in the context of the contract (Rosenfeld, 2001).

Finally, the relationships within the network are based on the collaboration of its members and aim at the increment of their competitive advantage. The members of the cluster develop relationships based on mutual trust and share a common business vision, which includes the development of the whole region (Cooke, 2001). Table 1 (Voulgaridou, 2008) summarizes the differences between enterprise networks and clusters, as discussed above.

As stated in introduction, existence of clusters acts as a nest for the development of virtual enterprise networks and one form of expansion for highly sophisticated virtual enterprise networks is the formation of collaborative commerce. Collaborative commerce (c-commerce) is a term that has emerged to describe a fundamental shift in the way companies interact. It is a set of techniques allowing companies to better manage their extended enterprise. It consists of cross-enterprise capabilities that leverage new technologies to allow an enterprise to manage, more effectively, today's complex partner network through improved sharing of business processes, decision making, workflow and data with key trade partners (Deloitte Research, 2002). Essentially, it concerns the coming together of collaborators using IT, such as the Internet, to integrate a company's business processes with those of its customers and suppliers and exploit opportunities as they arise.

C-commerce makes it possible for firms, especially SMEs, to take advantage of the benefits offered by a cluster and become more competitive by choosing a business strategy around IT, which adds value to the whole supply chain (Li et al., 2005). The adoption of c-commerce increases business agility and enables business partners to operate complex transactions and share advanced and updated information. However, c-commerce is not just a technology issue. It concerns a company's entire system; it is about building improved capabilities and integrating relationships with key players in the value chain (suppliers, business partners, customers, etc.). C-commerce eliminates the notion of vertical integration and enhances partnering, collaboration, corporate reengineering and the development of strategic alliances. Collaborative Commerce has emerged as a unifying, more effective way to integrate relationships, processes, people, workflow, and technologies of organizations.

Figure 1. Impact of c-commerce on business performance: percentage of improvement

C-commerce has the ability to revolutionize the way clusters do business and provide competitive advantage to their members by (Deloitte Research, 2002; Johnston, 1998):

- Lowering transaction costs
- Reducing communication costs and response times
- Developing new capabilities
- Further improving networking
- Sharing real-time information
- Aligning operations
- Enhancing flexibility
- Increasing customer satisfaction and
- Improving planning through better network visibility

Figure 1 represents the impact of c-commerce on strategic and operational performance, based on the answers given by respondents on a survey conducted by Deloitte Research (2002).

Integration, automation and collaboration are the key elements that ensure partners' communication while advanced web technologies are needed to support this new business model (Park, Suh & Lee, 2004). Beyond simple online buying and selling, c-commerce needs efficient back-office operations and software systems that support collaboration. Enterprise Resource Planning (ERP) systems promote collaboration among key departments and functions within an enterprise, while business-to-business (B2B) strategies and web technologies have made it possible for partners to work together by effectively integrating their ERP systems.

As a conclusion, clusters provide a concentration of related companies to engage collectively in a market and encourage them to participate in electronic and collaborative commerce. The advent of the information technology, led companies and especially small and medium enterprises (SMEs) to realize that in order to remain competitive new approaches are needed. In this context, clusters and collaborative networks supported by Information Technologies (IT) became an apparent solution.

Multicriteria Decision Analysis and Supplier Selection

In increasingly competitive and globalised markets, companies are constantly under pressure to find ways in order to cut their costs and increase customer's satisfaction. Since a qualified and reliable supplier is a key element in reducing material costs and achieving on-time deliveries, supplier selection is increasingly recognized as a critical decision in supply chain management (Dahel, 2003). Evidence drawn from current literature proves that supplier evaluation and selection is a complicated matter because of the large number of criteria needed to be considered (Bayazit, 2006). The evaluation and selection of suppliers is a typical multicriteria decision making (MCDM) problem, involving both qualitative and quantitative criteria. More than half of the papers reviewed for the aims of the current study examine the use of different decision making methods and tools for supplier selection. The decision making methods reported for supplier selection can be categorized into five broad categories: traditional multiple criteria decision making (MCDM), mathematical programming, artificial intelligence, expert systems, and multivariate statistical analysis. Most of the authors seem to agree that the supplier selection problem is further aggravated due to the need for multiple criteria, the conflicting objectives of the criteria, the involvement of many alternatives (due to increasing competition and globalization) and the numerous internal and external constraints imposed by the purchasing process (Weber, Current & Desai, 2000). A point of differentiation of this study against others is the fact that the whole decision process takes place within a collaborative cluster and therefore specialized criteria, other than the ones used in the typical supplier selection problem, are involved.

Analytic Network Process with Benefits, Opportunities, Cost and Risks

The Analytic Network Process is a multicriteria decision analysis approach developed by Tomas Saaty (2000). It allows the simultaneous inclusion of tangible and intangible criteria and it incorporates feedback and interdependent relationships among decision criteria and alternatives

ANP is a well-known technique and since its introduction, it has been recognized by scholars and widely used in various decision analysis processes. The literature review (79 articles in 51 journals) performed by the authors, concerning the implementations of the ANP revealed its dominance on strategic decisions and supplier selection, as shown in Figure 2.

Technically, the ANP model consists of clusters and elements. A cluster in ANP should not be confused with the cluster as an enterprise formation. ANP clusters are just sets that group elements of

Figure 2. Distribution of ANP articles by research area

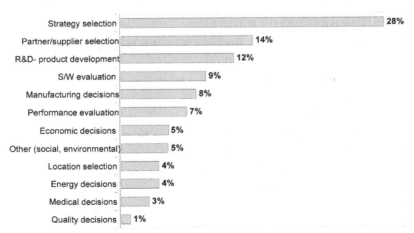

the same kind (criteria). The dominance or 'relative importance of influence' is the core concept. Judgments are provided based on the fundamental AHP scale by answering the question (Saaty, 2005): Which of the two elements Y, Z influences a third element X more with respect to the control criterion? The control criterion can be regarded as the overall goal of the problem. Taking into account the control criterion is very important so that all pairwise comparisons are considered with respect to the same criterion and thus making synthesis meaningful. A control criterion is an important way to keep human thought focused when answering the question of dominance and gives the possibility for, first, decomposing a complex problem with a variety of influences and second pulling it back together by using the weights of these influences (Kirytopoulos et al., 2009). In decision-making, there are conflicting criteria, such as criteria in benefits (B) versus those in costs (C), and criteria in opportunities (O) versus those in risks (R). The general theory of ANP enables decision makers to deal with these BOCR merits (benefits, opportunities, costs and risks), by introducing the notion of negative priorities for Costs and Risks, along with the rating of the alternatives. The four initially individual merits are synthesized at the end, providing a single outcome which indicates the best possible decision. In short, ANP suggests the development of four control hierarchies (sub-networks): Benefits, Opportunities, Cost And Risks (BOCR). Through these networks one can evaluate the alternatives, following the same procedure as in simple ANP networks (not clustered as BOCR). Under the ANP - BOCR concept, pairwise comparison questions ask which alternative is most beneficial or has the best opportunity under each sub-criterion/detailed criterion in benefits and opportunities subnetworks (Saaty, 2004). On the other hand, the pairwise comparison questions ask which alternative is riskiest or costliest under each

sub-criterion/detailed criterion in risks and costs subnets. The weights of alternatives are combined first according to the weights of subcriteria/ detailed criteria for each subnet. Then, the results are synthesized in order to get the overall ranking of the alternatives and obtain the final answer. Saaty (2003) proposed five ways to combine the scores of each alternative under B, O, C and R. The relative priority, P_i, for each alternative "i" can be estimated through five different equations (approaches). These approaches are:

1. Additive approach

$$P_i = bB_i + oO_i + c\left[(1\,/\,C_i)_{normalised}\right] + r\left[(1\,/\,R_i)_{normalized}\right]$$

(1)

2. Probabilistic additive approach

$$P_i = bB_i + oO_i + c(1 - C_i) + r(1 - R_i)$$

(2)

3. Subtractive approach

$$P_i = bB_i + oO_i - cC_i - rR_i$$

(3)

4. Multiplicative Priority Powers approach

$$P_i = B_i^b O_i^o \left[(1\,/\,C_i)_{normalised}\right]^c \left[(1\,/\,R_i)_{normalized}\right]^r$$

(4)

5. Multiplicative approach

$$P_i = B_i O_i\,/\,C_i R_i$$

(5)

where B_i, O_i, C_i and Ri represent the synthesized results of alternative *i* under merits B, O, C and R, respectively and b, o, c and r are normalized weights of merits B, O, C and R, respectively. Finally, sensitivity analysis needs to be performed on the final outcome. Sensitivity analysis is concerned with 'what-if' scenarios to find out how stable to changes the final answer is. Sensitivity analysis is used for checking if these changes reverse the order of the alternatives. A more detailed description of the ANP method, along with the implementation steps are presented in the Case Study section.

CASE STUDY: THE PARAPHARMACEUTICAL COLLABORATIVE CLUSTER

The parapharmaceutical cluster presented in this chapter is geographically located in south and central Greece and consists of four basic business entities (Kirytopoulos, Leopoulos & Voulgaridou, 2008):

- Parapharmaceutical manufacturing companies producing OTC (Over The Counter) pharmaceutical products, such as sterilised gloves, disposable syringes, products for personal and dental care etc. These products need to meet tight specifications and restrictions, as defined by the relevant legislation.
- Wholesalers, who store and distribute products, act as links between the parapharmaceutical manufacturing companies and the points of sales (pharmacies or brand pharmacies) by buying from the first and distributing products to the latter.
- Stores which are allowed to sell drugs and related products, namely pharmacies and brand pharmacies.
- The Service Provider, which is responsible for managing the parapharmaceutical network and the maintenance of the information technology (IT) systems that support the cluster operation. From a strategic point of view, the role of the service provider is to aggregate the needs

of the pharmacies and negotiate with the suppliers (parapharmaceutical manufacturing companies and wholesalers), achieving economies of scale.

As in most cases, the parapharmaceutical cluster was built up spontaneously by the local business players who pinpointed the opportunity for growth and prosperity through a cluster arrangement. In order to enhance their collaboration, the initial group of companies made important investments in IT, exchanged corporate data through web-based infrastructures and engaged collectively in various business activities (see following subsections). Moreover, they developed partnerships with academic institutions in order to access innovation and technical knowledge. The identification of the parapharmaceutical network as a cluster came later as a result of academic research on these structures and public authorities' initiatives to recognize and support innovative networks to boost creative capacity and competitiveness. Determining the types of industries and firms that constitute a cluster and whether that cluster has achieved competitive advantage is a highly subjective process, but it is also a process in which no "right" or "wrong" answers exist (York County Economic Development Corporation, 2004). As a result many methodologies (both quantitative and qualitative) have been proposed by the researchers. Because of its subjectivity, cluster analysis is often misunderstood and misused. Cluster analysis is not a classification system. It is a process for understanding the relationship among cluster-actors and their relative strength in the overall economy. There is also a tendency to rely too much on numbers, but in practical terms, the numbers themselves are only relative measures and often fail to describe the complex cluster environment, where relationships, strategies and policies cannot be easily quantified. Based on the above, for the characterization of the parapharmaceutical network as a cluster, the widely accepted qualitative method of experts' opinion has been used. Table

Table 2. Characteristics of enterprise clusters

Enterprise Clusters' characteristics	Parapharmaceutical network	Comments
Geographical proximity	√	Members are located in south and central Greece
Interconnection of members	√	Members are interconnected through traditional means, IT and web-based systems (refer to following subsections)
Diffusion of information and technology	√	E-commerce platform IT systems Collaborative Risk Management Decision support policies Common business goals (refer to following subsections)
Informal relationships with related industries, associated institutions etc.	√	Service providers IT companies Universities
Coexistence of collaborative and competitive relationships	√	Collaboration among members in a vertical level and competition among suppliers-members and among pharmacies
Learning culture	√	Promotion activities Training activities Value-added activities (refer to following subsections)

2 summarizes the characteristics that render the parapharmaceutical network as a cluster.

The following subsections describe the core business processes of our case cluster.

Purchasing Processes

An important strategy of the collaborative cluster is the separation of the purchasing orders into two main categories:

- Flow Orders
- Negotiation Orders

Flow orders refer to system-to-system electronic transactions. Pharmacies create the order in their ERP system, according to their inventory policy, and then upload it, as a batch file with a predefined format (refer to figure 3), to a common shared application. Then suppliers access these files and download the order files, which then incorporate into their ERP systems. The tech-nological integration of the parapharmaceutical members and the unified coding system permit an easy and real-time exchange of information regarding orders' data, delivery times, invoicing and order tracking. Figure 3 presents the basic processes of the electronic flow orders.

Within the flow order category one can usually find branded products that the customers ask specifically from the pharmacy (e.g. a specific brand of shampoo). On the other hand, negotiation orders are usually selected for products that the customer has no preference in brands, such as bandage, cotton, etc. As far as the negotiation orders are concerned, they are managed as a project and executed by the service provider, through a web-based application which allows electronic submission. The e-negotiation application of the parapharmaceutical collaborative cluster has the ability to map complex negotiation structures, including multiple stages of negotiations with more than one bidding parameter, such as price, delivery time, additional offers and payment terms.

Figure 3. Basic processes of the electronic flow orders

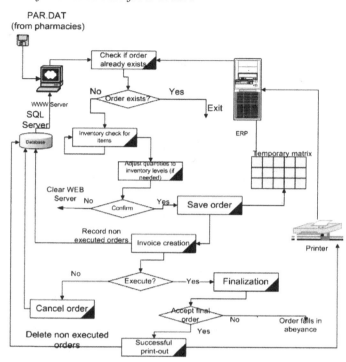

The system architecture is depicted in Figure 4. The steps for the execution of the negotiation orders are as follows:

- Initially, the service provider specifies the content of the negotiation regarding the category of the products and its time limit. As a result, a negotiation scenario is formed and uploaded on the web-based application.
- The pharmacies, members of the cluster, are then able to download the scenarios and import them into their ERPs.
- Consequently, the ERP system creates a purchase suggestion based on the inventory levels. Afterwards, pharmacists are able to process the order and decide upon the products and the desired quantities. The final order is then uploaded on the wed-based application.
- As soon as the scenarios' time limit is reached, the service provider concentrates

the orders placed by the pharmacies and creates a batch order, categorized by products' codes and quantities.

- Then, the suppliers, members of the cluster, by using their username and password, enter the web-based application and download order information and import it into their ERPs.
- Further, they process the order and submit their offer (discount on wholesale price) by uploading it on the web application.
- The service provider is then responsible to evaluate the offers and accept, decline or renegotiate. As soon as the negotiation is finished and the supplier is selected, the service provider sends the invoice to the wholesaler, who performs the physical distribution of the orders.

- The service provider receives, finally, a general discount for the whole order. After holding a certain commission, the

Figure 4. The system architecture for Web-based negotiations

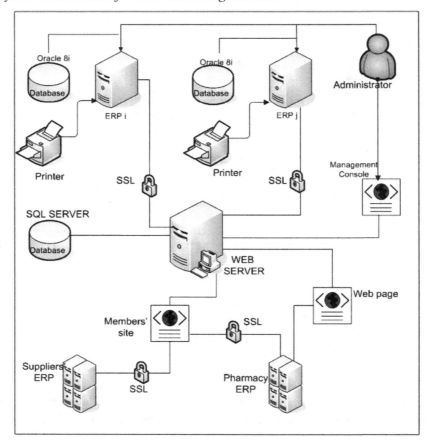

service provider shares the rest of the discount achieved to each pharmacy, in direct analogy with the volume of their order.

IT Support Activities

An advanced IT support is offered to the members of the collaborative cluster by the service provider, summarized as follows (Leopoulos, Kirytopoulos & Voulgaridou, 2006):

- Technical support, upon request, is provided to each member both by remote assistance and physical presence at the pharmacies.

- Updates and upgrades are uploaded on the web-based system for the pharmacist to download.
- New modules or services installed on their systems are supported by an easy to use manual or by further training activities if necessary.
- Finally, the service provider informs the pharmacists about the release of new IT functionalities available.

Promotion Activities

The service provider is also responsible for the creation of various promotional activities in order to enhance the marketing policy of the cluster's members, such as POS supplier visits, open exhibitions, market studies, media marketing etc.

Value-Adding Activities

The service provider also offers additional services in order to boost the performance of the pharmacists and achieve customers' satisfaction. In short these services include:

- Merchandising activities: the service provider recommends, based on the principles of category management, optimal product display and shelf organization.
- Training activities: selected salespersons perform advanced seminars in order to help pharmacists ameliorate their sales qualifications.
- Additional services: the pharmacy expands its role from a single point of sales to an advanced consulting unit. As a result, pharmacists will be able to provide guidance on products of health and beauty or even nutrition advises and information on relevant products.

Management of Risk within the Collaborative Cluster

The parapharmaceutical collaborative cluster has developed a process and a tool in order to manage its operational and business risks. Specifically, a risk database is installed and managed by the service provider, which allows the identification, analysis, mitigation and monitoring of risks. Based on the reports, generated by the database, the members of the collaborative cluster are able to better manage their operations and support their decisions.

Problem Description

As already mentioned, decision making plays a vital role for the operation of the collaborative cluster under study. The service provider has to decide which members will receive more support or promotion or value-adding activities and in general, decision making is a daily and strategically important activity. One of the most significant decisions the Service Provider has to take during day to day operation is the selection of suppliers' offers for a particular negotiation order. Such a decision has to take into consideration all aspects/criteria required and thus constitutes a multicriteria decision making problem. Due to the unique nature of the enterprise clusters' structure, where the members not only cooperate but also compete, there is a need to consider both criteria that apply to any supplier selection process (e.g. cost, quality, delivery time) and criteria that refer to partnership (e.g. relationships, joint problem solving). The particularity of the cluster case comes from the fact that the ideal choice should, on one hand, be in favour of the buyers, in terms of price and quality and on the other hand, should take into account the members' relationships in order to preserve the state of equilibrium and stability. In order to cope with this complex decision problem, the authors propose a comprehensive framework, based on the ANP - BOCR approach.

Proposed ANP - BOCR Model

The model applies the ANP - BOCR technique to the problem of selecting the best offer for a particular parapharmaceutical negotiation order. In the specific negotiation order that we place under study, three different suppliers participate (disguised): Supplier 1 is a big international company, Supplier 2 a new local production company with important investments in IT technology and involvement in cluster's collaborative activities and Supplier 3 a traditional company having close relationships with the parapharmaceutical collaborative cluster. The ANP - BOCR processes were implemented by using Super Decisions Software created by Saaty (2004) to alleviate the mathematical burden. The methodology includes the following steps:

Step 1- Model construction: First the service provider managers were interviewed by the authors about the critical factors that need to be taken into consideration in order to choose among the different suppliers' offers. These factors were validated through interviews with other parapharmaceutical supply chain members and were initially compiled as a long catalogue with overlapping data and redundancies. Next, these factors were reviewed

and categorized under the ANP - BOCR merits. As far as the relationships among the clusters and the elements of the model are concerned, the service provider managers where interviewed and the interdependences were identified. As mentioned above, ANP deals systematically with all kinds of feedback and interactions (inner and outer dependence). When elements are linked exclusively to elements in another cluster, the model shows only outer dependence. When elements are linked to elements within the same cluster, there is an inner dependence. The resulting ANP - BOCR subnets are illustrated in Figure 5.

Every subnet consists of the Alternatives cluster and clusters containing the criteria under each merit. Specifically, the *Benefits* subnet includes two clusters, namely the 'Profile', for

Figure 5. Subnets under BOCR merits

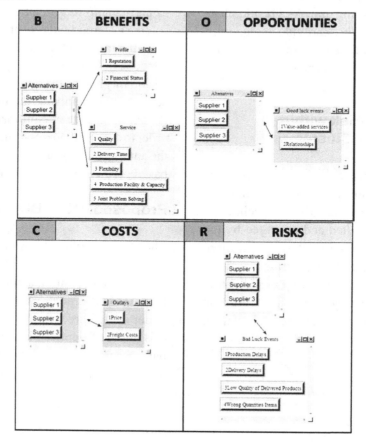

the evaluation of suppliers' the reputation and financial status and the 'Service' for the evaluation of suppliers' quality, delivery time, flexibility, production facility and capacity, joint problem solving. The *Costs* subnet includes the price and the freight costs of each supplier. The *Opportunities* subnet is described by the 'Good luck events' cluster, which takes into account the possibility of each supplier to ameliorate its relationships with the collaborative clusters member and the level of value-added services that it could provide. Finally, the *Risks* subnet takes into account the threats of purchasing by the suppliers under evaluation, an important perspective of business partnerships (Leopoulos & Kirytopoulos, 2002). Collaborative cluster decision makers can retrieve this data from the risk database, managed by the service provider.

Step 2- Clusters' and elements' pairwise comparisons: After the model was constructed, an additional meeting between the authors and the service provider's managers took place, during which the managers were asked to respond to a series of pairwise comparisons among clusters and among elements, by applying Saaty's 1–9 scale (Saaty, 1980). "Super Decisions" software is able to calculate the inconsistency ratio for each comparison matrix, so the most consistent value for the entries can be determined. The inconsistency measure is useful for identifying possible errors in judgments as well as actual inconsistencies in the judgments themselves. For example, if A is more important than B and B is more important than C, C cannot be more important than A. In general, the inconsistency ratio should be less than 0.1. The criteria under the benefit and opportunity subnets were compared by asking which element provides more benefit/opportunity. For costs and risks the question was modified as 'Which criterion causes higher cost/risk?' After all comparisons took place, the weights of the clusters and elements were calculated, forming the clusters priority matrix and the unweighted super-matrix under ANP - BOCR

subnets, respectively. The weighted super-matrix was obtained by multiplying the elements of the unweighted super-matrix by the appropriate cluster weight. Specifically, the values in the cluster matrix were used to weight the unweighted super-matrix by multiplying the value in the cell of the cluster matrix times the value in each cell in the component of the unweighted super-matrix to produce the weighted super-matrix. Finally, the Limit matrix was derived by multiplying the weighted super-matrices by themselves, which accounts for variable interaction, until the system's row values converge to the same value for each column of the matrices. Tables 3 and 4 (appendix) present the weighted super-matrix and the limit matrix of the benefit subnet. The weights of the alternatives under the ANP - BOCR merits are illustrated in Figure 6.

Step 3- Computation of the overall score for each alternative: For the specific decision problem and according to the service provider managers, the

Figure 6. Weights of the alternatives under ANP - BOCR merits

Benefits				
Name	Graphic	Ideals	Normals	Raw
Supplier 1		1.000000	0.399246	0.199623
Supplier 2		0.984241	0.392954	0.196477
Supplier 3		0.520481	0.207800	0.103900

Opportunities				
Name	Graphic	Ideals	Normals	Raw
Supplier 1		0.199244	0.098554	0.049277
Supplier 2		0.822431	0.406807	0.203403
Supplier 3		1.000000	0.494639	0.247320

Costs				
Name	Graphic	Ideals	Normals	Raw
Supplier 1		1.000000	0.333333	0.166667
Supplier 2		1.000000	0.333333	0.166667
Supplier 3		1.000000	0.333333	0.166667

Risks				
Name	Graphic	Ideals	Normals	Raw
Supplier 1		0.212689	0.155245	0.077622
Supplier 2		0.157334	0.114840	0.057420
Supplier 3		1.000000	0.729915	0.364957

ANP - BOCR merits were not equally important and needed to be weighted. In order to achieve so, pairwise comparisons of all merits were performed with respect to the control criterion (evaluate suppliers). The final priorities of the ANP - BOCR merits are shown in Figure 7.

The results were synthesized in order to get the overall ranking of the alternatives and obtain the final answer. The final synthesis was made by using both the additive and multiplicative formula, as described in section 'ANALYTIC NETWORK PROCESS WITH BENEFITS, OPPORTUNITIES, COSTS AND RISKS' and the final priorities of the alternatives are presented in Figure 8.

Step 4- Sensitivity analysis on the final outcome: Sensitivity analysis deals with 'what-if' kind of questions to determine whether the final answer is stable to changes (experiments) in the inputs, either judgments or priorities.

It was interesting to determine whether these changes alter the order of the alternatives. The priorities of alternatives were plotted on the y axis, with respect to the different experiments/priorities (x-axis). Figure 9 depicts the sensitivity graph of the parapharmaceutical model for each merit and the priorities that alter the ranking of the alternatives. For example the Benefits chart indicates that the ranking of the alternatives alters when the priorities Benefits priorities converge to 1.

Figure 7. Priorities of the ANP - BOCR merits

Benefits	0.286214
Costs	0.060175
Opportunities	0.154508
Risks	0.499103

Figure 8. Final priorities of the alternatives

Name	Graphic	Ideals	Normals	Raw
Supplier 1		0.771010	0.346089	0.746379
Supplier 2		1.000000	0.448877	0.968054
Supplier 3		0.456770	0.205034	0.442178

Figure 9. Sensitivity analysis

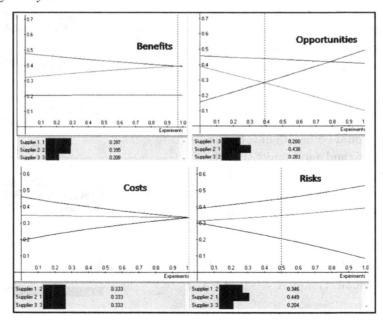

CONCLUSION

Decision making and risk management in collaborative commerce and clusters comprise the core research area of this study. C-commerce and clusters are increasingly attracting the attention of companies and policy makers as they represent efficient structures for stimulating the competitiveness, productivity and innovation of their members. Despite these benefits, the concept of clusters bears also some limitations. An important obstacle is that small enterprises have significant difficulties to fund IT investments due to initial capital needed to support a cluster initiative. There seems to be a critical mass that must be achieved before a firm reaches the right combination of financial resources, technical abilities and strategic competence to implement collaborative commerce practices. Furthermore, when cluster firms rely on few buyers or on the activity of a limited number of companies, they may fail if the latter move or disappear, even if they themselves are still competitive. To avoid these pitfalls, a trusted and respected relationship with partners coupled with appropriate technology seems to be necessary.

However, the aforementioned drawbacks were absent in the case study of the Greek parapharmaceutical industry described in this chapter. Specific circumstances (funding opportunities provided by the EC) forced dominant parties of the cluster (manufacturing companies and wholesalers) to assist the weaker ones (pharmacies). As a result, the service provider managed to raise funds from the major players, as well as to exploit European funding for small and very small enterprises.

Due to the unique nature of the enterprise clusters' structure, where the members not only cooperate but also compete, the decision making can be a complex issue. The core objective and contribution of this study is the provision of a framework for the decision making process within these structures. The multicriteria decision making problem examined here was the evaluation of suppliers in a collaborative cluster environment. The method used to support the decision process is the Analytic Network Process – Benefits, Opportunities, Costs and Risks (ANP-BOCR) model that can alleviate rather complex problems, encompassing various conflicting criteria. The ANP - BOCR approach, as part of this method, enables the decision maker to visualize the impact of various conflicting criteria in the final outcome and documents the evaluation results in such way that they can be communicated to various stakeholders.

For the parapharmaceutical c-cluster example, the results indicate that among the four sets of criteria, namely Benefits, Opportunities, Costs and Risks, the decision making process is dominated by Risks and Benefits (refer to Figure 7), confirming the dynamic and conflicting nature of these enterprise structures. Moreover, the ANP - BOCR method managed to handle the conflicting criteria, inherent in the supplier evaluation process and provided a rational synthesis in order to reveal the 'best' alternative. More specifically, although for each ANP - BOCR merit a different alternative was the most dominant (Supplier 1 for benefits, Supplier 3 for opportunities, etc., refer to Figure 6) the ranking of the merits and the synthesis of the results, determined Supplier 2 as the 'best' alternative for the problem under study. This finding also explains why decision making in such an environment is so complex and suggests that each time a different perspective is imposed to the model, a different result will be produced. However, the proposed approach succeeds in synthesizing the four different perspectives (merits of the ANP – BOCR model) and supports final decision making by the user. The model has been illustrated here for three distinct suppliers but it is capable of comparing any number, inevitably increasing the level of complexity.

The ANP - BOCR approach proposed by this study bears also a few limitations (Voulgaridou, Kirytopoulos & Leopoulos, 2008). The most important is the fact that the outcome of the model depends on the inputs provided by the service provider managers. Moreover, the formation of the pairwise comparison matrices is a time-consuming and complex task, while inconsistency may also occur, leading to doubtful or wrong results. Thus, it would be wise to use decision analysis experts that may assist the decision maker in the whole process.

FURTHER RESEARCH DIRECTIONS

This study raises several important issues that could spark further research, such as the evaluation of the model and its implementation in additional case studies drawn from related industries. Such an endeavor might be beneficial and result in developing a generic system that could support the decision makers and reveal the significance of certain alternatives, criteria and elements.

In addition, a comparison of the results to other models' outcomes would be also useful. Although, as stated in this chapter, the proposed model is, in theory, one of the most suitable for this specific business environment, other models may provide similar results. For example, ELECTRE methods seem to deal well with supplier evaluation problems and lately, research trends show an increasing preference to hybrid models (e.g. ANP and goal programming).

Moreover, collaborative commerce and enterprise clusters are considerably new concepts and need to be further investigated. Collaborative commerce requires important investments in IT, along with advanced technical know-how. In parallel it should be examined under which circumstances, clusters might become an obstacle to further development of their members.

There is a belief that in the context of rapidly changing technology, cluster firms become more vulnerable if they are locked in old technologies and if they do not become flexible enough to adapt to these changes, constrained by their cultural particularities. Culture often proves to be the stated reason for failure when adopting new technology and the framework proposed by the present study presupposes an unconditional trusted and respected relationship among partners, an assumption that not always holds true. Thus, research endeavors towards how mutual trust can be enriched in cluster environments should be considered of great importance.

ACKNOWLEDGMENT

The authors greatly appreciate the help of the book editor, Dr. Stavros Ponis for his insights and useful comments that greatly improved the quality of this chapter. They also would like to thank the anonymous reviewers for their constructive comments.

REFERENCES

Akkermans, H., Bogerd, P., Yucesan, E., & van Wassenhove, L. (2003). The impact of ERP on supply chain management; Exploratory findings from a European Delphi study. *European Journal of Operational Research, 146*(2), 284–301. doi:10.1016/S0377-2217(02)00550-7

Bayazit, O. (2006). Use of analytic network process in vendor selection decisions, *Benchmarking. International Journal (Toronto, Ont.), 13*(5), 566–579.

Cairncross, F. (1997). The Death of Distance, London: Orion Business Books.

Camarinha-Matos, L., Afsarmanesh, H., Galeano, N., & Molina, A. (2009). Collaborative networked organizations – Concepts and practice in manufacturing enterprises. *Computers & Industrial Engineering*, *57*(1), 46–60. doi:10.1016/j.cie.2008.11.024

Camarinha-Matos, L. M., Afsarmanesh, H., Garita, C., & Lima, C. (1998). Towards an architecture for virtual enterprises. *Journal of Intelligent Manufacturing*, *9*, 189–199. doi:10.1023/A:1008880215595

Chan, F., & Kumar, N. (2007). Global supplier development considering risk factors using fuzzy extended AHP-based approach. *Omega*, *35*(4), 417–431. doi:10.1016/j.omega.2005.08.004

Christopher, M. (1992). Logistics and Supply Chain Management. London: Pitman.

Cooke, P. (2001). Knowledge Economies: Clusters, Learning & Co-operative Advantage. London: Routledge.

Cooke, P. (2001). Knowledge Economies: Clusters, Learning & Co-operative Advantage. London: Routledge.

Cooper, M., Lambert, D., & Pugh, J. (1997). Supply Chain Management: More than a new name for logistics. The International Journal of Logistics Management, 8(1), 1-14. In Coyole, D. (1997). The Weightless Word: Strategies for Managing the Digital Economy, London: Capstone.

Coyole, D. (2001). Paradoxes of Prosperity: Why the New Capitalism Benefits All. London: Texere Publishing.

Dahel, N. (2003). Vendor selection and order quantity allocation in volume discount environments, *Supply Chain Management. International Journal (Toronto, Ont.)*, *8*(4), 334–342.

Doz, Y., & Hamel, G. (1998). Alliance Advantage: The Art of Creating Value Through Partnering, Cambridge, MA: Harvard Business School Press.

Fujita, M., Krugman, P., & Venables, A. (2000). The Spatial Economy: Cities, Regions and International Trade. Cambridge, MA: MIT Press

Gadde, L., & Håkansson, H. (2001) *Supply Network Strategies*. Chichester, UK: John Wiley & Sons..

Gray, J. (1998). False Dawn: The Delusions of Global Capitalism. London: Granta Books.

Guerrieri, P., & Pietrobelli, C. (2000, June 15-17). Models of Industrial Distincts Evolution and Changes in Technological Règimes. *DRUID Summer Conference*, Denmark, pp. 1-19.

Håkansson, H., & Snehota, I. (1998). The burden of relationships or who's next? In Thurnbull, P. (ed.) Network dynamics in international marketing. Oxford: Elsevier Science.

Hallikas, J., Karvonen, I., Pulkkinen, U., Virolainen, V.-M., & Tuominen, M. (2004). Risk management processes in supplier networks. *International Journal of Production Economics*, *90*(1), 47–58. doi:10.1016/j.ijpe.2004.02.007

Harland, M. (1996). Supply Chain Management: Relationships, Chains and Networks. *British Journal of Management*, (March): 63–80. doi:10.1111/j.1467-8551.1996.tb00148.x

Håkansson, H., & Johanson, J. (1993). The Network as a Governance Structure. Interfirm Cooperation beyond Markets and Hierarchies. In Grabher, G. (ed.), *The Embedded Firm*, London: Routledge.

Hu, J., & Su, D. (2007). EJB-MVC oriented supplier selection system for mass customization. *Journal of Manufacturing Technology Management*, *18*(1), 54–71. doi:10.1108/17410380710717643

Johnston, D. (1998). Open networks, electronic commerce and the global information infrastructure. *Computer Standards & Interfaces, 20*, 95–99. doi:10.1016/S0920-5489(98)00042-7

Kirytopoulos, K., Leopoulos, V., & Voulgaridou, D. (2008). Supplier selection in pharmaceutical industry: An analytic network process approach. Benchmarking: An International Journal, 15(4), 494-516.Krugman, P. (1997). Pop Internationalism. Cambridge, MA: MIT Press

Kirytopoulos, K., Voulgaridou, D., Panopoulos, D., & Leopoulos, V. (2009). Project termination analysis in SMEs: Making the right call. *International Journal of Management and Decision Making, 10*(1-2), 69–90. doi:10.1504/IJMDM.2009.023915

Leopoulos, V., & Kirytopoulos, K. (2002). Methodology for risk management in systems development. In *Proceedings of the Recent Advances in Computers, Computing and Communications*, 13-18. Leopoulos, V., Kirytopoulos, K. & Voulgaridou, D. (2006). Electronic alliances and the (para)pharmaceutical supply chain: Identification of risks. *WSEAS Transactions on Systems 5*(1), 279-284.

Li, M., Wang, J., Wong, Y., & Lee, K. (2005). A collaborative application portal for the mould industry. *International Journal of Production Economics, 96*(2), 233–247. doi:10.1016/j.ijpe.2004.04.007

Marsden, C. (1997). Corporate Citizenship. *Faith in Business, 1*(4)

Martinus, K., Rowe, M., Burn, J., & Walker, E. (2005, June 30-July 1). Beyond Clusters - Collaborative Commerce and Clustering. *CRIC Cluster conference, Beyond Cluster- Current Practices & Future Strategies*, Ballarat, Australia.

O'Brien, R. (1992). Global Financial Integration: The end of Geography? London: Pinter.

Ohmae, K. (1995). The End of Nation State: The Rise of Regional Economies. London: Harper Collins.

Park, H., Suh, W., & Lee, K. (2004). A role-driven component-oriented methodology for developing collaborative commerce systems. *Information and Software Technology, 46*(12), 819–837. doi:10.1016/j.infsof.2004.02.002

Perona, M., & Miragliotta, G. (2003). Complexity management and supply chain performance assessment. A field study and a conceptual framework. *International Journal of Production Economics, 90*(1), 103–115. doi:10.1016/S0925-5273(02)00482-6

Pfohl, H., & Buse, P. (2000). Inter-Organizational Logistics Systems in Flexible Production Networks. An Organizational Capabilities Perspective. *International Journal of Production & Logistics Management, 30*(1), 388–401.

Porter, M. (1985). Competitive Advantage of Nations. New York: The Free Press.

Porter, M. (1998). Clusters and the new economics of competition. *Harvard Business Review, November/December.*

Reve, T. (1990). The Firm as a Nexus of Internal and External Contracts.In M. Aoki, B. Gustafsons, and O. Williamson, (eds), The Firm as a Nexus of Treaties. London: Sage.

Ritchie, B., & Brindley, C. (2001). The Information-Risk Conundrum. *Journal of Marketing Intelligence and Planning, 19*(1), 29–37. doi:10.1108/02634500110363781

Rosenfeld, S. (2001, March 29-30), Backfitting into Clusters: retrofitting public policies. *Symposium for Integration Pressures: Lessons from Around the Word*, Harvard University.

Rowe, M., Burn, J., & Walker, E. (2005, June 30-July 1). Small and Medium Enterprises Clustering and Collaborative Commerce – a social issues perspective. *CRIC Cluster conference. Beyond Cluster- Current Practices & Future Strategies.* Ballarat, Australia.

Saaty, T. (1980). The Analytic Hierarchy Process, New York: McGraw-Hill.

Saaty, T. (2000). Fundamentals of Decision Making with the Analytic Hierarchy Process. Pittsburg, PA: RWS Publications.

Saaty, T. (2003). Negative priorities in the analytic hierarchy process. *Mathematical and Computer Modelling, 37*(9-10), 1063–1075. doi:10.1016/S0895-7177(03)00118-3

Saaty, T. (2004). Super Decisions Software. Pittsburg, PA: RWS Publications.

Saaty, T. (2005). Theory and Applications of the Analytic Network Process.Pittsburgh, PA: RWS Publications.

Scott, A. (1998). Regions and the Word Economy. Oxford, UK: Oxford University Press.

Scott, A. (2001). Global City Regions: Trends, Theory and Policy. Oxford, UK: Oxford University Press.

Tatsiopoulos, I., Ponis, S., & Hadzilias, E. (2004). An E-Releaser of Production Orders in the Extended Enterprise. *Production Planning and Control Journal, 15*(2), 119–132. doi:10.1080/09537280410001662547

Trends Business Research (2001). *Business Clusters in the UK- A First Assessment,* A report for the Department of Trade and Industry, DTI pub 5257.

Voulgaridou, D. (2008). *Decision support based on risk for project-based procurements of enterprise clusters.* Doctoral Dissertation, National Technical University of Athens.

Voulgaridou, D., Kirytopoulos, K., & Leopoulos, V. (2009). An analytic network process approach for sales forecasting. [ORIJ]. *OPERATIONAL RESEARCH: An International Journal, 9*(1), 35–53.

Weber, C., Current, J., & Desai, A. (2000). An optimization approach to determining the number of vendors to employ *Supply Chain Management. International Journal (Toronto, Ont.), 5*(2), 90–98.

York County Economic Development Corporation. (2004). *Industry Cluster Analysis Baseline Report (1995 – 2001 data),* Retrieved March 28, from http://www.ycedc.org/images/ClusterAnalaselineReport.pdf

ADDITIONAL READINGS

Colgman, C., & Baker, C. (2003). A Framework for Assessing Cluster Development. *Economic Development Quarterly, 17*(4), 352–366. doi:10.1177/0891242403256667

Coyole, D. (1997). The Weightless Word: Strategies for Managing the Digital Economy, London: Capstone.

Das, T., & Teng, B.-S. (2000). A resource-based theory of strategic alliances. *Journal of Management, 26*(1), 31–61. doi:10.1016/S0149-2063(99)00037-9

De Boer, L., Labro, E., & Morlacchi, P. (2001). A review of methods supporting supplier selection. *European Journal of Purchasing & Supply Management, 7,* 75–89. doi:10.1016/S0969-7012(00)00028-9

Dickson, G. (1966). An analysis of vendor selection systems and decisions. *Journal of Purchasing, 2*(1), 5–17.

Doumpos, M., & Zopounidis, C. (Eds.). (2002) Multicriteria Decision Aid Classification Methods. Dordrecht, The Netherlands: Kluwer Academic Publishers.

Duranton, G., & Puga, D. (2000). Diversity and Specialisation in Cities: Why, Where and When Does it Matter? *Urban Studies (Edinburgh, Scotland)*, *37*(3), 533–555. doi:10.1080/0042098002104

Enright, M. (1996). Regional Clusters and Economic Development: A Research Agenda. In U. Staber, N. Schaefer, & B. Sharma (eds.), Business Networks: Prospects for Regional Development, Berlin: Walter de Gruyter.

Enterprise Directorate – General (2002). *Final Report of the Expert Group on Enterprise Clusters and Networks*. In the framework of Multi-annual Programme for Enterprise Entrepreurnship.

Feser, E. (1998). Old and New Theories of Industry Clusters' in Clusters and Regional Specialisation: On Geography, Technology and Networks, ed. M. Steiner, London: Pion.

Feser, E., & Bergman, E. (2000). National Industry Cluster Templates: A Framework for Regional Cluster Analysis. *Regional Studies*, *34*(1), 1–20. doi:10.1080/00343400050005844

Figueira, J., Greco, S., & Ehrgott, M. (2005) Multiple Criteria Decision Analysis: state of the art surveys. New York: Springer Science & Business Media, Inc.

Forlani, R., & Mullins, J. (2000). Perceived risks and choices in entrepreneurs: new venture decisions. *Journal of Business Venturing*, *15*(1), 305–322. doi:10.1016/S0883-9026(98)00017-2

Greco, S., Matarazzo, B., & Slowinski, R. (1999). Multicriteria Decision Making: Advances in MCDM Models, Algorithms, Theory, and Applications. Boston: Kluwer academic Publishers.

Krugman, P. (1998). What's new about the new economic geography? *Oxford Review of Economic Policy*, *14*(2). doi:10.1093/oxrep/14.2.7

Lambert, D. (Ed.). (2006). Supply Chain Management: Process, Partnerships, Performance, 2nd edition. Sarasota, FL: Supply Chain Management Institute.

Leopoulos, V., & Kirytopoulos, K. (2002). Methodology for risk management in systems development. *Recent Advances in Computers. Computer Communications*, 13–18.

Leopoulos, V., & Kirytopoulos, K. (2004). Risk Management: a competitive advantage in the purchasing function. *Production Planning and Control, special issue: Purchasing and e-procurement*, *15*(7), 678-687.

Leopoulos, V., Kirytopoulos, K., & Manadrakis, C. (2006). Risk management for SMEs: Tools to use and how. *Production Planning and Control*, *17*(3), 322–332. doi:10.1080/09537280500285136

Luger, M., & Goldstein, H. (1991). Technology in the Garden: Research Parks and Regional Economic Development. Chapel Hill, NC: University of North Carolina Press.

Malmberg, A., & Power, D. (2003, June 12-14). (How) Do (Firms in) Clusters Create Knowledge? *DRUID Summer Conference 2003 on Creating, Sharing and Transferring Knowledge. The role of geography, institutions and organizations*. Copenhagen, Denmark.

Markusen, A. (1996). Sticky Places in Slippery Space: A Typology of Industrial Districts. *Economic Geography*, *72*(2), 293–314. doi:10.2307/144402

OECD. (1999). Boosting Innovation: The Cluster Approach, Paris: OECD.

OECD. (2004). Business Clusters: Promoting Enterprises in Central and Eastern Europe, OECD-Local Economic and Employment Development (LEED) Programme, Paris.

Pardalos, P., Siskos, Y., & Zopounidis, C. (Eds.). (1995). Advances in Multicriteria Analysis. Dordrecht, The Netherlands: Kluwer Academic Publishers.

Porter, M. (2000). Clusters and Government Policy. *Wirtschaftspolitische Bldtter*, *47*(2), 144–154.

Pouder, R., & St. John, C. (1996). Hot spots and blind spots: Geographical clusters of firms and innovation. *Academy of Management Review*, *21*, 1192–1225. doi:10.2307/259168

Rentizelas, A., Tziralis, G., & Kirytopoulos, K. (2007). Incorporating uncertainty in optimal investment decisions. World Review of Entrepreneurship. *Management and Sustainable Development*, *3*(3-4), 273–283.

Vincke, P. (1992). Multicriteria Decision-Aid. Chichester, UK: John Wiley & Sons.

APPENDIX

Table 3. Weighted matrix of benefits subnet

		Alternatives			Profile		Service				
		Sup-plier 1	Sup-plier 2	Sup-plier 3	1Reputa-tion	2Fi-nancial Status	1Qual-ity	2De-livery Time	3Flex-ibility	4 Pro-duction Facility & Ca-pacity	5Joint Prob-lem Solv-ing
Alterna-tives	Sup-plier 1	0.000	0.000	0.000	0.691	0.731	0.558	0.297	0.091	0.691	0.081
	Sup-plier 2	0.000	0.000	0.000	0.218	0.188	0.320	0.540	0.455	0.218	0.577
	Sup-plier 3	0.000	0.000	0.000	0.091	0.081	0.122	0.163	0.455	0.091	0.342
Profile	1 Repu-tation	0.071	0.095	0.048	0.000	0.000	0.000	0.000	0.000	0.000	0.000
	2 Fi-nancial Status	0.071	0.048	0.095	0.000	0.000	0.000	0.000	0.000	0.000	0.000
Service	1 Quality	0.237	0.124	0.142	0.000	0.000	0.000	0.000	0.000	0.000	0.000
	2 Deliv-ery Time	0.129	0.205	0.092	0.000	0.000	0.000	0.000	0.000	0.000	0.000
	3 Flex-ibility	0.075	0.124	0.192	0.000	0.000	0.000	0.000	0.000	0.000	0.000
	4 Pro-duction Facility & Ca-pacity	0.372	0.054	0.066	0.000	0.000	0.000	0.000	0.000	0.000	0.000
	5 Joint Problem Solving	0.044	0.350	0.365	0.000	0.000	0.000	0.000	0.000	0.000	0.000

Table 4. Limit matrix of benefits subnet

		Alternatives			Profile		Service				
		Sup-plier 1	Sup-plier 2	Sup-plier 3	1Reputa-tion	2Fi-nancial Status	1Qual-ity	2De-livery Time	3Flex-ibility	4 Pro-duction Facility & Ca-pacity	5Joint Prob-lem Solv-ing
Alterna-tives	Sup-plier 1	0.200	0.200	0.200	0.200	0.200	0.200	0.200	0.200	0.200	0.200
	Sup-plier 2	0.196	0.196	0.196	0.196	0.196	0.196	0.196	0.196	0.196	0.196
	Sup-plier 3	0.104	0.104	0.104	0.104	0.104	0.104	0.104	0.104	0.104	0.104
Profile	1 Repu-tation	0.038	0.038	0.038	0.038	0.038	0.038	0.038	0.038	0.038	0.038
	2 Fi-nancial Status	0.034	0.034	0.034	0.034	0.034	0.034	0.034	0.034	0.034	0.034
Service	1 Quality	0.086	0.086	0.086	0.086	0.086	0.086	0.086	0.086	0.086	0.086
	2 Deliv-ery Time	0.076	0.076	0.076	0.076	0.076	0.076	0.076	0.076	0.076	0.076
	3 Flex-ibility	0.059	0.059	0.059	0.059	0.059	0.059	0.059	0.059	0.059	0.059
	4 Pro-duction Facility & Ca-pacity	0.092	0.092	0.092	0.092	0.092	0.092	0.092	0.092	0.092	0.092
	5 Joint Problem Solving	0.115	0.115	0.115	0.115	0.115	0.115	0.115	0.115	0.115	0.115

Chapter 13
Risk Assessment in Virtual Enterprise Networks:
A Process–Driven Internal Audit Approach

Nikolaos A. Panayiotou
National Technical University of Athens, Greece

Stylianos Oikonomitsios
CIA, Consultant, Greece

Christina Athanasiadou
Ernst & Young, Greece

Sotiris P. Gayialis
National Technical University of Athens, Greece

ABSTRACT

In today's business environment, supply chains involve a number of autonomous organizations. Agility, effectiveness and efficiency of these supply chains can be achieved by forming virtual enterprise networks. The nature of supply chain processes with inter-organizational activities, involving different enterprises in a virtual enterprise network, increases the need for control in a well-designed and structured manner. Internal Audit activities and controls can help virtual organizations to improve and operate in a more efficient manner. This chapter proposes a methodological approach for the design of the Internal Audit function for risk assessment and control identification of inter-organizational supply chain processes, using business process modelling techniques and an internal audit–oriented enterprise modelling tool. A case study in the auditing of the supply chain processes in a virtual enterprise network demonstrates the application of the suggested methodology and tool.

INTRODUCTION

According to recently formulated definitions of the Institute Of Internal Auditors (IIA) (IIA, 2009;

Bou-Raad, 2000), Internal Audit is an independent, objective assurance and consulting activity designed to help the organization to improve and operate in a more efficient manner. Although the role of Internal Audit in business process improvement is emphasized in the aforementioned definitions, com-

DOI: 10.4018/978-1-61520-607-0.ch013

mon business practice shows a partial orientation towards financial and accounting analysis and control (Fadzil et al., 2005), while the application of Internal Audit to deal with efficiency and effectiveness is often overlooked. Internal Audit, in both its assurance and its consulting roles, contributes to the management of risk in a variety of ways. Its core role with regard to enterprise risk management is to provide objective assurance to the board on the effectiveness of risk management. Indeed, research has shown (IIA, 2004) that board directors and internal auditors agree that the two most important ways that internal audit provides value to the organization are in providing objective assurance that the major business risks are being managed appropriately and that the risk management and internal control framework is operating effectively.

The ever-increasing complexity of business processes and services demands business supply chains which involve a number of autonomous organizations. Competitive markets require that these supply chains are agile, effective and efficient. This can be achieved by forming dynamic virtual enterprise networks. Difficulties with deploying these networks are immense and organizations may not be prepared to cope with the changing nature of risk arising from such a strategic shift. The nature of supply chain processes with inter-organizational and cross-functional activities, involving different enterprises in a virtual network, increases the need for efficient and effective control in a well-designed and structured manner.

The evolution of internal auditing provides a basis for risk mitigation efforts within the supply chain processes. No longer focused on providing a check over accounting transactions, the internal auditor now applies risk-based auditing methods to management activities that span the enterprise. This enterprise-wide view makes internal auditing primed to analyze risk associated with operating highly interconnected supply chain networks (Hallikas & Varis, 2009). Internal auditors can identify

problems that cross organizational boundaries. They can take the responsibility to provide objective assurance in the evaluation and improvement of risk management, identifying and reporting problems that can impact the economic health of the members of a virtual enterprise network (Fike, 2005).

In this chapter a specific methodological approach for the mitigation of risks in virtual enterprise networks is proposed. This approach assists the design of an Internal Audit process for risk assessment and control identification, using business process modelling techniques. Moreover, specific templates are suggested for risk assessment and control identification connected with the existing organizational and inter-organizational processes and activities of the supply chain in the enterprise network. An internal audit–oriented enterprise modelling tool is developed to support the risk assessment and the control identification. The proposed methodology tries to assist business process improvement and quality enhancement in the enterprise supply chain and supports the extended role of Internal Audit as a facilitator of change towards the enterprises network's business objectives. It is intended to provide a structured set of methods and tools in order to maximize efficiency in virtual networks. A case study in the auditing for risk assessment and control identification related to risks of the supply chain processes in a virtual enterprise network demonstrates the application of the suggested methodology and tool.

The organization of the chapter is as follows. The next section outlines the theoretical assumptions of the concepts of Internal Audit and introduces the relation of business process modelling and internal audit controls in the context of inter-organizational processes and activities in the supply chain. Then, the proposed methodology for process driven internal audit in virtual enterprise networks is described. Next, the supportive enterprise modelling tool is presented. The case study section presents the implementation of the methodology and the proposed tool for process driven internal audit in a virtual enterprise network. A concluding section outlines the implications of the research and its practical usefulness.

BACKGROUND

In the past, business organizations often operated in "stand-alone mode" or relied on rather static networks of cooperating organizations. Nowadays, competition has become fiercer, fueled by developments like the globalization of business, shortening time-to-market requirements, and increased market transparency. Products and services are on the one hand of quickly increasing complexity, and on the other hand subject to increasingly frequent modifications and replacements (Grefen et al., in press). To comply with these market settings, organizations have to shift their priority to flexibility and ability to change if they want to survive (Pieper et al., 2004).

An enterprise can been defined as a dynamic set of interacting elements, including technical processes, organizational processes, technical functions, departments, business centers, and subsystems such as finance, production, marketing, and management. An element of an enterprise serves multiple roles, and interacts with other elements and with the environment. Elements of an enterprise include men, machines, buildings, inflow of materials and orders, outflow of goods and services, monetary values, human relations, and management. Elements and inter-relationships can be dynamic. The arrangement of elements and management of resources in order to operate in an efficient manner may be quite complex (Temponi et al., 2009).

In addition, changes are forced to enterprises by various events such as global competition, workforce changes, new technology, and continuously changing customers' preferences. Enterprises must harmonize structure and deal with competition in an increasingly complex and vaguely understood business environment. As a result, dynamically established cooperation between organizations is more and more required in order to meet market demands. Consequently, we see the emergence of new business models that are focused on these new business abilities and rely on intensive collaboration between autonomous business entities based on dynamic partnering. This new business form is called a virtual enterprise (Grefen et al, 2009). Operating in frequently changing markets implies that virtual enterprises cannot have a stable character over time. The partners that are involved in the provision of a shared process are changing continuously according to the requirements of the customer and the processes. In that case, a virtual enterprise is being created in a dynamic way addressing the needs and requirements of the customer and the individual partners (Ouzounis & Tschammer, 2001), based on circumstances given.

In practice, relationships between collaborating business partners with relation to supply chain in a virtual network are regulated by a set of rules. These rules are sometimes the object of a business agreement between supply chain partners (Gaudreault et al., 2009). A virtual enterprise network is mainly determined by the selection of the partners that collaborate in it and by the inter-organizational process links that are woven between the partners. Taking into consideration that links between elements and parties of a virtual enterprise network are complex, it is important to apply internal controls in these networks for risk management purposes.

The relationship between internal control and risk management remained blurry in the literature for many years (Spira & Page, 2003). Blackburn (1999) argues that control is a subset of risk management and explains the connection of risk management with the business objectives. In simpler words, business objectives are reached with the realization of business processes and risks can be identified in these business processes. The identified risks are managed and controlled and business process improvement is achieved, so the new role of Internal Audit in connection with business objectives and strategy is explained.

In 1947, the Statement of Responsibilities of Internal Audit, defined Internal Auditing as an 'independent appraisal function established within an organization to examine and evaluate in activities as a service to the organization' (Trotman, 1983). Initially, the objective of the function was to assist members of the organization in the effective discharge of their responsibilities. The emphasis of the role was aimed at evaluating the correctness of financial transactions (Bou-Raad, 2000).

The introduction of Information Technology and Electronic Commerce to business practices led to the redefinition of the Internal Auditor's role introducing the parameter of the assurance services. Year by year, the Internal Audit profession is not relying solely on audits of financial reports but it is moving towards other value-added services (Bou-Raad, 2000). The swift of the Internal Auditor's role is expressed in a new definition provided by the Institute of Internal Auditors in Australia, according to which Internal Auditing is an independent, objective, assurance and consulting activity designed to add value and improve an organization's operations (Parkinson, 1999). As a result of the new definition, control is not the only focus of Internal Audit, but there is also an emphasis on risk management, governance and control processes. Respectively, similar definitions are evidenced by the Committee Of Sponsoring Organizations of the Treadway Commission (COSO) Report of the USA, the Cadbury Report of the UK, the Criteria of Control Board (COCO) audit reports in Canada and the King Report on Corporate Governance of South Africa (McNamee & Selim, 1999).

The evolution of internal auditing provides a basis for risk management efforts within the business processes. In this context, an Internal Audit process will do more than just provide information (Schleifer & Greenawalt, 1996). It will also interpret, synthesize and analyze infor-mation to help management identify trends and business challenges. Furthermore, management will increasingly rely on Internal Audit to provide a conclusion on the effectiveness of the control environment and on the alignment of the control framework within the business.

The broader approach to Internal Audit has afforded an opportunity for claiming its expertise in the crucial area of risk management. In other words, it is suggested that Internal Audit is a key component of good corporate governance practice. However this opportunity has not been fully realized and exploited by Internal Auditors, who must have an in-depth understanding of business processes in order to be able to manage risk and define controls trying to assess these risks. Audits are a tool with widespread use throughout industry, for example, in financial, quality, technical, safety, project management, human resource and purchasing situations carried out by experts in the related processes (Bayley, 1983; Evans & Dale, 1989; Hoare, 1987; Kelly, 1988; Sayle, 1988; Torrington, 1987). Some companies with an established Internal Audit process for many years have already tried to include specialists such as engineers and marketers to give a broader operational perspective on auditing and risk management (Blackburn, 1999).

The increased importance of business processes and activities for Internal Auditing has already been recognized in many case studies and surveys, most of which are connected with quality systems. For example, a survey carried out in manufacturing companies in New Zealand (Hawkes & Adams, 1995) suggests that Internal Auditors in manufacturing companies change their role and responsibilities in response to TQM initiatives. Generally, this change in focus involves a move away from financial auditing and internal control compliance checks to a primary focus on quality systems reviews. Many firms have established Internal Audit processes in conjunction with the introduction of quality management programmes and ISO certification. This suggests that quality review requirements of the ISO 9000 series of standards (BSI, 1987), together with the continuous improvement philosophy of TQM, have provided opportunities, as well as challenges, for Internal Audit. In the context of the ISO 9000 quality management system series of standards, quality auditing is a tool to ensure that procedures meet the requirement of the standard and are properly implemented. A good Internal Audit program should also ensure that senior managers are aware of significant shortcomings in their systems. Audits, therefore, constitute an essential element of the quality improvement tool kit and an effective control mechanism for the organization. In the wider business context, management audits can be used to critically assess any business process and provide evidence on which to base action. The major work in the field of management auditing is that of Sayle (1988), who provides a comprehensive approach to auditing and quality improvement. The formal basis for quality auditing is also outlined in ISO 10011 (BSI, 1991), which supplements the ISO 9000 (BSI, 1987) series of quality management standards.

A lot of papers in the literature refer to the use of Enterprise Modelling techniques such as IDEF-0, GRAI, Data Flow Diagrams or ARIS methods, to name only some of them (NIST, 1993; Kelly, 1988; Tatsiopoulos et al., 2001; Panayiotou et al., 2006) in Business Process Reengineering initiatives or in the improvement of quality systems. In the area of supply chain management, the role of Business Process Management has been empowered, as researchers view the supply chain as a whole and promote customer focus, supplier partnerships, cooperation and information sharing and process improvement (McAdam & McCormack, 2001). The existing relationships between different partners in the inter-organizational supply chain and the inter-departmental and cross-functional nature of the processes involved (De Toro & McVabe, 1997) highlight the need to control, monitor and improve work methods.

Although many scientists refer to the importance of approaches such as reengineering, continuous improvement, benchmarking and enterprise modelling in the management of supply chain (Trkman et al., 2007), only few of them, (Hyland & Beckett, 2002; Carnaghan, 2006) examine the use of such techniques combined with the Internal Audit view.

Mapping of risks is suggested as essential to the internal audit department's supply chain risk mitigation efforts. This mapping consists of understanding and defining supply chain risk and identifying the controls for risk assessment. This approach tries to recognize the causal impacts across the supply chain where an insignificant disruption builds upon itself creating a significant disruption that impacts the organization's ability to deliver goods and services at anticipated costs. A classic example is demand amplification (bullwhip effect) across supply chain partners where stable demand manifests into erratic order and production behavior (Spekman and Davis, 2004). Enterprise modelling techniques which incorporate risk-based auditing methods can be applied for mapping of risks and controls in supply chain processes with inter-organizational and cross-functional activities.

A PROPOSED METHODOLOGY FOR PROCESS-DRIVEN INTERNAL AUDIT

The methodological approach proposed for the planning and execution of the Internal Audit work is focused on the identification of risks and the definition of the related controls of the enterprises involved in the network and consists of four stages:

- Stage 1: Strategic Analysis focused on the identification of strategic risks for the enterprises, especially those affecting the virtual enterprise network

- Stage 2: Process analysis of the processes to be audited according to the prioritisation enabled by the strategic risk analysis
- Stage 3: Process risk assessment and controls identification related to risks
- Stage 4: Controls assessment and Internal Audit execution.

In this chapter, emphasis is put on stages 2, 3 and partially on stage 4, as the intention is to present the integration of the process modelling technique in the Internal Audit process applied in inter-organizational supply chain management for risk assessment purposes. Moreover, the purpose is to introduce the contribution of the process modelling technique to the documentation of processes, the identification of significant process level risks and controls in place to manage these risks and the development of Internal Audit programs that can be used for controlling purposes.

The use of the business process modelling technique for the documentation of supply chain processes and the identification of internal controls enhances the Internal Auditor's process improvement efforts through:

- Easy identification of controls in place to manage the process-level risks
- Structured evaluation of internal controls' design, as it is easy to identify controls missing or not properly designed
- Easy identification of major controls already in place to manage significant risks, to be included in-scope of the Internal Audit's evaluation of controls' operating effectiveness (if these are operating as designed and intended).

The proposed approach is presented in Figure 1, and its stages are further described in the text below.

Stage 1: Strategic Analysis

Strategic Analysis provides an initial understanding of the network enterprises' strategy and the environment, in which they operate, identifies and assesses the strategic risks of the network as a whole and the key processes related to those risks. The purpose is to develop the Internal Audit Plan, which defines the scope of the work of Internal Audit within a given period of time (i.e. annually) focusing on the areas/ key processes with significant risk. Through strategic analysis, business risks can be linked to the strategic objectives of the enterprise network and key business processes can be linked to business risks that threaten these objectives. Strategic Analysis is undertaken to:

- Gain a high-level understanding of the business, its markets and external forces.
- Understand and identify the strategic objectives and strategies in place to achieve these objectives and assess their reasonableness. This is achieved through discussion with management, review of enterprises' information (history, organizational charts, business and strategic plans, vision/ mission statements, Board of Directors' meeting minutes, etc), review of industry business models and use of strategic analysis tools such as PEST analysis, Porter's Five Forces Analysis and the Balanced Scorecard.
- Understand and assess the general risk areas that can threaten the achievement of these objectives. Management involvement is critical in the identification of strategic risks and the establishment of the criteria to be used for the assessment of significance of those risks. The significance and ranking of the risks identified is determined by considering two factors: the potential impact of the risks and the likelihood that the risks will occur.

Figure 1. Internal audit process methodological approach

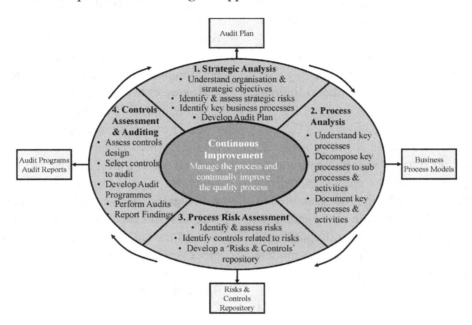

• Identify the existing organizational structures and the key processes to support the achievement of these objectives and manage these risks. All responses to risks at the strategic level must be associated with key business processes (strategic, core and supportive management processes and subprocesses). To identify the key processes, discussion and interviews with management are performed.

As a result of this analysis, key strategic risks and related business processes are identified and prioritized in order to develop the appropriate Audit Plan. Strategic risks may be identified in different enterprises of the network; the Plan will include all risks identified and considered significant, as long as they are related to the processes under examination. The Plan includes the key processes and risks to be evaluated and tested, defining the scope of the work of the Internal Audit within a specific period of time.

Stage 2: Process Analysis

The second stage of the methodological approach analyses the key business processes identified in stage 1 and included in the Audit Plan. The analysis of the process involves the definition of its objectives and a detailed investigation of the sub-processes and activities from which it is composed, resources used and information flows. For this purpose, interviews are conducted with the process owners and other persons involved, in order to obtain an understanding of each key business process, sub-process and activity.

Once understanding of the key processes is gained, the processes documentation follows, using the hierarchical modelling technique of business process models. Each process/ subprocess and activity is presented as a combination of inputs and outputs. Each sub-process is identified by a reference number linked to the "parent" process, and each activity is also identified by a reference number linked to "parent" sub-process. It should be stated that, at this point, the controls for each activity have not yet been recognized.

The business process diagrams presenting the activities carried out by the enterprises involved in the network are accompanied by a narrative description, which includes:

- The sub-process objective
- The scope of the sub-process
- The persons involved in the sub-process (internal and external)
- The reference number of each activity, linked to the "parent" sub-process
- The activities to which the sub-process is decomposed and detailed description of each activity
- The documents and records used/ maintained.

The template used for the narrative description of the sub-processes, is shown in Figure 2.

Stage 3: Process Risk Assessment

Process Risk Assessment follows the same steps to that used in the Strategic Risk Assessment, however, this stage goes one step further to look also at controls that are in place to manage those risks. It is very important that the strategic risks identified at the Strategic Risk Assessment stage be considered at the Process Risk Assessment level.

Process Risk Assessment is using the activities represented in the business process models of the lowest level for the identification of risks, which threaten the achievement of process objectives and the mapping of the controls that are in place to manage these risks. Risks are identified at the activity-level through review of data obtained during discussion with process owners and review of business process diagrams. As process owners and staff usually have a better understanding of the network enterprises' environment, it is normal to involve them in the process of risk identification. Process-level risks are documented and each risk is linked to one or more activities. It should be stated, however, that it may not always be possible to provide a one-to-one link between the risks and the activities since some activities may be exposed to external uncontrollable sources of risk.

Once the risks are identified, the significance of risks (high, medium, low) is assessed considering the impact of not achieving the business objectives and their likelihood of occurrence. This assessment will help to identify and document controls that are in place to address these risks adequately. After this step, controls in place to manage those

Figure 2. Process description template

PROCESS:		A0. <<PROCESS NAME>>
SUB-PROCESS:		A1. <<Sub-process Name>>
PROCESS OBJECTIVE:		<<Process objective description>>
SCOPE:		<<Sub-process scope>>
ENTITIES INVOLVED:		♦ <<Departments, people, external parties involved in the sub-process>>
Ref No	ACTIVITY	DESCRIPTION
A1.1	<<Activity>>	<<Activity Description>>
A1.2		
DOCUMENTS/ RECORDS:		♦ <<Documents/ records used in the sub-process>>

risks are identified and mapped on the business process diagrams. Each control has a reference number in order to be easily linked to a risk and the activity to which it is connected. A detailed description of each control is also documented in the risks and controls repository presented in Figure 3.

The risks and controls repository are used to:

- Present the link between the activities represented in the business process diagrams, their risks and the related controls
- Ensure that controls are identified for all areas of risk
- Provide a basis for the identification of control design weaknesses (i.e. absence of controls) and the selection of controls to be tested for their operating effectiveness based on the significance of the risks they manage.

Stage 4: Controls Assessment - Audit Execution

The documentation of the controls using the proposed tools assists auditors to assess the effectiveness of the internal controls' design and operating effectiveness. Business process diagrams include risk and controls as linking objects to the process activities. The risks for which controls

do not exist are recognized, defining either that there is a control weakness or that the risk is at an acceptable level and management agreed not to mitigate it (due to high cost of implementing a control or due to the possibility to reduce the available opportunities for gain). The auditor reviews known controls against identified risks to establish the extent of residual risk and identifies any other controls, which may cover the same risk and further reduce the residual risk. The next step is to assess the operating effectiveness of the identified and documented controls. Management is involved in the selection of the controls to be evaluated (through detailed testing of controls) based on the significance of risk. The audit work will focus then on these controls during the audit execution. In order to perform the audit, detailed audit steps are defined.

For the detailed testing of controls it is important to document all testing activities. The risks and controls repository can be easily extended to act as an Internal Audit program/ checklist as presented in Figure 4, for performing tests of controls and recording the results of testing.

The audit program that will be used in the audit includes:

- The reference number of the activity to which the selected controls are linked
- The selected internal controls to be tested per sub-process and activity

Figure 3. Risks & controls repository

RISKS AND CONTROLS REPOSITORY					
Ref No	Activities	Risks	Risk Assessment (H/M/L)	Control Ref No	Internal Controls
A1	<<SUB-PROCESS>>				
A1.1	<<Activity>>	<<Risk 1>>	H	C-A1-1	<<Control 1>>
		<<Risk 2>>	M	C-A1-2	<<Control 2>>
A1.2	<<Activity>>		L	C-A1-3	<<Control 2>>
			H	C-A1-4	<<Control 2>>

- The steps that should be followed in order to perform the test of each control
- The significance of risks managed by the selected controls as assessed in stage 3.

During the audit the following information will be completed:

- The description of the results the control is operating and possible finding after the test is performed (operating inefficiencies)
- The actions proposed to be taken in order to improve the controls
- A statement on whether the results of the audit should be reported to management
- The reference number of the working papers obtained during the audit execution that can be used in the future to support and evidence the results of the controls audit.

Once the testing has been performed, the results and the recommendations for the improvement of processes and internal controls are documented into the Internal Audit report and are communicated to management in order to decide further actions.

A SUPPORTIVE ENTERPRISE MODELLING TOOL

In order to support the suggested methodological approach for the design of a process-driven Internal Audit function for risk assessment and control identification, a proposed enterprise modelling tool was constructed using the Sybase PowerDesigner enterprise modelling software. Business Process Model (BPM) method was used for the construction of process diagrams. This modelling method is proprietary of the Sybase PowerDesigner software tool and describes the various tasks and processes of a business and how the partners interact with these tasks and processes (Sybase, 2008). The existing method of Business Process Model (BPM) was modified in order to incorporate the internal audit view. More specifically, a new method was developed with the following functionality:

- The business processes are designed using the rules of Business Process Models. According to these, a process can be decomposed in sub-processes in different hierarchical levels, and, in activities in the lowest level of detail. Every process,

Figure 4. Internal audit program template

AUDIT PROGRAM							
Ref No	Internal Controls	Audit Steps	Current Controls Description/ Finding	Recommendation	Risk (H/M/L)	Reportable Finding (Y/N)	W/P Ref
A1	<<SUB-PROCESS>>						
A1.1	<<Activity>>						
C-A1-1	<<Control 1>>	▪ <<Audit Step 1>> ▪ <<Audit Step 2>>			H	Y	
C-A1-2	<<Control 1>>	▪ <<Audit Step 1>> ▪ <<Audit Step 2>>			M	N	

sub-process and activity has a unique code number. The organizational units performing the activities are also modelled as well as the information flow between the different activities performed by specific organizational roles.

- The risks are connected to activities and are represented with arrows. Every risk can be classified as low, medium or high in an attribute of the arrow. One risk can lead to one or more controls, which are represented as cylinders. At the same time it is possible for more than one risk to lead to the same control. A control has a unique code number, a description, as well as analytical instructions for the checks that have to be performed.

A simple representation of the suggested method is presented in Figure 5.

The database functionality of Sybase PowerDesigner combined with the newly introduced internal audit-related objects permit the generation of reports that cover the suggested documents of the methodological approach presented in Figures 2, 3 and 4. More specifically, the process descriptions can be automatically generated (as the description is simply an attribute that can be retrieved by the customised report), as well as the risks and controls repository and the internal audit program. An important feature of the tool is the capability that offers to the auditor to define the audit scope. Typical criteria that can be easily used in order to select a specific area for audit of the supply chain are the following:

- Selected process or range of processes.
- Selected sub-process or range of sub-processes.
- Selected activity or range of activities.
- Selected organizational units.
- Selected classification of risk (low, medium, high).
- Combination of the above.

The suggested enterprise modelling tool can support Stages 2, 3 and part of Stage 4 of the proposed methodological framework, enabling the easy and structured analysis of the processes to be audited, the definition of risks and controls in relation with the corresponding activities and the generation of the audit plans.

CASE STUDY: PROCESS-DRIVEN INTERNAL AUDIT IN THE SUPPLY CHAIN IN A VIRTUAL ENTERPRISE NETWORK

The application of the proposed methodological approach for the design of a process-driven Internal Audit function for risk assessment and control identification of related risks is described in the following paragraphs, where the supply chain process in a virtual enterprise network operating in the electronics sector is analyzed. This process is considered to be very important by management, as it affects the production of one of the most important product families that brings more than fifty percent of enterprise network's turnover on an annual basis. Some activities are performed by sub-contractors and others are performed internally in the organization.

The cooperation of the networked enterprises includes distinguishing operational characteristics that are very important and call for careful internal audit in many of its activities such as the production scheduling, the production process and materials control. The need for coordination between the enterprises involved in the network as well as their frequent interaction add in the complexity of auditing and increase the administrative cost of controlling.

In order to achieve risk assessment in an efficient way, and manage internal audit of the important and complex supply chain process, the suggested methodological approach and enterprise modelling tool were used. As a first step, the busi-

Figure 5. Indicative objects of the proposed internal audit modelling method

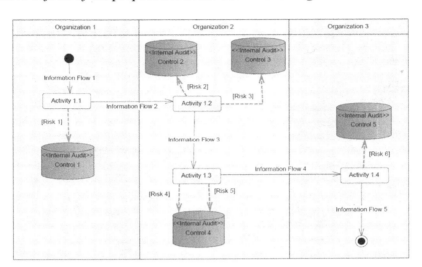

ness process model was generated as described in Stage 2 of Figure 1. An indicative business model of the process (which was minimised for presentation purposes in this chapter) is depicted in Figure 6.

The tool supports the inclusion of activity descriptions within the diagram, a functionality, which permits the automatic process description generation afterwards. A sample of the report generated by the tool has been included in Appendix 1.

The use of enterprise modelling promoted the better and more structured comprehension of the process and its important aspects. The identification of discrete activities enabled the easier identification of risks related to them. As a result, the business process diagram was expanded in order to incorporate the internal audit view, by including all the recognised risks and controls. Figure 7 depicts part of the expanded business model related to the process model of Figure 6. In the example of Figure 7, subcontracting orders creation activities are presented. These activities are performed by the production planning and purchasing departments of one of the members of the virtual enterprise. Then, the released subcontracting orders are forwarded to one or more subcontractors of the network. The vari-

ous controls of the subcontracting orders creation activities ensure the mitigation of risks which can affect the effectiveness of the production phases to subcontractors, and consequently the effectiveness and efficiency of the whole supply chain.

The modelling of risks and controls permitted the creation of a related repository in the database of the tool, in the way it is described in Stage 3 of the approach. Appendix 2 includes the report of risks and controls for each activity of the supply chain process of the case study. Furthermore, for each control, more analytical instructions concerning the checks that have to be performed by the auditor are maintained in a related attribute of each control object. This functionality enables the generation of specific audit programs according to the criteria selected by the auditor. For example, in Appendix 3, it can be seen that an audit program was filtered, including only the controls connected with high risks of activities in the supply chain process. In this way, the audit execution included in Stage 4 is supported. The maintenance of the generated models permits the repetitive use of the repository content, increasing the productivity and the effectiveness of the auditor in his/ her audit missions.

Figure 6. Supply chain process

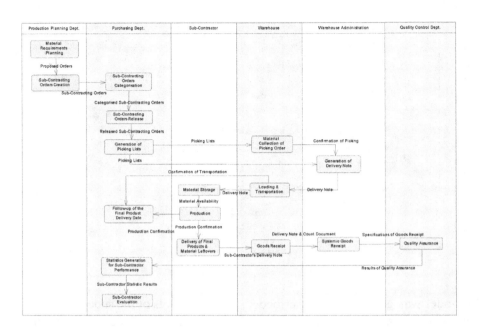

FUTURE RESEARCH DIRECTIONS

Internal auditors need to be out in the front, leading the business units with regards to the internal control system and focusing on strategic business objectives. It is essential to establish internal audit activity as a vital business operation in a virtual enterprise network rather than an observation activity, waiting for events to happen and deal with the impacts they have (Fadzil et al, 2005). Internal auditor should act as a management consultant, independent professional and business partner in a virtual enterprise network, where smaller firms join forces to undertake a project that cannot be efficiently handled by individual firms.

Business process improvement requires periodically changes in planning, organizing, staffing and directing inside the enterprises. Internal auditor's approach needs to be dynamic and adapt to the continual development of the virtual enterprise network.

The supportive process modelling tool is characterized by the process orientation, the central administration of all the information concerning the internal audit of the supply chain process in a single database, as well as the use of a common method for the representation of the related objects. The proposed set of tools and methods can substantially increase the productivity of the auditor. A further important enhancement of the enterpise modelling tool could include the modelling of the audit findings in different process instances. Such an enhancement could permit the statistical exploitation of the findings with the use of a fully integrated internal audit database, offering, at the same time, an easy-to-use enterprise modelling front-end.

Based on the fact that today's business climate is characterized by high uncertainty, globalization of business, outsourcing, shorter product lifecycles and high customer expectations, effective supply chain management can help enterprises quickly generate greater market value, operate more efficiently on a long-term basis, improve cost structures, enhance the balance sheet, and respond quickly both to turmoil and to opportunity.

Figure 7. Business process model with risks & controls

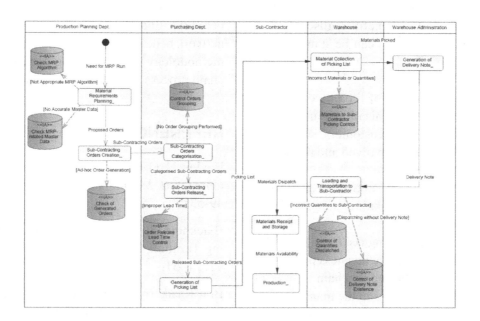

This paper sets guidelines for enterprise modelling of supply chain processes. Even though the modelling tool, as processes become more complex, may be expensive and time-consuming upon implementation, the benefits of risk reduction and improvements in enterprises operations will outweigh the costs. The modelling tool not only provides solutions to supply chain potential issues but it also provides a structure for the virtual enterprise network to develop and enhance an effective supply chain management strategy.

CONCLUSION

The nature of supply chain processes with inter-organizational and cross-functional activities, involving different enterprises in a virtual network, increases the need for efficient and effective control. The importance of Internal Audit activities and controls is very high for risk management purposes in virtual enterprise networks. The

realisation of internal audit in a purely financial manner cannot guarantee efficient and effective results in control, problem solving and continuous process improvement, three important goals of virtual enterprise networks operation. Business process management with the use of enterprise modelling techniques can enhance the effectiveness of an internal audit system. The appraisal of the effectiveness of the existing controls in the supply chain function can be supported by methods including an internal audit view incorporated in the typical activity, organizational and information views. '

The proposed methodological framework supports the whole lifecycle of the internal audit process, from the strategic definition of the important business processes to the internal audit control and the feedback to strategy. The stages of business process analysis, process risk assessment, control assessment and auditing are supported by a proposed enterprise modelling tool which is an extended version of business process modelling method including the internal audit view through the connection of risks and controls to activities. The most important benefits realised by the proposed approach and tool can be summarised as follows:

- Better understanding of the processes under review, the organizational units and the partners (such as customers, suppliers, subcontractors etc.) involved and the information exchanged.
- Analysis of virtual network enterprises' processes, formulating supply chain function
- Mapping of the existing risks and controls connected with specific business processes and activities of the supply chain.
- Improved effectiveness in the management of the internal audit missions through the filtering of activities, risks and controls during the audit preparation phase.
- Improved efficiency of the internal audit process through the use of the suggested enterprise-modelling tool, which automatically generates the appropriate audit plans based on the selection of the desired scope in the audit mission by the auditor.
- Easy inclusion of the proposed (and accepted) improvements in the processes or creation of new necessary controls.
- Facilitation of the report generation process, after the conclusion of the audit mission.

The proposed methodology and its application in the case study prove that enterprise modelling techniques which incorporate risk-based auditing methods can be applied for risk assessment and control in supply chain processes with inter-organizational and cross-functional activities. The process orientation, the central administration of all the information concerning the internal audit of the supply chain process in a single database and the use of a common method for the representation

of the related objects can substantially enhance risk management efforts in virtual enterprise networks. Enterprises participating in the virtual network benefit from application of the proposed methodology and modelling tool, since supply chain process optimization is achieved.

REFERENCES

Bayley, H. (1983). A Review of Technical Audit. *Chartered Mechanical Engineer, November*, 49-53.

Blackburn, S. (1999). Managing Risk and Achieving Turnbull Compliance . *Accountants Digest*, *417*, 1–51.

Bou-Raad, G. (2000). Internal Auditors and a Value-Added Approach: The New Business Regime. *Managerial Audit Journal*, *15*(4), 182–186. doi:10.1108/02686900010322461

BSI. (1987). BS 5750: ISO 9000 Quality Systems Standards. London: British Standards Institution (BSI).

BSI. (1991). BS 7229: ISO 10011 Guide to Quality Systems Auditing. London: British Standards Institution (BSI).

Carnaghan, C. (2006). Business process modelling approaches in the context of process level audit risk assessment: An analysis and comparison . *International Journal of Accounting Information Systems*, *7*(2), 170–204. doi:10.1016/j.accinf.2005.10.005

De Toro, I., & McCabe, T. (1997). How to Stay Flexible and Elude Fads . *Quality Progress*, *30*(3), 55–60.

Evans, E. F., & Dale, B. G. (1989). The Use of Audits in Purchasing . *International Journal of Physical Distribution & Materials Management*, *18*(7), 15–23.

Fadzil, F. H., Haron, H., & Jantan, M. (2005). Internal auditing practices and internal control system . *Managerial Auditing Journal, 20*(8), 844–866. doi:10.1108/02686900510619683

Fike, R. L. (2005). *Supply chain risk management: redefining the audit function within a large industrial company*. Master Thesis of Engineering in Logistics, Massachusetts Institute of Technology, Engineering Systems Division.

Gaudreault, J., Frayret, J.-M., & Pesant, G. (2009). Distributed search for supply chain coordination . *Computers in Industry, 60*(6), 441–451. doi:10.1016/j.compind.2009.02.006

Grefen, P., Eshuis, R. Mehandjiev, N., Kouvas, G., & Weichhart, G. (in press). Cross Work: Internet-Based Support for Process-Oriented Instant Virtual Enterprises. *IEEE Internet Computing, 13*(6).

Grefen, P., Eshuis, R., Mehandjiev, N., Kouvas, G., & Weichhart, G. (2009). Dynamic business network process management in instant virtual enterprises . *Computers in Industry, 60*(2), 86–103. doi:10.1016/j.compind.2008.06.006

Hallikas, J., & Varis, J. (2009). Risk Management in Value Networks. In G. A. Zsidisin, & B. Ritchie (Eds), Supply Chain Risk: A Handbook of Assessment, Management, and Performance (pp. 35-52), New York: Springer.

Hawkes, L., & Adams, M. B. (1995). Total Quality Management and the Internal Audit: Empirical Evidence . *Managerial Auditing Journal, 10*(1), 31–36. doi:10.1108/02686909510077361

Hoare, D. (1987) Succeeding by Self-audit, *Management Today, April*, 94-95.

Hyland, P., & Beckett, R. (2002). Learning to compete: the value of internal benchmarking. *Benchmarking: An International Journal, 9*(3), 293–304. doi:10.1108/14635770210429036

IIA. (2004). The role of internal audit in enterprise-wide risk management, Position Statement, *Institute of Internal Auditors (IAA)*, London. Retrieved July 13, 2009, from www.theiia.org/iia/download.cfm?file=283

IIA. (2009). Definition of Internal Auditing, *Institute of Internal Auditors (IAA)*. Retrieved July 13, 2009, from http://www.theiia.org/guidance/standards-and-guidance/ippf/definition-of-internal-auditing

Kelly, A. (1988). Maintenance Systems Auditing - An Aid to Effective Maintenance Management. *Maintenance, September/October*, 6-12.

McAdam, R., & McCormack, D. (2001). Integrating Business Process for Global Allignment and Supply Chain Management. *Business Process Management Journal, 7*(2), 113–130. doi:10.1108/14637150110389696

McNamee, D., & Selim, G. (1999). The Next Step in Risk Management. *The Internal Auditor, 56*(3), 35–38.

NIST. (1993) Integration Definition for Function Modelling (IDEF-0) (Publication 183), Federal Information Processing Standard (FIPS), Gaithersburg, MD: Computer Systems Laboratory, National Institute of Standard and Technology (NIST).

Ouzounis, V., & Tschammer, V. (2001, October 3-5). Towards Dynamic Virtual Enterprises. In *Proceedings of the First IFIP Conference I3E 2001, Towards the e-Society: E-Commerce. E-Business, and E-Government*, Zurich, Switzerland: Kluwer Academic Publishers.

Panayiotou, N., Athanasiadou, C., & Economitsios, S. (2006). Using Enterprise Modelling Techniques in the Internal Audit Process Design Towards Continuous Improvement. In Scientific Anniversary Volume in Honor of Professor Emeritus K. N. Dervitiostis, University of Piraeus, Greece.

Parkinson, M. (1999, October 20) *Presentation for Internal Auditing*. Presented at the Institute of Internal Auditors Educators Symposium, Sydney, Australia.

Pieper, R., Kouwenhoven, V., & Hamminga, S. (2004). Beyond the Hype: e-Business Strategy in Leading European Companies. The Netherlands: Van Haren Publishing.

Sayle, A. J. (1988) Management Audits, 2nd ed. London: Allen J. Sayle Ltd.

Schleifer, L., & Greenawalt, M. (1996). The internal auditor and the critical thinking process . *Managerial Auditing Journal*, *11*(5), 5–13. doi:10.1108/02686909610120479

Spekman, R. E., & Davis, E. W. (2004). Risky business: expanding the discussion on risk and the extended enterprise . *International Journal of Physical Distribution & Logistics Management*, *34*(5), 414–433. doi:10.1108/09600030410545454

Spira, L. F., & Page, M. (2003). Risk Management, The Reinvention of Internal Control And the Changing Role of Internal Audit . *Accounting, Auditing & Accountability Journal*, *16*(4), 640–661. doi:10.1108/09513570310492335

Sybase (2008) *Sybase PowerDesigner Business Process Model User's Guide*, Version 12, Sybase Inc., USA. Retrieved July 10, 2008, from http://www.sybase.com.

Tatsiopoulos, I. P., Panayiotou, N. A., & Ponis, S. T. (2001, May) *A Modelling & Evaluation Methodology for E-Commerce BPR*. Paper presented at the 4th SME SME International Conference, May 14-16, 2001, Aalborg University, Denmark.

Temponi, C., Bryant, M. D., & Fernandez, B. (2009). Integration of business function models into an aggregate enterprise systems model . *European Journal of Operational Research*, *199*(3), 793–800. doi:10.1016/j.ejor.2008.08.007

Torrington, D. P., & Hall, L. A. (1987) Personnel Management: A New Approach. Upper Saddle River, NJ: Prentice-Hall.

Trkman, P., Stemberger, M. I., & Groznik, A. (2007). Process Approach to Supply Chain Integration, *Supply Chain Management* . *International Journal (Toronto, Ont.)*, *12*(2), 116–128.

Trotman, E. (1983) The Role of The Internal Auditor, Professional Development for the Australian Society of Accountants, Australia.

ADDITIONAL READINGS

Anderson, U. (2003). Assurance and Consulting Services. In A.D. Bailey Jr., A.A. Gramlin & S. Ramamoorti (Eds.), Research Opportunities in Internal Auditing (pp. 97-124), The Institute of Internal Auditors Research Foundation, Altamonte Springs, Florida.

Arend, R. J., & Wisner, J. D. (2005). Small business and supply chain management: is there a fit? *Journal of Business Venturing*, *20*(3), 403–436. doi:10.1016/j.jbusvent.2003.11.003

Black, J. A., & Edwards, S. (2000). Emergence of virtual or network organizations: fad or feature . *Journal of Organizational Change Management*, *13*(6), 567–576. doi:10.1108/09534810010378588

Cai, J., Liu, X., Xiao, Z., & Liu, J. (2009). Improving supply chain performance management: A systematic approach to analyzing iterative KPI accomplishment . *Decision Support Systems*, *46*(2), 512–521. doi:10.1016/j.dss.2008.09.004

Chandrashekar, A., & Schary, P. B. (1999). Toward the Virtual Supply chain: The Convergence of IT and Organization. *The International Journal of Logistics Management*, *10*(2), 27–40. doi:10.1108/09574099910805978

Chopra, S. (2003). Designing the distribution network in a supply chain. *Transportation Research Part E, Logistics and Transportation Review, 39*(2), 123–140. doi:10.1016/S1366-5545(02)00044-3

Duane, I. R., & Webb, J. W. (2007). A multi-theoretic perspective on trust and power in strategic supply chains. *Journal of Operations Management, 25*(2), 482–497. doi:10.1016/j.jom.2006.05.004

Gong, O., Lai, K. K., & Wang, S. (2008). Supply chain networks: Closed Jackson network models and properties. *International Journal of Production Economics, 113*(2), 567–574. doi:10.1016/j.ijpe.2007.10.013

Handfield, R. B., & Bechtel, C. (2002). The role of trust and relationship structure in improving supply chain responsiveness. *Industrial Marketing Management, 31*(4), 367–382. doi:10.1016/S0019-8501(01)00169-9

Hult, G. T. M., Ketchen, D. J. Jr, & Nichols, E. L. Jr. (2003). Organizational learning as a strategic resource in supply management. *Journal of Operations Management, 21*(5), 541–556. doi:10.1016/j.jom.2003.02.001

Hurtubise, S., Olivier, C., & Gharbi, A. (2004). Planning tools for managing the supply chain. *Computers & Industrial Engineering, 46*(4), 763–779. doi:10.1016/j.cie.2004.05.018

Lau, H. C. W., Chin, K. S., Pun, K. F., & Ning, A. (2000). Decision supporting functionality in a virtual enterprise network . *Expert Systems with Applications, 19*(4), 261–270. doi:10.1016/S0957-4174(00)00038-5

Lau, H. C. W., Wong, C. W. Y., Ngai, E. W. T., & Hui, I. K. (2003). Quality management framework for a virtual enterprise network: a multi-agent approach. *Managing Service Quality, 13*(4), 300–309. doi:10.1108/09604520310484716

Lu, L., & Wang, G. (2008). A study on multi-agent supply chain framework based on network economy. *Computers & Industrial Engineering, 54*(2), 288–300. doi:10.1016/j.cie.2007.07.010

Manthou, V., Vlachopoulou, M., & Folinas, D. (2004). Virtual e-Chain (VeC) model for supply chain collaboration. *International Journal of Production Economics, 87*(3), 241–250. doi:10.1016/S0925-5273(03)00218-4

Meade, L., & Sarkis, J. (1998). Strategic analysis of logistics and supply chain management systems using the analytical network process. *Transportation Research Part E, Logistics and Transportation Review, 34*(3), 201–215. doi:10.1016/S1366-5545(98)00012-X

Nagurney, A. (2009). A system-optimization perspective for supply chain network integration: The horizontal merger case . *Transportation Research Part E, Logistics and Transportation Review, 45*(1), 1–15. doi:10.1016/j.tre.2008.02.003

Nagurney, A., Cruz, J., Dong, J., & Zhang, D. (2005). Supply chain networks, electronic commerce, and supply side and demand side risk. *European Journal of Operational Research, 164*(1), 120–142. doi:10.1016/j.ejor.2003.11.007

Nagurney, A., & Matsypura, D. (2005). Global supply chain network dynamics with multicriteria decision-making under risk and uncertainty . *Transportation Research Part E, Logistics and Transportation Review, 41*(6), 585–612. doi:10.1016/j.tre.2005.07.002

Ostrovsky, M. (2008). Stability in Supply Chain Networks . *The American Economic Review, 98*(3), 897–923. doi:10.1257/aer.98.3.897

Peck, H., & Juttner, U. (2000). Strategy and Relationships: Defining the Interface in Supply Chain Contexts. *The International Journal of Logistics Management, 11*(2), 33–44. doi:10.1108/09574090010806146

Pickett, K. (2003) The internal auditing handbook. West Sussex, UK: John Wiley & Sons Ltd.

Ramamoorti, S., Bailey, A. D. Jr, & Traver, R. O. (1999). Risk assessment in internal auditing: a neural network approach . *International Journal of Intelligent Systems in Accounting Finance & Management, 8*(3), 159–180. doi:10.1002/(SICI)1099-1174(199909)8:3<159::AID-ISAF169>3.0.CO;2-W

Robson, K., Humphrey, C., Khalifa, R., & Jones, J. (2007). Transforming audit technologies: Business risk audit methodologies and the audit field . *Accounting, Organizations and Society, 32*(4-5), 409–438. doi:10.1016/j.aos.2006.09.002

Sarens, G. (2009). Internal Auditing Research: Where are we going? *International Journal of Auditing, 13*(1), 1–7. doi:10.1111/j.1099-1123.2008.00387.x

Stefanovic, D., Stefanovic, N., & Radenkovic, B. (2009). Supply network modelling and simulation methodology . *Simulation Modelling Practice and Theory, 17*(4), 743–766. doi:10.1016/j.simpat.2009.01.001

Strader, T. J., Lin, F.-R., & Shaw, M. J. (1998). Information infrastructure for electronic virtual organization management . *Decision Support Systems, 23*(1), 75–94. doi:10.1016/S0167-9236(98)00037-2

Sutton, S. G., & Hampton, C. (2003). Risk assessment in an extended enterprise environment: redefining the audit model. *International Journal of Accounting Information Systems, 4*(1), 57–73. doi:10.1016/S1467-0895(03)00010-1

Tage, S.-L., & Prabir, B. (2002). *Challenges of Integration in Supply Chain Networks: An European Case Study* (ACES Working Paper 2002.1). Pittsburgh, PA: University of Pittsburgh.

Thompson, K. (2005). Virtual Enterprise Networks allow business scale through virtual collaboration. *Virtual Collaboration Networks, 34.* Retrieved July 10, 2009, from http://www.bioteams.com/2005/07/11/virtual_enterprise_networks.html

Tseng, M.-L., Chiang, J. H., & Lan, L. W. (2009). Selection of optimal supplier in supply chain management strategy with analytic network process and choquet integral . *Computers & Industrial Engineering, 57*(1), 330–340. doi:10.1016/j.cie.2008.12.001

Zgodavova, K., Kosc, P., & Kekale, T. (2001). Learning before doing: utilising a co-operative role play for quality management in a virtual organization . *Journal of Workplace Learning, 13*(3), 113–119. doi:10.1108/13665620110388415

APPENDIX A

Table 1. Process description example

Code	Activity Name	Organisation Unit	Description
A07.03.01	Material Requirements Planning	Production Planning Dept.	The Production Planner of the companies runs MRP once every fifteen days in order to generate proposed production order, proposed sub-contracting orders and purchase requisitions. The algorithm of MPR takes into account the BOMs, the production routings, the inventory availability, as well as the lead times of the suppliers and sub-contractors.
A07.03.02	Sub-Contracting Orders Creation	Production Planning Dept.	The proposed orders and requisitions generated by the MRP are accepted by the Production Planner, changed or rejected by the production planner who must take into account soft company-related issues. The result of the activity is the creation of sub-contracting orders, which are automatically forwarded to the buyer of the Purchasing Department through the Existing ERP system.
A07.03.03	Sub-Contracting Orders Grouping	Purchasing Dept.	The buyer of the Purchasing Department collects the sub-contracting orders and groups them accordingly based on the common requirements and the demanded dates of delivery.
A07.03.04	Sub-Contracting Orders Release	Purchasing Dept.	The buyer of the Purchasing Department generates the proposed sub-contracting orders, which are released after the approve of the Purchase Manager. The sub-contracting orders are sent by e-mail to the sub-contractor with an automatic process through the ERP system.

APPENDIX B

Table 2. Risks & controls repository for the activities of the supply chain process (process a07.03)

Activity	Risk	Risk Assessment	Control
A07.03.01 Material Requirements Planning	The algorithm used is not the appropriate one, generating wrong sub-contracting proposed orders	Low Risk	C07.03-01 Check of the material requirements planning algorithm
A07.03.01 Material Requirements Planning	The algorithm used does not use accurate master data, generating wrong sub-contracting proposed orders	Medium Risk	C07.03-02 Check on the accuracy of master data: ■ Material Master ■ Bills of Materials ■ Routings ■ Vendor Master
A07.03.02 Sub-Contracting Orders Creation	No formal sub-contracting orders are generated and sub-contracting is carried out on an ad-hoc basis	Low Risk	C07.03-03 Check of the generated sub-contracting orders
A07.03.03 Sub-Contracting Orders Grouping	Grouping is not carried out in order to collect all the sub-contracting orders related to the same sub-contractor	High Risk	C07.03-04 Control of the sub-contracting orders grouping process

Activity	Risk	Risk Assessment	Control
A07.03.04 Sub-Contracting Orders Release	The proposed sub-contracting orders delay to be transformed to released orders	Low Risk	C07.03-05 Check on the lead time of the transformation from order creation to order release
A07.03.05 Generation of Picking Lists	The necessary material for transportation to the sub-contractor is not collected	Low Risk	C07.03-06 Check of the transformation routine of the released orders to picking lists
A07.03.06 Material Collection	The materials included in the picking lists are not collected	Medium Risk	C07.03-07 Check the physically collected materials compared with the picking list
A07.03.06 Material Collection	Different materials from these on the packing lists are collected	Medium Risk	C07.03-08 Check the physically collected materials compared with the picking list
A07.03.07 Generation of Delivery Note	The delivery note quantities do not agree with the real quantities	Medium Risk	C07.03-09 Check of the delivery notes accuracy
A07.03.08 Loading & Transportation	The wrong materials have been loaded to the track for delivery to the sub-contractor	Medium Risk	C07.03-10 Check of the loaded quantities compared to the quantities of the delivery notes
A07.03.09 Material Storage	The materials stored in the sub-contractor's warehouse cannot be monitored in the IT system of the company	Low Risk	C07.03-11 Monitoring of the available inventory in the sub-contractor's premises through the IT system and physical counting
A07.03.10 Production	The production process is not the agreed one	High Risk	C07.03-12 Production process walk-through
A07.03.11 Follow-up of the Final Products Delivery Date	The agreed delivery dates are not kept	High Risk	C07.03-13 Check of the operation of the follow-up activity
A07.03.11 Follow-up of the Final Products Delivery Date	The service level agreement of the contract with the sub-contractor are not kept	High Risk	C07.03-14 Check of the existing service level agreements in the contracts with the sub-contractors
A07.03.12 Delivery of Final Products & Material Leftovers	Delivery is not performed according to the conditions agreed with the sub-contractor	Medium Risk	C07.03-15 Check of the delivery conditions compared with the conditions agreed with the sub-contractor
A07.03.13 Goods Receipt	The products quantities do not agree with the quantities expected	Medium Risk	C07.03-16 Check of the quantities delivered compared with the quantities ordered
A07.03.13 Goods Receipt	The returned raw materials do not agree with the quantities expected based on the BOMs	High Risk	C07.03-17 Check of the quantities returned compared with the quantities that should be returned according to BOMs
A07.03.13 Goods Receipt	The products and raw material delivered do not agreed with the quantities of the delivery note	High Risk	C07.03-18 Check of the quantities delivered compared with the quantities of the delivery note
A07.03.14 Systemic Goods Receipt	The sub-contracting orders do not close	High Risk	C07.03-19 Check on the status of the sub-contracting orders in the IT system
A07.03.14 Systemic Goods Receipt	Costing of the final products is not accurate	High Risk	C07.03-20 Check of the final product costing process
A07.03.14 Systemic Goods Receipt	The real material and product movements are not accurately transferred to the Information System	High Risk	C07.03-21 Check of material movement transactions and inventory locations accuracy
A07.03.15 Quality Assurance	Quality assurance is not performed	High Risk	C07.03-22 Check of the quality assurance process
A07.03.15 Quality Assurance	The quality of sub-contracting work is not satisfactory	High Risk	C07.03-23 Check of the quality problems of the final products

Activity	Risk	Risk Assessment	Control
A07.03.15 Quality Assurance	Claims are not performed for problematic products	High Risk	C07.03-24 Check of the claims process for problematic situations recognised by quality assurance
A07.03.16 Statistics Generation for Sub-Contractor Performance	Statistics are not generated for sub-contractor performance	Low Risk	C07.03-25 Check on the existence of statistics analysis of former sub-contractors performance
A07.03.16 Statistics Generation for Sub-Contractor Performance	Statistics generated for sub-contractor performance are not accurate	Medium Risk	C07.03-26 Check of the statistics generation process
A07.03.17 Sub-Contractor Evaluation	Sub-contracting evaluation is not performed	High Risk	C07.03-27 Check on the adherence of the company to the evaluation process
A07.03.17 Sub-Contractor Evaluation	The criteria used for sub-contractor evaluation are not set properly	Medium Risk	C07.03-28 Check on the criteria used for the evaluation of the sub-contractor performance
A07.03.17 Sub-Contractor Evaluation	Claims are not monitored in order to be used for sub-contractor evaluation	High Risk	C07.03-29 Check of the claims process and monitoring of the claims value

APPENDIX C

Table 3. Audit programme example for the supply chain process (high risks)

Control Code	Control Name	Control Description Text
C07.03-04	Control of the sub-contracting orders grouping process	For three different days of the last three months, where sub-contracting orders have been created, the groupings created are checked compared with the existing released orders.
C07.03-12	Production process walk-through	For two active sub-contractors, a thorough walk-through of the production process in their premises is carried out in order to confirm the agreed production process. Available documentation for the sub-contractors' production process as well as the necessary master data must be used.
C07.03-13	Check of the operation of the follow-up activity	For all the sub-contracting orders of five selected days, the information completed in the IT system by the purchasing department during the follow-up activity is checked.
C07.03-14	Check of the existing service level agreements in the contracts with the sub-contractors	For all the existing contracts with sub-contractors, the existence of specific service level agreements is checked. Then, for ten different cases of follow-up, it is checked whether the follow-up process was performed promptly.
C07.03-17	Check of the quantities returned compared with the quantities that should be returned according to BOMs	For five cases of goods received, the quantities of returned material are confirmed compared to these included in the BOMs. In the case of differences of more than five percent, further investigation in co-operation with the sub-contractor is carried out in order to identify possible changes in the production orders or data entry errors.
C07.03-18	Check of the quantities delivered compared with the quantities of the delivery note	Real-time check in five cases of goods receipt is performed in order to check the accuracy of the information included in the delivery notes and the execution of the appropriate activities by the employees in the case of differences.
C07.03-19	Check on the status of the sub-contracting orders in the IT system	For three selected dates (one being the date of control), the existing open sub-contracting orders are identified. From these, the ones that should have been closed are identified.

Control Code	Control Name	Control Description Text
C07.03-20	Check of the final product costing process	For five different cases of products, the cost calculation of the previous month is examined. Special care is needed to be taken in order to find out that the cost of sub-contracting is added to the final products.
C07.03-21	Check of material movement transactions and inventory locations accuracy	In five cases of goods receipts by sub-contractors, the related material movements are checked and the inventory levels are monitored. Moreover, for three selected cases, inventory balances are checked in order to identify possible negative inventories.
C07.03-22	Check of the quality assurance process	Real-time check in five cases of goods receipt is performed in order to check the conformance with the existing ISO process of quality assurance that must be followed in every case of goods receipt.
C07.03-23	Check of the quality problems of the final products	In five real-time checks, the process of quality assurance is checked concerning the quality assurance buffer, the sampling, the marking and the recording of the results.
C07.03-24	Check of the claims process for problematic situations recognised by quality assurance	In two real-time checks with quality problems, the process of generation of claims is checked.
C07.03-27	Check on the adherence of the company to the evaluation process	Study of the evaluation files of three sub-contractors in order to check the adherence of the company to the evaluation process.
C07.03-29	Check of the claims process and monitoring of the claims value	The value of claims of the last six months grouped by sub-contractor is analysed with the check of the related report. In two real-time checks with quality problems, the process of generation of claims is checked.

Chapter 14

Avoiding Risks Related with Strategic Pricing in Virtual Enterprise Networks:
An Agent Based Approach

Christos Manolarakis
Athens Information Technology, Greece

Ioannis T. Christou
Athens Information Technology, Greece

Gregory Yovanof
Athens Information Technology, Greece

ABSTRACT

In this chapter we describe an effort to capture market dynamics of consumer products via Agent-based Models and apply the findings in the context of risk management focused in Virtual Enterprise Networks. The developed tool can help significantly leverage risks associated with price wars, or other aggressive strategies the players in a given market may choose to follow. It can also significantly improve purchasing/procurement and production planning decisions by better estimating (for the short-term of course) the variability in demand that will be experienced by a new price for a given product, thus optimizing supply chain operations and minimizing the logistics risks often associated with marketing campaigns. Finally, the tool can also be used to estimate the short-term profitability and break-even point for a proposed new product introduced by a Virtual Enterprise in an existing market, information that greatly minimizes risks related to the introduction of new products in the market, and then to estimate the optimal introductory price for the new product.

INTRODUCTION

Analysis of complex systems and decision making in such complex environments as today's volatile markets is an extremely demanding challenge in terms of data required, processes and personnel, with results often really founded on little more than the top decision maker's instincts. Tools for monitoring and studying interacting behaviors of system components could, therefore, possibly

DOI: 10.4018/978-1-61520-607-0.ch014

provide a better insight into the market dynamics at least for the short-term (Gilbert, 2008). The aim of the research described in this chapter is to support enterprises participating in a Virtual Enterprise venture (or a Supply Chain network) in assessing their strategic pricing process and thus relax all (or some of) the risks inherent in the pricing function. Virtual Enterprises (VE) arose as a prominent trend in the notion of cooperative synergies among businesses. A business formation may be outsourcing cooperative schemes leveraging the power of supply chains or even business consortiums sharing common vision or market targets (Camarinha et al., 2007). The use of Agent Based Modeling Systems (ABMS) techniques to represent such formations is widely used in the literature as a means of absorption of the inhering complexity which includes knowledge transfer, cooperative strategic decisions and information sharing.

ABMS is essentially a tool for managing complex systems by using advanced techniques such as mathematical modeling and discrete-event simulation to produce a new way to discover strategic, tactical and operational business solutions (North et. al., 2007). The basic advantage of Agent Based Modeling in comparison to the existing traditional modeling techniques such as statistical modeling, risk analysis, optimization, or system dynamics, is that it can capture non linear interactions that are common in the problems addressed in the industries and markets without having to explicitly consider the underlying mathematical structure that governs the system behavior. Emergent behavior is after all, an aggregate result of usually non-linear interactions. Another major advantage of ABMS is that it can be used to investigate not only what happened in a given business situation but also what might have happened. Once an Agent Based Model has been tuned to capture the real–life events that occurred in the immediate past, it can be used for sensitivity analysis by running what–if scenarios with slight perturbations of one or more of the

world parameters of the model. The ability to build what-if scenarios is of fundamental importance to making business decisions both in the short and in the medium term. Uncovering unexpected issues through a trial and error process in real life may be extremely costly or simply infeasible. Agent models on the other hand, can be used to quickly explore many different possibilities in order to select the "best" one found.

In order to support the pricing functions of a VE or SCN, we designed and built a configurable simulation environment for running what-if scenarios in consumer product markets with well-established dynamics. Consumer product sales estimates are derived from major e-commerce sites' sales-ranking data, and these distributions are then fed to the agent-based simulation environment so as to derive a consumer behavior model for the given market. The system utilizes a Simulated Annealing process to learn the optimal parameters determining the consumers' perceptual value distribution. Once the system has learned a set of parameters that accurately predict the sales distribution for the given market, it can be used as a strategic forecasting tool, in predicting market share or revenue growth in the face of price changes in any of the competing products in the market. We demonstrate the use of the tool in two case-studies of consumer electronics products. One case-study, that of the MP3 player market was chosen as a ground-truth validation test-case, because the dynamics of this market have been studied fairly well and the market reached its equilibrium state some time ago, meaning that any tool for supporting decision making regarding pricing in this market should give results close to the actual stable empirical observations that have been collected for this market. The second case-study, namely the smart-phones market, was selected because one of the major players in this market, Nokia, exhibits many characteristics of a Virtual Enterprise in its organization, while at the same time it is a company known for its exceptional supply chain management. Nokia's handling of the fire at the Philips microchip plant in Alburquerque, New Mexico, in 2000, the now classic case of supply chain disruption, has changed forever the dynamics of the mobile phone industry. And, while the fire affected both Ericsson, the Swedish manufacturer that kept the lead in the mobile phone market at the time, and Nokia, both companies took a very different approach toward the incident, and in hindsight, clearly displayed how to and how not to handle supply chain disruptions. As a result of that, the incident turned disaster cost the Swedish company $400 million in lost sales, and it had to quit the mobile-phone business, leaving Nokia to cement its position as the European (and, subsequently, global) market leader.

BACKGROUND

The industry and especially businesses that produce consumer products are always eager to discover patterns and triggers that drive and influence consumer behavior. By acquiring such information, better strategic decisions can be made that efficiently capture the various behavioral schemes consumers exhibit. The decision to buy a product -especially when this is offered in a fully competitive market- is an inherently complex process, as the consumer faces a number of external factors which must be taken into consideration, and accordingly inline those with their preferences. Consumer behavior analysis is a branch of micro-economic theory that targets precisely this problem, and attempts to explain –in a broad sense- how consumers behave, assuming some *rationality hypotheses* hold. To deal with those complex interactions, researchers started using agent-based models to represent consumer entities as agents.

Janseen and Jager (1999) used agent based models to describe the so called "lock-in" phenomenon, a situation where a specific technology or product dominates in a certain market so that

the customers *perceive* that they are locked and no longer have a "switch" option to buy products offered by competitor sellers. Obvious examples of companies whose products at least for some time reached lock-in position are Microsoft Windows, Microsoft Office, Sony camcorders etc. Also, lock-in effects exist for combinations of products from the same vendor; for example, the camera bodies of many camera vendors will only work with lenses manufactured from the camera body vendor and their partners. The Lock-in effect essentially creates such high barriers to entry for competitors, that the seller of the lock-in product/ service obtains an effective monopoly position in the market. The simulation model developed follows a cellular automata approach in order to describe the local interactions of agents, so the consumption is a cellular automation process. Two problem instances are examined such as the "lock-in" effect for similar products and the same for alternative products. The results of their survey offer some insights about the lock-in patterns' occurrences, both globally and for spatial lock-ins of the consumats (the term used in their research to map the consumers).

Chevalier et al (2002) used publicly available data on the sales ranks of about 20,000 books to derive quantity proxies at the two leading online booksellers, Amazon.com and Barnes & Noble's. By mapping the gathered information to the corresponding prices they estimated elasticities for the demand faced by both sellers along with a consumer price index for the online books. The results revealed spectacular changes to price sensitivity and the bias of the retailed based books CPI index due to the introduction of online bookstores. In our research we approach actual sales estimation using similar techniques and assumptions including the gathering of sales rank data of the MP3 and smartphones devices respectively along with the distributional assumption made in order to feasibly transform sales ranking data into actual sales.

Agent based modeling techniques were used

in the study of Izquierdo and Izquierdo (2007) to explore consumer behavior under the effects of market quality and variability. The core of the study though is not the exploration of the reasons that drive the consumer behavior but to illustrate how quality uncertainty may harm markets, ending in market failure. The core agents used in their model include the seller agents and buyer agents. Both of them in each session may have unary interaction in terms of products exchanged. The sellers have a minimum sales price so in each trading session the seller offers her items only if the price for the product is equal or higher in comparison to minimum set. On the other hand the buyer entities are based on a reservation price and a multiplier, representing the buyer's expected quality for the product, which shapes the demand function. By applying certain rules to extract the quality perceived by the buyers for specific products according to their past experiences, as well as the perceptions of others in their social network, the authors conclude with some useful propositions about individual learning in dynamic models. Furthermore the authors verified the commonsense intuition that quality expectations for a product may vary among buyers and moreover, that their individual past experiences in combination with product quality variability may hurt market sales. On the other hand, information sharing among buyers through social networks, may decrease those damage effects in the market as buyers with low esteem for a certain product may reevaluate their positioning against product's quality due to their social links.

In our study we expand such techniques not only to simulate the behavior of the input system and extract its characteristics but also to develop a supportive tool for risk management in Virtual Enterprise networks. Currently, there have been recognized four types of risks in Virtual Enterprise Networks (Hudsal, 2009), which include supply-side risks, operational risks, external risks and demand-side risks. We are mostly dealing with the last type of risks considering that understanding

the way consumers perceive products or services offered can further explain demand fluctuation or reactions and thus improve risk management related with the demand-side of a VE.

PREDICTING DEMAND VIA CONSUMER PERCEPTION ANALYSIS

The VE concept was one of the most successful ones among several business organizational models that the information era brought along with the spread of the business activities globally and the multi dimensional competition. One of the main benefits that the VE model has brought about is the fact that virtual entrepreneurship entails lesser risk for the individual firm since risk is spread across the network (Cardoso et al., 2005). The advantages are major, as interacting businesses share entrepreneurial accommodation at the same time that they preserve their unique business identity and competencies. They deal with constant change and disruptive innovation by shaping new strategic schemas and partnerships.

In this particular work we aim to provide a VE with information containing a *detailed description of how a product or service is perceived by customers and what would be any probable reactions market wise (buy versus not buy) regarding changes in price, technology or even design.* Provision of behavioral and adoption data associated with specific products and services may increase the effectiveness of business decisions on behalf of the VE and further lead to risk minimization for new to the market product launches. Having such information on hand, decision makers can determine optimal pricing policies for the products produced by the VE. On the other hand, without such information, a decision maker can make catastrophic decisions, for example by raising the price of the product at the same time that demand is elastic and a competitor adds more features to their product and lowers their price, thus stripping the decision maker of a significant portion of their prior market share.

There are many examples of products or services that became success stories or they were pushed to exit because of their positioning. Positioning of products and services plays a critical role in the marketing strategy that a company pursues and every decision regarding that should be considered strategic. Abstractly seen, the term "Product Positioning" or "Market Positioning [of a product/service]" refers to the place or position a product or service occupies in the consumer's mind. Usually it is related to the concept of differentiation, as it's not rare that two similar products (brands) can hold distinctive position in the consumer's mind and that is where the strategic character of the term lies. Furthermore the way a brand will be positioned affects subsequently the entire vector's parameters specific to a product or services including pricing, distribution channels and marketing decisions.

Consumers buy products in most cases by deciding on the basis of two pillar parameters, namely what is cheaper, or better. But defining "better" without bias is very hard most of the times, as the product's physical characteristics are not always those that determine the threshold of a decision to buy. This is the essence of branding, which in turn is what marketing is all about. Thus we understand that differentiation and the root strategies that drive it play the pivotal role in shaping in the consumer's mind what constitutes "better".

The core of positioning lies on the notion of market segmentation. Consumers usually can be segmented to different cohorts according to their different needs and wants and their different expectations from a product or service. Positioning aims at grouping together specific products or services in appropriate segments of population so that each specific segment's needs and requirements are met by the products within that segment. As a result for a specific need, there are multiple products that are positioned differently and may

differ in physical terms or simply perceptually (as a result of strong branding campaigns). The distinction in physical terms, taking an example from the automobile industry, may refer to four wheel drive vehicles that mostly serve the need for off road driving in comparison to the common two wheel drive vehicles of low horsepower which serve mostly the need for cheap transportation. As we can see the same industry produces products that from a broad aspect serve as means of transport but their physical differences conclude in a different positioning to the corresponding market segments.

Although physical positioning plays a stellar role in the product's success to meet the needs and wants of the consumers it may not always be the prominent factor. As it was mentioned above, positioning is the overall perception that the consumer draws in their mind for a specific product or service. Sometimes consumers don't even know or are interested to know of a chosen product's special characteristics as their selection is based on the perception that the selected product (regardless of its internal characteristics) is better for them. In most cases the decision to buy is heavily influenced by the presentation layer of the product (the product's marketing campaign and strategy). The brand together with look-and-feel features including packaging, are often the factors that push the customers to buy one product over the other. Thus a successful marketing campaign may position differently the exact same product in terms of emphasizing different physical characteristics and make it a "blockbuster".

In order to achieve a successful product positioning, marketers should first determine the bundle of competitive products that already exist in the market they want to enter or reposition. Then they should determine the attributes vector of perception influencing factors for the specific products and collect perceptions from customers for already existing products or similar products for knowledge gathering. All the above steps in combination with the current position of the product (if already exists) assemble in the so called perceptual grid which is a mapping of the perceptual based classification of product or service taxonomies regarding a specific need (Mullins et al. (2006).

In order to generate and depict the perceptual mapping, consumer perception regarding an attributes vector is gathered per product or its representative brand. Then the results are depicted versus a two dimensional grid (in the case of a bi-attribute vector) or in a multidimensional grid. The graphical output creates a perceptual map, which can be used as a driver to product positioning for new entries or repositioning of already existing products. While building the perceptual map, considering price as one of the two or more attributes may result in an uninformative perceptual grid if all products have the same price, something that may happen only in a perfectly competitive market. In our case studies, we have seen that price gaps between the selected products were significant and influential to the buyers' decision.

There are many benefits from using perceptual mapping. They help recognize market segments regarding the specific attributes. Having the segments-specified clusters of brands or products evolve may indicate the best medians to position the product in the cluster or the segment. Furthermore, the representation of the market competition for the specific perceptual attributes gives a reasonable picture of the existing competitive landscape, i.e. the positions of the competitors and their strength. The analysis of the perceptual grid ends with a well stated product positioning statement followed by specific value proposition. Marketers who do not consider the described process often end-up in product ill-positioning, value proposition overlapping in comparison to already existing products and sometimes to the cannibalization (if not purposely) of their own products. In this study we try to offer a comprehensive tool that can help marketing decision makers understand product positioning by integrating

consumer product perception information with actual sales estimated data.

In the following, we describe the details of the algorithms used to infer demand for a particular product under competition from close (but not perfect) substitutes.

AGENT-BASED MODELING AND SIMULATION

In this work, our methodology for system representation is based on the use of Agent Based Modeling. Although agent based models are widely used in the literature of virtual enterprises to represent the interconnections and interactions amongst business entities (agent) for our research we use it to represent the surrounding shell of the VE's which is the market and specifically the consumers, regarding the perceptual positioning of product and services. Agent Based Modeling and Simulation, as already stated in the introduction, is a well established technique used to represent the operational characteristics of systems and furthermore to create knowledge based on this representation. The creation of knowledge is the cumulative result between complexity and its analysis under the ABMS notion. But how can ABMS deal with complexity and create value on that?

The new trends that are currently encountered in most organizations include mass usage of information technology, new ways to manage inventories, the verticality of the production schemes along with expansion and globalization; these trends create a complex to manage and operate system. Consequently, the markets where these organizations participate are getting all the more complex by diminishing the analytical capabilities of the traditional tools. Many times leaders failed to make the right choices because unexpected interactions within their decision space took place. Thus there is an obvious need to capture or draw behaviors or facts that may emerge through complex and/or unexpected interactions.

The concept of ABMS combines a number of science disciplines including object oriented programming (OOP) and discrete event simulation. The latter is used to describe a sequence of events under a simulation concept while object oriented programming represents the programmable entities as objects with specific attributes and relations. ABMS uses rules that create the framework under which its components interact. Sometimes ABMS is confused with Artificial Intelligence (AI). AI aims in creating artifacts that exhibit intelligent behavior, whereas ABMS may use those artifacts as its constituent parts of the developed framework (Weiss, 1999). Introducing agent based modeling as an analysis tool can capture information in a fine grained level. Furthermore ABMS can support different levels of decision making especially when those decisions have to be taken in fast changing environments.

Agents are individual entities that exhibit specific behavior and have certain responsibilities. They are able to learn and adapt their behavior accordingly (Wooldridge et. Al., 1995). The adaptation is produced when agents process the incoming information or when they interact with other agents. The construction of an agent based model is the most prominent part as it provides the base source of information of the expected so –called emergent phenomena. Wrong perception of the system being modeled or corrupted knowledge about agents along with lack of supportive data may lead to wrong conclusions and consequently the model will not be validated. Thus, basic prerequisites for every modeler are the concentration of all the available data about the system being modeled and valid information about the possible interactions between agents if any exist.

Each agent is declared OOP-wise as an object with specific attributes, variables and behaviors. The attributes can be considered as the constant characteristics of the agent (e.g. age, profession, marital status). Variables may change their value,

as they are declarative factors of the status or the condition of each corresponding agent. The behavior supports the logic of the agent and is triggered by a variety of events, which may or may not include interaction with other agents. One of the major triggering factors in agent based modeling is randomness. Like real life situation when many events are triggered by random event alike in agent based modeling randomness is used to cover such scenario or in some other cases to fill the gap of the lack of data. Random generation also is very supportive to the notion that the majority of the decisions made are probabilistic. The combination between attributes and variables takes place only when the underlying logic is modeled.

An agent can be triggered either by internal or external events or factors. For example suppose that we are modeling demand for products with high demand elasticity. Consider also an external parameter / factor called "economic crisis" to enter the system. What we expect from the consumer agents is to sharply drop demand for those products as their demand is very elastic and subject to economic cycle perturbations. In most cases the scope of external factors is global and affects the majority of the agents in the model. Furthermore agents may trigger new or different behavior by internal factors or events. Such factors are mainly part of each agent's profile and may be for example the preference vector for a specific category of products. In our research we use such internal factors as determinants of the agent's decision to buy. Internal factors actually can be seen under the hood of utility function. The bigger the outcome of the utility function from a resulting state the bigger the preference of the agent to stay at that state.

There are many examples of a wide use of agent-based models. In most developed countries the deregulation of the electricity markets by their privatization led to the need of models able to handle the new operational scheme. Many supply firms bid into a market under a new regulatory framework. The models developed so far are trying to anticipate the resulting effects so as to guarantee smooth inter-actions between electricity suppliers and purchasers to check or predict price changes or to control the environmental impact of such change.

The simulations are able to represent the day to day transactional activities between the stakehold-ers that generate new strategies and learn from the past. Some of the techniques that those models use include reinforcement learning, which actually enables the agent to find the policy that maximizes its utility. More specifically, in the case of the electricity markets the supplier agents by defining a pricing scheme to follow from a pre configured list bid their price for a certain amount of electricity supply. If the purchasing agents accept this bid, the strategy is tagged with a specific probability that increases if the specific choice turns to be profitable in similar circumstances or decreases when the opposite effects are considered.

There are many ad-hoc programming tools that support the development of agent based models. Those include object oriented program-ming languages such as Java, Objective C, C#, C++ along with a number o hybrid languages designed for agent modeling including Repast, Netlogo, Starlogo, JADE, Mason and many oth-ers. Whatever language the modeler would select to develop the model the following features of the component agents should be met in order to be characterized as an Agent Based Model. The agents should exhibit:

- *Memory: The agents should remember pre-vious states and consider their preferences and perceptions before acting.*
- *Performance: The agents should be equipped with a set of behaviors able to per-form which include*
- *Motion:* The ability to move within the in-teraction space
- *Communication:* Agents should be able to send and receiving messages, thus interact-ing between each others.
- *Action: Translated either in motion or*

communication or both.
- *Perception: Having a feeling of their actual state and their surrounding environment.*
- *Policy: In game theory a policy is defined by the set of possible actions on behalf of the policy carrier. Likewise, agents are car-riers of such policies including strategic decisions that aim to maximize their utility function. Policies include specific rules and heuristics given their specific presentation and history.*

DATA SOURCES, DATA GATHERING & ALGORITHMIC TECHNIQUES

In Virtual Enterprises, information exchange is a critical success factor for the overall network. Network business entities should be provided with current and valid information to drive them to reliable and robust decision making actions. As mentioned in the previous section our research effort aims to provide a robust informational framework that captures and propagates customer product perception behavior.

In order to describe and model customers' mar-ket perception, we customized a number of data mining techniques to feed and further train some ad hoc algorithmic procedures. The data gathering process was one of our major impediments to that direction as consumer product detailed statistics is highly nontrivial to obtain. In the absence of such data, we experimented with web mining techniques in order to get the required information implicitly by extracting data distributional patterns from products' popularity in e-commerce sites.

The most common metric of product popular-ity publicly exposed is the sales ranking metric of a product in a particular e-commerce web site. We used this metric in our research, extracting it using web-mining techniques in combination with the available Amazon's web services APIs. Amazon.com provides web services that clients can consume to get all the information needed to extract sales ranking for each product they are interested. Thus, by submitting each product's unique identifier, which can be found under the ASIN notation in the product's linked page, it is possible to acquire the desired information by parsing the XML document returned by the API. By automating the script to run every one-hour (according to Amazon's information update policy for popular items) a statistically significant amount of hourly sales ranking data can be accumulated. In the following paragraph we expand our description of mining Amazon's mass data sources by focusing on components reference constituting Amazon's Web-Services and further explanation of the data extraction process.

SPECIFIC DETAILS ON MINING CONSUMER DEMAND AND PERCEPTIONS USING AMAZON WEB SERVICES

The typical user interface for anyone who purchases products through Amazon.com includes a page with product description and a bundle of special information such as price, sales ranking, reviews and its classification product wise. All these product descriptive data are publicly available via Amazon Web Services which is a bundle of services, a suite targeting a variety of distinct areas of interest. The suite includes the following major services:

1. Amazon E-Commerce Service (ECS) exposes Amazon's product data and e-commerce functionality. This allows developers, web site owners and merchants to leverage the data and functionality that Amazon uses to power its own e-commerce business.
2. Amazon Historical Pricing Web service gives developers programmatic access to over three years of sales data for books, music, videos, and DVDs (as sold by third-party sellers on Amazon.com). Sellers can use Amazon Historical Pricing to make informed decisions on pricing and purchasing.
3. Amazon Mechanical Turk provides a Web services API for computers to integrate Artificial Intelligence directly into their processing.
4. Alexa Web Information Service provides developers with a platform able to host requests for historical usage data of web sites and related to them links. The service is offered under charge in a pay as you go basis.
5. Amazon Simple Queue Service used to offer a scalable-hosted queue for buffering messages between distributed application components.

The study documented here used the ECS 4.0 service to retrieve the desired information. Although there are already APIs offered by Amazon that help developers to access the desired information for the purposes of the specific study we developed proprietary code that gave us all the toolset needed to parse XML format-based information exposed through Amazon's web services.

At a high level, the web mining process we applied can be described as follows. We first define the array of products that is of interest to us and for which we want to collect real time sales rank information. Then we iterate through all the array elements, and for each element, the procedure calls the specific web service from Amazon found at http://webservices.amazon.com/onca/xml?Service=AWSECommerceService&SubscriptionId=<UserUniqueIdentifierobtainedbyregisteringintheAWS>&Operation=ItemLookup&ItemId=<Oneoftheselectedproducts>&ResponseGroup=SalesRank

The returned page is broken down by reading the XML elements using a parser that implements SAX (chosen as a model because of its speed) by also defining a number a special call back functions to handle events during parsing. The parsed information is stored (actually the sales rank and the time stamp) and then transformed to an approximation of the actual sales figures following the process described in the beginning of the next section.

Whether the offered APIs are used directly, or within proprietary code developed for that purpose, there are two major steps to be taken to access that information. The first prerequisite to gain access to the specific services is an account creation in the Amazon Web Services site (aws. amazon.com). The account creation is followed by a unique assignment of access key identifiers which are the keys to uniquely identify the sender of a request to the AWS web service. As already mentioned before, the Amazon E-commerce service exposes massive amounts of data about all the items sold through Amazon's site in all of its locales. The Amazon Web sites enable product sales from Amazon plus many other vendors. The products available through the Amazon E-Commerce Service (ECS) draw from this huge inventory and include a majority of the products available on an Amazon Web site. ECS is available for all of the Amazon sites: US (amazon. com),UK (amazon.co.uk),Germany (amazon. de), Japan (amazon.co.jp), France (amazon.fr), Canada (amazon.ca).

ACTUAL PRODUCT SALES APPROXIMATION

As mentioned previously the metric used to gain a reliable data approximation was Amazon's sales rank. *Sales rank is the number of products in the specific product segment or category that are positioned higher (in sales rank) in comparison to the actual position of the selected product.* Thus a sales rank #345 of product "A" in Electronics means that there are 344 products that exhibit more sales than "A" in that segment. One major task is then to translate the observed sales ranking of each product into a measure of sales quantity. To do so,

we need to know the probability distribution of the products' sales-rank. A standard distributional assumption for this type of rank data is a Pareto distribution. If X is a random variable that follows a Pareto distribution (Brakman et al.,1999), then the probability that X is greater than some number x is given by Eq. 1

$$\Pr\{X > x\} = \left(\frac{x}{x_m}\right)^{-k} \tag{1}$$

for all $x \geq x_m$, where x_m is the (necessarily positive) minimum possible value of X, and k is a positive parameter. The most important parameter is k, the shape parameter that indicates the relative frequency of large observations. If k is 2, for example, the probability of an event decreases in the square of the size. With a value of 1, it decreases linearly.

In order to estimate the sales of each device from its Sales-Rank, assuming the distribution of product sales in the "Electronics" category of Amazon follows the Pareto distribution, *we compute for each device, the sales volume that is most likely to yield the rank that is observed for the device.* Assuming therefore that a device has rank r, in a category that has D products and follows a Pareto distribution with parameters x_m, k we seek to find the sales volume x_p that maximizes the probability that there are exactly r products with higher sales than x_p and D-r products with sales less than x_p. This probability is computed as

$$f(x) = \Pr\{X_1 > x \wedge \ldots X_r > x \wedge X_{r+1} \leq x \wedge \ldots X_D \leq x\} = \left[\left(\frac{x}{x_m}\right)^{-k}\right]^r \left[1 - \left(\frac{x}{x_m}\right)^{-k}\right]^{D-r}$$

To compute the maximizing value x_p we set the first derivative of $f(x)$ to zero, which yields

$$f'(x) = \frac{k}{x_m}\left[(D-r)\left(\frac{x}{x_m}\right)^{-kr-k-1}\left(1 - \left(\frac{x}{x_m}\right)^{-k}\right)^{D-r-1} - r\left(\frac{x}{x_m}\right)^{-kr-1}\left(1 - \left(\frac{x}{x_m}\right)^{-k}\right)^{D-r}\right] = 0$$

and solving for x we get $x^k = x_m^k \dfrac{D}{r}$ which gives the optimal estimated value for sales

$$x_p = x_m \left(\frac{D}{r} \right)^{\frac{1}{k}}$$

Notice that this implies that the maximizing value x_p satisfies $\Pr\{X > x\} = \dfrac{r}{D}$ which can be interpreted as follows: the best estimate for *the sales of a product that has rank r, is found by setting the probability of the sales being more than the estimate equal to the fraction of products with sales higher or equal to the product*. This statement is true *only* for a Pareto distribution, and not necessarily for other power-law distributions (e.g. Zipf distribution).

We now have to estimate the parameters of the Pareto distribution in the target category of Amazon. This is easily done when we know the sales of *any* two products in the particular category, by simply solving a resulting system of two non-linear equations with two unknowns $\left(x_m \text{ and } k \right)$. This results in an estimate of the market share for each product in the market categories. These estimates form the target sales distributions to be learnt from an Agent Model Simulation.

LEARNING THE STATISTICAL DISTRIBUTIONS THAT POSITION PRODUCTS ON THE CONSUMER PERCEPTUAL MAP

Having sales information for each product in a competitive market and a reasonable estimate of the value of each product's attribute – inferred from statistical analysis and other data-gathering techniques including web mining of reports, reviews, questionnaires etc.- leads to a reasonable positioning of each product on the perceptual map (grid).

However, this map by itself is not sufficient for answering important decision making problems such as the optimal pricing scheme that a company should adopt for its products. To answer such a question, one needs to know the elasticity of the market –even in the short-term. Market elasticity would be readily available if the underlying causes driving consumer behavior were known. We chose to model consumer behavior using as dimensions (major factors) the following product attributes: Brand loyalty (B), Features available (F), Price of the product (P), and Design of the product (D). The selection of the mentioned parameters was based on the frequency that each of them appeared in different device benchmarking and comparison sites used in the scope of our research. Regarding the price we followed the most prominent assumption that is considered in economics that consumers are rational. In the simplest possible scheme, we consider that the buyers' population is generated from a stochastic process that gives values to independent random variables characterizing each of these independent attributes. Each random variable follows a normal distribution whose parameters must be estimated. Then, according to our model, each consumer buys the product that is closest to their preference vector, assuming of course that it is close enough, and the distance between them does not exceed a threshold. Learning the parameters of each distribution, together with a rule that decides "which product is closest to a given customer preferences" is the next task to solve. Despite its simplicity, an analytical solution to this naïve problem does not exist. We resort to a combination of Agent-based Modeling and Simulation and Optimization techniques to solve this estimation problem. As there are several techniques for solving non-linear optimization problems, we mention in brief the most important ones. They are all search methods for locating a high-quality local optimum of a given objective function.

Table 1. Corresponding terminology in statistical physics and combinatorial/non-linear optimization (haykin, 1999)

Physics	Combinatorial/non-linear Optimization
Sample	Problem Instance
State	Configuration
Energy	Cost function
Temperature	Control parameter
Ground-State-Energy	Minimum cost
Ground-State-Configuration	Optimal Configuration

Simulated Annealing

Simulated annealing is well known technique suitable for solving combinatorial and non-linear optimization problems. The target is, as always, to minimize the cost function of a system that may exhibit multiple local optima. The simulated annealing algorithm was inspired from metallurgy and more specifically resembles the way metals restructure via the annealing process. At high temperatures, when metals are in liquid condition the system is considered to be in a disordered state. As the metal goes through the annealing process and the temperature is falling (cooling) the system approaches to the lowest possible energy state. Thus the system ends to a frozen ground for T=0 which is translated to the thermodynamic equilibrium point. In theory, given enough iterations and a slow enough cooling schedule, the algorithm converges to the global optimum. The operational description of the process has as follows.

Given that the system is in a thermodynamic energy state E at temperature T, the annealing process perturbs it, resulting in a new energy state. If the change in the energy dE is negative the new state is accepted, otherwise it's accepted with a probability given by the Boltzmann's factor $e^{-dE/T}$. The above process is repeated, and every time the temperature decrements according to an annealing schedule, until the end point of T=0 is reached. In the algorithm, the thermodynamic energy state must be replaced with the value of the user function to optimize. In the table below we show the correspondence between statistical physics and combinatorial optimization; the algorithmic description follows.

Genetic Algorithms

The family of search algorithms/heuristics which essentially attempt to optimize a function by evaluating and modifying a current candidate set can be related with many scientific disciplines such as statistical physics and biology. The most representative such combination between biology and local heuristics is the research area known as Genetic Algorithms (GA). The main components of a Genetic Algorithm are the population of abstract representation of potential solutions that result in a set of possible or candidate solution. Genetic Algorithms aim to find better solutions amongst the previously mentioned candidate solutions (Whitley,1994). Genetic algorithms generate randomly an initial population of individuals that constitute a generation, in a parallelism to biology. The algorithm evaluates the fitness of each individual in the population according to pre-defined fitness function that has to be in a close correspondence to the actual cost function that one wishes to optimize. Based on the evaluation results, certain individuals from the current generation are selected for "mating" with a probability of selection proportional to their fitness (Schmitt et al.,2004)–in an analogy with

Figure 1. The simulated annealing algorithm

```
function SIMULATED ANNEALING (schedule) returns a solution state

Inputs: schedule, a hash representation of discrete time into temperature

local variables : current, a score in memory
                  next , a score in memory
                  T, the temperature that controls the downward probabilistic steps


current ← INITIAL_STATE
For t←1 to ∞ do
T← schedule(t)
If T=0 then return current
next ←a randomly selected successor of current
ΔE← VALUE[next]-VALUE[current]
If ΔE>0 then current ←next
else current ← next only with probability e^{-ΔE/T}
```

the principle of "natural selection" in the theory of evolution-, in which the selected individuals are recombined –using a mechanism known as crossover- and/or mutated, resulting in a new population or generation. The algorithm iterates using the newly generated population and continues until some stopping criteria are reached which may be the satisfaction of a threshold value in the fitness function or a specific number of iterations to have concluded.

Tabu Search

Another search algorithm belonging in the family of local search algorithms is Tabu Search (TS). Tabu Search is a meta-heuristic algorithm used to solve non-linear optimization problems. It was widely used in the field of operations research and is another alternative to hill climbing solutions (Cvijovic et al., 1995). The algorithm is based on the representation of the human short-term memory, and tracks a list of n visited states that cannot be visited again until a number of iterations is reached (Glover, 1994). This type of short-term memory is also called "recency-based" memory and the list that holds the visited states is called "tabu-list". Moving from one state to another is

usually based on a local search algorithm that has to respect however the tabu search procedure rules mentioned above.

Scatter Search

Finally, recent advancements in Tabu Search generated a variant called Scatter Search. The latter enables principles and strategies that are not included and applied by other evolutionary methods and exhibits great performance in the solution of complex optimization problems. To link scatter search with the as above described Tabu search we should underline the fact that they both share common characteristics. Specifically, scatter search makes use of the very successful notion of the short-term memory introduced in the TS. The major operational feature of the scatter search algorithm is that combines already existing solutions the so-called reference set to generate new ones (Glover, 1994). Every new solution is a linear combination of two other already existing solutions. The idea resembles the processes of combining decision rules in order to develop new strategies methodology widely used to solve the job shop category of scheduling problems. Furthermore, scatter search builds not only on the notion of combining rules but expands the idea to the combination of constraints. The new generated valid inequalities' descendants of the initial constraint set constitute the so-called surrogate constraints (Glover, 1977).

ALGORITHMIC DETAILS

The logic behind the developed algorithm is to provide managers and decision makers with a practical tool to apply a variety of business scenarios in the context of sensitivity analysis. Thus, the stakeholders may experiment with price perturbations and monitor the reaction of users to them given that the system has already trained and learned the distribution of user preferences on the basis of product perception. Providing decision makers with information regarding the elasticity of their market audience to price fluctuations, allows them to draw strategic decisions for new product positioning, effective pricing and stress testing of the market to different price levels for a specific product feature vector. Furthermore it could also help someone discover niches in an existing market as among other functionalities the system locates users on a perceptual map canvas. A detailed description of the system's operational characteristics follows.

The exact algorithm, shown in Figure 2 assumes that a customer (represented by an Agent in the model) buys the product that best matches his/her preferences where a match is computed as the weighted Root Mean Square (RMS) of differences between the customer's value of the product along each dimension and the overall rating of the product for the corresponding dimension. If the match value exceeds a certain threshold (to be computed by the algorithm) the agent does not buy the product. It is clear therefore, that many generated agents in the model won't buy any product, as they are all not good enough matches for their needs.

In each major iteration, the system computes a proposed Gaussian distribution for customers' perceptual values along each dimension –i.e. Brand Loyalty, Product Design, and Product Features- except (P)rice because it is assumed that when all else is equal, customers prefer lower price and so the distribution for price preferences of agents is $N(5,0.5)$ to account for some customers that may not choose a product on account of its cheap price (a phenomenon well established in literature, where consumers may not select a cheaper product in order to avoid being considered "stingy" by their friends and family). Therefore, the system randomly sets mean and standard deviation values for 3 distributions, each representing the distribution of consumer preferences for each attribute of the product. The system also sets randomly weights w_D, w_B, w_F and w_P for each dimension. Then, a fixed number of agents are generated and their perceptual values for the four product dimensions are drawn from the proposed Gaussian distribution for each dimension. Using these values, the agent finds the product that best matches their own attribute values, and if the match is close enough, they buy the product. After all agents have made a purchasing decision, the market share of each product is computed. This market-share distribution is then compared against the target distribution computed as described in paragraph 2.1, and the weighted RMSE score of the proposed distribution is computed. This score then serves as the objective function value for a Simulated Annealing procedure that attempts to learn the best parameters of the Gaussian Distributions for the three product dimensions considered together with the weights of these dimensions and the threshold for purchase decision; *the objective function is therefore a function of eleven variables corresponding to the distribution parameters and associated weights, and the threshold value for making a purchase.*

Once the system has learnt the optimal parameters that produce a market share distribution of

Figure 2. The perceptual market mapping (Per.Ma.Ma) algorithm

```
ALGORITHM PER.MA.MA
BEGIN
Read product defined ratings
IF is_experiment_run THEN
            IF exist changes in prices THEN
                        Apply changes
            ELSE
                        Use predefined ratings
            ENDIF
ELSE
            Use predefined ratings
ENDIF
            Open buffer streams
            Open writing streams
Empty global best memory, Empty scores memory, Empty parameters memory
Delete pointers vectors, output files
WHILE temperature > -1
            IF it is the first run THEN
                                    Initialize the distribution parameters
                        ELSE
                                    Add a randomly generated differential factor to each and every one of the distribution parameters
                        ENDIF
                        FOREACH customer-agent
                                    Trigger agent behavior
                                    Get the customer's rating
                                    Create an array of sums of the squared differences for all the products
                                    Take the minimum of them
                                    IF the minimum value <=1
                                                Buy the respective product
                                    ELSE
                                                Ignore the existing products
                                    ENDIF
                        ENDFOR
                        Get the fitting error as distances between observed sales & sales generated by the system
                        IF is-first-run THEN
                                    Set as best score the current score
                                    Insert results and parameters in the respective memory arrays parameters
                        ELSE
                                    IF new-score < score-in-memory THEN
                                                Replace the existing parameters in memory with
                                                these that the pointer of the specific score shows
                                                IF new-score< best-score THEN
                                                            Replace the global-best scores
                                                ENDIF
                                                ELSE
                                                IF random-uniform [0, 1]<exp(score in memory- new- score) / T THEN
                                                            Replace existing parameters in memory with
                                                            these that the pointer of the specific score shows
                                                ENDIF
                                                Decrease temperature by 1 degree
                                                IF temperature=1 THEN
                                                            Compare with the existing global best
                                                            IF new-score<global-best THEN
                                                                        Replace all parameters to point to these of the global best
                                                            ENDIF
                                                ENDIF
                                                Report the results and statistics
                                                Update histograms and graphics
                                    ENDIF
                        ENDIFELSE
            ENDIF
ENDWHILE
Report total results, Close buffer streams, Close writing streams
END
```

the various products that is close enough to the estimated one, the system can be used for what-if scenario analysis and risk management. In particular, the system user can modify the ratings along a product's dimensions (the most obvious being price) and see the effects of this change in the market-share and total sales in the model, by running an agent simulation with the given (learnt) parameters. For example, the user can reduce the price of one product by 10%, and see how elastic demand for the particular product is –in the face of no other changes in the market. Or, *the user can modify several ratings of more than one product at once and see the effect of all these simultaneous changes in the market-share distributions of the products, together with the effect on product profitability and sustainability.*

The software development was based on Netlogo (Wilensky, 2004) which is a cross-platform multi-agent programmable model environment (Gilbert, 2008) especially designed for implementing agent based modeling. Netlogo is enhanced with a graphical interface builder and advanced tools such as systems dynamics modeler. The model structure as any agent-based model developed in Netlogo consists of three parts. The first part includes the variables declaration and any agents' breeds that will be used for the model. The second part includes the setup procedure that is responsible for setting up the model environment before each execution by putting the system in its initial native state. Finally the execution part which includes all the procedures, those are responsible for the agents behavior and system updates as well as for the graphics and user-messages production.

The system also provides a real time updated graph of the sales per device, a reactive perceptual mapping and a distribution graph of customers in comparison to the price rating given; its Graphical User Interface is shown in figures 3 and 4.

JUSTIFICATION OF THE ALGORITHM

The model assumes that consumers' perceptions of the value of each product along each of the four dimensions (except for price dimension) considered can be modeled as random variables

*Figure 3. The **MP3 8GB** predicted market distribution after a hypothetical price-war where all players reduce prices significantly*

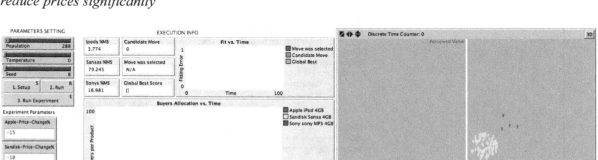

drawn from a Gaussian uni-variate distribution whose (μ, σ) parameters are to be determined. The algorithm implements a stochastic search for the optimal parameters of the distribution of customers along a multi-dimensional space assuming the independence and normality of the distribution of values along dimension. One could argue that the dimensions considered are not independent; for example, brand loyalty is not built independent of product quality or pricing; branding of products is a long process and, like trust, is hard to build but easy to break if the perception of the user about the factors on which the brand is based changes due to usually objective criteria. For example, if a brand that advertises durability of its products gradually starts loosing this quality, consumers will immediately notice and defect. The damage to the brand may almost nullify all previous marketing efforts. Nevertheless, in the short-term, which is the length of time for which our tools predictions are valid for, one could say that these dimensions are close enough to being independent. The

next issue to consider regards the validity of the results of the algorithm; in particular, it is quite possible that there are many different distribution and weight combinations that together with appropriate thresholds minimize the error in the observed market share distribution of the various products and the computed market distribution, i.e. there may be multiple global optimizers that minimize the distribution error. The question is then how can one validate the conclusions about market elasticity that the algorithm offers, based on the global optimizer the system has reached. Empirically, *we have observed that the landscape of distributional error is not flat, but on the contrary it is quite steep, with a unique global minimizer;* also, the results of the algorithm can be validated against management intuition of the marketplace characteristics: i.e. if the Per.Ma.Ma results indicated that the major factor driving consumer purchase behavior in the MP3 market is product features, that conclusion would need to be carefully re-evaluated as the MP3 products

Figure 4. A typical screenshot of the GUI developed for the scope of the research. consider the price experimenting options per company on the left.

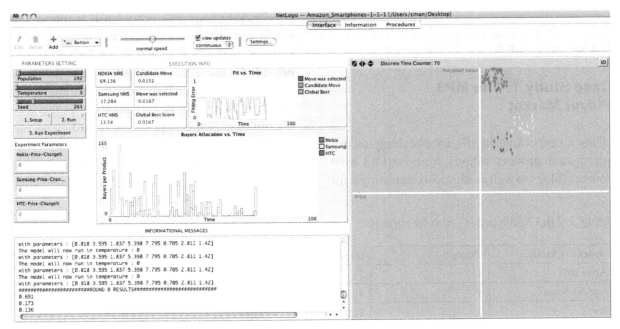

Table 2. Mp3 4gb market segment ratings

Dimension Product	(D)esign	(F)eatures	(P)rice	(B)rand Loyalty
Apple iPod	**5**	**5**	**2**	**4**
SanDisk Sansa	3	4	4	3
Sony	2	4	2	3

considered are rather similar in offered features. It is also possible to validate results using a more complex and time-consuming procedure. One can run the algorithm at one particular point in time, and then wait until another player changes the price of their product or makes any other move that causes their product's position on the perceptual map to move. At that point, the predictions of the system can be validated, if the system correctly predicts the re-distribution of the market-share because of the new positions, or invalidated if the system fails to accurately predict this re-distribution. In any case, the two position maps of the market can be fed into the system in order to compute a distribution of customers' perceptions on the map so that the total error in market share distribution for both instances of the product positions (before and after seller makes change in product attributes) is minimized.

CASE STUDIES

Case Study 1: The MP3 Player Market

Using Competitive Intelligence techniques, we aggregated product ratings from various web sources (blogs as well as Amazon.com ratings) for each product and normalized them in the interval [0…5], with 0 being the worst, and 5 being the best. The products' ratings are as shown in Table 2 and Table 3 respectively for the 4GB and the 8GB market segments.

The model developed so far successfully distributes any given population in both the 4GB and the 8GB market. Furthermore according to several runs the model exhibits essential match in real-world population distribution and the same for in-segment distribution. The model is both stable and precise, as the results deviations between several runs are not very significant. The summarized distributions of the population per segment are shown in table 4.

The GUI for the system for this case-study is shown in Figure 3 below. Once the system has been trained and created the perceptual map for the market-place (shown in the right-most window) the user may run what-if scenarios by modifying the current price of any product in the map by a certain percentage (in the text-boxes provided in the left-most middle pane of the GUI) and hitting the "Run Experiments" button above the text-boxes. The system then shows the new distribution of the population according to the new position of the products on the map. This newly computed distribution determines the new (hypothesized) market shares of each player after

Table 3. Mp3 8gb market segment ratings

Dimension Product	(D)esign	(F)eatures	(P)rice	(B)rand Loyalty
Apple iPod	4	3	1	3
SanDisk Sansa	4	4	5	2
Sony	2	4	3	3

Table 4. Computed population distribution per company & per storage category

Company Segments	Storage Segments	4GB		8GB	
		Observed	Per.Ma.Ma Error:0.0022	Observed	Per.Ma.Ma Error:0.0161
Apple		0.9615	0.96	0.2517	0.157
SanDisk		0.0358	0.04	0.6700	0.609
Sony		0.0027	0	0.0783	0.235

the percentile price changes have occurred, thus giving an answer to a question such as, "what will happen to my market share if product B's price drops 10%?".

Case Study 2: The Smart-Phone Market

In the following case study we will try to exhibit how information is drawn for a specific market and how value can be added to a potential VE user of the proposed system. By exploiting the derived information VE's may move with a series of strategic value creative decisions such as the launching of a new smartphone device that currently is not captured by the market and thus not associated with specific positioning in the perceptual mapping of the corresponding market. Moreover as currently great focus on devices' complementary services is given (like the iTunes service for iPods) such information should give the stimulus to develop another complementary market in the formation of VE supporting the regarding devices in analogy of the perceptual map drawn for the products under study. Obviously the advantages may be

numerous as business synergies across VE's take place. Furthermore the prominent issue for every potential VE is to create value by understanding and elaborating on unseen market needs and not adding value on existing offers. The information is presented in a way that scenario based expansions may be accommodated, and in particular, by propagating the new perceptual mapping according to price changes.

The smart-phones market was selected because of some attractive characteristics of the key players in it. In particular, the share of smart-phones in mobile phone markets has increased spectacularly the last few years as the convergence of various technologies in one single device offers multiple features at a lower price. We tried to experiment by selecting three prominent models that recently launched in the European market by Nokia, Samsung and HTC respectively. Both offer similar features, all operate under the "touch screen" concept and are sold more or less at the same price range. A summarized view of the products selection is given in table 5.

To come up with a reasonable estimate of users' perceptions of the various product attributes,

Table 5. Product description per company selection

Company	Description
Samsung	Samsung SGH-I900 Omnia black Smart-phone (Navi-Vollversion D-A-CH, 8GB, UMTS/HSDPA, 5MP)
Nokia	Nokia 5800 XpressMusic blue (GPS, WLAN, HSDPA, UMTS, EDGE, MP3, 3,2 MP)
HTC	HTC P3700 Touch Diamond (Touch-Screen, GPS, UMTS) Smart-phone

we aggregated product ratings from various web sources (blogs as well as Amazon.com ratings) for each product and normalized them in the interval [0...5], with 0 being the worst, and 5 being the best. The products' ratings are as shown in Table 6 and Table 7 respectively for the selected smart-phones.

The model developed, successfully distributed any given population market. Furthermore according to several runs the model exhibits essential match in real-world population distribution and the same for in-segment distribution. The model is both stable and precise, as the results deviations between several runs are not very significant. The summarized distributions of the population per segment and the corresponding results given by the Perceptual Market Mapping algorithm (Per. Ma.Ma) are shown in table 4.

In the following figure, we show the GUI of the system configured for smart-phone market research.

CONCLUSION

Agent Based Modeling is a tool that allows the description and simulation of the evolution or interactions of social structures. The tool described in this study approaches consumer behavior under the perspective of their perception for consumer products. Products nominally satisfying the same need, as the mp3 audio reproduction devices satisfy the need for music, and the smartphones for communication and a bundle of many other complementary and supportive activities, because they are seen under different perceptual lenses, drive consumers to different market decisions.

The study shows how to get a new insight on consumer segmentation regarding a specific product type. Thus, not only the actual segmentation can be represented in terms of the perceptual mapping techniques but also marketing scenarios can be drawn. The algorithm developed and trained with actual market data learns the distributional parameters of the market's population. Then, using these parameters, price strategic scenarios or irrational user reactions can be evaluated, without the need for explicit "market trial-and-error". Therefore, a company can avoid risks associated with changing its pricing strategies as well as compute near-optimal counter-strategies in case of price-wars initiated by opponents. By being able to predict early that a forced price change is inevitable, the company will have additional time available to adapt its supply chain to account for the cost savings necessary to implement the price discount, and/or to better schedule its procurement and purchasing activities and even its production

Table 6. Smart-phone market segment ratings

Dimension Product	(D)esign	(F)eatures	(P)rice	(B)rand Loyalty
Nokia	5	4	4	5
Samsung	5	3	2	3
HTC	4	4	3	2

Table 7. Computed population distribution per company

Company	Observed	Per.Ma.Ma
Nokia	0.6923	0.6914
Samsung	0.1852	0.1728
HTC	0.1225	0.1358

and scheduling plans. Especially in the case of Virtual Enterprises forming to introduce a new product in an existing market, the tool can be invaluable in assisting managers determine the market share that the new product is likely to get, once its attribute vector has been set. Setting an attribute vector for a new product implies setting values for the Design, Features, Brand-Loyalty and Price attributes. A reasonable value for Brand Loyalty would be close to 0 because both the product and the company offering it are supposedly new. Values for the rest of the attributes can be estimated by determining how close the newly introduced product is to existing products in each of these dimensions (e.g. if a competitor product has a value for Design equal to 4 and the new product is superior in its design, then it should get a value of 4.5 or 5 on this dimension). Once the new product is positioned in the perceptual map, a new experiment using the distribution of customers' perceptions computed from the initial training phase will lead to an estimate of the market share that the product will have during its introduction in the market. Such information, drastically reduces the risks associated with the launch of the product (in particular, the product's profitability and break-even point can be reliably estimated and this information directly leads to near-optimal decisions regarding the introduction or not of the product in the market and its initial market price).

Furthermore, the study also shows how hidden information can be extracted implicitly using mass information modules and applications such as the one offered by Amazon Web Services. The data extraction making distributional assumptions can be further enhanced with combination of the ranking information with customer reviews and supplier information. Furthermore new assumptions can be made based on the number of devices that should be sold, per category, in order to change the ranking position of the product.

The models developed represent with great efficiency the real world findings for the consumer behavior with respect to MP3 and smartphones market, considering the market of the selected products, and even offers a closer insight via the agents interaction, helping us understand prominent issues in the product life-cycle theory. Usually the pioneering player in a market gets the most of the share but as the market enters the growth phase new players prosper to steal market share.

FUTURE RESEARCH DIRECTION

As already mentioned, regarding the validation of the results of the algorithm, we note that the results can be validated against management intuition of the marketplace characteristics: i.e. if the Per.Ma.Ma results indicated that the major factor driving consumer purchase behavior in the MP3 market is product features, that conclusion would need to be carefully re-evaluated as the MP3 products considered are rather similar in offered features. We are working on a methodology to validate results using a more complex and time-consuming procedure, but hopefully exhibiting more robustness. One can run the algorithm at one particular point in time, and then wait until another player changes the price of their product or makes any other move that causes their product's position on the perceptual map to move. At that point, the predictions of the system can be validated, if the system correctly predicts the re-distribution of the market-share because of the new positions, or invalidated if the system fails to accurately predict this re-distribution. In any case, the two position maps of the market can be fed into the system in order to compute a distribution of customers' perceptions on the map so that the total error in market share distribution for both instances of the product positions (before and after seller makes change in product attributes) is minimized.

Finally, by enhancing further the model with data referring to the technological S-curve of the products, a new dimension to the behavioral space of the model can be added. The agents will then base their selection not only according to a static evaluation of the market positioning of the products, but also in a continuously evolving space where the changes in value proposition for each product will exert a different degree of influence on their final choice.

REFERENCES

Brakman, S., Garretsen, H., Van Marrewijk, C., & van den Berg, M. (1999). The return of Zipf: Towards a further understanding of the rank-size distribution. *Journal of Regional Science*, 39739–39767.

Camarinha-Matos, L. M., & Afsarmanesh, H. (2007). A Comprehensive Modeling Framework for Collaborative Networked Organizations. *Journal of Intelligent Manufacturing*, *18*, 529–542. doi:10.1007/s10845-007-0063-3

Cardoso, H. L., & Oliveira, E. (2005). *Virtual Enterprise Normative Framework within Electronic Institutions*. Retrieved June 6, 2009, from http://paginas.fe.up.pt/~eol/PUBLICATIONS/2005/esaw_post.PDF

Chevalier, J., & Goolsbee, A. (2003). Measuring prices and price competition online: Amazon and Barnes & Noble.com. *Quantitative Marketing and Economics*, *1*(2), 203–222. doi:10.1023/A:1024634613982

Cvijovic, D., & Klinowski, J. (1995). Taboo search - an approach to the multiple minima problem. *Science*, *267*, 664–666. doi:10.1126/science.267.5198.664

Gilbert, N. (2008). Agent Based Models: Quantitative Applications in the Social Sciences. Thousand Oaks, CA: SAGE Publications.

Glover, F. (1977). Heuristics for Integer Programming Using Surrogate Constraints. *Decision Sciences*, *8*(1), 156–166. doi:10.1111/j.1540-5915.1977.tb01074.x

Glover, F. (1994a). Genetic Algorithms and Scatter Search: Unsuspected Potentials. *Statistics and Computing*, *4*, 131–140. doi:10.1007/BF00175357

Glover, F. (1994b). Tabu Search for Nonlinear and Parametric Optimization (with links to genetic algorithms). *Discrete Applied Mathematics*, *49*, 231–255. doi:10.1016/0166-218X(94)90211-9

Goldstone, R. L., & Janssen, M. A. (2005). Computational models of collective behavior. *Trends in Cognitive Sciences*, *9*(9), 424–430. doi:10.1016/j.tics.2005.07.009

Haykin, S. (1999). Neural Networks A Comprehensive Foundation. Upper Saddle River, NJ: Prentice Hall.

Hudsal J. (2009). *From Risk Supply Chains to Risks in Virtual Enterprise Networks: Ideas, Concept and a Framework*. MTIP 2009 (Submitted Abstract)

Izquierdo, S. S., & Izquierdo, L. R. (2007). The impact of quality uncertainty without asymmetric information on market efficiency. *Journal of Business Research*, *60*(8), 858–867. doi:10.1016/j.jbusres.2007.02.010

Kirkpatrick, S., Gelatt, C. D., & Vecchi, M. P. (1983). Optimization by Simulated Annealing. *Science New Series*, *220*(4598), 671–680.

Mullins, W., & Larreche, B. (2006). Marketing Strategy A Decision Focused Approach. New Delhi, India: Tata McGraw-Hill.

North, M., & Macal, C. (2007). Managing Business Complexity: Discovering Strategic Solutions with Agent-Based Modeling and Simulation. New York: Oxford University Press.

Schmitt, L. M. (2004). Theory of Genetic Algorithms. *Theoretical Computer Science, 259*, 1–61. doi:10.1016/S0304-3975(00)00406-0

Weiss, G. (1999). Mutiagent systems: A modern approach to distributed artificial intelligence. Cambrigde, MA: MIT Press.

Whitley, D. (1994). A genetic algorithm tutorial. *Statistics and Computing, 4*, 65–85. doi:10.1007/BF00175354

Wilensky, U. (2004). *NetLogo Scatter model*. Retrieved from http://ccl.northwestern.edu/netlogo/models/Scatter Evanston, IL: Center for Connected Learning and Computer-Based Modeling, Northwestern University.

Wooldridge, M., & Jennings, N. R. (1995). Intelligent Agents: Theory and Practice. *The Knowledge Engineering Review, 10*, 115–152. doi:10.1017/S0269888900008122

ADDITIONAL READINGS

Choi, K.-H., Kim, D.-S., & Doh, Y.-H. (2007, December). Multi-agent-based task assignment system for virtual enterprises. *Robotics and Computer-integrated Manufacturing, 23*(6), 624–629. doi:10.1016/j.rcim.2007.02.003

Dawid, H. (2006). Agent-based models of innovation and technological change, In L. Tesfatsion, & K.L. Judd, Elsevier (eds.),Handbook of Computational Economics, Volume 2.

Izquierdo, L. R., Izquierdo, S. S., Gotts, N. M., & Polhill, J. G. (2007). Transient and asymptotic dynamics of reinforcement learning in games. *Games and Economic Behavior, 61*(2), 259–276. doi:10.1016/j.geb.2007.01.005

Jo, C., Chen, G., & Choi, J. (2004). A new approach to the BDI agent-based modeling. In *Proceedings of the 2004 ACM Symposium on Applied Computing* (Nicosia, Cyprus, March 14 - 17, 2004). SAC '04. ACM, New York, 1541-1545.

Lau, H. C. W., Chin, K. S., Pun, K. F., & Ning, A. (2000, November). Decision supporting functionality in a virtual enterprise network. *Expert Systems with Applications, 19*(4), 261–270. doi:10.1016/S0957-4174(00)00038-5

LeBaron, B. (2001). Evolution and time-horizons in an agent-based stock market. *Macroeconomic Dynamics, 5*(2), 225–254. doi:10.1017/S1365100501019058

Lee, W. B., & Lau, H. C. W. (1999). Multi-agent modelling of dispersed manufacturing network . *International Journal of Expert System with Application, 16*(3), 297–306. doi:10.1016/S0957-4174(98)00078-5

Macal, C. M., & North, M. J. (2007, September 12). Agent-based modeling and simulation: desktop ABMS. In *Proceedings of the 39th Conference on Winter Simulation: 40 Years! the Best Is Yet To Come*. Washington D.C., Winter Simulation Conference. (pp. 95-106). Piscataway, NJ: IEEE Press.

Macal, C. M., & North, M. J. (2008, December 7-10). Agent-based modeling and simulation: ABMS examples. In *Proceedings of the 40th Conference on Winter Simulation*, Miami, FL, S. Mason, R. Hill, L. Mönch, and O. Rose, (Eds). Winter Simulation Conference, 101-112.

Martinez, M. T., Fouletier, P., Park, K. H., & Favrel, J. (2001, December). Virtual enterprise – organisation, evolution and control. *International Journal of Production Economics, 74*(1-3), 225–238. doi:10.1016/S0925-5273(01)00129-3

Min Huang, W. H., Yang, I. H., Wang, X., & Lau, H. C. W. (2008, November). A fuzzy synthetic evaluation embedded tabu search for risk programming of virtual enterprises. *International Journal of Production Economics*, *116*(1), 104–114. doi:10.1016/j.ijpe.2008.06.008

Roche, C., Fitouri, S., Glardon, R., & Pouly, M. (1998). The potential of multi-agent systems in virtual manufacturing enterprises. In *Proceedings of 9th International Workshop on Database and Expert Systems Applications*, (pp. 913-918).

Russel, S., & Norvig, P. (2003). Artificial Intelligence A Modern Approach. Upper Saddle River, NJ: Prentice Hall.

Xu, W., Wei, Y., & Fan, Y. (2002, April 11). Virtual enterprise and its intelligence management. *Computers & Industrial Engineering*, *42*(2-4), 199–205. doi:10.1016/S0360-8352(02)00053-0

Zhou, Q., & Besant, C. B. (1999). Information management in production planning for a virtual enterprise. *International Journal of Production Research*, *37*(1), 207–218. doi:10.1080/002075499192011

Zipf, G. K. (1949). Human Behavior and the Principle of Least Effort: an Introduction to Human Ecology. Cambridge, MA: Addison-Wesley

Compilation of References

AAIRM. (2002). A risk management standard. London: The Institute of Risk Management.

Abecassis, C. (2006). Integrating Design and Retail in the Clothing Value Chain: An Empirical Study of the Organisation of Design. International *Journal of Operations and Production Management, 26*(4), 412–428. doi:10.1108/01443570610650567

Aberdeen Group. (2005). *The Supply Risk Management Benchmark Report*. Boston: Aberdeen Group.

Abrahamson, M. (2008). The Role of Logistics in Corporate Strategy. In Arlbjørn, J. S., Halldorson, A., Jahre, M., & Spens, K. (Eds.), *Northern Lights in Logistics & Supply Chain Management* (pp. 49–63). Copenhagen, Denmark: CBS Press.

Abram, T. (2009). The hidden values of it risk management. *Information Systems Audit and Control Association (ISACA) Journal*, (2), 40-45.

Abramovitz, M., & David, P. A. (1996). Technological Change, Intangible Investments and Growth in the Knowledge-based Economy: The US Historical Experience. In D. Foray & B.A. Lundvall (eds), Employment and Growth in the Knowledge-based Economy. Paris: OECD.

Adams, T. J., Austin, S. P., Soprano, R. S., & Stiene, L. M. (2002). Assessing the transition to production risk. *Program Manager, September*, 10-21.

Agrawal, V., & Seshadri, S. (1999). Risk intermediation in supply chains. *Journal IIE Transactions, 32*, 819–831.

Ahuja, G. (2000). Collaboration networks, structural holes, and innovation: A longitudinal study. *Administrative Science Quarterly, 45*, 425–455. doi:10.2307/2667105

Ahuja, M. K., & K. M. Carley (1998) .Network structure in virtual organizations. *Journal of Computer- Mediated Communication 3*(4): Special Issue on Virtual Organizations.

Akerlof, G. A. (1970). The Markets for "Lemons": Quality Uncertainty and the Market Mechanism . *The Quarterly Journal of Economics*, (August): 488–500. doi:10.2307/1879431

Akkermans, H., Bogerd, P., Yucesan, E., & van Wassenhove, L. (2003). The impact of ERP on supply chain management; Exploratory findings from a European Delphi study . *European Journal of Operational Research, 146*(2), 284–301. doi:10.1016/S0377-2217(02)00550-7

Albert, R., Jeong, H., & Barabasi, A.-L. (2000). Error and attack tolerance of complex networks. *Nature, 406*, 378–382. doi:10.1038/35019019

Alexopolous, C., & Seila, A. F. (1998). Output data analysis. In J. Banks (Ed.), Handbook of Simulation: Principles, Methodology, Advances, Applications, and Practice (pp. 225-272). New York: John Wiley and Sons.

Allen, M. K., & Emmelhainz, M. A. (1984). Decision support systems: an innovative aid to managers . *Journal of Business Logistics, 5*(2), 128–143.

Amaratunga, D., & Baldry, D. (2001). Case study methodology as a means of theory building: performance measurement in facilities management organizations. *Work Study, 50*(3), 95–104. doi:10.1108/00438020110389227

Amit, R., & Schoemaker, P. J. H. (1993). Strategic Assets and Organizational Rent. *Strategic Management Journal, 14*, 33–46. doi:10.1002/smj.4250140105

Angeloudis, P., Bichou, K., & Bell, M. G. H. (2007). Security and Reliability of the Liner Container-Shipping Network: Analysis of Robustness using a Complex Network Framework . In Bichou, K., Bell, M. G. H., & Evans, A. (Eds.), *Risk Management in Port Operations*. London: Informa.

Anon. (2009). *Northern Ireland cluster facilitators forum: case study*. Retrieved July 20, 2009, from http://www.bioteams.com/etc_ven_case_study.pdf

Antonelli, C. (2007). The Business Governance of Localized Knowledge. *Industry and Innovation, 13*(3), 227–261. doi:10.1080/13662710600858118

Appelqvist, P., & Gubi, E. (2005). Postponed variety creation: case study in consumer electronics retail . *International Journal of Retail & Distribution Management., 33*(10), 734–748. doi:10.1108/09590550510622281

Argote, L., Beckamn, S., & Epple, D. (1990). The Persistence and Transfer of Learning in Industrial Settings. *Management Science, 36*(2). doi:10.1287/mnsc.36.2.140

Asbjørnslett, B. (2008). Assessing the Vulnerability of Supply Chains . In Zsidisin, G. A., & Ritchie, B. (Eds.), *Supply Chain Risk: A Handbook of Assessment, Management and Performance*. New York: Springer.

Aven, T. (2008). Risk analysis: Assessing uncertainties beyond expected values and probabilities. West Sussex, UK: John Wiely and Sons, Ltd.

Bachmann, R. (2001). Trust, power and control in trans-organizational relations. *Organization Studies, 22*(2), 337–365. doi:10.1177/0170840601222007

Baiman, S., Fischer, P. E., & Rajan, M. V. (2001). Performance measurement and Design in supply chains . *Management Science, 47*(1), 173–188. doi:10.1287/mnsc.47.1.173.10673

Bain, J. S. (1968). Industrial organization. New York: Wiley.

Balasubramanian, R. (2001). Concurrent Engineering – A Powerful Enabler of Supply Chain Management. *Quality Progress, 34*(6), 47–53.

Banks, J. (1998). Principles of simulation. In J. Banks (Ed.), Handbook of Simulation: Principles, Methodology, Advances, Applications, and Practice (pp. 3-30). New York: John Wiley and Sons.

Barabasi, A.-L., & Albert, R. (1999). Emergence of scaling in random networks. *Science, 286*, 509–512. doi:10.1126/science.286.5439.509

Barabasi, A.-L., & Bonabeau, E. (2003). Scale-Free Networks. *Scientific American*, (May): 50–59.

Barbini, F. M. (2003). Innovative Trade Fairs for Incubating Virtual Enterprises. In L. M. Camarinha-Matos, L.M. and Afsarmanesh, H. (eds.). Processes and Foundations for Virtual Organizations. Boston: Kluwer Academic Publishers.

Barbini, F. M., & D'Atri, A. (2005). How Innovative are Virtual Enterprises? In Bartmann D, Rajola F, Kallinikos J, Avison D, Winter R, Ein-Dor P, Becker J, Bodendorf F, Weinhardt C eds. *Proceedings of the Thirteenth European Conference on Information Systems*, 1091-1102, Regensburg, Germany.

Barley, B. (2003). Project Risk Management. New York: McGraw-Hill.

Barley, S. R. (1996). Technicians in the workplace: ethnographic evidence for bringing work into organizational studies. *Administrative Science Quarterly, 41*(3), 404–441. doi:10.2307/2393937

Barney, J. (1991). Firm Resources and Sustained Competitive Advantage . *Journal of Management, 17*(1), 99–120. doi:10.1177/014920639101700108

Barney, J. (2001). Resource-based theories of competitive advantage: a ten-year retrospective on the resource-based view. *Journal of Management, 27*(6), 643–650. doi:10.1177/014920630102700602

Bass, F. M. (1969). A new product growth model for consumer durables. *Management Science, 15*(5), 215–227. doi:10.1287/mnsc.15.5.215

Battini, D., & Persona, A. (2007). Towards a use of network analysis: quantifying the complexity of Supply Chain Networks. *Int. J. Electronic Customer Relationship Management, 1*(1), 75–90. doi:10.1504/IJECRM.2007.014427

Baum, J. A. C., Calabrese, T., & Silverman, B. S. (2000). Don't go it alone: alliance network composition and startups' performance in Canadian biotechnology. *Strategic Management Journal, 21*, 267–294. doi:10.1002/(SICI)1097-0266(200003)21:3<267::AID-SMJ89>3.0.CO;2-8

Bayazit, O. (2006). Use of analytic network process in vendor selection decisions, *Benchmarking . International Journal (Toronto, Ont.), 13*(5), 566–579.

Bayley, H. (1983). A Review of Technical Audit. *Chartered Mechanical Engineer, November*, 49-53.

Beach, R., Muhleman, A., Price, D., Paterson, A., & Sharp, J. (2000). A review of manufacturing flexibility. *European Journal of Operational Research, 122*, 41–57. doi:10.1016/S0377-2217(99)00062-4

Beamon, B. M. (1999). Measuring supply chain performance. *International Journal of Operations & Production Management, 19*(3), 275–292. doi:10.1108/01443579910249714

Beck, U. (1992). *Risk Society*. London: Sage.

Beck, U. (1999). *What is Globalization?* Cambridge, UK: Polity Press.

Beesley, L. (2004). Multi-level complexity in the management of knowledge networks. *Journal of Knowledge Management, 8*(3), 71–100. doi:10.1108/13673270410541051

Bell, D. C., Atkinson, J. A., & Carlson, J. W. (1999). Centrality measures for disease transmission networks. *Social Networks, 21*, 1–21. doi:10.1016/S0378-8733(98)00010-0

Bell, D. G., Giordano, R., & Putz, P. (2002). Inter-firm sharing of process knowledge: exploring knowledge markets. *Knowledge and Process Management, 9*(1), 12–22. doi:10.1002/kpm.131

Bello, D. C., Lohtia, R., & Sangtani, V. (2004). An institutional analysis of supply chain innovations in global marketing channels. *Industrial Marketing Management, 33*, 57–64. doi:10.1016/j.indmarman.2003.08.011

Berger, C. M. (1987). Communicating under uncertainty. In M. E. Roloff, & G. R. Miller (eds), Interpersonal Processes: New Dimensions in Communications Research, (pp. 39–62). Newbury Park, CA: Sage.

Berger, P. L., & Luckmann, T. (1966). The social construction of reality. London: Allen Lane The Penguin Press

Berman, J. (2006). *3PL conslidation market is going strong*. Retrieved from http://www.logisticsmgmt.com/article/334621-3PL_consolidation_market_is_going_strong.php

Berry, M. (1998). Strategic planning in small high-tech companies. *Long Range Planning, 31*(3), 455–466. doi:10.1016/S0024-6301(98)80012-5

Bessant, J., & Venables, T. (2008) Creating Wealth from Knowledge. Cheltenham, UK: Edward Elgar Publishing Ltd.

Bhatt, G. D. (2000). Information dynamics, learning and knowledge creation in organizations. *The Learning Organization, 7*(2), 89–98. doi:10.1108/09696470010316288

Bhatt, G. D. (2001). Knowledge management in organizations: examining the interaction between technologies, techniques and people. *Journal of Knowledge Management, 5*(1), 68–75. doi:10.1108/13673270110384419

Bickhoff, N., Böhmer, C., Eilenberger, G., Hansmann, K.-W., Niggemann, M., & Ringle, C. (2003). *Mit Virtuellen Unternhemen zum Erfolg - Ein Quick-Check für Manager*. Berlin, Germany: Springer.

Bienstock, C. C. (1996). Sample size determination in logistics simulations. *International Journal of Physical Distribution & Logistics Management., 26*(2), 43–50. doi:10.1108/09600039610113191

Bienstock, C. C., & Mentzer, J. T. (1999). An experimental investigation of the outsourcing decision for motor carrier transportation. *Transportation Journal., 39*(1), 42–59.

Birtwistle, G., Siddiqui, N., & Fiorito, S. S. (2003). Quick response: perception of UK fashion retailers. *International Journal of Retail & Distribution Management, 31*(2), 118–128. doi:10.1108/09590550310462010

Blackburn, S. (1999). Managing Risk and Achieving Turnbull Compliance . *Accountants Digest, 417*, 1–51.

Blackhurts, J., Wu, T., & O'Grady, P. (2005). Pcdm a decision support modelling methodology for supply chain, product and process design decision. *Journal of Operations Management, 23*(3), 325–343. doi:10.1016/j.jom.2004.05.009

Blackler, F. (1995). Knowledge, knowledge work and organizations: an overview and interpretations. *Organization Studies, 16*(6), 1021–1046. doi:10.1177/017084069501600605

Blaikie, N. (2000). Designing social research: the logic of anticipation. Cambridge, UK: Polity Press.

Blecker, T., & Neumann, R. (2000). Interorganizational Knowledge Management - Some Perspectives for Knowledge oriented Strategic Management in Virtual Organizations, In Y. Malhotra (Ed), Knowledge Management and Virtual Organizations. Hershey, PA: Idea Group Publishing

Bogataj, D., & Bogataj, M. (2007). Measuring the supply chain risk and vulnerability in frequency space. *International Journal of Production Economics, 108*, 291–301. doi:10.1016/j.ijpe.2006.12.017

Bolisani, E., & Oltramari, A. (2009, February 17-18). *Capitalizing flows of knowledge: models and accounting perspectives*, paper presented at the 4th International Forum on Knowledge Asset Dynamics – IFKAD, University of Glasgow.

Bolisani, E., & Scarso, E. (1999). Information Technology Management: a Knowledge-Based Perspective. *Technovation, 19*, 209–217. doi:10.1016/S0166-4972(98)00109-6

Bolstorff, P., & Rosenbaum, R. (2003). *Supply chain excellence: a handbook for dramatic improvement using SCOR mode*.New York: Amakon.

Booker, S., Gardner, J., Steelhammer, L., & Zumbakyte, L. (2004). What is your risk appetite? The risk-it model. *Information Systems Audit and Control Association (ISACA) . Journal, 35*(2), 38–43.

Borgatti, S. P., & Li, X. (2009). On social network analysis in a supply chain context. *Journal of Supply Chain Management, 45*(2), 5–22. doi:10.1111/j.1745-493X.2009.03166.x

Borodzicz, E. (2005). Crisis & security management. Atrium, UK: John Wiley & Sons Ltd.

Bostrom, A., French, S., & Gottlieb, S. (Eds.). (2008). Risk assessment, modeling and decision support: Strategic directions. Heidelberg, Germany: Springer-Verlag.

Boudreau, J. W., & Ramstad, P. M. (1997). Measuring intellectual capital: learning from financial history. *Human Resource Management, 36*(3), 343–356. doi:10.1002/(SICI)1099-050X(199723)36:3<343::AID-HRM6>3.0.CO;2-W

Bou-Raad, G. (2000). Internal Auditors and a Value-Added Approach: The New Business Regime. *Managerial Audit Journal, 15*(4), 182–186. doi:10.1108/02686900010322461

Bowersox, D. J., & Closs, D. J. (1996). Logistical Management: The Integrated Supply Chain Processes. New York: McGraw-Hill.

Bowersox, D. J., Closs, D. J., & Stank, T. P. (2000). Ten Mega-Trends That Will Revolutionize Supply Chain Logistics. *Journal of Business Logistics, 21*(2), 1–16.

Boyce, J., & Jennings, D. (2002). Information assurance: Managing organizational IT security risks. Woburn, MA: Butterworth-Heinemann.

Boyer, S. (2004). SCADA: supervisory control and data acquisition. Research Triangle Park, NC: Instrument Society of America.

Brakman, S., Garretsen, H., Van Marrewijk, C., & van den Berg, M. (1999). The return of Zipf: Towards a further understanding of the rank-size distribution. *Journal of Regional Science, 39739*–39767.

Brass, D. J. (1984). A structural analysis of individual influence in an organization. *Administrative Science Quarterly, 29*, 518–539. doi:10.2307/2392937

Brass, D. J. (1995). A social network perspective on human resources management. *Research in Personnel ang . Human Resource Management, 13*, 39–79.

Brindley, C., & Ritche, B. (2004). Introduction. In C. Brindley (Ed.), Supply chain risk (pp. 1-13). Hampshire, UK: Ashgate.

Broder, J. (2006). Risk analysis and the security survey. Burlington, MA: Butterworth-Heinemann Elsevier.

Brotby, W. (2006). Information security governance: Guidance for boards of directors and executive management. Rolling Meadows, IL: IT Governance Institute.

Brown, B. (April, 2008). *Critical steps to reduce the risks associated with using external consultants on your projects.* Paper presented at Project Summit & Business Analyst World, Philadelphia, PA.

Brown, J. S., & Duguid, P. (1991). Organizational learning and communities of practice: toward a unified view of working, learning and innovation. *Organization Science, 2*(1), 40–57. doi:10.1287/orsc.2.1.40

Brown, J. S., & Duguid, P. (2000). The social life of information. Boston, MA: Harvard Business School Press.

Brown, J. S., & Duguid, P. (2001). Knowledge and Organization: a social practice perspective. *Organization Science, 12*(2), 198–213. doi:10.1287/orsc.12.2.198.10116

Browne, J., & Zhang, J. (1999). Extended and virtual enterprises-similarities and differences. *International Journal of Agile Management Systems, 1*(1), 30–36. doi:10.1108/14654659910266691

BSI. (1987). BS 5750: ISO 9000 Quality Systems Standards. London: British Standards Institution (BSI).

BSI. (1991). BS 7229: ISO 10011 Guide to Quality Systems Auditing. London: British Standards Institution (BSI).

Bucklin, L. P. (1965). Postponement, speculation and the structure of distribution channels. *JMR, Journal of Marketing Research, 2*(1), 26–31. doi:10.2307/3149333

Budros, A. (1999). A conceptual framework for analyzing why organizations downsize. *Organization Science, 10*(1), 69–82. doi:10.1287/orsc.10.1.69

Bukh, P. N., Larsen, H. T., & Mouritsen, J. (2001). Constructing intellectual capital statements. *Scandinavian Journal of Management, 17*, 87–108. doi:10.1016/S0956-5221(00)00034-8

Burgess, M., Canwright, G., & Engo-Monsen, K. (2003). A graph theoretical model of computer security. *International Journal of Information Security, 3*(2), 70–85. doi:10.1007/s10207-004-0044-x

Burkett, M. J. (2006). Design for Supply: An Evolutionary Path. *Supply Chain Management Review, 10*(8), 11–16.

Burkhardt, M. E., & Brass, D. J. (1990). Changing patterns or patterns of change: The effect of a change in technology on social network structure and power. *Administrative Science Quarterly, 35*, 104–127. doi:10.2307/2393552

Busby, J., & Zhang, H. (2008). How the subjectivity of risk analysis impacts project success. *Project Management Journal, 39*(3), 86–96. doi:10.1002/pmj.20070

Busi, M., & Mc Ivor, R. (2008). Setting the outsourcing research agenda: the top-10 most urgent outsourcing areas. *Strategic Outsourcing: An International Journal, 1*(3), 185–197. doi:10.1108/17538290810915263

Buzacott, J. (1982). *The fundamental principles of flexibility in manufacturing systems.* Paper presented at the meeting of the International Conference of Flexible Manufacturing Systems. Amsterdam: Elsevier.

Buzon, L., Bouras, A., & Ouzrout, Y. (2004). Knowledge Exchange in a Supply Chain Context . In Camarinha-Matos, L. M. (Ed.), *Virtual Enterprises and Collaborative Networks* (pp. 145–152). Boston: Springer. doi:10.1007/1-4020-8139-1_16

Byrne, J. (1993). The virtual corporation. *Business Week*, 98–102.

Byrne, J. A. (1993, February 8). *The Virtual Corporation.* Business Week.

Caddy, I. (2000). Intellectual assets and liabilities. *Journal of Intellectual Capital*, *2*(1), 129–146. doi:10.1108/14691930010377469

Caddy, I., Guthrie, J., & Petty, R. (2001). Managing orphan knowledge: current Australasian best practice. *Journal of Intellectual Capital*, *2*(4), 384–397. doi:10.1108/14691930110409679

Cairncross, F. (1997). The Death of Distance, London: Orion Business Books.

Calantone, R., Dröge, C., & Vickery, S. (2002). Investigating the manufacturing–marketing interface in new product development: does context affect the strength of relationships? *Journal of Operations Management*, *20*(3), 273–287. doi:10.1016/S0272-6963(02)00009-8

Camacho, J., Guimera, R., & Amaral, L. A. N. (2002). Robust patterns in food web structure. *Physical Review Letters*, 88.

Camarinha-Matos, L. M. (2002). *Virtual Organizations in Manufacturing: Trends and challenges*. International Conference on Flexible Automation and Intelligent Manufacturing 2002, Dresden, Germany

Camarinha-Matos, L. M. (Ed.). (2004). Virtual enterprises and collaborative networks. Norwell, MA: Kluwer Academic Publisher. Dallas, G. (Ed.). (2004). Governance and risk. New York: McGraw-Hill companies Inc.

Camarinha-Matos, L. M., & Afsarmanesh, H. (2003). Elements of a Base VE Infrastracture. *Journal of Computers in Industry*, *51*(2), 139–163. doi:10.1016/S0166-3615(03)00033-2

Camarinha-Matos, L. M., & Afsarmanesh, H. (2003). Elements of a base VE Infrastructure. *Computers in Industry*, *51*(2), 139–163. doi:10.1016/S0166-3615(03)00033-2

Camarinha-Matos, L. M., & Afsarmanesh, H. (2007). A Comprehensive Modeling Framework for Collaborative Networked Organizations. *Journal of Intelligent Manufacturing*, *18*, 529–542. doi:10.1007/s10845-007-0063-3

Camarinha-Matos, L. M., Afsarmanesh, H., Garita, C., & Lima, C. (1998). Towards an architecture for virtual enterprises. *Journal of Intelligent Manufacturing*, *9*, 189–199. doi:10.1023/A:1008880215595

Camarinha-Matos, L., Afsarmanesh, H., Galeano, N., & Molina, A. (2009). Collaborative networked organizations – Concepts and practice in manufacturing enterprises. *Computers & Industrial Engineering*, *57*(1), 46–60. doi:10.1016/j.cie.2008.11.024

Canbolat, Y. B., Gupta, G., Matera, S., & Chelst, K. (2005). Analyzing risk in sourcing design and manufacture of components and subsystems to emerging markets. Paper presented at the annual conference of the Decision Sciences Institute, San Francisco.

Cannon, D., Bergmann, T., & Pamplin, B. (2006). CISA certified information systems auditor study guide. New York: Wiley Publishing, Inc.

Capo-Vicedo, J., Capo-Vicedo, J., Exposito-Langa, M., & Tomas-Miquel, J.-V. (2008). Creation of interorganizational networks of small and medium enterprises: virtual netchain concept. *The ICFAI Journal of Business Strategy.*, *5*(4), 23–39.

Cardoso, H. L., & Oliveira, E. (2005). *Virtual Enterprise Normative Framework within Electronic Institutions*. Retrieved June 6, 2009, from http://paginas.fe.up.pt/~eol/PUBLICATIONS/2005/esaw_post.PDF

Carnaghan, C. (2006). Business process modelling approaches in the context of process level audit risk assessment: An analysis and comparison. *International Journal of Accounting Information Systems*, *7*(2), 170–204. doi:10.1016/j.accinf.2005.10.005

Cavinato, J. (2004). Supply chain logistics risks; From the back room to the board room. *International Journal of Physical Distribution & Logistics Management*, *34*(5), 383–387. doi:10.1108/09600030410545427

Cavinato, J. L. (2004). Supply chain logistics risks. *International Journal of Physical Distribution & Logistics Management*, *34*(5), 383–388. doi:10.1108/09600030410545427

Chailkin, S., & Lave, J. (1993). Understanding practice. Cambridge, UK: Cambridge University Press.

Chan, F., & Kumar, N. (2005). Global supplier development considering risk factors using fuzzy extended AHP-based approach. *The International Journal of Management Science, 35*, 417–431.

Chan, F., & Kumar, N. (2007). Global supplier development considering risk factors using fuzzy extended AHP-based approach. *Omega, 35*(4), 417–431. doi:10.1016/j.omega.2005.08.004

Chan, K. C. (1994). Learning for total quality. *The Learning Organization, 1*(1), 17–22. doi:10.1108/09696479410053403

Chang, Y., & Makatsoris, H. (2001). Supply chain modeling using simulation. *International Journal of Simulation, 2*(1), 24–30.

Chanvas, J. (2004). Risk analysis in theory and practice. London: Elsevier Inc.

Chapell, A., & Peck, H. (2005). The application of a six sigma methodology to military supply chain processes. in *Operations and Global Competitiveness: Proceedings of the Euroma Conference*, (pp. 809–818).

Chen, X., & Zhang, J. (2008). Supply chain risk analysis by using jump-diffusion model. In *Proceedings of the 2008 Winter Simulation Conference*, 638-646.

Chen, Y., & Seshadri, S. (2006). Supply chain structure and demand risk. *Journal of IFAC, 42*, 1291–1299. doi:10.1016/j.automatica.2005.11.008

Chesbrough, H. W., & Teece, D. J. (2009, March 3). When is Virtual Virtuous? Organizing for Innovation. *Strategic Management of Intellectual Capital. Harvard Business Review*, 27–36.

Chevalier, J., & Goolsbee, A. (2003). Measuring prices and price competition online: Amazon and Barnes & Noble.com. *Quantitative Marketing and Economics, 1*(2), 203–222. doi:10.1023/A:1024634613982

Child, J., Faulkner, D., & Tallman, S. B. (2005a). Networks . In *Cooperative Strategy* (pp. 145–163). Oxford, UK: Oxford University Press.

Child, J., Faulkner, D., & Tallman, S. B. (2005b). The Virtual Corporation . In *Cooperative Strategy* (pp. 164–189). Oxford, UK: Oxford University Press.

Childe, S. J. (1998). The extended enterprise-a concept of co-operation. *Production Planning and Control, 9*(4), 320–327. doi:10.1080/095372898234046

Chiles, T. H., & McMackin, J. F. (1996). Integrating variable risk preferences, trust, and transaction cost economics. *Academy of Management Review, 21*(1), 73–99. doi:10.2307/258630

Choi, S., Whinston, A., & Stahl, D. (1997). Economics of Electronic Commerce. Indianapolis, IN: Macmillan

Choi, T. Y., & Kim, Y. (2008). Structural embeddedness and supplier management: A network perspective. *Journal of Supply Chain Management, 44*(4), 5–13. doi:10.1111/j.1745-493X.2008.00069.x

Choi, T. Y., & Krause, D. R. (2006). The supply base and its complexity: Implications for transaction costs, risks, responsiveness, and innovation. *Journal of Operations Management, 24*(5), 637–652. doi:10.1016/j.jom.2005.07.002

Choi, T., Y., & Hong, Y. (2002). Unveiling the structure of supply networks: case studies in Honda, Acura, and DaimlerChrysler. *Journal of Operations Management, 20*, 469–493. doi:10.1016/S0272-6963(02)00025-6

Choo, C. W. (1998). The knowing organization: how organizations use information to construct meaning, create knowledge and make decisions. Oxford, UK: Oxford University Press.

Chopra, S., & Sodhi, M. (2004). Managing risk to avoid supply-chain breakdown. *MIT Sloan Management Review, 46*(1), 53–61.

Christley, R. M., Pinchbeck, G. L., Bowers, R. G., Clancy, D., French, N. P., & Bennett, R. (2005). Infection in Social Networks: Using Network Analysis to Identify High-Risk Individual. *American Journal of Epidemiology, 162*(10), 1024–1031. doi:10.1093/aje/kwi308

Christopher, M. (1992). Logistics and Supply Chain Management. London: Pitman.

Christopher, M. (2003). *Creating resilient Supply Chains: A practical guide*. Bedford, UK:Cranfield University.

Christopher, M. (2005). Logistics and Supply Chain Management, Creating Value Adding Networks - 3rd Edition, London: Prentice Hall.

Christopher, M. (2005). Managing risk in the supply chain . In *Logistics and Supply Chain Management* (3rd ed., pp. 231–258). Harlow, UK: Prentice Hall.

Christopher, M., & Lee, H. (2004). Mitigating supply chain risk through improved confidence. *International Journal of Physical Distribution & Logistics Management*, *34*(5), 388–396. doi:10.1108/09600030410545436

Christopher, M., & Lee, H. L. (2001). Supply chain confidence: the key to effective supply chains through improved visibility and reliability. Global Trade Management, November, 1–10.

Christopher, M., & Peck, H. (1997). Managing logistics in fashion markets. *The International Journal of Logistics Management*, *8*(2), 63–74. doi:10.1108/09574099710805673

Christopher, M., & Peck, H. (2003). Marketing Logistics - 2nd Edition. Oxford, UK: Butterworth Heinemann.

Christopher, M., & Peck, H. (2004). Building the resilient supply chain. *The International Journal of Logistics Management*, *15*, 1–14. doi:10.1108/09574090410700275

Christopher, M., & Rutherford, C. (2004) .Creating Supply Chain Resilience through Agile Six Sigma. *CriticalEye*, *Jun-Aug*, 24-28.

Christopher, M., & Towill, R. D. (2000). Supply Chain Migration From Lean and Functional to Agile and Customised. *Supply Chain Management: An International Journal*, *5*(4), 206–213. doi:10.1108/13598540010347334

Christopher, M., Aitken, J., & Towill, D. (2002). Understanding, Implementing and Exploiting Agility and Leanness. *International Journal of Logistics*, *5*(1), 59–74. doi:10.1080/13675560110084139

Chu, S., Keogh, E., Hart, D., & Pazzani, M. (2002). Iterative deepening dynamic time warping for time series. In *Proceedings of the 2nd SIAM International Conference on Data Mining*. 195-212.

Cisic, D., Komadina, P., & Hlaca, B. (2007). Network analysis of the Mediterranian port supply chain structures. *Journal of Maritime Studies*, *21*(1), 211–220.

Clemons, E. (2000, June 13). Gauging the power play in the new economy. *Financial Times*.

Cohen, W. M., & Levinthal, D. A. (1989). Innovation and Learning: the Two Faces of R&D. *The Economic Journal*, *99*(397), 569–596. doi:10.2307/2233763

Cohen, W. M., & Levinthal, D. A. (1990). Absorptive capacity: a new perspective on learning and innovation. *Administrative Science Quarterly*, *35*(2), 128–152. doi:10.2307/2393553

Coleman, B. J., & Jennings, K. M. (1998). The UPS strike: Lessons for Just-In-Timers. *Production and Inventory Management Journal*, *39*(4), 63–68.

Collin, J., & Lorenzin, D. (2006). Plan for supply chain agility at Nokia: Lessons from the mobile infrastructure industry. *International Journal of Physical Distribution & Logistics Management*, *36*(6), 418–430. doi:10.1108/09600030610677375

Combs, B. (1999). *The pseudo-internal intruder: A New access oriented intruder category*. Unpublished doctoral dissertation, University of Virginia, Virginia, USA.

Cooke, P. (2001). Knowledge Economies: Clusters, Learning & Co-operative Advantage. London: Routledge.

Cooper, M., Lambert, D., & Pugh, J. (1997). Supply Chain Management: More than a new name for logistics. The International Journal of Logistics Management, 8(1), 1-14. In Coyole, D. (1997). The Weightless Word: Strategies for Managing the Digital Economy, London: Capstone.

Cornish, M. (2007). The business continuity planning methodology . In Hiles, A. (Ed.), *The Definitive Handbook of Business Continuity Management* (pp. 105–118). Chichester, UK: John Wiley & Sons.

Cousins, P. D. (2002). A Conceptual Model for Managing long-term inter-organisational relationships. *European*

Journal of Purchasing and Supply Management, 8, 71–82. doi:10.1016/S0969-7012(01)00006-5

Cousins, P. D., Lamming, R. C., Lawson, B., & Squire, B. C. (2008). Strategic Supply Management: Principles, theories and practice. Harlow, UK: Pearson Education Limited.

Cox, G. (2005), Cox Review of Creativity in Business: Building on the UK's Strengths, London: HMSO.

Coyole, D. (2001). Paradoxes of Prosperity: Why the New Capitalism Benefits All. London: Texere Publishing.

Crabtree, B. F., & Miller, W. L. (1999). Doing qualitative research. Thousand Oaks, CA, Sage Publications.

Craighead, C. W., Blackburst, J., Rungtusanatham, M. J., & Handfield, R. B. (2007). The Severity of Supply Chain Disruptions: Design Characteristics and Mitigation Capabilities. *Decision Sciences, 38*(1), 131–156. doi:10.1111/j.1540-5915.2007.00151.x

Craighead, C. W., Blackhurst, J., Rungtusanatham, M. J., & Handfield, R. B. (2007). The Severity of Supply Chain Disruptions: Design Characteristics and Mitigation Capabilities. *Decision Sciences, 38*(1), 131–156. doi:10.1111/j.1540-5915.2007.00151.x

Cranfield (2003). Creating Resilient Supply Chains: A Practical Guide. *Report produced by the Centre of Logistics and Supply Chain Management, Cranfield School of Management. Research Funded by Department for Transport.*

Crouhy, M., Galai, D., & Mark. R. (2006). *The essentials of risk management.* New York: The McGraw-Hill.

Cucchiella, F., & Gastaldi, M. (2006). Risk management in supply chain: a real option approach. *Journal of Manufacturing Technology Management, 16,* 700–720. doi:10.1108/17410380610678756

Cunha, M. M., & Putnik, G. (2006). *Agile Virtual Enterprises: Implementation and Management Support.* Hershey, PA: Idea Group Publishing.

Cvijovic, D., & Klinowski, J. (1995). Taboo search - an approach to the multiple minima problem. *Science, 267,* 664–666. doi:10.1126/science.267.5198.664

D'Atri, A., & Motro, A. (2002). VirtuE: Virtual Enterprises for Information Markets. In *Proc. European Conference on Information Systems*, Gdansk, Poland.

Dahel, N. (2003). Vendor selection and order quantity allocation in volume discount environments, *Supply Chain Management . International Journal (Toronto, Ont.), 8*(4), 334–342.

Dally, W., & Towles, B. (2004). Principles and practices of interconnection networks. San Francisco: Morgan Kaufmann.

Dant, T. (1991). Knowledge, ideology and discourse: a sociological perspective. London: Routledge.

Darby, J., & Kindinger, J. (September, 2000). *Risk factor analysis—A new qualitative risk management tool.* Paper presented at Project Management Institute annual seminar & Symposium, Houston,TX.

Das, S. K., & Abdel-Malek, L. (2003). Modelling the flexibility of order quantities and lead-times in supply chains. *International Journal of Production Economics, 85,* 171–181. doi:10.1016/S0925-5273(03)00108-7

Das, T. K., & Teng, B. S. (1996). Risk types and inter-firm alliance structures. *Journal of Management Studies, 33,* 827–843. doi:10.1111/j.1467-6486.1996.tb00174.x

Das, T. K., & Teng, B. S. (1999). Managing risks in strategic alliances . *The Academy of Management Executive, 13*(4), 1–13.

Das, T. K., & Teng, B. S. (2001). Relational risks and its personal correlates in strategic alliances . *Journal of Business and Psychology, 15*(3), 449–465. doi:10.1023/A:1007874701367

Das, T. K., & Teng, B. S. (2001). Trust, control and risk in strategic alliances: an integrated framework. *Organization Studies, 22*(2), 251–283. doi:10.1177/0170840601222004

Davidow, W. H., & Malone, M. (1992). *The Virtual Corporation.* New York: HarperBusiness.

Davis, C., Schiller, M., & Wheeler, K. (2006). IT auditing: Using controls to protect information assets. Emeryville, CA: McGraw-Hill Osborne Media.

Dawidow, W. H., & Malone, M. S. (1993). *The Virtual Corporation*. New York: HarperBusiness.

De Haes, S., & Grembergen, W. (2009). Enterprise governance of information technology: Achieving strategic alignment and value. New York: Springer.

De Loach, J. W. (2000). *Enterprise-wide Risk Management: Strategies for linking risk and opportunity.* London: Financial Times/Prentice Hall.

De Toro, I., & McCabe, T. (1997). How to Stay Flexible and Elude Fads . *Quality Progress*, *30*(3), 55–60.

Deleris, A., & Erhun, F. (2005). Risk Management in Supply Networks Using Monte-Carlo Simulation. In *Proceedings of the 2005 Winter Simulation Conference*, (pp. 1643-1649).

Deloach, J. W. (2000). Enterprise-wide risk management: Strategies for linking risk and opportunity Upper Saddle River, NJ: Prentice Hall

Demirkan, H., & Cheng, H. (2006). The risk and information sharing of application services supply chain. *European Journal of Operational Research*, *187*, 765–784. doi:10.1016/j.ejor.2006.03.060

Deng, Z., Solvang, B., & Solvang, W. D. (2000). *Collaboration and Co-ordination of Virtual Supply Chain via Electronic Networking*. Paper presented at The 16h IFIP World Computer Congress, Beijing, China.

DeSanctis, G., & Monge, P. (1999). Introduction to the Special Issue: Communication Processes for Virtual Organizations. *Organization Science*, *10*(6), 693–703. doi:10.1287/orsc.10.6.693

Desbarats, G. (1999). The innovation supply chain. *Supply Chain Management*, *4*(1), 7–17. doi:10.1108/13598549910254708

Design Council. (2004/2005). Design in Britain Internal Report by the Design Council.

Design Council. (2005). *Brown Backs Design*. Retrieved from www.design-council.org

Desouza, K., & Awazu, Y. (2004). Markets in Know-How. Business Strategy Review, (Autumn), 59-65

Deutsch, M. (1969). Conflicts: productive and destructive. *Journal of the Social Sciences*, *25*, 7–41.

Dhar, R., & Glazer, R. (2003, May). Hedging Customers. *Harvard Business Review*, 86–92.

Dhebar, A. (1993). Managing the quality of quantitative analysis. *Sloan Management Review*, *34*(2), 69–75.

Dirks, K. T., & Ferrin, D. L. (2001). The role of trust in organizational settings. *Organization Science*, *12*(4), 450–467. doi:10.1287/orsc.12.4.450.10640

Doyle, S. A., & Broadbridge, A. (1999). Differentiation by design: the importance of design in retailer repositioning and differentiation . *International Journal of Retail & Distribution Management*, *27*(2), 72–82. doi:10.1108/09590559910258571

Doz, Y. L. (1996). The evolution of cooperation in strategic alliances: initial conditions or learning processes. *Strategic Management Journal*, *17*, 55–83. doi:10.1002/(SICI)1097-0266(199601)17:1<55::AID-SMJ788>3.0.CO;2-B

Doz, Y., & Hamel, G. (1998). Alliance Advantage: The Art of Creating Value Through Partnering, Cambridge, MA: Harvard Business School Press.

Drucker, P. F. (1999). *Management Challenges for the 21st Century*. Oxford, UK: Butterworth Heinemann.

DTI. (2003). Competing in the Global Economy: The Innovation Challenge. London: Department of Trade and Industry

Duarte, D. L., & Snyder, N. T. (1999). *Mastering Virtual Teams: Strategies, Tools, and Techniques that Succeed*. San Francisco: Jossey-Bass.

Duclos, L. K., Vokurka, R. J., & Lummus, R. R. (2003). A conceptual model of supply chain flexibility. *Industrial Management & Data Systems*, *103*(5/6), 446–456. doi:10.1108/02635570310480015

Dukerich, J., Kramer, R., & McLean-Parks, J. (1998). The dark side of organizational identification. In Whetten, D. A., & Godfrey, P. C. (eds), Identity in organizations: building theory through conversations (p. 245-256). London: Sage Publications.

Dyer, J. H. (1997). Effective interfirm collaboration: How firms minimize transaction costs and maximize transaction value. *Strategic Management Journal*, *18*(7), 535–556. doi:10.1002/(SICI)1097-0266(199708)18:7<535::AID-SMJ885>3.0.CO;2-Z

Dyer, J. H. (2000). *Collaborative Advantage: Winning through Extended Enterprises Supplier Networks*. Oxford, UK: Oxford University Press.

Easterby-Smith, M., Araujo, L., & Burgoyne, J. (1999). Organizational learning and the learning organization: developments in theory and practice. London: Sage Publications.

Ebel, H., Mielsch, L.-I., & Bornholdt, S. (2002). Scale free topology of e-mail networks. *Physical Review*, 66.

Edvisson, L., & Malone, M. S. (1997). Intellectual Capital. London: Piatkus Publications.

Eisenhardt, K. M. (1989). Building theories from case study research. *Academy of Management Review*, *14*(4), 532–550. doi:10.2307/258557

Ekwall, D. (2009). Managing the Risk for Antagonistic Threats against the Transport Network. Unpublished PhD thesis, University of Borås, Sweden.

Elkins, D., Handfield, R. B., Blackburst, J., & Craighead, C. W. (2005). 18 Ways to Guard Against Disruption. Supply Chain Management Review, 46.

Elkins, D., Kulkarni, D., & Tew, J. (2008). Identifying and assessing supply chain risk. In B. Handfield & K. McCormack (Eds.), Supply chain risk management: minimizing disruptions in global sourcing (pp. 51-56). London: Auerbach Publications.

Embleton, P. R., & Wright, P. C. (1998). A practical guide to successful outsourcing. *Empowerment in Organizations*, *6*(3), 94–106. doi:10.1108/14634449810210832

Engelhardt-Nowitzki, C., & Zsifkovits, H. (2007). Complexity-induced supply chain risks – interdependencies between supply chain risks and complexity management. In W. Kersten & T. Blecker (Eds.), Managing risks in supply chains (pp. 37-56). Berlin, Germany: Verlag.

Erikson, K. (1990). On work and alienation. In Erikson, K. & Valls, P. (eds), The nature of work: sociological perspectives (pp.19-35). New Haven, CT: Yale University.

Evans, E. F., & Dale, B. G. (1989). The Use of Audits in Purchasing. *International Journal of Physical Distribution & Materials Management*, *18*(7), 15–23.

Evans, J., & Olson, D. (1998). Introduction to Simulation and Risk Analysis. Upper Saddle River, New Jersey: Prentice-Hall.

Fadzil, F. H., Haron, H., & Jantan, M. (2005). Internal auditing practices and internal control system . *Managerial Auditing Journal*, *20*(8), 844–866. doi:10.1108/02686900510619683

Faisal, M. N., Banwet, D. K., & Shankar, R. (2006). Mapping supply chains on risk and customer sensitivity dimensions . *Industrial Management & Data Systems*, *106*(6), 878–895. doi:10.1108/02635570610671533

Faisal, M., Banwet, D., & Shankar, R. (2007). Quantification of risk mitigation environment of supply chains using graph theory and matrix methods. *European Journal of Industrial Engineering*, *1*, 22–39. doi:10.1504/EJIE.2007.012652

Ferdows, K., Lewis, M., & Machuca, J. A. D. (2004). Zara. *Supply Chain Forum* . *International Journal (Toronto, Ont.)*, *4*(2), 62–67.

Fike, R. L. (2005). *Supply chain risk management: redefining the audit function within a large industrial company*. Master Thesis of Engineering in Logistics, Massachusetts Institute of Technology, Engineering Systems Division.

Filos, E., & Ouzounis, V. K. (2003). Virtual Organisations Technologies, Trends, Standards and the Contribution of the European RTD Programmes. *International Journal of Computer Applications in Technology*, Special Issue . *Applications in Industry of Product and Process Modelling Using Standards*, *18*(1), 6–26.

Finch, P. (2004). Supply chain risk management. *Supply Chain Management: An International Journal*, *9*(2), 183–196. doi:10.1108/13598540410527079

Finch, S. (2009). An upsdide to the downturn. *CPO Agenda, Spring.*

Fine, C. H. (1998). Clockspeed: Winning industry control in the age of temporary advantage. Reading, MA: Perseus Books.

Fine, C. H., & Whitney, D. E. (1996). Is the make-buy decision process a core competence? Working paper no. 3875-96, February, MIT Center for Technology, Policy, and Industrial Development, Cambridge, MA.

Fisher, M. L. (1997). What is the right supply chain for your product? *Harvard Business Review, 75*(2), 105–116.

Fishman, G. S., & Kiviat, P. J. (1968). The statistics of discrete event simulation. *Simulation, 10*(4), 185–195. doi:10.1177/003754976801000406

Fitzgerald, L., Johnston, R., Brignall, S., Silvestro, R., & Voss, C. (1991). Performance Measurement in Service Business. London: Chartered Institute of Management Accountants.

Flynn, D. (2003). *Information Systems Requirements: Determination and Analysis* (2nd ed.). New York: Mc Graw-Hill.

Foray, D. (2004). The Economics of Knowledge. Boston: MIT Press.

Ford, D., Cotton, B., Farmer, D., Gross, A., & Wilkinson, I. (1993). 'Make-or-buy decisions and their implications. *Industrial Marketing Management, 22*(3), 207–214. doi:10.1016/0019-8501(93)90007-T

Forrester, J. W. (1961). *Industrial Dynamics.* Waltham, MA: Pegasus Communications.

Foucault, M. (1980) The Archaeology of Knowledge, London: Polity Press

Fowler, D. (1999). Virtual private networks. San Francisco: Morgan Kaufmann Publishers Inc.

Franke, U. (2000). The Knowledge Based view (KBV) of the Virtual Web, the Virtual Corporation and the Net Broker. In Y. Malhotra (Ed), Knowledge Management and Virtual Organizations, Hershey, PA: Idea Group Publishing

Franks, J. (2000). Supply Chain Innovation. *Work Study, 49*(4), 152–155. doi:10.1108/00438020010330484

Franz, M., Freudenthaler, K., Kameny, M., & Schoen, S. (2002). The development of the Siemens Knowledge Community Support, In T.H. Davenport & and G.J.B. Probst, (Eds.), Knowledge Management Case Book, (147-159), New York: Wiley and Sons.

Fricker, R. D. Jr, & Goodhart, C. A. (2000). Applying a bootstrap approach for setting reorder points in military supply systems. *Naval Research Logistics, 47*(6), 459–478. doi:10.1002/1520-6750(200009)47:6<459::AID-NAV1>3.0.CO;2-C

Fujita, M., Krugman, P., & Venables, A. (2000). The Spatial Economy: Cities, Regions and International Trade. Cambridge, MA: MIT Press

Fuller, J. B., O'Conner, J., & Rawlinson, R. (1993). Tailored logistics: the next advantage . *Harvard Business Review, 71*(3), 87–98.

Gadde, L., & Håkansson, H. (2001) *Supply Network Strategies.* Chichester, UK: John Wiley & Sons..

Gaonkar, R. S., & Viswanadham, N. (2007). Analytical Framework for the Management of Risk in Supply Chain. *IEEE Transactions on Automation Science and Engineering, 4*(2), 265–273. doi:10.1109/TASE.2006.880540

Garber, R., & Sarkar, S. (2007). Want a more flexible supply chain? *Supply Chain Management Review, 62,* 28–33.

Gaudreault, J., Frayret, J.-M., & Pesant, G. (2009). Distributed search for supply chain coordination . *Computers in Industry, 60*(6), 441–451. doi:10.1016/j.compind.2009.02.006

Georgantzas, N. C. (2001). Virtual enterprise network: the fifth element of corporate governance. *Human Systems Management., 20*(3), 171–189.

Gerwin, D. (1987). An agenda for research on the flexibility of manufacturing processes. *International Journal of Operations & Production Management, 7*(1), 38–49. doi:10.1108/eb054784

Gerwin, D. (1993). Manufacturing flexibility: a strategic perspective. *Management Science*, *39*(4), 395–410. doi:10.1287/mnsc.39.4.395

Gilbert, N. (2008). Agent Based Models: Quantitative Applications in the Social Sciences. Thousand Oaks, CA: SAGE Publications.

Gilley, K. M., & Rasheed, A. (n.d.). Making more by doing less: An analysis of outsourcing and its effect on firm performance. *Journal of Management*, *26*(4), 763–790. doi:10.1016/S0149-2063(00)00055-6

Gillham, B. (2000). Case study research methods. London & New York: Continuum Editions.

Giunipero, L. C., & Eltantawy, R. A. (2004). Securing the upstream supply chain: a risk management approach. *International Journal of Physical Distribution & Logistics Management*, *34*(9), 698–713. doi:10.1108/09600030410567478

Glover, F. (1977). Heuristics for Integer Programming Using Surrogate Constraints. *Decision Sciences*, *8*(1), 156–166. doi:10.1111/j.1540-5915.1977.tb01074.x

Glover, F. (1994a). Genetic Algorithms and Scatter Search: Unsuspected Potentials. *Statistics and Computing*, *4*, 131–140. doi:10.1007/BF00175357

Glover, F. (1994b). Tabu Search for Nonlinear and Parametric Optimization (with links to genetic algorithms). *Discrete Applied Mathematics*, *49*, 231–255. doi:10.1016/0166-218X(94)90211-9

Goldman, S. L., Nagel, R. N., & Preis, K. (1995). *Agile Competitors and Virtual Organizations - Strategies for Enriching the Customer*. New York: Van Nostrand Reinhold.

Goldstone, R. L., & Janssen, M. A. (2005). Computational models of collective behavior. *Trends in Cognitive Sciences*, *9*(9), 424–430. doi:10.1016/j.tics.2005.07.009

Good, W. J., & Hatt, P. K. (1952). Methods in social research. New York: Mc Graw Hill.

Goranson, H. (1999). The agile virtual enterprise: Cases, metrics, tools. New York: Quorum Books.

Goranson, H. T. (1999). *The agile virtual enterprise: cases, metrics, tools*. Westport, CT: Quorum Books.

Grabowski, M., & Roberts, K. H. (1997). Risk mitigation in large scale systems: Lessons from high reliability organizations. *California Management Review*, *39*, 152–162.

Grabowski, M., & Roberts, K. H. (1999). Risk mitigation in virtual organizations. *Organization Science*, *10*(6), 704–721. doi:10.1287/orsc.10.6.704

Grandori, A., & Soda, G. (1995). Inter-firm networks: antecedents, mechanisms and forms. *Organization Studies*, *16*(2), 183–214. doi:10.1177/017084069501600201

Grant, K. A. (2007). Tacit knowledge revisited – We can still learn from Polanyi. *Electronic Journal of Knowledge Management*, *5*(2), 173–180.

Grant, R. M. (1996). Toward a Knowledge-Based Theory of the Firm. *Strategic Management Journal*, *17*(Winter), 109–122.

Gray, J. (1998). False Dawn: The Delusions of Global Capitalism. London: Granta Books.

Grefen, P., Eshuis, R. Mehandjiev, N., Kouvas, G., & Weichhart, G. (in press). Cross Work: Internet-Based Support for Process-Oriented Instant Virtual Enterprises. *IEEE Internet Computing*, *13*(6).

Grefen, P., Eshuis, R., Mehandjiev, N., Kouvas, G., & Weichhart, G. (2009). Dynamic business network process management in instant virtual enterprises . *Computers in Industry*, *60*(2), 86–103. doi:10.1016/j.compind.2008.06.006

Grembergen, W. (Ed.). (2003). Strategies for information technology governance. Hershy, PA: Idea Group Publishing.

Grossman, S. J., & Hart, O. D. (1986). The Costs and Benefits of Ownership: A Theory of Vertical and Lateral Integration. *The Journal of Political Economy*, *94*(4), 691–719. doi:10.1086/261404

Guerrieri, P., & Pietrobelli, C. (2000, June 15-17). Models of Industrial Distincts Evolution and Changes in Technological Règimes. *DRUID Summer Conference*, Denmark, pp. 1-19.

Gulati, R. (1995). Does familiarity breed trust? The implications of repeated ties for contractual choice in alliances. *Academy of Management Journal, 38*(1), 85–112. doi:10.2307/256729

Gulati, R., & Wang, L. (2003). Size of the Pie and Share of the Pie: Implications of Structural Embeddedness for Value Creation and Value Appropriation in Joint Ventures. *Research in the Sociology of Organizations, 20,* 209–242. doi:10.1016/S0733-558X(02)20008-7

Gulati, R., Khanna, T., & Nohria, N. (2004). Unilateral commitments and the importance of process in alliances. *Sloan Management Review,* 61–74.

Gunasekaran, A., & Ngai, E. W. T. (2004). Virtual supply-chain management. *Production Planning and Control, 15*(6), 584–595. doi:10.1080/09537280412331283955

Gunasekaran, A., Patel, C., & Tirtiroglu, E. (2001). Performance measures and metrics in a supply chain environment. *International Journal of Operations & Production Management, 21*(1-2), 71–87. doi:10.1108/01443570110358468

Gustavsson, S. O. (1984). Flexibility and productivity in complex production processes. *International Journal of Production Research, 22*(5), 801–808. doi:10.1080/00207548408942500

Hakansson, H. (1989). Corporate technological behaviour: cooperation and networks. London: Routledge.

Hakansson, H., & Johanson, J. (1988). Formal and informal cooperation strategies in international industrial networks. In Contractor, F. J., & Lorange, P. (eds), Cooperative strategies in international business. Lexington, UK: Lexington Books.

Håkansson, H., & Johanson, J. (1993). The Network as a Governance Structure. Interfirm Cooperation beyond Markets and Hierarchies. In Grabher, G. (ed.), *The Embedded Firm*, London: Routledge.

Håkansson, H., & Snehota, I. (1998). The burden of relationships or who's next? In Thurnbull, P. (ed.) Network

dynamics in international marketing. Oxford: Elsevier Science.

Halaris, C., Kerridge, S., Bafoutsou, G., Mentzas, G., & Kerridge, S. (2003). An Integrated System Supporting Virtual Consortia in the Construction Sector. *Journal of Organizational Computing and Electronic Commerce, 13*(3/4), 243–265. doi:10.1207/S15327744JOCE133&4_06

Hale, R., & Whitlam, P. (1997). Towards the virtual organization. London: McGraw Hill International.

Hall, H. (2001, April). *Social exchange for knowledge exchange*. Paper presented in the Conference "Managing Knowledge: conversations and critiques", Leicester University Management Center, UK.

Hallikas, J., & Varis, J. (2009). Risk Management in Value Networks. In G. A. Zsidisin, & B. Ritchie (Eds), Supply Chain Risk: A Handbook of Assessment, Management, and Performance (pp. 35-52), New York: Springer.

Hallikas, J., Karvonen, I., Pulkkinen, U., Virolainen, V.-M., & Tuominen, M. (2004). Risk management processes in supplier networks. *International Journal of Production Economics, 90*(1), 47–58. doi:10.1016/j.ijpe.2004.02.007

Hallikas, J., Virolainen, V.-M., & Tuominen, M. (2002). Risk analysis and assessment in network environments: A dyadic case study. *International Journal of Production Economics, 78*(1), 45–55. doi:10.1016/S0925-5273(01)00098-6

Halman, J. M., & Keizer, J. A. (1994). Diagnosing risks in product-innovation project. *International Journal of Project Management, 12*(2), 75–81. doi:10.1016/0263-7863(94)90013-2

Hamel, G. (1991). Competition for competence and inter-partner learning with international strategic alliances. *Strategic Management Journal, 12,* 83–103. doi:10.1002/smj.4250120908

Handfield, R. B., & Bechtel, C. (2002). The role of trust and relationship structure in improving supply chain responsiveness. *Industrial Marketing Management, 31,* 367–382. doi:10.1016/S0019-8501(01)00169-9

Handy, C. (1995). Trust and the virtual organization: how do you manage people whom you do not see? *Harvard Business Review*, *73*, 40–48.

Hardy, G. (2006). New roles for board members on IT. *Governance Journal*, *13*(151), 11–14.

Harland, C., & Knight, L. (2005). Outsourcing: Assessing the Risks and Benefits for Organizations, Sectors and Nations. *International Journal of Operations & Production Management*, *25*(9), 831–850. doi:10.1108/01443570510613929

Harland, C., Brenchley, R., & Walker, H. (2003). Risk in supply networks. *Journal of Purchasing and Supply Management*, *9*, 51–62. doi:10.1016/S1478-4092(03)00004-9

Harland, M. (1996). Supply Chain Management: Relationships, Chains and Networks . *British Journal of Management*, (March): 63–80. doi:10.1111/j.1467-8551.1996.tb00148.x

Harringan, K. R. (1984). Formulating vertical integration strategies. *Academy of Management Review*, *9*, 638–652. doi:10.2307/258487

Harringan, K. R. (1984). Matching vertical integration strategies to competitive conditions. *Strategic Management Journal*, *7*, 535–555.

Harrison, A., & van Hoek, R. (2008). *Logistics Management and Strategy: Competing Through The Supply Chain*. London: Prentice Hall.

Harrison, J. S., & John, C. H. (1996). Managing and partnering with external stakeholders . *The Academy of Management Executive*, *10*(2), 46–57.

Hart, P., & Saunders, C. (1997). Power and trust: Critical factors in the adoption and use of electronic data interchange. *Organization Science*, *8*(1), 23–42. doi:10.1287/orsc.8.1.23

Hartman, B., Flinn, D. J., & Beznosov, K. (2001). Enterprise security with EJB and CORBA. New York: John Wiley & Sons.

Hassan, M., & Jain, R. (2003). High performance TCP/IP networking. Upper Saddle River, NJ: Prentice Hall.

Hawkes, L., & Adams, M. B. (1995). Total Quality Management and the Internal Audit: Empirical Evidence . *Managerial Auditing Journal*, *10*(1), 31–36. doi:10.1108/02686909510077361

Hayes, R. H., & Wheelwright, S. C. (1979). The dynamics of process-product life cycles . *Harvard Business Review*, *57*(22), 127–136.

Hayes, R. H., & Wheelwright, S. C. (1984). Restoring Our Competitive Edge: Competing Through Manufacturing. New York: Wiley

Haykin, S. (1999). Neural Networks A Comprehensive Foundation. Upper Saddle River, NJ: Prentice Hall.

Hendricks, K. B., & Singhal, V. R. (2005). An empirical analysis of the effect of supply chain disruptions on long-run stock price performance and equity risk of the firm. *Production & Operations Management.*, *14*(1), 35–52.

Hendricks, K. B., & Singhal, V. R. (2005). Association Between Supply Chain Glitches and Operating Performance. *Management Science*, *51*(5), 695–711. doi:10.1287/mnsc.1040.0353

Hendry, J. (1995). Culture, community and networks: the hidden cost of outsourcing. *European Management Journal*, *13*(2), 193–200. doi:10.1016/0263-2373(95)00007-8

Hennet, J., Mercantini, J., & Demongodin, I. (2008). Toward an integration of risk analysis in supply chain assessment. In *Proceedings of the 20th European Modelling & Simulation Symposium*, (pp. 255-260).

Henriksson, K. (1999). The collective dynamics of organizational learning. Lund, Sweden: Lund University Press.

Hillson, D. (2008). Why risk includes opportunity. *The Risk Register Journal of PMI's Risk Management Special Interest Group*, *10*(4), 1–3.

Hoare, D. (1987) Succeeding by Self-audit, *Management Today, April*, 94-95.

Hocker, J. L., & Wilmot, W. W. (1985). Interpersonal Conflict. 2nd edition, Dubuque, IA: William C. Brown.

Holland, W., & Sodhi, M. (2004). Quantifying the effect of batch size and order errors on the bullwhip effect using simulation. *International Journal of Logistics: Research & Applications.*, *7*(3), 251–261.

Holsapple, C. W. (2003). Knowledge and its Attributes. In C.W. Holsapple (Ed.), Handbook of Knowledge Management (pp. 165-188). Berlin, Germany: Springer-Verlag

Holsapple, J., & Jones, K. (2005). Exploring Secondary Activities of the Knowledge Chain. *Knowledge and Process Management*, *12*(1), 3–30. doi:10.1002/kpm.219

Hoogervorst, J. (2009). Enterprise governance and enterprise engineering. Diemen, The Netherlands: Springer.

Hu, J., & Su, D. (2007). EJB-MVC oriented supplier selection system for mass customization . *Journal of Manufacturing Technology Management*, *18*(1), 54–71. doi:10.1108/17410380710717643

Huang, G. Q., Zhang, X. Y., & Liang, L. (2005). Towards integrated optimal configuration of platform products, manufacturing processes and supply chains. *Journal of Operations Management*, *23*(3/4), 267–290. doi:10.1016/j.jom.2004.10.014

Huang, M., Ip, W. H., Yang, H., Xingwei, W., & Lau, H. C. W. (2008). A fuzzy synthetic evaluation embedded tabu search for risk programming of virtual enterprises. *International Journal of Production Economics*, *116*(1), 104–114. doi:10.1016/j.ijpe.2008.06.008

Hudsal J. (2009). *From Risk Supply Chains to Risks in Virtual Enterprise Networks: Ideas, Concept and a Framework.* MTIP 2009 (Submitted Abstract)

Huisman, M., & van Duijn, M. A. J. (2005). Software for social network analysis . In Carrington, P. J. (Eds.), *Models and Methods in Social Network Analysis*. New York: Cambridge University Press.

Humphreys, E. (2007). Implementing the ISO/IEC 27001 information security management system standard. Norwood, MA: Artech House Publishers.

Husdal, J. (2008). *Does location matter?* Paper presented at the International Conference on Flexible Supply Chains in a Global Economy, Molde, Norway.

Husdal, J. (2009). *Does location matter? Supply chain disruptions in sparse transportation networks.* Paper presented at the TRB Annual Meeting, Washington, DC.

Hyland, P., & Beckett, R. (2002). Learning to compete: the value of internal benchmarking. *Benchmarking: An International Journal*, *9*(3), 293–304. doi:10.1108/14635770210429036

Iandoli, L., & Zollo, G. (2007), Organizational Cognition and Learning. Building Systems for the Learning Organization. Hershey, PA: IGI Global Publishing.

IIA. (2004). The role of internal audit in enterprise-wide risk management, Position Statement, *Institute of Internal Auditors (IAA)*, London. Retrieved July 13, 2009, from www.theiia.org/iia/download.cfm?file=283

Inkpen, A. C., & Tsang, E. W. K. (2005). Social capital, networks and knowledge transfer . *Academy of Management Review*, *30*(1), 146–165.

ISO. (2009). ISO/FDIS 31000 Risk management - Principles and guidelines. *International Standards Organization (ISO) Technical Managemnt Board.* Retrieved May 30, 2009, from http://www.iso.org/iso/iso_catalogue/catalogue_tc/catalogue_detail.htm?csnumber=43170

IT Governance Institute 'ITG'. (2008). Enterprise value: Governance of IT investments - The Val IT framework 2.0. Rolling Meadows, IL: Information Systems Audit and Control Association, (ISACA).

Izquierdo, S. S., & Izquierdo, L. R. (2007). The impact of quality uncertainty without asymmetric information on market efficiency. *Journal of Business Research*, *60*(8), 858–867. doi:10.1016/j.jbusres.2007.02.010

Jagdev, H. S., & Browne, J. (1998). The extended enterprise —a context for manufacturing. *Production Planning and Control*, *9*(3), 216–245. doi:10.1080/095372898234190

Jagdev, H. S., & Thoben, K. D. (2001). Anatomy of enterprise collaborations . *Production Planning and Control*, *12*(5), 437–451. doi:10.1080/09537280110042675

Jarillo, J. C. (1988). On strategic networks. *Strategic Management Journal*, *9*, 31–41. doi:10.1002/smj.4250090104

Jarrillo, J. C. (1988). Strategic Networks: Creating the Borderless Organisation. Oxford, UK: Butterworth-Heinemann.

Jarvenpaa, S. L., & Leidner, D. E. (1999). Communication and trust in global virtual teams. *Organization Science, 10*, 791–815 (also published as Communication and trust in global virtual teams, *Journal of Computer Mediated Communication, 3*[4], June 1998)

Jarvenpaa, S. L., Shaw, T. R., & Staples, D. S. (2004). Toward Contextualized Theories of Trust: The Role of Trust in Global Virtual Teams. *Information Systems Research, 15*(3), 250–267. doi:10.1287/isre.1040.0028

Jeong, H., Tombor, B., Albert, R., Oltvai, Z. N., & Barabasi, A.-L. (2000). The large-scale organization of metabolic networks. *Nature, 407*, 651–654. doi:10.1038/35036627

Jiang, B., Frazier, V., & Prater, E. L. (2006). Outsourcing effects on firms' operational performance: An empirical study. *International Journal of Operations & Production Management, 26*(12), 1280–1300. doi:10.1108/01443570610710551

Johnson, M. (1997). Outsourcing (in brief). Boston: Butterworth Heinemann Editions. Israel, J. (1971). Alienation. New York: Allyn and Bacon Editions.

Johnson, M. E. (2001). Learning from toys: lessons in managing supply chain risk from the toy industry. *California Management Review, 43*(3), 106–124.

Johnston, D. (1998). Open networks, electronic commerce and the global information infrastructure. *Computer Standards & Interfaces, 20*, 95–99. doi:10.1016/S0920-5489(98)00042-7

Jordan, E., & Silcock, L. (2005). Beating IT risks. West Sussex, UK: John Wiely and Sons, Ltd.

Jorion, P. (2007), Financial Risk Manager Handbook. New York: Wiley.

Jütner, U., Peck, H., & Christopher, M. (2003). Supply Chain Risk Management: Outlining an Agenda for Future Research. *International Journal of Logistics: Research and Applications, 6*(4), 197–210.

Juttner, U. (2005). Supply Chain Risk Management Understanding the Business Requirements from a Practitioner Perspective. *The International Journal of Logistics Management, 16*, 120–141. doi:10.1108/09574090510617385

Juttner, U. (2005). Supply chain risks management: understanding the business requirements from a practitioner perspective. *Journal of Logistics Management, 16*(1), 120–141. doi:10.1108/09574090510617385

Kaihara, T. (2003). Supply Chain Management Multi-agent based supply chain modelling with dynamic environment. *International Journal of Production Economics, 85*(2), 263–269. doi:10.1016/S0925-5273(03)00114-2

Kajüter, P. (2003). Risk Management in Supply Chains. In Seuring, S., Müller, M., Goldbach, M., & Schneidewind, U. (Eds.), *Strategy and Organization in Supply Chains*. Heidelberg, Germany: Physica.

Kanter, R. M., & Mayers, P. S. (1991). Interorganizational bonds and intraorganizational behavior: how alliances and partnerships change the organizations forming them. In Etzioni, A. & Lawrence P. (eds), Socio-Economics: towards a new synthesis. New York: Armonk

Kaplan, J. (2002, January 14). The realities of outsourcing. *Network World*, 12-13.

Kaplan, S. (1997). The words of risk analysis. *Risk Analysis, 17*(4), 407–417. doi:10.1111/j.1539-6924.1997.tb00881.x

Karningsih, P. D., Kayis, B., & Kara, S. (2007). *Risk Identification in Global Manufacturing Supply Chain*. Jakarta, Indonesia: University of Indonesia.

Katzy, B. R., & Dissel, M. (2001). A toolset for building the virtual enterprise. *Journal of Intelligent Manufacturing, 12*(2), 121–131. doi:10.1023/A:1011248409830

Katzy, B., & Schuh, G. (1998). The Virtual Enterprise. In Molina, A., Kusiak, A., & Sanchez, J. (Eds.), *Handbook of Life Cycle Engineering - Concepts, Methods and Tools*. Dordrecht, UK: Kluwer Academic Publishers.

Kayworth, T., & Leidner, D. (2000). The global virtual manager: a prescription for success. *Eur. Managmt J., 18*(2), 183–194. doi:10.1016/S0263-2373(99)00090-0

Keebler, J. S. (2006). Rigor in logistics and supply chain models. Paper presented at the annual meeting of the Council of Supply Chain Management Professionals, San Antonio, TX.

Kelly, A. (1988). Maintenance Systems Auditing - An Aid to Effective Maintenance Management. *Maintenance, September/October*, 6-12.

Keqiang, W., Zhaofeng, Z., & Dongchuan, S. (2008). *Structure analysis of supply chain networks based on complex network theory*. Paper presented at the Fourth International Conference on Semantics, Knowledge and Grid.

Kersten, W., Boger, M., Hohrath, P., & Spath, H. (2006). Supply chain risk management: development of a theoretical and empirical framework. In W. Kersten & T. Blecker (Eds.), Managing risks in supply chains (pp. 3-17). Berlin, Germany: Verlag.

Khan, O., Christopher, M., & Burnes, B. (2008). The impact of product design on supply chain risk: a case study. *International Journal of Physical Distribution and Logistics Management*, 38(5), 412–432. doi:10.1108/09600030810882834

Kincade, D. H., Regan, C., & Gibson, F. Y. (2007). Concurrent engineering for product development in mass customization for the apparel industry . *International Journal of Operations & Production Management*, 27(6), 627–649. doi:10.1108/01443570710750295

Kinder, T. (2003). Go with the flow-a conceptual framework for supply relations in the era of the extended enterprise. *Research Policy*, 32(3), 503–523. doi:10.1016/S0048-7333(02)00021-5

Kindinger, J. (2002). *A systems approach to project risk management*. Paper presented at the 6th International Conference on Probabilistic Safety Assessment and Management, Puerto Rico, USA.

King, N. (2004), Using interviews in qualitative research, In Cassell, C., &Symon, G. (eds.), Essential guide to qualitative methods in organizational research, Thousand Oaks, CA: Sage Publications. (pp. 11-22).

Kirkpatrick, S., Gelatt, C. D., & Vecchi, M. P. (1983). Optimization by Simulated Annealing. *Science New Series*, 220(4598), 671–680.

Kirytopoulos, K., Leopoulos, V., & Voulgaridou, D. (2008). Supplier selection in pharmaceutical industry: An analytic network process approach. Benchmarking: An International Journal, 15(4), 494-516.Krugman, P. (1997). Pop Internationalism. Cambridge, MA: MIT Press

Kirytopoulos, K., Voulgaridou, D., Panopoulos, D., & Leopoulos, V. (2009). Project termination analysis in SMEs: Making the right call. *International Journal of Management and Decision Making*, 10(1-2), 69–90. doi:10.1504/IJMDM.2009.023915

Kissani, I. (2006). Reliability improvement in supply chain design under demand and supply uncertainties. In W. Kersten & T. Blecker (Eds.), Managing risks in supply chains (pp. 57-75). Berlin, Germany: Verlag.

Kleindorfer, P. R., & Saad, G. H. (2005). Managing Disruption Risks in Supply Chains . *Production and Operations Management*, 14(1), 53–68.

Klimov, R., & Merkuryev, J. (2008). Simulation model for supply chain reliability evaluation. *Journal: Technological and Economic Development of Economy*, 14, 300–311. doi:10.3846/1392-8619.2008.14.300-311

Knight, F. (1965). Risk, Uncertainty and Profit. New York: Harper & Row.(first published 1921).

Kogan, K., & Tapiero, C. (2007) Supply chain games: operations management and risk valuation. New York: Springer.

Korman, A. K. (1970). Towards a hypothesis of work behaviour. *The Journal of Applied Psychology*, 56, 31–41. doi:10.1037/h0028656

Koste, L. L., & Malhotra, M. K. (1999). A theoretical framework for analyzing the dimensions of manufacturing flexibility. *Journal of Operations Management*, 18(1), 75–93. doi:10.1016/S0272-6963(99)00010-8

Kotler, P., & Rath, G. A. (1984). Design: A Powerful but Neglected Strategic Tool . *The Journal of Business Strategy*, 5(2), 16–21. doi:10.1108/eb039054

Kovács, G. L., & Paganelli, P. (2003). A planning and management infrastructure for large, complex, distributed projects—beyond ERP and SCM. *Computers in Industry*, *51*(2), 165–183. doi:10.1016/S0166-3615(03)00034-4

Kraljic, P. (1983). Purchasing Must Become Supply Management. *Havard Business Review (September-October)*.

Krishnan, V., & Ulrich, K. (2001). Product development decisions: a review of the literature. *Management Science*, *47*(1), 52–68. doi:10.1287/mnsc.47.1.52.10665

Kumar, A. (2004). Mass customization: metrics and modularity. *International Journal of Flexible Manufacturing Systems*, *16*(4), 287–312. doi:10.1007/s10696-005-5169-3

Kumar, K., & Dissel, H. G. V. (1996). Sustainable Collaboration: Managing Conflict and Cooperation in Interorganizational Systems. *Management Information Systems Quarterly*, *20*(3), 279–300. doi:10.2307/249657

Kumar, V., Fantazy, A., & Kumar, U. (2006). Implementation and management framework for supply chain flexibility. *Journal of Enterprise Information Management*, *19*(3), 303–319. doi:10.1108/17410390610658487

Kumpe, E., & Bolwjin, P. T. (1988)... *Harvard Business Review*, 75–81.

Kunreuther, H. (2006). Risk and reaction: Dealing with interdependencies. *Harvard International Review: Global Catastrophe*, *28*(3), 17–23.

Kunreuther, H. (2008). *The weakest link: Risk management strategies for dealing with interdependencies* (Working Paper # 2008-10-13). Philadelphia, PA: University of Pennsylvania, the Wharton School.

Kupke, S., & Lattemann, C. (2007). The strategic virtual corporation: bridging the experience gap. *International Journal of Web Based Communities*, *3*(1), 4–15. doi:10.1504/IJWBC.2007.013770

Kwak, Y. (2003, September). *Perception and practice of project risk management*. Paper presented in the Project Management Institute Global Congress North America, Baltimore, MD.

Lambert, D. M., & Pohlen, T. L. (2001). Supply Chain metrics. *International Journal of Logistics Management*, *12*(1), 1–19. doi:10.1108/09574090110806190

Lamming, R. C. (1993). Beyond partnership - Strategies for innovation and lean supply. London: Prentice-Hall.

Lamming, R., C., Johnsen, T., Zheng, J., & Harland, C. (2000). An intial classifcation of supply networks. *International Journal of Operations & Production Management*, *20*(6), 675–691. doi:10.1108/01443570010321667

Landeghem, H., & Vanmaele, H. (2002). Robust planning: a new paradigm for demand chain planning. *Journal of Operations Management*, *20*, 769–783. doi:10.1016/S0272-6963(02)00039-6

Lane, P. J., & Lubatkin, M. (1998). Relative absorptive capacity and inter-organizational learning. *Strategic Management Journal*, *19*, 461–477. doi:10.1002/(SICI)1097-0266(199805)19:5<461::AID-SMJ953>3.0.CO;2-L

Lankford, W. M., & Parsa, F. (1999). Outsourcing: a primer. *Management Decision*, *37*(4), 310–316. doi:10.1108/00251749910269357

Lau, H. C. W., & Lee, W. B. (2000). On a responsive supply chain information system. *International Journal of Physical Distribution & Logistics Management*, *30*(7/8), 598–610. doi:10.1108/09600030010346242

Lave, J., & Wenger, E. (1991). Situated learning. Legitimate peripheral participation. Cambridge, UK: Cambridge University Press.

Law, A. M. (2005). How to build valid and credible simulation models. Winter Simulation Conference. pp. 24-32, Orlando, Fl. Retrieved April 1, 2009, from http://www.informs-sim.org/wsc05papers/004.pdf.

Law, A. M. (2006). Simulation Modeling and Analysis. New York: McGraw-Hill.

Lazonick, W., & O' Sullivan, M. (2000). Maximizing shareholder value: a new ideology for corporate governance. *Economy and Society*, *29*(1), 13–35. doi:10.1080/030851400360541

Lazzarini, S. G., Chaddad, F. R., & Cook, M. L. (2001). Integrating supply chain and network analyses: The study of netchains. *Journal of Chain and Network Science.*, *1*(1), 7–22. doi:10.3920/JCNS2001.x002

Lee, H. L. (2004). The Triple-A Supply Chain. *Harvard Business Review*, *82*(10), 102–112.

Lee, H. L., & Sasser, M. (1995). Product universality and design for supply chain. *Production Planning and Control*, *6*(3), 270–277. doi:10.1080/09537289508930279

Lee, H. L., Billington, C., & Carter, B. (1993). Hewlett-Packard Gains Control of Inventory and Service through Design for Localization. *Interfaces*, *23*(4), 1–11. doi:10.1287/inte.23.4.1

Lee, H. L., Padmanabhan, V., & Whang, S. (1997). Information distortion in a supply chain: The bullwhip effect. *Management Science*, *43*(4), 546. doi:10.1287/mnsc.43.4.546

Lee, H., & Whang, S. (2003). Higher supply chain security with lower cost: lessons from total quality management. Working paper, Graduate School of Business, Stanford University.

Lefebvre, L. A., & Lefebvre, E. (2002). E-commerce and virtual enterprises: issues and challenges for transition economies. *Technovation*, *22*, 313–323. doi:10.1016/S0166-4972(01)00010-4

Leonard, D., & Sensiper, S. (1998). The role of tacit knowledge in group innovation. *California Management Review*, *40*(3), 112–132.

Leopoulos, V., & Kirytopoulos, K. (2002). Methodology for risk management in systems development. In *Proceedings of the Recent Advances in Computers, Computing and Communications*, 13-18. Leopoulos, V., Kirytopoulos, K. & Voulgaridou, D. (2006). Electronic alliances and the (para)pharmaceutical supply chain: Identification of risks. *WSEAS Transactions on Systems* 5(1), 279-284.

Levinson, D. (1973). Role, personality and social structure in the organizational setting. In Salaman, G., & Thompson, K. (eds), People in organizations, (pp. 222-237). Milton Keynes, UK: Open University Press.

Lewicki, R. J., McAllister, D. J., & Bies, R. J. (1998). Trust and Distrust: New Relationship & Realities. *Academy of Management Review*, *23*(3), 438–454. doi:10.2307/259288

Lewis, C. D. (1970), Scientific Inventory Control. New York: American Elsevier Publishing Company.

Lewis, J. D. (1999). *Trusted Partners: How Companies Build Mutual Trust and Win Together.* New York: Free Press.

Li, H., & Xiao, R. (2006). A multi-agent virtual enterprise model and its simulation with Swarm.

Li, M., Wang, J., Wong, Y., & Lee, K. (2005). A collaborative application portal for the mould industry. *International Journal of Production Economics*, *96*(2), 233–247. doi:10.1016/j.ijpe.2004.04.007

Li, X., & Barnes, I. (2008). Proactive supply risk management methods for building a robust supply selection process when sourcing from emerging markets. *Strategic Outsourcing: An International Journal*, *1*(3), 252–267. doi:10.1108/17538290810915308

Liebowitz, J., Montano, B., McCaw, D., & Rednik, K. (2000). The Knowledge Audit . *Journal of Knowledge and Process Management*, *7*(1), 208–212.

Lientz, B., & Larssen, L. (2006). Risk management for IT projects. Oxford, UK: Butterworth-Heinemann.

Lillehagen, F., & Karlsen, D. (2001). Visual extended enterprise engineering and operation-embedding knowledge management and work execution. *Production Planning and Control*, *12*(2), 164–175. doi:10.1080/09537280150501266

Lin, A., & Patterson, D. (2006). An Investigation in to the barriers to Introducing Virtual Enterprise Networks. Wang, W. Y. C., Heng M. S. H., Chau P. Y. K. (eds.), Supply Chain Management: Issues in the Era of Collaboration and Competition, Hershey, PA: IGI Global Publishing.

Lin, J. (2000). Vertical integration versus outsourcing: a knowledge based reconciliation. In *Proceedings of the Midwest Academy of Management Conference.*

Loebbecke, C., & van Fenema, P. C. (2000). Virtual Organizations that Cooperate and Compete: Managing the Risks of Knowledge Exchange. In Y. Malhotra (Ed), Knowledge Management and Virtual Organizations, Hershey, PA: Idea Group Publishing.

Lonsdale, C. (1999). Effectively managing vertical supply relationships: a risk management model for outsourcing. *Supply Chain Management: An International Journal, 4*(4), 176–183. doi:10.1108/13598549910284499

Lorange, P., & Roos, J. (1992). Strategic alliances: formation, implementation, and evolution. Cambridge, MA: Blackwell.

Lovkvist-Andersen, A., Olson, R., Ritchey, T., & Stenstrom, M. (2004) Developing a Generic Design Basis (GDB) model for extraordinary societal events using computer-aided morphological analysis. Retrieved April 10, 2009, from www.swemorph.com

Lummus, R. R., Duclos, K. L., & Vokurka, R. J. (2005). Delphi study on supply chain flexibility. *International Journal of Production Research, 43*(4), 1–13.

Lummus, R. R., Duclos, L. K., & Vokurka, R. J. (2003). Supply Chain Flexibility: Building a New Model. *Global Journal of Flexible Systems Management, 4*(4), 1–13.

Madsen, E. S., Riis, J. O., & Waehrens, B. V. (2008). The Knowledge Dimension of Manufacturing Transfers: A Method for Identifying Hidden Knowledge. *Strategic Outsourcing: An International Journal, 1*(3), 198–209. doi:10.1108/17538290810915272

Magretta, J. (1998). The Power of Vertical Integration: an Interview with Dell Computer's Michael Dell. *Harvard Business Review, 76*(2), 73–84.

Majima, T., Katuhara, M., & Takadama, K. (2007). Analysis on transport networks of railway, subway and waterbus in Japan. *Studies in Computational Intelligence, 56*, 99–113. doi:10.1007/978-3-540-71075-2_8

Makukha, K., & Gray, R. (2004). Logistics partnerships between shippers and logistics service providers: the relevance of strategy. *International Journal of Logistics: Research & Applications., 7*(4), 361–377.

Malhotra, Y. (Ed.). (2000). Knowledge Management and Virtual Organizations. Hershey, PA: Idea Group Publishing.

Malykhina, E. (2005). The real time imperative. *Information Week, 3*(January), 1020, 43.

Manuj, I., & Mentzer, J. T. (2008). Global supply chain risk management. *Journal of Business Logistics., 29*(1), 133–155.

Manuj, I., Mentzer, J. T., & Bowers, M. R. (2009). Enhancing the rigor of computer-based simulation research in logistics and supply chain management. *International Journal of Physical Distribution and Logistics Management., 39*(3), 172–201. doi:10.1108/09600030910951692

March, J. G., & Shapira, Z. (1987). Managerial Perspectives on Risk and Risk Taking. *Management Science, 33*(11), 1404–1418. doi:10.1287/mnsc.33.11.1404

Marsden, C. (1997). Corporate Citizenship. *Faith in Business, 1*(4)

Martinez, M. T., Fouletier, P., Park, K. H., & Favrel, J. (2001). Virtual enterprise – organisation, evolution and control. *International Journal of Production Economics, 74*(1-3), 225–238. doi:10.1016/S0925-5273(01)00129-3

Martinus, K., Rowe, M., Burn, J., & Walker, E. (2005, June 30-July 1). Beyond Clusters - Collaborative Commerce and Clustering. *CRIC Cluster conference, Beyond Cluster-Current Practices & Future Strategies,* Ballarat, Australia.

Mason-Jones, R., & Towill, D. R. (1998). Shrinking the supply chain uncertainty circle. *IOM Control, 24*(7), 17–22.

Masson, R., Iosif, L., MacKerron, G., & Fernie, J. (2007). Managing complexity in agile global fashion industry supply chains. *International Journal of Logistics Management, 18*(2), 238–254. doi:10.1108/09574090710816959

Mather, H. (1992). Design for Logistics (DFL) - The Next Challenge for Designers . *Production and Inventory Management Journal, 33*(1), 7–11.

Mayer, R. C., Davis, J. H., & Schoorman, F. D. (1995). An Integrative Model of Organizational Trust . *Academy of Management Review, 20*(3), 709–734. doi:10.2307/258792

Maznevski, M., & Chudoba, K. (2001). Bridging space over time: global virtual team dynamics and effectiveness. *Organization Science, 11*(5), 473–492. doi:10.1287/orsc.11.5.473.15200

Mc Ivor, R. (2000). A Practical Framework for Understanding the Outsourcing Process. *Supply Chain Management: An International Journal, 5*(1), 22–36. doi:10.1108/13598540010312945

Mc Manus, S., Seville, E., Brunsdon, D., & Vargo, J. (2007). *Resilience Management: A Framework for Assessing and Improving the Resilience of Organisations (No. 2007/01)*. Christchurch, New Zealand: Resilient Organisations.

McAdam, R., & McCormack, D. (2001). Integrating Business Process for Global Allignment and Supply Chain Management. *Business Process Management Journal, 7*(2), 113–130. doi:10.1108/14637150110389696

McAllister, D. J. (1995). Affect and cognition based trust as foundations for interpersonal cooperation in organizations. *Academy of Management Journal, 38*, 24–59. doi:10.2307/256727

McCumber, J. (2004). Assessing and managing security risk in IT systems: A structured methodology. Boca Raton, FL: Auerbach Publications.

McDermott, R., & O'Dell, C. (2001). Overcoming cultural barriers to sharing knowledge. *Journal of Knowledge Management, 5*(1), 76–85. doi:10.1108/13673270110384428

McDonough, E., Kahn, K., & Barczak, G. (2001). An Investigation of the Use of Global, Virtual, and Collocated New Product Development Teams. *Journal of Product Innovation Management, 18*(2), 110–120. doi:10.1016/S0737-6782(00)00073-4

McKnight, D. H., Cummings, L. L., & Chervany, N. L. (1998). Initial Trust Formation in New Organizational Relationships. *Academy of Management Review, 23*(3), 473–490. doi:10.2307/259290

McNamee, D., & Selim, G. (1999). The Next Step in Risk Management. *The Internal Auditor, 56*(3), 35–38.

Mehra, A., Kilduff, M., & Brass, D. (2001). The social networks of high and low-self monitors: Implications for workplace performance. *Administrative Science Quarterly, 46*, 121–146. doi:10.2307/2667127

Melnyk, A., Rodrigues, A., & Ragatz, G. (2008). Using simulation to investigate supply chain disruptions. In G. Zsidisin (Ed.), Supply chain risk: A handbook of assessment, management and performance (pp. 104-122). New York: Springer.

Memon, N., & Larsen, H. L. (2006). *Structural analysis and destabilizing terrorist networks.* Paper presented at the International Conference on Data Mining.

Mendonça, E., & Giménez, C. (2007). Drivers and sources of supply flexibility: an exploratory study. *International Journal of Operations & Production Management, 27*(10), 1115–1136. doi:10.1108/01443570710820657

Menken, I., & Blokdijk, G. (2008). Virtualization: The complete cornerstone guide to virtualization best practices. Brisbane, Australia: Emereo Pty Ltd.

Mentzer, J. T., & Gomes, R. (1991). The strategic planning model: a PC-based dynamic, stochastic, simulation dss generator for managerial planning. *Journal of Business Logistics., 12*(2), 193–219.

Mentzer, J. T., Dewitt, W., Keebler, J. S., Min, S., Nix, N. W., Smith, C. D., & Zacharia, Z. G. (2001). Defining supply chain management. *Journal of Business Logistics., 22*(2), 1–26.

Merriam-Webster online (n.d.). Retrieved September 4, 2009, from http://www.merriam-webster.com/dictionary/innovation

Meulbroek, L. (2002). The promise and challenge of integrated risk management. *Risk Management & Insurance Review, 5*(1). doi:10.1111/1098-1616.00006

Meulbrook, L. (2000). Total strategies for company-wide risk control . *Financial Times (North American Edition)*, 9.

Meyerson, D., Weick, K. E., & Kramer, R. M. (1996). Swift Trust and Temporary Groups In *Trust in Organizations*, Thousand Oaks, CA: Sage Publications. Also presented at the conference of Trust in organizations, held at the Graduate School of Business, Stanford University, May 14-15th, 1994.

Miles, M. B., & Huberman, A. M. (1994). Qualitative data analysis, Thousand Oaks, CA, Sage Publications.

Miles, R. E., & Snow, C. C. (1984). Fit failure and the hall of fame . *California Management Review, 26*(3), 10–28.

Milgate, M. (2001). Alliances, outsourcing and the lean organization. Praeger.

Millar, J., Demaid, A., & Quintas, P. (1997). Trans-organizational Innovation: A Framework for Research. *Technology Analysis and Strategic Management, 9*(4), 399–418. doi:10.1080/09537329708524294

Miller, K. D. (1992). A Framework for Integrated Risk Management in International Business. *Journal of International Business Studies, 23*(2), 311–331. doi:10.1057/palgrave.jibs.8490270

Misawa, K., & Hattori, K. (1998). R&D outsourcing to create core competence. *Kenkyu Kaihatsu Manejimento, 8*(6), 4-13. Translated by J. K. Keaton, Retrieved from http://www.jkl.org/rd_research

Mishler, E. G. (1991). Representing discourse: the rhetoric of transcription. *Journal of Narrative and Life History, 1*, 255–280.

Mitchell, V. W. (1995). Organizational risk perception and reduction – a literature review. *British Journal of Management, 6*, 115–133. doi:10.1111/j.1467-8551.1995.tb00089.x

Mitroff, I., & Alpasan, M. (2003). Preparing for evil. *Harvard Business Review, 81*(4), 109–115.

Mizruchi, M. S., & Marquis, C. (2006). Egocentric, sociocentric, or dyadic? Identifying the appropriate level of analysis in the study of organizational networks. *Social Networks, 28*, 187–208. doi:10.1016/j.socnet.2005.06.002

Moeller, R. (2008, April). *Enterprise risk management and the project manager.* Paper presented at Project Summit & Business Analyst World, Philadelphia, PA.

Monckza, R. M., Trent, R. J., & Handfield, R. (2005). Purchasing & supply chain management (3 ed.). Mason, Ohio: Thomson South-Western.

Monge, P. R., & Contractor, N. S. (2003). *Theories of Communication Networks.* New York: Oxford University Press.

Moore, K. G. (2002). Six sigma: driving supply at Ford. Supply Chain Management Review, (July/August), pp.38–43.

Morey, D., Maybury, M., & Thuraisingham, B. (Eds.). (2000). Knowledge Management: classic and contemporary works. Cambridge, MA: The MIT Press.

Morgan, C. (2004). Structure, speed and salience: performance measurement in the supply chain. *Business Process Management Journal, 10*(5), 522–536. doi:10.1108/14637150410559207

Morris, S. A., Marshall, T. E., & Rainer, R. K. (2002). Impacts of User Satisfaction and Trust on Virtual Team Members. *Information Resources Management Journal, 15*(2), 22–30.

Morrow, D., Wilkerson, T., & Davey, M. (2009). SCOR for Supply Chain Risk Management. Retrieved March 14, 2009, from http://www.supply-chain.org/

Moses, A., & Par, A. (2008). Dimensions of change in make or buy decision processes. *Strategic Outsourcing: An International Journal, 1*(3), 230–251. doi:10.1108/17538290810915290

Mowery, D. C., Oxley, J. E., Silverman, B. (1996). Strategic alliances and interfirm knowledge transfer. *Strategic Management Journal, 17* (Winter Special Issue), 77-91.

Mowshowitz, A. (1994). Virtual Organization: A Vision of Management in the Information Age. *The Information Society, 10*, 267–288.

Mowshowitz, A. (1997). Virtual Organization. *Communications of the ACM, 40*(9), 30–37. doi:10.1145/260750.260759

Mowshowitz, A. (2002). *Virtual Organization, Toward a Theory of Societal Transformation Stimulated by Information Technology*. Westport, UK: Quorum Books.

Mullins, W., & Larreche, B. (2006). Marketing Strategy A Decision Focused Approach. New Delhi, India: Tata McGraw-Hill.

Mun, J. (2006). Modeling risks: applying Monte Carlo simulation, real options analysis, forecasting, and optimization techniques. Atrium, UK: John Wiley & Sons Ltd.

Myerson, J. (Ed.). (2001). Enterprise systems integration. Boca Raton, FL: Auerbach Publications.

Nagurney, A., & Matsypura, D. (2005). Global supply chain network dynamics with multicriteria decision-making under risk and uncertainty [Electronic version]. *Journal of Transportation research, 41*, 585-612.

Nahapiet, J., & Goshal, S. (1998). Social capital, intellectual capital and the organizational advantage. *Academy of Management Review, 23*(2), 242–266. doi:10.2307/259373

Narain, R., Yadav, R. C., Sarkis, J., & Cordeire, J. J. (2000). The strategic implications of flexibility in manufacturing systems. *International Journal of Agile Management Systems, 2*(3), 202–213. doi:10.1108/14654650010356112

Neaigus, A., Friedman, S. R., Curtis, R., DesJarlais, D. C., Furst, S. T., & Jose, B. (1994). The relevance of drug injectors' social and risk networks for understanding and preventing HIV infection. *Social Science & Medicine, 38*, 67–78. doi:10.1016/0277-9536(94)90301-8

Neely, A., Gregory, M., & Platts, K. (1995). Performance measurement system design. *Manufacturing Engineering Group, 15*(4), 80–116.

Newman, M. (2004). Firewalls: keeping the big, bad world out of your firm. *San Fernando Valley Business Journal, 9*(18), 21–22.

Newman, M. E. J. (Ed.). (2007). *The mathematics of networks*. Ann Arbor, MI: Center for the Study of Complex Systems.

Niemann, K. (2008). From Enterprise architecture to IT governance: Elements of effective IT management. Wiesbaden, Germany: Vieweg & Sohn verlag.

Niemeyer, A., Pak, M., & Ramaswamy, S. (2003) Smart tags for your supply chain. *McKinsey Q., 4* Available online at: http://premium.mckinseyquarterly.com

NIST. (1993) Integration Definition for Function Modelling (IDEF-0) (Publication 183), Federal Information Processing Standard (FIPS), Gaithersburg, MD: Computer Systems Laboratory, National Institute of Standard and Technology (NIST).

Nohria, N., & Eccles, R. G. (1992). Networks and organizations. Boston, MA: Harvard Business Press.

Nolan, R. L., & Croson, D. C. (1995). *Creative Destruction: A Six-Stage Process for Transforming the Organization*. Boston: Harvard Business School Publishing.

Nonaka, I. (1994). A dynamic theory of organizational knowledge creation. *Organization Science, 5*(1), 14–37. doi:10.1287/orsc.5.1.14

Nonaka, I., & Takeuchi, H. (1995). The knowledge creating company: how Japanese companies create the dynamics of innovation. Oxford, UK: Oxford University Press.

Nooteboom, B., Berger, H., & Noorderhaven, N. (1997). Effects of trust and goverence on relational risk. *Academy of Management Journal, 40*(2), 308–338. doi:10.2307/256885

Norman, A., & Lindroth, R. (2004). Categorization of Supply Chain Risk and Risk Management . In Brindley, C. (Ed.), *Supply Chain Risk* (pp. 14–27). Aldershot, UK: Ashgate.

Norrman, A., & Jansson, U. (2004). Ericsson's proactive supply chain risk management approach after a serious sub-supplier accident. International . *Journal of Physical Distribution & Logistics Management, 34*, 434–456. doi:10.1108/09600030410545463

Norrman, A., & Lindroth, R. (2004). Categorization of supply chain risk and risk management. In C. Brindley (Ed.), Supply chain risk (pp. 14-27). Hampshire, UK: Ashgate. Jahns, C., Hartmann, E. & Moder, M. (2006). Managing supply risks: a system theory approach to supply early warning systems. In W. Kersten, & T. Blecker (Eds.), Managing risks in supply chains (pp. 195-212). Berlin,Germany: Verlag.

Nortel Networks. (2004). Enabling real-time communications effectiveness for today's virtual enterprise. Research Triangle Park, NC: Nortel Networks.

North, D. C. (1990). Institutions, institutional change and economic performance. Cambridge, UK: Cambridge University Press.

North, M., & Macal, C. (2007). Managing Business Complexity: Discovering Strategic Solutions with Agent-Based Modeling and Simulation.New York: Oxford University Press.

O' Brien, R. (1992). Global Financial Integration: The end of Geography? London: Pinter.

O'Hehir, M. (2007). What is business continuity planning (BCP) stratetgy? In Hiles, A. (Ed.), *The Definitive Handbook of Business Continuity Management* (pp. 27–46). Chichester, UK: John Wiley & Sons.

O'Neal, C. (1993). Concurrent engineering with early supplier involvement: a cross functional challenge . *International Journal of Purchasing and Materials Management, 29*(2), 3–9.

O'Neill, H., & Sackett, P. (1994). The Extended Manufacturing Enterprise Paradigm . *Management Decision, 32*(8), 42–49. doi:10.1108/00251749410069453

O'Rourke, M. (2004). Protecting your reputation. *Risk Management*(April).

Office of Government Commerce (OGC). (2002). Management of risk: Guidance for practitioners. London: Office of Government Commerce, Stationary office.

Ohmae, K. (1995). The End of Nation State: The Rise of Regional Economies. London: Harper Collins.

Oke, A., & Maltz, A. (2009). Criteria for sourcing from developing countries. *Strategic Outsourcing:An International Journal, 2*(2), 145–164. doi:10.1108/17538290910973367

Olifer, N., & Olifer, V. (2006). Computer networks: Principles, technologies and protocols for network design. West Sussex, UK: John Wiley and Sons, Ltd.

Oliver, D. (2009). An introduction to the business model for information security. Rolling Meadows, IL: Information Systems Audit and Control Association, (ISACA).

Orr, J. (1990). Sharing knowledge, celebrating identity: war stories and community memory in a service culture. In Middleton, D. S., & Edwards, D. (eds), Collective remembering: memory in society. Thousand Oaks, CA: Sage Publications.

Osborn, R.N., & Hagedoorn, J.G. (1998). Embedded patterns of international alliance formation . *Organization Studies, 19*(5), 617–638. doi:10.1177/017084069801900404

Ouzounis, V., & Tschammer, V. (2001, October 3-5). Towards Dynamic Virtual Enterprises. In *Proceedings of the First IFIP Conference I3E 2001, Towards the e-Society: E-Commerce*. E-Business, and E-Government, Zurich, Switzerland: Kluwer Academic Publishers.

Paik, S. K., & Bagchi, P. (2007). Understanding the causes of the bullwhip effect in a supply chain. *International Journal of Retail and Distribution Management, 35*(4), 308–324. doi:10.1108/09590550710736229

Panayiotou, N., Athanasiadou, C., & Economitsios, S. (2006). Using Enterprise Modelling Techniques in the Internal Audit Process Design Towards Continuous Improvement. In Scientific Anniversary Volume in Honor of Professor Emeritus K. N. Dervitiostis, University of Piraeus, Greece.

Panteli, N., & Sockalingam, S. (2005). Trust and conflict within virtual inter-organizational alliances: a framework for facilitating knowledge sharing. *Decision Support Systems*, 39, 599–617. doi:10.1016/j.dss.2004.03.003

Park, H., Suh, W., & Lee, K. (2004). A role-driven component-oriented methodology for developing collaborative commerce systems. *Information and Software Technology*, 46(12), 819–837. doi:10.1016/j.infsof.2004.02.002

Park, K. H., & Favrel, J. (1999). Virtual enterprise — Information system and networking solution. *Computers & Industrial Engineering*, 37(1-2), 441–444. doi:10.1016/S0360-8352(99)00113-8

Parkinson, M. (1999, October 20) *Presentation for Internal Auditing.* Presented at the Institute of Internal Auditors Educators Symposium, Sydney, Australia.

Patell, J. M. (1987). Cost Accounting, Process Control, and Product Design: A Case Study of the Hewlett-Packard Personal Office Computer Division. *Accounting Review*, 62(4), 808–839.

Paulson, U. (2004). Supply chain risk management. In C. Brindley (Ed.), Supply chain risk (pp. 79-96). Hampshire, UK: Ashgate.

Paulsson, U. (2004). Supply Chain Risk Management. In Brindley, C. (Ed.), *Supply Chain Risk*. London: Ashgate.

Paulsson, U. (2007). *On Managing Disruption Risks in the Supply Chain - the DRISC Model.* Unpublished PhD dissertation, Lund University, Lund, Sweden.

Peck, H. (2003). *Creating Resilient Supply Chains: A practical guide.* Cranfield, UK: Cranfield School of Management Publications.

Peck, H. (2005). Drivers of supply chain vulnerability: an integrated framework. *International Journal of Physical Distribution & Logistics Management*, 35(3/4), 210–229. doi:10.1108/09600030510599904

Pedersen, J. D., & Berg, R. J. (2001). Supporting partner selection for Virtual Enterprises. In Mo, J., & Nemes, L. (Eds.), *Global Engineering, Manufacturing and Enterprise Networks* (pp. 95–102). Dordrecht, UK: Kluwer Academic Publishers.

Peltier, R. (2005). Information security risk analysis. Boca Raton, FL: Taylor and Francis.

Peña, I. (2002). Knowledge networks as parts of an integrated knowledge management approach. *Journal of Knowledge Management*, 6(5), 469–478. doi:10.1108/13673270210450423

Perona, M., & Miragliotta, G. (2003). Complexity management and supply chain performance assessment. A field study and a conceptual framework. *International Journal of Production Economics*, 90(1), 103–115. doi:10.1016/S0925-5273(02)00482-6

Petersen, K. P., Handfield, R. B., Lawson, B., & Cousins, P. D. (in press). Buyer dependency and relational capital formation: The mediating effects of socialization processes and supplier integration. *Journal of Supply Chain Management*.

Pfohl, H., & Buse, P. (2000). Inter-Organizational Logistics Systems in Flexible Production Networks. An Organizational Capabilities Perspective. *International Journal of Production & Logistics Management*, 30(1), 388–401.

Pieper, R., Kouwenhoven, V., & Hamminga, S. (2004). Beyond the Hype: e-Business Strategy in Leading European Companies. The Netherlands: Van Haren Publishing.

Pike, R., & Neale, B. (1999). Corporate finance and investment: decisions and strategies. Upper Saddle River, NJ: Prentice-Hall.

Pires, S. R. I., Bremer, C. F., De Santa Eulalia, L. A., & Goulart, C. P. (2001). Supply chain and virtual enterprises: comparisons, migration and a case study. *International Journal of Logistics: Research and Applications*, 4(3), 297–311.

PMI. (2008). A Guide to project management body of knowledge. Newtown square, PA: Project Management Institute.

Pollock, N., & Cornford, J. (2004). ERP systems and the university as "unique" organization. *Information Technology & People*, 17(1), 31–52. doi:10.1108/09593840410522161

Porter, M. (1985). Competitive Advantage of Nations. New York: The Free Press.

Porter, M. (1998). Clusters and the new economics of competition. *Harvard Business Review, November/December.*

Porter, M. E. (1985). Competitive Advantage: Creating and Sustaining Superior Performance, New York: The Free Press.

Poston, T. (2006, April 25). *Thinking inside the box*, BBC News, 2006/04/25. Retrieved April 8, 2009, from http://news.bbc.co.uk/go/pr/fr/-/1/hi/business/4943382.stm

Potter, A., & Disney, S. M. (2006). Bullwhip and batching: an exploration. *International Journal of Production Economics, 104*(2), 408–418. doi:10.1016/j.ijpe.2004.10.018

Power, M. (2004). The Risk Management of Everything: Rethinking the Politics of Uncertainty. London: Demos.

Power, M. J., Desouza, K. C., & Bonifazi, C. (2006). The Outsourcing Handbook: How to implement a successful outsourcing process. Philadelphia: Kogan Page.

Power, M., Bonifazi, C., & DeSouza, K. C. (2004). The Ten Outsourcing Traps to Avoid. *The Journal of Business Strategy, 25*(2), 37–42. doi:10.1108/02756660410525399

Prahalad, C. K., & Hamel, G. (1994). Strategy as a field of study: Why search for a new paradigm? *Strategic Management Journal, 15*, 5–16.

Preiss, K. (1999). Modelling of knowledge flows and their impact. *Journal of Knowledge Management, 3*(1), 36–46. doi:10.1108/13673279910259376

Pritsker (1998). Principles of simulation modeling. In J. Banks (Ed.), Handbook of Simulation: Principles, Methodology, Advances, Applications, and Practice (pp. 31-51). New York: John Wiley and Sons.

Purdy, L., & Safayeni, F. (2000). Strategies for supplier selection: A framework for potential advantages and limitations. *IEEE Transactions on Engineering Management, 47*(4), 435–443. doi:10.1109/17.895339

Putnik, G. (Ed.), & Cunha, M. (Ed.). (2005). Virtual enterprise integration: technological and organizational perspectives. Hershy, PA: Idea Group Publishing.

Quinn, J. B. (1992). Intelligent Enterprise. New York: Free Press.

Quinn, J. B. (1999). Strategic Outsourcing: Leveraging Knowledge Capabilities . *Sloan Management Review, 40*(4), 9–22.

Quintas, P. (2002). Managing knowledge in the new century. In Little, S., Quintas, P., Ray, T. (eds), Managing knowledge: an essential reader. London: The Open University in Association with Sage Publications.

Raelin, J. A. (1997). A model of work-based learning. *Organization Science, 8*(6), 563–578. doi:10.1287/orsc.8.6.563

Ragatz, G. L., Handfield, R. B., & Scannel, T. V. (1997). Success factors for integrating suppliers into new product development . *Journal of Product Innovation Management, 14*(3), 190–202. doi:10.1016/S0737-6782(97)00007-6

Ramgopal, M. (2003). Project uncertainty management. *Coastal Engineering, 45*(12), 21–24.

Ramirez, D. (2008). IT risk management standards: The bigger picture. *Information Systems Audit and Control Association (ISACA) Journal, 2008*(4), 35-39.

Rasmussen, L. B., & Wangel, A. (2007). Work in the virtual enterprise – creating identities, building trust and sharing knowledge. *AI & Society, 21*, 184–199. doi:10.1007/s00146-005-0029-y

Reid, R. L., Tapp, J. B., Liles, D. H., Rogers, K. J., & Johnson, M. E. (1996, August 18-20). An integrated management model for virtual enterprises: vision, strategy and structure. In *Proceedings of the International Conference on Engineering and Technology Management*, IEMC 96, Vancouver BC.(pp. 522–527)

Renn, O. (2008). Risk governance: Coping with uncertainty in a complex world, London, UK: Earthscan Publications Ltd

Renn, O., & Walker, K. (Eds.). (2007). Global risk governance: Concept and practice using the IRGC framework. Dordrecht, The Netherlands: Springer.

Reve, T. (1990). The Firm as a Nexus of Internal and External Contracts.In M. Aoki, B. Gustafsson, and O. Williamson, (eds), The Firm as a Nexus of Treaties. London: Sage.

Rice, J. B., & Caniato, F. (2003). Building a secure and resilient supply network. *Supply Chain Management Review, 7*(5), 22–30.

Ritche, B., & Brindley, C. (n.d.). SCRM and performance – Issues and Challenges. In G. Zsidisin (Ed.), Supply chain risk: A handbook of assessment, management and performance (pp. 249-270). New York: Springer.

Ritchie, B., & Brindley, C. (2001). The Information-Risk Conundrum. *Journal of Marketing Intelligence and Planning, 19*(1), 29–37. doi:10.1108/02634500110363781

Rosenfeld, S. (2001, March 29-30), Backfitting into Clusters: retrofitting public policies. *Symposium for Integration Pressures: Lessons from Around the Word,* Harvard University.

Rosenfield, D. B., Copacino, W. C., & Payne, E. C. (1985). Logistics planning and evaluation when using 'what-if' simulation . *Journal of Business Logistics., 6*(2), 89–119.

Rothwell, R., & Gardiner, P. (1985). Invention, innovation, re-innovation and the role of the user. *Technovation, 3,* 167–186. doi:10.1016/0166-4972(85)90012-4

Rowbottom, U. (2004). Managing risk in global supply chains. *Supply Chain Practice, 6*(2), 16–23.

Rowe, M., Burn, J., & Walker, E. (2005, June 30-July 1). Small and Medium Enterprises Clustering and Collaborative Commerce – a social issues perspective. *CRIC Cluster conference. Beyond Cluster- Current Practices & Future Strategies.* Ballarat, Australia.

Roy, S., Sivakumar, K., & Wilkinson, I. F. (2004). Innovation Generation in Supply Chain Relationships: A Conceptual Model and Research Propositions. *Journal of the Academy of Marketing Science, 32*(1), 61–79. doi:10.1177/0092070303255470

Royal Society. (1992). Risk Analysis, Perception and Management. London: Royal Society.

Saaty, T. (1980). The Analytic Hierarchy Process, New York: McGraw-Hill.

Saaty, T. (2000). Fundamentals of Decision Making with the Analytic Hierarchy Process. Pittsburg, PA: RWS Publications.

Saaty, T. (2003). Negative priorities in the analytic hierarchy process. *Mathematical and Computer Modelling, 37*(9-10), 1063–1075. doi:10.1016/S0895-7177(03)00118-3

Saaty, T. (2004). Super Decisions Software. Pittsburg, PA: RWS Publications.

Saaty, T. (2005). Theory and Applications of the Analytic Network Process.Pittsburgh, PA: RWS Publications.

Sachan, A., & Datta, S. (2005). Review of supply chain management and logistics research. *International Journal of Physical Distribution & Logistics Management., 35*(9), 664–704. doi:10.1108/09600030510632032

Saenz, M. J., Barillas, D., & Lamban, M. P. (2008, July). *Innovation Strategies in Supply Chain Management and their relationship with Flexibility and Customer Service.* Paper presented at the meeting of the International Congress on Project Engineering, Zaragoza, Spain.

Sanchez, R. (1995). Strategic flexibility in product competition. *Strategic Management Journal, 16*(5), 135–159. doi:10.1002/smj.4250160921

Sankar, N. R., & Prabhu, B. S. (2001). Modified approach for prioritization failures in a system failure mode and effects analysis. *International Journal of Quality & Reliability Management, 18*(3), 324–335. doi:10.1108/02656710110383737

Santesmaes, M. (2005). Dyane, version 3, design and analysis of survey in social and market researches. Madrid, Spain: Piramide.

Sargent, R. G. (2007). Verification and validation of simulation models. In Proceedings of the 2007 Winter Simulation Conference, Washington, DC (pp. 124-37).

Retrieved April 1, 2009, from http://www.informs-sim.org/wsc07papers/014.pdf.

Sari, B. (2009). SME based virtual enterprises: Basics, concepts and methods. Saarbrücken, Germany: VDM Publishing.

Sari, B., Kilic, S. E., & Sen, D. T. (2007). Formation of Dynamic Virtual Enterprises and Enterprise Networks. *International Journal of Advanced Manufacturing Technology, 34*(11-12), 1246–1262. doi:10.1007/s00170-006-0688-y

Sari, B., Kilic, S. E., & Sen, D. T. (2008). AHP Model for the Selection of Partner Companies in Virtual Enterprises. *International Journal of Advanced Manufacturing Technology, 38*, 367–376. doi:10.1007/s00170-007-1097-6

Saris, W. E., & Gallhofer, I. (2007). Estimation of the effects of measurement characteristics on the quality of survey questions. *Survey Research Methods, 1*(1), 29–43.

Sarker, S., & Sahay, S. (2002). Information systems development by US–Norwegian virtual teams: implications of time and space. In *Proceedings of the Thirty-Fifth Annual Hawaii, International Conference on System, Sciences*, Hawaii, USA, pp. 1–10.

Sarker, S., Lau, F., & Sahay, S. (2001). Using an Adapted Grounded Theory Approach for Inductive Theory Building About Virtual Team Development. *The Data Base for Advances in Information Systems, 32*(1), 38–56.

Sayle, A. J. (1988) Management Audits, 2nd ed. London: Allen J. Sayle Ltd.

Scarborough, H. (1995). Blackboxes, hostages and prisoners. *Organization Studies, 16*(6), 991–1019. doi:10.1177/017084069501600604

Schekkerman, J. (2006). How to survive in the jungle of enterprise architecture frameworks. Victoria, BC: Trafford Publishing.

Schlarman, S. (2009). IT risk exploration: The IT risk management taxonomy and evolution. *Information Systems Audit and Control Association (ISACA) Journal, 2009*(3), 27-30.

Schleifer, L., & Greenawalt, M. (1996). The internal auditor and the critical thinking process. *Managerial Auditing Journal, 11*(5), 5–13. doi:10.1108/02686909610120479

Schmitt, L. M. (2004). Theory of Genetic Algorithms. *Theoretical Computer Science, 259*, 1–61. doi:10.1016/S0304-3975(00)00406-0

Schwarz, S. (2008, April). *Projecting Risk from stakeholder analysis using RACI*. Paper presented at Project Summit & Business Analyst World, Philadelphia, PA.

Scott, A. (1998). Regions and the Word Economy. Oxford, UK: Oxford University Press.

Scott, A. (2001). Global City Regions: Trends, Theory and Policy. Oxford, UK: Oxford University Press.

Scott, J. (2005). Social Network Analysis (2 ed.). London: Sage Publications Ltd.

Seibert, S. E., Kraimer, M. L., & Liden, R. C. (2001). A social capital theory of career success. *Academy of Management Journal, 44*(2), 219–237. doi:10.2307/3069452

Sengupta, S. (2008). A Plan for Building a New Supply Chain. *Supply Chain Management Review, 12*(1), 46–52.

Seufert, A., von Krogh, G., & Back, A. (1999). Towards Knowledge Networking. *Journal of Knowledge Management, 3*(3), 180–190. doi:10.1108/13673279910288608

Shang, J. S., Li, S., & Tadikamalla, P. (2004). Operational design of a supply chain system using the taguchi method, response surface methodology, simulation, and optimization. *International Journal of Production Research, 42*(18), 3823–3849. doi:10.1080/00207540410001704050

Shannon, R. (1975). System simulation. The art and science. Upper Saddle River, NJ: Prentice-Hall.

Shapkin, A., & Shapkin, B. (2005). Risk theory and risk situation modelling. Moscow: Dashkov&Co.

Sharifi, H., Ismail, H. S., & Reid, I. (2006). Achieving Agility in Supply Chain Through Simultaneous 'Design of' and 'Design for' the Supply Chain . *Journal of Manufacturing Technology, 17*(8), 1078–1098. doi:10.1108/17410380610707393

Shaw, R. (1997). *Trust in the Balance*. San Francisco: Jossey-Bass.

Sheffi, Y. (2001). Supply chain management under the threat of international terrorism. *International Journal of Logistics Management*, *12*(2), 1–11. doi:10.1108/09574090110806262

Sheffi, Y. (2005). *The Resilient Enterprise - Overcoming Vulnerability for Competitive Advantage*. Cambridge, MA: MIT Press.

Silver, E. A., Pyke, D. F., & Peterson, R. (1998). Inventory Management and Production Planning and Scheduling. New York: Wiley.

Simões, D., & Soares, A. L. (2004). The Formation and Dissolution of Organizational Networks: A Knowledge Management Perspective . In Camarinha-Matos, L. M. (Ed.), *Virtual Enterprises and Collaborative Networks* (pp. 301–310). Boston: Springer. doi:10.1007/1-4020-8139-1_32

Simon, H. A. (1991). Bounded rationality and organizational learning. *Organization Science*, *2*(1), 125–134. doi:10.1287/orsc.2.1.125

Simonin, B. L. (1999). Ambiguity and the process of knowledge transfer in strategic alliances. *Strategic Management Journal*, *20*, 595–623. doi:10.1002/(SICI)1097-0266(199907)20:7<595::AID-SMJ47>3.0.CO;2-5

Simons, R. L. (1999). How risky is your company? *Harvard Business Review*, *77*(3).

Slack, N. (1983). Flexibility as a manufacturing objective . *International Journal of Operations & Production Management*, *3*(3), 4–13. doi:10.1108/eb054696

Smallman, C. (1996). Risk and organisational behaviour: a research model. *Disaster Prevention and Management*, *5*(2), 12–26. doi:10.1108/09653569610112880

Smeltzer, L. R., & Siferd, S. P. (1998). Proactive supply management: the management of risk. *International Journal of Purchasing and Materials Management*, *34*(1), 38–45.

Smith, K. G., Carroll, S. C., & Ashford, S. J. (1995). Intra and Interorganizational Cooperation: Toward a Research Agenda. *Academy of Management Journal*, *38*(1), 7–22. doi:10.2307/256726

Snow, C. S., Miles, R. E., Coleman, H. J., & Henry, H. J. (1992). Managing 21st Century Network Organizations. *Organizational Dynamics*, *20*(3), 5–21. doi:10.1016/0090-2616(92)90021-E

Sodhi, M. (2005). Management demand risk in tactical supply chain planning for a global consumer electronics company. *International Journal of Production and Operations Management*, *14*, 69–79.

Solvang, W. D. (2001). Architecture *for supply chain analysis and methodology for quantitative measurement of supply chain flexibility*. Unpublished PhD dissertation, NTNU, Trondheim, Norway.

Sparrowe, R. T., & Liden, R. C. (2001). Social networks and the performance of individuals and groups. *Academy of Management Journal*, *44*(2), 316–325. doi:10.2307/3069458

Spekman, R. E., & Davis, E. W. (2004). Risky business: expanding the discussion on risk and the extended enterprise . *International Journal of Physical Distribution & Logistics Management*, *34*(5), 414–433. doi:10.1108/09600030410545454

Spender, J. C. (1996). Making knowledge the basis of a dynamic theory of the firm. *Strategic Management Journal*, *17*, 45–62.

Spira, L. F., & Page, M. (2003). Risk Management, The Reinvention of Internal Control And the Changing Role of Internal Audit . *Accounting, Auditing & Accountability Journal*, *16*(4), 640–661. doi:10.1108/09513570310492335

Stake, R. E. (1994). Case studies. In Denzin, N. K. & Lincoln, Y.S. (eds), Handbook of qualitative research. Thousand Oaks, CA: Sage Publications.

Stanley, M. H. R., Amaral, L. A. N., Buldyrev, S. V., Leschhorn, H., Maass, P., & Salinger, M. A. (1996). Scaling behaviour in the growth of companies. *Nature*, *379*, 804–806. doi:10.1038/379804a0

Stauffer, D. (2003). *Supply chain risk: Deal with it.* Harvard Business Review.

Steinberg, R. (2005). Implementing ITIL: Adapting your it organization to the coming revolution in it service management. Victoria, BC: Trafford Publishing.

Stevenson, M., & Spring, M. (2007). Flexibility from a supply chain perspective: definition and review. *International Journal of Operations & Production Management*, *27*(7), 685–713. doi:10.1108/01443570710756956

Stewart, T. A. (1997). Intellectual Capital: the new wealth of organizations. London: Nicholas Brealey Publishing.

Stiglitz, J. (1999). Public Policy for a Knowledge Economy. *OECD Report*. Retrieved September 18, 2007 from http://www.worldbank.org/html/extdr/extme/knowledge-economy.pdf

Stiglitz, J. (2002). Information and the Change in the Paradigm in Economics. *The American Economic Review*, *92*(3), 460–501. doi:10.1257/00028280260136363

Sun, H., & Venuvinod, P. K. (2001). The Human Side of Holonic Manufacturing Systems . *Technovation*, *21*(6), 353–360. doi:10.1016/S0166-4972(00)00055-9

Sun, H., & Wu, J. (2005). Scale-free characterisitics of supply chain distribution networks. *Modern Physics Letters B*, *19*(17), 841–848. doi:10.1142/S0217984905008797

Supply Chain Council. (n.d.). *Supply-Chain Operations Reference-model*. Retrieved from www.supply-chain.org

Sveiby, K. E. (1997). The new organizational wealth: managing and measuring knowledge based assets. San Francisco: Berrett-Koehler.

Svensson, G. (2002). A conceptual framework of vulnerability in firms' inbound and outbound logistics flows. *International Journal of Physical Distribution & Logistics Management*, *32*, 110–134. doi:10.1108/09600030210421723

Sybase (2008) *Sybase PowerDesigner Business Process Model User's Guide*, Version 12, Sybase Inc., USA. Retrieved July 10, 2008, from http://www.sybase.com.

Sykes, S. R. (2006). Supply chain risk management - gaining a baseline grasp on an increasingly important challenge . *CSCMP Supply Chain Comment*, *40*(Jan/Feb), 12–13.

Szymankiewicz, J. (1994). Contracting out or Selling out? *Logistics Information Management*, *7*(1), 28–35. doi:10.1108/09576059410052368

Taiwana, A., & Keil, M. (2006). Functionality risk in information systems development: An empirical investigation. *IEEE Transactions on Engineering Management*, *53*(3), 412–425. doi:10.1109/TEM.2006.878099

Takac, P. F. (1993). Outsourcing Technology. *Management Decision*, *31*(1), 25–38. doi:10.1108/00251749310023157

Takeishi, A. (2002). Knowledge partitioning in the interfirm division of labor: the case of automotive product development. *Organization Science*, *13*(3), 321–338. doi:10.1287/orsc.13.3.321.2779

Tang, C. (2006). Perspectives in supply chain risk management. *International Journal of Production Economics*, *103*(2), 451–488. doi:10.1016/j.ijpe.2005.12.006

Tang, C., & Tomlin, B. (2008). How much flexibility does it take to mitigate supply chain risks? In G. Zsidisin (Ed.), Supply chain risk: A handbook of assessment, management and performance (pp. 155-174). New York: Springer.

Tang, C., & Tomlin, B. (2008). The power of flexibility for mitigation supply chain risks. *International Journal of Production Economics*, *116*, 12–27. doi:10.1016/j.ijpe.2008.07.008

Taps, S. B., & Steger-Jensen, K. (2007). Aligning supply chain design with manufacturing strategies in developing regions. Production Planning and Control, 18(6), 475–486. doi:10.1080/09537280701495021doi:10.1080/09537280701495021

Tarantino, A. (2008). The governance, risk, and compliance handbook. Hoboken, NJ: John Wiley and Sons Inc.

Tatsiopoulos, I. P., Panayiotou, N. A., & Ponis, S. T. (2001, May) *A Modelling & Evaluation Methodology for E-Commerce BPR*. Paper presented at the 4th SME SME International Conference, May 14-16, 2001, Aalborg University, Denmark.

Tatsiopoulos, I., Ponis, S., & Hadzilias, E. (2004). An E-Releaser of Production Orders in the Extended Enterprise. *Production Planning and Control Journal*, *15*(2), 119–132. doi:10.1080/09537280410001662547

Teece, D. J. (2001). Strategies for managing knowledge assets: the role of firm structure and industrial context. In Nonaka, I. & Teece D., Managing industrial knowledge: creation, transfer, utilization. London: Sage Publications.

Teece, D. J. (2003). Knowledge and Competence as Strategic Assets. In C.W. Holsapple (Ed.), Handbook of Knowledge Management (pp. 129-152). Berlin, Germany: Springer-Verlag.

Temponi, C., Bryant, M. D., & Fernandez, B. (2009). Integration of business function models into an aggregate enterprise systems model . *European Journal of Operational Research*, *199*(3), 793–800. doi:10.1016/j.ejor.2008.08.007

Theoharakis, V., & Serpanos, D. N. (Eds.). (2001). Enterprise networking: Multilayer switching and applications. London: Idea Group Publishing.

Thompson, J. (2003). Managing your virtual world: Internal controls for enterprise technology. *Government Finance Review*, *19*(4), 46–51.

Thompson, K. (2008). The networked enterprise: Competing for the future through virtual enterprise networks. Tampa, FL: Meghan-Kiffer Press.

Thompson, K. (2008). The Networked Enterprise: Competing for the Future Through Virtual Enterprise Networks. Tampa, FL: Meghan-Kiffer Press.

Thompson. (2009, March). *Collaborating for New Business*. Presented at Connecting Innovation, Brighton, UK. Retrieved June 29, from bioteams.com/2009/05/20/the_networked_enterprise.html

Tiwana, A. (2000). The knowledge management toolkit. Upper Saddle River, NJ: Prentice Hall.

Todeva, E. (2006). Business networks. Strategy and structure. London: Routledge.

Tomlin, B. (2006). On the value of Mitigation and Contingency Strategies for Managing Supply Chain Disruption Risks. *Management Science*, *52*(5), 639–657. doi:10.1287/mnsc.1060.0515

Torrington, D. P., & Hall, L. A. (1987) Personnel Management: A New Approach. Upper Saddle River, NJ: Prentice-Hall.

Towill, D. R., & Disney, S. M. (2008). Managing bullwhip-induced risks in supply chains. *International Journal of Risk Assessment & Management.*, *10*(3), 238–262. doi:10.1504/IJRAM.2008.021376

Tranfield, D., Denyer, D., & Smart, P. (2003). Towards a Methodology for Developing Evidence-Informed Management Knowledge by Means of Systematic Review. British Journal of Management, 14(3), 207–222. doi:10.1111/1467-8551.00375doi:10.1111/1467-8551.00375

Trends Business Research (2001). *Business Clusters in the UK- A First Assessment*, A report for the Department of Trade and Industry, DTI pub 5257.

Trkman, P., Stemberger, M. I., & Groznik, A. (2007). Process Approach to Supply Chain Integration, *Supply Chain Management* . *International Journal (Toronto, Ont.)*, *12*(2), 116–128.

Trotman, E. (1983) The Role of The Internal Auditor, Professional Development for the Australian Society of Accountants, Australia.

Tsai, M., Hung, S., & Han, C. (2006). Key risk factors for logistics outsourcing – a case of retailing industry in Taiwan. In W. Kersten & T. Blecker (Eds.), Managing risks in supply chains (pp. 179-192). Berlin, Germany: Verlag.

Tsoukas, H. (1996). The firm as a distributed knowledge system: a constructionist approach. *Strategic Management Journal*, *17*, 11–25.

Tsoukas, H., & Vladimirou, E. (2001). What is organizational knowledge? *Journal of Management Studies, 38*(7), 973–993. doi:10.1111/1467-6486.00268

Tuma, A. (1998). Configuration and coordination of virtual production networks . *International Journal of Production Economics, 56-57*(1), 641–648. doi:10.1016/S0925-5273(97)00146-1

Turban, E., Leidner, D., McLean, E., & Wetherbe, J. (2008). Information technology for management: Transforming organizations in the digital economy. Hoboken, NJ: John Wiley and Sons Inc.

Türke, R. (2008). Governance: Systemic foundation and framework. Heidelberg, Germany: Physica-Verlag.

Turnbull, P., Ford, D., & Cunningham, M. T. (1996). Interaction, relationships and networks in business markets: an evolving perspective. *Journal of Business and Industrial Marketing, 11*(3/4), 44–62. doi:10.1108/08858629610125469

Tyre, M., & Von Hippel, E. (1997). The Situative Nature of Adaptive Learning in Organizations. *Organization Science, 8*(1), 71–83. doi:10.1287/orsc.8.1.71

Ulrich, K. T., & Eppinger, S. D. (2000). Product design and development, New York: McGraw Hill.

UPS. (2006, April 18-19). *Innovation and Global supply chain'- conference summary.* Retrieved July 17, 2009, from http://longitudes08.com/Barcelona08/research/conference_materials/Chicago06_Summary.pdf

Upton, D. M. (1995). What really makes factories flexible? *Harvard Business Review, 73*(4), 74–81.

Uzzi, B. (1997). Social structure and competition in interfirm networks: The paradox of embeddedness. *Administrative Science Quarterly, 42*, 35–67. doi:10.2307/2393808

van de Ven, A. H. (1992). Suggestions for studying strategy process: a research note. *Strategic Management Journal, 13*, 169–191. doi:10.1002/smj.4250131013

Van Der Vorst, J. G. A. J., Beulens, A. J. M., De Wit, W., & Van Beek, P. (1998). Supply chain management in food chains: improving performance by reducing uncertainty. *International Transactions in Operational Research, 5*(6), 487–499. doi:10.1016/S0969-6016(98)00049-5

Van Hoek, R. (2003). Are you ready? Risk readiness tactics for the supply chain. Logistics Research Network, London: Institute of Logistics and Transport.

Van Hoek, R. I., & Chapman, P. (2006). From tinkering around the edge to enhancing revenue growth: supply chain-new product development, Supply Chain Management: an international journal, 11(5), 385-389.

Van Hoek, R. I., & Chapman, P. (2007). How to move supply chain beyond cleaning up after new product development, Supply Chain Management: an international journal, 12(4), 239-244.

Van Ryssen, S., & Hayes Godar, S. (2000). Going international without going international: multinational virtual teams. *J. Int. Managment, 6*, 49–60. doi:10.1016/S1075-4253(00)00019-3

Vanany, I., Zailani, S., & Pujawan, I. N. (2009). Supply Chain Risk Management: Literature Review and Future Research. *International Journal of Information Systems and Supply Chain Management, 2*(1), 16–33.

Vanson, S. (2001). Challenge of outsourcing human resources. Oxford, UK: Chandos Publishing.

Venkatraman, N., & Henderson, J. C. (1998). Real strategies for virtual organizing. *Sloan Management Review,* (Fall): 33–48.

Vickery, S., Calantone, R., & Drogue, C. (1999). Supply chain flexibility: an empirical study. *Journal of Supply Chain Management, 35*(3), 16–24. doi:10.1111/j.1745-493X.1999.tb00058.x

Von Hippel, E. (1994). Sticky information and the locus of problem solving: Implications for innovation. *Management Science, 40*(4), 429–439. doi:10.1287/mnsc.40.4.429

Vose, D. (2008). Risk analysis: A quantitative guide, West Sussex, UK: John Wiley and Sons, Ltd.

Voulgaridou, D. (2008). *Decision support based on risk for project-based procurements of enterprise clusters.* Doctoral Dissertation, National Technical University of Athens.

Voulgaridou, D., Kirytopoulos, K., & Leopoulos, V. (2009). An analytic network process approach for sales forecasting. [ORIJ]. *OPERATIONAL RESEARCH: An International Journal, 9*(1), 35–53.

Wagner, S. M., & Bode, C. (2006). An Empirical Investigation into Supply Chain Vulnerability. *Journal of Purchasing and Supply Management, 12*, 301–312. doi:10.1016/j.pursup.2007.01.004

Walewski, J., & Gibson, G. (2003). International project risk assessment: methods, procedures, and critical factor (Research. Rep. No. 31). Austin, Texas: The University of Texas at Austin, Construction Industry Studies Centre. Additional Readings Biske, T. (2008). SOA governance. Birmingham, UK: Packt Publishing.

Walker, G., & Weber, D. (1984). A Transaction cost approach to make or buy decisions. *Administrative Science Quarterly, 29*, 373–391. doi:10.2307/2393030

Wallace, M., & Webber, L. (2008). IT governance 2009: Policies & procedures. Gaithersburg, MD:Aspen Publishers Inc.

Walters, D. (2004). A Business Model for Managing the Virtual Enterprise . In Camarinha-Matos, L. M. (Ed.), *Virtual Enterprises and Collaborative Networks* (pp. 273–280). Boston: Springer. doi:10.1007/1-4020-8139-1_29

Walters, D. (2007). *Supply Chain Risk Management: Vulnerability and Resilience in Logistics.* London: Kogan Page.

Wang, E. T. G., Barron, T., & Seidmann, A. (1997). Contracting structures for custom software development: the impacts of informational rents and uncertainty of internal development and outsourcing. *Management Science, 43*(12), 1726–1744. doi:10.1287/mnsc.43.12.1726

Warkentin, M., Sugumaran, V., & Bapna, R. (2001). E-knowledge networks for inter-organizational collaborative e-business . *Logistics Information Management, 14*(1/2), 149–162. doi:10.1108/09576050110363040

Warnecke, H. (1993). *The Fractal Company: A Revolution in Corporate Culture.* New York: Springer-Verlag.

Warrier, S., & Shandrashekhar, P. (2006). Enterprise risk management from boardroom to shop floor. Paper presented in the Asia Pacific Risk and Insurance conference, Tokyo, Japan.

Wasserman, S., & Faust, K. (1994). *Social Network Analysis: Methods and Applications.* Cambridge, UK: Cambridge University Press.

Waters, D. (2007). *Supply Chain Risk Management: Vulnerability and Resilience in Logistics.* London: Kogan Page Limited.

Watts, D. J. (2004). *Six Degrees: The Science of a Connected Age.* London: Vintage Books.

Weber, C., Current, J., & Desai, A. (2000). An optimization approach to determining the number of vendors to employ *Supply Chain Management . International Journal (Toronto, Ont.), 5*(2), 90–98.

Weick, K. (1995) Sensemaking in organizations. Thousand Oaks: Sage Publications.

Weick, K. E. (1993). The collapse of sense making in organizations: The Mann Gulch disaster . *Administrative Science Quarterly, 38*, 628–652. doi:10.2307/2393339

Weiss, G. (1999). Mutiagent systems: A modern approach to distributed artificial intelligence. Cambrigde, MA: MIT Press.

Wenger, E. (1998). Communities of practice. Cambridge, UK: Cambridge University Press.

Wernerfeld, B. (1984). A resource based view of the firm. *Strategic Management Journal, 5*(2), 171–180. doi:10.1002/smj.4250050207

Westerman, G., & Hunter, R. (2007). IT risk: Turning business threats into competitive advantage. Boston, MA: Harvard Business School Publishing.

Wheeler, R. (1996). Double Lives and Emotional Labour in Legal Firms . *Human Relations, 32*(3), 190–207.

Whitley, D. (1994). A genetic algorithm tutorial. *Statistics and Computing, 4*, 65–85. doi:10.1007/BF00175354

Whitley, R. (1999). Divergent Capitalisms: the social structuring and change of business systems. Oxford, UK: Oxford University Press.

Wilding, R. (2007). The Mitigation of Supply Chain Risk. *Institute of Supply Management, 18*(8), 12–13.

Wilding, R. D. (2003). The 3 Ts of highly effective Supply Chains. Supply Chain Practice, 5(3), 30–41.

Wilensky, U. (2004). *NetLogo Scatter model*. Retrieved from http://ccl.northwestern.edu/netlogo/models/Scatter Evanston, IL: Center for Connected Learning and Computer-Based Modeling, Northwestern University.

Williamson, O. E. (1975). Markets and Hierarchies: Analysis and Antitrust Implications, New York: The Free Press.

Williamson, O. E. (1985). The economic institutions of capitalism. New York: Free Press.

Wilson, D., & McCutcheon, D. (2003), Industrial Safety and Risk Management. Edmonton, Canada: University of Alberta Press.

Wooldridge, M., & Jennings, N. R. (1995). Intelligent Agents: Theory and Practice. *The Knowledge Engineering Review, 10*, 115–152. doi:10.1017/S0269888900008122

Yakhlef, A. (2002). Towards a discursive approach to organisational knowledge formation. *Scandinavian Journal of Management, 18*, 319–339. doi:10.1016/S0956-5221(01)00015-X

Yin, R. (1989). Case study research: Design and methods (Rev. ed.). Newbury Park, CA: Sage Publishing.

Yin, R. K. (1994), Case Study Research: Design and Methods. Applied Social. Thousand Oaks, CA: Sage Publications.

Yoo, S. B., & Kim, Y. (2002). Web-based knowledge management for sharing product data in virtual enterprises.

International Journal of Production Economics, 75(1), 173–183. doi:10.1016/S0925-5273(01)00190-6

York County Economic Development Corporation. (2004). *Industry Cluster Analysis Baseline Report (1995–2001 data),* Retrieved March 28, from http://www.ycedc.org/images/ClusterAnalaselineReport.pdf

Zaheer, A., McEvily, B., & Perrone, V. (1998). Does trust matter? Exploring the effects of interorganizational and interpersoinal trust on performance. *Organization Science, 9*(2), 141–159. doi:10.1287/orsc.9.2.141

Zhang, C., & Zhang, C. (2007). Design and simulation of demand information sharing in a supply chain. *Simulation Modelling Practice and Theory, 15*(1), 32–46. doi:10.1016/j.simpat.2006.09.011

Zhang, Q., Vonderembse, M. A., & Lim, J.-S. (2002). Value chain flexibility: a dichotomy of competence and capability. *International Journal of Production Research, 40*(3), 561–583. doi:10.1080/00207540110091695

Zhang, Q., Vonderembse, M. A., & Lim, J.-S. (2005). Logistics flexibility and its impact on customer satisfaction. *The International Journal of Logistics Management, 16*(1), 71–95. doi:10.1108/09574090510617367

Zheng, J., Johnsen, T., Harland, C. M., & Lamming, R. C. (1998, September 3-5). Initial conceptual framework for creation and operation of supply networks. In *Proceedings of the 14th IMP Annual Conference.* Turku, Finland.

Zhuge, H. (2006). Knowledge flow network planning and simulation. *Decision Support Systems, 2*(2), 571–592. doi:10.1016/j.dss.2005.03.007

Zineldin, M., & Torbjorn, B. (2003). Strategic alliances: Synergies and challenges. *International Journal of Physical Distribution & Logistics Management, 33*(5), 449–464. doi:10.1108/09600030310482004

Zinn, W., & Bowersox, D. J. (1988). Planning physical distribution with the principle of Postponement. *Journal of Business Logistics., 9*(2), 117–136.

Zsidisin, G. (2003). Managerial perceptions of risk. *Journal of Supply Chain Management, 39*, 14–25. doi:10.1111/j.1745-493X.2003.tb00146.x

Zsidisin, G. A. (2003). A grounded definition of supply risk. *Journal of Purchasing and Supply Management, 9*, 217–224. doi:10.1016/j.pursup.2003.07.002

Zsidisin, G. A. (2003). Managerial perceptions of supply risk. *Journal of Supply Chain Management, 39*(1), 14–25. doi:10.1111/j.1745-493X.2003.tb00146.x

Zsidisin, G. A., & Ritchie, B. (2008). Supply chain risk. A Handbook of Assessment, Management and Performance. New York: Springer.

Zsidisin, G. A., Ellram, L. M., Carter, J. R., & Cavinato, J. L. (2004). An analysis of supply risk assessment techniques. *International Journal of Physical Distribution & Logistics Management., 34*(5), 397–413. doi:10.1108/09600030410545445

Zsidisin, G. A., Ellram, L. M., Carter, J. R., & Cavinato, J. L. (2004). An Analysis of Supply Risk Assessment Techniques. *International Journal of Physical Distribution and Logistics Management, 34*(5), 397–413. doi:10.1108/09600030410545445

Zsidisin, G. A., Melnyk, S. A., & Ragatz, G. L. (2005). An Institutional Theory Perspective of Business Continuity Planning For Purchasing And Supply Management. *International Journal of Production Research, 43*(16), 3401–3420. doi:10.1080/00207540500095613

Zsidisin, G. A., Panelli, A., & Upton, R. (2000). Purchasing organization involvement in risk assessments, contingency plans, and risk management: an exploratory study. *Supply Chain Management, 5*(4), 187. doi:10.1108/13598540010347307

Zsidisin, G., & Ritchie, B. (2008). Supply chain risk management – developments, issues and challenges. In G. Zsidisin (Ed.), Supply chain risk: A handbook of assessment, management and performance (pp. 1-11). New York: Springer.

Zwegers, A., Wubben, H., & Hartel, I. (2002). Relationship Management in Enterprise Networks. In V. Marik, L.M. Camarinha-Matos & H. Afsarmanesh (eds.), Knowledge and technology integration in production and services – Balancing knowledge and technology in product and service life cycle, (pp. 157-164). Boston: Kluwer Academic Publishers.

About the Contributors

Dr. **Stavros Ponis** has graduated from the School of Mechanical Engineering of the National Technical University Athens (NTUA) in 1996. His Master's thesis resulted in the design of a software module for enhancing the functionality of an expert system that aimed to assist enterprises in the selection of ERP software packages based on the mode of their production system's operation. Dr. Ponis also owns a PhD from NTUA (2003) which focuses on the elaboration of a business reference model to support the production management and logistics processes of Virtual Enterprises in the Apparel Industry. From 2006 to 2008, Dr. Ponis has worked on his post doc research on the fields of Knowledge Management and Logistics to support Virtual Enterprise Networks. In that context he acted as the main post doc researcher for the project "A Reference Model to Support Knowledge Logistics in a Virtual Enterprise Environment" funded by the Ministry of National Education and Religious Affairs (http://simor.ntua.gr/pythagoras/index.html). In the beginning of his career (1996), Dr. Ponis has worked as an IT Manager - for almost three years- on behalf of a leading apparel enterprise. Later on (2000-2001), he was involved in several targeted research projects on behalf of the Section of Industrial Management and Operational Research (SIMOR) of NTUA as a Researcher. On December 2001 he was appointed the position of Teaching and Research Associate in SIMOR. As from November 2005, he has been elected Lecturer in the scientific area of Supply Chain Management and he currently teaches a series of courses such as Supply Chain Management, Operations Research, E-Commerce, Management of Production Information Systems and ERP Systems to graduate and post graduate students of NTUA. Dr. Stavros Ponis has published more than fifty scientific papers in edited books, scientific journals, conference proceedings and the specialized in production management commercial press. After editing the book entitled "Managing Risk in Virtual Enterprise Networks: Implementing Supply Chain Principles", his publication short-term objectives include the authoring of a textbook to support production and logistics decision making with the use of spreadsheets and the editing of an Encyclopedia for Virtual Enterprises and Supply Chain Management. Dr. Ponis has also acted as an associate editor in two scientific journals and is currently a member of the Scientific Committee in several International Conferences. Dr. Ponis is an Expert Reviewer for two different EU research units, these being INFSO.E2: Technologies for Information Management and D5-ICT for Enterprise Networking. Up to now, and for the last five years, Dr. Ponis has monitored, evaluated and finally approved the works of two large European Projects with a budget sum of over seven million euros. Dr. Ponis also is an expert reviewer for the General Secretariat of Research and Development and the Greek Information Society S.A. Finally, Dr. Ponis' current research interests are resided in the areas of Production Planning and Control, Supply Chain Management, Business Process Modeling, Networked and Virtual Enterprises, and Information Systems that support all the above.

* * *

Christina C. Athanasiadou is a Manager in Risk Advisory Services at Ernst & Young Greece. She has a long experience in internal audit, internal controls system development and evaluation, procedures documentation and risk advisory services. In the past she has worked as a consultant at KPMG specialized in business organization, business process improvement and internal audit, and as an internal auditor at Geniki Bank member of Societe General Group. Christina has a Masters and a Bachelors degree in Production and Management Engineering from the Technical University of Crete. She is also a member of the Institute of Internal Auditors (International and Greek) and member of the Technical Chamber of Greece.

Ettore Bolisani has a degree in Electronic Engineering ("Laurea") and a Ph.D. in Innovation Studies at the University of Padua (Italy). He is Associate Professor at the Faculty of Engineering of the University of Padua. Prior to this position, he was Assistant Professor at the University of Trieste (Italy) and, in 1997, research fellow at PREST (University of Manchester - UK). His research centres on technology assessment and technology management, with an emphasis on Information and Communication Technologies and Knowledge Management. He has worked in several research projects funded by the European Union, by Italian public institutions, and private organisations. He is Editor of "Building the Knowledge Society on the Internet: Sharing and Exchanging Knowledge in Networked Environment" (2008), published by IGI Global. He is Chair of the 10th European Conference on Knowledge Management.

Alessandro Creazza, Ph.D., is currently a research assistant at Clog, Logistics Research Centre - Carlo Cattaneo LIUC University, and has participated in a research exchange program with Cranfield University School of Management in the Centre for Logistics and Supply Chain Management. His research interests are mainly focused on logistics and distribution network design and modelling, global supply chain management, logistics real estate and warehousing. Alessandro is an adjunct lecturer in Logistics and Supply Chain Management at Carlo Cattaneo LIUC University and at Politecnico di Milano, and in his working background he has been developing a wide experience in logistics network design and transport management. In addition, he regularly collaborates with the Italian Chamber of Commerce and with local government agencies, developing funded research projects on logistics management.

Dr. **Samir Dani** is a Senior lecturer in Operations Management in the Loughborough University Business School. His current research looks at methods to manage and mitigate supply chain risks, supply chain innovation and supply chain relationships. Samir also teaches and conducts research in operations management. Currently, Samir is a principal investigator on an EPSRC project investigating supply chain risk management in the food sector and is a co-investigator on EPSRC and IMCRC projects in the area of supply chain management and Lean systems. He has the experience of working as a researcher on EPSRC projects in a diverse range of management issues and has published in refereed academic journals and presented at International conferences. Prior to joining academia, Samir has worked in the automotive sector for 5 years.

Sotiris P. Gayialis is a teaching and research associate at the Sector of Industrial Management & Operational Research of National Technical University of Athens (NTUA). In the past he has worked as a consultant and later on, he was involved in research projects as a researcher at NTUA. He has graduated from the School of Mechanical Engineering of the National Technical University Athens in 1997.

His diploma thesis aimed at the process redesign of the Greek Public Procurement System. He holds a PhD (2009) at NTUA in the field of Logistics. His research interests and publications are related in the areas of Supply Chain Management, Business Process Reengineering, Enterprise Modelling, Risk Management, Decision Support Systems and Management Information Systems.

Jan Husdal has since 2005 been a Research Scientist at Møreforsking Molde/Molde Research Institute in Molde, Norway, where he works on cost-benefit evaluations of infrastructure projects. Previously, he served as a government adviser in community vulnerability assessment and crisis management for more than 15 years. He holds a BSc in Civil Engineering from Norway (1985) and an MSc with distinction in Geographic Information Science from the University of Leicester, UK (2000). Since 2004 he has served as a member on the program committee on European Policy and Research with the Association for European Transport, served as a referee for Transportation Science and Transport Policy, and presented papers on supply chain risk and transportation vulnerability at a number of conferences. He is the founder a husdal.com, a personal Internet gateway to journal articles, research papers, books, websites and other resources related to his research interests, supply chain risk and transportation vulnerability.

Dr. **Omera Khan** is a Lecturer in Logistics & Supply Chain Management at the University of Manchester and Visiting Professor to a number of institutions across the UK, Sweden and Dubai. Prior to this post Omera was a post- doctoral Research Fellow in the Centre for Logistics and Supply Chain Management at Cranfield School of Management. Omera's research focus is on Supply Chain Risk Management, Design-Led Risk Management for the Supply Chain, Agile Supply Chains, Global Sourcing and Managing the Risks of Offshore Manufacturing. Omera has conducted several research projects on the topics of supply chain risk management and the risks of global sourcing, which have been commissioned by government institutions, research councils and companies.

Dr. **Epaminondas Koronis** is a graduate of Athens University of Economics and Business and holds a Masters and a PhD from Warwick Business School, UK. He has published papers and studies in the areas of Knowledge Management, Corporate Reputation and Organizational Crises while he has worked as a Research Fellow at Warwick Business School and as the academic Director of Mediterranean University College - Business School. He is currently a partner and Director of Research at Reputation Lab, a Research & Consultancy firm and an Adjunct Lecturer at Mediterranean University College's MBA Program.

Konstantinos Kirytopoulos holds a Mechanical Engineering Diploma and a PhD on Project Risk Management. He works as an Assistant Professor at the University of the Aegean (Greece) and cooperates with the industry in the fields of project management (mainly construction, oil and pharmaceutical industry), decision making and risk management. His main research interests are also focusing on the aforementioned fields. As a researcher he has published a significant amount of papers at international conferences and journals. More information can be obtained at www.kirytopoulos.eu

Ruslan Klimov earned his master's degree in information technology from Riga Technical University in 2005. Next year he became a researcher in the Department of Modelling and Simulation of Riga Technical University. Being a member of Latvian Simulation Society, he focused his professional interests on the application of simulation to risk handling in supply chains. At this time he also started his Doctoral thesis "Simulation-based supply chain risk management". In 2008 he participated in local university projects of operational IT risk management concept development for Latvian monetary and financial institutions. In 2009 Ruslan Klimov started his professional activity in Latvian Railway daughter company "JSC VRC Zasulauks".

Maria Pilar Lamban qualified from the University of Zaragoza, Spain as an Industrial Engineer, where she also obtained a post graduate degree in Industrial Organization. Nowadays she is professor in the Manufacturing Engineering and Design Department at the University of Zaragoza and she is adjunct professor in Zaragoza Logistics Center. She is finishing her Doctorate in a research line related to calculating product cost and control in the supply chain under uncertainty and she is researching in a framework to measure the performance in a supply chain. She has participated in several conferences about these topics, she has published various articles and participated in many projects related to supply chain management.

Vrassidas Leopoulos is a member of the Industrial Management and OR Section of the National Technical University of Athens (NTUA). He has been active for several years as a professional production engineer in both industrial and consulting firms. He studied Mechanical and Industrial Engineering at NTUA (1980) and followed post-graduate studies in Paris Ecole Des Mines, Ensae, Universite Paris IX (Dauphine). He holds a PhD (1985) in Petri – Nets simulation technique earned from the aforementioned University. His research interests cover risk management, decision management and e-business. He has undertaken or supervised many applied projects in the Greek industry concerning project management, risk management, e-business and ERP implementation.

Dr. **Ila Manuj** is an Assistant Professor of Logistics at the Department of Marketing and Logistics, University of North Texas, Denton. She holds a Ph.D. in Business Administration with a major in Logistics from the University of Tennessee, Knoxville. Her research interests are in the areas of risk and complexity management in global supply chains. She has published in *Journal of Business Logistics and International Journal of Physical Distribution and Logistics Management*, co-authored a book chapter, and presented at several national and international conferences. She has worked with CARE (India), a not-for-profit social development organization. She earned her master's degree in International Business from Indian Institute of Foreign Trade, New Delhi (India) and bachelor's degree in Management Sciences from Lucknow University, Lucknow (India).

Yuri Merkuryev is Full Professor and Head of Department of Modelling and Simulation at Riga Technical University, Latvia. His professional interests include methodology and practical application of discrete-event simulation, simulation-based gaming, supply chain modelling and management, as well as education in the areas of modelling & simulation and logistics management. He authors about 300 scientific publications, including 6 books, and serves at editorial boards of Simulation: Transactions of The Society for Modeling and Simulation International; International Journal of Simulation and Process Modelling; Simulation & Gaming: An Interdisciplinary Journal of Theory, Practice and Research. Prof. Merkuryev regularly participates in organising international conferences in the area of modelling and simulation. He was General Chair of European Conference on Modelling and Simulation, ECMS'2005. Prof. Merkuryev is habilitated doctor of engineering, corresponding member of Latvian Academy of Sciences, president of Latvian Simulation Society, EUROSIM board member, SCS senior member, and BCS chartered fellow.

Eva Navarro is Mechanical Engineer from the University of Zaragoza (Spain). In 2007, after she finished her degree, she decided to move to The Netherlands in order to study Commercial Engineering in the Hogeschool Zeeland University. After finishing this degree, she decided to focus her professional career in the logistics area, so she started a Master in Logistics and Supply Chain Management in Zaragoza Logistics Center, where she has developed an empirical research on flexibility in this area. Currently, she is developing her professional career in logistics service providers companies, known by their excellence in supply chain practices.

Stylianos Oikonomitsios graduated from the National Technical University of Athens in 2003, as a Mechanical Engineer with a specialization in Production Engineering. He is a CIA (Certified Internal Auditor-2006) and he holds also the CCSA (Certification in Control Self Assessment-2009) designation. In addition, he is an MBA candidate. He joined KPMG in January 2005 as an Advisor in the Risk Advisory Services. In October 2006 he was promoted to Senior Advisor and in October 2008 to Supervising Senior Advisor. He has significant experience in internal audit. He has worked in projects concerning Internal Auditing, Risk Assessment, Internal Control System Development, Review/ Evaluation of Internal Audit Procedures, Process Mapping, Business Process Planning and Reengineering and SOx (sec.404) Implementation and Testing.

Nikolaos A. Panayiotou is a Lecturer at the Sector of Industrial Management & Operational Research of National Technical University of Athens (NTUA). In the past he has worked as a consultant at KPMG specialised in Business Process Reengineering, Business Process Improvement, Business Plans and Human Resources Management. He has graduated from the School of Mechanical Engineering of the National Technical University Athens. He holds a MBA at University of Lancaster (UK) and a PhD (1999) at NTUA. His research interests and publications are related in the areas of Operational Research, Systems Analysis, E-Business, Business Process Reengineering, Process Simulation and Information Systems.

María Jesús Sáenz received her Doctorate in Manufacturing and Design Engineering and her Master's in Industrial Engineering from the University of Zaragoza, Spain. She is currently the Director of the scmLAB, Professor at the MIT-Zaragoza International Logistics Programme (Zaragoza Logistics Center), Research Affiliate at the MIT Center for Transportation and Logistics and Tenured Professor at the School of Engineering of the University of Zaragoza. She is the former Academic Director of the Zaragoza Logistics Center and the Director of the Spanish National Center of Excellence in Logistics. Her research interests centre on supply chain collaboration and project management. She has acted as the Main Coordinator in several international research projects. She has also conducted different research and development projects for companies around supply chain management innovation. She is the co-author of several books on these subjects and has published a number of articles in relevant international journals.

Dr. **Burak Sari** is a research fellow in the Technology and Innovation Management (TIM) research group, Leiden Institute of Advanced Computer Science (LIACS). His research inspiration is based on new ways of working derived from key innovative concepts such as virtuality and collaboration facilitated by advanced information and communication technologies (ICT). This led his research agenda to focus on virtual collaboration at team and organizational levels, virtual enterprises and virtual product development teams.

Mohammad Ali Hussein Shalan acquired a B.Sc. in Electrical Engineering and a Master in Telecommunication Engineering from University of Jordan in the years 1995 and 2005 respectively, with a research focused on Transmission Control Protocol (TCP) networking performance. A Professional Engineer, with 14 years of international experience in telecommunications, networking, information systems, project management, risk analysis, audit and governance, working currently as an information systems manager for a leading Saudi business group.

Dr. **Brian Squire** is Senior Lecturer in Operations and Supply Chain Management at Manchester Business School, The University of Manchester. Brian's research straddles the fields of operations and strategic supply management. He is particularly interested in product and process innovations such as the rise of mass customisation and modularisation, and how firms create and protect value through network capabilities. He is principal investigator on an EPSRC funded project looking at supply chain risk management and is actively involved with a range of public and private sector organisations on both research and commercial projects. His publications have appeared in journals including Production and Operations Management, British Journal of Management and International Journal of Operations and Production Management.

I. P. Tatsiopoulos is a Professor in Production Planning and Control and Manufacturing Information Systems in SIMOR/NTUA. He holds a Degree in Mechanical and Electrical Engineering with emphasis in industrial engineering from NTU Athens (1978) and a Ph.D. in Operations Management and O.R. from the University of Lancaster, England (1983). He has served as editor of various scientific journals, head of SIMOR, governmental committees and institutions, as long as coordinator of several national and EU funded projects. Among his varied academic interests, he recently focuses on strategic competitive management, computer-aided production management, logistics and the design and implementation of knowledge management systems.

Dr. **Juri Tolujew** was a lecturer and then assistant professor at the Technical University of Riga from 1976 to 2001. Since 2001, he has been a Research Manager at the Fraunhofer Institute for Factory Operation and Automation IFF in Magdeburg. He earned his Habilitation in Simulation Technology from Otto von Guericke University Magdeburg in 2001. Since 2005, he has also been a member of the faculty of the Institute of Logistics and Material Handling Systems at Otto von Guericke University Magdeburg. In recent years Dr. Tolujew has been intensively working on two fields of research. On the one hand, he employs models to generate data streams for operational logistic with the goal of developing and validating solutions for event management and early warning systems. On the other hand, he is further developing the paradigm of mesoscopic flow system simulation and modeling he formulated himself.

Dimitra Voulgaridou holds an Electrical and Computer Engineer Dimploma and a PhD on Decision Support for Supply Chain Management. She works as a research and teaching associate at National Technical University of Athens and at University of Aegean. Her main research interests cover decision support, supply chain management, project management and ERP systems.

Index

W